Lecture Notes in Computer Science 6791

Commenced Publication in 1973
Founding and Former Series Editors:
Gerhard Goos, Juris Hartmanis, and Jan van Leeuwen

Timo Honkela   Włodzisław Duch
Mark Girolami   Samuel Kaski (Eds.)

Artificial Neural Networks and Machine Learning – ICANN 2011

21st International Conference
on Artificial Neural Networks
Espoo, Finland, June 14-17, 2011
Proceedings, Part I

 Springer

Volume Editors

Timo Honkela
Aalto University School of Science
Department of Information and Computer Science
P.O. Box 15400, 00076 Aalto, Finland
E-mail: timo.honkela@aalto.fi

Włodzisław Duch
Nicolaus Copernicus University
School of Physics, Astronomy and Informatics
Department of Informatics
ul. Grudziadzka 5, 87-100 Torun, Poland
E-mail: wduch@is.umk.pl

Mark Girolami
University College London
Department of Statistical Science
1-19 Torrington Place, London, WC1E 7HB, UK
E-mail: girolami@stats.ucl.ac.uk

Samuel Kaski
Aalto University School of Science
Department of Information and Computer Science
P.O. Box 15400, 00076 Aalto, Finland
E-mail: samuel.kaski@aalto.fi

ISSN 0302-9743   e-ISSN 1611-3349
ISBN 978-3-642-21734-0   ISBN 978-3-642-21735-7 (eBook)
DOI 10.1007/978-3-642-21735-7
Springer Heidelberg Dordrecht London New York

Library of Congress Control Number: 2011929230

CR Subject Classification (1998): I.2, F.1, I.4, I.5, J.3, H.3

LNCS Sublibrary: SL 1 – Theoretical Computer Science and General Issues

Typesetting: Camera-ready by author, data conversion by Scientific Publishing Services, Chennai, India

Printed on acid-free paper

Springer is part of Springer Science+Business Media (www.springer.com)

Preface

The International Conference on Artificial Neural Networks (ICANN) is the annual flagship conference of the European Neural Network Society (ENNS). The idea of ICANN is to bring together researchers from two worlds: information sciences and neurosciences. The scope is wide, ranging from machine learning algorithms to models of real nervous systems. The aim is to facilitate discussions and interactions in the effort toward developing more intelligent artificial systems and increasing our understanding of neural and cognitive processes in the brain.

In 2011, ICANN returned to its roots after 20 years (for more information, see the ENNS website www.e-nns.org). The very first ICANN in 1991 was organized on the premises of Helsinki University of Technology on its beautiful campus in Espoo, Finland. For ICANN 2011, we invited all neural network researchers worldwide to join us in celebrating this 20th anniversary of ICANN and to see the latest advancements in our fast progressing field.

ICANN 2011 had two basic tracks: brain-inspired computing and machine learning research, with Program Committee chairs from both worlds and a thorough reviewing system. The conference structure was built around plenary talks given by renowned scientists described briefly in the following section.

- Thomas Griffiths (University of California, Berkeley, USA) is the Director of the Computational Cognitive Science Lab and the Institute of Cognitive and Brain Sciences at the University of California, Berkeley. They develop, for instance, mathematical models of higher level cognition, including probabilistic reasoning, learning causal relationships, acquiring and using language, and inferring the structure of categories.
- Riitta Hari (Aalto University, Finland) is an internationally recognized and respected neuroscientist. She was newly appointed as Academician of Science, a title that can be held by only 12 scientists at a time in Finland. She has developed methods and applications of human brain imaging and contributed decisively to the progress of this branch of science. Prof. Hari's current focus is on the brain basis of social interaction.
- Geoffrey Hinton (University of Toronto, Canada), the first winner of the David E. Rumelhart Prize, has provided many influential contributions to the area of artificial neural networks and adaptive systems. A non-exhaustive list of the areas where he has contributed substantial inventions includes back-propagation algorithm, Boltzmann machines, distributed representations, time-delay neural networks, and mixtures of experts. Prof. Hinton was the founding director of the Gatsby Computational Neuroscience Unit at University College London.
- Aapo Hyvärinen (University of Helsinki, Finland) is widely known for his contributions to the theory and applications of independent component analysis. His recent work also includes research on natural image statistics. He has

published in the major journals in the areas of neural networks and machine learning and his books have been translated into Japanese and Chinese.

– John Shawe-Taylor (University College London, UK) is Head of Department of Computer Science, and the scientific coordinator of the Network of Excellence in Pattern Analysis, Statistical Modelling and Computational Learning (PASCAL). His main research area is statistical learning theory, but his contributions range from neural networks and machine learning to graph theory. He is the co-author of two very successful books on the theory of support vector machines and kernel methods.

– Joshua Tenenbaum (Massachusetts Institute of Technology, USA) is a prominent researcher in the area of computational cognitive science. With his research group, he explores topics such as learning concepts, judging similarity, inferring causal connections, forming perceptual representations, and inferring mental states of other people.

A special plenary talk, shared with the co-located WSOM 2011, Workshop on Self-Organizing Maps, was given by Teuvo Kohonen, Academician of Science. He has introduced several new concepts to neural computing including theories of distributed associative memory and optimal associative mappings, the learning subspace method, the self-organizing maps (SOM), the learning vector quantization (LVQ), the adaptive-subspace SOM (ASSOM) in which invariant-feature filters emerge. Academician Teuvo Kohonen was the initiator and Chair of the first ICANN conference in 1991.

The technical program of ICANN 2011 consisted of 106 oral or poster presentations that highlighted key advances in the areas of neural networks and statistical machine learning research. The overall quality of the contributions can be considered high, also due to the high rejection rate. Approximately only every fourth submission was accepted to be presented orally in the conference. In addition to the regular conference sessions, one day was devoted to five workshops on topics related to theory and applications of brain-inspired computing and statistical machine learning. Two of the workshops were related to special challenges. A mind reading competition on MEG data was sponsored by the PASCAL network of excellence. The META-NET network of excellence sponsored a workshop on the use of context in machine translation.

The organizers had a chance to welcome the participants to the new Aalto University School of Science. From the beginning of 2010, the 100-year-old Helsinki University of Technology changed its name and form. It merged with Helsinki School of Economics and University of Art and Design Helsinki into Aalto University, becoming the second largest university in Finland. The conference was organized at Aalto University School of Science and the nearby Dipoli Congress Center. Both are centrally located in Otaniemi, Espoo, 15 minutes west of Helsinki. Otaniemi features a unique mix of world-class research organizations, academic institutions and over 800 companies from start-ups to multinational corporations operating around a compact campus. Otaniemi has been twice selected by the EU as one of the most innovative regions in Europe. It is a community of over 32,000 people with 16,000 students and 16,000 technology professionals.

We warmly thank all the authors of the contributed papers, workshop organizers and presenters. We also gratefully acknowledge the contribution of the plenary speakers whose presentations formed the backbone of the conference. We express our gratitude to the highly respected international Area Chairs and members of the Program Committee whose role was instrumental for the success of the conference. The Area Chairs, Program Committee members and the reviewers ensured a timely and thorough evaluation of the papers.

We are grateful to the members of the Executive Committee whose contributions were essential in ensuring the successful organization of the conference. Erkki Oja as the General Chair led the conference organizations with his great experience. Amaury Lendasse, the Local Chair, kept all details of the organization under control. Mari-Sanna Paukkeri committed a lot of work to compile the proceedings. Ilari Nieminen took care of numerous details in the arrangements, especially related to the review process and compilation of the proceedings. Laura Kainulainen efficiently handled the matters related to registrations in collaboration with the Aalto University staff. Jaakko Peltonen, the Publicity Chair, made sure that the conference was announced in all major forums. Alexander Ilin took good care of the workshop organizations. Francesco Corona as the Finance Chair ensured that the budget stayed in balance. Yoan Miche contributed in several practical areas in the arrangements including the Web. Ricardo Vigário was responsible for the social program and, in particular, the arrangements of the conference dinner. Tommi Vatanen organized the activities of the conference assistants and helped in preparing the evening program.

We are grateful to Microsoft Research whose representatives provided us with free access to their Conference Management Tool and helped in setting up the system. Last but not least, we would like to thank Springer for their co-operation in publishing the proceedings in the prestigious *Lecture Notes in Computer Science* series.

April 2011   Timo Honkela
                                                        Włodzisław Duch
                                                          Mark Girolami
                                                          Samuel Kaski

Organization

ICANN 2011 was held during June 14–17, 2011, organized by the Department of Information and Computer Science, Aalto University School of Science. The head of the department is Professor Olli Simula, who is a long-term member of the ENNS Executive Committee.

Executive Committee

General Chair — Erkki Oja (Aalto University, Finland)

Program Chairs — Włodzisław Duch (Nicolaus Copernicus University, Poland)

Mark Girolami (University College London, UK)

Timo Honkela (Aalto University, Finland)

Samuel Kaski (Aalto University, Finland)

Local Chair — Amaury Lendasse (Aalto University, Finland)

Publicity Chair — Jaakko Peltonen (Aalto University, Finland)

Area Chairs

Peter Auer (Austria)
Christian Bauckhage (Germany)
Wray Buntine (Australia)
Vince Calhoun (USA)
Antonius Coolen (UK)
Fernando Morgado Dias (Portugal)
Barbara Hammer (Germany)
Giulio Jacucci (Finland)
Kristian Kersting (Germany)
Neil Lawrence (UK)
Te-Won Lee (USA)
Mikko Kurimo (Finland)
Hiroshi Mamitsuka (Japan)
Klaus-Robert Müller (Germany)
Klaus Obermayer (Germany)
Cheng Soon Ong (Switzerland)

Jan Peters (Germany)
Marios Polycarpou (Cyprus)
Jose Principe (USA)
Volker Roth (Switzerland)
Craig Saunders (UK)
Masashi Sugiyama (Japan)
Alan Stocker (USA)
Ron Sun (USA)
Alfred Ultsch (Germany)
Peter Tino (UK)
Koen Van Leemput (USA)
Michel Verleysen (Belgium)
Jean-Philippe Vert (France)
Ole Winther (Denmark)
Chang Yoo (Korea)

Program Committee and Referees

Luis Alexandre (Portugal)
Paul Aljabar (UK)
Tanel Alumae (Estonia)
Mauricio Álvarez (UK)
Elisabeth Andre (Germany)
Alessia Annibale (UK)
Ana Antunes (Portugal)
Bruno Apolloni (Italy)
Ebru Arisoy (Turkey)
Beghdadi Azeddine (France)
Vineeth Balasubramaniam (USA)
Peter Battaglia (USA)
Luba Benuskova (New Zealand)
Ulysses Bernardet (Spain)
Monica Bianchini (Italy)
Ginestra Bianconi (USA)
Michael Biehl (The Netherlands)
Benjamin Blankertz (Germany)
Jamie Blundel (UK)
Antoine Bordes (Canada)
Abdeslam Boularias (Canada)
Mikio Braun (Germany)
Sebastien Bubeck (France)
Samuel Bulo (Italy)
Guido Caldarelli (Italy)
Cristina Campi (Finland)
Tonatiuh Peña Centeno (UK)
Michal Cernansky (Slovakia)
Jung-Hsien Chiang (Taiwan)
Jens Christian Claussen (Germany)
James Cussens (UK)
Jesse David (Belgium)
Lieven De Lathauwer (Belgium)
Andrea De Martino (Italy)
Yannick Deville (France)
Dotan Di Castro (Israel)
Jan Drugowitsch (France)
Lan Du (Australia)
Carl Ek (Sweden)
Deniz Erdogmus (USA)
Igor Farkas (Slovakia)
Jason Farquhar (The Netherlands)
Santo Fortunato (Italy)

Gernot Fink (Germany)
Benoit Frenay (Belgium)
Artu Garcez (UK)
Phil Garner (Switzerland)
Shuzhi Sam Ge (Singapore)
Mohammad Ghavamzadeh (France)
Fausto Giunchiglia (Italy)
Tobias Glasmachers (Switzerland)
Geoff Goodhill (Australia)
Dan Grollman (Switzerland)
Moritz Grosse-Wentrup (Germany)
Hirotaka Hachiya (Japan)
David Hardoon (UK)
Kohei Hatano (Japan)
Sebastien Helie (USA)
Ricardo Henao (Denmark)
James Hensman (UK)
Tom Heskes (The Netherlands)
Antti Honkela (Finland)
Naira Hovakimyan (USA)
Matthew Howard (UK)
Guang-Bin Huang (Singapore)
Zakria Hussain (UK)
Alexander Ilin (Finland)
Robert Jacob (USA)
Matjaz Jogan (USA)
Shivaram Kalyanakrishnan (USA)
Kittipat Kampa (USA)
Bert Kappen (The Netherlands)
Juha Karhunen (Finland)
Matthias Kaschube (USA)
Dietrich Klakow (Germany)
Stefanos Kollias (Greece)
Vera Kurkova (Hungary)
Ville Kyrki (Finland)
Jorma Laaksonen (Finland)
Harri Lahdesmäki (Finland)
Stéphane Lallich (France)
Georg Langs (France)
Jan Larsen (Denmark)
Robert Leeb (Switzerland)
Amaury Lendasse (Finland)
Weifeng Liu (USA)

Jyrki Lötjönen (Finland)
Mantas Lukosevicius (Germany)
Zhiyuan Luo (UK)
Mathew Magimai Doss (Switzerland)
Amir Madany Mamlouk (Germany)
Danilo Mandic (UK)
Naoki Masuda (Japan)
Bjoern Menze (USA)
Alessio Micheli (Italy)
Kazushi Mimura (Japan)
Tetsuro Morimura (Japan)
Morten Mørup (Denmark)
Alexander Mozeika (UK)
Christian Müller (Germany)
Shinichi Nakajima (Japan)
Sriraam Natarajan (USA)
Tim Nattkemper (Germany)
Yizhao Ni (UK)
Matthias Nickles (UK)
Nikolay Nikolaev (UK)
Ann Nowe (Belgium)
Ronald Ortner (Austria)
Erhan Oztop (Japan)
Sebastian Pannasch (Germany)
Ulrich Paquet (UK)
Il Park (USA)

Emilio Parrado (Spain)
Elzbieta Pekalska (UK)
Jaakko Peltonen (Finland)
Andrew Philippides (UK)
Justus Piater (Austria)
Alex Pouget (USA)
Novi Quadrianto (Australia)
Sabrina Rabello (USA)
Achim Rettinger (USA)
Alexis Roche (Switzerland)
Michael Rohs (Germany)
Fabrice Rossi (France)
Volker Roth (Switzerland)
Mert Sabuncu (USA)
Jun Sakuma (Japan)
Scott Sanner (Australia)
Ignacio Santamaria (Spain)
Murat Saraclar (Turkey)
Jagannathan Sarangapani (USA)

Mikkel Schmidt (Denmark)
Gerwin Schalk (USA)
Markus Schläpfer (Switzerland)
Benoit Scherrer (USA)
Mikkel Schmidt (Denmark)
Gabriele Schweikert (Germany)
Sambu Seo (Germany)
Sohan Seth (USA)
Vesa Siivola (Finland)
Sören Sonnenburg (Germany)
Emilio Soria-Olivas (Spain)
Alessandro Sperduti (Italy)
Jochen Steil (Germany)
Marc Strickert (Germany)
Taiji Suzuki (Japan)
Csaba Szepesvari (Canada)
Ichiro Takeuchi (Japan)
Michael Tangermann (Germany)
Franck Thollard (France)
Christian Thurau (Germany)
Michalis Titsias (UK)
Jussi Tohka (Finland)
Ryota Tomioka (Japan)
Antonios Tsourdos (UK)
Koji Tsuda (Japan)
Laurens van der Maaten
    (The Netherlands)
Carmen Vidaurre (Germany)
Ricardo Vigário (Finland)
Silvia Villa (Italy)
Nathalie Villa-Vialaneix (France)
Draguna Vrabie (USA)
Shinji Watanabe (Japan)
Markus Weimer (Germany)
Stefan Wermter (Germany)
Heiko Wersing (Germany)
Daan Wierstra (Switzerland)
Nick Wilson (UK)
Zhao Xu (Germany)
Zenglin Xu (Germany)
Makoto Yamada (Japan)
Yoshihiro Yamanishi (Japan)
Zhirong Yang (Finland)
Massimo Zancanaro (Italy)
Xinhua Zhang (Canada)
Shanfeng Zhu (China)

Table of Contents – Part I

Table of Contents – Part II

Transformation Equivariant Boltzmann Machines

Jyri J. Kivinen and Christopher K.I. Williams

Institute for Adaptive and Neural Computation
School of Informatics, University of Edinburgh, UK
j.j.kivinen@sms.ed.ac.uk, ckiw@inf.ed.ac.uk

Abstract. We develop a novel modeling framework for Boltzmann machines, augmenting each hidden unit with a latent transformation assignment variable which describes the selection of the transformed view of the canonical connection weights associated with the unit. This enables the inferences of the model to transform in response to transformed input data in a *stable and predictable* way, and avoids learning multiple features differing only with respect to the set of transformations. Extending prior work on translation equivariant (convolutional) models, we develop translation *and rotation* equivariant restricted Boltzmann machines (RBMs) and deep belief nets (DBNs), and demonstrate their effectiveness in learning frequently occurring statistical structure from artificial and natural images.

Keywords: Boltzmann machines, transformation equivariant representations, convolutional structures, transformation invariance, steerable filters, image modeling.

1 Introduction

We consider the problem of using DBN architectures to model the structure occurring in natural images. One of the desiderata for a computer vision system is that if the input image is transformed (e.g. by a translation of two pixels left), then the inferences made by the system should co-transform in a stable, and predictable way; this is termed *equivariance*. This behavior has been motivational in the development of steerable filters [1], and we argue that obtaining such transformation equivariant representations is important for the architectures that we are considering as well. *Translational* equivariance is readily built in by a convolutional architecture as found in neural networks [2,3], and more recently for RBMs see e.g. [4]. However, there are additional transformations that should be taken into account: in this paper we focus on equivariance with respect to in-plane *rotations*. Building in such property is important to avoid the system having to learn rotated versions of the same patterns at all levels in the network. For example in Fig. 2 of [4] many of the learned filters/ filter combinations shown are rotated versions of each other. The goal of this paper

T. Honkela et al. (Eds.): ICANN 2011, Part I, LNCS 6791, pp. 1–9, 2011.

is to build a DBN architecture that is translation and rotation equivariant. To do this we introduce a novel kind of rotational/steerable unit for Boltzmann machines, as described in section 2.

One of the inspirations for this paper is the work of Fidler and Leonardis [5], in which conjunctions of edge and bar (sine and cosine) Gabor features are built up into more complex patterns that occur frequently in the input image ensemble. Their architecture is translation and rotation invariant. However, their method does not define a generative model of images, but rather performs a layerwise grouping of features from layer $\ell - 1$ to create features at layer ℓ. This means that it is heavily dependent on various thresholds used in the learning algorithm, and also that it is unable to carry out bottom-up/top-down inference in the face of ambiguous input or missing data. We show how such translation and rotation invariant groupings arise naturally in a fully-specified multi-layer generative model.

2   Building in Transformation Equivariance

We first discuss the rotation-equivariant restricted Boltzmann machine (STEER-RBM) model which has one hidden layer; this hidden layer contains the 'steerable' units which are a particular feature of our architecture. Next in section 2.2 we describe a translation equivariant version of the model, and finally in section 2.3 generalize this to a deep belief net, which is the multi-hidden-layer generalization of the translation and rotation equivariant model.

2.1   Rotation Equivariant RBMs

The key feature of the STEER-RBM is the construction of the stochastic steerable hidden units, each of which combines a binary-valued activation variable h_j turning the unit on/off with an associated discrete-valued rotation variable r_j taking on possible states $k = 1, \ldots K$, whose effect is to in-plane rotate the weights of the unit by $360(k-1)/K$ degrees. Let $W_j(\cdot, 1)$ be the canonical pattern of weights connecting hidden unit h_j to visible units $\mathbf{v}$ under no rotation. The transformed weights $W_j(\cdot, k)$ for rotation k are derived from the canonical view using geometrical knowledge of in-plane rotations, so that

$$W_j(\cdot, k) = \mathbf{R}^{(k)} W_j(\cdot, 1) \quad \Rightarrow \quad W_j(i, k) = \sum_{\ell=1}^{D} R^{(k)}(i, \ell) W_j(\ell, 1), \qquad (1)$$

where $\mathbf{R}^{(k)}$ is a *fixed* $D \times D$ transformation matrix applying an in-plane rotation of $360(k-1)/K$ degrees, and D denotes the number of pixels/visible units in $\mathbf{v}$. Note that by choosing K large we can approximate rotations to any desired accuracy. An example of this rotation in action is shown in the top row of Figure 1. In our implementation, we bilinearly interpolate the weights into their new locations, such that each of the elements in the rotated view is computed as a convex combination of (maximally) four neighboring rotated canonical weights, each of which have been rotated about the center of the canonical weights plane[1]. Thus each row of the rotation matrices contains maximally four non-zero elements which sum to one.

Given this architecture, the joint probability density of a STEER-RBM model consisting of visible units $\mathbf{v}$ and binary hidden units $(\mathbf{h}, \mathbf{r})$ is given by the Boltzmann-distribution $p(\mathbf{v}, \mathbf{h}, \mathbf{r} \mid \theta) \propto \exp\{-\mathrm{E}(\mathbf{v}, \mathbf{h}, \mathbf{r} \mid \theta)\}$ with the following energy, assuming continuous, conditionally Gaussian units:[2]

$$\mathrm{E}(\mathbf{v}, \mathbf{h}, \mathbf{r} \mid \theta) = \sum_i \frac{v_i^2 - 2av_i}{2\sigma^2} - \sum_j h_j b_j - \frac{1}{\sigma} \sum_j h_j \sum_i v_i W_j(i, r_j) \qquad (2)$$

where $\theta = \{\mathbf{a}, \mathbf{b}, \mathbf{W}, \sigma\}$ consist of hidden unit biases $\mathbf{b}$, visible unit biases $\mathbf{a}$, connection weights $\mathbf{W}$, and the standard deviation of the Gaussian conditional distributions of the visible units σ. The energy function for binary visible units can be obtained by removing the quadratic term v_i^2, and setting σ to unity. As $W_j(i, r_j) = \sum_{k=1}^{K} \delta(k, r_j) W_j(i, k)$, the model defines a mixture of RBMs, but in contrast with the implicit mixture RBM model of [6], there is parameter sharing between the mixture components due to rotation equivariance. Although we have described the RBMs of above, extensions of other energy-based models to use rotational units could be also considered, such as conditionally full-covariance Gaussian models [7].

2.2   Rotation and Translation Equivariant RBMs

To learn models for whole images, a translation equivariant extension of the STEER-RBM is used, assuming a reduced connectivity structure so that a hidden unit h_j is connected to a subset of visible units specified by a receptive field system, and parameter sharing is used so that the responses of units to a stimulus are translation equivariant. We call the hidden units sharing these parameters a *feature plane*. To extend convolutional RBMs, the STEER-RBM also adds input rotation equivariance to hidden unit activation. Thus we consider a weight kernel ω_α for feature plane α, which is sufficient to define the connection weights between the hidden units in feature layer α and the visible units. The energy function for the convolutional STEER-RBM is then

$$\mathrm{E}(\mathbf{v}, \mathbf{h}, \mathbf{r} \mid \theta) = \sum_i \frac{v_i^2 - 2av_i}{2\sigma^2} - \sum_{\alpha, j} h_{\alpha j} \left(b_\alpha + \frac{1}{\sigma} \sum_{\ell \in \mathrm{N}_{\alpha j}} v_\ell \, \omega_\alpha(d(j, \ell), r_{\alpha j}) \right) \qquad (3)$$

where a is visible unit layer bias, b_α is the bias for hidden unit feature plane α, $\mathrm{N}_{\alpha j}$ indexes the visible units within the receptive field of hidden unit $h_{\alpha j}$, σ defines the standard deviation of the univariate Gaussian conditional distribution

---

[1] To avoid boundary artifacts with non-circular receptive fields, one can zero pad the canonical weights plane such that each of the rotated canonical weights are within the boundaries defined by the extended plane for any rotation angle.

[2] The joint probability density of the visible units conditional on the hidden units and model parameters factorizes as a multivariate spherical-covariance Gaussian.

$p(v_i \mid \mathbf{h}, \mathbf{r}, \theta)$, and $d(j,i)$ computes the spatial-offset dependent index of the weight kernel weight that is used to connect hidden unit h_j to v_i.

2.3   Rotation and Translation Equivariant Deep Belief Nets

To learn higher-level patterns from images, we follow the DBN approach of [8], stacking multiple layers of convolutional STEER-RBMs on top of each other. In this model, each of the hidden units in a higher level STEER-RBM is connected to a subset of the hidden units in each of the feature planes in the hidden layer below, again via by a receptive field system. As both the higher and lower level units are rotational, we now need a *triply* indexed weight parameter $w_{\ell-1_\beta}^{\ell\alpha}(j,m,k)$ which connects a unit in feature plane α in layer ℓ to feature plane β in layer $\ell-1$ below. Here j denotes the spatial offset, while m and k index the rotational states in the lower and higher layers respectively. Thus the energy function between layers ℓ and $\ell-1$ is of the following form:

$$E\left(\mathbf{h}^{\ell-1}, \mathbf{r}^{\ell-1}, \mathbf{h}^\ell, \mathbf{r}^\ell \mid \theta^\ell\right) = -\sum_\beta b_\beta^{\ell-1} \sum_i h_{\beta i}^{\ell-1} - \sum_\alpha b_\alpha^\ell \sum_j h_{\alpha j}^\ell$$
$$-\sum_\alpha \sum_j h_{\alpha j}^\ell \sum_\beta \sum_{i \in N_{\alpha j}^\ell} h_{\beta i}^{\ell-1} w_{\ell-1_\beta}^{\ell\alpha}(d(j,i), r_{\beta i}^{\ell-1}, r_{\alpha j}^\ell). \quad (4)$$

The computation of the transformed weights for these higher hidden layers has to be different from that of the first layer, since changing the rotational state of a higher level pattern needs to rotate the lower level rotational states/patterns accordingly. The transformations for each feature can be again done by knowledge using fixed transformation operators, by first in-plane rotating the lower-level rotation-specific canonical weight matrix slices, and then circularly shifting the dimensions of the resulting matrix. The non-canonical view of a level ℓ weight kernel can be thus written as follows:

$$w_{\ell-1_\beta}^{\ell\alpha}(j,m,k) = \sum_{\rho=1}^K \mathbf{S}^{(k)}(\rho,m) \sum_\delta R^{(k)}(j,\delta) w_{\ell-1_\beta}^{\ell\alpha}(\delta,\rho,1), \quad (5)$$

where $\mathbf{S}^{(k)}$ is a *fixed* $K \times K$ binary matrix applying a circular shift (of $k-1$ shifts) forward to the columns of $\mathbf{R}^{(k)} w_{\ell-1_\beta}^{\ell\alpha}(\cdot,\cdot,1)$.

3   Inference and Learning in the Models

As with standard RBMs, the conditional distributions of the hidden units are independent given $\mathbf{v}$ for the convolutional STEER-RBM. Thus we have for (3) that $p(\mathbf{h},\mathbf{r} \mid \mathbf{v},\theta) = \prod_\alpha \prod_j p(h_{\alpha j} \mid \mathbf{v},\theta)\, p(r_{\alpha j} \mid h_{\alpha j},\mathbf{v},\theta)$, where

$$p(h_{\alpha j} \mid \mathbf{v},\theta) = \frac{\sum_{k=1}^K \exp\left\{h_{\alpha j}\left(b_\alpha + \frac{1}{\sigma}\sum_{\ell \in N_{\alpha j}} v_\ell w_\alpha(d(j,\ell),k)\right)\right\}}{K + \sum_{k=1}^K \exp\left\{b_\alpha + \frac{1}{\sigma}\sum_{\ell \in N_{\alpha j}} v_\ell w_\alpha(d(j,\ell),k)\right\}}, \quad (6)$$

$$p(r_{\alpha j} \mid h_{\alpha j} = 1, \mathbf{v}, \theta) = \frac{\exp\left\{b_\alpha + \frac{1}{\sigma}\sum_{\ell \in N_{\alpha j}} v_\ell w_\alpha(d(j, \ell), r_{\alpha j})\right\}}{\sum_{k=1}^{K} \exp\left\{b_\alpha + \frac{1}{\sigma}\sum_{\ell \in N_{\alpha j}} v_\ell w_\alpha(d(j, \ell), k)\right\}}. \qquad (7)$$

The key quantity in this computation is $a_{\alpha j}(k) = \sum_{\ell \in N_{\alpha j}} v_\ell\, w_\alpha(d(j, \ell), k)$ which computes the dot product of the visible variables in $N_{\alpha j}$ with weight kernel w_α at rotation k. (6) evaluates a nonlinear combination of these quantities summed over k compared to K in order to compute $p(h_{\alpha j} \mid \mathbf{v}, \theta)$. Similarly in (7) $p(r_{\alpha j} \mid h_{\alpha j} = 1, \mathbf{v}, \theta)$ is computed based on the relative strengths of the $a_{\alpha j}(k)$ terms. For a multi-layer network a crude approximation to full inference is to sample from the learned STEER-RBMs layerwise from bottom to top. More sophisticated alternatives are possible, such as the up-down algorithm described in [8], or e.g. some other Markov chain Monte Carlo sampling methods.

As usual with DBNs we learn the parameters of the models layer-wise. We have used stochastic gradient-descent based methods to train the models in the experiments, optimizing an objective function consisting of a data fit term, plus a term that encourages sparsity[3]. For a datafit term based on the log likelihood L, the gradient wrt a parameter θ is given by $\frac{\partial L}{\partial \theta} = \langle\frac{\partial E}{\partial \theta}\rangle^+ - \langle\frac{\partial E}{\partial \theta}\rangle^-$, where $\langle \cdot \rangle^+$ denotes expectation with the training data clamped, and $\langle \cdot \rangle^-$ the unclamped phase. In fact we generally use the contrastive divergence CD-1 approximation to the negative phase. To understand how the model learns under optimization, it is instructive to consider the partial derivatives of the energy function with respect to the canonical features. Assuming the model of (3), we have that

$$\frac{\partial E(\mathbf{v}, \mathbf{h}, \mathbf{r} \mid \theta)}{\partial w_\alpha(\delta, 1)} = -\frac{1}{\sigma}\sum_j h_{\alpha j} \sum_{\ell \in N_{\alpha j}} v_\ell\, R^{(r_{\alpha j})}(d(j, \ell), \delta). \qquad (8)$$

This has the effect of multiplying the visible pattern in $N_{\alpha j}$ by $(\mathbf{R}^{(r_{\alpha j})})^T$. As this is a close approximation to applying a reverse rotation, patterns which are detected to be present in a non-canonical orientation, are rotated 'back' into the canonical view, in which the feature-specific canonical statistics are then updated. The learning is similar for the higher layer models, where the alignment also takes into account the lower unit's rotation assignment. Partial derivatives with respect to the biases take the standard forms.

4 Experiments

We first learnt RBM models (3) from a set of whitened natural images [9] using CD-1 learning[4]. Fig. 1 (left, top) shows the type of feature consistently learnt

---

[3] Non-sparsity is penalized proportional to a sum of feature-plane specific cross-entropies, each between a Bernoulli target distribution, and the distribution recording the average probability of a unit being off or on at the plane, similar to [6].

[4] σ was set close to the data standard deviation. The total target activation for sparsity encouragement was 0.1.

Rotational Views of a Feature   3 Features

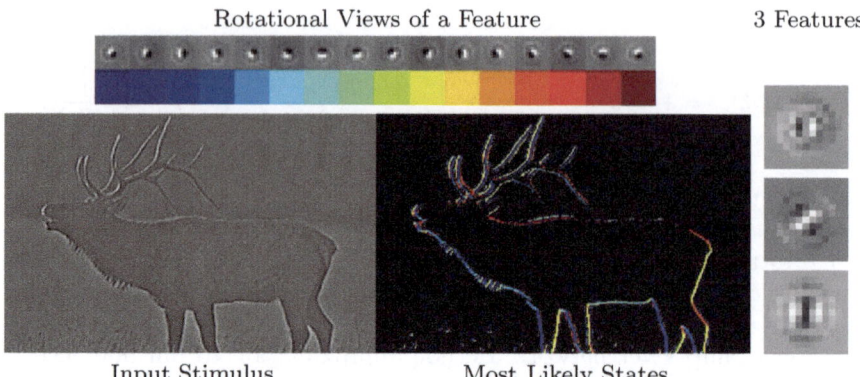

Input Stimulus   Most Likely States

Fig. 1. Left-top: Learned feature at various orientiations (with receptive field diameter = 9). Left-bottom: Whitened natural image region, and most likely unit states (colour-coded according to rotation). Right: Weights of the learned set of 3 features.

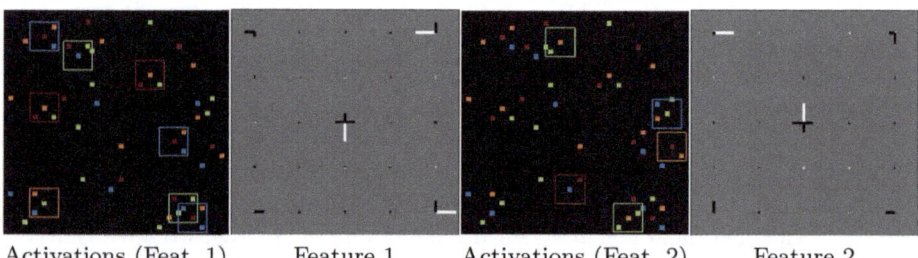

Activations (Feat. 1)   Feature 1   Activations (Feat. 2)   Feature 2

Fig. 2. Features learned from rotation colour-coded ($\rightarrow$, $\uparrow$,$\leftarrow$,$\downarrow$) artificial data containing rotated, randomly placed instances of two rotational shapes, in clutter. Panels 1 and 3 show the data, with the respective higher level features denoted by bounding boxes of the units' receptive field size centered on the unit location, and coloured according to the rotation assignment. In panels 2 and 4 the 5×5 canonical weight kernels are visualized using oriented black/white line segments, placed to start from an evenly spaced grid. The grid locations denote the spatial offsets for the weight kernels weights, the different orientations index the lower-level rotational states, the segment lengths denote the weight magnitude, and colour denoting the sign with black denoting a negative, and white denoting positive a weight. (Essentially this extends the Hinton plot to deal with (multi-way-)oriented weights).

as the most significant, at various rotations. This is an "edge detector", similar to the features found e.g. in [4] at various orientations. The bottom row shows a natural image patch, and most likely states colour-coded according to orientation, at each location. The responses occur at edge-like structures; notice the steady rotational response change, e.g. while tracing the outline of the central object. We have also trained this model with several feature planes; results using three are shown (right). To validate the higher-layer learning we first considered modeling artificial rotational pattern data simulating first-layer responses. Fig. 2 shows input patterns; the four colours denote four different orientation

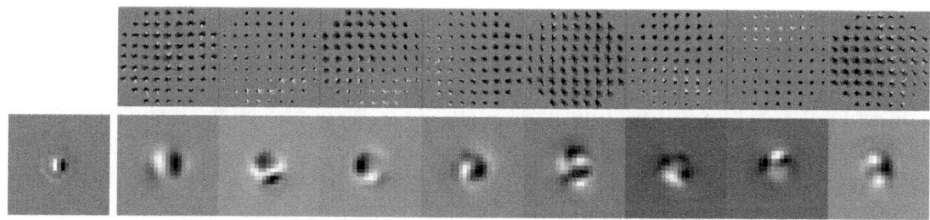

Fig. 3. (Top) The second layer weights (displayed as in Fig. 2) for 8 second-layer features. (Bottom) The first panel shows the first-layer basis feature; the other panels show the (linearly combined) first layer basis projections of the 8 features.

responses. There are two patterns in the noisy data, one consisting of 3 active inputs, and the other of 2. These are successfully learned, see panels 2 and 4, and the caption for more details. We have also applied the learning to the natural images, using the single edge-like feature in the first layer. The results (see Fig. 3) show this yields higher-order conjunctions of this feature, such as extended and curved edges, and intersections. Note that these features are similar to SIFT-descriptors [10], but in a generative framework.

5   Related Work

We have discussed above the work of Fidler and Leonardis [5]. The work of Zhu *et. al.* [11] is similar to [5], except that there is a top-down stage to the learning process (but not in the given the inference algorithm) to fill in missing parts of the hierarchy. Both papers use hand-crafted algorithms for detecting groupings of lower-level features, involving various thresholds. In contrast we formulate the problem as a standard DBN learning algorithm, but build in transformation equivariance. One advantage of the DBN is that it is naturally set up for bottom-up/top-down inference in the face of ambiguity or missing data.

The orientation-adapted Gaussian scale mixture (OAGSM) model [12] describes how a Gaussian model for a wavelet coefficient responses corresponding to an image patch can be augmented with latent variables to handle signal amplitude and dominant orientation. This allows e.g. modelling of oriented texture at arbitrary rotations. The learned edge filters at the first level of our model are analogous to the wavelet responses, while our second level units model the correlations between the coefficients. However, note (i) that the OAGSM model is only a model for patches not entire images, and (ii) that it does not provide a mixture model over the types of higher-level regularity, e.g. lines, corners, T-junctions etc. On the other hand the real-valued modelling of wavelet coefficients by OAGSM is more powerful than the binary activations of units in the STEER-DBN.

Our goal is to build in equivariance to known (translational and rotational) transformations. In contrast Memisevic and Hinton [13] describe how to *learn* transformations based on pairs of training images using factored 3-way Boltzmann machines. Such a network could be used in to identify rotated versions of a given pattern, e.g. by fixing a reference version of the pattern and inferring the transformation. However, it seems rather excessive to learn the machinery for this when it can be built in. Our work should not be confused with the directional unit Boltzmann machine (DUBM) network of Zemel *et al* [14]. Although DUBM units contain a rotational variable, this is not used to model relative rotations of subcomponents. For example in [15] the authors present a convolutional architecture where the rotational variable denotes the phase of an oscillator, relating to the theory of binding-by-synchrony.

6   Discussion

As we have shown, the STEER-DBN architecture handles translation and rotation invariances. The other natural transformation to consider is image scaling. However, this can be relatively easily handled by the standard computer vision method of downsampling the input image by various factors, and applying the similar processing to each scale. Higher layers at a given scale can also take inputs from various scales. Alternatively one could introduce scaling assignment variables for each unit similar to the ones for rotation, scaling the features.

Other future work includes learning more hidden layers, and using more expressive bottom-layer models, such as those allowing dependent Gaussian distributions for the visibles conditional on the hidden units [7].

Acknowledgements. JJK is partially funded by a SICSA studentship. This work is supported in part by the IST Programme of the European Community, under the PASCAL2 Network of Excellence, IST-2007- 216886. This publication only reflects the authors' views.

References

1. Simoncelli, E.P., Freeman, W.T., Adelson, E.H., Heeger, D.J.: Shiftable multi-scale transforms. IEEE Trans. IT 38, 587–607 (1992)
2. Waibel, A., Hanazawa, T., Hinton, G.E., Shikano, K., Lang, K.: Phoneme recognition using Time Delay Neural Networks. IEEE Trans. ASSP 37, 328–339 (1989)
3. LeCun, Y., Bottou, L., Bengio, Y., Haffner, P.: Gradient-based learning applied to document recognition. Proc. IEEE 86, 2278–2324 (1998)
4. Lee, H., Grosse, R., Ranganath, R., Ng, A.Y.: Convolutional deep belief networks for scalable unsupervised learning of hierarchical representations. In: ICML (2009)
5. Fidler, S., Leonardis, A.: Towards scalable representations of visual categories: Learning a hierarchy of parts. In: CVPR (2007)
6. Nair, V., Hinton, G.E.: 3D object recognition using deep belief nets. In: NIPS 22 (2009)
7. Ranzato, M., Mnih, V., Hinton, G.E.: Generating more realistic images using gated MRF's. In: NIPS 23 (2010)
8. Hinton, G.E., Osindero, S., Teh, Y.W.: A fast learning algorithm for deep belief nets. Neural Comp. 18, 1527–1554 (2006)

9. Olshausen, B.A., Field, D.J.: Emergence of simple-cell receptive field properties by learning a sparse code for natural images. Nature 381, 607–609 (1996)
10. Lowe, D.G.: Distinctive image features from scale–invariant keypoints. IJCV 60, 91–110 (2004)
11. Zhu, L., Lin, C., Huang, H., Chen, Y., Yuille, A.: Unsupervised structure learning: Hierarchical recursive composition, suspicious coincidence and competitive exclusion. In: ECCV (2008)
12. Hammond, D., Simoncelli, E.P.: Image modelling and denoising with orientation-adapted Gaussian scale mixtures. IEEE Trans. IP 17, 2089–2101 (2008)
13. Memisevic, R., Hinton, G.E.: Learning to represent spatial transformations with factored higher-order Boltzmann machines. Neural Comp. 22, 1473–1492 (2010)
14. Zemel, R.S., Williams, C.K.I., Mozer, M.C.: Lending direction to neural networks. Neural Networks 8, 503–512 (1995)
15. Mozer, M.C., Zemel, R.S., Behrmann, M., Williams, C.K.I.: Learning to segment images using dynamic feature binding. Neural Comp. 4, 650–665 (1992)

Improved Learning of Gaussian-Bernoulli Restricted Boltzmann Machines

KyungHyun Cho, Alexander Ilin, and Tapani Raiko

Department of Information and Computer Science
Aalto University School of Science, Finland
firstname.lastname@aalto.fi

Abstract. We propose a few remedies to improve training of Gaussian-Bernoulli restricted Boltzmann machines (GBRBM), which is known to be difficult. Firstly, we use a different parameterization of the energy function, which allows for more intuitive interpretation of the parameters and facilitates learning. Secondly, we propose parallel tempering learning for GBRBM. Lastly, we use an adaptive learning rate which is selected automatically in order to stabilize training. Our extensive experiments show that the proposed improvements indeed remove most of the difficulties encountered when training GBRBMs using conventional methods.

Keywords: Restricted Boltzmann Machine, Gaussian-Bernoulli Restricted Boltzmann Machine, Adaptive Learning Rate, Parallel Tempering.

1 Introduction

Conventional restricted Boltzmann machines (RBM) [1,17] define the state of each neuron to be binary, which seriously limits their application area. One popular approach to address this problem is to replace the binary visible neurons with the Gaussian ones. The corresponding model is called Gaussian-Bernoulli RBM (GBRBM) [8]. Unfortunately, training GBRBM is known to be a difficult task (see, e.g. [9,11,12]).

In this paper, we propose a few improvements to the conventional training methods for GBRBMs to overcome the existing difficulties. The improvements include another parameterization of the energy function, parallel tempering learning, which has previously been used for ordinary RBMs [6,5,3], and the use of an adaptive learning rate, similarly to [2].

2 Gaussian-Bernoulli RBM

The energy of GBRBM [8] with real-valued visible neurons $\mathbf{v}$ and binary hidden neurons $\mathbf{h}$ is traditionally defined as

$$E(\mathbf{v}, \mathbf{h}|\theta) = \sum_{i=1}^{n_v} \frac{(v_i - b_i)^2}{2\sigma_i^2} - \sum_{i=1}^{n_v}\sum_{j=1}^{n_h} W_{ij} h_j \frac{v_i}{\sigma_i} - \sum_{j=1}^{n_h} c_j h_j, \qquad (1)$$

where b_i and c_j are biases corresponding to hidden and visible neurons, respectively, W_{ij} are weights connecting visible and hidden neurons, and σ_i is the standard deviation associated with a Gaussian visible neuron v_i (see e.g. [11]).

T. Honkela et al. (Eds.): ICANN 2011, Part I, LNCS 6791, pp. 10–17, 2011.

The traditional gradient-based update rules are obtained by taking the partial derivative of the log-likelihood function $\log \sum_{\mathbf{h}} \exp(-E(\mathbf{v}, \mathbf{h}|\theta))$, in which the hidden neurons are marginalized out, with respect to each model parameter. However, training GBRBMs even using well-defined gradients is generally difficult and takes long time (see, e.g., [11,12]). One of the main difficulties is learning the variance parameters σ_i, which are, unlike other parameters, are constrained to be positive. Therefore, in many existing works, those parameters are often fixed to unity [9,11,15].

3   Improved Learning of Gaussian-Bernoulli RBM

3.1   New Parameterization of the Energy Function

The traditional energy function in (1) yields somewhat unintuitive conditional distribution in which the noise level defined by σ_i affects the conditional mean of the visible neuron. In order to change this, we use a different energy function:

$$E(\mathbf{v}, \mathbf{h}|\theta) = \sum_{i=1}^{n_v} \frac{(v_i - b_i)^2}{2\sigma_i^2} - \sum_{i=1}^{n_v} \sum_{j=1}^{n_h} W_{ij} h_j \frac{v_i}{\sigma_i^2} - \sum_{j=1}^{n_h} c_j h_j. \tag{2}$$

Under the modified energy function, the conditional probabilities for each visible and hidden neurons given the others are

$$p(v_i = v|\mathbf{h}) = \mathcal{N}\left(v \mid b_i + \sum_j h_j W_{ij}, \sigma_i^2\right),$$

$$p(h_j = 1|\mathbf{v}) = \mathrm{sigmoid}\left(c_j + \sum_i W_{ij} \frac{v_i}{\sigma_i^2}\right),$$

where $\mathcal{N}(\cdot \mid \mu, \sigma^2)$ denotes the Gaussian probability density function with mean μ and variance σ^2. The update rules for the parameters are, then,

$$\nabla W_{ij} = \left\langle \frac{1}{\sigma_i^2} v_i h_j \right\rangle_d - \left\langle \frac{1}{\sigma_i^2} v_i h_j \right\rangle_m, \tag{3}$$

$$\nabla b_i = \left\langle \frac{1}{\sigma_i^2} v_i \right\rangle_d - \left\langle \frac{1}{\sigma_i^2} v_i \right\rangle_m, \tag{4}$$

$$\nabla c_j = \langle h_j \rangle_d - \langle h_j \rangle_m, \tag{5}$$

where a shorthand notations $\langle \cdot \rangle_d$ and $\langle \cdot \rangle_m$ denote the expectation computed over the data and model distributions accordingly [1].

Additionally, we use a different parameterization of the variance parameters: $\sigma_i^2 = e^{z_i}$. Since we learn log-variances $z_i = \log \sigma_i^2$, σ_i is naturally constrained to stay positive. Thus, the learning rate can be chosen with less difficulty. Under the modified energy function, the gradient with respect to z_i is

$$\nabla z_i = e^{-z_i} \left(\left\langle \frac{1}{2}(v_i - b_i)^2 - \sum_j v_i h_j w_{ij} \right\rangle_d - \left\langle \frac{1}{2}(v_i - b_i)^2 - \sum_j v_i h_j w_{ij} \right\rangle_m \right).$$

3.2 Parallel Tempering

Parallel tempering (PT) learning. However, applying the same methodology to GBRBM is not straightforward: For example, a naive approach of multiplying σ_i with the temperature results in the base model with zero variances for the visible neurons, or scaling the energy function by temperature would yield infinite variances. Here, we follow the methodology of [3].

In order to overcome this problem, we propose a new scheme for constructing the intermediate models with inverse temperatures β such that

$$W_{ij}^{(t)} = \beta W_{ij}, \qquad\qquad b_i^{(t)} = \beta b_i + (1 - \beta)m_i,$$

$$c_j^{(t)} = \beta c_j, \qquad\qquad \sigma_i^{(\beta)} = \sqrt{\beta \sigma_i^2 + (1 - \beta)s_i^2},$$

where W_{ij}, b_i and c_j are the parameters of the current model, and m_i and s_i^2 are the overall mean and variance of the i-th visible component in the training data.

The intermediate model is thus an interpolation between the base model and the current model, where the base model consists of independent Gaussian variables fitted to the training data.

3.3 Adaptive Learning Rate

Many recent papers [2,16,7] point out that training RBM is sensitive to the choice of learning rate η and its scheduling. According to our experience, GBRBM tends to be even more sensitive to this choice compared to RBM. It will be shown later that, if the learning rate is not annealed towards zero, GBRBM can easily diverge in the late stage of learning.

The adaptive learning rate proposed in [2] addresses the problem of automatic choice of the learning rate. The adaptation scheme proposed there is based on an approximation of the likelihood that is valid only for small enough learning rates. In this work, we use the same adaptive learning rate strategy but we introduce an upper-bound for the learning rate so that the approximation does not become too crude.

4 Experiments

In all the experiments, we used the following settings. The weights were initialized to uniform random values between $\pm\frac{1}{n_v + n_h}$. Biases b_i and c_j were initialized to zero and variances σ_i to ones. Adaptive learning rate candidates (see [2]) were $\{0.9\eta, \eta, 1.1\eta\}$, where η is the previous learning rate. In PT learning, we used 21 equally spaced $\beta \in \{0, 0.05, \ldots, 1\}$, and in CD learning, we used a single Gibbs step.

4.1 Learning Faces

The CBCL data [13] used in the experiment contains 2,429 faces and 4,548 non-faces as training set and 472 faces and 23,573 non-faces as test set. Only the faces from the training set of the CBCL data were used.

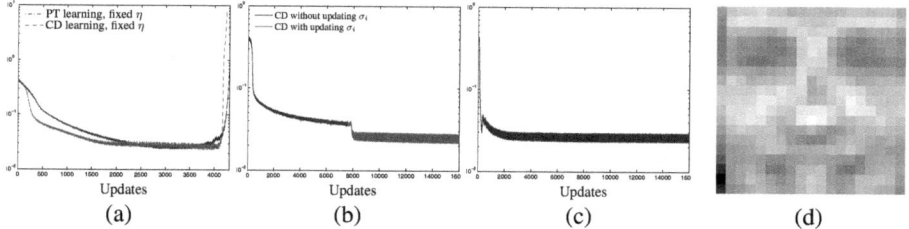

Fig. 1. (a)-(c): The reconstruction errors obtained by training GBRBM using a learning rate fixed to 0.001 (a), with the adaptive learning rate while updating variances from the 650-th epoch using CD learning (b) and using PT learning (c). (d): Visualization of the learned variances.

In the first experiment, we trained two GBRBMs with 256 hidden neurons using both CD and PT learning with the learning rate fixed to 0.001 while updating all parameters including σ_i^2. As can be observed from Fig. 1(a), learning diverged in both cases (CD and PT learning), which is manifested in the increasing reconstruction error. This result confirms that GBRBMs are sensitive to the learning rate scheduling. The divergence became significant when the variances decreased significantly (not shown in Fig. 1(a)), indirectly indicating that the sensitivity is related to learning the variances.

Learning Variances is Important. We again trained GBRBMs with 256 hidden neurons by CD and PT learning. The upper-bound and the initial learning rate were set to 0.01 and 0.0001, respectively.

Initially, the variances of the visible neurons were not updated, but fixed to 1. The training was performed for 650 epochs. Afterwards, the training was continued for 1000 epochs, however, with updating variances.

Fig. 2(a) shows the learned filters and the samples generated from the GBRBM after the first round of training. The reconstruction error nearly converged (see the blue curve of Fig. 1(b)), but it is clear to see that both the filters and the samples are very noisy. However, the continued training significantly reduced the noise from the filters and the samples, as shown in Fig. 2(b).

From Fig. 1(b), it is clear that learning variances decreased the reconstruction error significantly. The explanation could be that the GBRBM has learned the importance, or noisiness, of pixels so that it focuses on the important ones.

The visualization of the learned variances in Fig. 1(d) reveals that important parts for modeling the face , for example, eyes and mouth, have lower variances while those of other parts are higher. Clearly, since the important parts are rather well modeled, the noise levels of corresponding visible neurons are lower.

Parallel Tempering. In order to see if the proposed scheme of PT learning works well with GBRBM, an additional experiment using PT learning was conducted under the same setting, however, now updating the variances from the beginning.

The observation of Fig. 1(c) suggests that learning variances from the beginning helps. It is notable that the learning did not diverge as the adaptive learning rate could anneal the learning rate appropriately.

The samples were generated from the trained GBRBM. Comparing the samples in the right figures of Fig. 2(a)–(c) suggests that the GBRBM trained using PT learning

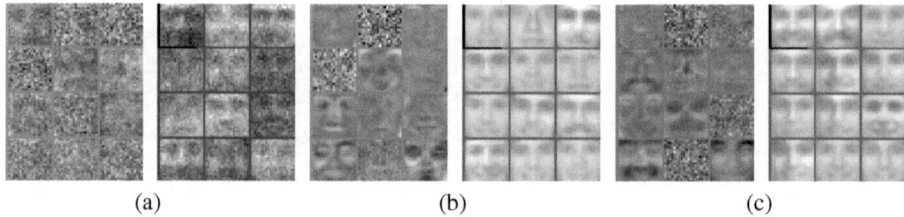

(a)   (b)   (c)

Fig. 2. Example filters (left) and samples (right) generated by GBRBM trained using CD learning without updating variances (a), continued with updating variances (b), and trained using PT learning with updating variances from the beginning (c). 12 randomly chosen filters are shown, and between each consecutive samples 1000 Gibbs sampling steps were performed.

provides more variety of distinct samples, which indirectly suggests that the better generative model was learned by PT learning.

4.2   Learning Natural Images

CIFAR-10 data set [11] consists of three-channel (R, G, B) color images of size 32×32 with ten different labels.

Learning Image Patches. In this experiment, the procedure proposed in [14] is roughly followed which was successfully used for classification tasks [11,12,4]. The procedure, first, trains a GBRBM on small image patches.

Two GBRBMs, each with 300 hidden neurons, following the modified energy function were trained on 8×8 images patches using CD and PT learning for 300 and 200 epochs, respectively.

Fig. 3 visualizes the filters learned by the GBRBMs. Apparently, the filters with the large norms mostly learn the global structure of the patches, whereas those with smaller norms tend to model more fine details. It is notable that this behavior is more obvious in the case of PT learning, whereas in the case of CD learning, the filters with the small norms mostly learned not-so-useful global structures.

The learned variances σ_i^2 of different pixels i were distributed in [0.0308 0.0373] and [0.0283 0.0430] in case of CD and PT learning. In both cases, they were smaller than those of the training samples s_i^2, lying between 0.0547 and 0.0697. This was expected and is desirable [11].

Classifying Natural Images. The image patches were preprocessed with independent component analysis (ICA) [10] and were transformed to vectors of 64 independent components each. Then, they were used as training data for GBRBMs. GBRBMs had 200 or 300 binary hidden neurons, and were trained by persistent CD learning [18] with a fixed learning rate $\eta = 0.005$ and variances fixed to one. The minibatch of size 20 was used, and we denote this model ICA+GBRBM.

Afterwards, 49 patches were extracted from each image in a convolutional way, and the hidden activations were obtained for each patch. Those activations were concatenated to form a feature vector which was used for training a logistic regression classifier.

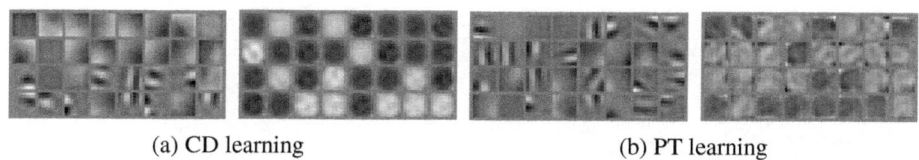

        (a) CD learning   (b) PT learning

Fig. 3. (a) two figures visualize 128 filters with the largest norms and 128 filters with the smallest norms of the GBRBM trained using CD learning, and (b) same figures obtained from PT learning

The best classification accuracy of 63.75% was achieved with ICA+GBRBM having 64 independent components and 300 hidden neurons after training the GBRBM for only about 35 epochs. The obtained accuracy is comparable to the accuracies from the previous research. Some of them using the variants of RBM include 63.78% by GBRBM with whitening [11], and 68.2% obtained by the mean and covariance RBM with principal component analysis [14].

Also, slightly worse accuracies were achieved when the raw pixels of the image patches were used. Using the filters obtained in the previous experiment, 55.20% (CD) and 57.42% (PT) were obtained. This suggests that it is important to preprocess samples appropriately.

Learning Whole Images. Due to the difficulty in training GBRBM, only data sets with comparably small dimensions have been mainly used in various recent papers. In case of CIFAR-10 the GBRBM was unable to learn any meaningful filters from whole images in [11].

In this experiment, a GRBM with 4000 hidden neurons was trained on whole images of CIFAR-10. It was expected that learning the variances, which became easier due to the proposed improvements, would encourage GBRBM to learn interesting interior features. CD learning with the adaptive learning rate was used. The initial learning rate and the upper-bound were set to 0.001. The training lasted for 70 epochs, and the minibatch of size 128 was used.

As shown in Fig. 4(a) the filters with the large norms tend to model the global features such as the position of the object, whereas the filters with the smaller norms model fine details, which coincides with the filters of the image patches. It is notable that the visualized filters do not possess those global, noisy filters (see Fig. 2.1 of [11]).

This visualization shows that the proposed improvements in training GBRBMs prevents the problem raised in [12] that a GBRBM easily fails to model the whole images by focusing mostly on the boundary pixels only.

Also, according to the evolution of the reconstruction error in Fig. 4(c), the learning proceeded stably. The red curve in the same plot suggests that the adaptive learning rate was able to anneal the learning rate automatically.

Looking at Fig. 4(b), it is clear that the GBRBM was able to capture the essence of the training samples. The reconstructed images look like the blurred versions of the original ones while maintaining the overall structures. Apparently, both the boundary and the interior structure are rather well maintained.

Fig. 4. (a): Two figures visualize 16 filters each with the largest norms (left) and the least norms (right) of the GBRBM trained on the whole images of CIFAR-10. (b): Two figures visualize original images (left) and their reconstructions (right). (c): The evolution of the reconstruction error and the learning rate.

5   Discussion

Based on the widely used GBRBM, we proposed a modified GBRBM which uses a different parameterization of the energy function. The modification led to the perhaps more elegant forms for visible and hidden conditional distributions given each other and gradient update rules.

We, then, applied two recent advances in training an RBM, PT learning and the adaptive learning rate, to a GBRBM. The new scheme of defining the tempered distributions for applying PT learning to GBRBM was proposed. The difficulty of preventing the divergence of learning was shown to be addressed by the adaptive learning rate with some practical considerations, for example, setting the upper bound of the learning rate.

Finally, the use of GBRBM and the proposed improvements were tested through the series of experiments on realistic data sets. Those experiments showed that a GBRBM and the proposed improvements were able to address the practical difficulties such as the sensitivity to the learning parameters and the inability of learning meaningful features from high dimensional data.

Despite these successful applications of GBRBM presented in this paper, training GBRBM is still more challenging than training a RBM. Further research in improving and easing the training is required.

Acknowledgements. This work was supported by the summer internship and the honours programme of the department, by the Academy of Finland and by the IST Program of the European Community, under the PASCAL2 Network of Excellence. This publication only reflects the authors' views.

References

1. Ackley, D.H., Hinton, G.E., Sejnowski, T.J.: A learning algorithm for Boltzmann machines. Cognitive Science 9, 147–169 (1985)
2. Cho, K.: Improved Learning Algorithms for Restricted Boltzmann Machines. Master's thesis, Aalto University School of Science (2011)

3. Cho, K., Raiko, T., Ilin, A.: Parallel tempering is efficient for learning restricted boltzmann machines. In: Proceedings of the International Joint Conference on Neural Networks (IJCNN 2010), Barcelona, Spain (July 2010)
4. Coates, A., Lee, H., Ng, A.Y.: An Analysis of Single-Layer Networks in Unsupervised Feature Learning. In: NIPS 2010 Workshop on Deep Learning and Unsupervised Feature Learning (2010)
5. Desjardins, G., Courville, A., Bengio, Y.: Adaptive Parallel Tempering for Stochastic Maximum Likelihood Learning of RBMs. In: NIPS 2010 Workshop on Deep Learning and Unsupervised Feature Learning (2010)
6. Desjardins, G., Courville, A., Bengio, Y., Vincent, P., Delalleau, O.: Parallel Tempering for Training of Restricted Boltzmann Machines. In: Proceedings of the Thirteenth International Conference on Artificial Intelligence and Statistics, pp. 145–152 (2010)
7. Fischer, A., Igel, C.: Empirical analysis of the divergence of Gibbs sampling based learning algorithms for restricted Boltzmann machines. In: Diamantaras, K., Duch, W., Iliadis, L.S. (eds.) ICANN 2010. LNCS, vol. 6354, pp. 208–217. Springer, Heidelberg (2010)
8. Hinton, G.E., Salakhutdinov, R.R.: Reducing the Dimensionality of Data with Neural Networks. Science 313(5786), 504–507 (2006)
9. Hinton, G.: A Practical Guide to Training Restricted Boltzmann Machines. Tech. Rep. Department of Computer Science, University of Toronto (2010)
10. Hyvärinen, A., Karhunen, J., Oja, E.: Independent Component Analysis, 1st edn. Wiley Interscience, Hoboken (2001)
11. Krizhevsky, A.: Learning multiple layers of features from tiny images. Tech. Rep. Computer Science Department, University of Toronto (2009)
12. Krizhevsky, A.: Convolutional Deep Belief Networks on CIFAR-2010. Tech. Rep. Computer Science Department, University of Toronto (2010)
13. MIT Center For Biological and Computation Learning: CBCL Face Database #1, http://www.ai.mit.edu/projects/cbcl
14. Ranzato, M.A., Hinton, G.E.: Modeling pixel means and covariances using factorized third-order Boltzmann machines. In: CVPR, pp. 2551–2558 (2010)
15. Salakhutdinov, R.: Learning Deep Generative Models. Ph.D. thesis, University of Toronto (2009)
16. Schulz, H., Müller, A., Behnke, S.: Investigating Convergence of Restricted Boltzmann Machine Learning. In: NIPS 2010 Workshop on Deep Learning and Unsupervised Feature Learning (2010)
17. Smolensky, P.: Information processing in dynamical systems: foundations of harmony theory. In: Parallel Distributed processing: Explorations in the Microstructure of Cognition, Foundations, vol. 1, USA, pp. 194–281. MIT Press, Cambridge (1986)
18. Tieleman, T.: Training restricted Boltzmann machines using approximations to the likelihood gradient. In: Proceedings of the 25th International Conference on Machine Learning, ICML 2008, pp. 1064–1071. ACM Press, New York (2008)

A Hierarchical Generative Model of Recurrent Object-Based Attention in the Visual Cortex

David P. Reichert, Peggy Series, and Amos J. Storkey

School of Informatics, University of Edinburgh,
10 Crichton Street, Edinburgh, EH8 9AB, UK
{d.p.reichert@sms.,pseries@inf.,a.storkey@}ed.ac.uk

Abstract. In line with recent work exploring Deep Boltzmann Machines (DBMs) as models of cortical processing, we demonstrate the potential of DBMs as models of object-based attention, combining generative principles with attentional ones. We show: (1) How inference in DBMs can be related qualitatively to theories of attentional recurrent processing in the visual cortex; (2) that deepness and topographic receptive fields are important for realizing the attentional state; (3) how more explicit attentional suppressive mechanisms can be implemented, depending crucially on sparse representations being formed during learning.

1 Introduction

A Deep Boltzmann Machine (DBM) is a hierarchical, probabilistic, sampling based neural network that learns representations from which it generates or predicts the data it sees, utilizing recurrent processing. Though introduced in a machine learning context [1], these properties make the DBM an interesting model of processing in the cortex (cf. e.g. [2,3]). In earlier work, we showed how the DBM can model homeostasis induced hallucinations [4]. Here, we demonstrate in a proof of concept how aspects of object-based attention can be modeled with a DBM as well – not in terms of saliency maps or eye movements, but in terms of what happens throughout the cortical hierarchy during the act of paying attention to an object in a visual scene. In that sense, this work can be understood as modeling in particular *covert* attention. It relates to approaches such as Selective Tuning [5] and others (e.g. [6,7]), but is unique in capturing facets of attention in a framework implementing aforementioned general properties.

We qualitatively elucidate on the following aspects of theories of attentional processing in the cortex: First, the notion of a fast feed-forward (FF) sweep followed by subsequent recurrent processing, the latter being essential for perceiving objects when scenes are cluttered [8]; second, that, in directing attention to an individual object in a scene, an attractor state is assumed which binds together and emphasizes aspects of that object represented throughout the cortical hierarchy, suppressing representations of competing objects [9,5]; third, the hypothesis that scene representations in the cortex are inherently such that higher stages represent primarily one object at a time, unlike lower stages such as V1 where the whole image is encoded in terms of low-level features [10].

T. Honkela et al. (Eds.): ICANN 2011, Part I, LNCS 6791, pp. 18–25, 2011.

Our main focus is the biological application, but on the technical side we show how deepness of the architecture and restricted receptive fields are important for realizing the attentional state, making the DBM robust against noise not seen in training. Finally, we explore additional suppressive attentional mechanisms to cope with problems beyond toy data, and argue that sparse representations could be critical to that end.

2   Setup

For brevity we only give a short overview of the model. See [1] on DBMs, and [4] on our specific setup, including additional neuroscientific motivation.

A DBM consists of several layers of stochastic neuronal units $\mathbf{x}$, usually with binary states, connected via symmetric weights $\mathbf{W}$, with no lateral connections within a layer to simplify computations. The lowest layer $\mathbf{x}^{(0)}$ contains the visible units representing the data the model is trained on, such as images. Higher layers $\mathbf{x}^{(k)}, k > 0$, consist of hidden units which learn to represent and generate the data. Together, these layers model the cortical stages of processing. The probability for a unit i to switch on is given by a sigmoid activation function,

$$P(x_i^{(k)} = 1 | \mathbf{x}^{(k-1)}, \mathbf{x}^{(k+1)}) = \frac{1}{1 + \exp(-B_i^{(k)} - T_i^{(k)})}, \tag{1}$$

with bottom-up input $B_i^{(k)} := \sum_l w_{li}^{(k)} x_l^{(k-1)} + b_i^{(k)}$ and top-down input $T_i^{(k)} := \sum_m w_{im}^{(k)} x_m^{(k+1)} + t_i^{(k)}$, which includes biases $b_i^{(k)}$ and $t_i^{(k)}$.[1]

The joint probability that the system assumes a state $\mathbf{x}$ is characterized by an energy function E,

$$P(\mathbf{x}) \propto \exp(-E(\mathbf{x})) \quad \text{with} \quad E(\mathbf{x}) = \sum_k -\mathbf{x}^{(k)T} \mathbf{W}^{(k)} \mathbf{x}^{(k+1)} - \mathbf{x}^{(k)T} (\mathbf{b}^{(k)} + \mathbf{t}^{(k)}). \tag{2}$$

2.1   Data Sets and Plain DBM vs. RRF-DBM

Basic training works such that each hidden layer learns to generate the activities of the layer below, utilizing simple local Hebbian weight updates. We use the following data sets (Figure 1a-e): A toy dataset consisting of simple shapes at random image positions (*shapes*), and two variations thereof containing either multiple such shapes (*multi-shapes*) or clutter (*shapes+clutter*). And, the *MNIST* data set of handwritten digits, popular in machine learning, and a clutter variation (*MNIST+clutter*), using digits separated into 60,000 training and 10,000 test cases. We also compare two architectures: A plain DBM, and a more biologically inspired version where weights are restricted to be localized, realizing receptive fields that increase in size in higher hidden layers (dubbed RRF-DBM

---

[1] Two sets of biases are obtained when training the DBM layer-wise. We do not merge them as they contribute separately to bottom-up and top-down input in section 4.

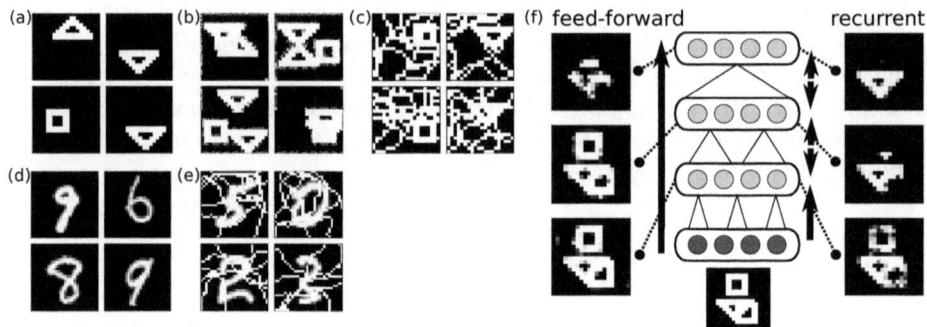

Fig. 1. (*a-e*) Data sets: (*a* and *d* for training). (*a*): *shapes* (squares, triangles and upside-down triangles). (*b*): *multi-shapes*. (*c*): *shapes+clutter*. (*d*): *MNIST*. (*e*): *MNIST+clutter*. (*f*): Projections of internal states across hidden layers in the RRF-DBM. The visibles are clamped to an image (bottom). After the initial bottom-up FF sweep (left), lower layers represent most of the image and the highest layer's state is unspecific. After 50 recurrent cycles (right), the highest layer has assumed an object specific state, and feed-back also biases the lower states toward the object.

for restrict. rec. field DBM).[2] Finally, a softmax label unit was attached to the top layer to allow for classification of the images [11].

3 Relation to Attentional Theories

Some theories pose that the aim of attentional processing is to form representations that are specific to one object at a time, especially in higher cortical areas [10,5]. We thus trained the models on individual objects only (shapes or digits), but then tested them on the various cluttered data sets to see whether information about individual objects is retrieved in the highest hidden layer even when scenes are complex in ways not seen in training. To decode what is being represented in a hidden layer individually, we performed what we call top-down projections [4]: Given the layer's states, the activations of layers below are computed subsequently in a pure feed-back manner until a reconstructed image is obtained.[3] Using the reconstructed image from the top layer and its label unit, we analyzed whether the individual object was represented by computing classification and squared reconstruction errors with regards to that object.

---

[2] Three hidden layers. The RRF-DBM had its number of units increased as necessary to compensate for the lower number of free parameters in the weights. No. of units: Shapes data sets: 500/500/500 (plain DBM), 26x26/26x26/26x26 (RRF-DBM). MNIST: 500/500/2000 (plain DBM), 28x28/28x28/43x43 (RRF-DBM). Receptive field sizes: 7x7/13x13/26x26. Pre-training: CD-1 for shapes, SAP (see [1]) for MNIST. No training of full DBM. Biases were initialized to -4, see section 4.

[3] This corresponds to generating from the top module in a Deep Belief Net, applied here in any hidden layer. Deterministic activations are used instead of samples.

When the model is run (performing Gibbs sampling on the joint probability), its state performs a random walk in the energy landscape along basins of attraction, which embody meaningful representations obtained during training. Because the latter are specific to individual objects by construction, the model assumes (stochastic) attractor states representing the objects being attended to [9,5], as shown below.

Finally, the notions of a fast FF sweep and subsequent recurrent processing naturally fit into the DBM framework as well: During normal inference, processing in a DBM is recurrent in that each hidden layer is sampled taking as input the states of both adjacent layers (the top layer only receives input from below). Hidden layers can be sampled sequentially in cycles spanning the hierarchy. For the initialization however it makes sense to perform a pure bottom-up FF pass [1], ignoring respective higher layer states, as initial states there are meaningless. We found classification and reconstruction performance to be reasonable after just the initial FF pass on non-cluttered data sets. For cluttered images however, subsequent recurrent processing was important to achieve better object specific representations, in line with what is suggested for the cortex [8,5].

3.1   Experiments: Inspection of the Hidden States

The plain DBM and the RRF-DBM were trained on the individual shapes or digits data sets, and then tested on the variations. To elucidate on what happens in the architecture during inference, an example case is displayed in Figure 1f. Here, the RRF-DBM had learned to represent individual shapes and is now run on an image of the *multi-shapes* set. Plotted are the decoded states of the three hidden layers both after the initial FF sweep and after 50 recurrent cycles. It becomes apparent that after the FF sweep, the hidden layer states are rather noisy, but the subsequent recurrent processing enables the top layer to form a clearer representation of an individual shape, allowing both for a localization of the object in image space and an improved classification.

We indeed find a shift from representing most of the scene in lower layers to representing the individual object in the highest layer. Representations are biased towards the attended object even in lower layers, but this results from feed-back from higher layers, as can be seen in the example by comparing the reconstructions of the first two hidden layers after the FF sweep and after recurrent processing. Only after the latter has taken place, involving feed-back from the topmost layer, are the representations biased toward the individual shape. In fact, when we removed the topmost layer of the RRF-DBM, no object specific state was assumed. This is partially because, due to the receptive field sizes, only the topmost layer has learned that training images only ever contained one shape. However, the deepness of the architecture plays a role in itself as well: We found that even for the plain DBM, a model with two hidden layers instead of three with the same total number of units performed worse (e.g. 43% vs. 22% classification error on *multi-shapes*). We argue that, with higher layers being further removed from the data in terms of processing steps, there is more flexibility for the model to assume its preferred states when the data is noisy.

Finally, we point out that while the presented effect has some resemblance to how a Hopfield network can retrieve memories from noisy initializations, the DBM is a much richer model than a Hopfield net, both in a biological and a machine learning sense (see [4]). In particular, in the DBM, *latent*, hierarchical representations are retrieved from a continuously presented image, rather than memorized images from a noisy initialization.

3.2   Experiments: Quantitative Evaluation

To evaluate the object specificity of the top layer states, classification and re-construction errors were computed for the plain and RRF-DBM on the various cluttered data sets (Figure 2). For the *multi-shapes* set,[4] which is complex and novel relative to what the models had been trained on, the errors are rather high after the FF sweep, but drop profoundly after subsequent recurrent processing cycles (e.g. classification error drops from about 50% to about 20% for the plain DBM). This is true for both plain and RRF-DBM, the latter performing some-what worse. For the noisy *shapes+clutter* set, performance is even worse after the FF sweep, with classification near chance. For the RRF-DBM, recurrent processing again helps greatly. Conversely, the plain DBM basically fails com-pletely for this data set to retrieve the shape from the clutter. We thus conclude that at least for certain types of noise, restricted receptive fields make the DBM decidedly more robust (independently reported also in [12]).

On the other hand, for the *MNIST+clutter* set, which is based on somewhat more difficult data, recurrent processing barely improves the performance over the FF sweep. This will be addressed in the next section.

4   Top-Down Suppression on Sparse Representations

Recurrent processing did not improve perception for *MNIST+clutter*. In ad-dressing the underlying problem we can further clarify the issue of attentional processing in the architecture. Basically, the recurrent interactions in effect en-able the higher layers to override image content according to what they prefer to represent. Having learned to represent individual objects, attentional selection can take place of for example one shape and suppression of others in the *multi-shapes* set. However, unlike simple toy shapes, the digits in MNIST vary much more in appearance. When presented with, for example, a digit 9 among clutter, the model should override the image representation in lower layers as to suppress the clutter. However, another way of reconciling the higher layers' expectation with the image could be to 'hallucinate' additional clutter to make the 9 into an 8. Suppression or imagination of image content are equally possible, and we find both when we decode the hidden states for *MNIST+clutter* (not shown).

Thus, while the top-down influence in the DBM can be seen as implementing Hierarchical Bayesian Inference [2], for attentional top-down selection specifically we need mechanisms that increase the signal-to-noise ratio (signal being what

---

[4] Errors were computed w.r.t. whichever of the three shapes was reconstructed best.

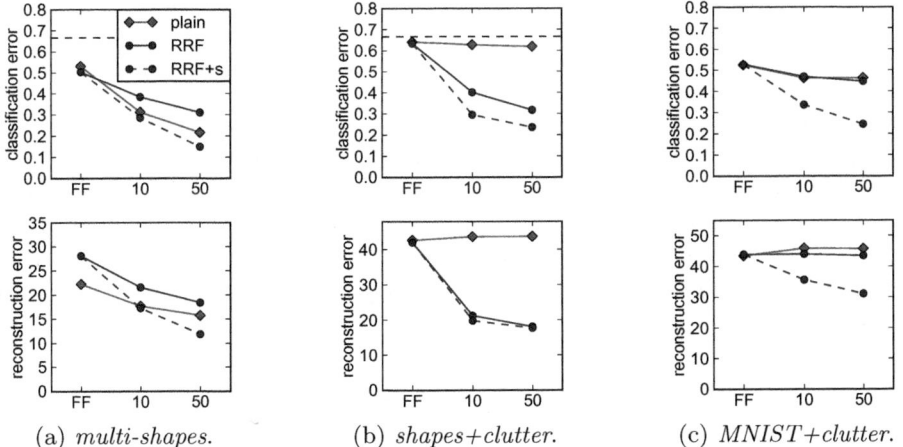

Fig. 2. Classification and reconstruction errors from top layer states for the three test sets. In each figure, scores are plotted for the plain DBM, RRF-DBM, and RRF-DBM with attentional suppression (section 4), taken after the FF sweep and after 10 or 50 subsequent recurrent cycles. Dashed lines denote chance classification error (0.9 for MNIST). $(a)+(b)$: For the shapes sets, recurrent processing improves performance markedly, moreso with suppression. For the *shapes+clutter* set, the restricted receptive fields of the RRF-DBM are essential to retrieve the shape. (c): For *MNIST+clutter*, the additional suppressive mechanism is necessary to achieve improvement.

is being attended to) without necessarily *changing* the content of the signal qualitatively, suppressing represented information related to the noise without 'hallucinating' additional content.

Two issues present in a standard DBM need to be overcome to that end: First, in a completely distributed representation, where the image is essentially encoded in the whole state vector $\mathbf{x}$, it is not clear how $\mathbf{x}$ is to be modified to achieve a suppression of image information localized to a certain part of image space. This is addressed by virtue of using the localized receptive fields, ensuring that units in lower layers only encode local information. The second issue is that switching an individual unit off (or on) does not necessarily correspond to suppressing information: For example, the unit could have inhibitory weights to the image. Indeed, we observed that for RRF-DBMs initialized with zero mean weights and biases, the learned representations are such that units tend to turn *off* when one of the shapes/digits is in their receptive fields.

To overcome the second issue, we initialized the unit biases to negative values at the beginning of training. This lead to a breaking of symmetry between units being on and off, and particularly to units being only sparsely activated throughout training.[5] In essence they thus learned representations where they only turn on if something 'out of the ordinary' happens. In that sense, a unit

---

[5] We found that this simple way of enforcing sparsity worked best for the problem at hand, compared to e.g. using a regularization on the gradient.

conveys much more information by being on than by being off, and suppression of a unit can indeed be seen as effecting a suppression of represented information. With negatively initialized biases, units would indeed only turn on when some object (part) was in their receptive fields.[6]

With such sparse representations established, we explore a heuristic suppressive mechanism to enhance the attentional processing: Where top-down input $T_i^{(k)}$ to a unit i in hidden layer k is suppressive, i.e. $< 0.$, that input is multiplied by a factor $\zeta^{(k)}$ ($\geq 1.$). This effectively allows higher layers to suppress states in lower layers if they do not match their predictions. The modified top-down input $\tilde{T}_i^{(k)}$ is thus $= \zeta^{(k)} T_i^{(k)}$ if $T_i^{(k)} < 0$, $= T_i^{(k)}$ otherwise, so that the probability for a unit to switch on is now given as:

$$P(x_i^{(k)} = 1 | \mathbf{x}^{(k-1)}, \mathbf{x}^{(k+1)}) = \frac{1}{1 + \exp(-B_i^{(k)} - \tilde{T}_i^{(k)})}. \tag{3}$$

The RRF-DBM experiments were repeated with the suppressive mechanism active in the intermediate hidden layers[7] over 50 recurrent cycles (Figure 2). The performance increased in all cases. Particularly, for *MNIST+clutter*, recurrent processing with suppression now improved the scores markedly over the initial FF sweep.

4.1   Spatial vs. Object-Based Attention

So far we have modeled object-based attention, where higher layers can make use of learned patterns in the hidden states to emphasize object specific representations. However, the topographic sparse representations in the RRF-DBM also make it possible to apply suppressive spatial spotlights directly in the hidden layers, for example to control the internal state of the model to focus on selected objects in the *multi-shapes* set. Shortly, testing the RRF-DBM with Gaussian spotlights directed towards chosen shapes in the images, classification error computed w.r.t. the selected shapes was 18%, which is comparable to the scores reported in Figure 2 (plain DBM 22%, RRF-DBM + suppression 15%), where the models were free to select any shape in an image. Hence, spatial attention can be used to bias the internal state towards regions of the image.

5   Conclusion

We demonstrated in this proof of concept work how the DBM model, which uniquely embodies several properties of interest in the computational neuroscience community, can be related to theories of attentional recurrent processing

---

[6] Of course, this results from pixels being mostly off in the images. However, in the light of the argument, the images should themselves be understood as stand-ins for sparse representations of images, for instance the output of edge detectors, rather than as 'black and white' images.

[7] $\zeta^{(k)}$ adjusted manually for each data set and layer. Values ranged from 1 to 5.

in the cortex. We also elucidated on a special role of sparse representations for attentional information selection, which allowed us to explore novel mechanisms for suppressing irrelevant information. In the long run, cortical models will need to integrate sensory signals from multiple modalities with planning and motor control. We believe that accounting for attentional processing, which in the broader sense organizes information into relevant and irrelevant and routes it between cortical submodules in a task dependent fashion, will be crucial.

Acknowledgments. We thank Y. Tang, N. Heess, J. Tsotsos, G. Hinton and the anon. reviewers for comments, and the EPSRC, MRC and BBSRC for funding.

References

1. Salakhutdinov, R., Hinton, G.: Deep Boltzmann machines. In: Proceedings of the 12th International Conference on Artificial Intelligence and Statistics (AISTATS), vol. 5, pp. 448–455 (2009)
2. Lee, T.S., Mumford, D.: Hierarchical Bayesian inference in the visual cortex. Journal of the Optical Society of America A 20(7), 1434–1448 (2003)
3. Fiser, J., Berkes, B., Orban, G., Lengyel, M.: Statistically optimal perception and learning: from behavior to neural representations. Trends in Cognitive Sciences 14, 119–130 (2010)
4. Reichert, D.P., Series, P., Storkey, A.J.: Hallucinations in Charles Bonnet Syndrome induced by homeostasis: a Deep Boltzmann Machine model. Advances in Neural Information Processing Systems 23, 2020–2028 (2010)
5. Tsotsos, J.K., Rodriguez-Sanchez, A.J., Rothenstein, A.L., Simine, E.: The different stages of visual recognition need different attentional binding strategies. Brain Research 1225, 119–132 (2008)
6. Deco, G., Rolls, E.T.: A neurodynamical cortical model of visual attention and invariant object recognition. Vision Research 44(6), 621–642 (2004)
7. Chikkerur, S., Serre, T., Tan, C., Poggio, T.: What and where: A bayesian inference theory of attention. Vision Research (2010), PMID: 20493206
8. Lamme, V.A., Roelfsema, P.R.: The distinct modes of vision offered by feedforward and recurrent processing. Trends in Neurosciences 23(11), 571–579 (2000), PMID: 11074267
9. Serences, J.T., Yantis, S.: Selective visual attention and perceptual coherence. Trends in Cognitive Sciences 10(1), 38–45 (2006), PMID: 16318922
10. Rensink, R.A.: The dynamic representation of scenes. Visual Cognition 7(1), 17 (2000)
11. Hinton, G.E., Osindero, S., Teh, Y.: A fast learning algorithm for deep belief nets. Neural Computation 18(7), 1527–1554 (2006)
12. Tang, Y., Eliasmith, C.: Deep networks for robust visual recognition. In: Proceedings of the 27th Annual International Conference on Machine Learning, Haifa, Israel, pp.1055–1062 (2010)

ℓ_1-Penalized Linear Mixed-Effects Models for BCI

Siamac Fazli[1], Márton Danóczy[1], Jürg Schelldorfer[2], and Klaus-Robert Müller[1]

[1] Berlin Institute of Technology, Franklinstr. 28/29, 10587 Berlin, Germany
[2] ETH Zürich,Rämistrasse 101, 8092 Zürich, Switzerland
fazli@cs.tu-berlin.de, marton@cs.tu-berlin.de,
schell@stat.math.ethz.ch, klaus-robert.mueller@tu-berlin.de

Abstract. A recently proposed novel statistical model estimates population effects and individual variability between subgroups simultaneously, by extending Lasso methods. We apply this ℓ_1-penalized linear regression mixed-effects model to a large scale real world problem: by exploiting a large set of brain computer interface data we are able to obtain a subject-independent classifier that compares favorably with prior zero-training algorithms. This unifying model inherently compensates shifts in the input space attributed to the individuality of a subject. In particular we are now able to differentiate *within-subject* and *between-subject variability*. A deeper understanding both of the underlying statistical and physiological structure of the data is gained.

1   Introduction

When measuring experimental data we typically encounter a certain inbuilt heterogeneity: data may stem from distinct sources that are all additionally exposed to varying measuring conditions. Such so-called group, respectively individual effects need to be modeled separately within a global statistical model. Note that here the data is not independent: a part of the variance may come from the individual experiment, while another may be attributed to a *fixed* effect. Such mixed-effects models [9] are known to be useful whenever there is a grouping structure among the observations, e.g. the clusters are independent but within a cluster the data may have a dependency structure. Note also that mixed-effects models are notoriously hard to estimate in high dimensions, particularly, if only few data points are available.

In this paper we will for the first time use a recent ℓ_1-penalized estimation procedure [10] for high-dimensional linear mixed-effects models in order to estimate the mixed effects that are persistent in experimental data from neuroscience. This novel method builds upon Lasso-type procedures [11], assuming that the number of potential fixed effects is large and that the underlying true fixed-effects vector is sparse. The ℓ_1-penalization on the fixed effects is used to achieve sparsity.

We will study Brain Computer Interfaces (BCI) [5], where we encounter high variability both between subjects and within repetitions of an experiment for the

T. Honkela et al. (Eds.): ICANN 2011, Part I, LNCS 6791, pp. 26–35, 2011.

same subject. The novel approach splits up the overall inherent variance into a within-group and a between-group variance and therefore allows us to model the unknown dependencies in a meaningful manner. While this is a conceptual contribution to adapt the mixed effects model for BCI, our paper also contributes practically. Due to the more precise modeling of the dependency structure we cannot only quantify both sources of variance but also provide an improved ensemble model that is able to serve as a one-size-fits-all BCI classifier – the central ingredient of a so-called zero-training BCI [6]. In other words we can minimize the usually required calibration time for a novel subject – where the learning machine adapts to the new brain – to practically zero.

2 Statistical Model

In this work we employ a so-called linear mixed-effects model [9], due to the dependence structure inherent to the two sources of variability: within-subject (dependence) and between-subject (independence). The classical linear mixed-effects framework has two limiting issues: (1) it cannot deal with high-dimensional data (i.e. the total number of observations is smaller than the number of explanatory variables) and (2) fixed-effects variable selection gets computationally intractable if the number of fixed-effects covariates is very large. By using a Lasso-type concept [11] these limits can be overcome in the present method [10], thus allowing application in the real world as we will see in the next sections.

2.1 Model Setup

Let $i = 1, \ldots, N$ be the number of subjects, $j = 1, \ldots, n_i$ the number of observations per subject and $N_T = \sum n_i$ the total number of observations. For each subject we observe an n_i-dimensional response vector y_i. Moreover, let X_i and Z_i be $n_i \times p$ and $n_i \times q$ covariate matrices, where X_i contains the fixed-effects covariates and Z_i the corresponding random-effects covariates. Denote by $\beta \in \mathbb{R}^p$ the p-dimensional fixed-effects vector and by $b_i, i = 1, \ldots, N$ the q-dimensional random-effects vectors. Then the linear mixed-effects model can be written as ([9])

$$y_i = X_i\beta + Z_ib_i + \varepsilon_i \qquad i = 1, \ldots, N \quad , \tag{1}$$

where we assume that $i)$ $b_i \sim \mathcal{N}_q(0, \tau^2 I_q)$, $ii)$ $\varepsilon_i \sim \mathcal{N}_{n_i}(0, \sigma^2 I_{n_i})$ and $iii)$ that the errors ε_i are mutually independent of the random effects b_i.

From (1) we conclude that

$$y_i \sim \mathcal{N}_{n_i}(X_i\beta, \Lambda_i(\sigma^2, \tau^2)) \quad \text{with} \quad \Lambda_i(\sigma^2, \tau^2) = \sigma^2 I_{n_i} + \tau^2 Z_i Z_i^\mathsf{T}. \tag{2}$$

It is important to point out that assumption $i)$ is very restrictive. Nevertheless, it is straightforward to relax this assumption and assume that $b_i \sim \mathcal{N}_q(0, \Psi)$ for a general (or possible structured) covariance matrix Ψ. For the data described in the next section, assumption $i)$ seems to hold.

2.2 ℓ_1-penalized Maximum Likelihood Estimator

Since we have to deal with a large number of covariates, it is computationally not feasible to employ the standard mixed-effects model variable selection strategies. To remedy this problem, in [10] a Lasso-type approach is proposed by adding an ℓ_1-penalty for the fixed-effects parameter β. This idea induces sparsity in β in the sense that many coefficients $\beta_j, j = 1, \ldots, p$ are estimated exactly zero and we can perform simultaneously parameter estimation and variable selection. Consequently, from (2) we derive the following objective function

$$S_\lambda(\beta, \sigma^2, \tau^2) := -\frac{1}{2}\sum_{i=1}^{N}\left\{\log|\Lambda_i| + (y_i - X_i\beta)^\mathsf{T}\Lambda_i^{-1}(y_i - X_i\beta)\right\} - \lambda\sum_{k=1}^{p}|\beta_k| \quad , \tag{3}$$

where β_1 is the unpenalized intercept and λ a nonnegative regularization parameter. Hence, estimating the parameters β, σ^2 and τ^2 is carried out by maximizing $S_\lambda(\beta, \sigma^2, \tau^2)$:

$$\hat\beta, \hat\sigma^2, \hat\tau^2 = \operatorname*{argmax}_{\beta, \sigma^2, \tau^2} S_\lambda(\beta, \sigma^2, \tau^2) \quad . \tag{4}$$

It is worth noting that $S_\lambda(\beta, \sigma^2, \tau^2)$ is a non-concave function, which implies that we can not apply a convex solver to maximize (3).

2.3 Prediction of the Random-Effects

The prediction of the random-effects coefficients $b_i, i = 1, \ldots, N$ is done by the maximum a posteriori (MAP) principle. Given the parameters β, σ^2 and τ^2, it follows by straightforward calculations that the MAP estimator for $b_i, i = 1, \ldots, N$ is given by $b_i = [Z_i^\mathsf{T} Z_i + \sigma^2/\tau^2 I_q]^{-1} Z_i^\mathsf{T}(y_i - X_i\beta)$. Since the true parameters β, σ^2 and τ^2 are not known, we plug in the estimates from (4). Hence the random-effects coefficients are estimated by

$$\hat b_i = [Z_i^\mathsf{T} Z_i + \hat\sigma^2/\hat\tau^2 I_q]^{-1} Z_i^\mathsf{T}(y_i - X_i\hat\beta). \tag{5}$$

2.4 Model Selection

The optimization problem in (4) is applied to a fixed tuning parameter λ. In practice, the solution of (4) is calculated on a grid of λ values. The choice of the optimal λ-value is then achieved by minimizing a criterion, i.e. a k-fold cross-validation score or an information criteria. We use the Bayesian Information Criterion (BIC) defined as

$$-2\ell(\hat\beta, \hat\sigma^2, \hat\tau^2) + \log N_T \cdot \hat{df}_\lambda \quad , \tag{6}$$

where $\hat{df}_\lambda = |\{1 \leq j \leq p; \hat\beta_j \neq 0\}|$ denotes the number of nonzero fixed regression coefficients and $\ell(\hat\beta, \hat\sigma^2, \hat\tau^2)$ denotes the likelihood function following from the model assumptions in (1). The BIC works well in the simulation examples presented in [10] and is computationally fast.

2.5   Computational Implementation

With τ and σ fixed, the cost function (3) is equivalent to an ℓ_1-penalized linear regression after whitening by the covariances Λ_i:

$$\hat{\beta} = \operatorname*{argmin}_{\beta | \tau, \sigma} \sum_{i=1}^{N} \left\| \Lambda_i^{-1/2} \left(X_i \beta - y_i \right) \right\|_2^2 + 2\lambda \sum_{k=1}^{p} |\beta_k| \qquad (7)$$

We solve the resulting convex optimization problem for β with fixed σ and τ using the orthant-wise limited memory quasi-Newton algorithm [1]. As suggested in [10], the optimization is performed over a grid of (σ^2, τ^2) to find the global optimum of all parameters. Preliminary analysis indicates that a so called random-intercept (i.e. one bias per group) is appropriate for our data, i.e., $Z_i = \mathbf{1}_{n_i}$ and $b_i \in \mathbb{R}$. Then, in the context of (1), σ^2 corresponds to the *within-subject variability* and τ^2 to the *between-subject variability*. By estimating σ^2 and τ^2 we are able to allocate the variability in the data to these two sources.

3   Available Data and Experiments

We use two different datasets of BCI data to show different aspects of the validity of our approach. The first consists of 83 BCI experiments (sessions) from 83 individual subjects and each session consists of 150 trials. Our second dataset consists of 90 sessions from only 44 subjects. The number of trials of a single session varies from 60 trials to 600 trials. In other words, our first dataset can be considered to be *balanced* in the number of *trials per subjects* and *sessions per subject*. Our second dataset is *unbalanced* in this sense. As one may expect, the balanced data is more suitable for building a zero-training classifier and enables us to obtain a 'clean' model. However, the unbalanced dataset enables us to examine how individual sessions of the same subject affect the estimation of our model and leads to a more thorough understanding of the underlying processes. Each trial consists of one of two predefined movement imaginations, being left and right hand, i.e. data was chosen such that it relies only on these 2 classes, although originally three classes were cued during the calibration session, being left hand (L), right hand (R) and foot (F). 45 EEG channels, which are in accordance with the 10-20 system, were identified to be common in all sessions considered. The data were recorded while subjects were immobile, seated on a comfortable chair with arm rests. The cues for performing a movement imagination were given by visual stimuli, and occurred every 4.5-6 seconds in random order. Each trial was referenced by a 3 second long time-window starting at 500 msec after the presentation of the cue. The experimental procedure was designed to closely follow [3].

3.1   Generation of the Ensemble

The ensemble consists of a large redundant set of subject-dependent common spatial pattern filters and their matching classifiers (LDA). Each dataset is first

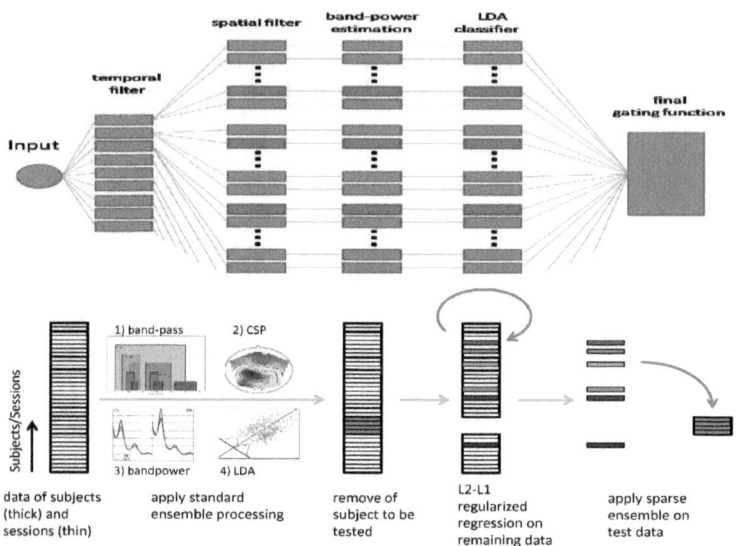

Fig. 1. Two flowcharts of the ensemble method. The red patches in the top panel illustrate the inactive nodes of the ensemble after sparsification.

preprocessed by 18 predefined temporal filters (i.e. band-pass filters) in parallel (see upper panel of Figure 1). A corresponding spatial filter and linear classifier is obtained for every dataset and temporal filter. Each resulting Common Spatial Pattern (CSP)-Linear Discriminant Analysis (LDA) couple can be interpreted as a potential basis function. Finding an appropriate weighting for the classifier outputs of these basis functions is of paramount importance for the accurate prediction. This processing was done by leave-one-subject-out cross-validation, i.e. the session of a particular subject was removed, the algorithm trained on the remaining trials (of the other subjects) and then applied to this subject's data (see lower panel of Figure 1).

The μ-rhythm (9-14 Hz) and synchronized components in the β-band (16-22 Hz) are macroscopic idle rhythms that prevail over the postcentral somatosensory cortex and precentral motor cortex, when a given subject is at rest. Imaginations of movements as well as actual movements are known to suppress these idle rhythms contralaterally. However, there are not only subject-specific differences of the most discriminative frequency range of the mentioned idle-rhythms, but also session differences thereof. We identified 18 neurophysiologically relevant temporal filters, of which 12 lie within the μ-band, 3 in the β-band, two in between μ- and β-band and one broadband $7-30$Hz. In all following performance related tables we used the percentage of misclassified trials, or 0-1 loss. Common spatial patterns (CSP) is a popular algorithm for calculating spatial filters, used for detecting event-related (de-) synchronization (ERD/ERS), and is considered to be the gold-standard of ERD-based BCI systems [2]. The CSP algorithm maximizes the variance of right hand trials, while simultaneously minimizing the variance for left hand trials. Given the two covariance matrices Σ_1 and Σ_2, of size *channels × concatenated timepoints*, the CSP algorithm returns the matrices W and D. W is a matrix of projections, where the i-th row has a relative variance of d_i for trials of class 1 and a relative variance of $1 - d_i$ for trials of class 2. D is a diagonal matrix with entries $d_i \in [0, 1]$, with length n, the number of channels: $W\Sigma_1 W^\mathsf{T} = D$ and $W\Sigma_2 W^\mathsf{T} = I - D$. Best discrimination is provided by filters with very high (emphazising one class) or very low eigenvalues (emphazising the other class), we therefore chose to only include projections with the highest 2 and corresponding lowest 2 eigenvalues for our analysis.

3.2 Validation

The subject-specific CSP-based classification methods with automatically, subject-dependent tuned temporal filters (termed reference methods) are validated by an 8-fold cross-validation, splitting the data chronologically. The chronological splitting for cross-validation is a common practice in EEG classification, since the non-stationarity of the data is thus preserved [5]. To validate the quality of the ensemble learning we employed a leave-one-subject out cross-validation (LOSO-CV) procedure, i.e. for predicting the labels of a particular subject we only use data from other subjects.

4 Results

4.1 Subject-to-Subject Transfer

As explained in Section 3, we use our first balanced dataset to find a zero-training subject-independent classifier. The left part of Figure 2 shows the results of fitting an ℓ_1-regularized least-squares regression model to fit a) a linear model with one bias and b) a mixed-effects model with one bias per subject. We are able to enhance the classification by use of the mixed-effects model.

As can be seen in Figure 3 (left panel) the LMM method needs less features per subject ($N_{\mathrm{LMM}} \approx 310$) as compared to estimating only one bias ($N_{\ell_1} \approx 500$). Besides from selecting less features in total, the LMM chose a higher fraction of features with low self-prediction errors. This is shown in the top panel, where we display the cumulative sum of features, sorted by increasing self-prediction accuracy. To visualize differences between weight vectors resulting from the LOSO-CV procedure, the right panel displays these vectors, projected to two dimensions. The matrix of Euclidean distances between all pairs of weights was embedded into a 2×83-dimensional space and projected onto the resulting point cloud's first two principal axes for visualization. In the middle part of Figure 3 we compare the performance of our method on the basis of individual subjects with other methods and perform t-tests to examine their statistical significance. The p-values are included within the figure. As the most simple baseline we chose

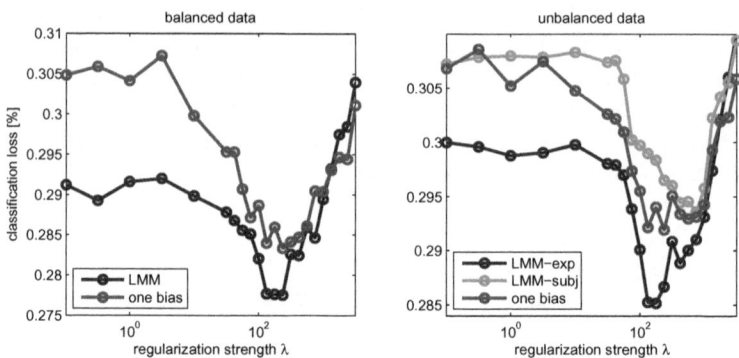

Fig. 2. The figures show the mean classification loss over subjects for the *balanced* dataset (left) and the *unbalanced* dataset (right) as a function of the regularization strength λ. The linear mixed-effects (LMM) approach is compared to classical ℓ_1 regularized least squares regression (one bias). LMM-subj estimates one bias per subject and LMM-exp one bias per experiment (session).

broadband $(7 - 30$ Hz) filtered and Laplacian filtered power features of motor related channels. As can be seen on the top left side of Figure 3 our method performs very favorably. LMM improves classification performance for 89.2% of the subjects considered with high significance. Furthermore, we compare with a recently proposed second-generation zero-training procedure [6] and achieve a significant improvement. Finally, we compare our method to the subject-dependent, cross-validated classifier loss, derived from the data themselves. A per se unfair comparison. Given that the subject-dependent classifier is not significantly better ($p = 0.93$), we may state, that we are on par.

4.2 Session-to-Session Transfer

To investigate how the results of the method can be understood in terms of individual subjects and their (possibly multiple) sessions, we validated the method in two ways. First we allow each experiment to have an individual bias. In the second approach, we allow only one bias per subject, i.e. multiple experiments/sessions from the same subject will be grouped. The results are shown in the right panel of Figure 4. They indicate a substantially higher between-group-variability if we allow biases for each experiment. This does not only confirm knowledge from previous publications, that the transfer of classifiers from sessions to sessions required a bias correction [8], but also underlines the validity of our approach in the sense that we are able to capture a meaningful part of the variability which would otherwise be ignored as noise. As can be seen in Figure 4, a substantial fraction of the variability can be attributed to within-subject differences.

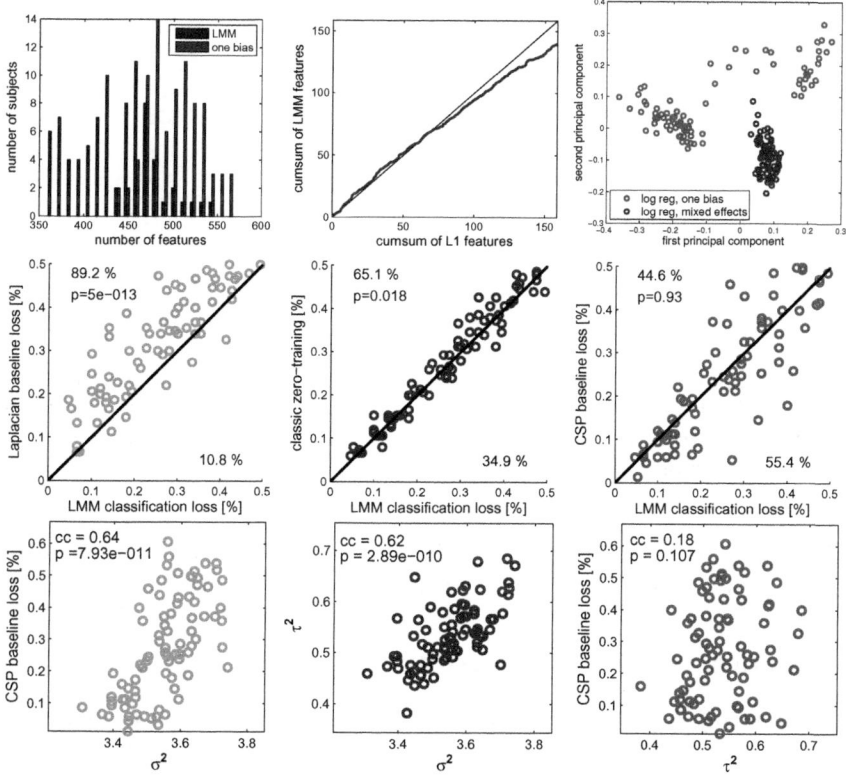

Fig. 3. Top: Scatter plots, comparing LMM with various baselines on a subject level. center left: histogram of the number of active features for all subjects. center middle: cumulative sum of features, sorted by 'self prediction'. center right: Variability between classifier weights b of the two models for each of the $N = 2 \times 83$ LOSO-training runs using the best regularization strength. Bottom: The three scatterplots show relations between $\sigma.^2$, τ^2 and the baseline cross-validation misclassification for every subject. cc stands for correlation coefficient and p stands for paired t-test significance.

4.3 Relation of Baseline Misclassification to σ^2 and τ^2

Using standard methods for ERD-related BCI decoding [4], we obtain a mean classification loss for each subject within our *balanced* dataset, based on the cross-validation of band-pass and spatially filtered features. In lowest part of Figure 3 we examine the relationship between this *baseline loss* and the *within-subject variability* $\sigma.^2$ and *between-subject variability* $\tau.^2$. The *baseline loss* and σ^2 have a strong positive correlation, with high significance. This makes intuitive sense: a dataset that is well classifyable should also exhibit low variance of its residuals. We furthermore examine the relation of τ^2 and σ^2 and find a strong positive relation. Interestingly we do not find a significant relation between the

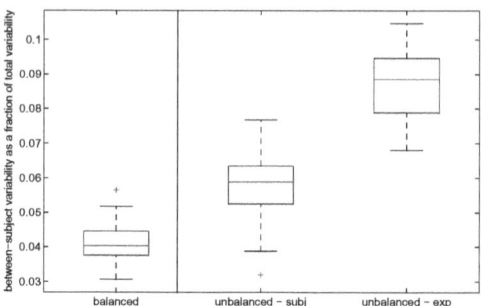

Fig. 4. The figure shows the magnitude of between-subject variability as a fraction of total variability. On the left: Results for the first *balanced* dataset. One the right: Results for the *unbalanced* dataset. *subj* stands for estimating one bias per subject and *exp* for estimating one bias per experiment.

baseline loss and τ^2. In other words it is not possible to draw conclusions about the quality of a subject's data by the variance of its assigned biases.

5   Discussion and Conclusions

When analyzing experimental data, it is of generic importance to quantify variation both across the ensemble of acquired data and within repetitions of measurements. In this paper we have applied a recent sparse modeling approach from statistics [10] based on a so-called ℓ_1-penalized linear mixed-effects model and proposed its first time use for a large real world data set, leading to a novel BCI zero-training model (see also [8,6]). The novel statistical model not only gave rise to a better overall prediction, but it furthermore allowed to quantify the differences in variation more transparently and also interpretably. By attributing some of the total variability, in other methods considered as noise, to differences between subjects, we are now able to obtain a solution that is sparser and at the same time superior in prediction accuracy. Our statistical framework can be applied to a large number of scientific experiments from many different domains, where inter-dependencies of input space exist. We have shown that our approach leads to more robust feature selection, is superior in its classification accuracy and may well find its way into a broader scientific context (for more details, please refer to [7]).

References

1. Andrew, G., Gao, J.: Scalable training of L_1-regularized log-linear models. In: Proceedings of the 24th international conference on Machine learning (ICML 2007), pp. 33–40. ACM Press, New York (2007)
2. Blankertz, B., Curio, G., Müller, K.R.: Classifying single trial EEG: Towards brain computer interfacing. In: Diettrich, T.G., Becker, S., Ghahramani, Z. (eds.) Advances in Neural Inf. Proc. Systems (NIPS 2001), vol. 14, pp. 157–164 (2002)

3. Blankertz, B., Dornhege, G., Krauledat, M., Müller, K.R., Kunzmann, V., Losch, F., Curio, G.: The Berlin Brain-Computer Interface: EEG-based communication without subject training. IEEE Trans Neural Syst. Rehabil. Eng. 14, 147–152 (2006)
4. Blankertz, B., Tomioka, R., Lemm, S., Kawanabe, M., Müller, K.R.: Optimizing spatial filters for robust EEG single-trial analysis. IEEE Signal Proc. Magazine 25(1), 41–56 (2008)
5. Dornhege, G., Millán, J.R., Hinterberger, T., McFarland, D., Müller, K.R. (eds.): Toward Brain-Computer Interfacing. MIT Press, Cambridge, MA (2007)
6. Fazli, S., Grozea, C., Danoczy, M., Blankertz, B., Popescu, F., Muller, K.R.: Subject independent EEG-based BCI decoding. In: Advances in Neural Information Processing Systems 22, pp. 513–521. MIT Press, Cambridge (2009)
7. Fazli, S., Danóczy, M., Schelldorfer, J., Müller, K.R.: ℓ_1-penalized Linear Mixed-Effects Models for high dimensional data with application to BCI. Neuroimage (2011), (in press)
8. Krauledat, M., Tangermann, M., Blankertz, B., Müller, K.R.: Towards zero training for brain-computer interfacing. PLoS ONE 3, e2967 (2008)
9. Pinheiro, J.C., Bates, D.M.: Mixed-Effects Models in S and S-Plus. Springer, New York (2000)
10. Schelldorfer, J., Bühlmann, P.: Estimation for high-dimensional linear mixed-effects models using ℓ_1-penalization. arXiv preprint 1002.3784 (2010)
11. Tibshirani, R.: Regression shrinkage and selection via the lasso. Journal of the Royal Statistical Society B 58, 267–288 (1996)

Slow Feature Analysis - A Tool for Extraction of Discriminating Event-Related Potentials in Brain-Computer Interfaces

Sven Dähne, Johannes Höhne, Martijn Schreuder, and Michael Tangermann

Machine-Learning Department, Berlin Institute of Technology,
Berlin, Germany
{sven.daehne,johannes.hoehne,martijn.schreuder,
michael.tangermann}@tu-berlin.de

Abstract. The unsupervised signal decomposition method Slow Feature Analysis (SFA) is applied as a preprocessing tool in the context of EEG based Brain-Computer Interfaces (BCI). Classification results based on a SFA decomposition are compared to classification results obtained on Principal Component Analysis (PCA) decomposition and to those obtained on raw EEG channels. Both PCA and SFA improve classification to a large extend compared to using no signal decomposition and require between one third and half of the maximal number of components to do so. The two methods extract different information from the raw data and therefore lead to different classification results. Choosing between PCA and SFA based on classification of calibration data leads to a larger improvement in classification performance compared to using one of the two methods alone. Results are based on a large data set (n=31 subjects) of two studies using auditory Event Related Potentials for spelling applications.

Keywords: Slow Feature Analysis, SFA, Dimensionality Reduction, EEG, Brain-Computer Interface, BCI, Principal Component Analysis, PCA, Event-Related Potentials, ERP, Auditory Evoked Potentials, AEP.

1 Introduction

The analysis of Event Related Potentials (ERP) of the human Electroencephalogram (EEG) provides introspection into the attentional status of the processing of internal or external events. For Brain-Computer Interfaces (BCIs), the online analysis of ERPs with machine learning methods [2] is a means to distinguish attended target stimuli from non-attended (non-target) stimuli. By focusing his/her attention to a subset of all e.g. visual or auditory stimuli presented, a BCI user performs a multiclass decision in order to control e.g. a text entry system or other applications.

Compared to other application domains, the signal-to-noise ratio (SNR) of EEG data used for BCI is rather poor. As the dimensionality of EEG data is rather large and the number of training samples available for the estimation of

T. Honkela et al. (Eds.): ICANN 2011, Part I, LNCS 6791, pp. 36–43, 2011.

good hyperparamters is typically low, the machine learning problems in BCI are challenging. As dimensionality reduction methods can alleviate this problem, they are widely used in BCI [2] and EEG research in general [6]. Widely used methods are the Principal Component Analysis (PCA) and variants of the Independent Component Analysis (ICA) [5]. Applied for the spatial filtering of EEG, they can reduce the signal dimensionality enormously.

A relatively new decomposition method, Slow Feature Analysis (SFA) [8], is motivated by the idea that different processes in the human brain act on distinctively different time scales. SFA decomposes a multivariate signal with respect to its temporal variation. The result of SFA is a set of purely spatial filters that each extract a univariate signal that is decorrelated from the signals of all other filters and varies with a different speed compared to the others. Blaschke et. al. [3] have shown that SFA can be regarded as a special case of temporal ICA.

As this work is the first application of SFA to EEG data, its suitability for spatial filtering of EEG is tested and compared to PCA preprocessing. Offline evaluation is performed for data from 31 subjects that participated in an auditory ERP paradigm for a BCI speller.

2   Methods

2.1   Data

The EEG data used for analysis stems from two separate auditory oddball ERP BCI studies [4] [7], (PASS2D data set and AMUSE data set, respectively).

In both studies EEG was recorded using a 63 channel layout and 1000 Hz sampling rate. The data was low-pass filtered to 40 Hz and down sampled to 100 Hz prior to analysis. Epochs were extracted between -150 ms and 800 ms relative to stimulus onset.

Both experiments consisted of a calibration phase and an online spelling phase. Experimental details of the PASS2D study (with corresponding AMUSE values given in parenthesis) are as follows: number of stimulus epochs in calibration phase = 3402 (4320), number of stimulus epochs in online phase = 11987 (8100), target to non-target ratio 1:8 (1:5), number of participants = 10 (21).

2.2   Decomposition Methods

The basic EEG model assumes that the surface potential measured on the scalp at a time t, denoted by $\mathbf{x}(t)$, is a linear superposition of a number of components with individual time courses $s_i(t)$ and fixed field patterns:

$$\mathbf{x}(t) = \mathbf{A}\mathbf{s}(t) + \mathbf{n}(t), \tag{1}$$

where $\mathbf{s}(t) = (s_1(t), s_1(t), \ldots)^T$ contains the time course of the components, $\mathbf{A} = (\mathbf{a}_1, \mathbf{a}_2, \ldots)$ contains the respective field patterns in the columns, and $\mathbf{n}(t)$ is noise. The index i runs from 1 to the number of recording channels.

This model can be inverted to yield a *decomposition* of the recorded data into an estimate of the component time courses and field patterns:

$$\hat{\mathbf{s}}(t) = \mathbf{W}^T \mathbf{x}(t), \tag{2}$$

where the estimated component time courses are extracted with *spatial filters* contained in the columns of $\mathbf{W} = [\mathbf{w}_1, \mathbf{w}_2, \ldots]$, i.e. $\hat{s}_i(t) = \mathbf{w}_i^T \mathbf{x}(t)$. An estimate of the field patterns can be obtained from $\mathbf{W}$ as well.

The generative model allows for a back projection of selected components from component space to EEG sensor space. If one splits up $\hat{\mathbf{s}}(t)$ into the time courses of the discriminative, respectively non-discriminative, components such that $\hat{\mathbf{s}}(t) = \hat{\mathbf{s}}_d(t) + \hat{\mathbf{s}}_{nd}(t)$, then it follows that

$$\mathbf{x}(t) = \hat{\mathbf{A}}\left(\hat{\mathbf{s}}_d(t) + \hat{\mathbf{s}}_{nd}(t)\right) = \mathbf{x}_d(t) + \mathbf{x}_{nd}(t), \tag{3}$$

i.e. one obtains the separation into discriminative and non-discriminative EEG in the original sensor space ($\mathbf{x}_d(t)$ and $\mathbf{x}_{nd}(t)$). $\hat{\mathbf{s}}_d(t)$ is obtained from $\hat{\mathbf{s}}(t)$ by replacing the non-discriminative component time courses with zeros. $\hat{\mathbf{s}}_{nd}(t)$ is created accordingly.

Typically the vectors $\mathbf{w}_i$ are selected to maximize (or minimize) a certain objective function. Different objectives have led to different decomposition methods, such as the well known PCA and the relatively new SFA [8].

PCA finds a set of filters that maximize the variance of the decomposed signal. The spatial filters $\mathbf{w}_i$ found by PCA are the eigenvectors of the data covariance matrix $\mathbf{C}$. PCA can be computed very fast and is a simple, yet powerful, tool in data exploration and dimensionality reduction.

SFA in its linear form finds a set of filters that minimize the temporal variation of the decomposed signal. In other words, SFA maximizes temporal slowness, or smoothness, of the components. However, it does so without temporal filtering, i.e. no smoothing in the time domain is allowed. Appropriate constraints ensure that the component signals are mean-free, have unit variance, and are decorrelated. The temporal variation is defined as the mean variance of the first temporal derivative of the SFA components. Thus, SFA minimizes the following measure:

$$\left\langle \dot{s}_i^2 \right\rangle_t = \left\langle (\mathbf{w}_i^T \dot{\mathbf{x}})^2 \right\rangle_t = \mathbf{w}_i^T \dot{\mathbf{C}} \mathbf{w}_i, \tag{4}$$

where $\dot{\mathbf{C}}$ is the second moment matrix of the time derivative of the data. Including the unit variance constraint in the objective leads to the $\mathbf{w}_i$ as the solution of the generalized eigenvalue problem [1]

$$\dot{\mathbf{C}} \mathbf{w}_i = \lambda_i \mathbf{C} \mathbf{w}_i. \tag{5}$$

The resulting SFA components are ordered according to temporal variation from slowest to fastest. For this linear case of SFA, the computation of the SFA components is very fast, because the problem reduces to an eigenvalue decomposition.

2.3 Component Selection, Feature Extraction and Classification

PCA and SFA decompositions were estimated on the raw EEG post-stimulus epochs of the calibration data. The time course of a PCA/SFA component epoch was reduced to three samples by averaging over three non-overlapping intervals within the epoch. The borders of these intervals were determined automatically for each time course via a simple heuristic that uses class labels.

The number of components used for further feature extraction and classification, here denoted by N_c, was determined using a 10-fold chronological split cross-validation on the calibration data. Within each fold, the training data was used to estimate the PCA/SFA components and to select intervals of their time courses. Then the components were sorted in descending order according to their class discriminability. Classification performance of the test data was assessed for N_c running from 1 to 63. In order to keep the input dimensionality low and to avoid over-fitting, not the N_c with maximal performance was chosen but the N_c that sufficed to reach 95% of maximal classification performance.

Thus, the final dimensionality of the classifier input is given by $3 \cdot N_c$. The classifier we applied was regularized Fisher Discriminant Analysis (shrinkage FDA) on extracted features [2].

We compared four different preprocessing conditions for ERP classification: raw EEG channels (i.e. no preprocessing), PCA, SFA, and *best x-val*. The method *best x-val* is a combination of the PCA and SFA condition: We first computed classification performance on the calibration data for PCA and the SFA separately. Then the decomposition method that yielded the best performance on the calibration data was applied to the online-data. The procedures for feature extraction and classification were the same in all conditions. Estimation of PCA/SFA components, selection of components (selection of raw channels in condition 1), selection of intervals, and classifier training was done on the calibration data. The resulting decompositions, component subsets, intervals, and classifier weights were fixed and applied to the online data.

3 Results

Figure 1 shows the field patterns and ERPs of the two most class-discriminative PCA and SFA components of subject VPob. The increase in classification performance was highest for this subject (over 30% absolute increase for PCA and SFA compared to raw channels). Note that because the polarity of the weight vectors $\mathbf{w}_i$ is arbitrary, the sign of the field patterns and time courses is arbitrary too. Here we corrected the sign such that the maximum response for target stimuli is positive. The units of the time courses are arbitrarily scaled and therefore omitted. The two most discriminative ERPs of the PCA/SFA components show the largest class difference late in their time courses (i.e. with peaks between 400 and 500 ms). However, also early discriminative intervals are present in PCA as well as SFA components. The field patterns tend to have their foci in central regions of the scalp. One has to be careful with their interpretation, because the indi-

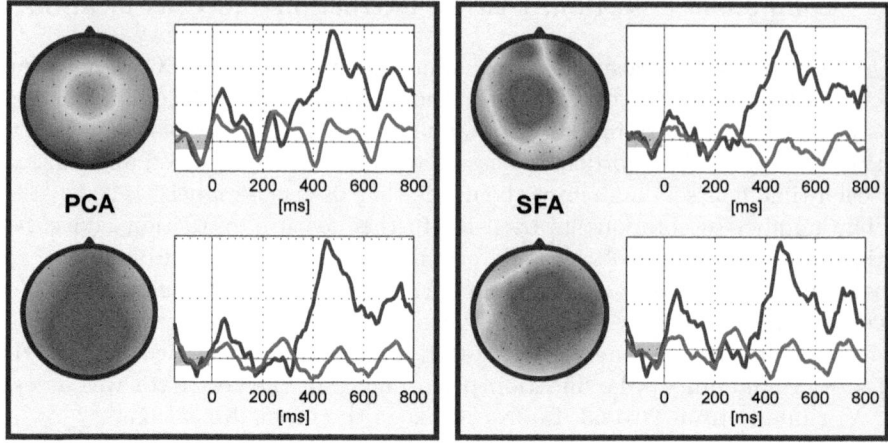

Fig. 1. Most discriminative components obtained by PCA and SFA, and their class-wise average responses (ERPs) for one subject. The blue line is the response for targets, the green line for non-target stimuli.

vidual PCA/SFA components not necessarily correspond to physiological EEG components. See section 4 for further notes on this point.

In figure 2 we depict the online-spelling data classification results of the different methods in several scatter plots. Each point in a scatter plot in the figure corresponds to the classification performances obtained for a single subject. The color of each point in plots **a** to **c** indicates N_c (the number of components) of the method on the y axis for this particular subject, as determined by cross-validation. Black stars indicate significant differences between the methods on the x and y axis when compared with a t-test, one star for $p < 0.05$ and two stars for $p < 0.01$. P-values are also given in upper left corner of each scatter plot.

In scatter plots **a** and **b** of figure 2 we compare the classification performance of the decomposition methods PCA and SFA (y axis, respectively) to classification using raw EGG channels (x axis). Both methods applied as preprocessing show a large performance increase compared to using no preprocessing. PCA, for example, improves classification performance for 26 out of 31 (84%). SFA yielded an improved classification in all but one subject (97%). In plot **c** of the same figure, we compare the performance of PCA with that of SFA. Here no statistically signifcant improvement for one method over the other can be observed. SFA worked better in 13 subjects, while PCA was better in 15 out of the 31 subjects. For 3 subjects the performance was the same.

The scatter plots **d**, **e**, and **f** of figure 2 compare the method *best x-val* to raw channels, PCA, and SFA. The color code used in these scatter plots indicates whether PCA or SFA was chosen as the *best x-val* method. For *best x-val* versus raw channels, we found that performance was better for 29 of the 31 subjects and equally good in the remaining two. In the ideal case, in which the calibration data performance accurately predicts the performance on the online data, all

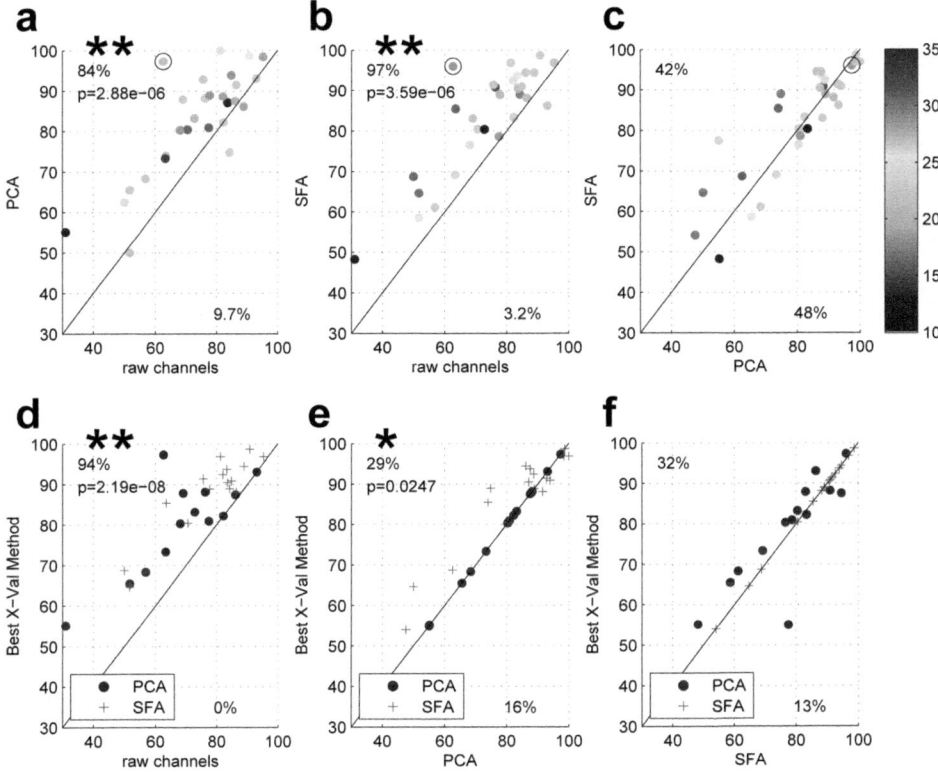

Fig. 2. Online classification performance. See text for detailed description.

points in scatter plots **e** and **f** should either lie above the diagonal or directly on it. However, for some subjects (9 out of 31) the choice for either PCA or SFA was wrong. The respective other method yielded better online classification. Those subjects are the red points underneath the diagonal in scatter plot **e** and the blue points underneath the diagonal in plot **f** of figure 2.

In figure 3 we show the grand average ERPs of the original EEG signal ($\mathbf{x}(t)$) and the EEG signal that would be observed for the discriminative subset of PCA/SFA components ($\mathbf{x}_d(t)$, see also equation 3). The average was taken over the subjects of the PASS2D study (mean over N=10 subjects). In this figure $\mathbf{x}_d(t)$ was created using the method *best x-val* and the set of components that was chosen after cross-validation. For $\mathbf{x}(t)$ and $\mathbf{x}_d(t)$, the figure shows the grand average target and non-target ERP time course of the central electrode Cz, scalp distribution of voltage averaged over three consecutive intervals separately for target and non-target stimuli, and discriminative power of the same intervals (AUC). Corresponding plots and scalp maps have the same color scale. The intervals from which the scalp plots were created are indicated with differently colored background in the time course of Cz. The figure shows that on average $\mathbf{x}_d(t)$ contains almost all of the event-related structure that was originally

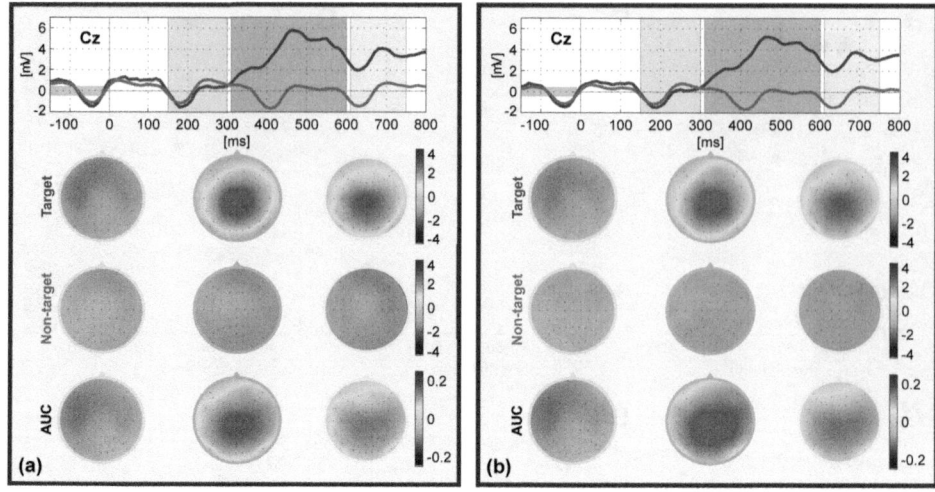

Fig. 3. Grand average ERPs and discriminative power of $\mathbf{x}(t)$ and $\mathbf{x}_d(t)$ (**a** and **b**, respectively). See equation 3 and text for detailed explanation.

contained in the original signal $\mathbf{x}(t)$. While the average amplitude is slightly lower for target epochs in $\mathbf{x}_d(t)$, the discriminative power has actually increased somewhat as can be observed in the scalp plots in the bottom rows of the plots.

4   Discussion

We have shown, that a subset of the extracted PCA/SFA components suffices to capture the ERP structure very well. However, it is generally not the case that any single PCA/SFA component corresponds to physiologically known EEG components, such as the P300 for example. By definition, the number of components obtained from any linear decomposition technique is equal to the number of EEG recording channels. This and the fact that physiological EEG components are likely to change in various aspects over the course of an experiment (latency and amplitude of time courses, shape of the field pattern, etc.) leads to an artificial break-up of physiological EEG components into several PCA/SFA components if they can be detected at all. Hence one has to be careful when interpreting obtained field patterns like the ones shown in figure 1.

After projecting discriminative PCA/SFA components back into EEG channel space, we found that the class-discriminability of the back projected EEG signal is elevated compared to the class-discriminability of the original EEG recordings. Hence, classification would be better when performed on the back projected EEG channels. However, doing the classification in the discriminative subspace of the decomposition method is even more beneficial because the number of dimensions is greatly reduced and thus features of the class distributions (such as their covariance structure) can be approximated better. The employed linear classifier LDA relies on an estimate of class-specific covariance structure and can therefore perform better if input dimensionality is reduced.

One other interesting question that needs to be investigated is why exactly SFA works for some subjects better than PCA and vice-versa. So far we have not been able to find consistent evidence which would aid in answering this question. This is still a matter of ongoing research.

In our analysis we have replicated the course of action that was taken during the actual BCI experiments: components were estimated, features extracted, and classifiers trained on calibration data only. The data of which classification results are reported was not used in model selection or training. Therefore we believe that our results bear strong relevance for future BCI studies. This however, remains to be shown with upcoming experiments.

Acknowledgments. We would like to thank Klaus-Robert Müller for valuable discussions. This work is supported by the European ICT Programme Project FP7-224631 and by GRK 1589/1.

References

1. Berkes, P., Wiskott, L.: Slow feature analysis yields a rich repertoire of complex cell properties. Journal of Vision 147, 579–602 (2005)
2. Blankertz, B., Lemm, S., Treder, M.S., Haufe, S., Müller, K.-R.: Single-trial analysis and classification of ERP components – a tutorial. NeuroImage (2010) (in press)
3. Blaschke, T., Berkes, P., Wiskott, L.: What is the relationship between slow feature analysis and independent component analysis? Neural Computation 18(10), 2495–2508 (2006)
4. Höhne, J., Schreuder, M., Blankertz, B., Tangermann, M.: Two-dimensional auditory P300 Speller with predictive text system. In: Conf. Proc. IEEE Eng. Med. Biol. Soc., pp. 4185–4188 (2010)
5. Kachenoura, A., Albera, L., Senhadji, L., Comon, P.: Ica: a potential tool for bci systems. IEEE Signal Processing Magazine, 25(1), 57–68 (2008)
6. Makeig, S., Jung, T.P., Bell, A.J., Ghahremani, D., Sejnowski, T.J.: Blind separation of auditory event-related brain responses into independent components. Proc. Natl. Acad. Sci. U.S.A. 94, 10979–10984 (1997)
7. Schreuder, M., Blankertz, B., Tangermann, M.: A New Auditory Multi-class Brain-Computer Interface Paradigm: Spatial Hearing as an Informative Cue. PLoS ONE 5(4) (2010)
8. Wiskott, L., Sejnowski, T.J.: Slow feature analysis: unsupervised learning of invariances. Neural Computation 14(4), 715–770 (2002)

Transforming Auto-Encoders

Geoffrey E. Hinton, Alex Krizhevsky, and Sida D. Wang

Department of Computer Science, University of Toronto
{geoffrey.hinton,akrizhevsky,sidawang88}@gmail.com

Abstract. The artificial neural networks that are used to recognize shapes typically use one or more layers of learned feature detectors that produce scalar outputs. By contrast, the computer vision community uses complicated, hand-engineered features, like SIFT [6], that produce a whole vector of outputs including an explicit representation of the pose of the feature. We show how neural networks can be used to learn features that output a whole vector of instantiation parameters and we argue that this is a much more promising way of dealing with variations in position, orientation, scale and lighting than the methods currently employed in the neural networks community. It is also more promising than the hand-engineered features currently used in computer vision because it provides an efficient way of adapting the features to the domain.

Keywords: Invariance, auto-encoder, shape representation.

1 Introduction

Current methods for recognizing objects in images perform poorly and use methods that are intellectually unsatisfying. Some of the best computer vision systems use histograms of oriented gradients as "visual words" and model the spatial distribution of these elements using a crude spatial pyramid. Such methods can recognize objects correctly without knowing exactly where they are – an ability that is used to diagnose brain damage in humans. The best artifical neural networks [4,5,10] use hand-coded weight-sharing schemes to reduce the number of free parameters and they achieve local translational invariance by subsampling the activities of local pools of translated replicas of the same kernel. This method of dealing with the changes in images caused by changes in viewpoint is much better than no method at all, but it is clearly incapable of dealing with recognition tasks, such as facial identity recognition, that require knowledge of the precise spatial relationships between high-level parts like a nose and a mouth. After several stages of subsampling in a convolutional net, high-level features have a lot of uncertainty in their poses. This is generally regarded as a desireable property because it amounts to invariance to pose over some limited range, but it makes it impossible to compute precise spatial relationships.

This paper argues that convolutional neural networks are misguided in what they are trying to achieve. Instead of aiming for viewpoint invariance in the activities of "neurons" that use a single scalar output to summarize the activities

T. Honkela et al. (Eds.): ICANN 2011, Part I, LNCS 6791, pp. 44–51, 2011.

of a local pool of replicated feature detectors, artifical neural networks should use local "capsules" that perform some quite complicated internal computations on their inputs and then encapsulate the results of these computations into a small vector of highly informative outputs. Each capsule learns to recognize an implicitly defined visual entity over a limited domain of viewing conditions and deformations and it outputs both the probability that the entity is present within its limited domain and a set of "instantiation parameters" that may include the precise pose, lighting and deformation of the visual entity relative to an implicitly defined canonical version of that entity. When the capsule is working properly, the probability of the visual entity being present is locally invariant – it does not change as the entity moves over the manifold of possible appearances within the limited domain covered by the capsule. The instantiation parameters, however, are "equivariant" – as the viewing conditions change and the entity moves over the appearance manifold, the instantiation parameters change by a corresponding amount because they are representing the intrinsic coordinates of the entity on the appearance manifold.

One of the major advantages of capsules that output explicit instantiation parameters is that they provide a simple way to recognize wholes by recognizing their parts. If a capsule can learn to output the pose of its visual entity in a vector that is linearly related to the "natural" representations of pose used in computer graphics, there is a simple and highly selective test for whether the visual entities represented by two active capsules, A and B, have the right spatial relationship to activate a higher-level capsule, C. Suppose that the pose outputs of capsule A are represented by a matrix, T_A, that specifies the coordinate transform between the canonical visual entity of A and the actual instantiation of that entity found by capsule A. If we multiply T_A by the part-whole coordinate transform T_{AC} that relates the canonical visual entity of A to the canonical visual entity of C, we get a prediction for T_C. Similarly, we can use T_B and T_{BC} to get another prediction. If these predictions are a good match, the instantiations found by capsules A and B are in the right spatial relationship to activate capsule C and the average of the predictions tells us how the larger visual entity represented by C is transformed relative to the canonical visual entity of C. If, for example, A represents a mouth and B represents a nose, they can each make a prediction for the pose of the face. If these predictions agree, the mouth and nose must be in the right spatial relationship to form a face. An interesting property of this way of performing shape recognition is that the knowledge of part-whole relationships is viewpoint-invariant and is represented by weight matrices whereas the knowledge of the instantiation parameters of currently observed objects and their parts is viewpoint-equivariant and is represented by neural activities [12].

In order to get such a part-whole hierarchy off the ground, the "capsules" that implement the lowest-level parts in the hierarchy need to extract explicit pose parameters from pixel intensities. This paper shows that these capsules are quite easy to learn from pairs of transformed images if the neural net has direct, non-visual access to the transformations. In humans, for example, a saccade causes

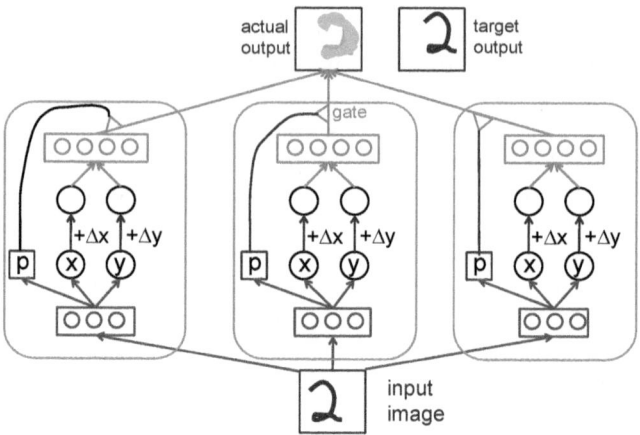

Fig. 1. Three capsules of a transforming auto-encoder that models translations. Each capsule in the figure has 3 recognition units and 4 generation units. The weights on the connections are learned by backpropagating the discrepancy between the actual and target outputs.

a pure translation of the retinal image and the cortex has non-visual access to information about eye-movements.

2   Learning the First Level of Capsules

Once pixel intensities have been converted into the outputs of a set of active, first-level capsules each of which produces an explicit representation of the pose of its visual entity, it is relatively easy to see how larger and more complex visual entities can be recognized by using agreements of the poses predicted by active, lower-level capsules. But where do the first-level capsules come from? How can an artificial neural network learn to convert the language of pixel intensities to the language of pose parameters? That is the question addressed by this paper and it turns out that there is a surprisingly simple answer which we call a "transforming auto-encoder". We explain the idea using simple 2-D images and capsules whose only pose outputs are an x and a y position. We generalize to more complicated poses later.

Consider the feedforward neural network shown in figure 1. The network is deterministic and, once it has been learned, it takes as inputs an image and desired shifts, Δx and Δy, and it outputs the shifted image. The network is composed of a number of separate capsules that only interact at the final layer when they cooperate to produce the desired shifted image. Each capsule has its own logistic "recognition units" that act as a hidden layer for computing three numbers, x, y, and p, that are the outputs that the capsule will send to higher levels of the vision system. p is the probability that the capsule's visual entity is

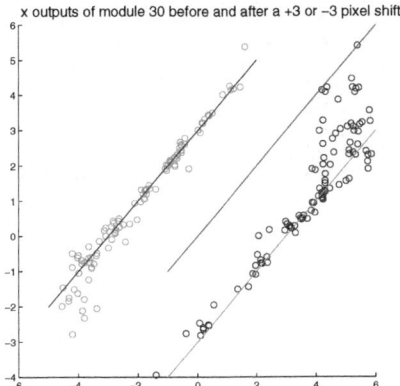
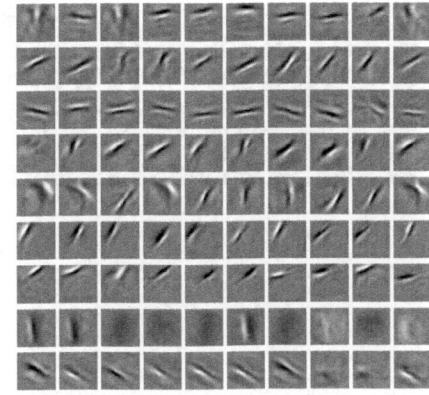

Fig. 2. Left: A scatterplot in which the vertical axis represents the x output of one of the capsules for each digit image and the horizontal axis represents the x output from the same capsule if that image is shifted by +3 or −3 pixels in the x direction. If the original image is already near the limit of the x positions that the capsule can represent, shifting further in that direction causes the capsule to produce the wrong answer, but this does not matter if the capsule sets its probability to 0 for data outside its domain of competence. **Right:** The outgoing weights of 10 of the 20 generative units for 9 of the capsules.

present in the input image. The capsule also has its own "generation units" that are used for computing the capsule's contribution to the transformed image. The inputs to the generation units are $x + \Delta x$ and $y + \Delta y$, and the contributions that the capsule's generation units make to the output image are multiplied by p, so inactive capsules have no effect.

For the transforming auto-encoder to produce the correct output image, it is essential that the x and y values computed by each active capsule correspond to the actual x and y position of its visual entity and we do not need to know this visual entity or the origin of its coordinate frame in advance.

As a simple demonstration of the efficacy of the transforming auto-encoder, we trained a network with 30 capsules each of which had 10 recognition units and 20 generation units. Each capsule sees the whole of an MNIST digit image. Both the input and the output images are shifted randomly by -2, -1, 0, +1, or +2 pixels in the x and y directions and the transforming auto-encoder is given the resulting Δx and Δy as an additional input. Figure 2 shows that the capsules do indeed output x and y values that shift in just the right way when the input image is shifted. Figure 2 shows that the capsules learn generative units with projective fields that are highly localized. The receptive fields of the recognition units are noisier and somewhat less localized.

2.1 More Complex 2-D Transformations

If each capsule is given 9 real-valued outputs that are treated as a 3×3 matrix A, a transforming auto-encoder can be trained to predict a full 2-D affine

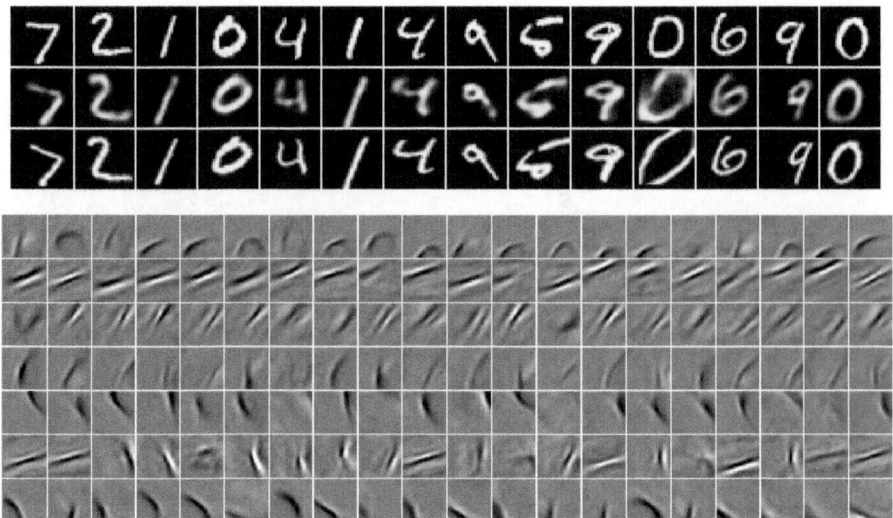

Fig. 3. Top: Full affine transformations using a transforming auto-encoder with 25 capsules each of which has 40 recognition units and 40 generation units. The top row shows input images; the middle row shows output images and the bottom row shows the correctly transformed output images. **Bottom:** The output weights of the first 20 generation units of the first 7 capsules for this transforming auto-encoder.

transformation (translation, rotation, scaling and shearing). A known transformation matrix T is applied to the output of the capsule A to get the matrix TA. The elements of TA are then used as the inputs to the generation units when predicting the target output image.

2.2 Modeling Changes in 3-D Viewpoint

A major potential advantage of using matrix multiplies to model the effects of viewpoint is that it should make it far easier to cope with 3-D. Our preliminary experiments (see figure 4) used computer graphics to generate stereo images of various types of car from many different viewpoints. The transforming auto-encoder consisted of 900 capsules, each with two layers (32 then 64) of rectified linear recognition units [8]. The capsules had 11x11 pixel receptive fields which were arranged on a 30x30 grid over the 96x96 image, with a stride of 3 pixels between neighbouring capsules. There was no weight-sharing. Each capsule produced from its layer of 64 recognition units a 3x3 matrix representation of the 3-D orientation of the feature that it was tuned to detect, as well as a probability that its implicitly defined feature was present. This 3x3 matrix was then multiplied by the real transformation matrix between the source and target images, and the result was fed into the capsule's single layer of 128 generative rectified linear units. The generation unit activities were multiplied by the capsule's "feature presence" probability and the result was used to increment the intensities in

Fig. 4. Left: Input, output and target stereo-pairs for training data. **Right:** Input, output and target stereo-pairs for car models not seen during training.

a 22x22 patch of the reconstructed image centered at the center of the capsule's 11x11 receptive field. Since the data consisted of stereo pairs of images, each capsule had to look at an 11x11 patch in both members of the stereo pair, as well as reconstructing a 22x22 patch in both members.

3 Discussion

Using multiple real-values is the natural way to represent pose information and it is much more efficient than using coarse coding[3], but it comes at a price: The only thing that binds the values together is the fact that they are the pose outputs of the same capsule so it is not possible for a capsule to represent more than one instance of its visual entity at the same time. It might seem that the inability to allow several, simultaneous instances of the same visual entity in the same limited domain is a serious weakness and indeed it is. It can be ameliorated by making each of the lowest-level capsules operate over a very limited region of the pose space and only allowing larger regions for more complex visual entities that are much less densely distributed. But however small the region, it will always be possible to confound the system by putting two instances of the same visual entity with slightly different poses in the same region. The phenomenon known as "crowding" [9] suggests that this type of confusion may occur in human vision.

From a pure machine learning perspective, providing the network with additional external inputs that specify the way in which the image has been transformed may appear unnecessary because this information could, in principle, be computed from the two images [7]. However, this information is often readily available and it makes the learning much easier, so it is silly not to use it. Specifying a global transformation of the image is *much* easier than explicitly specifying the poses of features because it can be done without making any committment to what visual entity should be extracted by each capsule or what intrinsic coordinate frame should be used when representing the pose of that visual entity.

A capsule bears some resemblance to a local pool of units in a convolutional neural network, because many of the recognition units have quite similar receptive fields in slightly different positions. There is a very important difference, however, in the way in which the outputs of all the recognition units are encapsulated for use by higher levels. In a convolutional pool, the combined output after subsampling is typically the scalar activity of the most active unit in the pool [11]. Even if the location of this unit is used when creating the reconstruction required for unsupervised learning, it is not used by higher levels [5] because the aim of a convolutional net is to make the activities translation invariant. Also, even if the location that is used for reconstruction were to be passed to higher levels, it would only have integer-valued coordinates. A capsule makes much better use of the outputs of the recognition units by using them to compute precise position coordinates which are accurate to a small fraction of a pixel. In this respect it resembles a steerable filter [2], but unlike most steerable filters it learns the receptive fields of the recognition units to optimize the accuracy of the computed coordinates and it also learns what visual entity to represent. Replicated copies of exactly the same weight kernel are far from optimal for extracting the pose of a visual entity over a limited domain, especially if the replication must cover scale and orientation as well as position.

Transforming auto-encoders also have an interesting relationship to Kalman filters. The usual way to apply Kalman filters to data in which the dynamics is a non-linear function of the observations is to use an "extended" Kalman filter that linearizes the dynamics about the current operating point. This often works quite well but it is clearly a hack. If we view the input and desired output images as temporally adjacent, the transforming auto-encoder is a more principled way to use a linear dynamical model. The recognition units learn to map the input to a representation in which the dynamics really are linear. After the poses of the capsules have been linearly transformed, the generation units map back to the observation domain. By measuring the error in the observation domain, we avoid the need to compute determinants that keep track of the extent to which errors have been compressed or expanded in moving between domains.

If we eliminate the extra input that gives the transforming auto-encoder direct knowledge of the transformation, we can model the small transformations between adjacent time-frames as zero-mean Gaussian noise. This reduces the transforming auto-encoder to a much less powerful learning method that is only able to find "slow features" that do not change much between successive images.

A model proposed in [1] uses a very different learning procedure to learn a similar representation to the transforming auto-encoder. The locally invariant probabilities that capsules compute resemble the outputs of their complex cells and the equivariant instantiation parameters resemble the outputs of their simple cells. They learn without using knowledge of transformations, but they only learn instantiation parameters that are linear functions of the image.

A transforming auto-encoder can force the outputs of a capsule to represent *any* property of an image that we can manipulate in a known way. It is easy, for example, to scale up all of the pixel intensities. If a first-level capsule outputs a number that is first multiplied by the brightness scaling factor and then used to scale the outputs of its generation units when predicting the brightness-transformed output, this number will learn to represent brightness and will allow the capsule to disentangle the probability that an instance of its visual entity is present from the brightness of the instance. If the direction of lighting of a scene can be varied in a controlled way, a capsule can be forced to output two numbers representing this direction but only if the visual entity is complex enough to allow the lighting direction to be extracted from the activities of the recognition units.

References

1. Berkes, P., Turner, R.E., Sahani, M.: A structured model of video reproduces primary visual cortical organisation. PLoS Computational Biology 5(9), 1–16 (2009)
2. Freeman, W., Adelson, E.: The design and use of steerable filters. IEEE Transactions on Pattern Analysis and Machine Intelligence 13(9), 891–906 (1991)
3. Hinton, G.E.: Shape representation in parallel systems. In: Proc. 7th International Joint Conference on Artificial Intelligence, vol. 2, pp. 1088–1096 (1981)
4. LeCun, Y., Bottou, L., Bengio, Y., Haffner, P.: Gradient-based learning applied to document recognition. Proceedings of the IEEE 86(11), 2278–2324 (1998)
5. Lee, H., Grosse, R., Ranganath, R., Ng, A.: Convolutional deep belief networks for scalable unsupervised learning of hierarchical representations. In: Proc. 26th International Conference on Machine Learning (2009)
6. Lowe, D.G.: Object recognition from local scale-invariant features. In: Proc. International Conference on Computer Vision (1999)
7. Memisevic, R., Hinton, G.: Learning to represent spatial transformations with factored higher-order boltzmann machines. Neural Comp. 22, 1473–1492 (2010)
8. Nair, V., Hinton, G.E.: Rectified linear units improve restricted boltzmann machines. In: Proc. 27th International Conference on Machine Learning (2010)
9. Pelli, D.G., Tillman, K.A.: The uncrowded window of object recognition. Nature Neuroscience 11, 1129–1135 (2008)
10. Ranzato, M., Huang, F., Boureau, Y., LeCun, Y.: Unsupervised learning of invariant feature hierarchies with applications to object recognition. In: Proc. Computer Vision and Pattern Recognition Conference (CVPR 2007). IEEE Press, Los Alamitos (2007)
11. Riesenhuber, M., Poggio, T.: Hierarchical models of object recognition in cortex. Nature Neuroscience 2, 1019–1025 (1999)
12. Zemel, R.S., Mozer, M.C., Hinton, G.E.: Traffic: Recognizing objects using hierarchical reference frame transformations. In: Touretzky, D.S. (ed.) Advances in Neural Information Processing Systems, pp. 266–273. Morgan Kauffman, San Mateo (1990)

Stacked Convolutional Auto-Encoders for Hierarchical Feature Extraction

Jonathan Masci, Ueli Meier, Dan Cireşan, and Jürgen Schmidhuber

Istituto Dalle Molle di Studi sull'Intelligenza Artificiale (IDSIA)
Lugano, Switzerland
{jonathan,ueli,dan,juergen}@idsia.ch

Abstract. We present a novel convolutional auto-encoder (CAE) for unsupervised feature learning. A stack of CAEs forms a convolutional neural network (CNN). Each CAE is trained using conventional on-line gradient descent without additional regularization terms. A max-pooling layer is essential to learn biologically plausible features consistent with those found by previous approaches. Initializing a CNN with filters of a trained CAE stack yields superior performance on a digit (MNIST) and an object recognition (CIFAR10) benchmark.

Keywords: convolutional neural network, auto-encoder, unsupervised learning, classification.

1 Introduction

The main purpose of unsupervised learning methods is to extract generally useful features from unlabelled data, to detect and remove input redundancies, and to preserve only essential aspects of the data in robust and discriminative representations. Unsupervised methods have been routinely used in many scientific and industrial applications. In the context of neural network architectures, unsupervised layers can be stacked on top of each other to build deep hierarchies [7]. Input layer activations are fed to the first layer which feeds the next, and so on, for all layers in the hierarchy. Deep architectures can be trained in an unsupervised layer-wise fashion, and later fine-tuned by back-propagation to become classifiers [9]. Unsupervised initializations tend to avoid local minima and increase the network's performance stability [6].

Most methods are based on the *encoder-decoder* paradigm, e.g., [20]. The input is first transformed into a typically lower-dimensional space *(encoder)*, and then expanded to reproduce the initial data *(decoder)*. Once a layer is trained, its code is fed to the next, to better model highly non-linear dependencies in the input. Methods using this paradigm include stacks of: Low-Complexity Coding and Decoding machines (LOCOCODE) [10], Predictability Minimization layers [23,24], Restricted Boltzmann Machines (RBMs) [8], auto-encoders [20] and energy based models [15].

In visual object recognition, CNNs [1,3,4,14,26] often excel. Unlike patch-based methods [19] they preserve the input's neighborhood relations and

T. Honkela et al. (Eds.): ICANN 2011, Part I, LNCS 6791, pp. 52–59, 2011.

spatial locality in their latent higher-level feature representations. While the common fully connected deep architectures do not scale well to realistic-sized high-dimensional images in terms of computational complexity, CNNs do, since the number of free parameters describing their shared weights does not depend on the input dimensionality [16,18,28].

This paper introduces the *Convolutional Auto-Encoder*, a hierarchical unsupervised feature extractor that scales well to high-dimensional inputs. It learns non-trivial features using plain stochastic gradient descent, and discovers good CNNs initializations that avoid the numerous distinct local minima of highly non-convex objective functions arising in virtually all deep learning problems.

2 Preliminaries

2.1 Auto-Encoder

We recall the basic principles of auto-encoder models, e.g., [2]. An auto-encoder takes an input $\mathbf{x} \in \mathcal{R}^d$ and first maps it to the latent representation $\mathbf{h} \in \mathcal{R}^{d'}$ using a deterministic function of the type $\mathbf{h} = f_\theta = \sigma(Wx + b)$ with parameters $\theta = \{W, b\}$. This "code" is then used to reconstruct the input by a reverse mapping of f: $\mathbf{y} = f_{\theta'}(h) = \sigma(W'h + b')$ with $\theta' = \{W', b'\}$. The two parameter sets are usually constrained to be of the form $W' = W^T$, using the same weights for encoding the input and decoding the latent representation. Each training pattern x_i is then mapped onto its code h_i and its reconstruction y_i. The parameters are optimized, minimizing an appropriate cost function over the training set $\mathcal{D}_n = \{(x_0, t_0), ..., (x_n, t_n)\}$.

2.2 Denoising Auto-Encoder

Without any additional constraints, conventional auto-encoders learn the identity mapping. This problem can be circumvented by using a probabilistic RBM approach, or sparse coding, or *denoising auto-encoders* (DAs) trying to reconstruct noisy inputs [27]. The latter performs as well as or even better than RBMs [2]. Training involves the reconstruction of a clean input from a partially destroyed one. Input x becomes corrupted input $\bar{x}$ by adding a variable amount v of noise distributed according to the characteristics of the input image. Common choices include binomial noise (switching pixels on or off) for black and white images, or uncorrelated Gaussian noise for color images. The parameter v represents the percentage of permissible corruption. The auto-encoder is trained to *denoise* the inputs by first finding the latent representation $\mathbf{h} = f_\theta(\bar{x}) = \sigma(W\bar{x} + b)$ from which to reconstruct the original input $\mathbf{y} = f_{\theta'}(h) = \sigma(W'h + b')$.

2.3 Convolutional Neural Networks

CNNs are hierarchical models whose convolutional layers alternate with subsampling layers, reminiscent of simple and complex cells in the primary visual cortex [11]. The network architecture consists of three basic building blocks to be stacked and composed as needed. We have the convolutional layer, the max-pooling layer and the classification layer [14]. CNNs are among the most successful models for supervised image classification and set the state-of-the-art in many benchmarks [13,14].

3   Convolutional Auto-Encoder (CAE)

Fully connected AEs and DAEs both ignore the 2D image structure. This is not only a problem when dealing with realistically sized inputs, but also introduces redundancy in the parameters, forcing each feature to be global (i.e., to span the entire visual field). However, the trend in vision and object recognition adopted by the most successful models [17,25] is to discover localized features that repeat themselves all over the input. CAEs differs from conventional AEs as their weights are shared among all locations in the input, preserving spatial locality. The reconstruction is hence due to a linear combination of basic image patches based on the latent code.

The CAE architecture is intuitively similar to the one described in Sec. 2.2, except that the weights are shared. For a mono-channel input x the latent representation of the k-*th* feature map is given by

$$h^k = \sigma(x * W^k + b^k) \tag{1}$$

where the bias is broadcasted to the whole map, σ is an activation function (we used the scaled hyperbolic tangent in all our experiments), and $*$ denotes the 2D convolution. A single bias per latent map is used, as we want each filter to specialize on features of the whole input (one bias per pixel would introduce too many degrees of freedom). The reconstruction is obtained using

$$y = \sigma(\sum_{k \in H} h^k * \tilde{W}^k + c) \tag{2}$$

where again there is one bias c per input channel. H identifies the group of latent feature maps; $\tilde{W}$ identifies the flip operation over both dimensions of the weights. The 2D convolution in equation (1) and (2) is determined by context. The convolution of an $m \times m$ matrix with an $n \times n$ matrix may in fact result in an $(m+n-1) \times (m+n-1)$ matrix (full convolution) or in an $(m-n+1) \times (m-n+1)$ (valid convolution). The cost function to minimize is the mean squared error (MSE):

$$E(\theta) = \frac{1}{2n} \sum_{i=1}^{n} (x_i - y_i)^2. \tag{3}$$

Just as for standard networks the backpropagation algorithm is applied to compute the gradient of the error function with respect to the parameters. This can be easily obtained by convolution operations using the following formula:

$$\frac{\partial E(\theta)}{\partial W^k} = x * \delta h^k + \tilde{h}^k * \delta y. \tag{4}$$

δh and δy are the deltas of the hidden states and the reconstruction, respectively. The weights are then updated using stochastic gradient descent.

3.1   Max-Pooling

For hierarchical networks in general and CNNs in particular, a max-pooling layer [22] is often introduced to obtain translation-invariant representations. Max-pooling down-samples the latent representation by a constant factor, usually taking the maximum value over non overlapping sub-regions. This helps improving filter selectivity, as the activation of each neuron in the latent representation is determined by the "match" between the feature and the input field over the region of interest. Max-pooling was originally intended for fully-supervised feed-forward architectures only.

Here we introduce a max-pooling layer that introduces sparsity over the hidden representation by erasing all non-maximal values in non overlapping sub-regions. This forces the feature detectors to become more broadly applicable, avoiding trivial solutions such as having only one weight "on" (identity function). During the reconstruction phase, such a sparse latent code decreases the average number of filters contributing to the decoding of each pixel, forcing filters to be more general. Consequently, with a max-pooling layer there is no obvious need for L1 and/or L2 regularization over hidden units and/or weights.

3.2   Stacked Convolutional Auto-Encoders (CAES)

Several AEs can be stacked to form a deep hierarchy, e.g. [27]. Each layer receives its input from the latent representation of the layer below. As for deep belief networks, unsupervised pre-training can be done in greedy, layer-wise fashion. Afterwards the weights can be fine-tuned using back-propagation, or the top level activations can be used as feature vectors for SVMs or other classifiers. Analogously, a CAE stack (CAES) can be used to initialize a CNN with identical topology prior to a supervised training stage.

4   Experiments

We begin by visually inspecting the filters of various CAEs, trained in various setups on a digit dataset (MNIST [14]) and on natural images (CIFAR10 [13]). In Figure 1 we compare 20 7×7 filters (learned on MNIST) of four CAEs of the same topology, but trained differently. The first is trained on original digits (a), the second on noisy inputs with 50% binomial noise added (b), the third has an additional max-pooling layer of size 2×2 (c), and the fourth is trained on noisy inputs (30% binomial noise) and has a max-pooling layer of size 2×2 (d). We add 30% noise in conjunction with max-pooling layers, to avoid loss of too much relevant information. The CAE without any additional constraints (a) learns trivial solutions. Interesting and biologically plausible filters only emerge once the CAE is trained with a max-pooling layer. With additional noise the filters become more localized. For this particular example, max-pooling yields the visually nicest filters; those of the other approaches do not have a well-defined shape. A max-pooling layer is an elegant way of enforcing a sparse code required to deal with the overcomplete representations of convolutional architectures.

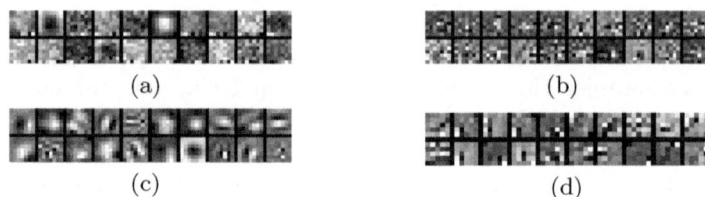

Fig. 1. A randomly selected subset of the first layer's filters learned on MNIST to compare noise and pooling. (a) No max-pooling, 0% noise, (b) No max-pooling, 50% noise, (c) Max-pooling of 2x2, (d) Max-pooling of 2x2, 30% noise.

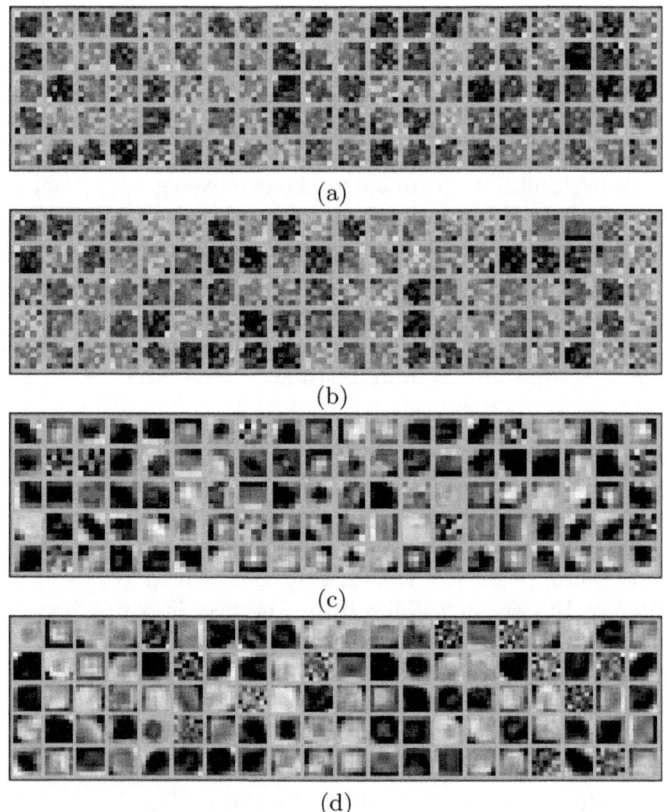

Fig. 2. A randomly selected subset of the first layer's filters learned on CIFAR10 to compare noise and pooling (best viewed in colours). (a) No pooling and 0% noise, (b) No pooling and 50% noise, (c) Pooling of 2x2 and 0% noise, (d) Pooling of 2x2 and 50% noise.

When dealing with natural color images, Gaussian noise instead of binomial noise is added to the input of a denoising CAE. We repeat the above experiment on CIFAR10. The corresponding filters are shown in Figure 2. The impact of a max-pooling layer is striking (c), whereas adding noise (b) has almost no visual effect except on the weight magnitudes (d). As for MNIST, only a max-pooling layer guarantees convincing solutions, indicating that max-pooling is essential. It seems to at least partially solve the problems that usually arise when training auto-encoders by gradient descent. Another welcome aspect of our approach is that except for the max-pooling kernel size, no additional parameters have to be set by trial and error or time consuming cross-validation.

4.1 Initializing a CNN with Trained CAES Weights

The filters found in the previous section are not only interesting in themselves but also biologically plausible. We now train a CAES and use it to initialize a CNN with the same topology, to be fine-tuned for classification tasks. This has already shown to alleviate common problems with training deep standard MLPs, [6]. We investigate the benefits of unsupervised pre-training through comparisons with randomly initialized CNNs.

We begin with the well established MNIST benchmark [14] to show the effect of pre-training for subsets of various sizes. Classification results in Table 1 are based on the complete test set and the specified numbers of training samples. The network has 6 hidden layers: 1) convolutional layer with 100 5x5 filters per input channel; 2) max-pooling layer of 2x2; 3) convolutional layer with 150 5x5 filters per map; 4) max-pooling layer of 2x2; 5) convolutional layer of 200 maps of size 3x3; 6) a fully-connected layer of 300 hidden neurons. The output layer has a softmax activation function with one neuron per class. The learning rate is annealed during training. No deformations are applied to MNIST to increase the "virtual" number of training samples, which would reduce the impact of unsupervised pre-training for this problem that is already considered as good as solved. We also test our model on CIFAR10. This dataset is challenging because little information is conveyed by its 32 by 32 pixel input patterns. Many methods were tested on it. The most successful ones use normalization techniques to remove second order information among pixels [5,12], or deep CNNs [3]. Our method provides good recognition rates even when trained on "raw"

Table 1. Classification results on MNIST using various subsets of the full data

	1k	10k	50k
CAE [%]	**7.23**	**1.88**	**0.71**
CNN [%]	7.63	2.21	0.79
K-means (4k feat) [5][a]	-	-	0.88

[a] We performed this experiment using the code provide by the authors.

Table 2. Classification results on CIFAR10 using various subsets of the full data; comparison with other unsupervised methods

	1k	10k	50k
CAE [%]	**52.30**	**34.35**	21.80
CNN [%]	55.52	35.23	22.50
Mean-cov. RBM [21]	-	-	29.00
Conv. RBM [12]	-	-	21.10
K-means (4k feat) [5]	-	-	*20.40*

pixel information only. We add 5% translations only for supervised fine-tuning, and re-use the MNIST CNN architecture, except that the input layer has three maps, one for each color channel. Results are shown in Table 2. On CIFAR10 we obtain, to our knowledge, the best result so far for any unsupervised architecture trained on non-whitened data. Using raw data makes the system fully on-line and, additionally, there is no need to gather statistics over the whole training set. The performance improvement with respect to the randomly initialized CNN is bigger than for MNIST because the problem is much harder and the network profits more from unsupervised pre-training.

5   Conclusion

We introduced the Convolutional Auto-Encoder, an unsupervised method for hierarchical feature extraction. It learns biologically plausible filters. A CNN can be initialized by a CAE stack. While the CAE's overcomplete hidden representation makes learning even harder than for standard auto-encoders, good filters emerge if we use a max-pooling layer, an elegant way of enforcing sparse codes without any regularization parameters to be set by trial and error. Pre-trained CNNs tend to outperform randomly initialized nets slightly, but consistently. Our CIFAR10 result is the best for any unsupervised method trained on the raw data, and close to the best published result on this benchmark.

References

1. Behnke, S.: Hierarchical Neural Networks for Image Interpretation. LNCS, vol. 2766, pp. 1–13. Springer, Heidelberg (2003)
2. Bengio, Y., Lamblin, P., Popovici, D., Larochelle, H.: Greedy layer-wise training of deep networks. In: Neural Information Processing Systems, NIPS (2007)
3. Cireşan, D.C., Meier, U., Masci, J., Gambardella, L.M., Schmidhuber, J.: High-Performance Neural Networks for Visual Object Classification. ArXiv e-prints, arXiv:1102.0183v1 (cs.AI) (Febuary 2011)
4. Ciresan, D.C., Meier, U., Masci, J., Schmidhuber, J.: Flexible, high performance convolutional neural networks for image classification. In: International Joint Conference on Artificial Intelligence, IJCAI (to appear 2011)
5. Coates, A., Lee, H., Ng, A.: An analysis of single-layer networks in unsupervised feature learning. Advances in Neural Information Processing Systems (2010)
6. Erhan, D., Bengio, Y., Courville, A., Manzagol, P.A., Vincent, P.: Why Does Unsupervised Pre-training Help Deep Learning? Journal of Machine Learning Research 11, 625–660 (2010)
7. Fukushima, K.: Neocognitron: A self-organizing neural network for a mechanism of pattern recognition unaffected by shift in position. Biological Cybernetics 36(4), 193–202 (1980)
8. Hinton, G.E.: Training products of experts by minimizing contrastive divergence. Neural Comp. 14(8), 1771–1800 (2002)
9. Hinton, G.E., Osindero, S., Teh, Y.W.: A fast learning algorithm for deep belief nets. Neural Computation (2006)

10. Hochreiter, S., Schmidhuber, J.: Feature extraction through LOCOCODE. Neural Computation 11(3), 679–714 (1999)
11. Hubel, D.H., Wiesel, T.N.: Receptive fields and functional architecture of monkey striate cortex. The Journal of Physiology 195(1), 215–243 (1968), http://jp.physoc.org/cgi/content/abstract/195/1/215
12. Krishevsky, A.: Convolutional deep belief networks on CIFAR-2010 (2010)
13. Krizhevsky, A.: Learning multiple layers of features from tiny images. Master's thesis, Computer Science Department, University of Toronto (2009)
14. LeCun, Y., Bottou, L., Bengio, Y., Haffner, P.: Gradient-based learning applied to document recognition. Proceedings of the IEEE 86(11), 2278–2324 (1998)
15. LeCun, Y., Chopra, S., Hadsell, R., Ranzato, M., Huang, F.: A tutorial on energy-based learning. In: Bakir, G., Hofman, T., Schölkopf, B., Smola, A., Taskar, B. (eds.) Predicting Structured Data. MIT Press, Cambridge (2006)
16. Lee, H., Grosse, R., Ranganath, R., Ng, A.Y.: Convolutional deep belief networks for scalable unsupervised learning of hierarchical representations. In: Proceedings of the 26th International Conference on Machine Learning, pp. 609–616 (2009)
17. Lowe, D.: Object recognition from local scale-invariant features. In: The Proceedings of the Seventh IEEE International Conference on Computer Vision, vol. 2, pp. 1150–1157 (1999)
18. Norouzi, M., Ranjbar, M., Mori, G.: Stacks of convolutional Restricted Boltzmann Machines for shift-invariant feature learning. In: 2009 IEEE Conference on Computer Vision and Pattern Recognition, pp. 2735–2742 (June 2009), http://ieeexplore.ieee.org/lpdocs/epic03/wrapper.htm?arnumber=5206577
19. Ranzato, M., Boureau, Y., LeCun, Y.: Sparse feature learning for deep belief networks. In: Advances in Neural Information Processing Systems, NIPS 2007 (2007)
20. Ranzato, M., Fu Jie Huang, Y.L.B., LeCun, Y.: Unsupervised learning of invariant feature hierarchies with applications to object recognition. In: Proc. of Computer Vision and Pattern Recognition Conference (2007)
21. Ranzato, M., Hinton, G.E.: Modeling pixel means and covariances using factorized third-order boltzmann machines. In: Proc. of Computer Vision and Pattern Recognition Conference, CVPR 2010 (2010)
22. Scherer, D., Müller, A., Behnke, S.: Evaluation of pooling operations in convolutional architectures for object recognition. In: International Conference on Artificial Neural Networks (2010)
23. Schmidhuber, J.: Learning factorial codes by predictability minimization. Neural Computation 4(6), 863–879 (1992)
24. Schmidhuber, J., Eldracher, M., Foltin, B.: Semilinear predictability minimization produces well-known feature detectors. Neural Computation 8(4), 773–786 (1996)
25. Serre, T., Wolf, L., Poggio, T.: Object recognition with features inspired by visual cortex. In: Proc. of Computer Vision and Pattern Recognition Conference (2007)
26. Simard, P., Steinkraus, D., Platt, J.: Best practices for convolutional neural networks applied to visual document analysis. In: Seventh International Conference on Document Analysis and Recognition, pp. 958–963 (2003)
27. Vincent, P., Larochelle, H., Bengio, Y., Manzagol, P.A.: Extracting and Composing Robust Features with Denoising Autoencoders. In: Neural Information Processing Systems, NIPS (2008)
28. Zeiler, M.D., Krishnan, D., Taylor, G.W., Fergus, R.: Deconvolutional Networks. In: Proc. Computer Vision and Pattern Recognition Conference, CVPR 2010 (2010)

Error-Backpropagation in Networks of Fractionally Predictive Spiking Neurons

Sander M. Bohte

CWI, Life Sciences Group
Science Park 123, NL-1097XG Amsterdam, The Netherlands
sbohte@cwi.nl
http://www.cwi.nl/~sbohte

Abstract. We develop a learning rule for networks of spiking neurons where signals are encoded using fractionally predictive spike-coding. In this paradigm, neural output signals are encoded as a sum of shifted power-law kernels. Simple greedy thresholding can compute this encoding, and spike-trains are then exactly the signal's fractional derivative. Fractionally predictive spike-coding exploits natural statistics and is consistent with observed spike-rate adaptation in real neurons; its multiple-timescale properties also reconciles notions of spike-time coding and spike-rate coding. Previously, we argued that properly tuning the decoding kernel at receiving neurons can implement spectral filtering; the applicability to general temporal filtering was left open. Here, we present an error-backpropagation algorithm to learn these decoding filters, and we show that networks of fractionally predictive spiking neurons can then implement temporal filters such as delayed responses, delayed match-to-sampling, and temporal versions of the XOR problem.

1 Introduction

Real biological neurons compute in continuous time via the exchange of electrical pulses or *spikes*, and algorithmic descriptions of neural information processing in terms of spikes likely holds the key to resolving the scientific question of how biological spiking neurons work. The interest in the computational properties of spiking neurons was boosted in particular by findings from experimental and theoretical neuroscience [12,16], which suggested that the precise timing of individual spikes can be important in neural information processing. This has led to great debate, as the general assumption in neuroscience has always been that it is the neuron's spike rate that encodes information.

The notion of neural spike-time coding has resulted in the development of a number of spiking neural network approaches demonstrating that spiking neurons can compute using precisely times spikes similar to traditional neurons in neural networks [14,4,13]. Still, in spite of the successes of spiking neural networks, and the theoretical appeal of spike-time coding, it has remained a challenge to extend spike-based coding to computations involving longer timescales. Recurrent spiking neural network approaches can achieve longer memory, though

T. Honkela et al. (Eds.): ICANN 2011, Part I, LNCS 6791, pp. 60–68, 2011.

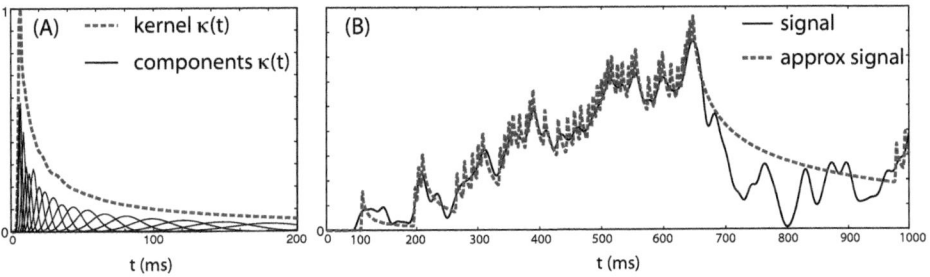

Fig. 1. (A) Power-law kernel (dashed blue) for $\beta = 0.8$, and Guassian components κ_k (B) Signal (black) approxiamated with a sum of power-law kernels (dashed blue)

they are notoriously hard to train [21]; edge-of-stability dynamical systems methods like reservoir computing show promise [11,5], although they require many neurons and spikes, and mostly disregard notions of spike-time coding.

Based on recent neuroscience findings [10], and reconciling the notions of both spike-time coding and spike-rate coding, we proposed a novel scheme for spike-based neural coding based on the observation that a mild derivative – a *fractional* derivative – of a signal can under certain conditions *be* a series of spikes [3]. In this framework, neural spiking is a statistically efficient means of encoding time-continuous signals. It does so by approximating the internally computed neural signal as sum of shifted kernels, where these kernels decay following a power-law (e.g. figure 1A). Power-law kernels provide much longer traces of past signals as compared to exponentially decaying kernels [7], and are thus much more suitable for computing temporal functions over behaviorally relevant timescales.

In this paper, we exploit key properties of the fractional-spike coding framework to learn functions over behaviorally relevant timescales. We capitalize on the fact that power-law kernels can be approximated for example using a weighted sum of exponential functions. We show that useful temporal filters can be learned by adapting these composite weights when decoding spike-trains *at the receiving synapse*. For this task, we derive error-backpropagation in the fractional spike-coding paradigm. With this learning rule we show that networks of fractionally predictive neurons can learn functions through time like delayed timer-functions and recall tasks like delayed-match-to-sample.

2 Fractionally Predictive Spiking Neurons

Starting from the standard Linear-nonlinear neuron model [2], an artificial neuron j computes an internal variable $y_j(t)$ as a function over the weighted sum of filtered inputs $x_j(t)$: $y_j(t) = \mathcal{F}(x_j(t))$ and $x_j(t) = \sum_{i \in \mathcal{J}} w_{ij} f_i(y_i(t))$, where $\mathcal{J}$ is the set of presynaptic neurons i to neuron j, and $f_i(y_i(t))$ denotes the (temporal) filter that computes $(f_i * y_i)(t)$.

As defined in [3], a fractionally predictive spiking neuron j approximates the internal signal $y_j(t)$ with $\hat{y}_j(t)$ as a sum of shifted power-law kernels centered at spike-times $\{t_i\}$:

$$y_j(t) \approx \hat{y}_j(t) = \sum_{t_j < t} \kappa(t - t_j).$$

The fractional derivative of order α of this approximation $\hat{y}_j(t)$ is just the spike-train $\{t_i\}$ when the kernel $\kappa(t)$ decays proportional to a power-law $\kappa(t) \propto t^{-\beta}$ when $\alpha = 1 - \beta$ [3]:

$$\frac{\partial^\alpha \hat{y}_j(t)}{\partial t^\alpha} = \sum_{t_j < t} \delta(t - t_j).$$

Such signal approximation $\hat{y}_j(t)$ can be achieved by computing the difference between the current signal estimation and the (emitted) future estimation (prediction) $\hat{y}(t)$, adding a spike t_i when this difference exceeds a threshold ϑ:

$$z(t) = y(t) - \hat{y}(t)$$
$$t_i = t \quad \text{if} \quad z(t) > \vartheta$$

With a single, positive threshold only positive signal deviations are transmitted, and for negative deviations the transmitted signal decays as $t^{-\beta}$ (closely matching actual spiking neuron behavior [15]). Such signal approximation is shown in figure 1B, where the height of the kernel κ is set to two times the threshold ϑ. Alternatively, the signal approximation can be precise up to ϑ if we use positive and negative spikes to signal respectively positive and negative deviations, for instance using two tightly coupled spiking neurons [3].

We use the fact that a power-law kernel $\kappa(t)$ can be approximated as a sum (or cascade) of different, weighted exponentially decaying functions $\kappa_k(t)$ [7]:

$$\kappa(t) \approx \sum_k \kappa_k(t),$$

as illustrated in figure 1A. This lets us rewrite $\hat{y}_i(t)$ as a sum of components $y_i^k(t)$:

$$\hat{y}_i(t) = \sum_{t_i < t} \sum_k \kappa_k(t - t_i) = \sum_k y_i^k(t).$$

At a receiving neuron j, a temporal filter κ_{ij} of the signal $\hat{y}_j(t)$ from neuron j can then be created by weighing these components with weights w_{ij}^k at the receiving synapse:

$$\kappa_{ij}(t) = \sum_k w_{ij}^k y_i^k(t).$$

and the neuron's input is thus computed as:

$$x_j(t) = \sum_{i \in \mathcal{J}} \sum_{t_i < t} \kappa_{ij}(t - t_i) = \sum_{i \in \mathcal{J}} w_{ij}^k y_i^k(t),$$

Note that for $w_{ij}^k = w_{ij} \forall k$, the input at neuron j decodes a weighted version of the output of presynaptic neurons i.

3   Learning in Networks of Fractionally Predictive Spiking Neurons

We consider a standard fully connected feedforward neural network, with input layer $\mathcal{I}$, hidden layer $\mathcal{H}$, and output layer O, populated with neurons i, j and m. We derive standard error-backpropagation learning rules for adjusting the components w_{ij}^k of the filtering kernels $\kappa_{ij}(t)$ for each connection in the network.

Given desired output activation pattern $s_k(t)$ for each output neuron k, we define a standard quadratic error measure in terms of the output $\hat{y}$:

$$E(t) = \sum_{m \in O} (s_m(t) - \hat{y}_m(t))^2$$

The goal is to adjust each weight w_{ij}^k (and w_{jm}^k) in the network so as to minimize the error over some time-period $[T, T']$:

$$\Delta w_{ij}^k \propto -\frac{\partial \sum_{t=T}^{T'} E(t)}{\partial w_{ij}^k} = \sum_{t=T}^{T'} \frac{\partial E(t)}{\partial w_{ij}^k},$$

(as the error-contributions are conditionally independent).

For the output layer, we have:

$$\frac{\partial E(t)}{\partial w_{jm}^k} = \frac{\partial E(t)}{\partial \hat{y}_m(t)} \frac{\partial \hat{y}_m(t)}{\partial x_m(t)} \frac{\partial x_m(t)}{\partial w_{jm}^k} = (s_m(t) - \hat{y}_m(t)) \, \mathcal{F}'(x_m(t)) y_j^k(t),$$

where $\mathcal{F}'(x_m(t))$ denotes the derivative $\partial \hat{y}_m / \partial x_m(t)$.

For weights in the hidden layer, the error-contributions become:

$$\frac{\partial E(t)}{\partial w_{ij}^k} = \sum_{m \in O} \frac{\partial E(t)_m}{\partial \hat{y}_m(t)} \frac{\partial \hat{y}_m(t)}{\partial x_m(t)} \sum_{k'} \frac{\partial x_m(t)}{\partial y_j^k(t)} \frac{\partial y_j^k(t)}{\partial \hat{y}_j(t)} \frac{\partial \hat{y}_j(t)}{\partial x_j(t)} \frac{\partial x_j(t)}{\partial w_{ij}^k}$$

$$= \sum_{m \in O} \left[(s_m(t) - y_m(t)) \mathcal{F}'(x_m(t)) \sum_{k'} w_{jm}^{k'} \right] \mathcal{F}'(x_j(t)) y_i^k(t).$$

Here, we take the transfer-function $\hat{y} = \mathcal{F}(x(t))$ to be piece-wise linear, with $\mathcal{F}(x(t)) = 0$ for $x(t) < 0$, and $\mathcal{F}(x(t)) \approx \alpha x(t)$ otherwise; a lack of input signals then automatically maps to a lack of output signals.

4   Experiments

We illustrate the efficacy of the derived error-backpropagation learning rule with some examples of behaviorally relevant temporal computations. Given a defined input-output relationship, we computed the respective approximation $\hat{y}(t)$ with power-law kernels, obtaining corresponding input-output spike-trains. We trained the network to minimize the error between the actual output and the desired output, both in terms of the respective power-law kernel approximation.

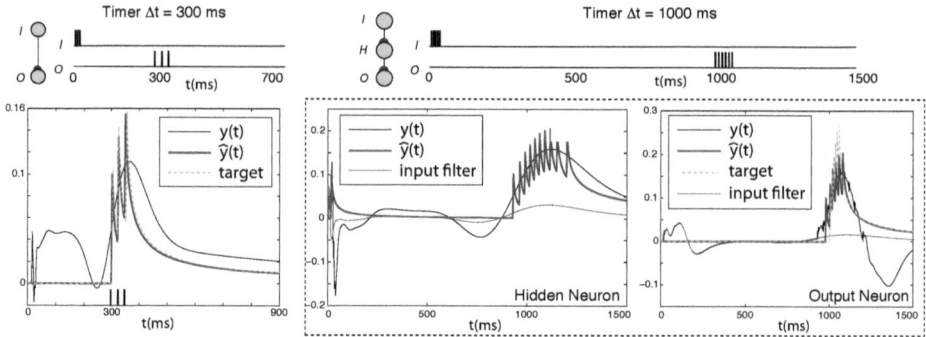

Fig. 2. Neural timers. Left: learning a 300ms delay directly from input. Top: input-target spike pattern. Bottom: Learned response after 400 epochs, with the kernel approximation $\hat{y}(t)$ matching the target output. Target (green dashed) and internal signal $y(t)$ (solid black) and signal kernel approximation $\hat{y}(t)$ (dashed blue). Right: learning a larger response at $\Delta t = 1000$ms, with an additional hidden neuron. Top: input-target spike pattern. Bottom: Learned response after 900 epochs, for the hidden neuron (center) and the output neuron (right). Shown in red is the developed temporal filter.

In all experiments, we use a power-law kernel with $\beta = 0.8$ (after [10]), which we approximate with 40 Gaussians, with centers μ_k distributed evenly over the log of the timeframe [5, 10000]ms, increasing variance σ_k as $\mu_k/5$. We used a greedy search heuristic to find the weighing of the individual gaussians such that their sum closely approximated the desired power-law decay. The learning rate was set at 0.01, and we considered the error over a time range of (0, 2000]ms (as all relevant patterns were defined within this range). It should be noted that in both hidden and output layer, the signal-approximation incurs a delay on the computed signal approximation equal to the rise-time of the kernel; in all figures (and in the error-computations), we subtracted this fixed delay for clarity. Setting the maximum kernel height $\kappa_M = 0.1$, we used a threshold $\vartheta = 0.5\kappa_M$. Weights were initialized such that input elicited some spikes in each hidden neuron. We trained the networks until the error was less than one "misplaced" spike.

Spiking neuron as timer. In figure 2, we show how a single fractionally predictive neuron can learn to give a precise delayed response. Given three input spikes at the start of the trial, the neuron responds with three carefully timed spikes some 300ms later. Such a direct input-output relation however was not sufficient to learn a precise mapping for substantially larger delays, such as 1,000ms. In the center and right figure, we show how the addition of a hidden neuron can help the output neuron to learn a delayed precise response. The hidden neuron computes a broad delay of about 900ms, and the output neuron then derives a much more precise response. Shown in red are also the effective temporal input filters that the respective neurons develop.

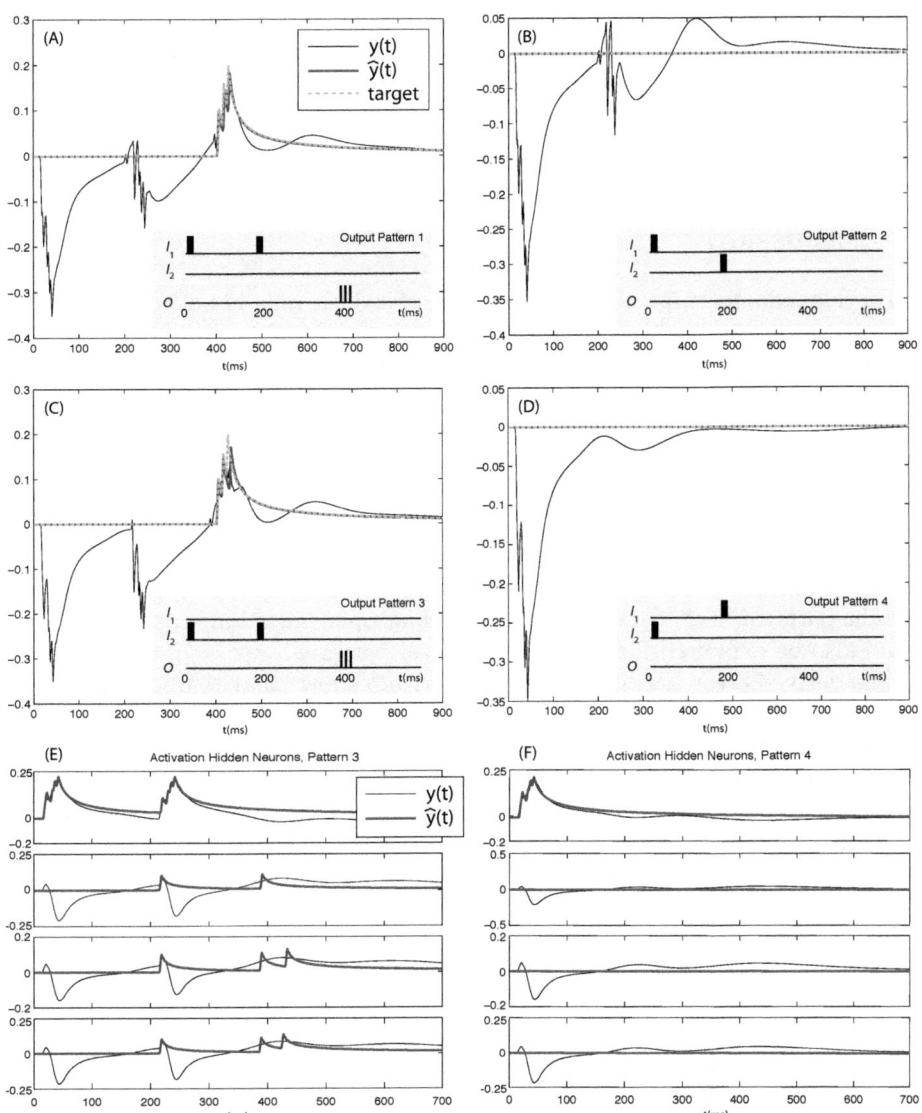

Fig. 3. Learning delayed match-to-sample. (A)-(D): the output neuron in a 2-4-1 network correctly learns the spike-responses $\hat{y}(t)$ to the four input-output patterns (inset boxes), in about 2000 epochs. (E)-(F): hidden neuron responses for patterns 3 and 4.

Delayed Match To Sample. Many behavioral tasks in some way require an animal to remember something it had experienced earlier: delayed match-to-sample tasks. We taught a simple version of this task. One of two input neurons emits a few spikes, and when the same input neuron spikes some 200ms later, the output neuron has to respond with an additional 200ms delay (see insets in figures 3A-D); if the other input neuron spikes, the output neuron has to remain silent. A network using four hidden neurons can successfully learns this task (figure 3), also for variations with more spikes and longer delays (not shown).

Delayed XOR. We were also able to train the network on various delayed temporal XOR problems similar to those in [4] (not shown for lack of space).

5 Discussion

We developed a learning algorithm for supervised learning in networks of spiking neurons using the fractionally predictive spike-coding paradigm from [3]. This coding paradigm allows for a natural signal encoding over multiple timescales, consistent with the self-similar statistical properties of natural signals [22]. It also allows for a natural reconciliation of spike-time coding and spike-rate coding as expressions of fractionally predictive spike-coding at different timescales. Within this paradigm, decoding of the fractional spike-code amounts to summing power-law kernels. As we noted in [3], such decoding allows for straightforward spectral filtering, as power-law kernels can be decomposed as a sum of exponential kernels with different time-constants; spectral filtering is achieved by decoding only certain parts of such composite kernels. The open question was whether this could also be exploited for learning temporal patterns.

The derived error-backpropagation algorithm shows that temporal filters can be learned in networks of fractionally predictive spiking neurons, for a number of tasks, over behaviorally relevant time-courses. Effectively, the exponentials that can be composed to a power-law kernel are used as time-delays. Such delays have been explored before in the context of spike-time coding [14,4,18], but only over small time-courses (tens of milliseconds), consistent with biologically observed axonal delays between neurons. Behaviorally relevant tasks operate typically over substantially longer timescales; and it is interesting to note that models of reinforcement learning [20,9] in fact similarly employ neurons receiving multiple delayed inputs to allow standard neural networks to learn sequential tasks, with some recent experimental results supporting this notion as well [1].

Neural coding over longer timescales is implicit in the fractionally predictive spike-coding paradigm, and corresponds at the encoding side to the physiologically well-established phenomenon of spike-rate adaptation. Our learning rule effectively conjectures that similar multiple-timescale machinery is effective *and tunable* at the receiving part of individual synapses. To some degree this must be true, as real neurons often have complex temporal receptive field dynamics, and many neurons exhibit sustained activity in response to a brief activation [8].

The learning rule presented here allows for learning input-output relations over different timescales: at short timescales, we can exactly learn relative spike-times; at longer timescales, we are no longer able to learn exact spike-times but instead learn approximate instantaneous spike-rates.

We used a single positive threshold spiking neuron model to approximate the internally computed signal into a sum of power-law kernels. This arrangement by necessity cannot encode signal decreases that are faster than the decay of the sum of power-law kernels. This could be remedied by arranging two neurons such that the signal is effectively approximated using both a positive and a negative threshold, as we did in [3]. We did not use such an arrangement here for three reasons, the first being simplicity. Secondly, power-law decay of a signal is, under certain conditions, consistent with an optimal Bayesian observer model [19], and thirdly the corresponding asymmetric detection of signal changes up versus down is well known in the psychophysical literature [6].

Having a standard supervised learning algorithm will allow us to further explore the fractionally predictive spike-coding paradigm in the context of recurrent neural networks, in particular reservoir computing. We are also working on developing the paradigm for reinforcement learning, as that is how most animals learn, and, as noted, that is also where the closest comparable modeling work has already taken place. Importantly, in the latter paradigm, methods like attention-gated reinforcement learning on average compute the error-backpropagation gradient [17], suggesting a direct link to the presented work.

References

1. Bernacchia, A., Seo, H., Lee, D., Wang, X.: A reservoir of time constants for memory traces in cortical neurons. Nature Neuroscience (2011)
2. Bishop, C.: Neural networks for pattern recognition. Oxford Univ. Press, Oxford (1995)
3. Bohte, S., Rombouts, J.: Fractionally predictive spiking neurons. In: Lafferty, J., Williams, C.K.I., Shawe-Taylor, J., Zemel, R., Culotta, A. (eds.) NIPS vol. 23, pp. 253–261 (2010)
4. Bohte, S., Kok, J., La Poutre, H.: Error-backpropagation in temporally encoded networks of spiking neurons. Neurocomputing 48(1-4), 17–37 (2002)
5. Buesing, L., Schrauwen, B., Legenstein, R.: Connectivity, dynamics and memory in reservoir computing with binary and analog neurons. Neural Comp. (in press)
6. DeWeese, M., Zador, A.: Asymmetric dynamics in optimal variance adaptation. Neural Computation 10(5), 1179–1202 (1998)
7. Drew, P., Abbott, L.: Models and properties of power-law adaptation in neural systems. Journal of Neurophysiology 96(2), 826 (2006)
8. Gnadt, J., Andersen, R.: Memory related motor planning activity in posterior parietal cortex of macaque. Experimental Brain Research 70(1), 216–220 (1988)
9. Ludvig, E., Sutton, R., Kehoe, E.: Stimulus representation and the timing of reward-prediction errors in models of the dopamine system. Neural Computation 20(12), 3034–3054 (2008)
10. Lundstrom, B., Higgs, M., Spain, W., Fairhall, A.: Fractional differentiation by neocortical pyramidal neurons. Nature Neuroscience 11(11), 1335–1342 (2008)
11. Maass, W., Natschläger, T., Markram, H.: Real-time computing without stable states: A new framework for neural computation based on perturbations. Neural Computation 14(11), 2531–2560 (2002)
12. Markram, H., Tsodyks, M.: Redistribution of synaptic efficacy between neocortical pyramidal neurons. Nature 382(6594), 807–810 (1996)
13. McKennoch, S., Voegtlin, T., Bushnell, L.: Spike-timing error backpropagation in theta neuron networks. Neural Computation 21(1), 9–45 (2009)

14. Natschläger, T., Ruf, B.: Spatial and temporal pattern analysis via spiking neurons. Network: Computation in Neural Systems 9(3), 319–332 (1998)
15. Pozzorini, C., Naud, R., Mensi, S., Gerstner, W.: Multiple timescales of adaptation in single neuron models. In: Front. Comput. Neurosci. Conference Abstract: Bernstein Conference on Computational Neuroscience (2010)
16. Rieke, F., Warland, D., Bialek, W.: Spikes: Exploring the Neural Code (1999)
17. Roelfsema, P., Van Ooyen, A.: Attention-gated reinforcement learning of internal representations for classification. Neural Computation 17(10), 2176–2214 (2005)
18. Schrauwen, B., Van Campenhout, J.: Extending spikeprop. In: Proceedings IJCNN 2004, vol. 1, IEEE, Los Alamitos (2005)
19. Snippe, H., van Hateren, J.: Recovery from contrast adaptation matches ideal-observer predictions. JOSA A 20(7), 1321–1330 (2003)
20. Suri, R., Schultz, W.: Learning of sequential movements by neural network model with dopamine-like reinforcement signal. Exp. Brain Res. 121(3), 350–354 (1998)
21. Tino, P., Mills, A.: Learning beyond finite memory in recurrent networks of spiking neurons. Neural Computation 18(3), 591–613 (2006)
22. Van Hateren, J.: Processing of natural time series of intensities by the visual system of the blowfly. Vision Research 37(23), 3407–3416 (1997)

ESN Intrinsic Plasticity versus Reservoir Stability

Petia Koprinkova-Hristova[1] and Guenther Palm[2]

[1] Bulgarian Academy of Sciences, Institute of System Engineering and Robotics,
Sofia, Bulgaria
pkoprinkova@icsr.bas.bg
[2] Institute of Neural Information Processing, University of Ulm, Ulm, Germany
guenther.palm@uni-ulm.de

Abstract. The work presented in this paper was inspired by similarities between intrinsic plasticity (IP) pre-training of the ESN reservoir and the common
RNN stability conditions derived from nonlinear control theory. The common
theoretical stability conditions were applied to the ESN structure. It was proven
that in fact IP training achieves a balance between maximization of entropy at
the ESN output and the concentration of that output distribution around the
pre-specified mean value. Thus the squeezing of the neuron nonlinearities is
produced not only by nonzero biases and translation of the ESN equilibrium
state but also by the chosen output distribution mean value. The numerical
investigations of different random reservoirs showed that the IP improvement
stabilizes even initially unstable reservoirs.

Keywords: Echo state network, intrinsic plasticity, stability.

1 Introduction

Nowadays applications of neural networks to modeling of complex dynamical systems and dependencies require fast and stable trainable recurrent neural network
(RNN) structures. Such a structure named "Echo state network" (ESN) [2, 3, 5] has
recently been proposed. It incorporates a dynamic recurrent reservoir and easily trainable output neurons. The ESN reservoir structure is randomly generated. There are no
universal recipes for reservoir generation [5] and all works in this direction are task
dependent. The only restriction is that it has to have so called "echo state property"
that means: the effect of its previous state and input to its output should vanish gradually in time, i.e. asymptotic stability. The usual recommendation for achieving the
echo state property is to generate a reservoir weight matrix with spectral radius below
one. However as it was mentioned in many works [5] this condition will not guaranty
ESN stable behavior in general. Another way to obtain proper behavior of the reservoir is to use a bias term [2, 6] that will move the operating point of the system in the
desired direction. In search of achieving rich reservoirs with a large diversity of states,
Ozturk et al. [6] proposed a method for placing the poles of the linearized ESN in
order to assure its stable behavior having at the same time a spectral radius close to
the stability boundary. This approach is based on average entropy maximization at the
ESN output. Another direction of work, also aimed at maximization of information

T. Honkela et al. (Eds.): ICANN 2011, Part I, LNCS 6791, pp. 69–76, 2011.

transmission trough the ESN (equivalent to its output entropy maximization), is called "intrinsic plasticity" (IP) [7, 8]. It is related to known biological mechanisms that change neural excitability according to the distribution of the stimuli. The authors proposed a gradient method for adjusting the biases and an additional gain adjustment aimed at achieving the desired distribution of outputs.

In fact maximization of entropy in both cases could be related to an increase of the ESN system stability since it is well known that any stable stationary state has a local maximum of entropy [4]. In the huge area of stability analysis of complex nonlinear systems there are theoretical developments that could be applied only by simulations, but they are not able to give mathematical rules for the construction of stable nonlinear systems as a whole. RNN stability was theoretically investigated in [1]. The authors proved that addition of a bias term to the neural activation functions allows restricting the sector of their nonlinearities thus improving system stability. Another common conclusion is that reservoir connection weights should be decreased. These two main results from [1] correspond very well to what was done in practice by the IP method [7, 8], although its motivation was slightly different. However all the works on IP reported that reservoir spectral radius increases thus causing danger to corrupt stability of the ESN. But in fact simulation investigations in this direction [8] showed much more stable behavior of IP pre-trained reservoirs in comparison to randomly generated ones.

The work presented in this paper was inspired by similarities between IP pre-training of ESN reservoir and the RNN stability conditions derived in [1]. The common stability conditions from [1] were applied to the ESN structure. It was proven that in fact IP training achieves balance between maximization of entropy at the ESN output and the concentration of the output distribution around the pre-specified mean value. Thus the squeezing of the neurons' nonlinearity sectors is provoked not only by nonzero biases and translation of the ESN equilibrium state, but also by the chosen output distribution mean value. The simulation investigations with different random reservoirs showed that the IP improvement stabilizes even initially unstable reservoirs.

2   Problem Statement

2.1   Echo State Networks as a Special Structure RNN

ESNs are a kind of recurrent neural networks that arise from so called "reservoir computing approaches" [5]. Their dynamics is describes as follows:

$$r(k) = f^{res}\left(W^{in}u(k) + W^{res}r(k-1)\right)$$
$$out(k) = f^{out}\left(W^{out}[u(k) \quad r(k)]\right)$$
(1)

Here, $u(k)$ is a vector of network inputs, $r(k)$ a vector of the reservoir neuron states; f^{out} is usually the identity function, W^{out} is a trainable $n_{out} \times (n_u + n_r)$ matrix (here

n_{out}, n_u and n_r are the dimensions of the corresponding vectors *out*, *u* and *r*); W^{in} and W^{res} are $n_r \times n_u$ and $n_r \times n_r$ matrices that are randomly generated and are not trainable. The neurons in the reservoir have a simple sigmoid output function f^{res} that is usually *tanh*.

Since the linear superposition of stable subsystems is also stable, here we'll consider only internal reservoir dynamics of (1). Following the state space transformation as in [1] the undisturbed dynamics (i.e. with zero input *u*) of the reservoir with addition of matrices for bias *b* and gain *a* terms as in [7] becomes:

$$x_1(k) = \tanh\left(a_1 W^{res} x_2(k) + b_1 \right), \quad x_1(k) = r(k)$$
$$x_2(k) = x_1(k-1)$$

$$(2)$$

Here a_1 and b_1 are diagonal matrices with $n_r \times n_r$ size containing the gains and biases of reservoir neurons. In matrix equation form system (2) becomes:

$$x(k) = Ax(k) + B\xi(k), \quad x(k) = col(x_1(k) \quad x_2(k)) \tag{3}$$

where:

$$A = \begin{pmatrix} 0 & 0 \\ I & 0 \end{pmatrix} \quad B = \begin{pmatrix} I & 0 \\ 0 & 0 \end{pmatrix} \quad \Theta = \begin{pmatrix} 0 & a_1 W^{res} \\ 0 & 0 \end{pmatrix} \quad b = \begin{pmatrix} b_1 \\ 0 \end{pmatrix}$$
$$\xi(k) = \tanh(\rho(k)) = \begin{pmatrix} \xi_1(k) \\ 0 \end{pmatrix} c, \quad \rho(k) = \Theta x(k) + b = \begin{pmatrix} \rho_1(k) \\ 0 \end{pmatrix}$$

$$(4)$$

For the system (3) in [1] theoretical stability conditions related to the sectors to which the nonlinearities ξ belong, and a special form of linear matrix inequality that includes matrices from (4), were proposed. Since the IP improvement of the reservoir influences only the matrices *a* and *b* we'll investigate further how this improvement influences the stability conditions for the system (3).

2.2 Intrinsic Plasticity Adaptation and Its Relation to ESN Reservoir Stability

The IP reservoir improvement proposed in [7, 8] is based on minimization of the Kullback-Leibler divergence D_{KL} as a measure for the difference between the actual $p(r)$ and the desired $p_d(r)$ distribution of reservoir neuron outputs *r*. Since the commonly used transfer function of neurons is the hyperbolic tangent, the proper target distribution that maximizes the information at the output according to [7] is the Gaussian one:

$$p_d(r) = \frac{1}{\sigma\sqrt{2\pi}} \exp\left(-\frac{(r-\mu)^2}{2\sigma^2} \right) \tag{5}$$

with the expected value μ and variance σ. Thus the D_{KL} becomes:

$$D_{KL}(p(r), p_d(r)) = \int p(r)\log\left(\frac{p(r)}{p_d(r)}\right) =$$
$$= -H(r) + \frac{1}{2\sigma^2}E\left((r-\mu)^2\right) + \log\frac{1}{\sigma\sqrt{2\pi}} \tag{6}$$

Here $H(r)$ is entropy, the last term is constant and the second one determines the deviation of the output from the desired mean value μ scaled by a constant proportional to the variance σ. Thus minimization of (6) will lead to compromise between entropy maximization and minimization of distance between μ and r. Since in [7] it was recommended to use Gaussian distribution with zero mean, in practice application of IP training gradient rules will tend to concentrate around zero and squeeze into the interval $[-3\,\sigma,\, 3\,\sigma]$ the reservoir outputs. This is done by adjustment of gain matrix a_l and bias matrix b_l in (2).

In [1] it was theoretically proven that a nonzero bias b_l leads to squeezing of the sectors of nonlinearities ξ from (3) and thus improves the stability of the system. Another stability condition from [1] is that the connection weights should be decreased. IP reservoir improvement rules in fact can do exactly this by adjustment of the bias and gain matrices. Of course it is hard to investigate theoretically the effect of IP on the reservoir parameters but numerical investigations of different randomly generated reservoirs in section 4 will definitely show that IP improves their stability.

3   Theoretical Stability Conditions for ESN

In order to investigate stability of the system (3) we first must find its equilibrium point z as follows:

$$z = Az + B\tanh(\Theta z + b) \tag{7}$$

So if $b=0$ the equilibrium is at the origin of the coordinate system in the state space. Otherwise it is moved in dependence on the vector b.

Hence for the nonzero biases we need to transform the system (7) into a new coordinate system $g=x-z$ with equilibrium at its origin as follows:

$$g(k) = Ag(k) + B\eta(k), \quad \eta(k) = \tanh(v(k)+c) - \tanh(c)$$
$$c = \Theta z + b \qquad\qquad v(k) = \Theta g(k) \tag{8}$$

According to [1] the nonlinearity $\eta(k)$ belongs to a narrower sector in comparison to the initial one of $\xi(k)$.

Following the stability criteria in [1], the system (8) is stable if we can find such positive definite matrices H and $\Gamma=diag\{\Gamma_i\}$ that fulfill the following linear matrix inequality (LMI):

$$(Ag + B\eta)^T H(Ag + B\eta) - y^T Hy +$$
$$(M\Theta y - \eta)^T \Gamma(\eta - N\Theta y) < 0 \tag{9}$$

Here the matrices $M=diag(m_i)$ and $N=diag(n_i)$ contain the upper and lower bounds of the nonlinearities η_i. Following the results of [1] the values of m_i are obtained as follows:

$$m_i = \max \frac{\eta_i(v)}{v} = \frac{\eta_i(v_0)}{v_0}, \quad \frac{\partial \eta_i(v)}{\partial v}\bigg/ v \bigg|_{v=v_0} = 0 \tag{10}$$

Having in mind that IP improvement tries to squeeze the output values of the reservoir into the interval $[-3\ \sigma,\ 3\ \sigma]$ we can conclude that the corresponding total neuron input must be in the interval $[arctanh(-3\ \sigma),\ arctanh(3\ \sigma)]$. Having in mind that because of nonzero bias the new coordinate system of i-th neuron nonlinearity η_i is moved to the point $(c_i,\ tanh(c_i))$ we can determine the new working interval of that nonlinearity to be $[c_i- arctanh(-3\ \sigma),\ c_i+ arctanh(3\ \sigma)]$. Hence following the formulas from [1] we can easily calculate the lower nonlinearity bounds n_i as follows:

$$n_i = \frac{\tanh(c_i + arctanh(3\sigma)) - \tanh(c_i)}{(c_i + arctanh(3\sigma)) + c_i} \tag{11}$$

Having in mind the special form of matrices (4) that are related to the ESN structure, the LMI (9) could be transformed into the form:

$$col(g_1 \quad g_2 \quad \eta_1)^T Lcol(g_1 \quad g_2 \quad \eta_1) < 0 \tag{12}$$

Since H is a symmetrical matrix and diagonal matrices M and N are also symmetric, they all can be divided into four block matrices as follows:

$$H = \begin{pmatrix} H_1 & H_2^T \\ H_2 & H_3 \end{pmatrix} \quad M = \begin{pmatrix} M_1 & 0 \\ 0 & M_2 \end{pmatrix} \quad N = \begin{pmatrix} N_1 & 0 \\ 0 & N_2 \end{pmatrix} \tag{13}$$

Hence the matrix L from (12) and its corresponding LMI (12) becomes:

$$\begin{pmatrix} -H_1 & -H_2^T & 0 \\ -H_2 & -H_3 - (a_1 W^{res})^T M_1 \Gamma_1 N_1 a_1 W^{res} & H_2 + (a_1 W^{res})^T M_1 \Gamma_1 \\ 0 & H_2^T + \Gamma_1 N_1 a_1 W^{res} & H_1 - \Gamma_1 \end{pmatrix} < 0 \tag{14}$$

The above matrix L can be presented as sum of two matrices L_1 and L_2 as follows:

$$L_1 = \begin{pmatrix} -H_1 & -H_2^T & 0 \\ -H_2 & -H_3 & 0 \\ 0 & 0 & 0 \end{pmatrix} \quad L_2 = \begin{pmatrix} 0 & 0 & 0 \\ 0 & -(a_1 W^{res})^T M_1 \Gamma_1 N_1 a_1 W^{res} & H_2 + (a_1 W^{res})^T M_1 \Gamma_1 \\ 0 & H_2^T + \Gamma_1 N_1 a_1 W^{res} & H_1 - \Gamma_1 \end{pmatrix} \tag{15}$$

Since H is positive definite by definition the first matrix L_1 is negative definite. Hence the ESN will be stable if we can find such positive definite matrices H and $\Gamma_1=diag(\gamma_i)$ that fulfill the following LMI:

$$\left(\begin{matrix} -\left(a_1W^{res}\right)^T M_1\Gamma_1 N_1 a_1W^{res} & H_2 + \left(a_1W^{res}\right)^T M_1\Gamma_1 \\ H_2^T + \Gamma_1 N_1 a_1W^{res} & H_1 - \Gamma_1 \end{matrix} \right) < 0 \tag{16}$$

Practically the IP training procedure influences the matrices a_1 and b_1. The first one is included in the above LMI and its influence on the ESN stability can be investigated directly. The second one influences in a more complex manner the upper and lower bounds of the nonlinearity sectors (i.e. diagonals of matrices M_1 and N_1) as follows: the bias term moves the working sector of neurons nonlinearities influencing the vector c from equations (8); further elements of vector c take part in equations (10) and (11) that calculate diagonal elements of these matrices. One possible way to investigate the overall influence of IP training on the ESN stability condition (16) is to solve that LMI with variable a_1, M_1 and N_1 thus finding their allowed stability regions. These regions can be compared with the obtained after IP training matrices a_1, M_1 and N_1. Another possible way is to train ESN with IP procedure and after that to compare stability of initial and trained ESNs. From the theoretical investigations in [1] it was concluded that the common recommendation for improving the RNN stability is to try to decrease the weights and to "squeeze" the sectors to which neurons nonlinearities belong, i.e. to decrease the values of a_1 and of the difference M_1-N_1. In the next section we'll investigate by simulations how IP improvement of the reservoir influences the ESN stability following the recommendations from [1].

4 Numerical Investigations of ESN stability

We generated several random reservoirs with four neurons, two inputs and different spectral radii (SR) varying from stable (0.6 and 0.9) to unstable (1.2) ones.

Table 1. Nonlinearities sector width change trough IP iterations

It.	SR=0.6				SR=0.9				SR=1.2			
	neuron No				neuron No				neuron No			
No	1	2	3	4	1	2	3	4	1	2	3	4
0	0.50	0.62	0.51	0.58	0.56	0.61	0.61	0.72	0.48	0.58	0.53	0.59
1	0.21	0.25	0.23	0.27	0.20	0.17	0.23	0.19	0.26	0.30	0.08	0.23
2	0.15	0.15	0.13	0.16	0.12	0.10	0.14	0.11	0.17	0.21	0.06	0.15
3	0.14	0.13	0.11	0.13	0.10	0.10	0.12	0.10	0.15	0.20	0.06	0.14
4	0.13	0.12	0.10	0.13	0.10	0.10	0.12	0.10	0.14	0.21	0.06	0.13
6	0.13	0.12	0.10	0.13	0.10	0.10	0.12	0.10	0.14	0.21	0.06	0.13

Table 2. Diagonals of matrices a_1 after IP training

SR=0.6				SR=0.9				SR=1.2			
neuron No				neuron No				neuron No			
1	2	3	4	1	2	3	4	1	2	3	4
0.39	0.31	0.35	0.28	0.35	0.46	0.27	0.33	0.35	0.47	0.66	0.29

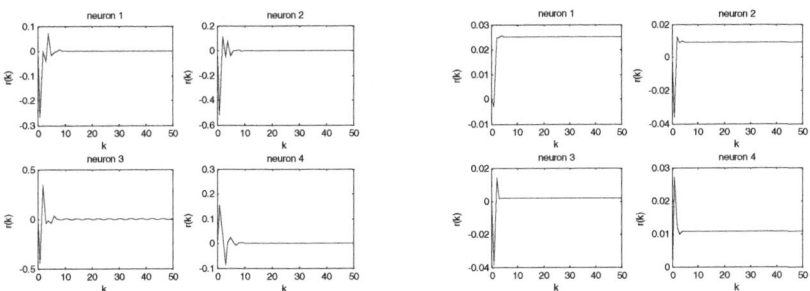

Fig. 1. Simulation of initial reservoir (left) with spectral radius 0.6 and IP trained reservoir (right) after 3rd iteration

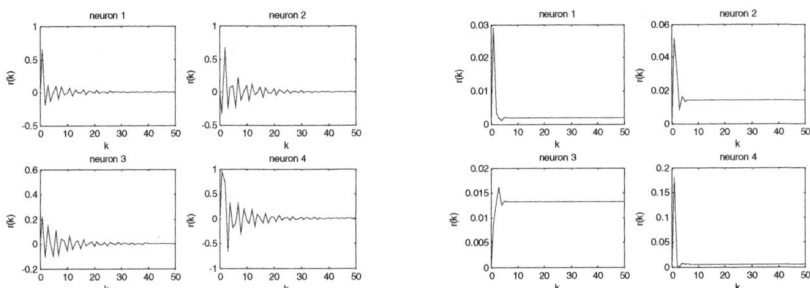

Fig. 2. Simulation of initial reservoir (left) with spectral radius 0.9 and IP trained reservoir (right) after 3rd iteration

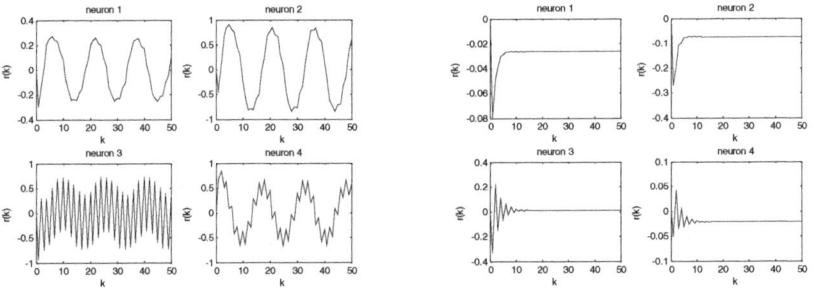

Fig. 3. Simulation of initial reservoir (left) with spectral radius 1.2 and IP trained reservoir (right) after 3rd iteration

The two inputs were randomly generated in the interval [-1, 1]. We used recommended in [7] mean and variance of the Gaussian distribution to be $\mu=0$ and $\sigma=0.1$ respectively. IP reservoir improvement was done in 5 iterations. We observed that after the 3rd iteration there are no significant parameter changes. Table 1 summarizes changes of sector nonlinearity widths. It can be seen that they become significantly narrow after the first IP iteration and after the 3rd iteration there are no considerable changes. Table 2 presents diagonal elements of matrices a_1 obtained after IP training. Their values below 1 guarantee decreasing of reservoir connection weights. The simulation results before and after 3rd iteration are shown on Figures 1, 2 and 3. As can be seen even highly unstable initial reservoirs become quite stable after IP improvement.

5 Conclusions

In the present paper we find a close relationship between IP improvement of ESN reservoir and stabilization of undisturbed reservoir dynamics. We showed that although IP training is aimed at maximization of entropy at ESN reservoir output and in spite of the concerns about increasing its spectral radius, in practice it stabilizes even initially unstable reservoirs. This is due to the two main necessary stability conditions for RNN derived in [1]: squeezing of the neurons' nonlinearity sectors and decreasing of the connection weights. The derived stability condition in the form of a linear matrix equation for the ESN structure as a special RNN allows numerical investigations of reservoir stability.

Acknowledgments. This work was partially supported by the Bulgarian National Science Fund under the Project No DDVU02/11.

References

1. Barabanov, N., Prokhorov, D.: Stability analysis of discrete-time recurrent neural networks. IEEE Trans. on Neural Networks 13(2), 292–303 (2002)
2. Jaeger, H.: Tutorial on training recurrent neural networks, covering BPPT, RTRL, EKF and the "echo state network" approach. GMD Report 159, German National Research Center for Information Technology (2002)
3. Jaeger, H.: Adaptive nonlinear system identification with echo state networks. In: Advances in Neural Information Processing Systems 15 (NIPS 2002), pp. 593–600. MIT Press, Cambridge (2003)
4. Haddad, W.M., Chellaboina, V.S., Nersesov, S.G.: Thermodynamics: A Dynamical System Approach. Princeton University Press, Princeton (2005)
5. Lukosevicius, M., Jaeger, H.: Reservoir computing approaches to recurrent neural network training. Computer Science Review 3, 127–149 (2009)
6. Ozturk, M., Xu, D., Principe, J.: Analysis and design of Echo state networks. Neural Computation 19, 111–138 (2007)
7. Schrauwen, B., Wandermann, M., Verstraeten, D., Steil, J.J., Stroobandt, D.: Improving reservoirs using intrinsic plasticity. Neurocomputing 71, 1159–1171 (2008)
8. Steil, J.J.: Online reservoir adaptation by intrinsic plasticity for back-propagation-decoleration and echo state learning. Neural Networks 20, 353–364 (2007)

Adaptive Routing Strategies for Large Scale Spiking Neural Network Hardware Implementations

Snaider Carrillo[1], Jim Harkin[1], Liam McDaid[1], Sandeep Pande[2], Seamus Cawley[2], and Fearghal Morgan[2]

[1] Intelligent Systems Research Centre (ISRC),
University of Ulster, Magee Campus, Derry, Northern Ireland
carrillo_lindado-s@email.ulster.ac.uk
[2] Bio-Inspired Electronics and Reconfigurable Computing Research Group (BIRC),
National University of Ireland, NUI Galway, Galway, Ireland
fearghal.morgan@nuigalway.ie

Abstract. This paper presents an adaptive Network-on-Chip (NoC) router, which forms part of an embedded mixed signal Spiking Neural Network (SNN) architecture called EMBRACE (Emulating Biologically-inspiRed ArChitectures in hardware). The novel adaptive NoC router provides the inter-neuron connectivity for EMBRACE, maintaining router communication and avoiding dropped router packets by adapting to router traffic congestion. The router also adapts to NoC traffic congestion or broken NoC connections (faults) by reconfiguring the routing topology to select an alternative route. Performance, power and area analysis of the proposed adaptive router using Synopsys Design Compiler (for TSMC 90nm CMOS technology) indicates a router throughput of 3.2Gbps on each of 5 available router channels, low router power consumption (1.716mW) and small router area (0.056mm^2). Router adaptive behaviour in the presence of applied real-time traffic congestion has been demonstrated on a Virtex II Pro Xilinx FPGA for a 4x2 router array. Results indicate the feasibility of using the proposed adaptive NoC router within a scalable EMBRACE hardware SNN architecture.

Keywords: Spiking neural networks, network-on-chip, inter-neuron scalability, EMBRACE architecture, adaptive routing, fault-tolerant, brain-inspired computing.

1 Introduction

Understanding and emulating the behaviour of the brain has received much attention not only from neuroscientists, but also from engineers and computer scientists [1]. Whilst neuroscientists are interested in biophysical models, engineers and computer scientists are more interested in harnessing the brain's powerful signal processing capability. The brain can provide extraordinary computational performance with low power consumption, compared to traditional computer paradigms such as the von Neumann computing approach. Neural processing is based on computational neuron models known as spiking neural networks (SNNs) [2].

T. Honkela et al. (Eds.): ICANN 2011, Part I, LNCS 6791, pp. 77–84, 2011.
© Springer-Verlag Berlin Heidelberg 2011

SNNs communicate by transmitting short transient pulses or spikes between neurons, via weighted synaptic connections. Synapses can have either an excitatory or inhibitory effect on a neuron's internal membrane potential. A spiking neuron will emit a spike when its potential exceeds a neuron-specific membrane potential threshold value. The computational power of SNNs is realised by the synaptic connections between neurons, the weights on these connections and the internal membrane potential threshold of each neuron. The brain is highly efficient in how it processes information and tolerates faults. Thus, the aforementioned attributes make SNNs suitable for implementing resilient classifiers and control applications, e.g. robotics controllers, due to their ability to provide a good solution in the presence of imprecise or unseen data.

The hope is to harness this efficiency and build artificial neural systems that can emulate the key information processing principles of the brain. However, existing approaches cannot provide the dense interconnect for the billions of neurons and synapses that are required. Software approaches are too slow to execute large scale SNN-based algorithms and do not scale efficiently to ever increasing neuron density. Therefore, it is necessary to look to new custom hardware architectures to address this scalability issue and to enable the deployment of brain-like embedded systems processors. A detailed review regarding artificial neural network hardware implementation can be found in [3].

Recently, the Network-on-Chip (NoC) interconnect paradigm [4] was introduced as a promising solution to solve the on-chip communication problems experienced in Systems-on-Chip (SoC) computing architectures, where generally high throughput and high interconnect capability is required. In general, NoC architectures are composed of a set of shared processing elements (PEs), routers and channels, which are arranged in a topology depending on the application. In the context of SNNs, these PEs refer to the neuron models attached to the NoC routers placed throughout the network. Channels are analogous to the synapses/axons of spiking neurons. The SNN topology in this case refers to the way spiking neurons are interconnected across the network. In this regard, the authors have investigated and proposed EMBRACE (Emulating Biologically-inspiRed ArChitectures in hardware) [5], [6], a scalable embedded hardware SNN device. The EMBRACE reconfigurable mixed-signal hardware SNN, which is still to be realised, incorporates a low-area/power, CMOS-compatible analogue neuron/synapse cell architecture and implements inter-neuron connectivity through the use of a digital, packet-based NoC communication architecture, which provides flexible, time-multiplexed communication channels, scalable interconnect and reconfigurability (see Fig. 1).

This paper presents an adaptive NoC router which provides the inter-neuron connectivity within the EMBRACE architecture. The novel adaptive NoC router maintains SNN communication and avoids dropped SNN packets by adapting to SNN traffic congestion in large scale hardware neural network-based computing systems. The router also adapts to NoC router congestion and broken router connections (faults) by reconfiguring the routing topology to select an alternative route. Performance, power and area analysis of the proposed adaptive router using Synopsys Design Compiler (for TSMC 90nm CMOS technology) indicates the feasibility of using the proposed adaptive NoC router within a scalable EMBRACE hardware SNN architecture.

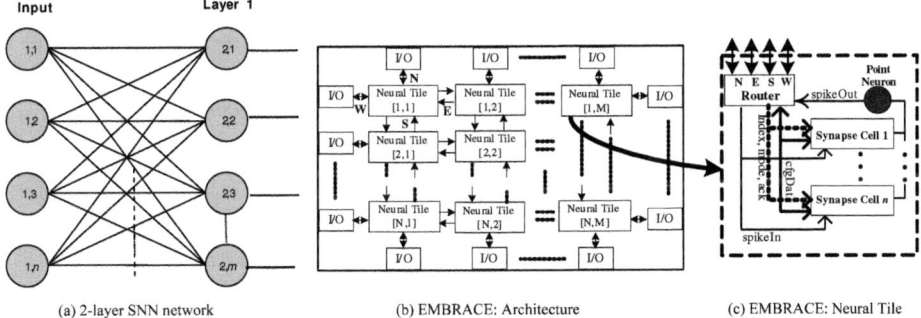

Fig. 1. EMBRACE Architecture: (a), (b) show a regular n x m topology and its corresponding 2D NoC implementation using EMBRACE. (c) shows the neural tile composed of a digital router and an analogue neural cell with its correspondent synapses (spikeIn) and axon (spikeOut).

The remainder of this paper is organised as follows: Section 2 details the proposed adaptive NoC router architecture. Section 3 presents experimental results obtained based on simulation and validated on a FPGA hardware implementation of the pro-pose router. Finally, Section 4 concludes the paper.

2   Adaptive NoC Router Architecture

This section presents the proposed adaptive NoC router architecture. An adaptive NoC router is beneficial when network traffic patterns are highly irregular [2]. The proposed NoC router is composed of 4 ports to facilitate north, east, south and west inter-router connectivity, and a fifth NoC-neural tile port.

The novelty of the proposed adaptive NoC router is its adaptive scheduler and rout-ing scheme (see Fig. 2a). These two capabilities offer the following advantages over traditional non adaptive routers: a) an adaptive arbitration policy module combines the fairness policy of the round-robin arbiter and the priority scheme of a first-come first-serve approach. This enables improved router throughput according to the traffic behaviour presented across the network, b) an adaptive routing scheme which facili-tates router adaptation, based on spike traffic patterns and a channel congestion detec-tor (CCD) to avoid traffic congestion.

Adaptive arbitration policy: A key property of an arbiter is its fairness in providing equal service to different network traffic requests. A spiking neuron traffic pattern is highly asynchronous and non-uniform [1]. The proposed adaptive router uses a hybrid arbitration policy which combines the strong fairness policy of the round-robin arbiter and the priority scheme of a first-come first-serve approach. The proposed adaptive arbitration policy uses a spike event register to store information regarding each spike event for each router input buffer, and five distributed control units, i.e. one for each port.

The proposed approach allows the scheduler to manage thread communication without incurring task-switching overhead. Only the input buffers that contain information are serviced, thus avoiding wasted clock cycles. Similarly when a heavy load traffic scenario occurs, all ports are serviced, based on the same approach as the round-robin.

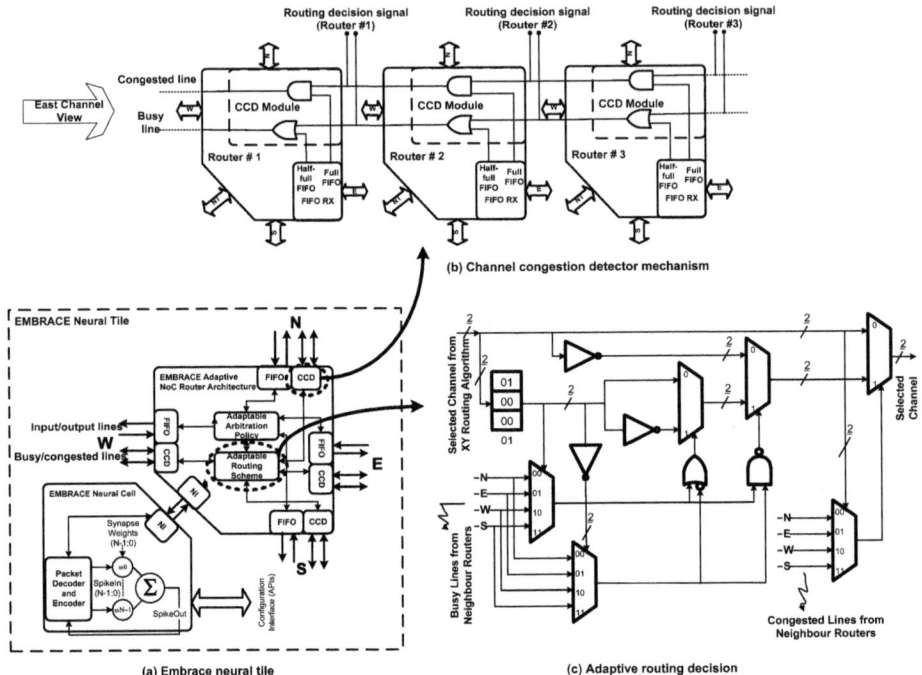

Fig. 2. Adaptive NoC router architecture overview

Adaptive routing module: The proposed adaptive routing scheme is composed of three main components, as follows (see Fig. 2): a) an XY routing algorithm, which receives the packet from the adaptable arbitration policy module, b) a channel congestion detector (CCD) which, based on the information received from neighbouring routers, selects an output port direction and passes this information to c) the adaptive routing decision module. The CCD provides a means of detecting the current state of traffic in any given direction. Three status types exist for each direction: *Free* (input FIFO is empty), *Busy* (by default this flag indicates that the input FIFO is half-full, but the user can setup a threshold for triggering the flag) or *Congested* (input FIFO is full). The CCD module can detect whether forward N, E, S or W channels are free, busy or congested. The adaptive routing decision module uses the output port direction provided by the XY routing algorithm, the state information provided by the CCD, and the output FIFO availability, to select an appropriate output port (see Fig. 2c).

3   Experiments and Results

This section presents results on the throughput capability, area utilisation and power consumption of the proposed adaptive router for varied SNN traffic loads, and benchmarks its performance against existing approaches. Additionally, experimental results for a 4x2 array of adaptive routers implemented on a Virtex II Pro Xilinx FPGA are also presented. A VHDL implementation of the proposed adaptive router architecture has been created in order to evaluate its performance. The testbench setup was inspired by [7] and verified in [6]. This setup proposed the attachment of terminal instruments such as counters and generators at each router port (see Fig. 3). The spike event generator defines the traffic pattern, packet length and the spike injection rate (i.e. the time between spike events). The spike event counter measures the SNN output spike rate and deduces the spike throughput and the number of unsuccessfully routed (dropped) spike packet.

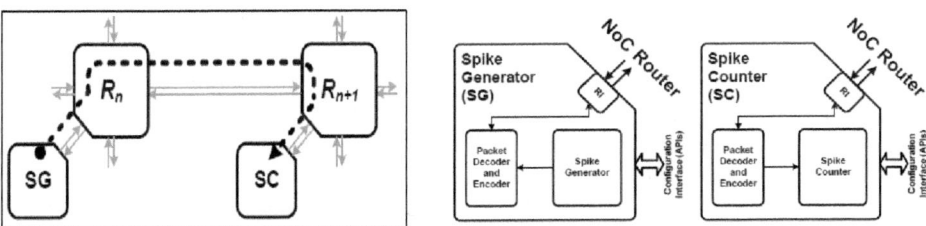

Fig. 3. Spike generator and spike counter internal architecture, NoC router connection ports and configuration interface

3.1   Traffic throughput

Several experiments have been carried out to assess the throughput of the proposed router. Fig. 4 illustrates the average adaptive router packet throughput with varying Spike Injection Rate (SIR), for a range of router channel formats. In addition, router performance has been compared to that of an earlier non-adaptive EMBRACE NoC router, which uses a round-robin scheme [4]. The main advantages of the proposed approach are in the following operational scenarios:

The first scenario is a situation where router ports are idle and the adaptive router is able to skips the idle ports. This avoids wasted clock cycles and provides increased packet throughput compared to the round-robin approach. For example, results shown in Fig. 4 illustrate equal performance, when either one or three ports are used at the same time, for both adaptive and non-adaptive at SIR = 20 (i.e. spike packet generated every 20 clock cycles). However, for SIR = 2, the proposed adaptive router achieves almost double the throughput compared to the non-adaptive router, as the proposed adaptive arbitration policy along with the adaptive routing scheme are able to handle the incoming packets, ignoring the idle ports. The previous scenario represents a typical traffic pattern for spiking neurons firing in burst mode [1].

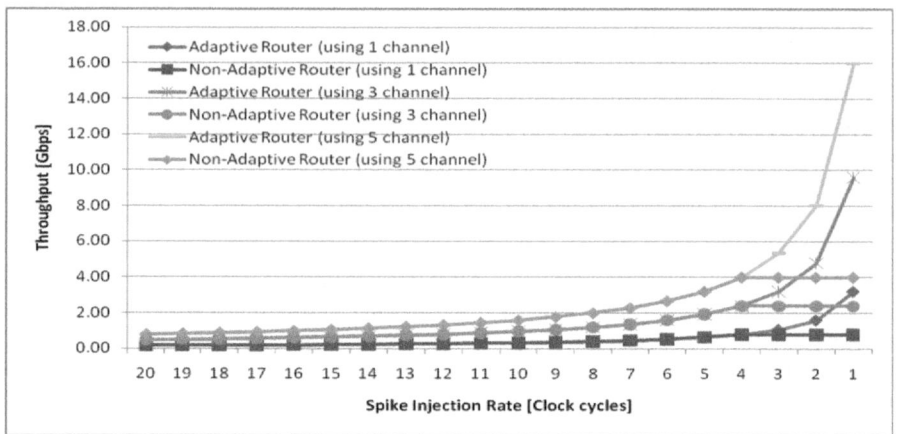

Fig. 4. Throughput for the proposed adaptive NoC router as a function of the spike injection rate under different traffic loads using different number of channel at the same time

The second scenario is when all router ports are busy, as the advantage in using the proposed adaptive router arises when the SIR is less or equal to the number of ports that need to be serviced before the arbiter grants the priority to the same port that emitted the spike previously. In addition, for both of the above scenarios, when the SIR value is less than or equal to the number of ports minus one (i.e. SIR = 4), the non-adaptive router reaches a maximum saturation level, i.e. the highest level of demand for which spike packet throughput equals demand. The spike packet generation frequency (SIR) becomes faster than the time given to the router to process the incoming packets. As demand is increased beyond saturation, the non-adaptive router can no longer handle all packets and it becomes impossible for the round-robin arbiter to service all ports efficiently. Thus, the unserviced router ports drop packets and the throughput remains constant [7].

3.2 Router Performance, Power and Area

Table 1 summarises the results of performance, power and area analysis of the proposed adaptive router, performed using Synopsys Design Compiler (for TSMC 90nm CMOS technology). Assumptions are an EMBRACE spike packet width is 32-bits, 100MHz system frequency, and a very high neuron firing rate causing a fully loaded NoC router. Results indicate a router throughput of 3.2Gbps on each of 5 available router channels (aggregate throughput of 16 Gbps), low router power consumption (1.716mW) and small router area (0.056mm^2). Table 1 also shows the trade-off between the depth of the input FIFO and the maximum throughput per router. In addition, Table 2 compares the performance of the proposed router with other existing approaches [8], [9], [10]. Table 2 highlights a high throughput of 16Gbps for the proposed adaptive NoC router whilst exhibiting a low power overhead of 1.716mW. Results for the proposed adaptive router offer an improvement of 11% and 93%, for packet throughput and power consumption respectively, compared to the state of the art [8].

Table 1. Synthesis summary for the proposed router based on the TSMC 90nm CMOS

Input FIFO [Depth]	Dynamic Power [mW]	Leakage Power [mW]	Total Power [mW]	Area Utilisation [mm²]	Throughput per Channel [Gbps]
1	0.846	0.070	0.916	0.028	2.688
2	1.096	0.083	1.179	0.035	2.816
3	1.269	0.097	1.366	0.042	2.944
4	1.422	0.116	1.538	0.050	3.072
5	1.591	0.125	1.716	0.056	3.200

Table 2. Comparison of the proposed router against other existing approaches

Project Reference	Quality of Service (QoS)	Congestion Mechanism	Throughput [Gbps]	Power [mW]
This work	Best Effort	Yes	16.000	1.716
Spinnaker [8]	Best Effort	Yes	14.400	27.000
Facets [9]	Best/Guaranteed Effort	No	6.100	NA
Theocharides. et al [10]	Best Effort	No	0.100	NA

3.3 Performance of FPGA-Based Adaptive NoC Router

A 4x2 array of the proposed adaptive NoC routers has been prototyped and demonstrated on a Virtex II Pro Xilinx FPGA device. The router maintains SNN communication and avoids dropped SNN packets by adapting to traffic congestion. Due to the adaptive decision module, the router also adapts to injected network faults (broken NoC connections) by reconfiguring the routing topology to select an alternative route. The FPGA hardware testing has demonstrated real-time traffic congestion control and a resulting sustained aggregate router throughput of 16 Gbps. Fig. 5 illustrates an FPGA prototype test scenario, with no congestion on the network. Router R[1,2] neural tile transmits spikes to the R[4,1] neural tile (using an XY routing algorithm). Fig 5 also illustrates two alternative routing topologies, configured by the adaptive router when the R[1,2] to R[4,1] link is congested or where a link fault is introduced.

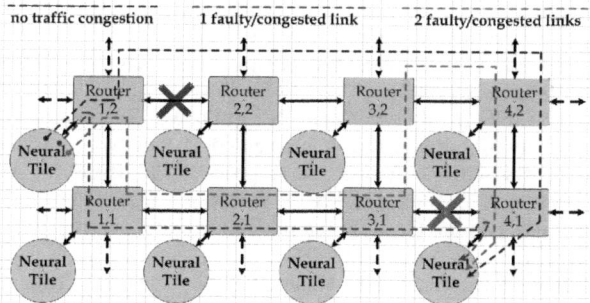

Fig. 5. A 4x2 array of NoC routers prototyped on a Virtex II Pro Xilinx FPGA to validate the proposed traffic congestion mechanism for the adaptive NoC router

4 Conclusion

The brain is highly efficient in how it processes information and tolerates faults. The basic processing units are neurons and synapses that are interconnected in a complex pattern. Computer scientist and engineers aim to harness this efficiency and build artificial neural systems that can emulate the key information processing principles of the brain. However, existing approaches cannot provide the dense interconnect for the billions of neurons and synapses that are required. In this regard, this paper has presented a novel adaptive NoC router architecture, to be used as an interconnection architecture within the mixed signal EMBRACE brain-inspired computation platform. Router adaptive behaviour in the presence of applied real-time traffic congestion has been demonstrated on a Virtex II Pro Xilinx FPGA for a 4x2 router array. Results are promising and establish the motivation to continue using the NoC paradigm as a way to overcome the interconnection problems for large scale hardware SNN implementation.

Acknowledgments. Snaider Carrillo Lindado is supported by a Vice-Chancellor's Research Scholarship (VCRS) from the University of Ulster.

References

1. Trappenberg, T.: Fundamentals of computational neuroscience. Oxford University Press, Oxford (2009)
2. Gerstner, W.: Spiking neuron models: Single neurons, populations, plasticity. Cambridge Univ. Pr., Cambridge (2002)
3. Misra, J., Saha, I.: Artificial neural networks in hardware: A survey of two decades of progress. Neurocomput. 74, 239–255 (2010)
4. Benini, L., De Micheli, G.: Networks on chips: a new SoC paradigm. Computer 35, 70–78 (2002)
5. Harkin, J., Morgan, F., McDaid, L., Hall, S., McGinley, B., Cawley, S.: A Reconfigurable and Biologically Inspired Paradigm for Computation Using Network-On-Chip and Spiking Neural Networks. International Journal of Reconfigurable Computing 2009, 1–13 (2009)
6. Cawley, S., Morgan, F., McGinley, B., Pande, S., McDaid, L., Carrillo, S., Harkin, J.: Hardware Spiking Neural Network Prototyping and Application. Journal of Genetic Programming and Evolvable Machines (2011) (in press)
7. Dally, W.J., Towles, B.: Principles and practices of interconnection networks. Morgan Kaufmann, San Francisco (2004)
8. Theocharides, T., Link, G., Vijaykrishnan, N., Irwin, M., Srikantam, V.: A generic reconfigurable neural network architecture implemented as a network on chip. In: Proceedings of IEEE International SOC Conference, 2004, pp. 191–194. IEEE, los Alamitos (2004)
9. Philipp, S., Schemmel, J., Meier, K.: A QoS network architecture to interconnect large-scale VLSI neural networks. In: 2009 International Joint Conference on Neural Networks, pp. 2525–2532. IEEE, Los Alamitos (2009)
10. Plana, L.A., Furber, S.B., Temple, S., Khan, M., Shi, Y., Wu, J., Yang, S.: A GALS Infrastructure for a Massively Parallel Multiprocessor. IEEE Design & Test of Computers 24, 454–463 (2007)

Self-Organizing Map for the Multi-Goal Path Planning with Polygonal Goals

Jan Faigl and Libor Přeučil

Czech Technical University in Prague - Department of Cybernetics
{xfaigl,preucil}@labe.felk.cvut.cz

Abstract. This paper presents a self-organizing map approach for the multi-goal path planning problem with polygonal goals. The problem is to find a shortest closed collision free path for a mobile robot operating in a planar environment represented by a polygonal map $\mathcal{W}$. The requested path has to visit a given set of areas where the robot takes measurements in order to find an object of interest. Neurons' weights are considered as points in $\mathcal{W}$ and the solution is found as approximate shortest paths connecting the points (weights). The proposed self-organizing map has less number of parameters than a previous approach based on the self-organizing map for the traveling salesman problem. Moreover, the proposed algorithm provides better solutions within less computational time for problems with high number of polygonal goals.

1 Introduction

A problem of finding a collision-free path for a mobile robot such that the robot visits a given set of goals is called the multi-goal path planning problem (MTP). The problem arises in various robotic tasks and one of them is an inspection task in which model of the robot work space is a priori known. A model can be a building plan that can be represented as the polygonal domain, i.e., a polygonal map with obstacles. In such a map, a goal can be a single point or a polygonal region. Goals represent places in the environment where a mobile robot takes measurements. A practical motivation for this type of problems are searching missions where a mobile robot has to inspect the environment to find an object of interest, e.g., victims in search&rescue missions [7].

The planning problem for point goals can be formulated as the well-known traveling salesman problem (TSP), and for which many self-organizing map (SOM) approaches have been proposed since the first work of Angéniol and Fort. In the case of polygonal goals, the problem formulation can be found as the safari route problem [8], or the zookeeper problem [2]. These problems can be solved in a polynomial time for particular restricted problem formulations, e.g., problems without obstacles, with a given starting point, and polygonal goals attached to the boundary. However, these problem variants can be formulated as the traveling salesman problem with neighborhoods (TSPN) [6]. Although approximation algorithms for restricted variants of the TSPN exist [3,1], in general, the TSPN is APX-hard and cannot be approximated with a factor $2 - \epsilon$, where $\epsilon > 0$, unless P=NP [9].

T. Honkela et al. (Eds.): ICANN 2011, Part I, LNCS 6791, pp. 85–92, 2011.

Here, it is worth to mention that SOM approaches for the TSP are focused on its Euclidean variant, i.e., distances between nodes and goals are determined as the Euclidean distances between two points. The main difference of the MTP is that a path between two goals (or node–goal path) has to be collision free; thus, geodesic paths (distances) avoiding the collision with obstacles have to be considered in the self-organizing procedure, which increases the complexity of the adaptation process.

In this paper, new SOM adaptation procedure for the MTP with polygonal goals is proposed. The approach follows standard SOM adaptation schema for the TSP that has been extended to the polygonal domain using approximate shortest path in [5]. The adaptation uses new winner selection procedure that finds and creates new neurons using a distance to a segment of the goal. Moreover, practical aspects of the adaptation process in the polygonal map are considered to decrease the computation burden of the adaptation. In addition, simplified adaptation rules based on [11] are used and together with the novel winner selection procedure they lead to less number of adaptation parameters. The proposed procedure is also able to deal with point goals. As such, it provides a unified way to solve various modifications of the MTP, which includes safari route problem and also the watchman route problem as a variant of the MTP where goals are polygons of a convex cover set of $\mathcal{W}$ [4].

2   Self-Organizing Map for Multi-Goal Path Planning with Polygonal Goals

The problem addressed in this paper can be defined as follows. Having a polygonal map $\mathcal{W}$ and a set of goals $\mathbf{G} = \{g_1, \ldots, g_n\}$, the problem is to find a closed shortest path such that the path visits at least one point of each goal $g_i \in \mathbf{G}$. A goal can be a single point, or a polygonal region, and all goals entirely lie in $\mathcal{W}$. A polygonal goal g is represented as a sequence of points $g = (p_1^g, \ldots, p_k^g)$, which forms a border of g represented as a set of straight line segments $\delta g = \{s_1^g, s_2^g, \ldots, s_k^g\}$, where s_i^g is a straight line segment inside $\mathcal{W}$, $s_i^g = (p_i^g, p_{i+1}^g)$ for $0 \leq i < k$, and $s_k^g = (p_k^g, p_1^g)$.

The proposed adaptation procedure is based on two-layered competitive neural network. The input layer consists of two dimensional input vector. An array of output units is the second layer, and it forms a uni-dimensional ordered structure. The neuron's weights represent coordinates of a point in $\mathcal{W}$, which is called node, and denoted as ν in this paper. Connected nodes form a ring that represents the requested path. In SOM for the TSP (for example [10]), goals are presented to the network in a random order and neurons compete to be the winner using the Euclidean distances between them and the goal. Then, the winner node is adapted towards the presented goal. However, in the MTP, a collision free path has to be determined because of obstacles in $\mathcal{W}$. The adaptation process may be considered as a node movement along the node–goal path towards the goal, i.e., the node (neuron's weights) is placed on the path closer to the goal while it travels distance according to the neighbouring function f.

An approximation of the shortest path may be used for the node–goal path determination [5].

Novel winner selection procedure is proposed to address polygonal goals. The procedure is based on consideration of the ring as a sequence of straight line segments in $\mathcal{W}$. Again, due to obstacles in $\mathcal{W}$, such a sequence is found using an approximate shortest path between two points (point–point path) in $\mathcal{W}$ [4].

Let the ring r be a sequence of line segments $r = (s_1^r, s_2^r, \ldots, s_l^r)$. The winner node is found as a "closest" point of the ring to the set of segments representing the goal g. The exact shortest path between two segments in $\mathcal{W}$ is substituted by the following approximation. First, the Euclidean distance between the segments s_i^r and s_j^g is determined; thus, two points on the segments are found, $p_r \in s_i^r$ and $p_g \in s_j^g$. The point–point path for these points is found to approximate the shortest path between two segments in $\mathcal{W}$. So, a pair (p_r, p_g) with the minimal length of the approximate shortest path between p_r and p_g is the result of the winner selection procedure. The point p_r is used for creating new node if a node with the same coordinates is not already in the ring. The found point p_g at the goal segment is used as a point goal towards which nodes are adapted using the point–point path. In the case of a point goal g, a similar procedure is used for approximating shortest segment–point path and p_g is the point goal itself.

The adaptation is an iterative stochastic procedure starting with an initial creation of m nodes, where $m = 2n$ and n is the number of goals. The neurons' weights are set to form a small circle around the first goal g_1, or around the centroid of g_1 for the polygonal goal. The used neighbouring function is $f(\sigma, d) = exp(-d^2/\sigma^2)$ for $d < 0.2m$, and $f(\sigma, d) = 0$ otherwise, where σ is the learning gain (the neighbouring function variance) and d is the distance of the adapted node from the winner node measured in the number of nodes (the cardinal distance). The adaptation process performs as follows.

1. *Initialization:* For a set of n goals $\mathbf{G}$ and a polygonal map $\mathcal{W}$, create $2n$ nodes around the centroid of the first goal. Let the initial value of the leaning gain be $\sigma = 10$, and adaptation parameters be $\mu = 1$, $\beta = 10^{-5}$, and $i = 1$.
2. *Randomizing:* Create a random permutation of goals $\Pi(\mathbf{G})$.
3. *Winner Selection:* For a goal $g \in \Pi(\mathbf{G})$ and the current ring r as a path in $\mathcal{W}$ find the pair (p_r, p_g) using the proposed winner selection procedure. Create a new node ν with coordinates p_r if such a node does not already exist. A node at the coordinates p_r is the winner node $\nu^\star$.
4. *Adapt:* If g is a point goal or $\nu^\star$ is not inside the polygonal goal g:
   – Let the current number of nodes be m, and N be a set of $\nu^\star$'s neighborhoods in the cardinal distance less than or equal to $0.2m$.
   – Move $\nu^\star$ along approximate shortest path $S(\nu^\star, p_r)$ towards p_r by the distance $|S(\nu^\star, p_r)|/\mu$, where $|S(.,.)|$ is the length of the approximate path.
   – Move nodes $\nu \in N$ for which $\mu f(\sigma, d) < \beta$ towards p_r along $S(\nu, p_r)$ by the distance $|S(\nu, p_r)|\mu f(\sigma, d)$, where f is the neighbouring function and d is the cardinal distance of ν to $\nu^\star$.
   Remove g from the permutation, $\Pi(\mathbf{G}) = \Pi(\mathbf{G}) \setminus \{g\}$, and if $|\Pi(\mathbf{G})| > 0$ go to Step 3.

5. *Ring regeneration:* Create a new ring as a path in $\mathcal{W}$ using only the winner nodes of the current adaptation step, i.e., remove all other nodes. Make nodes from the endpoints of $s^r \in r$ that do not correspond to the winners, i.e., nodes correspond to the sequence of path's vertices.
6. *Update adaptation parameters:* Set $i = i+1$, $\sigma = (1-0.001i)\sigma$, and $\mu = 1/\sqrt[4]{i}$.
7. *Termination condition:* If all polygonal goals have particular winner inside the polygonal goal, and if all point goals have the winner in a sufficient distance, e.g., less than 10^{-3}, or $\sigma < 10^{-4}$ Stop the adaptation. Otherwise go to Step 2.
8. *Final path construction:* Use the last winners to determine the final path using point–point approximate path in $\mathcal{W}$.

It is clear that the proposed adaptation procedure considering ring as a collision free path in $\mathcal{W}$ with the closest ring–goal segments selection is more computationally demanding than a consideration of node–goal points, which does not require determination of shortest path between two nodes. The adaptation performed only if $\mu f(\sigma, d) < \beta$ (called $\beta - condition$ rule) decreases the computational burden without significant influence to the solution quality. Also the used evolution of σ, μ [11] provides fast convergence. However, it decreases the solution quality in few cases in comparison to Somhom's parameters [10] used in [5,4]. An experimental comparison of these algorithms is presented in Section 3.

Regarding the necessary parameters settings the main advantage of the proposed procedure is that it does not require specific parameters tuning. Based on several experiments the procedure seems to be insensitive to changes of the initial values of σ and μ. Also the used size of the winner neighborhood ($0.2m$) provides the best trade-off between the solution quality and computational time.

It is worth to mention that the used approximation of the shortest path between two points (described in [4]) is more computationally demanding, and it is less precise than the node–goal path approximation. However, it requires less memory. It is because precomputed shortest paths from all map vertices to the goals are used in the node–goal path queries. Thus, lower memory requirements and a faster initialization are additional advantages of the proposed method.

3   Experiments

The proposed adaptation procedure has been experimentally verified in two sets of problems with polygonal goals, and compared with the SOM approach for the watchman route problem (WRP) [4]. The first set represents a "generalized" safari route problem, where convex polygonal goals, possibly overlapping each other, are placed in $\mathcal{W}$. The second set represents the WRP with restricted visibility range presented in [4]. Moreover, the proposed procedure has been compared with the SOM approach for the TSP in $\mathcal{W}$ [5] where goals are points.

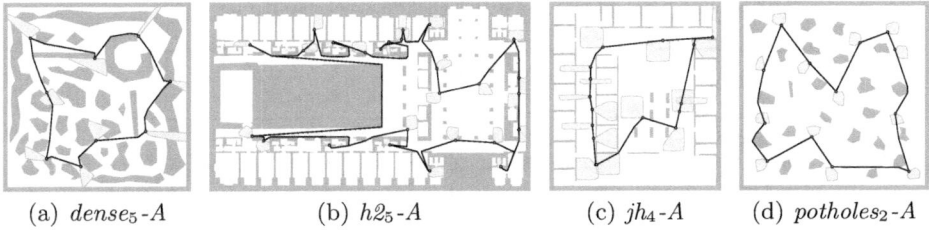

(a) $dense_5$-A   (b) $h2_5$-A   (c) jh_4-A   (d) $potholes_2$-A

Fig. 1. Selected solutions of the safari route problems, light polygons are goals, small disk at convex goal are the last winner nodes, black lines are found paths

The WRP algorithm adapts nodes towards centroids of the convex polygonal goals[1]. An alternate point is determined at the polygon border using node–centroid path to avoid placement of nodes too close to the polygon centroid, i.e., the node movement towards the centroid is stopped at the border. For the safari route problem, the WRP algorithm has been modified to do not consider the ring coverage, and to adapt nodes towards the determined alternate points. Besides, the WRP and the TSP algorithms has been modified to use the $\beta - condition$ rule and the Euclidean distance for pre-selection of winner nodes candidates, i.e., approximate node–goal path is determined only if the Euclidean node–goal distance is less than the distance of the current winner node candidate to the goal. These two modifications are technical, as they do not affect the solution quality; however, they decrease the computational burden several times.

The examined algorithms have been implemented in C++, compiled by the G++ 4.2.1 with the -O2 optimization, and executed within the same computational environment using single core of the i7-970 CPU at 3.2 GHz, and 64-bit version of the FreeBSD 8.2. Thus, the presented average values of the required computational times T can be directly compared.

The SOM algorithms are randomized, and therefore, each problem has been solved 50 times, and the average length of the path L, the minimal found path length L_{min}, and the standard deviation in percents of L denoted as $s_L\%$ are used as the quality metrics. Reference solutions from [4,5] are used for the WRPs and the TSPs, and the solution quality is measured as the percent deviation to the reference path length of the average path length, $PDM = (L-L_{ref})/L_{ref}\cdot100\%$, and as the percent deviation from the reference of the best solution, $PDB = (L_{min}-L_{ref})/L_{ref}\cdot100\%$. All presented length values are in meters. The number of goals is denoted as n in the presented tables.

The experimental results for the safari route problems are presented in Table 1 and selected best solutions found by the proposed algorithm are depicted in Figure 1. The proposed procedure provides better solutions for most of the problems. The procedure is more computationally demanding for complex environments like the problem h2$_5$-A because shortest paths have many segments. This is also the case of the jh$_{10}$-coverage problem, which is an instance of the WRP with many overlapping convex goals.

---

[1] In [4], triangles of a triangular mesh are used to support determination of ring coverage, which is not necessary for safari route problems.

Table 1. Experimental results for the safari route problems

Problem	n	SOM for WRP [4]				Proposed			
		L	$s_L\%$	L_{min}	T [s]	L	$s_L\%$	L_{min}	T [s]
dense-small	35	114.2	3.45	105.63	0.34	113.7	3.99	102.80	0.98
dense$_5$-A	9	62.6	1.96	60.66	0.14	59.0	2.77	58.05	0.23
h2$_5$-A	26	407.2	0.98	399.34	1.22	405.2	0.88	396.07	2.12
jh-rooms	21	88.3	0.76	87.84	0.13	88.1	0.10	87.83	0.15
jh$_{10}$-doors	21	67.6	1.34	66.11	0.16	63.7	1.43	61.99	0.15
jh$_{10}$-coverage	106	106.9	1.34	103.89	1.49	97.9	6.20	92.99	2.66
jh$_4$-A	16	61.1	1.86	58.71	0.33	57.3	1.32	56.59	0.32
jh$_5$-corridors	11	65.8	1.87	62.77	0.14	59.7	0.35	59.53	0.20
pb$_5$-A	7	275.8	4.47	265.29	0.31	271.7	4.36	264.70	0.31
potholes$_2$-A	13	71.9	1.91	70.37	0.04	71.6	2.08	70.09	0.08

Table 2. Experimental results for the WRP

Map	d [m]	n	L_{ref} [m]	SOM for the WRP [4]				Proposed				
				PDM	PDB	$s_L\%$	T [s]	PDM	PDB	L_{min}	$s_L\%$	T [s]
jh	inf	100	207.8	-52.67	-53.39	1.53	1.45	-53.71	-54.17	95.27	2.78	2.40
jh	10.0	108	207.3	-51.84	-53.02	3.27	1.95	-50.65	-54.02	95.30	6.89	2.64
jh	5.0	130	216.4	-48.67	-51.75	3.39	1.27	-51.54	-53.06	101.56	4.18	5.75
jh	4.0	169	219.9	-43.48	-46.34	3.22	2.97	-48.38	-49.42	111.22	2.71	9.21
jh	3.0	258	225.5	-27.92	-30.60	1.61	5.18	-35.04	-37.04	142.01	2.27	13.12
jh	2.0	480	281.9	-8.99	-11.09	1.06	20.68	-17.25	-19.85	225.91	1.64	23.16
jh	1.5	852	350.3	-3.81	-5.51	1.02	109.81	-14.56	-15.68	295.39	0.74	100.40
jh	1.0	1800	470.8	3.96	2.36	0.59	430.88	-9.06	-10.25	422.50	0.55	452.03
pb	inf	52	533.3	-18.11	-22.26	4.98	1.44	-16.18	-23.18	409.69	5.70	1.28
pb	10.0	111	612.7	-12.48	-14.86	3.92	2.57	-15.46	-17.94	502.78	4.73	3.46
pb	5.0	262	682.9	-7.35	-9.34	2.45	5.56	-7.01	-10.62	610.38	4.45	15.23
pb	4.0	373	720.1	-6.17	-8.78	3.25	16.80	-7.46	-10.09	647.41	3.16	20.37
pb	3.0	714	774.8	-5.62	-6.72	0.55	42.52	-3.04	-9.54	700.81	6.95	114.08
pb	2.0	1564	901.9	-2.88	-4.41	1.02	244.72	-0.30	-9.40	817.12	4.53	373.74
pb	1.5	2787	1115.9	1.03	0.07	0.54	997.68	-9.12	-12.12	980.59	2.27	1078.42
pb	1.0	6188	1564.2	2.55	1.90	0.41	5651.06	-12.52	-13.89	1346.87	0.78	3276.43
ta	inf	46	203.6	-30.99	-31.48	0.52	0.28	-33.67	-33.94	134.52	1.69	0.76
ta	10.0	70	202.6	-28.11	-28.80	0.28	0.41	-28.36	-28.89	144.08	1.45	1.63
ta	5.0	152	254.1	-15.68	-17.97	1.81	1.26	-19.61	-20.35	202.39	0.83	6.39
ta	4.0	209	272.2	-7.39	-9.91	1.36	3.69	-15.70	-16.65	226.90	0.85	11.64
ta	3.0	357	315.0	-6.28	-8.75	1.61	12.61	-13.46	-14.42	269.57	1.30	15.58
ta	2.0	757	408.3	1.09	-1.20	0.87	66.48	-10.97	-12.52	357.18	1.00	59.00
ta	1.5	1320	522.1	1.06	-1.18	0.97	194.25	-12.81	-13.63	450.92	0.59	251.08
ta	1.0	2955	743.6	5.21	3.80	0.57	1398.71	-12.45	-13.54	642.89	0.57	987.77

The results for the WRP are presented in Table 2, where d denotes the restricted visibility range. Also in this type of problems, the proposed procedure provides better solutions. Although the procedure is more computationally demanding for small problems, it provides significantly better results with less required computational time for problems with $d=1\ m$, which have many convex polygons. The results indicate that the proposed procedure scales better with

Table 3. Experimental results for the TSP

Problem	n	L_{ref} [m]	SOM for the TSP [5]				Proposed			
			PDM	PDB	$s_L\%$	T [s]	PDM	PDB	$s_L\%$	T [s]
jari	6	13.6	0.36	0.00	0.55	0.01	0.23	0.00	0.15	0.01
complex2	8	58.5	-0.00	-0.00	0.00	0.01	0.47	-0.00	1.60	0.02
m1	13	17.1	0.31	0.00	1.15	0.02	0.17	0.00	0.20	0.03
m2	14	19.4	9.52	0.00	3.50	0.03	10.76	5.32	3.16	0.04
map	17	26.5	5.92	0.73	4.39	0.05	6.87	0.73	4.37	0.07
potholes	17	88.5	4.58	2.37	2.17	0.06	5.56	2.37	2.48	0.06
a	22	52.7	0.89	0.31	1.00	0.09	1.58	0.31	2.37	0.11
rooms	22	165.9	1.02	0.00	0.86	0.11	0.12	0.00	0.11	0.15
dense4	53	179.1	15.04	8.33	3.16	0.68	18.17	9.00	2.38	0.68
potholes2	68	154.5	6.12	2.50	2.01	0.65	7.54	3.11	2.23	0.35
m31	71	39.0	6.71	2.29	1.53	1.41	8.72	4.80	1.64	1.00
warehouse4	79	369.2	5.97	2.42	2.13	1.92	8.47	2.87	2.68	0.81
jh2	80	201.9	1.94	0.48	0.64	0.95	2.04	0.67	0.66	0.71
pb4	104	654.6	1.06	0.01	1.34	1.53	1.95	0.51	3.05	0.84
ta2	141	328.0	2.97	1.69	0.69	2.27	3.69	2.19	0.75	1.11
h25	168	943.0	2.85	2.00	0.60	8.75	2.42	1.65	0.53	6.70
potholes1	282	277.3	6.84	4.91	1.02	10.47	6.97	4.19	0.91	2.71
jh1	356	363.7	4.02	2.74	0.56	22.29	4.32	3.23	0.46	7.05
pb1.5	415	839.6	2.60	1.12	2.25	24.13	10.40	1.47	5.21	6.62
h22	568	1 316.2	2.81	1.87	0.51	87.61	3.00	1.97	0.46	32.19
ta1	574	541.1	5.51	4.63	0.41	38.11	6.39	4.88	0.73	10.86

increasing number of goals. The reason for this is in the number of involved neurons. While the algorithm [4] derives the number from the number of goals, the proposed procedure dynamically adapts the number of neurons using shortest path in $\mathcal{W}$. Thus, for very large problems in the same map, additional neurons do not provide any benefit, and only increase the computational burden. The worse average results for the map pb, $d=3$ and $d=2$ are caused by the used point–point shortest path approximation, which provides unnecessary long paths in several cases. Nevertheless, the proposed procedure is able to find significantly better solutions, regarding the PDB, than the WRP algorithm [4].

The results for the TSP are presented in Table 3. The proposed procedure provides competitive results to the algorithm [5]. Worse average solutions are found for several problems. In these cases, the point–point path approximation provides longer paths than the point–goal path used in the TSP algorithm. The used schema of parameters evolution [11] leads to faster convergence, which "compensates" the more complex winner selection. However, the schema is the main reason for the worse performance of the proposed procedure than the TSP algorithm [5] with parameters' evolution [10].

4 Conclusion

Novel winner selection procedure for self-organizing maps has been proposed in this paper. The proposed adaptation procedure is able to deal with variants of the multi-goal path planning problem including the TSP, the WRP and the safari route problem. Moreover, the procedure can be considered as parameterless, as the number of neurons is determined during the adaptation process. It provides a unified approach to solve various routing problems in the polygonal domain $\mathcal{W}$.

Although the proposed algorithm provides outstanding results in many cases, both the required computational time and the solution quality may be improved as the former algorithms for the WRP and the TSP provide better results in particular problems. Both these aspects are related to the evolution of the adaptation parameters, e.g., σ, μ, or size of the winner node neighborhood. Besides, the utilized approximation may be improved. Shortest path approximation and investigation of adaptation schemata with different evolution of parameters are subjects of the further work.

Acknowledgments. The work presented in this paper has been supported by the Ministry of Education of the Czech Republic under the program "National research program II" by Project No. 2C06005.

References

1. de Berg, M., Gudmundsson, J., Katz, M.J., Levcopoulos, C., Overmars, M.H., van der Stappen, A.F.: Tsp with neighborhoods of varying size. Journal of Algorithms 57(1), 22–36 (2005)
2. Chin, W.-P., Ntafos, S.: The zookeeper route problem. Information Sciences: an International Journal 63(3), 245–259 (1992)
3. Dumitrescu, A., Mitchell, J.S.B.: Approximation algorithms for tsp with neighborhoods in the plane. Journal of Algorithms 48(1), 135–159 (2003)
4. Faigl, J.: Approximate Solution of the Multiple Watchman Routes Problem with Restricted Visibility Range. IEEE Transactions on Neural Networks 21(10), 1668–1679 (2010)
5. Faigl, J., Kulich, M., Vonásek, V., Přeučil, L.: An Application of Self-Organizing Map in the non-Euclidean Traveling Salesman Problem. Neurocomputing 74, 671–679 (2011)
6. Goodman, J.E., O'Rourke, J. (eds.): Handbook of Discrete and Computational Geometry. CRC Press LLC, Boca Raton (2004)
7. Kulich, M., Faigl, J., Přeučil, L.: Cooperative planning for heterogeneous teams in rescue operations. In: IEEE International Workshop on Safety, Security and Rescue Robotics (2005)
8. Ntafos, S.: Watchman routes under limited visibility. Computational Geometry: Theory and Applications 1(3), 149–170 (1992)
9. Safra, S., Schwartz, O.: On the complexity of approximating tsp with neighborhoods and related problems. Computational Complexity 14(4), 281–307 (2006)
10. Somhom, S., Modares, A., Enkawa, T.: A self-organising model for the travelling salesman problem. Journal of the Operational Research Society, 919–928 (1997)
11. Zhang, W., Bai, Y., Hu, H.P.: The incorporation of an efficient initialization method and parameter adaptation using self-organizing maps to solve the TSP. Applied Mathematics and Computation 172(1), 603–623 (2006)

Unlearning in the BCM Learning Rule for Plastic Self-organization in a Multi-modal Architecture

Mathieu Lefort, Yann Boniface, and Bernard Girau

LORIA, Campus Scientifique, BP 239, 54506 Vandœuvre-lès-Nancy Cedex, France
{mathieu.lefort, yann.boniface, bernard.girau}@loria.fr

Abstract. An agent moving in a real environment perceives it by numerous noisy sensors which provide some high dimensionality data with unknown topology. In order to interact in this complex and changing environment, according to the active perception theory, the agent needs to learn the correlations between its actions and the changes they induce in the environment. In the perspective of a bio-inspired architecture for the learning of multi-modal correlations, this article focuses on the ability to forget some previously learned selectivity in a model of perceptive map which spatially codes the sensor data. This perceptive map combines the Bienenstock Cooper Munro (BCM) learning rule, which raises a selectivity to a stimulus, with the neural field (NF) theory, which provides spatial constraints to self-organize the selectivities at the map level. The introduction of an unlearning term in the BCM learning rule (BCMu) improves the BCM-NF coupling by providing plasticity to the self-organization.

Keywords: BCM learning rule, dynamic neural fields, self-organization, unlearning, plasticity, multi-modality.

1 Introduction

Gibson has defined the notion of affordances which corresponds to the possible actions that an agent can perform with an object [7]. An object is then defined by the set of its affordances. The idea that actions take an essential part in the notion of object is also developed by O'Regan and Noë [14], who define an object as a sensory-motor invariant.

Human beings perceive the world by spatially distant sensors. However, their processing are interacting with each other, as illustrated in the ventriloquist effect [3] or in the Mc Gurk effect [12]. Merging the senses allows the brain to form a consistent perception of the world and to reduce the global noise of the sensors. For example, human reaction time is quicker for a consistent audio-visual stimulus than for a visual or an audio stimulus alone [9].

At a mesoscopic level, the cortex shows a generic structure all over its surface, composed of cortical columns (see [13] for an overview). In the functional view of the cortex, it is made up of several areas dedicated to a specific work.

T. Honkela et al. (Eds.): ICANN 2011, Part I, LNCS 6791, pp. 93–100, 2011.

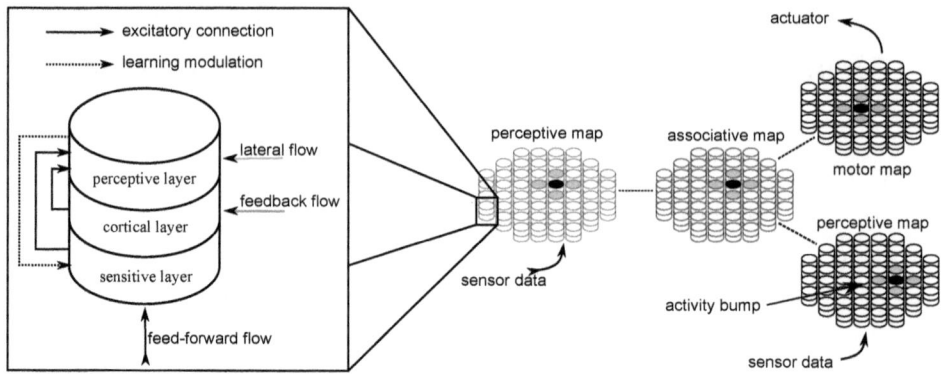

Fig. 1. (right) Example of use of the modular architecture with two sensors and one actuator. (left) Generic architecture of a cortical column in a perceptive map. The sensitive layer receives the feed-forward flow coming from the sensor, the cortical layer is connected to the associative map providing feedback from the multi-modal context and the perceptive layer codes the current perception by an activity bump, resulting from a lateral competition.

Perceptive areas compute a specific sensory flow, providing a spatial coding by self-organization, meaning that close neurons are sensitive to close stimuli, as the orientation coding in visual areas [4] or the tonotopic organization in the auditory cortex [15]. Associative areas merge perceptive flows and influence perceptions by feedback. This hierarchical view explains activities observed during the ventriloquist effect [3] but is questioned as multi-modal neurons were recently found in perceptive areas [5].

We have designed a multi-modal architecture to learn sensory-motor contingencies [11]. In this architecture, perceptive maps self-organize to map the sensor data topology in a two dimensional spatial coding, which is influenced to be consistent with the other perceptions. This self-organization is based on the coupling of neural fields with the BCM (Bienenstock Cooper Munro) learning rule. In this article, we focus on the addition of an unlearning term in the BCM equation to improve the efficiency of the neural field modulation and bring plasticity to the self-organization in order to better adapt to the multi-modal constraints.

In section 2, we briefly describe the main features of our multi-modal architecture and our perceptive map (for more details refer to [11,10]). In section 3, we introduce an unlearning term in the BCM equation that provides the forgetting of the discriminated stimulus if the modulation is not consistent. We illustrate the self-organization plasticity provided by the unlearning term in the experiment of section 4.

2   Model

2.1   General Architecture

Our architecture consists of interconnected perceptive and associative maps (see figure 1 right). Motor actions are represented by a perceptive map, that corresponds to the related proprioception. All maps have a generic two dimensional structure, to respect the cortex topology, composed of cortical columns with multiple layers. All computations and learning rules have local, continuous, decentralized and unsupervised properties.

Perceptive maps receive a sensory flow and provide a spatially localized activity bump representing the current perception. Sensor data topology is learned with a self-organization mechanism that provides generalization when coupled with the spatial coding. The associative map merges all perceptions to create a multi-modal context that, in return, influences each perception to be consistent. Thus, each perceptive map maps its sensor data flow so that its self-organization is consistent with the other maps. A sensory-motor correlation is represented by the set of the activity bump localizations, that is learned in the weights of the inter map connections.

2.2   Perceptive Map

Our model of perceptive map is composed of multilayer cortical columns (see figure 1 left). The sensitive layer uses the bio-inspired BCM learning rule [2], which is based on an hebbian rule with a sliding threshold between long term potentiation (LTP) and long term depression (LTD). This LTP/LTD sliding threshold induces competition between inputs, so that, applied to a stimuli flow, this rule has the property to autonomously develop a selectivity to one stimulus. The cortical layer is connected to the associative map and its activity represents the multi-modal influence. The perceptive layer uses neural fields [1,16] to filter its input, corresponding to the cortical and the sensitive informations. The perceptive activity represents the membrane potential of a discrete manifold, which evolves with a differential equation summing the input term with a lateral term, corresponding to an intra map connectivity with a difference of Gaussian shape, and a decay term, to suppress the activity in case of missing input. This lateral connectivity induces spatial competition that raises an activity bump where the input is spatially and temporally consistent. These spatial constraints are propagated to the organization of the sensitive layer, with the modulation of the sensitive activity by the perceptive one.

Thus, the coupling of the sensitive layer with the perceptive layer provides a self-organization of the selectivities of the sensitive layer that maps the sensor data topology. This self-organization can be influenced, by modifying the perceptive activity, to be consistent with the multi-modal context.

3   Unlearning

3.1   Motivation

The self-organization of the sensitive layer results from its continuous interaction loop with the perceptive layer. Although, the dynamic appears as a sequential process as the modulation can appear only when the sensitive layer begins to develop a selectivity. The perceptive modulation of the sensitive activity modifies

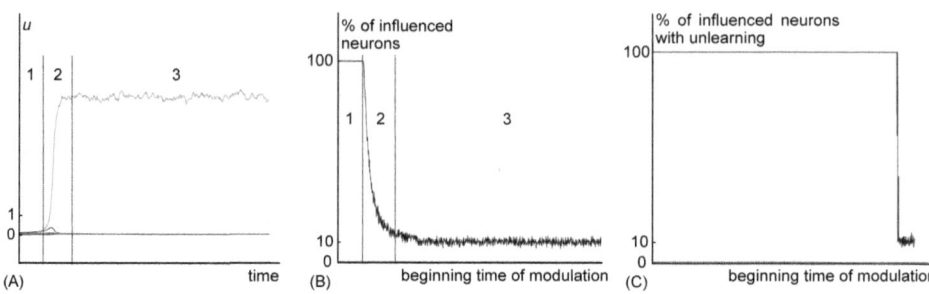

Fig. 2. Compared evolution dynamic of the activity for each stimulus (A), of the percentage of influenced neurons by an additive modulation as a function of its beginning time without unlearning (B) or with unlearning (C). These data are generated with ten orthogonal stimuli with a uniform probability of apparition.

the basins of attraction of the BCM learning rule to favor a specific stimulus. However, solutions of the BCM equation are stable so that the modulation is efficient only if the BCM equation is far from convergence. Thus, the efficiency of the sensitive activity modulation depends on the time of apparition of the perceptive activity (see figure 2).

More technically, the dynamic of the BCM learning rule can be split into three steps. In the first phase (1), the neuron have random weights so that activities are similar for each stimulus and the modulation is efficient. During the second phase (2), the threshold value increases and induces competition between inputs. As a consequence, the difference between the response value to the discriminated stimulus and the other one increases, leading to a decreasing efficiency of the modulation. The third phase (3) corresponds to a neuron that has developed a selectivity to the discriminated stimulus with a value equal to the inverse probability of its apparition. This selectivity is stable, and the modulation is no more efficient because of the important and stimulus dependent gap between activities (a neuron has 10% chance to be influenced, which corresponds to random chance as there are ten uniformly distributed stimuli).

Once the BCM learning rule has converged, this equilibrium is stable, so that the modulation has no more effect on it. This means that at the map level, the obtained self-organization is stable whatever the modulation. However, the self-organization needs to be plastic to adapt to the multi-modal constraints. Moreover, these constraints may change over time in case of addition, suppression or deterioration of a perceptive map. The idea is to modify the BCM learning rule, so that the selectivity of a stimulus is no more a stable point if the modulation is not consistent with its selectivity.

3.2   Equations

In the BCM learning rule, the activity u of a neuron is equal to the weighted sum of the stimulus $\mathbf{x}$ (equation (1)). The LTP/LTD sliding threshold θ is computed as the recent expectation of the square of the neuron activity (equation (2)).

The weight evolution is based on an hebbian rule using the LTP/LTD threshold (equation (3)).

$$u = \mathbf{w}.\mathbf{x} \tag{1}$$
$$\theta = E_\tau[u^2] \tag{2}$$
$$\Delta\mathbf{w} = \eta\mathbf{x}u(u - \theta) \tag{3}$$

To influence the neuron selectivity, its activity is modulated by an increasing function m of the perceptive layer activity s (equation (4)) [8]. The modulation is additive to be more efficient on non discriminated stimuli, whose neuron activity are nearby 0. We add an unlearning term in the evolution equation of $\mathbf{w}$ (equation (7)). The function $\hat{f}$ is a sigmoid that detects the lack of modulation (1 for no modulation and tending to 0 for a high one). Thus, the $\hat{f}(s)u^2$ term detects inconsistency between the current selectivity and modulation. β is a constant and χ is the recently expected modulation, so that unlearning is active only if the perceptive layer raises activity bumps. $w \times x$ stands for the term-by-term multiplication of the weight vector with the input vector. Thus, if the neuron is modulated and its selectivity is inconsistent with the modulation, its weights will decrease especially for the current stimulus.

$$u = \mathbf{w}.\mathbf{x} + m(s) \tag{4}$$
$$\theta = E_\tau[u^2] \tag{5}$$
$$\chi = E_{\tau'}[s] \tag{6}$$
$$\Delta\mathbf{w} = \eta(\mathbf{x}u(u - \theta) - \beta\chi\hat{f}(s)u^2\mathbf{w} \times \mathbf{x}) \tag{7}$$

3.3 Properties

The BCM equation with unlearning (BCMu) has three solutions that correspond to a non discriminated stimulus and to a discriminated one with or without consistent modulation. The stability of each nine couples of these three solutions is tested by adding a small perturbation of the weights and analyzing its evolution. This mathematical analysis[1] shows that the only stable points of the BCMu equation correspond to a selectivity to one stimulus that can be modulated or not. In the case of a modulated stimulus, the unlearning term is equal to 0 so that the stable point is the same as in the BCM learning rule (see [6] for more details). However, in the case of a non modulated stimulus, its value is limited by a fixed value. Thus, this stable point is no more stable if another stimulus is sufficiently modulated because of the competition between stimuli introduced by the LTP/LTD sliding threshold.

Practically, the BCMu learning rule raises a selectivity to a stimulus, that is forgotten if it does no longer fit the modulation. Thus, the selectivity becomes consistent with the modulation, whenever it appears and shows some

---

[1] See www.loria.fr/~lefortma/recherche/icann/annexes.pdf for the equations.

spatio-temporal continuity (see figure 2 (C)). At the map level, the sensitive self-organization is still stable but is plastic to the changes of the perceptive modulation that represents a consensus between the local sensation and the multi-modal constraints.

4   Results

The perceptive activity is artificially fixed, independently of the sensitive activity, and is equal to the spatial coding of the current stimulus corresponding to a specified self-organization (see figure 3). This activity may represent a consensus between local sensation and multi-modal constraints. This self-organization changes over time, representing a change in multi-modal constraints.

Figure 4 shows the comparative results between the self-organization that determines the perceptive activity and the obtained self-organization of the sensitive layer, using the BCM or the BCMu learning rule. The first self-organization is correctly learned by the perceptive map, with or without the unlearning term, meaning that the modulation is efficient on the sensitive self-organization. We can notice that the self-organization is slightly smoother with the use of the unlearning term.

Visually, the self-organization of the sensitive layer without unlearning appears 'frozen', whereas the BCMu rule succeeds in self-organizing the layer in accordance with the modulation changes (see figure 4 (A)). The value of the difference with respect to the fixed self-organization remains high when using the BCM rule, whereas it decreases with the BCMu rule until reaching a value close to the one obtained for the first fixed self-organization (see figure 4 (B)).

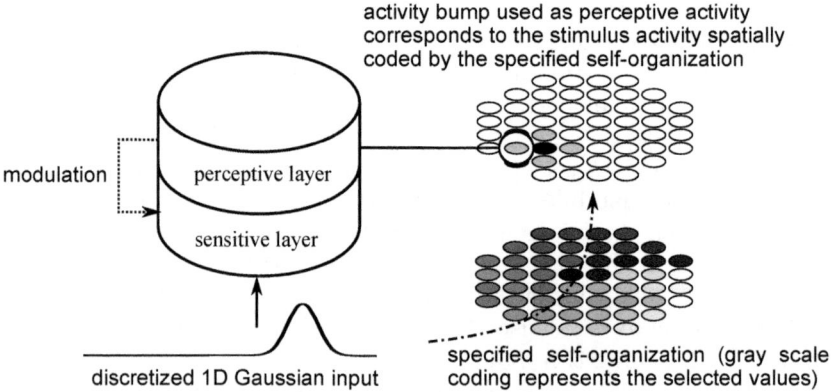

Fig. 3. Protocol used to test the plasticity of the self-organization to the multi-modal constraints. The multi-modal context is the current sensor data spatially coded by a defined self-organization.

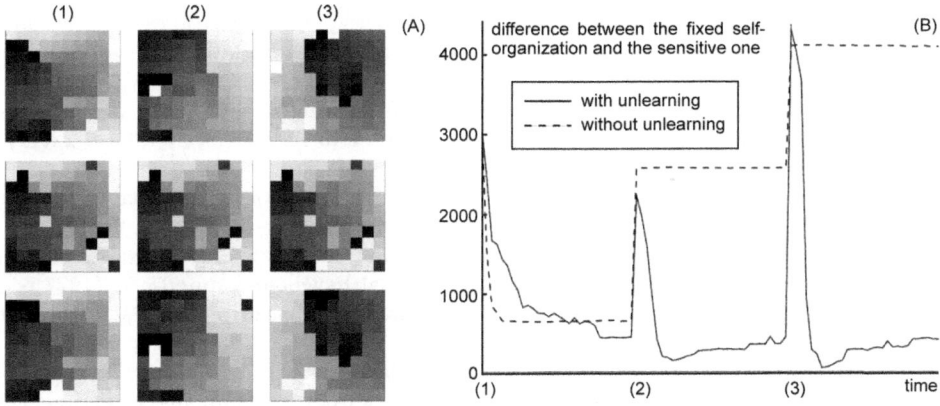

Fig. 4. (A) The selectivity of a column is represented in gray scale. Successive fixed self-organizations that provide the perceptive activity are shown in the first row. Sensitive self-organizations using the BCM learning rule (respectively BCMu) are in the second (respectively third) row. (B) Evolution of the sum over all columns of the difference between the selectivities of the fixed self-organization and the sensitive one. The peaks correspond to the change of fixed self-organization.

5   Conclusion

This article presents a forgetting mechanism for the BCM learning rule that consists in adding an unlearning term. This term induces a decreasing activity for the discriminated stimulus, if it is not consistent with the modulation received until it is limited by a constant term. Thus, with an efficient modulation, the only stable solution of this learning rule is the discrimination of a single stimulus which is consistent with the received modulation.

Our model of perceptive map for multi-modal association is based on the coupling of a sensitive layer which raises sensitive information with a perceptive layer which filters this information to raise a spatially localized activity, consistent with the other perceptions. The use of the BCM learning rule with unlearning (BCMu) in our perceptive map model provides plasticity to the self-organization of the sensitive layer. This plasticity is useful to adapt to the multi-modal constraints of a changing environment.

References

1. Amari, S.-I.: Dynamics of pattern formation in lateral-inhibition type neural fields. BiolCyb. 27, 77–87 (1977)
2. Bienenstock, E.L., Cooper, L.N., Munro, P.W.: Theory for the development of neuron selectivity: orientation specificity and binocular interaction in visual cortex. J. Neurosci. 2(1), 32–48 (1982)
3. Bonath, B., Noesselt, T., Martinez, A., Mishra, J., Schwiecker, K., Heinze, H.-J., Hillyard, S.A.: Neural basis of the ventriloquist illusion. Current Biology 17(19), 1697 (2007)

4. Bosking, W.H., Zhang, Y., Schofield, B., Fitzpatrick, D.: Orientation selectivity and the arrangement of horizontal connections in tree shrew striate cortex. Journal of neuroscience 17(6), 2112 (1997)
5. Cappe, C., Barone, P.: Heteromodal connections supporting multisensory integration at low levels of cortical processing in the monkey. Eur. J. Neurosci. 22(11), 2886–2902 (2005)
6. Cooper, L.N., Intrator, N., Blais, B.S., Shouval, H.Z.: Theory of Cortical Plasticity. World Scientific, Singapore (2004)
7. Gibson, J.J.: The theory of affordances. In: Shaw, R., Bransford, J. (eds.) Perceiving, Acting, and Knowing: Toward an Ecological Psychology, pp. 67–82 (1977)
8. Girod, T., Alexandre, F.: Effects of a modulatory feedback upon the bcm learning rule. In: CNS (2009)
9. Goldring, J.E., Dorris, M.C., Corneil, B.D., Ballantyne, P.A., Munoz, D.R.: Combined eye-head gaze shifts to visual and auditory targets in humans. Experimental Brain Research 111, 68–78 (1996)
10. Lefort, M., Boniface, Y., Girau, B.: Auto-organisation d'une carte de neurones BCM sous contrainte multimodale. In: 5ème Conférence française de Neurosciences Computationnelles - Neurocomp 2010, Lyon France (October 2010)
11. Lefort, M., Boniface, Y., Girau, B.: Self-organization of neural maps using a modulated BCM rule within a multimodal architecture. In: Proceedings of Brain Inspired Cognitive Systems 2010, Madrid Espagne (August 2010)
12. Mcgurk, H., Macdonald, J.: Hearing lips and seeing voices. Nature 264(5588), 746–748 (1976)
13. Mountcastle, V.B.: The columnar organization of the neocortex. Brain 120(4), 701 (1997)
14. O'Regan, J.K., Noë, A.: A sensorimotor account of vision and visual consciousness. Behavioral and Brain Sciences 24(05), 939–973 (2001)
15. Romani, G.L., Williamson, S.J., Kaufman, L.: Tonotopic Organization of the Human Auditory Cortex. Psychiatry 132, 650 (1975)
16. Rougier, N.P., Vitay, J.: Emergence of attention within a neural population. Neural Networks 19(5), 573–581 (2006)

Neuronal Projections Can Be Sharpened by a Biologically Plausible Learning Mechanism[*]

Matthew Cook[1],[**], Florian Jug[2], and Christoph Krautz[2],[***]

[1] Institute of Neuroinformatics,
University of Zurich and ETH Zurich, Switzerland
cook@ini.phys.ethz.ch
[2] Institute of Theoretical Computer Science,
ETH Zurich, Switzerland
{fjug,ckrautz}@inf.ethz.ch

Abstract. It is known that neurons can project topographically to their target area, and reciprocal projections back from the target area are typically aligned with the forward projection. However, the wide terminal arbors of individual axons limit the precision of such anatomical reciprocity. This leaves open the question of whether more precise reciprocal connectivity is obtainable through the adjustment of synaptic strengths. We have found that such a sharpening of projections can indeed result from a combination of biologically plausible mechanisms, namely Hebbian learning at synapses, continuous winner-take-all circuitry within areas, and homeostatic activity regulation within neurons. We show that this combination of mechanisms, which we refer to collectively as "sharp learning", is capable of sharpening inter-area projections in a variety of network architectures. Sharp learning offers an explanation for how precise topographic and reciprocal connections can emerge, even in early development.

Keywords: Self-organization, Early development, Recurrent networks.

1 Introduction

A recurring theme of inter-areal projections is that they are topographic in nature [1, 2], meaning that the relative positions of the terminal axonal arbors in the target area are arranged similarly to the relative positions of the somas in the source area. However, the terminal arbors often overlap significantly, with a single arbor covering from 5% to 30% of the total target area [3].

A natural question is whether the synaptic connections might provide more precise topographic connectivity than one would assume just by examining the morphology and assuming random connectivity [4] within the axonal and dendritic arbor regions.

---

[*] The authors are listed in alphabetic order.
[**] Supported by EU Project Grant FET-IP-216593.
[***] Supported by ETH Research Grant ETH-23 08-1.

T. Honkela et al. (Eds.): ICANN 2011, Part I, LNCS 6791, pp. 101–108, 2011.

Note that a precise projection does not necessarily imply small arbors. Even if non-precise connections are pruned during development, the remaining, precise synapses will still be distributed throughout the area where the original axonal arbor overlapped with dendritic arbors of target cells, as in Fig. 1(a,b). Thus the morphology alone cannot indicate whether such a sharpening process has occurred or not, and current anatomical knowledge does not yet include sufficient information on synaptic specificity of inter-areal projections [5, 6], leaving the question open.

The biologically plausible mechanisms that we use are Hebbian learning at synapses, continuous winner-take-all circuitry within areas, and homeostatic

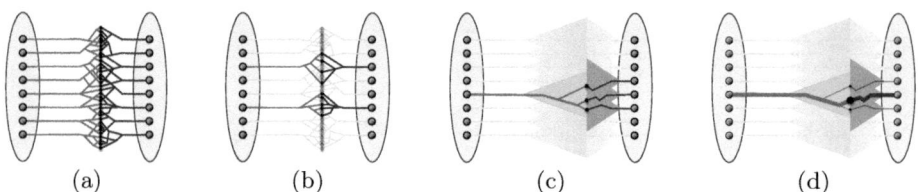

(a)   (b)   (c)   (d)

Fig. 1. (a) A precise projection between two areas (grey ellipses) without small arbors. The synapses (black dots) can be distributed throughout the area where the projecting cell's axonal arbor (left, red) overlaps with the dendritic arbor (right, blue) of the target cell. Although the arbors have a chaotic and unfocused morphology, the projection is in fact perfectly topographic, one-to-one connectivity. (b) The same picture with most arbors grayed out. Here it is easier to see how the synaptic connections are providing a perfectly precise projection. (c) When one area projects to another, the terminal axonal and dendritic arbors (symbolized as shaded triangles) allow each projecting neuron to reach a range of targets (three shown). (d) Learning mechanisms can effectively sharpen the projection by strengthening some synapses and weakening others. This is symbolized here by showing the connection of the most-aligned units as strengthened, while other connections are weakened, yielding the connectivity of (a). For visual clarity, these diagrams (a)-(d) are vast simplifications of real arbors, which contain thousands of synapses in three dimensions, often centered around the target soma. In reality a projection would not have to be one-to-one to be considered precise, but it would need to use synaptic specificity to prefer localized targets.

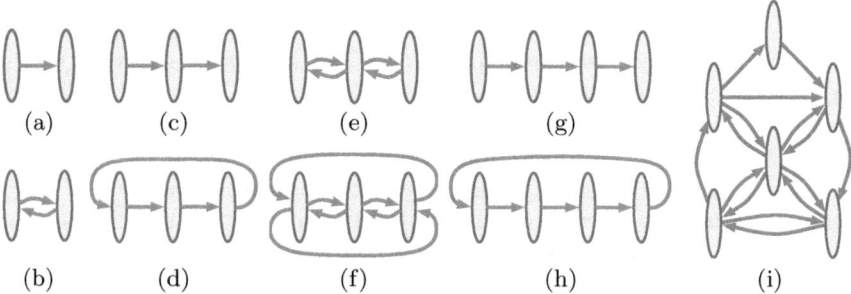

(a)   (c)   (e)   (g)

(b)   (d)   (f)   (h)   (i)

Fig. 2. Examples of inter-areal architectures where sharp learning is successful, including feed-forward paths and cycles (a,c,g,d,h), bidirectional paths and cycles (e,b,f), and an arbitrary complex structure (i)

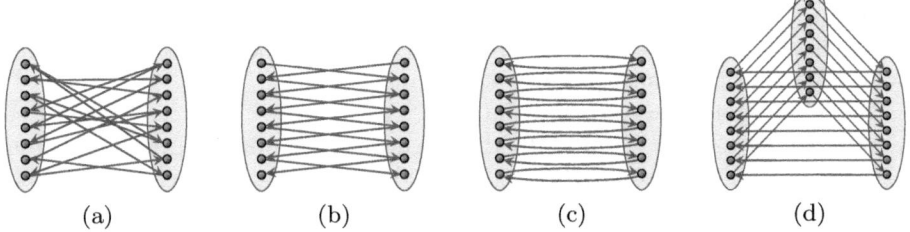

(a)	(b)	(c)	(d)

Fig. 3. Various types of connections. (a) Shows disordered connectivity, as would be expected with randomly connected synapses. Such randomness is often assumed when considering connectivity on a scale smaller than a dendritic arbor [4, 5]. (b) Shows skewed connectivity, as would be almost inevitable from a developmental program of chemotaxic axon growth attempting to form reciprocal connections. (c) Shows reciprocal connectivity, which is achieved by sharp learning. (d) Shows how this idea can be generalized to cycles of length three or more. Again, aligned connectivity is shown, as achieved by sharp learning. The arrows in each diagram represent the strongest connection. Nearby connections (not shown) are also present but weaker.

long-term activity regulation within neurons, as shown in Fig. 4. We find that this combination of mechanisms, which we refer to collectively as *sharp learning*, is capable of sharpening inter-areal projections in a variety of network architectures, such as those in Fig. 2. Furthermore, in networks with recurrently connected areas, sharp learning results in sharpened back projections being aligned with sharpened forward projections, as shown in Fig. 3(c,d).

Over the last decades, there have been countless models examining the training of weights between layers in a network. Our results are most closely related to the pioneering work of Willshaw and Malsburg, who modeled the development of unidirectional topographic retino-tectal projections in the frog [7].

2   Methods

Sharp learning takes place in the context of interacting groups of units that we refer to as *populations* or *areas*. The large-scale architecture of a network lies in

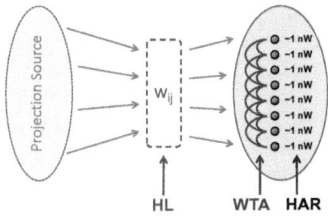

Fig. 4. Components of sharp learning: Hebbian learning (HL) between areas, winner-take-all (WTA) within areas, and homeostatic activity regulation (HAR) within units

the projections between these populations. These projections can be shown in a *projection diagram*, such as those shown in Fig. 2. One well-known projection diagram is that of Felleman and van Essen, showing the connectivity between cortical areas in the visual pathway of the macaque [8].

The populations are composed internally of *units*, which can be considered as corresponding either to an individual neuron, to a small neural microcircuit in the cortex [5], or to a tightly connected group of cells such as a cortical microcolumn [9].

Sharp learning is a combination of three strategies, as shown in Fig. 4 and Fig. 5. Synaptic connections between areas are controlled by Hebbian learning (HL), so that the weights reflect the correlation of typical network activity [10]. Local connections within an area (*lateral connections*) support continuous winner-take-all (WTA) dynamics [11], so neighboring units within an area exhibit similar activity patterns and noisy input is smoothed. Homeostatic activity regulation (HAR) within each unit modulates the Hebbian learning so that a unit does not become permanently active or inactive, but maintains a desired average activity level [12]. This makes sure that every unit is used, and that each unit is used in moderation.

It is worth noting that the presented components work on quite different time scales. The WTA dynamics operate on a short time scale, allowing the network to converge quickly. HAR and HL operate on a longer time scale, averaging over many inputs.

Winner-Take-All. The units within each of the populations are laterally interconnected so that each population is effectively a continuous winner-take-all circuit [11], meaning that the dynamics lead to a localized region of activity, similar to the encoding of a value by a population code [13]. The connection weight $w_{i,j}$ between units i and j is defined as

$$w_{i,j} = \gamma \cdot e^{-\frac{1}{2}(d(i,j)/\sigma)^2} - \delta, \tag{1}$$

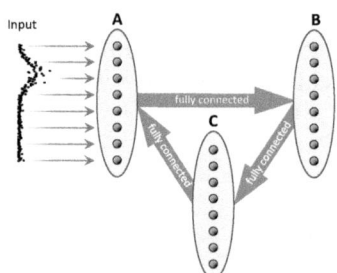

Sharp Learning Algorithm
1: initialize inter-areal weights randomly
2: **loop**
3:     initialize units with random activity
4:     draw and feed noisy input to **A**
5:     **repeat**
6:         do WTA update (eq. 1)
7:     **until** change in unit activities $< \epsilon$
8:     do HL (eq. 2) and HAR (eq. 3)
9: **end loop**

Fig. 5. The main loops in the sharp learning algorithm. The three-population ring architecture of Fig. 2(d) is shown, but the procedure is the same for all architectures. If lines 7 and 8 are swapped, then we refer to the modified algorithm as the "continuous learning" form of the algorithm.

where $d(i,j) = \min\{|i - j|, n - |i - j|\}$ gives the distance d between i and j, with n being the number of units in the population. In order to avoid boundary effects we let the distance measure wrap around. The parameters γ, σ, and δ specify the amplitude, the width, and the vertical displacement (i.e. the amount of lateral inhibition) of the Gaussian shape of the connection weights profile.

Hebbian Learning. The update of the weights $w_{i,j}^t$ depends on (i) the activities a_i^t and a_j^t of units i and j at time t (incremented in the outer loop of Fig. 5), and (ii) two global parameters α_l and α_d. The Hebbian learning rate α_l regulates the speed at which connections get learned and is usually set to a value smaller then α_d, the weight decay rate. The weights are updated according to:

$$w_{i,j}^{t+1} = (1 - \alpha_d) \cdot w_{i,j}^t + \alpha_l \cdot a_i^t \cdot a_j^t. \tag{2}$$

We perform Hebbian learning only on inter-areal weights. To speed up the running time of simulations it suffices to do these updates only after the WTA converged.

Homeostatic Activity Regulation. We use the following update formula for the homeostatic activity terms:

$$h_j^t = -c \cdot (\bar{a}_j^t - a_{\text{target}}), \tag{3}$$

where c is a scaling constant, a_{target} sets the desired activity level, and $\bar{a}_j^t$ is a running average of the activity of unit j, defined by

$$\bar{a}_j^t = (1 - \omega)\bar{a}_j^{t-1} + \omega a_j^t \tag{4}$$

where ω is the inverse time constant of the averaging.

Neural Units and Update Dynamics. At each discrete time step τ in the inner loop of Fig. 5, we update the activity level a_j^τ of each unit j. To do this, we first sum the activity levels of all units connected to unit j, weighted by their connection strengths. This sum includes both the lateral connectivity within the population as well as the connections coming from other populations. This sum is corrected by the homeostatic activity regulation term h_j^t. Finally we apply a non-linear function θ that restricts the activity level to the range $[0, 1]$. This yields

$$a_j^{\tau+1} = \theta(h_j^t + \sum_{i \in \Gamma_j^{\text{in}}} w_{i,j}^t \cdot a_i^\tau), \tag{5}$$

where Γ_j^{in} is the set of units connected to unit j, and θ is a logistic function

$$\theta(x) = \frac{1}{1 + e^{-m(x-s)}} \tag{6}$$

parameterized by m and s.

Note that the time τ in Equation 5 refers to iterations of the inner loop (lines 5-7 of Fig. 5), while the time t in Equations 2-4 refers to iterations of the outer loop (lines 2-9 of Fig. 5).

3   Results

We show in Fig. 6 the results of sharp learning applied to the network of Fig. 2(d), as described in Fig. 5. Below each connection matrix shown in Fig. 6 is a diagram of the projection represented by that matrix, showing an arrow to the strongest target for each projecting unit. As described above, the populations in the simulation use a wrap-around topology for the lateral connectivity (the continuous winner-take-all), which is the only place we induce any topology into the network. Using a wrap-around topology allows an arbitrary displacement to arise in each projection, while still being precisely topographic. One can also see

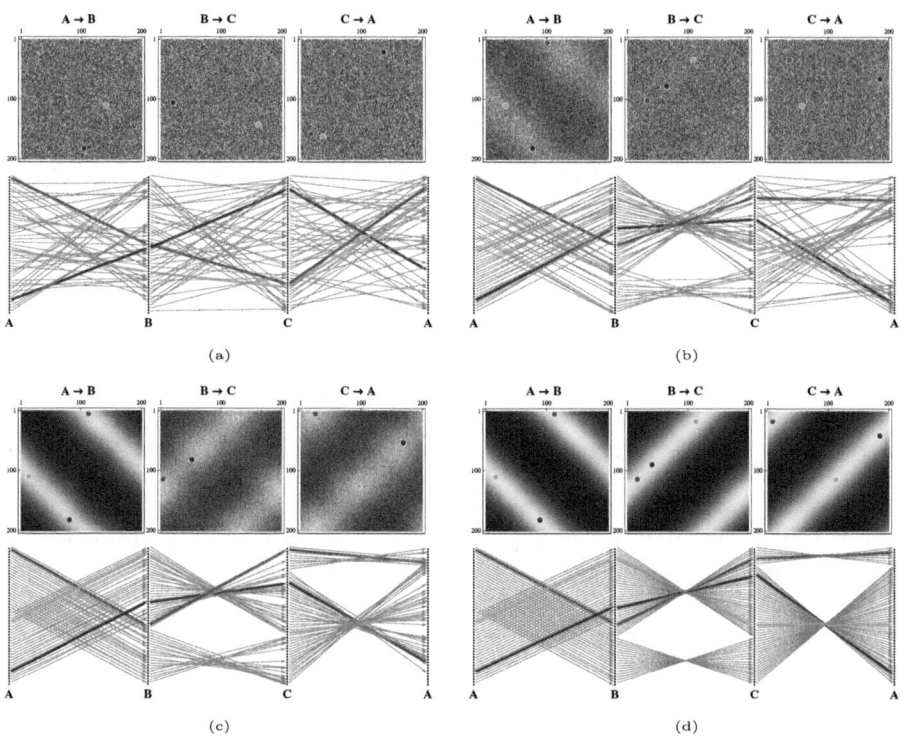

Fig. 6. The weight matrices of the example network of Fig. 5. **(a)** shows the random initial state of the network, **(b)** and **(c)** show the state of the network during learning, and **(d)** shows the state after learning has converged. The matrices are shown with low values dark and high values white. Below each matrix is a mapping showing which target element each source element is most strongly connected to. In (a-d), the first matrix shows the weights from population A (row) to population B (column), the second from B to C, and the third from C to A. The goal of our algorithm, as reached in (d), is that neighbors within a source population should project to neighboring destinations, and the circular path starting from any unit should come back to that unit. Three examples of such paths are highlighted in different colors.

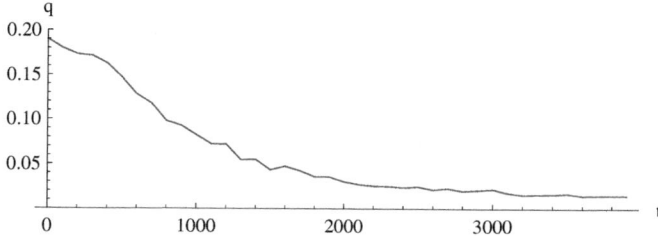

Fig. 7. Evolution of quality value q for the network of Fig. 5. The q-values give the mean squared error compared to a perfect topographic mapping between all connected populations of a network.

Table 1. Quality of sharp learning for the network architectures shown in Fig. 2. The quality q of a result is the root-mean-squared error in the position of the activity in each layer of the network, averaged over all possible positions of the peak of the input acitvity. The position of the activity in a layer is determined by considering the position of best fit of a Gaussian kernel, measured such that the size of the entire layer is 1. Due to the wrap around topology of the populations, the error is always between 0 and 0.5.

Networks shown in Fig. 2	(a)	(b)	(c)	(d)	(e)	(f)	(g)	(h)	(i)
Quality of sharp learning (q)	0.006	0.013	0.005	0.012	0.014	0.011	0.010	0.023	0.025

that the second and third matrices, once sharp learning has progressed, invert the ordering of the units within the population. The apparent discontinuities in the pattern of paths shown in Fig. 6(d) are in fact continuous, due to the wrap-around nature of the populations.

In Table 1 we compare the results of sharp learning for the network architectures shown in Fig. 2. For simulation each population contained 200 units. The q-values in the table give the mean squared error compared to a perfectly topographic mapping between all connected populations of a network.

Fig. 7 shows how the q-value evolves over the course of sharpening the projections in a network, for the network shown in Fig. 5. Other networks, even with layers of unequal size, behave comparably (data not shown).

4   Discussion

We have shown that sharp learning is able to effectively sharpen inter-areal projections in a variety of circumstances, using a combination of biologically plausible mechanisms.

To further confirm the biological plausibility of sharp learning it will be necessary to investigate the robustness of sharp learning with respect to inhomogeneities in the lateral connectivity within an area, as well as with respect to inhomogeneities in the homeostatic activity regulation and other parameters.

Another step towards biological plausibility would be to replace the mean-rate nodes used in our simulations by spiking units. This would require the transformation of the learning rules into a spike based equivalent.

We treat sharp learning here as a developmental process. We have also shown that a very similar procedure can learn data relationships fed to two populations in a network similar to the ones discussed here [14].

Since sharp learning can (i) help to create precise topographic connections, and (ii) subsequently be used to learn relationships by simply observing input fed to the network, we believe that sharp learning is a capable model of learning whose power has only started to be explored.

References

1. Price, D., Kennedy, H., Dehay, C., Zhou, L., Mercier, M.: The development of cortical connections. European Journal of Neuroscience 23, 910–920 (2006)
2. Essen, D., Zeki, S.: The topographic organization of rhesus monkey prestriate cortex. The Journal of Physiology 277, 193–226 (1978)
3. Kennedy, H., Salin, P., Bullier, J., Horsburgh, G.: Topography of developing thalamic and cortical pathways in the visual system of the cat. J. Comp. Neurol. 348(2), 298–319 (1994)
4. Braitenberg, V., Schütz, A.: Peters' rule and White's exceptions. In: Anatomy of the cortex: Statistics and geometry (Studies of brain function), pp. 109–111. Wiley, Chichester (1991)
5. Binzegger, T., Douglas, R., Martin, K.: A quantitative map of the circuit of cat primary visual cortex. The Journal of Neuroscience 24(39), 8441–8453 (2004)
6. Olshausen, B.A., Field, D.J.: How close are we to understanding V1? Neural Computation 17(8), 1665–1699 (2005)
7. Willshaw, D.J., van der Malsburg, C.: How patterned neural connections can be set up by self-organization. Proceedings of the Royal Society of London. Series B 194(1117), 431–445 (1976)
8. Felleman, D., Essen, D.V.: Distributed hierarchical processing in the primate cerebral cortex. Cerebral Cortex 1, 1–47 (1991)
9. Mountcastle, V.B.: Modality and topographic properties of single neurons of cat's somatic sensory cortex. Journal of Neurophysiology 20(4), 408–434 (1957)
10. Hebb, D.O.: The organization of behavior: A neuropsychological theory, p. 62. Wiley, Chichester (1949)
11. Douglas, R., Martin, K.: Recurrent neuronal circuits in the neocortex. Current Biology 17(3), R496–R500 (2007)
12. Turrigiano, G., Nelson, S.: Homeostatic plasticity in the developing nervous system. Nature Reviews Neuroscience 5, 97–107 (2004)
13. Georgopoulos, A., Kalaska, J., Caminiti, R., Massey, J.: On the relations between the direction of two-dimensional arm movements and cell discharge in primate motor cortex. The Journal of Neuroscience 2(11), 1527–1537 (1982)
14. Cook, M., Jug, F., Krautz, C., Steger, A.: Unsupervised learning of relations. In: Diamantaras, K., Duch, W., Iliadis, L.S. (eds.) ICANN 2010. LNCS, vol. 6352, pp. 164–173. Springer, Heidelberg (2010)

Explicit Class Structure by Weighted Cooperative Learning

Ryotaro Kamimura

IT Education Center, 1117 Kitakaname Hiratsuka Kanagawa 259-1292, Japan
`ryo@keyaki.cc.u-tokai.ac.jp`

Abstract. In this paper, we propose a new type of information-theoretic method called "weighted cooperative learning." In this method, two networks, namely, cooperative and uncooperative networks are prepared. The roles of these networks are controlled by the cooperation parameter α. As the parameter is increased, the role of cooperative networks becomes more important in learning. In addition, the importance of input units or variables is incorporated in the learning in terms of mutual information. We applied the method to the housing data from the machine learning database. Experimental results showed that weighted cooperative learning could be used to improve performance in terms of quantization and topographic errors. In addition, we could obtain much clearer class boundaries on the U-matrix by the weighted cooperative learning.

1 Introduction

In this paper, we propose a new type of information-theoretic method called "weighted cooperative learning." In this method, two networks, namely, cooperative and cooperative networks interact with each other. The uncooperative networks try to imitate cooperative networks as much as possible. Then, the roles of two networks are controlled by the cooperation parameter α. As the parameter α is increased, the role of cooperative networks becomes dominant. In addition, the importance of input units is considered by computing mutual information between competitive units and input patterns with attention to a specific input unit.

The computational procedure is composed of two phases. The first phase is comparable to the self-organizing maps (SOM), because we pay attention only to cooperation among neurons. One of the main difference is that our method is based upon soft competition among neurons and the degree of competition can freely be controlled. This property is essential to produce clearer class structure. In the conventional SOM, there have been many visualization techniques [5] to clarify class structure. One of the well-known techniques is the U-matrix [3] which is good at detecting the class boundaries visually. However, even if we use those conventional visualization techniques, it is difficult to see clear class boundaries on the map, in particular when the problems become complex. In our method, competition is freely controlled for different purposes. In this paper, we control the competition for better interpretation.

In the second phase, the degree of cooperation is controlled. This means that the roles of cooperative and uncooperative networks can be changed for different purposes. Our objective is to make class structure as clear as possible and for this purpose, the

T. Honkela et al. (Eds.): ICANN 2011, Part I, LNCS 6791, pp. 109–116, 2011.

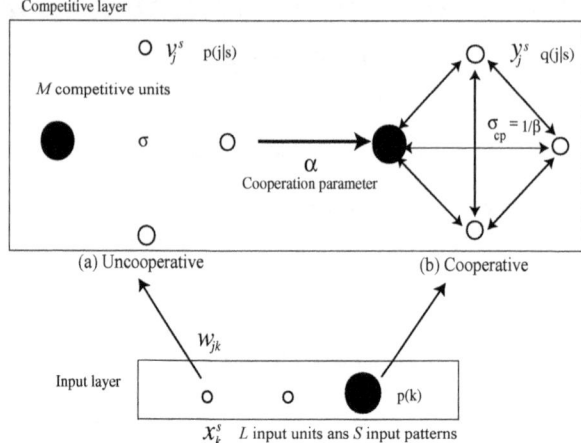

Fig. 1. Concept of uncooperative (a) and cooperative (b) network with the cooperation parameter α

degree of cooperation is controlled. In addition, we take into account the importance of input units or the information of input units for clearer representation. The importance is measured in terms of mutual information of input units and obtained information is used to make class structure as clear as possible.

2   Theory and Computational Methods

2.1   Cooperative Learning

Figure 1 shows a concept of cooperative learning, in which an uncooperative network or network without cooperation between units (a) tries to imitate the cooperative network or network with cooperation (b). In an uncooperative network, the firing probability of the jth competitive unit is defined by

$$p(j \mid s) = \frac{\exp\left\{-\frac{1}{2}(\mathbf{x}^s - \mathbf{w}_j)^T \mathbf{\Lambda}(\mathbf{x}^s - \mathbf{w}_j)\right\}}{\sum_{m=1}^{M} \exp\left\{-\frac{1}{2}(\mathbf{x}^s - \mathbf{w}_m)^T \mathbf{\Lambda}(\mathbf{x}^s - \mathbf{w}_m)\right\}}, \tag{1}$$

where $\mathbf{x}^s$ and $\mathbf{w}_j$ denote the L-dimensional input and weight vectors and the klth element of the scaling matrix $(\Lambda)_{kl}$ is defined by

$$(\Lambda)_{kl} = \delta_{kl}\frac{p(k)}{\sigma^2}, \tag{2}$$

where $p(k)$ denotes the firing probability of the kth input unit and σ is a spread parameter.

For the cooperative network, we borrow the computational methods developed for the conventional self-organizing maps, and then we use the ordinary neighborhood kernel used for SOM, namely,

$$h_{jc} = \exp\left(\frac{\|\mathbf{r}_j - \mathbf{r}_c\|^2}{2\sigma_{nh}^2}\right), \tag{3}$$

where $\mathbf{r}_j$ and $\mathbf{r}_c$ denotes the position of the jth and cth unit on the output space. The cooperative outputs can be defined by the summation of all neighboring competitive units

$$y_j^s = \sum_{c=1}^{M} h_{jc} \exp\left\{-\frac{1}{2}(\mathbf{x}^s - \mathbf{w}_c)^T \mathbf{\Lambda}_{cp}(\mathbf{x}^s - \mathbf{w}_c)\right\}, \tag{4}$$

where M is the number of competitive units and the klth element of the scaling matrix $(\mathbf{\Lambda}_{cp})_{kl}$ is given by

$$(\mathbf{\Lambda}_{cp})_{kl} = \delta_{kl}\frac{p(k)}{\sigma_{cp}^2}, \tag{5}$$

where σ_{cp} is the spread parameter for the cooperative network. The conditional probability $q(j|s)$ of the firing of the jth competitive unit, given the sth input pattern, can be obtained by normalizing the competitive unit outputs y_j^s. To imitate cooperative networks by uncooperative ones, we must decrease the following KL divergence measure

$$I_{KL} = \sum_{s=1}^{S}\sum_{j=1}^{M} p(s)p(j \mid s) \log \frac{p(j \mid s)}{q(j \mid s)}, \tag{6}$$

where S is the number of input patterns. It is possible to directly differentiate this equation to have update rules. However, the final update rules become complicated. Instead of the direct differentiation, we introduce the free energy. The free energy can be defined by

$$F = -2\sigma^2 \sum_{s=1}^{S} p(s) \log \sum_{j=1}^{M} q(j|s) \exp\left\{-\frac{1}{2}(\mathbf{x}^s - \mathbf{w}_j)^T \mathbf{\Lambda}(\mathbf{x}^s - \mathbf{w}_j)\right\}. \tag{7}$$

Then, the free energy can be expanded as

$$F = \sum_{s=1}^{S} p(s) \sum_{j=1}^{M} p^*(j \mid s)\|\mathbf{x}^s - \mathbf{w}_j\|^2 + 2\sigma^2 \sum_{s=1}^{S} p(s) \sum_{j=1}^{M} p^*(j \mid s) \log \frac{p^*(j \mid s)}{q(j \mid s)} \tag{8}$$

where

$$p^*(j \mid s) = \frac{q(j \mid s) \exp\left\{-\frac{1}{2}(\mathbf{x}^s - \mathbf{w}_j)^T \mathbf{\Lambda}(\mathbf{x}^s - \mathbf{w}_j)\right\}}{\sum_{m=1}^{M} q(m \mid s) \exp\left\{-\frac{1}{2}(\mathbf{x}^s - \mathbf{w}_m)^T \mathbf{\Lambda}(\mathbf{x}^s - \mathbf{w}_m)\right\}}, \tag{9}$$

Now, it is easy to differentiate the free energy to have update rules. Suppose that input patterns are given with the same probabilities, and then we have

$$\mathbf{w}_j = \frac{\sum_{s=1}^{S} p^*(j \mid s)\mathbf{x}^s}{\sum_{s=1}^{S} p^*(j \mid s)}. \tag{10}$$

2.2   Weighted Cooperation

Now, we must compute the firing probability of the kth input unit $p(k)$. One of the easiest way is to suppose that all input units fire equally, namely,

$$\dot{p}(k) = \frac{1}{L}. \tag{11}$$

This type of learning is called "normal cooperation." On the other hand, it is quite natural to take into account the actual firing probabilities of input units. For this purpose, we use the procedure of information enhancement [1]. The information enhancement procedure has been used to compute mutual information between competitive units and input patterns with attention paid to a specific component.

Let us compute mutual information when the tth input unit is a target for enhancement, we have competitive unit outputs v_{jt}^s computed by

$$v_{jt}^s \propto \exp\left\{-\frac{1}{2}(\mathbf{x}^s - \mathbf{w}_j)^T \mathbf{\Lambda}_t (\mathbf{x}^s - \mathbf{w}_j)\right\}, \tag{12}$$

where the klth element of the scaling matrix $(\mathbf{\Lambda}_t)_{kl}$ is defined by

$$(\mathbf{\Lambda}_t)_{kl} = \frac{\delta_{kl}\delta_{kt}}{\sigma^2}. \tag{13}$$

We can normalize these outputs for probabilities,

$$p(j \mid s; t) = \frac{\exp\left\{-\frac{1}{2}(\mathbf{x}^s - \mathbf{w}_j)^T \mathbf{\Lambda}_t (\mathbf{x}^s - \mathbf{w}_j)\right\}}{\sum_{m=1}^{M} \exp\left\{-\frac{1}{2}(\mathbf{x}^s - \mathbf{w}_m)^T \mathbf{\Lambda}_t (\mathbf{x}^s - \mathbf{w}_m)\right\}}. \tag{14}$$

And we have

$$p(j; t) = \sum_{s=1}^{S} p(s)p(j \mid s; t). \tag{15}$$

By using these probabilities, we have enhanced information for the tth input unit

$$I_t = \sum_{s=1}^{S} \sum_{j=1}^{M} p(s)p(j \mid s; t) \log \frac{p(j \mid s; t)}{p(j; t)}. \tag{16}$$

We normalize this enhanced information by

$$r(t) = \frac{I_t}{\sum_{l=1}^{L} I_l}. \tag{17}$$

As this enhanced information is increased, the tth input variable contributes more to the organized responses of competitive units to input patterns. We use this normalized enhanced information to approximate the firing probability of input units, namely,

$$p(k) = r(k). \tag{18}$$

Because the distances between input patterns and connection weights are weighted by $p(k)$, the learning is called "weighted cooperation learning."

2.3 Controlling Cooperation and Computational Procedures

Because the uncooperative network tries to imitate the cooperative network, we consider the spread parameter σ_{cp} for the cooperative network as the base parameter. Then, by using a parameter α, we define the relation between two networks

$$\sigma = \alpha\sigma_{cp}. \tag{19}$$

For simplicity reason, the parameter α is supposed to be larger than or equal to one, and the parameter is called "cooperation parameter." When the cooperation parameter is one, the cooperative and uncooperative network are controlled by the same value of the spread parameter. As the cooperation parameter is increased, the effect of the cooperative networks becomes more apparent.

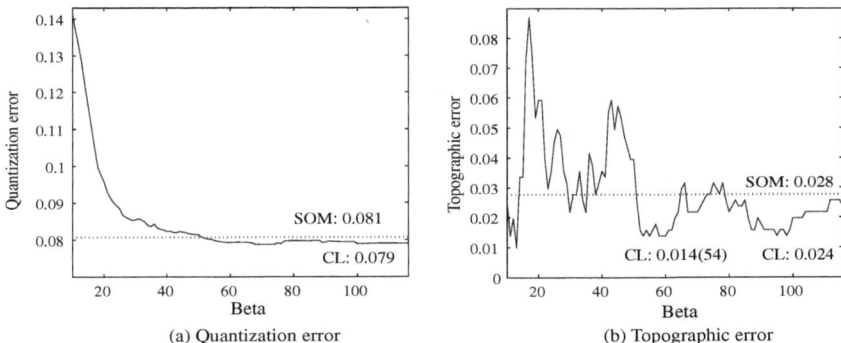

(a) Quantization error   (b) Topographic error

Fig. 2. Quantization errors (a) and topographic errors (b) as a function of the parameter β for the housing data

The computational procedure is composed of two phases[1]. In the first phase, only cooperation is considered where we try to obtain an optimal value of the spread parameter σ_{cp}. We suppose that uncooperative networks have no influence on learning. This situation can be described when the spread parameter σ becomes infinity and then the probability $p^*(j \mid s)$ becomes equivalent to $q(j \mid s)$ before learning. The actual parameter for the cooperation is the spread parameter σ_{cp} and it is defined by

$$\sigma_{cp} = \frac{1}{\beta}, \tag{20}$$

where β is larger than zero. When the parameter β is increased gradually, the spread parameter σ_{cp} becomes gradually decreased and has a possibility to reach its stable points, because the increment becomes smaller. When the parameter β is larger, the competition becomes more like the winner-take-all; and when the parameter is small, the competition becomes soft competition.

---

[1] In the cooperative network, the other parameter σ_{nh} in the neighborhood kernel should be determined. For simplicity reason, the neighborhood parameter is independently controlled.

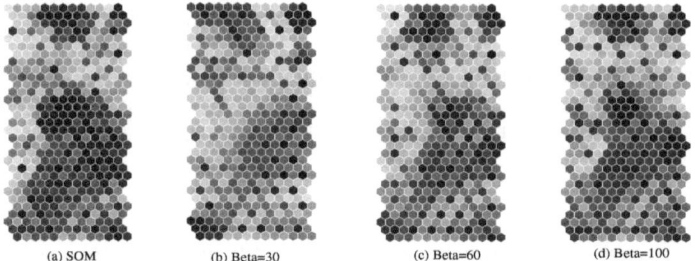

(a) SOM   (b) Beta=30   (c) Beta=60   (d) Beta=100

Fig. 3. U-matrices obtained by the conventional SOM (a) and the information-theoretic cooperative method (b)-(h) for the housing data

In the second phase, with the fixed value of the parameter β, we try to change the cooperation parameter α to obtain feature maps for better interpretation. The cooperation parameter α is larger, competitive units in the uncooperative networks respond more uniformly to input patterns and the cooperation networks play a more important role in learning.

3   Results and Discussion

We present experimental results on the housing data from the machine learning database[2] to show the good performance of our method. The number of input units and patterns are 14 and 506, respectively. We use the SOM toolbox developed by Vesanto et al. [4], because it is easy to reproduce final results in the present paper by using this package. The quantization error is simply the average distance from each data vector to its BMU(best-matching unit). The topographic error is the percentage of data vectors for which the BMU and the second-BMU are not neighboring units [2].

In the first place, we present the results in the first phase of learning. Figure 2(a) shows quantization errors as a function of the parameter β. As the parameter is increased, qunatization errors are gradually decreased and finally the error reaches its lowest point of 0.079 when the parameter β is 116. On the other hand, the error by the conventional SOM is 0.081. Thus, slight improvement can be seen by the cooperative learning, comparing with SOM. Figure 2(b) shows topographic errors as a function of the parameter β. The topographic errors fluctuate greatly when the parameter β is small. Then, the errors become lower than that by the conventional SOM. The lowest error of the cooperative learning is 0.014, when the parameter β is 54. Thus, the topographic errors are significantly reduced.

Figure 3 shows U-matrices by the conventional SOM and cooperative learning. Figure 3(a) shows the U-matrix by the conventional SOM. We can see boundaries in warmer color on the upper and left hand side of the matrix, though they are rather ambiguous. Figure 3(b) shows the U-matrix when the parameter β is 30. The wide boundary in warmer color on the upper side of the matrix appears. When the parameter is increased to 60 in Figure 3(c), the wide boundary become slimmer. Finally, when

---

[2] http://archive.ics.uci.edu/ml/

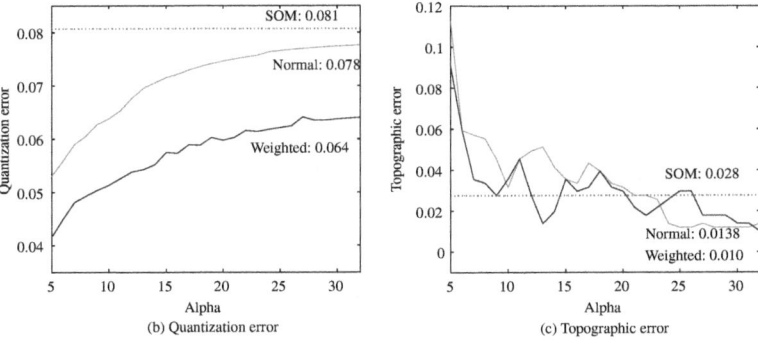

Fig. 4. Quantization errors (a) and topographic errors (b) as a function of the parameter α for the housing data

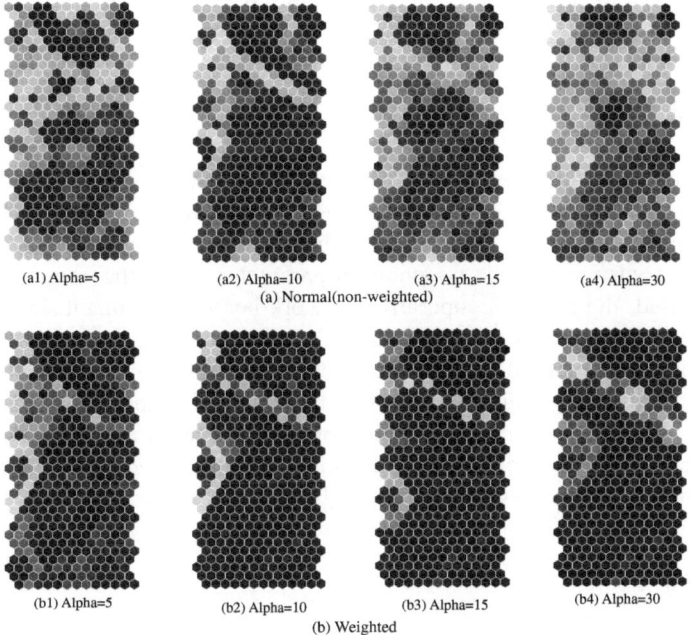

Fig. 5. U-matrices obtained by the normal learning (a) and the weighted learning (b)

the parameter is 100 in Figure 3(d), boundaries on the matrix show more clearly the boundaries obtained by the conventional SOM in Figure 3(a).

In the second phase of learning, the cooperation parameter α is changed with the fixed value of the other paramter β. Figure 4(a) shows quantization errors as a function of the cooperation parameter α in the second phase of learning. As can be seen in the figure, the errors are increased as the parameter is increased for both methods. However, we can see that errors by the weighted method are much lower than those by the normal method. Figure 4(b) shows topographic errors as a function of the parameter α.

The topographic errors fluctuate greatly compared with the quantization errors. Though the lowest error of 0.010 is obtained by the weighted method, the errors are almost equivalent for both methods.

Figures 5(a) and (b) show the U-matrices by the normal and weighted learning, respectively. As shown in the figure, by the both methods, obtained boundaries become clearer than those by the conventional SOM and the cooperative learning in Figure 3. However, we can say that class boundaries obtained by the weighted learning are much more explicit that those by the normal learning. When the cooperation parameter is five in Figure 5(a1), there are several minor boundaries around the major boundaries by the normal learning. However, with the weighted learning in Figure 5(b1), only major boundaries in warmer colors remain. When the cooperation parameter is ten in Figure 5(a1) and (a2), minor boundaries obtained by the normal learning disappear and only major boundary are clearly shown by the weighted learning. As the cooperation parameter is further increased from 15 in Figure 5(a3) and (b3) to 30 in Figure 5(a4) and (b4), the boundaries in warmer color become obscure by the normal learning, but by the weighted method, clear boundaries remain to be stable.

4   Conclusion

In this paper, we have proposed a new type of information-theoretic method called "weighted cooperative learning." In the method, uncooperative networks try to imitate cooperative networks as much as possible. The roles of cooperative and uncooperative networks are controlled by the cooperation parameter α. As the cooperation parameter is increased, the role of cooperative network become dominant. In addition, the importance of input units or variable is included by computing mutual information for each input unit. The method is applied to the housing data from the machine learning database. Experimental results showed that the cooperative and weighted cooperative learning show better performance than the conventional SOM in terms of quantization and topographic errors. In particular, the weighted cooperative learning succeeded in producing much clearer class boundaries for better interpretation.

References

1. Kamimura, R.: Information-theoretic enhancement learning and its application to visualization of self-organizing maps. Neurocomputing 73(13-15), 2642–2664 (2010)
2. Kiviluoto, K.: Topology preservation in self-organizing maps. In: Proceedings of the IEEE International Conference on Neural Networks, pp. 294–299 (1996)
3. Ultsch, A.: U*-matrix: a tool to visualize clusters in high dimensional data. Tech. Rep. 36, Department of Computer Science, University of Marburg (2003)
4. Vesanto, J., Himberg, J., Alhoniemi, E., Parhankangas, J.: SOM toolbox for Matlab. Tech. Rep. Laboratory of Computer and Information Science, Helsinki University of Technology (2000)
5. Vesanto, J.: SOM-based data visualization methods. Intelligent Data Analysis 3, 111–126 (1999)

Unsupervized Data-Driven Partitioning of Multiclass Problems

Hernán C. Ahumada, Guillermo L. Grinblat, and Pablo M. Granitto*

CIFASIS, French Argentine International Center for Information and Systems
Sciences, UPCAM (France) / UNR–CONICET (Argentina),
Bv. 27 de Febrero 210 Bis, 2000 Rosario, Argentina
{ahumada,grinblat,granitto}@cifasis-conicet.gov.ar

Abstract. Many classification problems of high technological value are
multiclass. In the last years, several improved solutions based on the
combination of simple classifiers were introduced. An interesting kind of
methods creates a hierarchy of sub-problems by clustering prototypes
of each one of the classes, but the solution produced by the clustering
stage is heavily influenced by the label's information. In this work we
introduce a new strategy to solve multiclass problems that makes more
use of spatial information than other methods. Based on our previous
work on imbalanced problems, we construct a hierarchy of subproblems,
but opposite to previous developments, based only on spatial information
and not using class labels at any time. We consider different clustering
methods (either agglomerative or divisive) for this task. We use an SVM
for each sub-problem (if needed, because in several cases the clustering
method directly gives a subset with samples of a single class). Using
publicly available datasets we compare the new method with several
previous approaches, finding promising results.

1 Introduction

Several interesting machine learning tasks can be posed as the problem of assigning a given example to one of a finite set of classes, usually known as a
multiclass classification problem. For example, a handwritten recognition system has to read a series of strokes in a device and to assign them to one of the
valid entries to the system. Other classical examples include text and speech
categorization [3], object recognition in machine vision [9] or cancer diagnosis
based on gene expression data [17]. Unfortunately, some of the most efficient
classifiers available nowadays were designed to handle only two classes (binary
classifiers), as for example Adaboost [8] or the Support Vector Machines (SVM)
[6]. The problem of extending these binary classifiers to multiclass problem efficiently has been the subject of several publications on the last years. For a
complete review see for example Lorena et al. [14].

Although the method discussed in this work can be applied to any binary classifier, we concentrate on its use with SVM, the classifier with more applications

---

* Work supported by ANPCyT grant 237.

T. Honkela et al. (Eds.): ICANN 2011, Part I, LNCS 6791, pp. 117–125, 2011.

in the last years. For SVM in particular some direct extensions to multiclass problems have been introduced, but unfortunately they do not produce accurate classifiers in most cases. For example, Weston and Watkins [21] proposed a new formulation of the SVM (WW–SVM from here on) that can solve a multiclass problem as a single optimization task. Crammer and Singer [5], on the other side, introduced a generalized notion of the margin of multiclass problems, with which they cast them as constrained optimization tasks with a quadratic objective function, leading to multiple optimization problems of reduced size. We call that method the CS–SVM.

Most published efficient strategies are based on reducing the multiclass problem to a set of binary ones. A kind of these methods is based on the principle that all classes are equivalent (we call them "flat strategies") and, in order to make a decision, each class is compared to all others in the same way. The most simple method is the "One–vs-All" or OVA method [18], in which a k–class problem is decomposed into k binary sub-problems consisting in separating one of the classes from the rest. Hastie and Tibshirani [10] suggested a different approach in which all $k(k-1)/2$ pairs of classes are compared to each other. This approach is called "One–vs-One" or OVO, and is usually considered to be more effective than the OVA approach [11], in particular for SVM.

Flat methods are simple to understand and implement, but they ignore useful information when solving the problem. For example, it is easy to see that some classes in a given problem could be so distant in the feature space that there is no need to train a particular classifier on them. Hierarchical strategies (HS) attempt to use some of the spatial information in the problem at hand. HS methods build a decision tree (or a decision directed acyclic graph [16]) with a binary classifier at each node, and one class at each leaf. HS methods differ in the way in which each binary classifier is created [7,20]. For example, Liu et al. [13] at each step split the classes in two subsets using the k-means clustering method [15] applied to the centroids of each class, and then train an SVM to learn to discriminate both groups. The procedure is iterated until each node contains a single class. The idea behind this method (called Adaptive Hierarchical Multi-class SVM or AHM–SVM) is to look at each step for the split with the biggest separation between both subsets. The number of binary classifiers created by AHM–SVM is low, $k-1$. Benabdeslem and Bennani [4] introduced a very similar procedure (which we will call ALHC–SVM), in which the k-means clustering is replaced with the average linkage hierarchical clustering method [12].

Both HS methods described before create a hierarchy of sub-problems based on prototypes of each one of the k classes. According to this, the solution produced by the clustering stage is heavily influenced by the label's information. Furthermore, they use a single prototype for each class, assuming that all classes are compact structures in the feature space. Unfortunately, real world datasets usually do not have this property, as we will show in some examples. In this work we introduce a new strategy to solve multiclass problems that makes use of even more spatial information than traditional HS methods. Based on the general idea of our previous algorithm for imbalanced problems [1], we construct a hierarchy of sub-problems, but opposite to previous developments, based only on spatial information and not using class labels at any time or a single prototype for each class. Our goal is to split the problem into a series of simple and natural sub-problems using a given clustering method (either agglomerative or divisive). Following, we apply an SVM to each sub-problem (if needed, because in several cases the clustering method directly gives a subset with samples of a single class).

2   The Unsupervised Partitioning Method for Multiclass Problems

The unsupervised partitioning method (UPM, from now on) follows the same principle that our previous REPMAC development for imbalanced problems [1]: To divide the multiclass problem intelligently into several sub-problems (clusters) in order to translate a big multiclass problem into a set of simpler and smaller sub-problems. The general strategy is simple, we first use a clustering method in order to produce a hierarchy of subproblems and then we train classifiers, when needed, to solve the simpler problems at the leaves of the decision tree.

2.1   Hierarchy Construction

In order to create the hierarchy of subproblems we applied in this work two different hierarchical clustering methods.

Divisive Clustering: On one side, following our previous work, we used a divisive method, recursively splitting the dataset in two with the well-known k-means clustering method [15] (KM from here on). Divisive clustering methods usually have a stopping criteria for the recursive process. In this case we stop the recursion if: i) all the datapoints in a clusters belong to the same class or ii) there are only two classes in the cluster or iii) there are less than S_p points in the cluster ($S_p = 15$ in this work). The first two conditions are easy to understand, the last one stops the splitting if the cluster has only a few datapoints and a further split should leave us with less points than needed to train efficiently a classifier at the given node.

Table 1. Details of the 4 datasets used in this work. The k column shows the number of classes, p column shows the number of inputs, train and test columns show the corresponding number of datapoints in each set.

Dataset	k	p	train	test
Pendigits	10	16	7494	3498
Letters	26	16	16000	4000
Satimage	6	36	4435	2000
Yeast	10	8	1113	371

Agglomerative Clustering: On the other side, we applied two well-known hierarchical clustering methods [19], which are agglomerative in nature: the Average Linkage (AL) and the Single Linkage (SL) strategies. In this case, the method builds a full hierarchy, starting from individual datapoints and ending with all the dataset in a single cluster. In order to use this hierarchy in the learning process we need to prune the resulting tree with the aim of having problems that can be solved at each leaf. According to this, starting from the root, we go down the tree and check at each node if any of the three stopping criteria explained above is met. When this is the case, we prune the tree at that node and replace the subtree with a leaf containing all the points in it.

Classifiers: At the final step, we use an appropriate method to assign classes to all the points at each leaf. If the cluster has only one class (criteria i was met) then we obviously assign that class to the leaf. If criteria ii was met (a binary problem) we fit directly a binary SVM [6] to the datapoints in the cluster. Finally, in the few cases in which the leaf was created by criteria iii we fit an OVO-SVM to the leaf.

Outliers Handling: Outliers, which by definition are isolated points of one class, are usually a problem for HS methods. At this first development stage we choose to ignore outliers: If at a given cluster there are less than O_{min} datapoints of a given class ($O_{min} = 4$ in this work) we consider them as outliers and do not count them when evaluating stopping criteria or training an SVM.

2.2   Classification of New Datapoints

Once we have the full decision tree, a new example is classified according to the following procedure: At each level of the tree (starting from the root), the example is assigned to one of the branches, according to the rules of the clustering method (for example, for divisive KM, looking for the nearest centroid or looking for the nearest neighbor for SL). The procedure is iterated until a leaf is reached, where the example is classified using the decision function associated to that leaf (a given class for pure nodes or an SVM in other cases).

3   Experimental Results

We evaluated the performance of the new UPM method using 4 different datasets, all obtained from the UCI repository [2]. In Table 1 we show their main characteristics. All 4 problems have several classes and different number of samples/features. Two datasets (Pendigits and Letters) are well balanced while the other two show classes with a low fraction of samples.

Experimental Setup: We selected for comparison several multiclass SVM methods that were already discussed in the Introduction. First, we included two direct multiclass SVM methods, the WW-SVM and the CS-SVM. Then we

Table 2. Comparison of the classification error for the four datasets used in this work

	WW	CS	OVO	ALHM	AHM	KM	SL	AL
Pendigits	0,078	0,081	0,048	0,135	0,127	0,050	0,029	0,067
Letters	0,283	0,253	0,144	0,285	0,271	0,156	0,130	0,140
Satimage	0,160	0,174	0,138	0,153	0,162	0,110	0,139	0,124
Yeast	0,402	0,512	0,394	0,412	0,461	0,434	0,442	0,431

Table 3. Number of SVMs used by each method

	OVO	ALHM	AHM	KM	SL	AL
Pendigits	45	9	9	35	6	14
Letters	325	25	25	280	199	203
Satimage	15	5	5	42	8	36
Yeast	45	9	9	31	9	33

considered a flat method, the OVO strategy. Finally, we included two HS methods, the AHM–SVM and the ALHC–SVM. In the case of the new UPM method we used the three clustering strategies discussed before, KM, SL and AL. In all cases we used linear SVMs as classifiers, with the C parameter selected by an internal CV using only the corresponding training data. As we have fixed external test sets for evaluation, for each dataset we produced a single run of each method, training with the corresponding subset and then applying the classifier to the test set.

Results: In Table 2 we show the corresponding error levels for all methods. In three out of four problems one of the versions of UPM gives the best result and in the Yeast dataset only the OVO strategy outperforms our new method. It is interesting to note that the traditional OVO method works better than all other previous methods in the four datasets.

Comparing the results of the three different strategies for constructing the hierarchy of subproblems in UPM, the divisive KM is superior in two cases and the agglomerative SL in the other two, while AL ends in between of both methods in 3 out of 4 cases.

In Table 3 we show the number of SVMs used by each method. The ALHM and AHM method use less classifiers than all UPM versions, but their performance is limited, as was shown in Table 2. On the other hand, UPM usually produces less classifiers than the OVO method. In particular, the SL strategy has the property of producing small clusters that usually have only one class (no classifier needed), leading always to the hierarchy with the minimum number of classifiers. Again, the AL strategy produces a solution that is located in the middle of the two other UPM strategies.

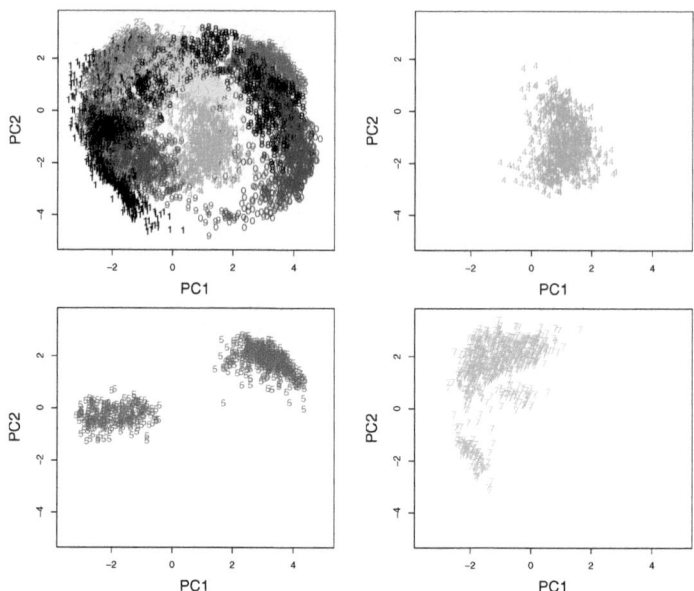

Fig. 1. PCA visualization of the Pendigits datasets. Top left: Full dataset. Others: Detail of three different classes.

Analysis: In Figure 1 we show the Pendigits dataset projected on the two first PCA components. In the top right panel we show the detail of a typical compact class (4), which has the spatial distribution that is assumed by the other HS strategies. However, as we show in the bottom panels of the same figure, classes 5 and 7 have a very different structure, with two well defined clusters each one. In Table 4 we show the error levels for some individual classes in this problem. For simple classes like 3 or 4 all methods show similar results. On the other hand, for more complex classes like 5 and 7 the new UPM strategy (in all 3 versions) clearly outperforms previous HS methods. In order to add evidence in this direction, we produced a new problem derived from the Pendigits dataset by joining classes 0 and 1 (the two most separated classes in Figure 1) in a unique class (called "0+1") and keeping the rest of the dataset unchanged. In the last row of Table 4 show the results of all methods for the new combined class. It is clear from the table that previous HS methods have increased considerably their error levels while the UPM strategy can easily cope with this problem.

The same effect can be seen in the Letters dataset. In Figure 2 we show PCA projections for two particular classes. In Table 5 we show the corresponding error levels for all methods. Again, it is clear from the table that the complex classes do not degrade the performance of UPM methods as they do with previous HS methods.

Table 4. Pendigits dataset: detail of error levels for some classes. Also, error level for an artificial class created by joining samples from classes 0 and 1.

Class	WW	CS	OVO	ALHM	AHM	KM	SL	AL
0	0.110	0.105	0.085	0.143	0.077	0.058	0.030	0.041
1	0.121	0.091	0.047	0.404	0.135	0.071	0.041	0.025
3	0.021	0.021	0.012	0.024	0.021	0.018	0.012	0.086
4	0.019	0.022	0.011	0.025	0.069	0.047	0.025	0.115
5	0.057	0.107	0.027	0.269	0.266	0.063	0.039	0.054
7	0.168	0.170	0.118	0.173	0.247	0.118	0.085	0.091
0 + 1	0.226	0.199	0.109	0.287	0.354	0.066	0.032	0.037

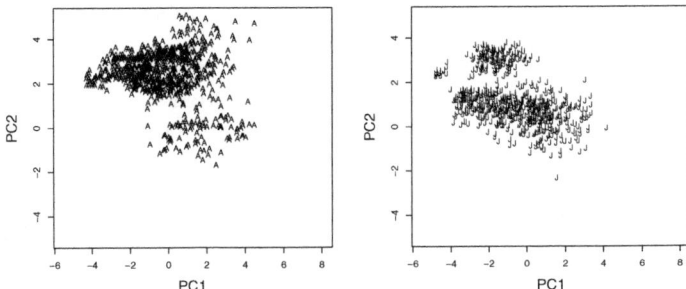

Fig. 2. PCA visualization of the Letters datasets, for two different classes, "A" (left) and "J" (right)

Table 5. Letters dataset: detail of error levels for classes A and J

Class	WW	CS	OVO	ALHM	AHM	KM	SL	AL
A	0.152	0.171	0.038	0.196	0.190	0.108	0.057	0.133
J	0.221	0.188	0.087	0.248	0.228	0.114	0.107	0.087

4   Conclusions

In this work we introduced UPM, a new strategy to deal with multiclass problems. The method has two steps, first it uses a clustering algorithm to construct a hierarchy of easier subproblems, and then it trains several SVMs to solve each individual subproblem. One of the advantages of the new method is that it usually produces clusters containing only one class, where no classifiers are needed.

Using four datasets we compared our new algorithm with 5 previous methods for multiclass problems. UPM showed the best results in 3 datasets, being second in performance in the fourth case.

We evaluated three different strategies for constructing the hierarchy, one divisive and two agglomerative. Overall, the AL strategy seems to be the most useful, as it shows good results in all cases with a limited number of classifiers.

However, when working with big datasets, the SL strategy could be preferred due to its low complexity compared with the other UPM methods.

We also showed that the UPM's unsupervised strategy is more efficient when facing the problem of classes with complex spatial structures than previous methods, like for example some classes of the Pendigits and Letters datasets.

We are currently extending the evaluation of the UPM method, including other datasets and classifiers.

References

1. Ahumada, H., Grinblat, G., Uzal, L., Granitto, P., Ceccatto, A.: Repmac: A new hybrid approach to highly imbalanced classification problems. In: 8th Int. Conference on Hybrid Intelligent Systems. pp. 386–391 (2008)
2. Asuncion, A., Newman, D.: UCI machine learning repository (2007), http://www.ics.uci.edu/~mlearn/MLRepository.html
3. Bahl, L., Jelinek, F., Mercer, R.: A maximum likelihood approach to continuous speech recognition. IEEE T. Pattern Anal. (2), 179–190 (2009)
4. Benabdeslem, K., Bennani, Y.: Dendogram-based SVM for Multi-Class Classification. J. Comput. Inform. Tech. 14(4), 283–289 (2006)
5. Crammer, K., Singer, Y.: On the algorithmic implementation of multiclass kernel-based vector machines. J Mach. Learn. Res. 2, 265–292 (2002)
6. Cristianini, N., Shawe–Taylor, J.: An Introduction to Support Vector Machines. Cambridge University Press, Cambridge (2000)
7. Fei, B., Liu, J.: Binary tree of SVM: a new fast multiclass training and classification algorithm. IEEE T. Neural Networ. 17(3), 696–704 (2006)
8. Freund, Y., Schapire, R.: A desicion-theoretic generalization of on-line learning and an application to boosting. In: Proc. of COLT, pp. 23–37 (1995)
9. Granitto, P., Verdes, P., Ceccatto, H.: Large-scale investigation of weed seed identification by machine vision. Comput. Electron. Agr. 47(1), 15–24 (2005)
10. Hastie, T., Tibshirani, R.: Classification by pairwise coupling. Ann. Stat. 26(2), 451–471 (1998)
11. Hsu, C.W., Lin, C.J.: A comparison of methods for multiclass support vector machines. IEEE T. Neural Networ. 13(2), 415–425 (2002)
12. King, B.: Step-wise clustering procedures. J. Am. Stat. Assoc. 69, 86–101 (1967)
13. Liu, S., Yi, H., Chia, L.T., Rajan, D.: Adaptive hierarchical multi-class SVM classifier for texture-based image classification. In: IEEE Int. Conf. on Multimedia and Expo, pp. 1–4 (2005)
14. Lorena, A.C., Carvalho, A.C., Gama, J.M.: A review on the combination of binary classifiers in multiclass problems. Artif. Intell. Rev. 30, 19–37 (2008)
15. McQueen, J.: Some methods for classification and analysis of multivariate observations. In: Proc. of the Fifth Berkeley Symposium on Mathematics, Statistics and Probability, pp. 281–297 (1967)
16. Platt, J., Cristianini, N., Shawe-Taylor, J.: Large margin dags for multiclass classification. In: Adv. in Neural Information Processing Systems, vol. 12, pp. 547–553 (2000)
17. Ramaswamy, S., Tamayo, P., Rifkin, R., et al.: Multiclass cancer diagnosis using tumor gene expression signatures. P. Natl. Acad. Sci. USA 98(26), 15149 (2001)

18. Rifkin, R., Klautau, A.: In defense of one-vs-all classification. J. Mach. Learn. Res. 5, 101–141 (2004)
19. Sneath, P.H.A., Sokal, R.R.: Numerical Taxonomy. W.H. Freeman and Company, San Francisco (1973)
20. Songsiri, P., Kijsirikul, B., Phetkaew, T.: Information-based dichotomization: A method for multiclass Support Vector Machines. In: IEEE Int. Joint Conference on Neural Networks, pp. 3284–3291 (2008)
21. Weston, J., Watkins, C.: Support vector machines for multi-class pattern recognition. In: 7th European Symposium On Art. Neural Networks, pp. 4–6 (1999)

Bounds for Approximate Solutions of Fredholm Integral Equations Using Kernel Networks

Giorgio Gnecco[1], Věra Kůrková[2], and Marcello Sanguineti[1]

[1] Department of Communications, Computer, and System Sciences (DIST)
University of Genoa, Via Opera Pia 13, 16145 Genova, Italy
{giorgio.gnecco,marcello}@dist.unige.it
[2] Institute of Computer Science, Academy of Sciences of the Czech Republic
Pod Vodárenskou věží 2, Prague 8, Czech Republic
vera@cs.cas.cz

Abstract. Approximation of solutions of integral equations by networks with kernel units is investigated theoretically. There are derived upper bounds on speed of decrease of errors in approximation of solutions of Fredholm integral equations by kernel networks with increasing numbers of units. The estimates are obtained for Gaussian and degenerate kernels.

Keywords: Radial and kernel networks, approximation of solutions of integral equations by kernel networks, model complexity.

1 Introduction

Fredholm integral equations play an important role in many problems in applied science. For example, they arise as restatements of differential problems with auxiliary boundary conditions in physics, particularly in potential theory and elasticity (see, e.g., [1, Chapter 4]). Although under reasonable assumptions there exists a formula describing their solutions, such formula is seldom of practical use. Instead of searching for exact solutions, many satisfactory techniques have been developed solving integral equations approximately (see, e.g., [2]). These techniques use various sets of approximating functions such as wavelets and radial-basis functions. Recently, perceptron networks [3] and Gaussian and multiquadric radial-basis functions (RBF) [4,5] have been used to find approximations of solutions of inhomogeneous Fredholm integral equations. In [5], the collocation method based on discretization of the domain was used to construct a cost functional, which was minimized over networks with incrementally increasing numbers of Gaussian radial units. The authors mentioned that in their numerical experiments "by increasing the number of RBFs (hidden-layer units), it is expected that a better approximation of the solution can be achieved, but the cost of computations will be increased."

In this paper, taking the hint from the experimental studies [3,4,5] we theoretically investigate dependence of approximation accuracy on the number of units in networks approximating solutions of Fredholm integral equations. We explore the trade-off between the accuracy of such approximate solutions and

T. Honkela et al. (Eds.): ICANN 2011, Part I, LNCS 6791, pp. 126–133, 2011.

the network complexity, by estimating the speeds of decrease of the approximation errors with increasing number of network units. We take advantage of results from nonlinear approximation theory of so called "variable-basis type" [6,7], which can be applied to networks with units from various "dictionaries" used in neurocomputing [8,9,10,11,12].

We consider two types of approximating networks. The first one is a one-hidden layer network with kernel units corresponding to the kernel of the equation; the second one has units generated by so-called "resolvent kernel". Our bounds show that the number of computational units required for a desired accuracy of approximation depends on the VC-dimension of the dictionary formed by such units, the Lebesgue measure of the domain where the solution is searched for, and the $\mathcal{L}^1$-norm of the function defining the equation. We apply our estimates to Gaussian and degenerate kernels, for which we estimate VC-dimensions of corresponding dictionaries.

The paper is organized as follows. In Section 2, we recall basic concepts and results on approximation by computational models with units from general dictionaries. In Section 3 we introduces Fredholm integral equations and discusses approaches to their approximate solutions. Sections 4 and 5 contain our estimates of accuracy of approximate solutions for dictionaries defined either by kernels of the equations or their associated resolvent kernels. Section 6 is a conclusion.

2   Approximation from a Dictionary

One-hidden layer networks with one linear output unit compute input-output functions from sets of the form

$$\operatorname{span}_n G := \left\{ \sum_{i=1}^n w_i g_i \,|\, w_i \in \mathbb{R}, g_i \in G \right\}, \tag{1}$$

where the set G is sometimes called a *dictionary* [13] and n is the *number of hidden units*. This number can be interpreted as a measure of *model complexity* of the network. Often, dictionaries are parameterized families of functions modelling computational units, i.e., they are of the form

$$G_K(X,Y) := \{K(\cdot,y) : X \to \mathbb{R} \,|\, y \in Y\}, \tag{2}$$

where $K : X \times Y \to \mathbb{R}$ is a function of two variables, an input vector $x \in X \subseteq \mathbb{R}^d$ and a parameter $y \in Y \subseteq \mathbb{R}^s$. When $X = Y$, we write briefly $G_K(X)$ and when $X = Y = \mathbb{R}^d$, we write merely G_K. In some contexts, K is called a *kernel*. However, the above-described computational scheme includes fairly general computational models, such as functions computable by perceptrons, radial or kernel units, Hermite functions, trigonometric polynomials, and splines. For example, with $K(x,y) = K(x,(v,b)) = \sigma(v \cdot x + b)$ and $\sigma : \mathbb{R} \to \mathbb{R}$ a sigmoidal function, the computational scheme (1) describes one-hidden-layer *perceptron networks*.

Estimates of model complexity of one-hidden layer networks can be obtained by inspection of upper bounds on rates of decrease of errors in approximation of families of functions of interest by sets $\mathrm{span}_n\, G$ with n increasing. Such rates have been studied in mathematical theory of neurocomputing for various types of computational units and norms measuring the errors such as Hilbert-space norms [14,15,6], $\mathcal{L}^p$-norms, $p \in (1,\infty)$ [16], and the supremum norm [17,18]. Typically, these estimates were derived for approximating sets of form

$$\mathrm{conv}_n\, G := \left\{ \sum_{i=1}^{n} w_i g_i \,|\, w_i \in [0,1], \sum_{i=1}^{n} w_i = 1, g_i \in G \right\} \tag{3}$$

and then extended to $\mathrm{span}_n\, G$.

We apply one of such upper bounds to the approximation of solutions of integral equations by kernel networks. To estimate accuracy of suboptimal solutions over the whole input domain uniformly, we use an upper bound on approximation error in the *supremum norm* $\|\cdot\|_{\sup}$ defined for a bounded function f on a set X as $\|f\|_{\sup} = \sup_{x \in X} |f(x)|$.

The upper bound is formulated in terms of the VC-dimension of the dictionary. Recall that the *Vapnik-Chervonenkis dimension (VC-dimension)* of a family F of real-valued functions on a set X is the maximum cardinality h of a set of points $\{y_i \in X \,|\, i = 1, \ldots, h\}$ that can be separated into two classes H_1 and H_2 in all 2^h possible ways, by using functions of the form $f(\cdot) - \alpha$, with $f \in F$ and $\alpha \in \mathbb{R}$, resp. [19]. In particular, if $f(y_i) - \alpha \geq 0$, then we say that (f, α) assigns y_i to the class H_1. Similarly, if $f(y_i) - \alpha < 0$, then (f, α) assigns y_i to the class H_2.

The next theorem is a slight reformulation of a theorem by Girosi [17]. It holds for functions with certain integral representations. For a kernel K and a function w in a space of functions on Y such that for each its element the integral (4) is defined, we denote by T_K the integral operator defined as

$$T_K(w)(x) := \int_Y w(y)\, K(x,y)dy. \tag{4}$$

Theorem 1. *Let $X \subseteq \mathbb{R}^d$, $K : X \times X \to \mathbb{R}$ be a bounded function with $\tau_K = \sup_{x,y \in X} |K(x,y)|$, h be the VC-dimension of $G_K(X)$, and g a function such that $g = T_K(w)$ for some $w \in \mathcal{L}^1(X)$. Then for every positive integer $n \geq h/2$*

$$\left\| g - \|w\|_{\mathcal{L}^1(X)} \mathrm{conv}_n(G_K(X) \cup -G_K(X)) \right\|_{\sup} \leq 4\tau_K \|w\|_{\mathcal{L}^1(X)} \sqrt{\frac{h \ln \frac{2en}{h} + \ln 4}{n}}$$

and $\left\| g - \mathrm{span}_n\, G_K(X) \right\|_{\sup} \leq 4\tau_K \|w\|_{\mathcal{L}^1(X)} \sqrt{\frac{h \ln \frac{2en}{h} + \ln 4}{n}}$.

3   Approximate Solutions to Fredholm Integral Equations

Solving the *inhomogeneous Fredholm integral equation of the second kind* associated with a subset X of $\mathbb{R}^d$, $\lambda \in \mathbb{R} \setminus \{0\}$, $K : X \times X \to \mathbb{R}$, and $f : X \to \mathbb{R}$ consists in finding a continuous function $\phi : X \to \mathbb{R}$ such that

$$\phi(x) - \lambda \int_X \phi(y)K(x,y)\, dy = f(x) \tag{5}$$

for all $x \in X$. If both K and f are continuous and X is compact, then it is well-known [20, Section 1.2] that the operator $T_K : \mathcal{C}(X) \to \mathcal{C}(X)$ defined in (4) is compact, so its sequence of eigenvalues $1/\lambda_i$ (ordered non increasingly) is either finite or convergent to 0 for $i \to +\infty$. By the well-known Fredholm Alternative Theorem (see, e.g., [20, Section 1.3]), when $1/\lambda$ is not an eigenvalue of T_K, there exists one and only one solution $\phi \in \mathcal{C}(X)$, which has the expression

$$\phi(x) = f(x) - \lambda \int_X f(y) R_K(x, y, \lambda) dy, \tag{6}$$

where $R_K : X \times X \times (\mathbb{R} \setminus \{0\})$ is continuous and called *resolvent kernel*. For each $\lambda \in \mathbb{R} \setminus \{0\}$, the function $R_K(\cdot, \cdot, \lambda)$ is bounded on $X \times X$. We denote by

$$G_{R_K}(X, \lambda) := \{R_K(\cdot, y, \lambda) \mid y \in X\} \tag{7}$$

the dictionary generated by the resolvent kernel R_K. Although (6) provides a way to solve equation (5) for every $f \in \mathcal{C}(X)$, it is seldom of practical use for a general kernel K. Several authors investigated approximation of solutions of (5) by perceptron [3] and Gaussian radial-basis function networks [5]. These computational models are known to be universal approximators (see, e.g., [21,22]) and thus any continuous solution of (5) on a compact domain in $\mathbb{R}^d$ can be arbitrarily well approximated by input-output functions of these models with accuracy increasing with growing model complexity.

For some kernels, in particular for the Gaussian one, even networks with units having a fixed width are universal approximators [23]. For such kernels, one can approximate arbitrarily well the solution of the equation (5) by input-output functions of the form $\mathrm{span}_n \, G_K(X)$. As solutions ϕ of this equation can be represented in terms of integrals with kernel K which can be approximated by Riemann sums, the difference $\phi - f$ can be approximated arbitrarily well by input-output functions of networks with units from the dictionary $G_K(X)$. Theorem 1 estimates rates of this approximation.

We estimate sup-norm errors in approximation by computational models with units from two types of dictionaries, considered in the next two sections, resp.:
1. the dictionary $G_K(X)$ generated by the kernel K of equation (5);
2. the dictionary $G_{R_K}(X, \lambda)$ generated by the resolvent kernel R_K associated with K (for cases when R_K has a simplified form).

To exploit Theorem 1, we need estimates of VC-dimensions of dictionaries $G_K(X)$. We consider two types of kernels. The first one is the *Gaussian kernel*

$$K(x, y) = e^{-\|x-y\|^2},$$

for which the VC-dimension of $G_K(X)$ is bounded from above by $d+1$. For each fixed width b, the VC-dimension of the dictionary generated by the Gaussian with this width $K(x, y) = e^{-b\|x-y\|^2}$ is less than or equal to the VC-dimension of Gaussian RBFs with varying widths and centers, which is equal to the VC-dimension of set of balls in $\mathbb{R}^d$. Dudley [24] proved that this VC-dimension is equal to $d+1$.

The second type of kernels are *degenerate* kernels [25, Section 2.3]

$$K(x, y) = \sum_{j=1}^{m} \xi_j(x) \eta_j(y), \tag{8}$$

where m is finite and $\{\xi_j\}$ and $\{\eta_j\}$ are two sets of linearly-independent functions on X. Degenerate kernels are of interest in applications because every $\mathcal{L}^2$ kernel can be arbitrarily well approximated by a sequence of degenerate kernels (with m increasing) [25, Section 2.6].

4 Bounds on Approximation Errors for Dictionaries Generated by Kernels of Integral Equations

In this section, we derive estimates of decrease of errors in approximation of solutions of integral equation by networks with units from dictionaries induced by the kernels of the equations. By μ we denote the Lebesgue measure on $\mathbb{R}^d$.

Theorem 2. *Let $X \subset \mathbb{R}^d$ be compact, $K : X \times X \to \mathbb{R}$ be a continuous kernel, $\lambda \neq 0$ be such that $\frac{1}{\lambda}$ is not an eigenvalue of T_K and $|\lambda| \, \| \int_X |K(\cdot, y)| dy \|_{\sup} < 1$. Then the solution ϕ of the equation (5) with f continuous satisfies*
(i) for the Gaussian kernel K and $n \geq (d+1)/2$

$$\|\phi - f - \operatorname{span}_n G_K(X)\|_{\sup}$$

$$\leq 4 \frac{|\lambda| \, \mu(X) \, \|f\|_{\sup}}{1 - \lambda \, \| \int_X |K(\cdot, y)| dy \|_{\sup}} \sqrt{\frac{(d+1)\ln(2en) + \ln 4}{n}}; \tag{9}$$

(ii) for a degenerate kernel K such that $K(x, y) = \sum_{j=1}^m \xi_j(x) \eta_j(y)$ for all $x, y \in X$, $\tau_K = \sup_{x,y \in X} |K(x, y)|$ and $n \geq (m+1)/2$

$$\|\phi - f - \operatorname{span}_n G_K(X)\|_{\sup}$$

$$\leq 4 \, \tau_K \frac{|\lambda| \, \mu(X) \, \|f\|_{\sup}}{1 - \lambda \, \| \int_X |K(\cdot, y)| dy \|_{\sup}} \sqrt{\frac{(m+1)\ln(2en) + \ln 4}{n}}. \tag{10}$$

Proof. The assumptions of Theorem 1 are satisfied with the choices $g = \phi - f$, $w = \lambda \phi$. It is easy to show that $\|w\|_{\mathcal{L}^1(X)} \leq \frac{|\lambda| \, \mu(X) \, \|f\|_{\sup}}{1 - \lambda \, \| \int_X |K(\cdot, y)| dy \|_{\sup}}$.

(i) in the case (i), the VC-dimension h of $G_K(X)$ is bounded from above by $d + 1$ (see [24]) and from below by 1, as $G_K(X)$ is nonempty. Note that the function $\beta(h, n) = h \ln \frac{2en}{h}$ in the upper bound from Theorem 1 is not monotone in h and bounded from above by $(d+1)\ln(2en)$. Then by Theorem 1, we get

$$\left\| \phi - f - \frac{|\lambda|\mu(X)\|f\|_{\sup}}{1 - \lambda \, \| \int_X |K(\cdot, y)| dy \|_{\sup}} \operatorname{conv}_n \left(G_K(X) \cup -G_K(X) \right) \right\|_{\sup}$$

$$\leq 4\tau_K \frac{|\lambda|\mu(X)\|f\|_{\sup}}{1 - \lambda \, \| \int_X |K(\cdot, y)| dy \|_{\sup}} \sqrt{\frac{(d+1)\ln(2en) + \ln 4}{n}}. \tag{11}$$

The statement follows by the inclusion

$$\frac{|\lambda| \, \mu(X) \, \|f\|_{\sup}}{1 - \lambda \, \| \int_X |K(\cdot, y)| dy \|_{\sup}} \operatorname{conv}_n \left(G_K(X) \cup -G_K(X) \right) \subset \operatorname{span}_n G_K(X). \tag{12}$$

(ii) In the case (ii), as the functions η_j are linearly independent, the set span $\mathcal{Y}$, where $\mathcal{Y} = \{\eta_1, \ldots, \eta_m\}$, has the dimension m. By [26, Theorem 1], the VC-dimension of span $\mathcal{Y}$ is bounded from above by $m + 1$. The VC-dimension h of $G_K(X)$ is bounded from above by $m + 1$, as $G_K(X) \subseteq$ span $\mathcal{Y}$, and from below by 1, since $G_K(X)$ is nonempty. Note that the function $\beta(h, n) = h \ln \frac{2en}{h}$ from the upper bound from Theorem 1 is not monotone in h and bounded from above by $(m + 1) \ln(2en)$. Then by Theorem 1 we get

$$\left\| \phi - f - \frac{|\lambda| \mu(X) \|f\|_{\sup}}{1 - \lambda \| \int_X |K(\cdot, y)| dy\|_{\sup}} \operatorname{conv}_n \left(G_K(X) \cup -G_K(X) \right) \right\|_{\sup}$$

$$\leq 4 \tau_K \frac{|\lambda| \mu(X) \|f\|_{\sup}}{1 - \lambda \| \int_X |K(\cdot, y)| dy\|_{\sup}} \sqrt{\frac{(m+1) \ln(2en) + \ln 4}{n}}. \tag{13}$$

The statement follows again by (12). $\qquad \square$

Theorem 2 shows that model complexity of a kernel network with units from the dictionary $G_K(X)$ approximating the difference between the solution ϕ of (5) and the function f depends on λ, τ_K, m, the sup-norm of f, and the sup-norm of the integral $\int_X |K(\cdot, y)| dy$ as a function of x. For every $x \in X$, this integral is bounded from above by τ_K times $\mu(X)$. So if $\lambda > 0$ and $\lambda \tau_K \mu(X) < 1$, we get $\frac{1}{1 - \lambda \| \int_X |K(\cdot, y)| dy\|_{\sup}} \leq \frac{1}{1 - \lambda \tau_K \mu(X)}$. Hence by Theorem 2 (i) we obtain the upper bound $\|\phi - f - \operatorname{span}_n G_K(X)\|_{\sup} \leq 4 \tau_K \frac{|\lambda| \mu(X) \|f\|_{\sup}}{1 - \lambda \tau_K \mu(X)} \sqrt{\frac{(d+1) \ln(2en) + \ln 4}{n}}$ and by Theorem 2 (ii) a similar estimate with d replaced by m.

5   Bounds on Approximation Errors for Dictionaries Generated by Resolvent Kernels

In this section, we derive an upper bound on decrease of approximation error with increasing number of computational units from the dictionary $G_{R_K}(X, \lambda)$ generated by the resolvent kernel R_K associated with K and the parameter λ.

Theorem 3. *Let $X \subset \mathbb{R}^d$ be compact, $K : X \times X \to \mathbb{R}$ be a continuous degenerate kernel such that $K(x, y) = \sum_{j=1}^m \xi_j(x) \eta_j(y)$ for all $x, y \in X$, $\lambda \neq 0$ be such that $\frac{1}{\lambda}$ is not an eigenvalue of T_K, and R_K be the resolvent kernel associated with K. Then the solution ϕ of the equation (5) with f continuous satisfies for every positive integer $n \geq (m + 1)/2$*

$$\|\phi - f - \operatorname{span}_n G_{R_K}(X, \lambda)\|_{\sup}$$

$$\leq 4 \sup_{x,y \in X} |R_K(x, y, \lambda)| |\lambda| \|f\|_{\mathcal{L}^1(X)} \sqrt{\frac{(m+1) \ln(2en) + \ln 4}{n}}. \tag{14}$$

Proof. The assumptions of Theorem 1 are satisfied with the choices $g = \phi - f$, $w = -\lambda f$, $K = R_K$, and $\|w\|_{\mathcal{L}^1(X)} = |\lambda| \|f\|_{\mathcal{L}^1(X)}$. To apply Theorem 1, we estimate the VC-dimension h of the dictionary $G_{R_K}(X, \lambda)$. As the kernel K of the integral equation (5) is degenerate, by [25, Section 2.3]) we get $R_K(x, y, \lambda)$

$= -\frac{1}{D(\lambda)} \sum_{k=1}^{m} [D_{1,k}(\lambda)\eta_1(y) + D_{2,k}(\lambda)\eta_2(y) + \ldots + D_{m,k}(\lambda)\eta_m(y)]\xi_k(x)$, where the $D_{i,k}(\lambda)$ are coefficients depending on λ (see, e.g., [25, pp. 56-57] for their expressions for $d = 1$). By similar arguments as in the proof of Theorem 2, the VC-dimension h of $G_{R_K}(X, \lambda)$ is bounded from above by $m+1$ and from below from 1, so $h \ln \frac{2en}{h} \leq (m+1) \ln(2en)$. Then, the statement follows from Theorem 1 and the inclusion $\|f\|_{\mathcal{L}^1(X)} \operatorname{conv}_n(G_{R_K}(X, \lambda) \cup -G_{R_K}(X, \lambda)) \subset \operatorname{span}_n G_{R_K}(X, \lambda)$. $\square$

Theorem 3 shows that the model complexity of a kernel network with resolvent kernel approximating the solution of the equation (5) depends on λ, the $\mathcal{L}^1$-norm of the function f, the number m of functions in the spectral representation of the degenerate kernel K, and on the supremum of R_K on $X \times X$. These estimates require a calculation of the resolvent kernel R_K which may not be always feasible.

6   Conclusions

Several authors [3,4,5] made experimental studies of approximation of solutions of Fredholm integral equations by neural networks. Taking the hint from such studies, we investigated properties of such approximate solutions theoretically. We derived estimates of speed of decrease of errors in approximation of solutions by kernel networks with increasing numbers of computational units. The upper bounds are formulated in terms of the VC-dimensions of dictionaries defined by kernels. Our results show that with increasing number of units, an arbitrarily close approximation can be achieved even if kernel models are not universal approximators. The estimates show that both the supremum norm and the $\mathcal{L}^1$-norm of the function f defining the integral equation $\phi(x) - \lambda \int_X K(x, y)\phi(y)dy = f(x)$ play crucial roles.

Acknowledgments. G. Gnecco and M. Sanguineti were partially supported by a PRIN grant from the Italian Ministry for University and Research, project "Adaptive State Estimation and Optimal Control". V. Kůrková was partially supported by GA ČR grant P202/11/1368 and the Institutional Research Plan AV0Z10300504. Collaboration of V. Kůrková with M. Sanguineti and G. Gnecco was partially supported by CNR - AV ČR project 2010-2012 "Complexity of Neural-Network and Kernel Computational Models".

References

1. Lovitt, W.V.: Linear Integral Equations. Dover, New York (1950)
2. Lonseth, A.T.: Sources and applications of integral equations. SIAM Review 19, 241–278 (1977)
3. Effati, S., Buzhabadi, R.: A neural network approach for solving Fredholm integral equations of the second kind. Neural Computing & and Applications (2010), doi:10.1007/s00521–010–0489–y
4. Alipanah, A., Esmaeili, S.: Numerical solution of the two-dimensional Fredholm integral equations by Gaussian radial basis function. J. of Comput. and Appl. Math (2009), doi:doi:10.1016/j.cam.2009.11.053

5. Golbabai, A., Seifollahi, S.: Numerical solution of the second kind integral equations using radial basis function networks. Appl. Math. and Comput. 174, 877–883 (2006)
6. Kůrková, V., Sanguineti, M.: Geometric upper bounds on rates of variable-basis approximation. IEEE Trans. on Inf. Th. 54, 5681–5688 (2008)
7. Gnecco, G., Kůrková, V., Sanguineti, M.: Some comparisons of complexity in dictionary-based and linear computational models. Neural Networks 24, 171–182 (2011)
8. Alessandri, A., Sanguineti, M.: Optimization of approximating networks for optimal fault diagnosis. Optim. Meth. and Soft. 20, 235–260 (2005)
9. Giulini, S., Sanguineti, M.: Approximation schemes for functional optimization problems. J. of Optim. Th. and Appl. 140, 33–54 (2009)
10. Gnecco, G., Sanguineti, M.: Accuracy of suboptimal solutions to kernel principal component analysis. Comput. Optim. and Appl. 42, 265–287 (2009)
11. Kainen, P.C., Kůrková, V., Sanguineti, M.: Complexity of Gaussian radial-basis networks approximating smooth functions. J. of Complexity 25, 63–74 (2009)
12. Kůrková, V., Sanguineti, M.: Approximate minimization of the regularized expected error over kernel models. Math. of Op. Res. 33, 747–756 (2008)
13. Gribonval, R., Vandergheynst, P.: On the exponential convergence of matching pursuits in quasi-incoherent dictionaries. IEEE Trans. on Inf. Th. 52, 255–261 (2006)
14. Jones, L.K.: A simple lemma on greedy approximation in Hilbert space and convergence rates for projection pursuit regression and neural network training. Ann. of Stat. 20, 608–613 (1992)
15. Barron, A.R.: Universal approximation bounds for superpositions of a sigmoidal function. IEEE Trans. on Inf. Th. 39, 930–945 (1993)
16. Darken, C., Donahue, M., Gurvits, L., Sontag, E.: Rate of approximation results motivated by robust neural network learning. In: Proc. 6th Annual ACM Conf. on Computational Learning Theory, pp. 303–309 (1993)
17. Girosi, F.: Approximation error bounds that use VC- bounds. In: Proc. Int. Conf. on Artificial Neural Networks, pp. 295–302 (1995)
18. Gurvits, L., Koiran, P.: Approximation and learning of convex superpositions. J. of Computer and System Sciences 55, 161–170 (1997)
19. Vapnik, V.N.: Statistical Learning Theory. Wiley, New York (1998)
20. Atkinson, K.: The Numerical Solution of Integral Equations of the Second Kind. Cambridge Univ. Press, Cambridge (1997)
21. Pinkus, A.: Approximation theory of the MLP model in neural networks. Acta Numerica 8, 143–195 (1999)
22. Park, J., Sandberg, I.W.: Approximation and radial-basis-function networks. Neural Computation 5, 305–316 (1993)
23. Mhaskar, H.N.: Versatile Gaussian networks. In: Proc. of IEEE Workshop of Nonlinear Image Processing, pp. 70–73 (1995)
24. Dudley, R.M.: Balls in $\mathbb{R}^k$ do not cut all subsets of k+2 points. Advances in Math. 31, 306–308 (1979)
25. Tricomi, F.G.: Integral Equations. Interscience, New York (1957)
26. Sontag, E.: VC dimension of neural networks. In: Bishop, C. (ed.) Neural Networks and Machine Learning, pp. 69–95. Springer, Berlin (1998)

An Improved Training Algorithm for the Linear Ranking Support Vector Machine

Antti Airola, Tapio Pahikkala, and Tapio Salakoski

University of Turku and Turku Centre for Computer Science (TUCS)
Joukahaisenkatu 3-5 B, Turku, Finland
{antti.airola,tapio.pahikkala,tapio.salakoski}@utu.fi

Abstract. We introduce an $O(ms + m\log(m))$ time complexity method for training the linear ranking support vector machine, where m is the number of training examples, and s the average number of non-zero features per example. The method generalizes the fastest previously known approach, which achieves the same efficiency only in restricted special cases. The excellent scalability of the proposed method is demonstrated experimentally.

Keywords: binary search tree, cutting plane optimization, learning to rank, support vector machine.

1 Introduction

The ranking support vector machine (RankSVM) [7,8], is one of the most successful methods for learning to rank. The method is based on regularized risk minimization with a pairwise loss function, that provides a convex approximation of the number of pairwise mis-orderings in the ranking produced by the learned model. Related learning algorithms based on the pairwise criterion include methods such as RankBoost [5], and RankRLS [11], among others. RankSVM has been shown to achieve excellent performance on ranking tasks such as document ranking in web search [8,3]. However, the scalability of the method leaves room for improvement. In this work we assume the so-called scoring setting, where each data instance is associated with a utility score reflecting its goodness with respect to the ranking criterion.

Previously, [9] has shown that linear RankSVM can be trained using cutting plane optimization very efficiently, when the number of distinct utility scores allowed is restricted. The introduced method has $O(ms + m\log(m) + rm)$ training complexity, where m is the number of training examples, s the average number of non-zero features per example, and r the number of distinct utility scores in the training set. A similar approach having same training complexity was also introduced by [3]. If r is assumed to be a small constant, the existing methods are computationally efficient. However, in the general case where unrestricted scores are allowed, if most of the training examples have different scores $r \approx m$ leading to $O(ms + m^2)$ complexity. This worst scale quadratic scaling limits the applicability of RankSVM in large scale learning.

T. Honkela et al. (Eds.): ICANN 2011, Part I, LNCS 6791, pp. 134–141, 2011.

In this work we generalize the work of [9] and present a training algorithm which has $O(ms + m \log(m))$ complexity even in the most general case, where arbitrary real-valued utility scores are allowed. The method is based on using binary search trees [2,4] for speeding up the evaluations needed in the optimization process. Our experiments show the excellent scalability of the method in practice, allowing orders of magnitude faster training times than the fastest previously known methods in case of unrestricted utility scores. Due to space constraints more detailed description of the method and related proofs are left to an upcoming journal extension of the work [1].

2   Learning Setting

Let D be a probability distribution over a sample space $\mathcal{Z} = \mathbb{R}^n \times \mathbb{R}$. An example $z = (\mathbf{x}, y) \in \mathcal{Z}$ is a pair consisting of an n-dimensional column vector of real-valued features, and an associated real-valued utility score. Let the sequence $Z = ((\mathbf{x}_1, y_1), \ldots, (\mathbf{x}_m, y_m)) \in \mathcal{Z}^m$ drawn according to D be a training set of m training examples. $X \in \mathbb{R}^{n \times m}$ denotes the $n \times m$ data matrix whose columns contain the feature representations of the training examples, and $\mathbf{y} \in \mathbb{R}^m$ is a column vector containing the utility scores in the training set.

Our task is to learn from the training data a ranking function $f : \mathbb{R}^n \to \mathbb{R}$. In the linear case such a function can be represented as $f(\mathbf{x}) = \mathbf{w}^T \mathbf{x}$, where $\mathbf{w} \in \mathbb{R}^n$ is a vector of parameters. Where the ranking task differs in the scoring setting from that of simple regression is that the actual values taken by the ranking function are typically not of interest. Rather, what is of interest is how well the ordering acquired by sorting a set of new examples according to their predicted scores matches the true underlying ranking. This is a reasonable criterion for example in the web search engines and recommender systems, where the task is to choose a suitable order in which to present web pages or products to the end user. A popular way to model this criterion is by considering the pairwise preferences induced by a ranking (see e.g. [6]). We say that an example z_i is preferred over example z_j, if $y_i > y_j$. In this case one would require from the ranking function that $f(\mathbf{x}_i) > f(\mathbf{x}_j)$. The performance of a ranking function can be measured by the pairwise ranking error defined as

$$\frac{1}{N} \sum_{y_i < y_j} H(f(\mathbf{x}_i) - f(\mathbf{x}_j)) , \tag{1}$$

where H is the Heaviside step function defined as

$$H(a) = \begin{cases} 1, & \text{if } a > 0 \\ 1/2, & \text{if } a = 0 \\ 0, & \text{if } a < 0 \end{cases}$$

and N is the number of pairs for which $y_i < y_j$. The equation (1) counts the number of swapped pairs between the true ranking and the one produced by f.

In some learning to rank settings instead of having a total order over all examples, the sample space is divided into disjoint subsets, and pairwise preferences are induced only from pairwise comparisons between the scores of examples in the same subset. An example of an application settings where this approach is commonly adopted is document retrieval, where data consists of query-document pairs, and the scores represent the utility of the document with respect to the associated user query [8]. Preferences are induced only between query-document pairs from the same query, never between examples from different queries. In such settings we can calculate (1) separately for each subset, and take the average value as the final error.

Minimizing (1) directly is computationally intractable, successful approaches to learning to rank according to the pairwise criterion typically minimize convex relaxations instead. The relaxation considered in this work is the pairwise hinge loss, which together with a quadratic regularizer forms the objective function of RankSVM.

3   Algorithm Description

The RankSVM optimization problem can be formulated as the unconstrained regularized risk minimization problem

$$\arg\min_{\mathbf{w}\in\mathbb{R}^n} \frac{1}{N} \sum_{y_i<y_j} \max(0, 1 + \mathbf{w}^{\mathrm{T}}\mathbf{x}_i - \mathbf{w}^{\mathrm{T}}\mathbf{x}_j) + \lambda\|\mathbf{w}\|^2, \tag{2}$$

where $\mathbf{w}$ is the vector of parameters to be learned, N is the number of pairs for which $y_i < y_j$ holds true, and $\lambda \in \mathbb{R}^+$ is a parameter. The first term is the empirical risk measuring how well $\mathbf{w}$ fits the training data, and the second term is the quadratic regularizer measuring the complexity of the hypotheses.

[9] proposed minimizing the RankSVM risk using cutting plane optimization. A more general treatment of this optimization approach, together with improved convergence analysis can be found in [12], where the method is known as the bundle method for regularized risk minimization. The cutting plane method needs $O(\frac{1}{\lambda\epsilon})$ iterations to converge to ϵ-accurate solution for convex nonsmooth loss functions, independent of the training set size [12]. By ϵ-accurate we mean that the difference between the regularized risk for the found solution, and for the optimal solution is smaller than a user defined parameter ϵ.

Due to space constraints detailed description of the cutting plane method is not possible here, but the central insight necessary for implementing fast training algorithms is as follows. On each iteration, given the current solution, the cutting plane method needs the value of the empirical risk, as well as that of its subgradient. For large dataset sizes it is these computations that dominate the runtime, since none of the other computations needed in the optimization are dependent on the sample size or dimensionality. To develop fast training methods a necessary and sufficient condition is to have an efficient algorithm for computing the risk, and its subgradient.

At first glance, it would appear that computing the empirical risk requires $O(m^2)$ comparisons between the training examples. However, as noted by [9,13], we can rewrite the empirical risk as

$$\frac{1}{N} \sum_{y_i < y_j} \max(0, 1 + \mathbf{w}^{\mathrm{T}}\mathbf{x}_i - \mathbf{w}^{\mathrm{T}}\mathbf{x}_j) = \frac{1}{N} \sum_{i=1}^{m}(c_i - d_i)\mathbf{w}^{\mathrm{T}}\mathbf{x}_i + c_i \qquad (3)$$

where c_i is the frequency how many times $y_i < y_j$ and $\mathbf{w}^{\mathrm{T}}\mathbf{x}_i > \mathbf{w}^{\mathrm{T}}\mathbf{x}_j - 1$, and d_i is the frequency how many times $y_i > y_j$ and $\mathbf{w}^{\mathrm{T}}\mathbf{x}_i < \mathbf{w}^{\mathrm{T}}\mathbf{x}_j + 1$. A subgradient with respect to $\mathbf{w}$ can be calculated as

$$\frac{1}{N} \sum_{i=1}^{m}(c_i - d_i)\mathbf{x}_i . \qquad (4)$$

Inner product evaluations, scalar-vector multiplications and vector summations are needed to compute (3) and (4). These take each $O(s)$ time.

Assuming that we know the values of c_i, and d_i for all $1 \leq i \leq m$, both the empirical risk and the subgradient require $O(ms)$ time.

[9] proposes an algorithm for computing these frequencies, and subsequently the loss and the subgradient. However, the work assumes that the range of possible utility score values is restricted to r different values, with r assumed to be a small constant. The method has the computational complexity $O(ms + m\log(m) + rm)$. If the number of allowed scores is not restricted, at worst case $r = m$ and the method has $O(ms + m^2)$ complexity, meaning quadratic behavior in m. In this work we present a more general algorithm, for which the time complexity of evaluating the loss and the subgradient is $O(ms + m\log(m))$ also in the most general case, where arbitrary real valued utility scores are allowed.

To formulate the algorithm we need for bookkeeping purposes a data structure which stores floating point numbers as elements. What is required is that if h is the current number of stored elements, it supports the following operations in $O(\log(h))$ time: insertion of a new element, and query to find out the number of values in the data structure with a larger/smaller value than the given query value. Finally, the data structure must allow the storage of duplicate values.

For logarithmic time insertion and computation of the desired order statistics, a suitable choice is a self-balancing search tree. Our implementation is based on the order statistics tree [4], which is a red-black tree [2] modified so that each node stores the size of the subtree, whose root node it is. Further, we modify the basic data structure to allow the insertion of several duplicate values to the same node. The self-balancing property is crucial, as it guarantees logarithmic worst case performance.

Algorithm 1 illustrates the $O(ms + m\log(m))$ time calculation for calculating the loss and the subgradient. First, the algorithm calculates the predicted scores for the training examples using the current model $\mathbf{w}$. Next, an index list π is created, where the indices of the training examples are ordered in an increasing order, according to the magnitudes of their predicted scores. Then, the algorithm calculates the frequencies needed in evaluating (3) and (4). In lines $7 - 12$ we

Algorithm 1. Subgradient and loss computation

Input: X, $\mathbf{y}$, $\mathbf{w}$, N
Output: a, loss
1   $\mathbf{p} \leftarrow X^{\mathrm{T}}\mathbf{w}$;
2   $\mathbf{c} \leftarrow m$ length column vector of zeros;
3   $\mathbf{d} \leftarrow m$ length column vector of zeros;
4   $\pi \leftarrow$ training set indices, sorted in ascending order according to $\mathbf{p}$;
5   $s \leftarrow$ new empty search tree;
6   $j \leftarrow 1$;
7   **foreach** $i \in \{1 \ldots m\}$ **do**
8      $k \leftarrow \pi[i]$;
9   **while** $(j \leq m)$ *and* $(\mathbf{p}[k] - \mathbf{p}[\pi[j]] > -1)$ **do**
10          $s.\mathrm{insert}(\mathbf{y}[\pi[j]])$;
11          $j \leftarrow j + 1$;
12      $\mathbf{c}[k] \leftarrow s.\mathrm{count\_larger}(\mathbf{y}[k])$;

13   $s \leftarrow$ new empty search tree;
14   $j \leftarrow m$;
15   **foreach** $i \in \{m \ldots 1\}$ **do**
16      $k \leftarrow \pi[i]$;
17   **while** $(j \geq 1)$ *and* $(\mathbf{p}[k] - \mathbf{p}[\pi[j]] < 1)$ **do**
18          $s.\mathrm{insert}(\mathbf{y}[\pi[j]])$;
19          $j \leftarrow j - 1$;
20      $\mathbf{d}[k] \leftarrow s.\mathrm{count\_smaller}(\mathbf{y}[k])$;

21   loss$\leftarrow \frac{1}{N}(\mathbf{p}^{\mathrm{T}}(\mathbf{c} - \mathbf{d}) + \mathbf{1}^{\mathrm{T}}\mathbf{c})$;
22   $\mathbf{a} \leftarrow \frac{1}{N}X(\mathbf{c} - \mathbf{d})$;

---

go through the examples in ascending order, as defined by the predicted scores. When considering a new example $\mathbf{x}_i$, the examples are scanned further, in lines $9-11$, to ensure that the true utility scores of such examples, for which, $\mathbf{w}^{\mathrm{T}}\mathbf{x}_i > \mathbf{w}^{\mathrm{T}}\mathbf{x}_j - 1$ holds true, are stored in the search tree. After this is ensured, the value of c_i is simply the number of scores in the search tree, for which $y_i < y_j$ holds. In lines $15 - 20$ we go through the examples in a reversed direction, and the values of d_i are calculated in an analogous manner. Once these values have been calculated, the loss and the subgradient can be evaluated as in (3) and (4). These operations are performed on lines 21 and 22 as vector-vector and matrix-vector operations, $\mathbf{1}$ represents a column vector of ones.

The computational complexity of the operation $X^{\mathrm{T}}\mathbf{w}$ needed to calculate the predicted scores is $O(ms)$. The cost of sorting the index list π according to these scores is $O(m \log(m))$. The $O(\log(m))$ time insertions on lines 10 and 18, as well as the $O(\log(m))$ time queries on lines 12 and 20 are each called exactly m times, leading to $O(m \log(m))$ cost.

The vector operations needed in calculating the loss have $O(m)$ complexity, and the matrix-vector multiplication necessary for computing the subgradient has $O(ms)$ complexity. Thus, the complexity of calculating the loss and the subgradient is $O(ms + m \log(m))$. The exact value of N can be computed in $O(m \log(m))$ by sorting the true utility scores of the training examples.

As discussed previously, in some ranking settings we do not have a global ranking over all examples. Instead, the training data may be divided into separate subsets, over each of which a ranking is defined. Let the training data set be divided into R subsets, each consisting on average of $\frac{m}{R}$ examples. Then we can calculate the loss and the subgradient as the average over the losses and subgradients for each subset. The computational complexity becomes $O(R * (\frac{m}{R}s + \frac{m}{R}\log(\frac{m}{R}))) = O(ms + m\log(\frac{m}{R}))$.

4   Computational Experiments

In the computational experiments we compare the scalability of the proposed $O(ms + m\log(m))$ time training algorithm to the fastest previously known approach. In addition, we compare our implementation to the existing publicly available RankSVM solvers. The considered data set contains a global ranking, and the utility scores are real valued. This means that $r \approx m$, and the number of pairwise preferences in the training sets grows quadratically with m.

We implement the proposed method, denoted as TreeRSVM, as well as a baseline method PairRSVM, which iterates over all pairs to compute the loss and the subgradient. The methods are implemented mostly in Python using the NumPy, SciPy and CVXOPT libraries, the most computationally demanding parts of the subgradient and loss computations are for both methods implemented in C language due to efficiency reasons.

In addition, we compare our method to the fastest publicly available previous implementations of RankSVM. The SVM^{rank} software is a C-language implementation of the method described in [9]. In theory SVM^{rank} and PairRSVM implement the same method, though the use of different quadratic optimizers, and the inclusion of certain additional heuristics within SVM^{rank}, mean that there may be some differences in their behavior. PRSVM implements in MATLAB a truncated Newton optimization based method for training RankSVM [3]. PRSVM optimizes a slightly different objective function than the other implementations, since it minimizes a squared version of the pairwise hinge loss.

TreeRSVM has $O(ms + m\log(m))$ training time complexity, whereas all the other methods have $O(ms + m^2)$ training time complexity. Therefore, TreeRSVM should on large datasets scale substantially better than the other implementations.

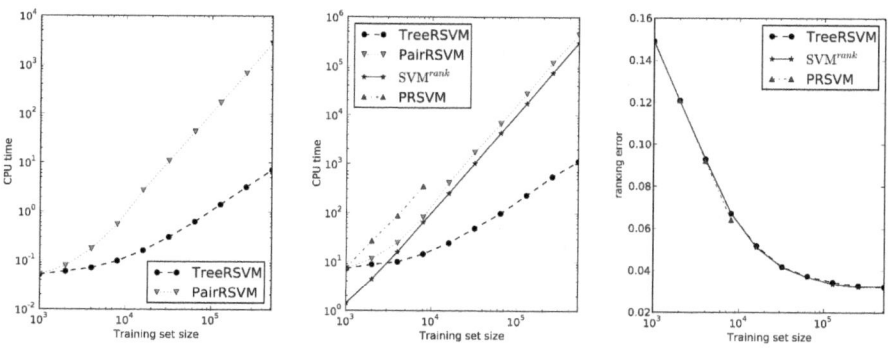

Fig. 1. Average iteration cost (left), runtimes (middle), test error plots (right)

Further, all the methods other than PRSVM have $O(ms)$ memory complexity due to cost of storing the data matrix. PRSVM has $O(ms + m^2)$ memory complexity, since it also forms a sparse data matrix that contains two entries per each pairwise preference in the training set. [3] also describe an improved version of PRSVM that has similar scalability as SVM^{rank}, but there is no publicly available implementation of this method.

The experiments are run on a desktop computer with 2.4 GHz Intel Core 2 Duo E6600 processor, 8 GB of main memory, and 64-bit Ubuntu Linux 10.10 operating system. For TreeRSVM, PairRSVM and SVM^{rank} we use the termination criterion $\epsilon < 0.001$, which is the default setting of SVM^{rank}. For PRSVM we use the termination criterion Newton decrement $< 10^{-6}$, as according to [3] this is roughly equivalent to the termination criterion we use for the other methods. SVM^{rank} and PRSVM use a regularization parameter C that is multiplied to the empirical risk term rather than λ, and do not normalize the empirical risk by the number of pairwise preferences N. Therefore, we use the conversion $C = \frac{1}{\lambda N}$, when setting the parameters.

We run scalability experiments on a data set constructed from the Reuters RCV1 collection [10], which consists of approximately 800000 documents. Here, we use a high dimensional feature representation, with each example having approximately 50000 tf-idf values as features. The data set is sparse, meaning that most features are zero-valued. The utility scores are generated as follows. First, we remove one target example randomly from the data set. Next, we compute the dot products between each example and the target example, and use these as utility scores. In effect, the aim is now to learn to rank documents according to how similar they are to the target document. Similarly to the scalability experiments in [3], we compute the running times using a fixed value for the regularization parameter, and a sequence of exponentially growing training set sizes. The presented results are for $\lambda = 10^{-5}$, and the training set sizes are from the range $[1000, 2000, \ldots 512000]$.

In Figure 1 are the experimental results. First, we plot the average time needed for subgradient computation by the TreeRSVM and the PairRSVM. It can be seen that the results are consistent with the computational complexity analysis, the proposed method scales much better than the one based on iterating over the pairs of training examples in subgradient and loss evaluations. Second, we compare the scalability of the different RankSVM implementations. As expected, TreeRank achieves orders of magnitude faster training times than the other alternatives. PRSVM could not be trained beyond 8000 examples due to large memory consumption. With 512000 training examples training SVM^{rank} took 83 hours, and training PairRSVM took 122 hours, whereas training TreeRSVM took only 18 minutes in the same setting. Finally, we plot the pairwise ranking errors, as measured on an independent test set of 20000 examples. PairRSVM is left out of the comparison, since it always reaches exactly the same solution as TreeRSVM. The results show that TreeRSVM and SVM^{rank} have similar performance as expected, as does PRSVM which optimizes a squared version of the pairwise hinge loss.

5   Conclusion

In this work we have introduced an improved training algorithm for the linear RankSVM, allowing efficient training also in case of unrestricted utility scores. The experiments demonstrate orders of magnitude improvements in training time on large enough data sets.

Acknowledgment. This work has been supported by the Academy of Finland.

References

1. Airola, A., Pahikkala, T., Salakoski, T.: Training linear ranking SVMs in linearithmic time using red-black trees. Pattern Recognition Letters (in press, 2011)
2. Bayer, R.: Symmetric binary B-trees: Data structure and maintenance algorithms. Acta Informatica 1, 290–306 (1972)
3. Chapelle, O., Keerthi, S.S.: Efficient algorithms for ranking with SVMs. Information Retrieval 13, 201–215 (2010)
4. Cormen, T.H., Leiserson, C.E., Rivest, R.L., Stein, C.: Introduction to Algorithms. MIT Press, Cambridge (2001)
5. Freund, Y., Iyer, R., Schapire, R.E., Singer, Y.: An efficient boosting algorithm for combining preferences. Journal of Machine Learning Research 4, 933–969 (2003)
6. Fürnkranz, J., Hüllermeier, E.: Preference learning. Künstliche Intelligenz 19(1), 60–61 (2005)
7. Herbrich, R., Graepel, T., Obermayer, K.: Support vector learning for ordinal regression. In: 9th International Conference on Articial Neural Networks, pp. 97–102. Institute of Electrical Engineers (1999)
8. Joachims, T.: Optimizing search engines using clickthrough data. In: Hand, D., Keim, D., Ng, R. (eds.) 8th ACM SIGKDD Conference on Knowledge Discovery and Data Mining, pp. 133–142. ACM Press, New York (2002)
9. Joachims, T.: Training linear SVMs in linear time. In: Eliassi-Rad, T., Ungar, L., Craven, M., Gunopulos, D. (eds.) 12th ACM SIGKDD Conference on Knowledge Discovery and Data Mining, pp. 217–226. ACM Press, New York (2006)
10. Lewis, D.D., Yang, Y., Rose, T.G., Li, F.: RCV1: A new benchmark collection for text categorization research. Journal of Machine Learning Research 5, 361–397 (2004)
11. Pahikkala, T., Tsivtsivadze, E., Airola, A., Boberg, J., Järvinen, J.: An efficient algorithm for learning to rank from preference graphs. Machine Learning 75(1), 129–165 (2009)
12. Smola, A.J., Vishwanathan, S.V.N., Le, Q.: Bundle methods for machine learning. In: McCallum, A. (ed.) Advances in Neural Information Processing Systems 20. MIT Press, Cambridge (2007)
13. Teo, C.H., Vishwanathan, S.V.N., Smola, A., Le, Q.V.: Bundle methods for regularized risk minimization. Journal of Machine Learning Research 11, 311–365 (2010)

Extending Tree Kernels with Topological Information

Fabio Aiolli, Giovanni Da San Martino, and Alessandro Sperduti

Dept. of Pure and Applied Mathematics, University of Padova,
via Trieste 63, 35121, Padova, Italy
{aiolli,dasan,sperduti}@math.unipd.it

Abstract. The definition of appropriate kernel functions is crucial for the performance of a kernel method. In many of the state-of-the-art kernels for trees, matching substructures are considered independently from their position within the trees. However, when a match happens in similar positions, more strength could reasonably be given to it. Here, we give a systematic way to enrich a large class of tree kernels with this kind of information without affecting, in almost all cases, the worst case computational complexity. Experimental results show the effectiveness of the proposed approach.

Keywords: kernel methods, tree kernels, machine learning.

1 Introduction

Kernel based methods are recognized to be very effective methods to cope with data in non vectorial form. Indeed, many real world applications exist where data are more naturally represented in structured form, including XML documents for information retrieval tasks, protein sequences in biology, and parse trees in natural language applications.

The design of this type of kernels is still a challenging problem as they should be expressive enough (avoiding the loss of relevant structural information) while remaining computationally not too demanding.

In this paper we focus on kernels for trees, for which several kernels have been defined in the last few years. As an example, consider the Subtree kernel (ST) [10] and the Subset tree kernel [2]: the former counts the number of matching proper subtrees and the latter kernel extends this space by also considering all subset trees. We noted that possibly relevant topological information about the relative position in the trees of the matching substructures is not typically taken into account in state-of-the-art kernels. In fact, common kernels for trees can be considered position invariant kernels, that is, features represent parts of the tree but do not maintain information about the position of the features in the original tree. Our intuition is that a more satisfactory notion of similarity on trees should give higher values to those structures which present the same features also in the same positions. One example of a kernel that incorporates this kind of information has been recently proposed in [1]. However, both the

T. Honkela et al. (Eds.): ICANN 2011, Part I, LNCS 6791, pp. 142–149, 2011.

type of topological information and the local kernels involved are different from the ones of the present paper (see section 3 for details).

Here we propose an operator which is applicable to a family of kernels for trees and is able to enrich these kernels with topological information while maintaining (with one exception) the same computational complexity in time. Experimental results obtained by this operator demonstrate its ability to improve the performance of baseline kernels on various datasets when topological information is really relevant for the domain at hand. More importantly, enriching fast tree kernels (such as the ST and SST kernels) allow them to reach accuracy values comparable to the ones of slower but more expressive tree kernels, such as the Partial Tree Kernel (PT) [7] even if enriched ST and SST kernels are faster to compute than PT.

The paper is organized as follows: section 2 gives a brief survey of kernels for trees. Section 3 describes an operator for extending tree kernels with topological information. Section 4 explains how to efficiently compute the novel kernels. Section 5 gives experimental evidence of the effectiveness of the extended kernels. Section 6 draws some conclusions and propose future extensions of the paper.

2   Kernels for Trees

This section describes some well known kernels for trees focusing on three of them which will be used as baselines in the experimental section: ST [10], SST [2] and PT [7] kernels. These kernels are all based on counting the number of parts (or substructures) which are shared by two trees. However, different kernels define in a different way the type of substructures that can be matched. Let us briefly present the them in decreasing order of expressivity. The PT kernel counts the number of matching *subtrees*, i.e. subsets of nodes of a tree (and edges that link them) which form a tree. The SST counts the number of matching *subset trees*, where subset trees are subtrees for which the following constraint is satisfied: either all of the children of a node belong to the subset tree or none of them. The ST kernel counts the number of matching *proper subtrees*, where proper subtrees are here defined as subtrees rooted at a node v and comprising all of its descendants. Note that all of the above kernels are members of the convolution kernel framework [4], that is they can be computed resorting to the following formula:

$$K(T_1, T_2) = \sum_{v_1 \in T_1} \sum_{v_2 \in T_2} C_{\mathcal{K}}(v_1, v_2), \tag{1}$$

where $\mathcal{K} \in \{ST, SST, PT\}$ (see below). $C(\mathcal{K})$ can be computed according to three rules: *i)* if the productions[1] at v_1 and v_2 are different then $C_{\mathcal{K}}(v_1, v_2) = 0$; *ii)* if the productions at v_1 and v_2 are the same, and v_1 and v_2 have only leaf children (i.e. they are pre-terminals symbols) then $C_{\mathcal{K}}(v_1, v_2) = \lambda$, where λ is an external parameter which causes a downweighting of the influence of larger

---

[1] A production is defined as the label of a node plus the labels of its children (if any).

substructure matches; iii) if the productions at v_1 and v_2 are the same, and v_1 and v_2 are not pre-terminals, then the value of $C_{\mathcal{K}}()$ depends on the kernel. If $\mathcal{K} = \mathcal{ST}$ then $C_{ST}(v_1, v_2) = \lambda \prod_{j=1}^{nc(v_1)} (C(ch_j[v_1], ch_j[v_2]))$, where $nc(v_1)$ is the number of children of v_1 and $ch_j[v]$ denotes the j-th child of node v. If $\mathcal{K} = \mathcal{SST}$ then $C_{SST}(v_1, v_2) = \lambda \prod_{j=1}^{nc(v_1)} (1 + C(ch_j[v_1], ch_j[v_2]))$. The computational complexity in time of the above kernels is $O(|T_1||T_2|)$, where $|T_i|$ is the number of nodes of the tree T_i. Nevertheless, a faster algorithm for computing the ST kernel has also been proposed in [10] with complexity in time $O(N \log N)$, where $N = \max\{|T_1|, |T_2|\}$. Finally, for the PT kernel we have a slightly more complex formulation, i.e.

$$C_{PT}(v_1, v_2) = \lambda \left(\mu^2 + \sum_{J_1, J_2, |J_1|=|J_2|} \mu^{d(J_1)+d(J_2)} \cdot \prod_{i=1}^{|J_1|} (1 + C_{PT}(chs_{v_1}[J_{1i}], chs_{v_2}[J_{2i}])) \right),$$

where $J_{11}, J_{12}, \ldots J_{21}, J_{22}, \ldots$ are sequences of indexes associated with the ordered sequences of children chs_{v_1} and chs_{v_2} respectively, J_{1i} and J_{2i} point to the i-th child in the two sequences and $|J_1|$ denotes the length of the sequence J_1. Finally, $d(J_1) = J_{1|J_1|} - J_{11}$ and $d(J_2) = J_{2|J_2|} - J_{21}$ (see [7] for details). The parameter μ penalizes subtrees built on subsequences of children that contain gaps. From this formulation one can see that the ST and SST kernels can be seen as special cases of the PT kernel. The Partial tree kernel can be evaluated in $O(\rho^3 |T_1||T_2|)$, where ρ is the maximum out-degree of the two trees.

3   Injecting Positional Information into Tree Kernels

Tree kernels, such as ST, SST, and PT, are position invariant kernels, i.e. any match between two subtrees $t_1 \in T_1$ and $t_2 \in T_2$ does not consider where t_1 and t_2 occur within T_1 and T_2, respectively. While this feature may turn useful to avoid too sparse kernels (kernels in which matches barely occur), it may generate an unsatisfactory kernel matrix from the point of view of structural similarity. This point is illustrated in Fig. 1 where $K_{ST}(T_1, T_3) = K_{ST}(T_2, T_3)$, while clearly a better representation of the similarity among the trees would prescribe the constraint $K(T_1, T_3) > K(T_2, T_3)$ to hold. Then, a nice tradeoff aiming at using

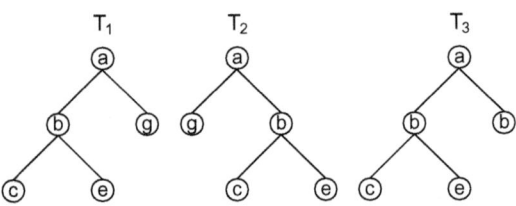

Fig. 1. Using the ST kernel we have $K_{ST}(T_1, T_3) = K_{ST}(T_2, T_3) = 3$, however it seems to be more reasonable to have $K(T_1, T_3) > K(T_2, T_3)$ since the matching subtrees (i.e. the leaf labeled **c**, the leaf labeled **e**, and the subtree **b(c,e)**) occur in the same positions within T_1 and T_3, while this is not the case for T_2

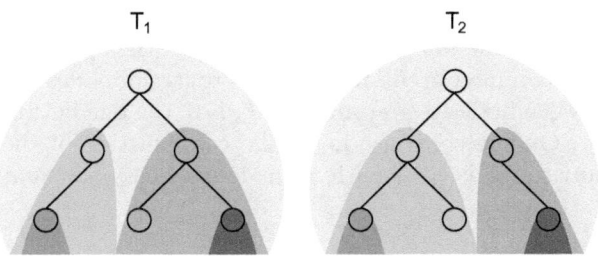

Fig. 2. A representation of which kernels $k()$ have to be computed to evaluate the kernel $K()$. Subtrees for which the kernel $k()$ is computed are the ones of the same color

this topological information while keeping low the sparsity of a kernel could be to extend the original feature space with new positional dependent features. We refer to the extended version of the kernels by applying the prefix PAK (Position Aware Kernel) to their names: PAK-ST, PAK-SST, PAK-PT. One simple way to do that is to define a kernel $K()$ which is the sum of local kernel $k()$ evaluations obtained for each pair of subtrees of the two trees sharing the same route. A route for a node $v \in T$, denoted by $\pi(v)$, is the sequences of indices of edges connecting the consecutive nodes in the path between $root(T)$, the root of the tree T, and v (for a more detailed description refer to [1]). The index of an edge is its position with respect to its siblings. The idea of the PAK extension is exemplified in Fig. 2 where the same color in the two trees correspond to those subtrees for which the kernel $k()$ have to be computed, i.e. those sharing the same route. Just to give an example, if we refer to trees T_1 and T_3 in Fig. 1, by using the ST kernel K_{ST}, we would have

$$K(T_1, T_3) = K_{ST}(\mathbf{c}, \mathbf{c}) + K_{ST}(\mathbf{e}, \mathbf{e}) + K_{ST}(\mathbf{b(c,e)}, \mathbf{b(c,e)}) + K_{ST}(\mathbf{g}, \mathbf{b}) + \\ + K_{ST}(\mathbf{a(b(c,e),g)}, \mathbf{a(b(c,e),b)}). \tag{2}$$

Each route has associated its depth $d(v)$ where $d(root(T)) = 1$ and $d(v)$ is $1 + d(parent(v))$. The formal definition of the kernel is the following:

$$K_k(T_1, T_2) = \sum_{v_1 \in T_1, v_2 \in T_2} \gamma^{d(v_1)} \delta\left(\pi(v_1), \pi(v_2)\right) k(t_{v_1}, t_{v_2}), \tag{3}$$

where $\delta()$ is a function whose value is 1 whether the two input routes are identical, 0 otherwise. When $\gamma = 0$ computing eq. (3) is equivalent to computing the baseline kernel.

Eq. (3) considers topological similarity while avoiding to have a too sparse kernel since the computation of the position invariant kernel between the two trees is included. Moreover, from a computational point of view, the repeated computation of the same kernel on subtrees can be done efficiently by reusing the already performed calculations. The kernel of eq. (3) is different from the ones described in [1] in both the local kernel (simple kernels on the nodes in [1] compared to tree kernels in this paper) and the kernel on the route considered.

Fig. 2 shows that the local kernel k between two subtrees is computed as many times as the length of the longest common prefix of their routes. For example in Fig. 1 the longest common prefix between the routes of nodes $\mathbf{e} \in T_1$ and $\mathbf{e} \in T_3$ is 2, the one between nodes $\mathbf{e} \in T_1$ and $\mathbf{e} \in T_2$ is 0, the one between nodes $\mathbf{e} \in T_1$ and $\mathbf{c} \in T_3$ is 1. On the contrary, in [1] the computation of the local kernel is repeated as many times as the length of the longest common suffix of the routes.

4   Algorithmic Issues

This section describes how to efficiently implement the kernel described in eq. 3. In fact, we will see that when using the SST or PT kernel as the "local" kernel k, the computational complexity of the extended kernel, i.e. eq. (3), is the same as the one of the local kernel. Unfortunately, the same idea would alter the complexity of ST, thus for the moment we'll focus on SST and PT.

Considering eq. (3), there are at most $n = \min(|T_1|, |T_2|)$ routes for which $\delta(\pi_{T_1}(v_1), \pi_{T_2}(v_2)) = 1$. A naive algorithm listing all the common routes and computing k for each of them, would have a complexity of $n \cdot Q$, where Q is the worst case complexity of the local kernel. Let us assume k is a convolution kernel, i.e. it can be written in the form of eq. (1). All C values can be computed in Q time, where $Q = O(|T_1| \cdot |T_2|)$ for SST and $Q = O(\rho^3 \cdot |T_1| \cdot |T_2|)$ for PT. We show that, by aggregating subsets of C values, it is actually possible to efficiently compute eq. (3). In fact, for each $v_1 \in T_1$ and $v_2 \in T_2$, let us define $S(v_1, v_2) = \sum_{v_2' \in t_{v_2}} C(v_1, v_2')$. By exploiting the recursive definition of C, it is easy to see that S can be computed as follows:

$$S(v_1, v_2) = C(v_1, v_2) + \sum_{j=1}^{nc(v_2)} S(v_1, ch_j(v_2)). \tag{4}$$

Note that, when v_2 is a leaf $nc(v_2) = 0$ and the second term of eq. (4) is 0. Assuming to have precomputed the C values, computing all of the S values related to a node v_1 requires $O(|T_2|)$. Thus computing all the S values for a pair of trees requires $O(|T_1| \cdot |T_2|)$, i.e. their computation does not affect the complexity of the SST and PT kernels. Plugging eq. (4) into eq. (3), we obtain:

$$K_k(T_1, T_2) = \sum_{v_1 \in T_1, v_2 \in T_2} \gamma^{d(v_1)} \delta(\pi(v_1), \pi(v_2)) \sum_{v_1' \in t_{v_1}} S(v_1', v_2). \tag{5}$$

Since, as already noted, there are at most $\min(|T_1|, |T_2|)$ common routes between T_1 and T_2 and those routes can be identified in $\min(|T_1|, |T_2|)$ steps by a simultaneous visit of both trees, the complexity of the kernel depends on the complexity of computing C and S values. Since the complexity of S is not greater than the complexity of computing C for SST and PT, the kernel we described in eq. (3) can be computed without altering the worst-case complexity of both kernels. The ST kernel has $O(N \log(N))$ time complexity [10], thus computing S values as described in this section, would alter the total complexity of the kernel. We have derived an algorithm for computing PAK-ST which is faster than $O(N^2)$, but it won't be described here due to lack of space.

5   Experiments

Experiments were performed to test the effectiveness of the proposed operator in conjunction with the ST, SST and the PT kernels. The SVM-Light software has been used for the experiments [5,8]. Our approach has been tested on the INEX 2005 dataset [3], the INEX 2006 dataset [3], the Propbank dataset [6].

The INEX 2005 dataset is a reduced version of the one used for the 2005 INEX competition [3] (for details of the preprocessing see [9]). It consists of 9, 640 xml documents describing movies from the IMDB database. The total number of tree nodes in the dataset is 247, 128, the average number of nodes in a tree is 25.63. The maximum outdegree of a node is 32. The task is an 11-class classification problem. The training and validation sets consist of 3397 and 1423 documents, respectively. The test set is formed by 4820 documents.

The INEX 2006 dataset [3] is derived from the IEEE corpus composed of 12000 scientific articles from IEEE journals in XML format. The total number of tree nodes in the dataset is 218, 537 and the average number of nodes in a tree is 18.05. The maximum outdegree of a tree is 66. In this case the training, validation and test sets consisted of 4237, 1816 and 6054 documents, respectively. The task is an 18-class classification problem.

The Propbank dataset [6] is derived from the Penn Tree Bank II dataset, which, in turns, consists of material from a set of Dow-Jones news articles. The corpus is divided into sections. In order to reduce the computational complexity of the task, we derived the training and validation sets from section 24 by selecting randomly, with uniform probability, a subset of 7000 and 2000 examples, respectively. The test set has been derived selecting randomly, with uniform probability, a subset of 6000 examples from section 23. The total number of tree nodes in the dataset are 209, 251 and the average number of nodes in a tree is 13.95. The maximum outdegree is 15. The task is a binary classification problem. The dataset is very unbalanced: the percentage of positive examples in each set is approximately 7%. Thus the F1 measure has been used for selecting the parameters on the validation set.

The procedure followed for the experiments on each dataset is the following. We first selected the best parameters of the baseline kernel on the validation set. Then, keeping them fixed, we applied the operator proposed in the paper selecting γ on the validation set. Finally, a model learned with the parameter setting on the union of the training and validation sets was tested on the test set. In the case of multiclass classification tasks, i.e. INEX 2005 and INEX 2006, the one against all methodology has been employed. Table 1 summarizes the results obtained. Note that the application of the operator always improves the accuracy of the baseline kernel on INEX 2005 and the improvement is impressive for the ST and SST kernels. For what concerns INEX 2006, in the case of ST and SST, adding positional information to the matchings does not improve

Table 1. Comparison between the classification error of ST, SST, PT and their version with the proposed operator. The columns represent the lowest classification error on validation and the corresponding classification error on the test set. The performance measure employed for the Propbank dataset is the F1. In bold the best result between the baseline and the PAK extension on the test set.

Kernel	INEX 2005		INEX 2006		Propbank	
	valid.	test	valid.	test	valid.	test
	error %	error %	error %	error %	F1 (error %)	F1 (error %)
ST	12.94	11.11	57.27	60.04	0.5078 (6.30)	0.5170 (6.60)
PAK-ST	3.52	**3.44**	57.27	60.04	0.5447 (5.85)	**0.5359** (6.23)
SST	12.51	11.17	57.72	60.40	0.5130 (5.60)	0.5420 (5.72)
PAK-SST	3.59	**3.31**	57.72	60.40	0.5431 (5.55)	**0.5477** (5.92)
PT	2.96	2.96	58.11	58.69	0.5488 (6.00)	0.5161 (7.00)
PAK-PT	2.96	**2.85**	57.55	58.85	0.5636 (5.65)	**0.5787** (6.07)

Table 2. Ratio between the execution times and the test errors or the F1 of the PAK extensions with respect to the baseline kernels

		PAK-ST			PAK-SST			PAK-PT		
		ST	SST	PT	ST	SST	PT	ST	SST	PT
INEX 2005	time	2.33	2.29	0.21	2.33	2.31	0.21	14.06	13.86	1.32
	err	0.30	0.30	1.16	0.29	0.28	0.29	0.25	0.25	0.96
INEX 2006	time	2.5	2.42	0.54	2.65	2.44	0.54	6.21	6.04	1.34
	err	1	0.99	1.02	1.01	1	1.03	0.98	0.97	1.01
Propbank	time	2.63	2.63	0.71	2.65	2.65	0.72	5.83	5.82	1.59
	err	1.03	0.98	1.03	1.05	1.01	1.06	1.12	1.06	1.12

the accuracy. The PT kernel improves its accuracy on the validation set, but it does not on the test set. This may be due to the fact that, in order to re-duce the time required for the whole experimentation, we do not reselect the c together with γ. The application of the operator improves the F1 of each of the baseline kernels for the Propbank dataset. Although the worst-case compu-tational complexity of PAK-SST and PAK-PT is the same with respect to the corresponding baselines, we computed the execution time overhead due to the PAK extension. The comparison has been performed with respect to the time (in seconds) required for computing the kernel matrices on a Intel(R) Xeon(R) 2.33GHz processor. All PAK extensions has been implemented as modules of the SVM-Light Software [8]. Table 2 reports the ratio between execution times and the ratio between test errors (F1 in the case of Propbank) of the PAK extensions with respect to the baseline kernels. While a ratio lower than 1 for the execution time or the test error means that the first method is better than the second, in the case of the F1, a ratio higher than 1 means that the first method is better than the second. Notice that the execution time ratios of both PAK-ST/PT and PAK-SST/PT are always lower than 1, thus PAK-ST and PAK-SST are faster, up to 4.76 times (0.21^{-1}), than PT. While being faster, PAK-SST has only slightly worse test error on INEX 2006, with ratio 1.03, and better performances on INEX 2005 and Propbank, (with ratios 0.29 and 1.06, respectively).

6   Conclusion and Future Work

In this paper we proposed a general operator for extending convolution tree kernels with positional features. It has quadratic computational complexity in time and thus does not alter the worst-case complexity of most of state-of-the-art tree kernels. Experimental results show that, when positional information is relevant for a specific task, this extension significantly improves on the baseline kernels. Moreover, less effective tree kernels, if enriched with topological information, may achieve accuracy values comparable to ones of the most effective tree kernels, while being faster to compute. Future works will study the injection of other kinds of relationships which can be defined on substructures and the application of the same operator to other convolution kernels.

References

1. Aiolli, F., Da San Martino, G., Sperduti, A.: Route kernels for trees. In: International Conference on Machine Learning, pp. 17–24 (2009)
2. Collins, M., Duffy, N.: New ranking algorithms for parsing and tagging: Kernels over discrete structures, and the voted perceptron. In: Proceedings of the Fortieth Annual Meeting on Association for Computational Linguistics, Philadelphia, PA, USA, pp. 263–270 (2002)
3. Denoyer, L., Gallinari, P.: Report on the XML mining track at INEX 2005 and INEX 2006: categorization and clustering of XML documents. ACM SIGIR Forum 41(1), 79–90 (2007)
4. Haussler, D.: Convolution kernels on discrete structures. Tech. Rep. UCSC-CRL-99-10, University of California, Santa Cruz (July 1999)
5. Joachims, T.: Making large-scale support vector machine learning practical, pp. 169–184. MIT Press, Cambridge (1999)
6. Kingsbury, P., Palmer, M.: From Treebank to PropBank. In: Proceedings of the 3rd International Conference on Language Resources and Evaluation, Las Palmas, Spain, pp. 1989–1993 (2002)
7. Moschitti, A.: Efficient convolution kernels for dependency and constituent syntactic trees. In: Proceedings of the European Conference on Machine Learning, pp. 318–329 (2006)
8. Moschitti, A.: Making tree kernels practical for natural language learning. In: Proceedings of EACL 2006, Trento, Italy (2006)
9. Trentini, F., Hagenbuchner, M., Sperduti, A., Scarselli, F., Tsoi, A.: A self-organising map approach for clustering of xml documents. In: Proceedings of the WCCI. IEEE Press, Vancouver (2006)
10. Vishwanathan, S., Smola, A.J.: Fast kernels on strings and trees. In: Proceedings of Neural Information Processing Systems 2002, pp. 569–576 (2002)

Accelerating Kernel Neural Gas

Frank-Michael Schleif, Andrej Gisbrecht, and Barbara Hammer

CITEC centre of excellence, Bielefeld University, 33615 Bielefeld, Germany
{fschleif,agisbrec,bhammer}@techfak.uni-bielefeld.de

Abstract. Clustering approaches constitute important methods for unsupervised data analysis. Traditionally, many clustering models focus on spherical or ellipsoidal clusters in Euclidean space. Kernel methods extend these approaches to more complex cluster forms, and they have been recently integrated into several clustering techniques. While leading to very flexible representations, kernel clustering has the drawback of high memory and time complexity due to its dependency on the full Gram matrix and its implicit representation of clusters in terms of feature vectors. In this contribution, we accelerate the kernelized Neural Gas algorithm by incorporating a Nyström approximation scheme and active learning, and we arrive at sparse solutions by integration of a sparsity constraint. We provide experimental results which show that these accelerations do not lead to a deterioration in accuracy while improving time and memory complexity.

1 Introduction

The dramatic growth in data generating applications and measurement techniques has created many high-volume data sets. Most of them are stored digitally and need to be efficiently analyzed to be of use. Clustering methods are very important in this setting and have been extensively studied in the last decades [9]. Challenges are mainly in time and memory efficient and accurate processing of such data with flexible and compact data analysis tools. The Neural Gas vector quantizer [13] (NG) constitutes a very effective prototype based clustering approach with a wide range of applications and extensions [21,10,1,23]. It is well known for its initialization insensitivity, making it a valuable alternative to traditional approaches like k-means. It suffers, however, from its focus on spherical or ellipsoidal clusters such that complex cluster shapes can only be represented based on an approximation with a very large number of spherical clusters. Alternative strategies dealing with more complex data manifolds or novel metric adaptation techniques in clusterings are typically still limited, unable to employ the full potential of a complex modeling [7,2]. The success of kernel methods in supervised learning tasks [20,19] has motivated recent extensions of unsupervised schemes to kernel techniques, see e.g. [22,3,17,5,6].

Kernelized neural gas (KNG) was proposed in [17] as a non-linear, kernelized extention of the Neural Gas vector quantizer. While this approach is quite promising it has been used only rarely due to its calculation complexity which

T. Honkela et al. (Eds.): ICANN 2011, Part I, LNCS 6791, pp. 150–158, 2011.
© Springer-Verlag Berlin Heidelberg 2011

is roughly in $O(N^2)$, with N as the number of points. Drawbacks are given by the storage of a large kernel matrix and the update of a combinatorial coefficient matrix, representing the prototypes implicitly. This makes the approach time and memory consuming already for small data sets.

Modern approaches in discriminative learning try to avoid the direct storage and usage of the full kernel matrix and restrict the underlying optimization problem to subsets thereof, see e.g. [16,20]. For unsupervised kernel methods comparably few work has been done so far to overcome the memory and time complexity for large data sets [12]. For the KNG approach no such strategy has been proposed at all up to our knowledge.

In this contribution, we extend KNG towards a time and memory efficient method incorporating a variety of techniques: The Nyström-Approximation of Gram matrices constitutes a classical approximation scheme [25,11], permitting the estimation of the kernel matrix by means of a low dimensional approximation. Further speedup can be achieved by using the explicit margin information to arrive at an active learning scheme. The high memory requirement which is caused by the implicit representation of prototypes in terms of feature vectors which, unlike for the supervised support vector machine, are usually not sparse, can be dealt with by incorporating sparsity constraints. Sparsity is a natural concept in the encoding of data [15] and can be used to obtain compact models. This concept has already been used in many machine learning methods [10,8] and different measures of sparsity have been proposed [15,8]. We integrate such a sparsity constraint into KNG.

In Section 2 we present a short introduction into kernels and give the notations used throughout the paper. Subsequently we present the KNG algorithm and the approximated variant, accelerated KNG (AKNG) by means of the Nyström approximation, active learning, and the additional sparsity constraint. We show the efficiency of the novel approach by experiments on several data sets. Finally, we conclude with a discussion in Section 4.

2   Preliminaries

We consider vectors $\mathbf{v}_j \in \mathbb{R}^d$, d denoting the dimensionality, n the number of samples. N prototypes $\mathbf{w}_i \in \mathbb{R}^d$ induce a clustering by means of their receptive fields which consist of the points $\mathbf{v}$ for which $d(\mathbf{v}, \mathbf{w_i}) \leq d(\mathbf{v}, \mathbf{w_j})$ holds for all $j \neq i$, d denoting a distance measure, typically the Euclidean distance.

A kernel function $\kappa : \mathbb{R}^d \times \mathbb{R}^d \to \mathbb{R}$ is implicitly induced by a feature mapping $\phi : \mathbb{R}^d \to \mathcal{F}$ into some possibly high dimensional feature space $\mathcal{F}$ such that

$$\kappa\left(\mathbf{v}_1, \mathbf{v}_2\right) = \left\langle \phi\left(\mathbf{v}_1\right), \phi\left(\mathbf{v}_2\right)\right\rangle_{\mathcal{F}} \tag{1}$$

holds for all vectors $\mathbf{v}_1$ and $\mathbf{v}_2$, where the inner product in the feature space is considered. Hence κ is positive semi-definite. Using the linearity in the Hilbert-space, we can express dot products of elements of the linear span of ϕ of the form $\sum_i \alpha_i \phi(\mathbf{v}_i)$ and images $\phi(\mathbf{v})$ via the form $\sum_i \alpha_i \kappa\left(\mathbf{v}_i, \mathbf{v}\right)$. This property is used in [17], to derive a kernelization of Neural Gas.

3   Neural Gas Algorithm

The Neural Gas (NG) algorithm is a type of vector quantizer providing a compact representation of the underlying data distributions [14]. Its goal is to find prototype locations $\mathbf{w}_i$ such that these prototypes represent the data $\mathbf{v}$, distributed according to $\mathcal{P}$, as accurately as possible, minimizing the energy function:

$$E_{NG}(\gamma) = \frac{1}{C(\gamma, K)} \sum_{i=1}^{N} \int \mathcal{P}(\mathbf{v}) \cdot h_\gamma(\mathbf{v}_i, \mathbf{W}) \cdot (\mathbf{v} - \mathbf{w}_i)^2 \, d\mathbf{v} \qquad (2)$$

with neighborhood function of Gaussian shape: $h_\gamma(\mathbf{v}_i, \mathbf{W}) = \exp(-k_i(\mathbf{v}, \mathbf{W})/\gamma)$. $k_i(\mathbf{v}, \mathbf{W})$ yields the number of prototypes $\mathbf{w}_j$ for which the relation $d(\mathbf{v}, \mathbf{w}_j) \leq d(\mathbf{v}, \mathbf{w}_i)$ is valid, i.e. the winner rank. $C(\gamma, K)$ is a normalization constant depending on the neighborhood range γ. The NG learning rule is derived thereof by stochastic gradient descent:

$$\triangle \mathbf{w}_i = \epsilon \cdot h_\gamma(\mathbf{v}_i, \mathbf{W}) \cdot (\mathbf{v} - \mathbf{w}_i) \qquad (3)$$

with learning rate ϵ. Typically, the neighborhood range γ is decreased during training to ensure independence of initialization and optimization of the quantization error. NG is a simple and highly effective algorithm for data clustering.

3.1   Kernelized Neural Gas

We now briefly review the main concepts used in Kernelized Neural Gas (KNG) as given in [17]. KNG optimizes the same cost function as NG but with the Euclidean distance substituted by a distance induced by a kernel. Since the feature space is unknown, prototypes are expressed implicitly as linear combination of feature vectors $\mathbf{w}_i = \sum_{l=1}^{n} \alpha_{i,l} \phi(\mathbf{v}_l)$, $\alpha_i \in \mathbb{R}^n$ is the corresponding coefficient vector. Distance in feature space for $\phi(\mathbf{v}_j)$ and $\mathbf{w}_i$ is computed as:

$$d_{i,j}^2 = \|\phi(\mathbf{v}_j) - \mathbf{w}_i\|^2 = \|\phi(\mathbf{v}_j) - \sum_{l=1}^{n} \alpha_{i,l} \phi(\mathbf{v}_l)\|^2 \qquad (4)$$

$$= k(\mathbf{v}_j, \mathbf{v}_j) - 2 \sum_{l=1}^{n} k(\mathbf{v}_j, \mathbf{v}_l) \cdot \alpha_{i,l} + \sum_{s,t=1}^{n} k(\mathbf{v}_s, \mathbf{v}_t) \cdot \alpha_{i,s} \alpha_{i,t} \qquad (5)$$

The update rules of NG can be modified by substituting the Euclidean distance by the formula (4) and taking derivatives with respect to the coefficients $\alpha_{i,l}$. The detailed equations are available in [17].

3.2   Nyström Approximation of the Kernel Matrix

As pointed out in [25] different strategies have been proposed to overcome the complexity problem caused by the kernel matrix in modern machine learning algorithms. One promising approach is the Nyström approximation.

It originates from the numerical treatment of integral equations of the form $\int \mathcal{P}(y)k(x,y)\phi_i(y)dy = \lambda_i\phi_i(x)$ where $\mathcal{P}(\cdot)$ is the probability density function, k is a positive definite kernel function, and $\lambda_1 \geq \lambda_2 \geq \ldots \geq 0$ and $\phi_1, \phi_2, \ldots$ are the eigenvalues and eigenfunctions of the integral equation. Given a set of i.i.d. samples $\{x_1, \ldots, x_q\}$ drawn from $\mathcal{P}(\cdot)$, the basic idea is to approximate the integral by the empirical average $1/q \sum_{j=1}^q k(x, x_j)\phi_i(x_j) \approx \lambda_i\phi_i(x)$ which can be written as the eigenvalue decomposition: $K\phi = q\lambda\phi$ where $K_{q \times q} = [K_{i,j}] = [k(x_i, x_j)]$ is the kernel matrix defined on X, and $\phi = [\phi_i(x_j)] \in \mathbb{R}^q$. Solving this equation we can calculate $\phi_i(x)$ as $\phi_i(x) \approx 1/(q\lambda) \sum_{j=1}^q k(x, x_j)\phi_i(x_j)$ which is costly. To reduce the complexity, one may use only a subset of the samples which is commonly known as the NyStöm method.

Suppose the sample set $V = \{\mathbf{v}_i\}_{i=1}^n$, with the corresponding $n \times n$ kernel matrix K. We randomly choose a subset $\mathbf{Z} = \{\mathbf{z}_i\}_{i=1}^q$ of landmark points and a corresponding kernel sub matrix $\mathbf{Q}_{q \times q} = [k(\mathbf{z}_i, \mathbf{z}_j)]_{i,j}$. We calculate the eigenvalue decomposition of this sub matrix: $\mathbf{Q}\phi_z = q\lambda_z\phi_z$ and obtain the corresponding eigenvector $\phi_z \in \mathbb{R}^q$ and the eigenvalue $q\lambda_z$. Subsequently we calculate the interpolation matrix $\hat{\mathbf{K}}_{n \times q} = [k(\mathbf{v}_i, \mathbf{z}_j)]_{i,j}$ to extend the result to the whole set V. We approximate the eigen-system of the full $K\phi_K = \phi_K\lambda_K$ by [24]:

$$\phi_K \approx \sqrt{\frac{q}{n}}\hat{\mathbf{K}}\phi_Z\lambda_{\mathbf{Z}}^{-1}, \lambda_K \approx \frac{n}{q}\lambda_{\mathbf{Z}}$$

K can be subsequently reconstructed as

$$K \approx \left(\sqrt{\frac{q}{n}}\hat{\mathbf{K}}\phi_Z\lambda_{\mathbf{Z}}^{-1}\right)\left(\frac{n}{q}\lambda_{\mathbf{Z}}\right)\left(\sqrt{\frac{q}{n}}\hat{\mathbf{K}}\phi_Z\lambda_{\mathbf{Z}}^{-1}\right)' = \hat{\mathbf{K}}\mathbf{Q}^{-1}\hat{\mathbf{K}}'$$

To integrate the Nyström approximation into KNG we only need to modify the distance calculation between a prototype $\mathbf{w}_i$ and a data point $\phi(\mathbf{v}_j)$ accordingly. The original update equation for the coefficient matrix in KNG reads as:

$$\alpha_{j,l}^{t+1} = \begin{cases} [1 - \epsilon \cdot h_\gamma(k_j(\phi(\mathbf{v}_i), \mathbf{W}))] \cdot \alpha_{j,l}^t & \text{if } \mathbf{v}_i \neq \mathbf{v}_l \\ [1 - \epsilon \cdot h_\gamma(k_j(\phi(\mathbf{v}_i), \mathbf{W}))] \cdot \alpha_{j,l}^t + \epsilon \cdot h_\gamma(k_j(\phi(\mathbf{v}_i), \mathbf{W})) & \text{if } \mathbf{v}_i = \mathbf{v}_l \end{cases}$$

with $t+1$ indicating the time step and $\mathbf{w}_k \in \mathbf{W}$ defined as in Eq. 4. The distance calculation using the Nyström approximation is done as follows: (6):

$$d_{\cdot,j} = K(j,j) - 2 \cdot T_{\cdot,j} + \text{diag}(\psi \cdot T') \tag{6}$$
$$\text{with } T_{i,\cdot} = ((\alpha_i \cdot \hat{\mathbf{K}}) \cdot \mathbf{Q}^{-1}) \cdot \hat{\mathbf{K}}' \tag{7}$$

where diag provides the main diagonal elements of the associated matrix. With Nyström-approximation the complexity is reduced to $O(q^2N)$ [24].

3.3 Sparse Coefficient Matrix

In [15] sparsity has been found to be a natural concept in the visual cortex of mammals. This work motivated the integration of sparsity concepts into many

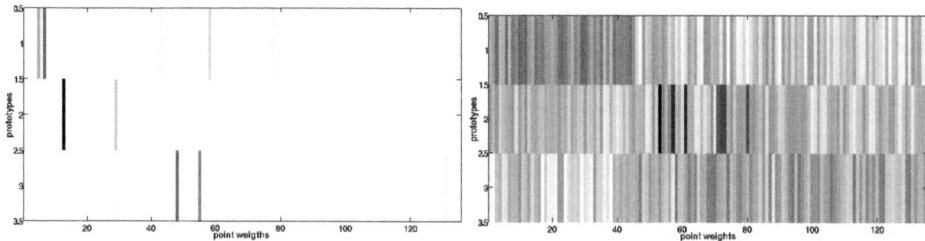

Fig. 1. Effect of the sparsity constraint for DS2 shown by means of the γ-matrix (normalized for better comparison) showing point weights (x-axis) for each prototype (y-axis). With sparsity left and without right. Dark values (1) indicated high loaded or high lighted data points for the considered prototype in the γ matrix. Data points with very low values (0) over all prototypes can be safely removed from the model.

machine learning methods to obtain sparse but efficient models. Here we will integrate sparsity as an additional constraint on the coefficient matrix α such that the amount of non-zero coefficients is limited. This leads to a compact description of the prototypes by means of sparse linear mixture models. We use the sparsity measure given in [15]. The sparsity $\mathbb{S}$ of a row of α is measured as

$$\mathbb{S}(\alpha_i) = -\sum_l S\left(\frac{\alpha_{i,l}}{\sigma}\right) \tag{8}$$

with σ as a scaling constant. The function S can be of different type, here we use $S(x) = \log(1 + x^2)$. We change the energy function of the KNG as follows

$$E_{KNG}(\gamma) = \frac{1}{C(\gamma, K)} \sum_{i=1}^{N} \int \mathcal{P}\left(\phi(\mathbf{v}) \cdot h_\gamma\left(\phi(\mathbf{v}_i), \mathbf{W}\right) \cdot \|\phi(\mathbf{v}) - \mathbf{w}_i\|^2 \, d\phi(\mathbf{v})\right.$$
$$-\beta \cdot \mathbb{S}(\alpha_i)$$

The updates for the coefficients of $\mathbf{w}_i$ are exactly the same as for the standard KNG using the Nyström formula to approximate the Gram matrix and including the additional term caused by the sparsity constrained

$$\frac{\partial \mathbb{S}}{\partial \alpha_{i,l}} = -\frac{2/\sigma^2 \cdot \alpha_{i,l}}{1 + (\alpha_{i,l}/\sigma)^2}$$

In addition, we enforce the constrained $\alpha_{i,l} \in [0,1]$ and $\sum_l \alpha_{i,l} = 1$ for better interpretability. The effect of the sparsity constraint on the UCI iris data is shown in Figure 3.3 with 1 prototype per class. The sparse model has an accuracy of $\approx 90\%$ whereas the original solution achieves only 86%.

3.4   Active Learning

The sparse coefficients α give rise to an active learning scheme in a similar manner as proposed in [18], leading to faster learning. The matrix α encodes

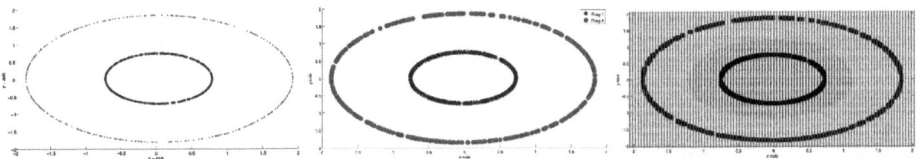

Fig. 2. Ring data set (left), post-labeled KGLVQ model (middle), the outer ring is red ('o'), the inner ring is blue ($\star$). The plot on the right shows the cluster boundaries of the model from the middle plot. The model was calculated without sparsity. It can be clearly seen that the A-KNG with an rbf kernel sucessfully separated these two clusters, with good cluster boundaries and a large margin between the two rings.

a weighting of the data-points. We take the column-wise mean of α as $\bar{\alpha}$ and calculate a threshold δ for each data-point indicating its relative importance for the learning. The average weight for a data-point in α is given as $\delta^* = \alpha_{i,j} = 1/N$, due to the normalization constraint. Weights close to this point are not sufficiently learned, such that they have not been deleted or emphasized so far. We transfer these weights to a skip probability for each data-point using:

$$\delta = 1/2 \cdot \exp\left(-\frac{(\bar{\alpha}_j - \delta^*)^2}{(2 \cdot std(\bar{\alpha})^2)}\right) \quad \text{with std - as the standard deviation} \quad (9)$$

This denotes the probability of the data-point to be skipped during learning. It should be noted, that at the beginning of the learning α is initialized randomly such that the probability of a data-point to be skipped is random; during learning only those points are likely to be skipped which are either not or most relevant for the model. In this line we roughly learn the model by considering an ϵ-tube around the cluster centers. However, by taking the probability concept *all* points are taken into account albeit with probably small probability.

4   Experiments

As a proof of concept, we start with a toy data set (DS1) and an RBF kernel. The data consist of 800 data points with 400 per ring in 2 dimensions (x/y) as shown in Figure 2. The first ring has a radius of $r = 10$ and the second $r = 4$, points are randomly sampled in $[0, 2\pi]$. The data set has been normalized in $N(0, 1)$. We also analyzed the ring data using the additional sparsity constraint. In the original model 53% of the weights, averaged over the prototypes are almost 0 (values $\leq 1e - 5$). In the sparsity approach we used σ^2 as the variance of the data scaled by 0.01 and $\beta = 1$ and obtained a model with about 75% of the points close to zero.

Following the work given in [12] we analyze several UCI benchmarks. We consider the well known iris data set (DS2), the Wisconsin Breast cancer data (WBC) (DS3), the Spam database (DS4), and Pima diabetes (DS5). Details about the data can be found in [4]. DS2 consists of 150 instances in three groups and is known to be almost linear separable by two hyperplanes. DS3 consists of

Table 1. Post labeled accuracy vs. runtime over 10 runs. For AK-NG and K-NG 10 cycles are calculated, each. Best results in bold, *-ed results are taken from [12].

Algorithm	Iris data	WBC	Spam	Pima diabetes
NG	91.7%/n.a.*	96.1%/n.a.*	68.4%/n.a. *	70.31%/7s
K-NG	90.0%/2.6s	91.7%/5.77s	**86.5%/350s**	71.74%/21s
AK-NG	92.6%/**0.14s**	92.1%/**0.73s**	84.42%/**2.9s**	**73.05%/0.94s**
K-Grower	**94.7%**/12.95s*	**97.0%**/807.17s*	81.3%/ $\gg$ 1000s*	n.a.
SUK-Grower	93.4%/47.95s*	96.8%/22.85s*	80.2%/44.83s*	n.a.

683 items. For this dataset non-linear supervised learning methods have been found to be very effective whereas linear approaches are not so effective. This motivates the assumption that kernelization might prove beneficial. The data set DS4 contains 1534 samples, and classification is difficult. The fifth data set (DS5) contains 768 samples. For each data set we used one prototype per expected group. The results are shown in Table 1.

All results are obtained using 10 cycles with a Nyström approximation of $1-10\%$ of the original kernel matrix, $\beta \in [0.001, 10]$, and the sparsity $\sigma \in [1, 100]$ determined on an independent test set. The value of the Nyström approximation is not very critical for the accuracy and mainly influences the runtime performance, whereas a too sparse solution can lead to a decrease in accuracy. Dataset D2,D3, and D5 are analyzed using an RBF kernel with a $\sigma^2 = \{1, 0.01, 0.1\}$ respectively, for DS4 we used a linear kernel. The other experimental settings have been chosen in accordance to [12] for compatibility. We also report two alternative state of the art clustering methods by means of core sets provided in [12], referred to as K-Grower and SUK-Grower. Analyzing the results given in Table 1 the AK-NG is significantly faster in calculating the clustering models than all other approaches with the same or only slightly less accuracy. Analyzing the optimizations separately for $DS3 - DS5$ we find: sparsity leads to a reduced memory consumption of $\approx 25\%(DS3), \approx 30\%(DS4)$ and $\approx 41\%(DS5)$ with respect to the unoptimized approach; Nyström approximation leads to a speedup of $\approx 1.6(DS3)$, $\approx 6.8(DS4)$ and $\approx 2(DS5)$ and the active learning strategy behaves similar. The effect of these optimizations has almost no effect on the accuracy, giving appropriate parameters as pointed out before.

5   Conclusions

In this paper we proposed an extension of kernelized neural gas with a significantly reduced model complexity and time complexity by incorporating the Nyström approximation and a sparsity constraint. We compared the efficiency of our approach with alternative state of the art clusterings with respect to clustering accuracy as well as efficiency. We found the AK-NG is similarly effective and significantly faster with respect to the considered approaches. So far, we tested the algorithm on UCI benchmarks, its application to real life very large data sets being the subject of ongoing work.

Acknowledgment. This work has been supported by the German Res. Found. (DFG), HA2719/4-1 (Relevance Learning for Temporal Neural Maps) and in the frame of the centre of excellence 'Cognitive Interaction Technologies'.

References

1. Ardizzone, E., Chella, A., Rizzo, R.: Color image segmentation based on a neural gas network. In: Marinaro, M., Morasso, P.G. (eds.) Proc. ICANN 1994, Int. Conf. on Artif. Neural Netw. vol. II, pp. 1161–1164. Springer, London (1994)
2. Arnonkijpanich, B., Hasenfuss, A., Hammer, B.: Local matrix adaptation in topographic neural maps. Neurocomputing 74(4), 522–539 (2011)
3. Ben-Hur, A., Horn, D., Siegelmann, H., Vapnik, V.: Support vector clustering. Journal of Machine Learning Research 2, 125–137 (2001)
4. Blake, C., Merz, C.: UCI repository of machine learning databases. Irvine, CA: University of California, Department of Information and Computer Science (1998), http://www.ics.uci.edu/mlearn/MLRepository.html
5. Filippone, M., Camastra, F., Massulli, F., Rovetta, S.: A survey of kernel and spectral methods for clustering. Pattern Recognition 41, 176–190 (2008)
6. Hammer, B., Hasenfuss, A.: Topographic mapping of large dissimilarity datasets. Neural Computation 22(9), 2229–2284 (2010)
7. Hastie, T., Tibshirani, R., Friedman, J.: The Elements of Statistical Learning. Springer, New York (2001)
8. Hoyer, P.: Non-negative Matrix Factorization with sparseness constraints. Journal of Machine Learning Research 5, 1457–1469 (2004)
9. Jain, A.K.: Data clustering: 50 years beyond K-means. PatRecL 31, 651–666 (2010)
10. Labusch, K., Barth, E., Martinetz, T.: Learning data representations with sparse coding neural gas. In: Verleysen, M. (ed.) Proceedings of the European Symposium on Artificial Neural Networks ESANN, pp. 233–238. d-side publications (2008)
11. Li, M., Kwok, J., Lu, B.L.: Making large-scale nyström approximation possible. In: Proc. of the Int. Conf. on Mach. Learn. (ICML) 2010 (2009)
12. Liang, C., Xiao-Ming, D., Sui-Wu, Z., Yong-Qing, W.: Scaling up kernel grower clustering method for large data sets via core-sets. Acta Automatica Sinica 34(3), 376–382 (2008)
13. Martinetz, T., Schulten, K.: A "Neural-Gas" network learns topologies. In: Kohonen, T., Mäkisara, K., Simula, O., Kangas, J. (eds.) Proc. International Conference on Artificial Neural Networks, Espoo, Finland, vol. I, pp. 397–402. North-Holland, Amsterdam (1991)
14. Martinetz, T.M., Berkovich, S.G., Schulten, K.J.: 'Neural-gas' network for vector quantization and its application to time-series prediction. IEEE Trans. on Neural Networks 4(4), 558–569 (1993)
15. Olshausen, B., Field, D.: Emergence of simple-cell receptive field properties by learning a sparse code for natural images. Letters to Nature 381, 607–609 (1996)
16. Platt, J.C.: Fast training of support vector machines using sequential minimal optimization, pp. 185–208. MIT Press, Cambridge (1999)
17. Qin, A.K., Suganthan, P.N.: A novel kernel prototype-based learning algorithm. In: Proc. of ICPR 2004, pp. 2621–2624 (2004)
18. Schleif, F.M., Hammer, B., Villmann, T.: Margin based active learning for lvq networks. Neurocomputing 70(7-9), 1215–1224 (2007)
19. Schlkopf, B., Smola, A.: Learning with Kernels. MIT Press, Washington (2002)

20. Shawe-Taylor, J., Cristianini, N.: Kernel Methods for Pattern Analysis and Discovery. Cambridge University Press, Cambridge (2004)
21. Strickert, M., Hammer, B.: Neural gas for sequences. In: Proc. International Workshop on Self-Organizing Maps (WSOM 2003), pp. 53–58. Kitakyushu (2003)
22. Tsang, I., Kwok, J.: Distance metric learning with kernels. In: Kaynak, O., Alpaydın, E., Oja, E., Xu, L. (eds.) ICANN 2003 and ICONIP 2003. LNCS, vol. 2714, pp. 126–129. Springer, Heidelberg (2003)
23. Walter, J.A., Martinetz, T.M., Schulten, K.J.: Industrial robot learns visuo-motor coordination by means of 'neural gas' network. In: Kohonen, T., Mäkisara, K., Simula, O., Kangas, J. (eds.) Artificial Neural Networks, vol. I, pp. 357–364. North-Holland, Amsterdam (1991)
24. Williams, C., Seeger, M.: Using the nystroem method to speed up kernel machines. Advances in Neural Information Processing Systems 13, 682–688 (2001)
25. Zhang, K., Tsang, I., Kwok, J.: Improved nyström low-rank approximation and error analysis o. In: Proc. of the Int. Conf. on Mach. Learn. (ICML 2010) (2009)

State Prediction: A Constructive Method to Program Recurrent Neural Networks

René Felix Reinhart and Jochen Jakob Steil

Research Institute for Cognition and Robotics (CoR-Lab) & Faculty of Technology
Bielefeld University, Universitätsstr. 25, 33615 Bielefeld, Germany
{freinhar,jsteil}@cor-lab.uni-bielefeld.de
http://www.cor-lab.de

Abstract. We introduce a novel technique to program desired state sequences into recurrent neural networks in one shot. The basic methodology and its scalability to large and input-driven networks is demonstrated by shaping attractor landscapes, transient dynamics and programming limit cycles. The approach unifies programming of transient and attractor dynamics in a generic framework.

Keywords: recurrent neural networks, input-driven dynamics, learning.

1 Introduction

It is a long outstanding question how to determine parameters of dynamical systems that shall display desired behaviors. Traditionally, data-driven parameter estimation for recurrent neural networks (RNNs) has been approached in one of the following contexts: (i) learning of associative memory networks mostly based on correlation matrices, or (ii) learning of general RNNs for approximation of input-output mappings by temporal generalizations of supervised backpropagation learning. Learning in the latter case is based on gradient descent with respect to some error criterion, which suffers from high computational load, bifurcations of the network dynamics during learning, and the typical gradient descent problems like vanishing gradients, local minima, etc. Research in this direction was widely concerned with minimizing the computational load and accelerating convergence of the gradient descent [1], but these efforts can not free learning by gradient descent in recurrent settings from its serious drawbacks.

One-shot learning of RNNs, like it is traditionally applied in the context of associative memory networks [2], is therefore attractive. However, attractor and sequence learning are strictly separated in these networks and learning does not easily generalize to input-driven settings. The combination of both one-shot learning of input-driven RNNs and shaping of transients in addition to desired attractor dynamics has not yet been accomplished.

We introduce a generic paradigm to program RNNs efficiently in one shot that applies to a wide range of neural network architectures. Based on the idea to program the state transitions of an observed system into a parameterized model, learning can be formulated as a simple regression problem and can be

T. Honkela et al. (Eds.): ICANN 2011, Part I, LNCS 6791, pp. 159–166, 2011.

accomplished efficiently in one shot without descending a gradient. This *state prediction* approach is applicable whenever state transitions can be formulated as linear system of equations with respect to the model parameters. Together with a trajectory-based sampling strategy, the method unifies programming of transient as well as attractor dynamics in a generic formulation. The combination of sampling desired sequences and one-shot learning solves three problems: First, bifurcations during learning are prevented. Second, shaping of transient and attractor behavior is unified, and third, linear regression is efficient to compute, yields the best parameter estimates with minimal norm and scales to complex network configurations. State prediction is related to the recently introduced regularization approach for input-driven RNNs [3], [4] and the approach taken by Jaeger in [5] to program the functionality of an external controller into a reservoir network. We present the principle of this previous work in a coherent framework for one-shot learning of input-driven RNNs.

2   State Prediction: A Constructive Approach

Consider a system with state $\mathbf{s}(k) \in \mathbb{R}^N$ at time step k that unfolds in time according to a mapping $\Phi : \mathbf{s}(k), \mathbf{u}(k) \mapsto \mathbf{s}(k+1)$, where $\mathbf{u}(k)$ are additional input signals. Assume one can sample typical flows $\{(\mathbf{s}_i(k), \mathbf{u}_i(k))\}_i$ of the system, where $k = 1, \dots, K_i$ for the i-th sequence. We model the observed system with the input-driven recurrent network dynamics

$$\mathbf{s}(k+1) = \sigma(\tilde{\mathbf{W}}\tilde{\mathbf{s}}(k)), \tag{1}$$

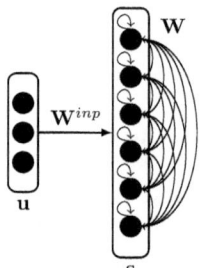

where σ is a nonlinear activation function, $\tilde{\mathbf{s}}(k) = (\mathbf{s}(k)^T, \mathbf{u}(k)^T, 1)^T$ is the combined input and system state, and $\tilde{\mathbf{W}} = (\mathbf{W}^T \ \mathbf{W}^{inpT} \ \mathbf{b})^T$ are the model parameters. The model is illustrated in Fig. 1. Typically, learning is approached by minimizing the error $E = 1/K \sum_k ||\mathbf{s}^*(k) - \mathbf{s}(k)||^2$, where the model parameters $\tilde{\mathbf{W}}$ are adapted in order to bring the sequence $\mathbf{s}(k)$ closer to the target sequence $\mathbf{s}^*(k)$. This error-based approach leads to recursive dependencies of the states on the weights, i.e. $\frac{\partial E(k)}{\partial w_{ij}} = -(s_i^*(k) - s_i(k))s_j(k-1)\sigma'(k)\frac{\partial s_i(k-1)}{\partial w_{ij}}$. In

Fig. 1. Input-driven recurrent neural network

contrast to the separation of the model dynamics and the target dynamics, the basic idea of *state prediction* is to find parameters $\tilde{\mathbf{W}}$ that explain the transitions between successive states $\mathbf{s}^*(k)$ and $\mathbf{s}^*(k+1)$ best, i.e. minimize

$$||\mathbf{s}^*(k+1) - \sigma(\tilde{\mathbf{W}}\tilde{\mathbf{s}}^*(k))|| \qquad \text{for } k = 1, \dots, K, \tag{2}$$

where $\tilde{\mathbf{s}}^*(t) = (\mathbf{s}^*(t)^T, \mathbf{u}(t)^T, 1)^T$. This formulation directly incorporates the sampled system transitions $\mathbf{s}^*(k), \mathbf{u}(k) \to \mathbf{s}^*(k+1)$ for parameter estimation which can be understood as state prediction parameterized by the input $\mathbf{u}(k)$.

The prediction is based on the observed state $\mathbf{s}^*(k)$, not on the dynamics of a partially trained model, which enables the constructive modeling of the sequence $\mathbf{s}^*(k)$ for $k = 1, \ldots, K$. To prevent the nonlinear activation function σ from cluttering the optimization of the model parameters $\tilde{\mathbf{W}}$, we rephrase the *state prediction problem* (2) as a linear system $\mathbf{a}^*(k+1) \equiv \sigma^{-1}(\mathbf{s}^*(k+1)) = \tilde{\mathbf{W}}\tilde{\mathbf{s}}^*(k)$. This linearization is possible if (i) σ is invertible and (ii) the observed data is transformed into the output range of σ. Condition (i) is fulfilled by all common sigmoidal activation functions like $tanh$, $atan$ or the logistic function. The second condition can be fulfilled without restriction for all bounded sequences. Collecting all R sampled trajectories in a matrix $\tilde{\mathbf{S}}^* = (\tilde{\mathbf{s}}_1^*(1), \ldots, \tilde{\mathbf{s}}_1^*(K_1{-}1), \ldots, \tilde{\mathbf{s}}_R^*(1), \ldots, \tilde{\mathbf{s}}_R^*(K_R{-}1))^T$, and the corresponding targets in $\mathbf{A}^* = \sigma^{-1}(\mathbf{s}_1^*(2), \ldots, \mathbf{s}_1^*(K_1), \ldots, \mathbf{s}_R^*(2), \ldots, \mathbf{s}_R^*(K_R))^T$, the optimal solution to the state prediction problem $||\mathbf{A}^* - \tilde{\mathbf{S}}\tilde{\mathbf{W}}^T||$ is $\tilde{\mathbf{W}}_{opt}^T = \left(\tilde{\mathbf{S}}^{*T}\tilde{\mathbf{S}}^* + \alpha\mathbb{1}\right)^{-1}\tilde{\mathbf{S}}^{*T}\mathbf{A}^*$, where α weights the contribution of a regularization constraint corresponding to a Gaussian prior distribution for the model parameters.

2.1 Sampling Dynamics for State Prediction

Programming dynamics by state prediction can be understood as a three-staged process: Observation of the desired system yields a data corpus which is used in a second step to determine the model parameters by solving the state prediction problem (2) by means of $\tilde{\mathbf{W}}_{opt}^T$. Then, the programmed model dynamics can be queried. One can substitute the first stage by synthesizing training data that represent the desired behavior. Observation of the desired dynamics is a key step and there are three basic ways how to sample dynamics for state prediction:

Sampling Velocities: Spatial sampling of states $\mathbf{s}$ with corresponding velocities $\mathbf{v}(\mathbf{s})$ of the system at that particular point in state space is one way to acquire training data. Simple integration yields the required pair of successive states $\mathbf{s}(k)$ and $\mathbf{s}(k{+}1) = \mathbf{s}(k){+}\mathbf{v}(\mathbf{s}(k))$. State transitions $\mathbf{s}(k) \to \mathbf{s}(k{+}1)$ can also be observed directly. Sampling velocities or state transitions means to observe the system dynamics stepwise for selected states and inputs. This approach elucidates the need for generalization: The programmed model has to operate also in areas of the state space where no training examples are present. A local modeling approach is hopeless because extrapolation is impossible. The network (1) models state transitions globally and thus can generalize the system behavior to novel states. However, sampling has to be done carefully, i.e. all important regions of the state space have to be included and the number of samples in each region should be sufficiently balanced. This is difficult for high-dimensional systems and therefore restricted sampling can be advantageous.

Sampling Attractor Conditions: Focussing on the target of implementing a specific behavior leads to the idea of sampling only particular conditions. For instance, attractor conditions can be easily formulated in terms of state prediction using that $\mathbf{s}(k{+}1) = \mathbf{s}(k)$ if $\mathbf{s}$ is an attractor state. This approach is typically applied to imprint memories into associative networks. Though conceptually curing the problem of sampling from the entire velocity field, there is a serious drawback: The differential equation is only sampled at special points in state space with zero velocity. Surrounding states $\mathbf{s} + \epsilon$ might not be attracted, i.e. the basin of attraction is too narrow and leaves space for spurious states.

Sampling Flows: A conceptually and practically appealing way of sampling dynamics is a trajectory-based approach. Simply record representative flows of the system. Recording or synthesizing exemplary state sequences (or a combination of both) solves the previous problems by collecting state transitions only at relevant regions of the state space while preventing degenerated sampling. In addition, learning from trajectories is biologically much more plausible. We demonstrate sampling of velocities and sampling of flows in the next sections.

3   Programming the Dynamics of a Single Neuron

We start with the minimal possible scenario and program the dynamics of a single neuron with $\sigma \equiv tanh$ and apply the sampling of velocities approach. We use no bias or inputs such that (1) has only one parameter w. The dynamics of the neuron can be *unistable*, i.e. a single globally and asymptotically stable fixed-point exists, or *bistable*, i.e. two fixed-points are separated by a saddle [8].

We create training data by sampling states s and their respective velocities $v(s)$ from a potential field $P(s) = -0.1 \sum_{i=1}^{2} (5(p_i - s)^2 + 1)^{-1}$ with two "charges" located in state space at p_1 and p_2. We move p_1 and $p_2 = -p_1$ from zero (potential field with a unique basin) to 0.7 (two detached basins) and train for each potential field a network model. We conduct the state prediction by modeling $s^* + v(s^*) = tanh(ws^*)$, where $v(s^*) = -\frac{\partial}{\partial s}P(s^*)$ are the respective velocities. We sample states and velocities near to the charges p_1 and p_2, and use $\alpha = 0$ for training.

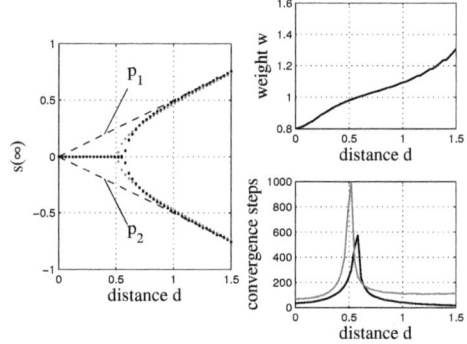

Fig. 2. Bifurcation of dynamics depending on the distance d of the potentials in the training data. Programmed network (black) and analytic dynamics (gray).

Fig. 2 (left) shows the attractor states $\bar{s} = s(\infty)$ of the programmed networks (black) and the potential field dynamics (gray) for different initial conditions as function of the distance $d = |p_1 - p_2|$ between the two charges. Note that the discrete dynamics given by $s(k+1) = s(k) + v(s(k))$ as well as the programmed network dynamics bifurcate at $d \approx 0.5$. The bifurcation introduces a saddle, i.e. is a saddle-node bifurcation, which explains the peak number of steps until convergence shown in Fig. 2 (bottom right). When both charges are separated further, this effect vanishes and the number of iterations until convergence decreases again. The weight of the programmed system is shown in Fig. 2 (top right) and also displays the point of bifurcation: When the weight surpasses unity, global asymptotic stability of the linearized system is not guaranteed anymore.

4   Programming Two Neuron Circuits

In this section, we focus on two neuron circuits without inputs and show that a variety of behaviors can be programmed into such circuits by simply providing some example sequences, i.e. sampling flows. The sequences are generated synthetically by a simple strategy: For each fixed-point attractor $\bar{\mathbf{s}}^*$, we select random perturbations $\epsilon_i \in \mathbb{R}^N$ and generate sequences by setting $\mathbf{s}_i^*(k) = \bar{\mathbf{s}}^* + (1 - k/K_i)^2 \epsilon_i$ with $k = 0, \ldots, K_i$. For each fixed-point, we typically use $K_i = 20$ for $i = 1, \ldots, 50$ and chose perturbations ϵ_i uniformly distributed in $[-0.2, 0.2]^2$. The neurons have $\sigma \equiv tanh$ and we use $\alpha = 0$ for training.

Table 1 shows various mappings from target sequences (2nd col.) to programmed dynamics (3rd col.). The network parameters are given in the forth column. For fixed-point attractors, the desired attractor positions (red dots) and the actual attractors of the programmed networks (green circles) show that the fixed-point conditions are accurately implemented by the networks. Generally, a few example sequences or even single sequences suffice to implement the desired behavior (see rows 4 and 5 in Table 1). Note that the training data does not only shape the dynamics in the limit case $k \to \infty$, i.e. the location of the attractor, but also the transient behavior as can be seen in case of the spiral pattern in the forth row of Table 1. In the second row of Table 1 we used $s_{i2}^*(k) = \bar{s}_2^* + (1 - k/K_i)^4 \epsilon_{i2}$ for training data generation. The trained network displays the changed speed of convergence along the second dimension. State prediction shapes both the transient dynamics and the behavior in the limit case, which is fundamentally different from learning of associative memories where auto- and temporal hetero-association are strictly separated.

We observe that all unistable systems have a spectral radius λ, the maximal absolute eigenvalue of $\mathbf{W}$, below unity. Bistability and cyclic attractors are indicated by spectral radii greater or close to unity. Note, however, that a spectral radius greater unity does not strictly imply loss of global stability if $\mathbf{b} \neq \mathbf{0}$.

5   Programming Input-Driven Network Dynamics

In a next step, we program the dynamics of an input-driven RNN that comprises a single input neuron and two internal neurons similar to the network structure shown in Fig. 1. We use the same parameters and generate training data as in Section 4, but this time we hide a sigmoidal structure in the training data which is only implicitly represented by the one dimensional network input u (see Fig. 3 (left)). The phase portraits of the trained network with exemplary flows are shown in Fig. 3 for input signals $u = 0$ (2nd col.) and $u = 0.2$ (3rd col.). The flows and velocities reveal that the network has a unique fixed-point for each input. Fig. 3 (right) shows the attractor states of the network for a fine-grained sampling of inputs in range $[0, 1]$. The sigmoidal structure is captured well by the parameterized network dynamics. In [3], [4], [5], the functioning of the state prediction approach is confirmed for large networks with multivariate and time-varying inputs.

Table 1. Programming networks with two neurons. The second column shows the training data and the third column shows the resulting phase portrait of the programmed network dynamics with exemplary flows. The desired fixed-point attractors are displayed by red dots and the actual attractors of the trained networks are shown as green circles. The forth column gives the actual network parameters and the spectral radius λ of the recurrent weights $\mathbf{W}$. We present rounded values for the network parameters which nonetheless describe very similar dynamics.

Description	Training Data	Phase Portrait	Parameters
Single fixed-point attractor			$\mathbf{W} = \begin{pmatrix} 0.8 & 0 \\ 0 & 0.84 \end{pmatrix}$ $\mathbf{b} = \begin{pmatrix} -0.05 \\ 0.06 \end{pmatrix}$ $\lambda = 0.84$
Single fixed-point attractor with modulated transients			$\mathbf{W} = \begin{pmatrix} 0.96 & 0 \\ 0 & 0.88 \end{pmatrix}$ $\mathbf{b} = \begin{pmatrix} -0.01 \\ 0.04 \end{pmatrix}$ $\lambda = 0.96$
Two fixed-point attractors			$\mathbf{W} = \begin{pmatrix} 1.04 & -0.01 \\ -0.04 & 0.94 \end{pmatrix}$ $\mathbf{b} = \begin{pmatrix} 0.005 \\ 0.002 \end{pmatrix}$ $\lambda = 1.05$
Single fixed-point attractor with spiral transients			$\mathbf{W} = \begin{pmatrix} 0.99 & 0.03 \\ -0.03 & 0.99 \end{pmatrix}$ $\mathbf{b} = \begin{pmatrix} 0 \\ 0 \end{pmatrix}$ $\lambda = 0.99$
Limit cycle			$\mathbf{W} = \begin{pmatrix} 1.02 & 0.03 \\ -0.03 & 1.02 \end{pmatrix}$ $\mathbf{b} = \begin{pmatrix} 0 \\ 0 \end{pmatrix}$ $\lambda = 1.02$

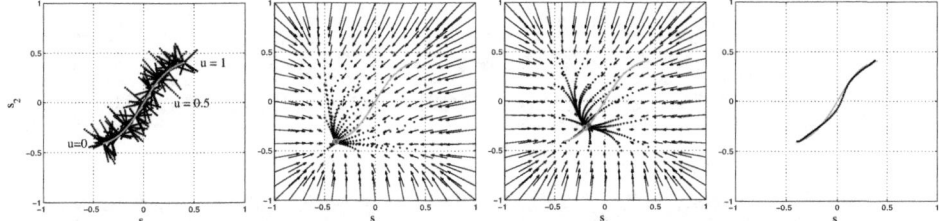

Fig. 3. Parameterized network dynamics programmed from training data (left). Phase portraits with flows for $u=0$ (2nd col.) and $u=0.2$ (3rd col.). The attractor states for $u \in \{0, 0.01, \ldots, 1\}$ approximate the shape present in the training data (right).

6   Storing Sequences in a Large Network

In this section, we demonstrate the scalability of the approach to recall long and high-dimensional sequences. We program a network with 784 neurons to recall two sequences of digit images taken from the MNIST database [6] (see Fig. 4 rows 1 and 5). In training, we present $\mathbf{s}^1(1) \equiv \mathbf{s}^1(11)$ and $\mathbf{s}^2(1) \equiv \mathbf{s}^2(11)$ to close the respective sequence loop. We scale the images into the range $[0.01, 0.99]^{784}$ and use $\sigma(a) = 1/(1 + exp(-a))$ as activation function and $\alpha = 0.1$ for training.

The second and sixth row in Fig. 4 show the generated state sequences of the trained network, where we initialized the network state with the first pattern of the respective sequence and then let it run freely. Note that the sequences are stably reproduced for hundreds of time steps which is confirmed by the instantaneous error plots in rows 4 and 8. Also, when the network is initialized with strongly corrupted states, the network is attracted to the trained limit cycles (see rows 3 and 7 in Fig. 4). This example shows that – in contrast to correlation-based learning of associative memory networks [2] – one-shot storage and robust recall of long sequences is possible with the state prediction approach.

7   Conclusion

At the advent of dynamical approaches to cognition (see [7] for instance), a lot of attention was directed to the qualitative behavior of RNNs. The main goal was to understand their dynamics, for instance by building up equivalence classes of dynamics and bifurcation manifolds [8], [9], and then construct networks with desired dynamics on demand. This approach is tightly bound to the analytic analysis of dynamical systems, which, unfortunately, is not feasible even for small networks and consequently restricts network construction. The state prediction paradigm in contrast is not restricted to small networks or by architectural assumptions like only piecewise constant inputs. The state prediction approach to program observed dynamics into a parameterized network model circumvents descending a gradient, is efficient to compute, and enables the one-shot construction of dynamical systems. Shaping of transient and attractor dynamics is unified by the state prediction paradigm in a generic framework.

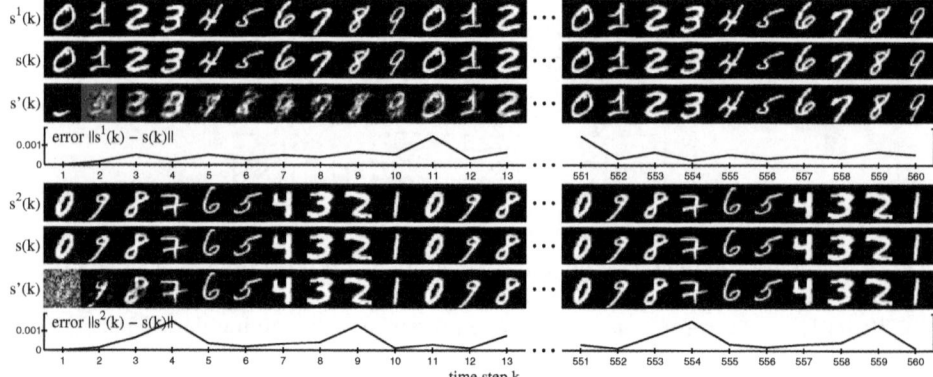

Fig. 4. Sequence generation. The 1st and 5th row show the target sequences $\mathbf{s}^1(k)$ and $\mathbf{s}^2(k)$. The 2nd and 6th row show the generated sequences, where $\mathbf{s}(1) = \mathbf{s}^1(1)$ and $\mathbf{s}(1) = \mathbf{s}^2(1)$, respectively. The corresponding instantaneous error is plotted in the 4th and 8th row. The 3rd and 7th row show the robustness against perturbations: The sequences are still recalled when occluding 75% of the initial state or adding noise.

Future work includes the theoretic analysis of the range of dynamics that can be implemented by state prediction. A necessary condition for successful learning is that the desired dynamics belong to the class of dynamics the network model spans. In addition, the sampled observations have to resemble the relevant dynamic behavior sufficiently well. In a next step, state prediction can be applied to networks with hidden representations: Features can be improved iteratively with respect to some criterion and then be programmed by state prediction.

References

1. Atiya, A.F., Parlos, A.G.: New Results on Recurrent Network Training. IEEE Trans. Neural Networks 11, 697–709 (2000)
2. Hopfield, J.J.: Neural Networks and Physical Systems with Emergent Collective Computational Abilities. Proc. Natl. Acad. Sci. USA 79, 2554–2558 (1982)
3. Reinhart, R.F., Steil, J.J.: A Constrained Regularization Approach for Input-Driven Recurrent Neural Networks. Differ. Equ. Dyn. Syst., 1–20 (2010)
4. Reinhart, R.F., Steil, J.J.: Reservoir Regularization Stabilizes Learning of Echo State Networks with Output Feedback. In: European Symp. on ANNs (2011)
5. Jaeger, H.: Reservoir Self-Control for Achieving Invariance Against Slow Input Distortions. Technical report, Jacobs University (2010)
6. Lecun, Y., Cortes, C., http://yann.lecun.com/exdb/mnist/
7. Beer, R.D.: Dynamical Approaches to Cognitive Science. Trends in Cognitive Sciences 4, 91–99 (2000)
8. Beer, R.D.: On the Dynamics of Small Continuous-Time Recurrent Neural Networks. Adaptive Behavior 3, 469–509 (1995)
9. Haschke, R., Steil, J.J.: Input Space Bifurcation Manifolds of Recurrent Neural Networks. Neurocomputing 64, 25–38 (2005)

Cluster Self-organization of Known and Unknown Environmental Sounds Using Recurrent Neural Network

Yang Zhang, Shun Nishide, Toru Takahashi,
Hiroshi G. Okuno, and Tetsuya Ogata

Graduate School of Informatics, Kyoto University,
Sakyo, Kyoto 606-8501, Japan

Abstract. Our goal is to develop a system that is able to learn and classify environmental sounds for robots working in the real world. In the real world, two main restrictions pertain in learning. First, the system has to learn using only a small amount of data in a limited time because of hardware restrictions. Second, it has to adapt to unknown data since it is virtually impossible to collect samples of all environmental sounds. We used a neuro-dynamical model to build a prediction and classification system which can self-organize sound classes into parameters by learning samples. The proposed system searches space of parameters for classifying. In the experiment, we evaluated the accuracy of classification for known and unknown sound classes.

Keywords: Environmental Sounds, Prediction, Classification, Neuro-dynamical Model.

1 Introduction

Recently, there have been a growing number of studies focusing on systems for classifying environmental sounds [1] [2]. Environmental sounds contain a large amount of information, such as those about the dynamic change in the environment. Recognition of environmental sounds is an indispensable ability for creating an autonomous system. Methods for classifying environmental sounds in previous studies are mainly based on statistical models [3] [4]. Studies show good performances that environmental sound classes are known (training data is composed of sounds from every sound class considered in the experiment).

The purpose of our study is to develop a system that enables robots working in real world to understand environmental sounds. Such systems require solving of the following two issues.

1. The model should be constructed from a small amount of sound samples as it is difficult to obtain a large number of learning sound samples due to durability of hardware.
2. The model should be capable of adapting to unknown sound classes as it is almost impossible to obtain all possible sound samples in advance.

T. Honkela et al. (Eds.): ICANN 2011, Part I, LNCS 6791, pp. 167–175, 2011.

We apply recurrent neural network as a dynamical system for the training model of environmental sounds. The dynamical system points out a new possibility for classifying unknown sounds. The concept of the dynamical system is to deal with sequence data by a fixed "rule" generated through training. The model would then infer the "rule" for the recognition and generation processes of unknown sounds. This capability is known as the generalization capability which provides the dynamical system the ability to deal with unknown data using few training data.

Studies have also been conducted to show the capability of dynamical systems to apply to sound classification and generation. Ogata et al. focuses on active sensing that exploits the dynamic features of an object [5]. They trained the parametric bias recurrent neural network (RNNPB) with sounds, arm trajectories, and tactile sensors generated while the robot moved/hit an object with its own arm [6]. The method appropriately configured unknown (untrained) objects in the PB space. Although the objectives of this study was not the classification of environmental sounds, it has shown an insight on how to apply dynamical systems for classifying known and unknown environmental sounds.

2   Environmental Sounds Classification System

2.1   Multiple Timescale Recurrent Neural Network (MTRNN)

In our model, we utilize the Multiple Timescale Recurrent Neural Network (MTRNN) [7], shown in Fig.1(a), for the dynamical system. The MTRNN is an extension of the continuous time recurrent neural network which acts as a prediction model to predict the next state as the output, from the current state as the input. The nodes of the MTRNN are composed of input/output nodes (IO), fast context nodes (Cf), and slow context nodes (Cs). The combination weights link nodes in a full connection manner except for those between IO and Cs.

In the MTRNN, each node possesses different changing rate controlled by time scale coefficients. More specifically, Cf have a high changing rate, which can help to generate dynamics, and Cs have a low changing rate, which can help the self-organizing gate to switch the structure of primitive sequence data. The function of fast context and slow context are illustrated in Fig.1(b). During the training process, each primitive sequence is encoded into the initial values of Cs. By selecting an arbitrary initial slow context value, the model can also generate novel primitive sequences.

The main calculations of the MTRNN are forward calculation and backward calculation (back propagation through time).

Forward calculating step: In this calculation, the MTRNN can predict the next state as the output with specified current state of IO and initial values of Cs.

Back propagation through time (BPTT) step: In this calculation, combination weights and initial values of Cs are updated for training the MTRNN to predict learning samples.

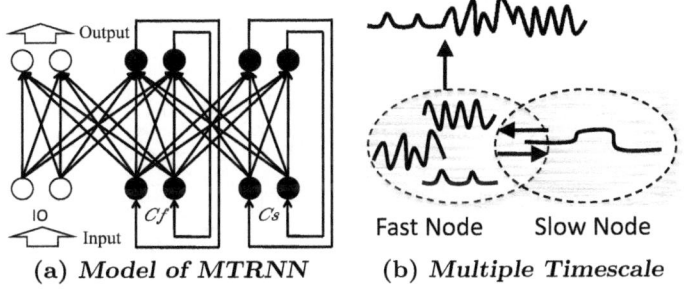

Fig. 1. Multiple Timescale Recurrent Neural Network

The three functions of the MTRNN (learning, recognition, and prediction) are conducted using the two calculations.

Learning: The MTRNN updates the combination weights and the initial values of Cs using training data through forward calculation and BPTT step until the output error converges. In this phase, sequence data used for training are self-organized in the Cs space.

Recognition: The MTRNN conducts forward calculation and BPTT as in the learning function. However, during BPTT, the output error is used only to update the initial values of Cs (i.e. combination weights are fixed in the BPTT step). Consequently, the process derives one point in the Cs space which represents the sequence data to be recognized.

Prediction: The initial values of the input and Cs are input into the MTRNN to associate the whole sequence data through forward calculation. As the input of each step, the output of the previous step is directly input into the MTRNN.

2.2   Environmental Sound Classification System

The classification system for environmental sounds is illustrated in Fig.2. Classification is conducted through four steps of the model (training, recognition, detection, and classification). The training and recognition steps are conducted using the learning and recognition functions of the MTRNN. We describe the detection and classification steps in the following subsections.

Detecting unknown sound classes. Detection of unknown sound classes is conducted by recognition and prediction functions of the MTRNN. The recognition function is first used to calculate the Cs value representing the sound sequence. The calculated Cs is then input into the MTRNN to associate the sound sequence through prediction. The prediction error is calculated by accumulating the absolute errors for each step of the predicted sequence and actual sequence. Prediction errors of unknown sounds are expected to be larger than

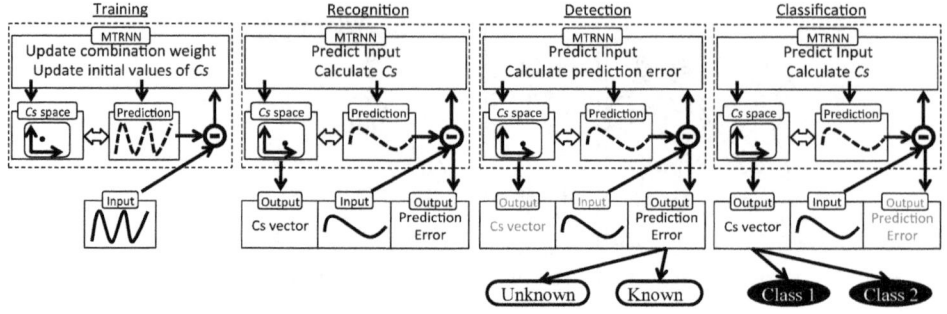

Fig. 2. Training and Classification of Proposed System

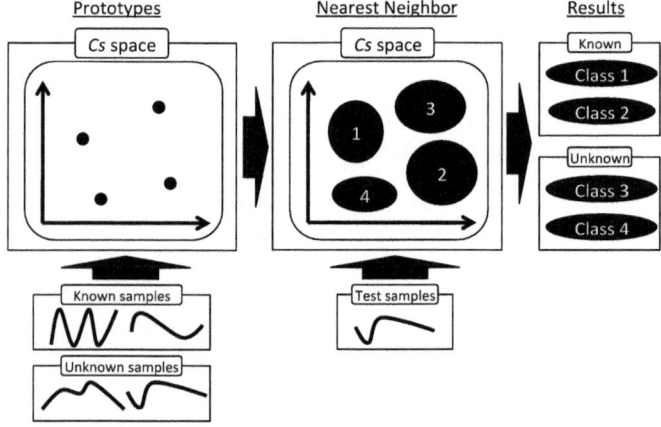

Fig. 3. Nearest Neighbor Algorithm for Sound Class Classification

for known (trained) sounds as the MTRNN is not trained with sounds from unknown classes. Therefore, unknown sound classes are classified by comparing the prediction error with a threshold value.

Classifying sound classes. Classification of sound classes is conducted based on the Cs value of the sequence. A detailed flow of classification is shown in Fig. 3.

First, several typical known and unknown sounds are selected and input into the MTRNN for recognition to calculate the Cs values. These Cs values are used as prototypes of nearest neighbor algorithm. Using these prototypes, the sound to be classified is evaluated based on the Euclidean distance between the sound and prototypes. The prototype with the smallest distance is selected and the sound is labeled as the sound class with the selected prototype.

3   Experiments

3.1   Condition

In the experiments, we used sounds from RWCP real environmental voice sound database to evaluate the performance of our system [8]. From the database, we selected 20 classes of sounds listed in Table 1. Each class is composed of 100 sound data. Four of the 100 data from each class were used for training the model. The Mel-frequency cepstral coefficient (MFCC, 12 dimensions) features with a 25-ms window and 10-ms interval were extracted from the sounds. The MFCC features were smoothed and normalized. Relatively long sounds were cut to create MFCC feature sequences with less than 150 steps. We conduced experiments by changing the threshold starting from 0 and increasing by 0.001. We present the result with the best classification performance.

The MTRNN was trained using the MFCC features of training sounds. The composition of the MTRNN is shown in Table 2. The process of the experiment is as follows.

1. Divide the twenty classes into four groups as shown in Table 1.
2. Select 11 sets of four-number groups {d1, d2, $\cdots$, d11} randomly.
3. Create inspection cross table constructed by class groups in Table 1 and 11 data groups. {(c1, c2, c3, c4), (c1, c2), (c1, c3), (c1, c4), (c2, c3), (c2, c4), (c3, c4)} × {d1, d2, $\cdots$, d11}

Table 1. Class Grouping for Cross Validation

Class Group	Class	Class Group	Class
c1	candybwl	c2	coin1
	coffmill		file
	crumple		pump
	dryer		punch
	horn		ring
c3	saw2	c4	shaver
	spray		tear
	stapler		toy
	string		trashbox
	whistle1		whistle2

Table 2. Composition of the MTRNN

The number of input nodes	12
The number of Cf nodes	20~40
The number of Cs nodes	5
The time scale of input nodes	2
The time scale of Cf nodes	5
The time scale of Cs nodes	10,000
Training times	50,000

3.2   Result

In this subsection, we present the result of detecting unknown sounds using prediction error and classifying known and unknown sound classes based on the self-organized Cs space.

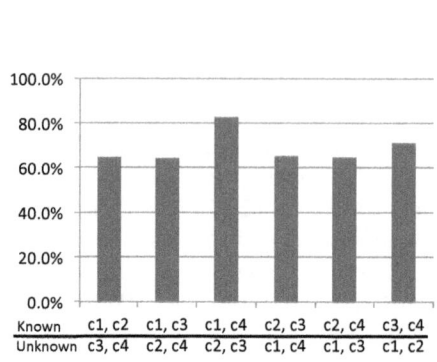
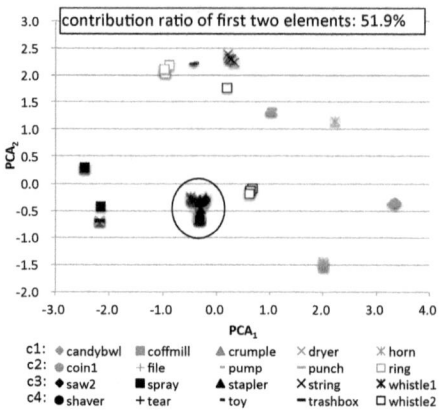

Fig. 4. Success Rate of Detection of Unknown Sounds

Fig. 5. Cs Space for Training Set $\{c1, c2, c3, c4 \times d1\}$

Detecting unknown sounds using prediction error
Subsection 2.2 describes the detection of unknown sound. Concretely, the sound is regarded as unknown one if its prediction error is larger than the threshold value. In subsection 3.1, the different threshold is set according to each class group. Figure 4 illustrates the results of average accuracy in detecting unknown sounds based on prediction error. The accuracy of each group is 63.9% in worst and 82.6% in best.

The Cs space
We present several results of the self-organized Cs spaces after learning in Fig.5 $\sim$ 7. (Classes enclosed by boxes are known sound classes.)

The Cs spaces shown in the figures are the results of principal component analysis (PCA) of the Cs values. We present the first two elements of five elements. The accumulated contribution ratio of first two elements of each Cs space is also shown in each figure.

From these figures, it is notable that the Cs values of each sound forms clusters of the same sound classes, denoting the effectivity of the MTRNN to self-organize sound sequences into the Cs space.

Classification of known and unknown sound classes
Figure 8 shows the average rates of classification in different combination of known and unknown classes. The error bar shows three times of standard error. From the results, it is notable that the success rate for 10 known classes significantly shows best performance.

3.3   Discussion

Comparing with GMM. If all target classes are fixed, stochastic method like GMM shows better classification performances than our method on neuro-

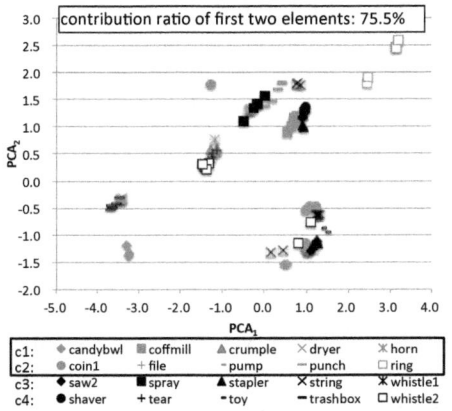

c1:	◆ candybwl	■ coffmill	▲ crumple	✕ dryer	✖ horn
c2:	● coin1	+ file	– pump	– punch	▫ ring
c3:	◆ saw2	■ spray	▲ stapler	✕ string	✻ whistle1
c4:	● shaver	+ tear	– toy	– trashbox	▫ whistle2

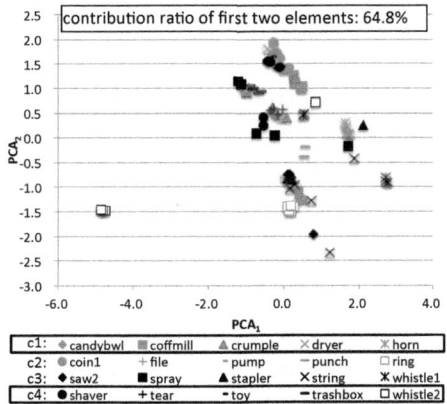

c1:	◆ candybwl	■ coffmill	▲ crumple	✕ dryer	✖ horn
c2:	● coin1	+ file	– pump	– punch	▫ ring
c3:	◆ saw2	■ spray	▲ stapler	✕ string	✻ whistle1
c4:	● shaver	+ tear	– toy	– trashbox	▫ whistle2

Fig. 6. Cs Space for Training Set $\{c1,$ $c2 \times d1\}$

Fig. 7. Cs Space for Training Set $\{c1,$ $c4 \times d1\}$

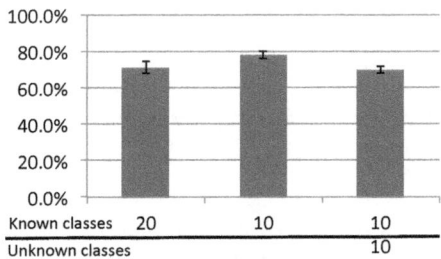

Fig. 8. Success Rate of Classification

dynamical systems (96.4% better in average). The main advantage of our method is that it can classify (generalize) unknown classes of sounds without any additional data and training phases.

Detection and classification of unknown sounds. We suggest that there is a trade-off relationship between the classification and the detection of unknown sounds. From Fig.4, (c1, c4) class group showed a good performance at detecting unknown sounds. Figure 7 shows the self-organized Cs space of (c1, c4) class group. Since the initial values of Cs on this space are not dispersed well, it is difficult for training (c1, c4) class groups to generalize the Cs space.

Scale of learning data and classification performance. More training samples can not lead a better performance (see Fig.8). In the figure, the 10-known-classes group shows the best classification performance. Actually, comparing with the Cs space of Fig.5 to Fig.6, the Cs space of (c1, c2) class group generates clear clusters whereas that of (c1, c2, c3, c4) class group generates clusters together. The prediction errors of (c1, c2, c3, c4) and (c1, c2) were almost the same. Increase of training samples makes the Cs space complex for classification.

Classifying unknown sounds. From the result of Fig.6 it is notable that unknown sounds are also self-organized in the Cs space. The result suggests the possibility of MTRNN to classify unknown sounds without the requirements of prototypes for unknown sound.

4   Conclusions

In this paper, we presented a prediction and classification system for environmental sounds using a neural-dynamical model. This system showed a new approach for classifying unknown environmental sounds using a small amount of samples.

For the evaluation experiment, we selected 20 classes from RWCP real environmental voice sound database, and trained the system using sequence data of Mel-frequency cepstrum coefficient (MFCC) features extracted from sounds. The results show the effectivity of the system to deal with both known and unknown sound classes.

In the discussion of comparing with GMM, GMM showed better accuracy than our system. As future work, we plan to investigate different features of sounds like Matching Pursuit [9] for improving performance of our system for more practical environments and sounds.

Acknowledgments. This research was supported by JST PRESTO (Information Environment and Humans), Grant-in-Aid for Creative Scientific Research (19GS0208), and Grant-in-Aid for Scientific Research (B) (21300076).

References

[1] Ashiya, T., Nakagawa, M.: A Proposal of a Recognition System for the Species of Birds Receiving Birdcalls: An Application of Recognition Systems for Environmental Sound. IEICE Transactions on Fundamentals of Electronics, Communications and Computer Sciences 76, 1858–1860 (1993)

[2] Exadaktylos, V., Silva, M., Aerts, J.-M., Taylor, C.J., Berckmans, D.: Real-time recognition of sick pig cough sounds. Computers and Electronics in Agriculture 63, 207–214 (2008)

[3] Sasaki, Y., Kaneyoshi, M., Kagami, S., Mizoguchi, H., Enomoto, T.: Daily sound recognition using pitch-cluster-maps for mobile robot audition. In: Proc. 2009 IEEE/RSJ International Conference on Intelligent Robots and Systems, pp. 2724–2729. IEEE Press, St. Louis (2009)

[4] Miki, K., Nishimura, T., Nakamura, S., Shikano, K.: Environmental Sound Discrimination Based on Hidden Markov Model. Information Processing Society of Japan SIG Notes 99, 79–84 (1999)

[5] Ogata, T., Ohba, H., Komatani, K., Tani, J., Okuno, H.G.: Extracting Multimodal Dynamics of Objects Using RNNPB. Journal of Robotics and Mechatronics, Special Issue on Human Modeling in Robotics 17, 681–688 (2005)

[6] Tani, J., Ito, M.: Self-organization of behavioral primitives as multiple attractor dynamics: A robot experiment. IEEE Transactions on Systems, Man, and Cybernetics A 33, 481–488 (2003)

[7] Yamashita, Y., Tani, J.: Emergence of Functional Hierarchy in a Multiple Timescale Neural Network Model: A Humanoid Robot Experiment. PLoS Comput Biol. 4, e1000220 (2008)

[8] Real World Computing Partnership, RWCP Sound Scene Database, http://tosa.mri.co.jp/sounddb/indexe.htm

[9] Yamakawa, N., Kitahara, T., Takahashi, T., Komatani, K., Ogata, T., Okuno, H.G.: Effects of modelling within- and between-frame temporal variations in power spectra on non-verbal sound recognition. In: Proc. 2010 International Conference on Spoken Language Processing, Makuhari, pp. 2342–2345 (2010)

Time-Dependent Series Variance Estimation via Recurrent Neural Networks

Nikolay Nikolaev[1], Peter Tino[2], and Evgueni Smirnov[3]

[1] Department of Computing, Goldsmiths College, University of London,
London SE14 6NW, United Kingdom
n.nikolaev@gold.ac.uk
[2] School of Computer Science, The University of Birmingham,
Birmingham B15 2TT, United Kingdom
p.tino@cs.bham.ac.uk
[3] Department of Computing, MICC-IKAT, Maastricht University,
Maastricht 6200 MD, The Netherlands
smirnov@micc.unimaas.nl

Abstract. This paper presents a nonlinear model for computing the time-dependent evolution of the variance in time series of returns on assets. First, we design a recurrent network representation of the variance, which extends the typically linear models. Second, we derive temporal training equations with which the network weights are inferred so as to maximize the likelihood of the data. Experimental results show that this dynamic recurrent network model yields results with improved statistical characteristics and economic performance.

1 Introduction

Subject of particular interest in finance is the time-dependent conditional variance in time series of returns on assets, known also as the volatility. A popular tool for capturing the latent variance in returns are the Generalized Autoregressive Conditional Heteroscedastic (GARCH) models [3]. GARCH models have already been enhanced by adding non-linearity using neural network formulations [2]. Non-linear GARCH models based on Recurrent Neural Networks (RNN) have also been proposed [5], [12], [9]. The RNN formulation offers two advantages: 1) RNN offer an adequate representation for the inherently recursive GARCH models because they are driven by external inputs as well as by internal temporal context signals; and 2) RNN enable derivation of analytical parameter estimation formula, leading to simple online training algorithms.

However, parameter fitting in such models does not explicitly account for time dependencies among the data, i.e. the gradient information (in gradient based training) is not propagated through time. Hence the models may not be fitted to their full potential of being dynamic machines that can learn time-dependent functions [13], [8]. Of course, the 'vanishing gradient' problem cannot be easily avoided in any RNN formulation (unless one uses specialized architectures such

T. Honkela et al. (Eds.): ICANN 2011, Part I, LNCS 6791, pp. 176–184, 2011.

as LSTM [6]). Nevertheless, propagation of error information, albeit to a limited time horizon, is desirable in fitting all parameterized state space models.

This paper presents an RNN-GARCH model for computing the dynamic evolution of the volatility of returns. First, we design a recurrent network representation for a zero-mean nonlinear GARCH model. Our restricted formulation captures only the volatility, unlike previous versions of GARCH using recurrent networks [12], [9]. Second, we derive temporal training equations with which the RNN-GARCH weights are inferred so as to maximize the model likelihood. The training rules use temporal derivatives obtained following the Real Time Recurrent Learning (RTRL) algorithm [13].

The developed RTRL training algorithm provides temporal derivatives of the log-likelihood function that are generalizations of the analytical (closed-form) derivatives [4] of linear GARCH models. While the analytical linear derivatives are typically used to compute the parameters in offline manner, the novel temporal derivatives are taken for online computations so as to reflect the stochastic nature of the sequentially arriving data. The temporal derivatives can also be used in offline manner in standard optimizers as demonstrated in this paper.

The efficacy of the proposed RNN-GARCH is studied on a benchmark currency exchange rates series. RNN-GARCH is compared with linear GARCH trained both in the maximum-likelihood (ML) [4] and Bayesian (with MCMC sampling) [7] frameworks. RTRL applied to RNN-GARCH results in slightly better macro characteristics (lower skewness and higher kurtosis), as well as in better economic performance (out-of-sample prediction of directional changes).

The remainder of this article is organized as follows. Section 2 provides the GARCH representation as a recurrent network. Section 3 gives the training algorithm for RNN-GARCH. Experimental results are reported in section 4. Finally, a brief conclusion is provided.

2   Nonlinear Dynamic GARCH Modelling

2.1   The GARCH(p,q) Model

The changes in the variance (volatility) of returns on assets constitute an unobserved process. The volatility is commonly represented as the standard deviation of the stochastic component of observable returns. Consider the mean adjusted log-returns from a series of prices (of stocks, currencies, etc.) S_t, that is $r_t = \log(S_t/S_{t-1}) - m$, assuming that $m = (1/T)\sum_{t=1}^{T} \log(S_t/S_{t-1})$. The dynamics of these log-returns can be described by the following simple heteroscedastic zero-mean GARCH(p,q) model [3]:

$$r_t = \varepsilon_t \sigma_t \tag{1}$$

$$\sigma_t^2 = \mu + \sum_{i=1}^{q} \alpha_i r_{t-i}^2 + \sum_{j=1}^{p} \beta_j \sigma_{t-j}^2 \tag{2}$$

where $\varepsilon_t \sim \mathcal{N}(0,1)$ is an i.i.d. normal random variable, and σ_t is the volatility.

Adopting $R_{t-1} = (r_1, r_2, ..., r_{t-1})$ to denote the past information up to time t, the moments of the return distribution are $E[r_t | R_{t-1}] = 0$ and $E[r_t^2 | R_{t-1}] = \sigma_t^2$. The parameter set of the model contains the mean level $\mu > 0$, the persistences β_j and the moving average coefficients α_i. The parameters are restricted to ensure positive variance ($\alpha_i \geq 0$, $\beta_j \geq 0$) and stationarity ($\sum_{i=1}^q \alpha_i + \sum_{j=1}^p \beta_j < 1$).

The distribution of the returns conditioned on the data up to time t reads

$$p(r_t | R_{t-1}) = \frac{1}{\sqrt{2\pi\sigma_t^2}} \exp\left(-\frac{r_t^2}{2\sigma_t^2}\right). \tag{3}$$

The GARCH model given by Eq. (1) and (2) has the capacity to describe the main features of the returns, namely their excess kurtosis, small autocorrelation and high persistence of the squared returns. However, linear GARCH models often fail to capture all these (desirable) features simultaneously.

2.2   The RNN-GARCH(p,q) Model

This research elaborates on an RNN-GARCH [12] that adds nonlinear terms to Eq. (1) and Eq. (2). The RNN accepts as external inputs the returns r_{t-i}^2 and the volatilities σ_{t-j}^2 as internal signals from its context.

The RNN-GARCH topology has a hidden layer and an output node that computes the volatility $h_t = \sigma_t^2$ (Figure 1). We use one hidden node to represent the linear part of the model Eq. (2), while the remaining hidden nodes are used to provide the nonlinear extension. The output node uses the absolute value function to produce positive volatility as suggested before [12].

Let us adopt the following notation for the inputs to the network at time t:

$$z_{t-l} = \begin{cases} 1.0, & \text{i.e. bias if } l = 0 \\ r_{t-l}^2, & \text{if } 1 \leq l \leq p \\ h_{t-l+p}, & \text{if } (p+1) \leq l \leq (p+q) \end{cases} \tag{4}$$

where p is the number of lagged inputs, and q are the recurrent connections.

These inputs feed the hidden nodes to compute the summations:

$$s_{k,t} = \sum_{l=0}^{p+q} w_{kl} z_{t-l} \tag{5}$$

where w_{kl} is the weight from the l-th source node to the k-th node.

The hidden nodes use the following activation functions:

$$u_{k,t} = g\left(s_{k,t}\right), \text{ and } g\left(s_{k,t}\right) = \begin{cases} s_{k,t}, & \text{linear part of the model} \\ \tanh(s_{k,t}), & \text{hyperbolic tangent} \end{cases} \tag{6}$$

As in neural net research, tanh can be suitably replaced by e.g. logistic sigmoid.

The output node uses the absolute valute function $f\left(s_{o,t}\right) = |s_{o,t}|$ to generate the output $h_t = \sigma_t^2$:

$$h_t = f\left(s_{o,t}\right) = f\left(\sum_{k=1}^K w_{ok} u_{k,t}\right)$$

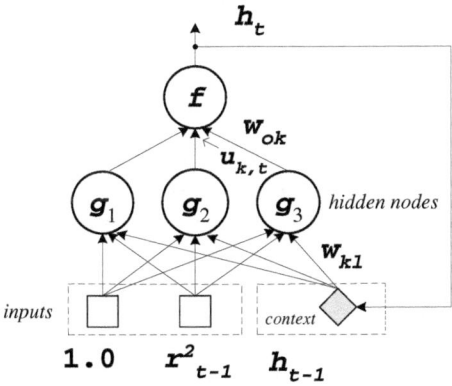

g_1 linear activation function
g_2, g_3 hyperbolic tangent activation functions
f absolute value function

Fig. 1. RNN-GARCH Model: a recurrent neural network interpretation of a nonlinear dynamic GARCH model

$$= f\left(\sum_{k=1}^{K} w_{ok} g\left(\sum_{l=1}^{p} w_{kl} r_{t-l}^2 + \sum_{l=p+1}^{p+q} w_{kl} h_{t-l+p} + w_{k0}\right)\right), \qquad (7)$$

where K is the number of hidden nodes in the network, and the weights w_{ok} connect the k-th hidden node to the network output.

3   Dynamic Training of RNN-GARCH

The learning problem can be formulated as follows: given a (training) series of returns $r_1, r_2, ..., r_{t,...}$, $1 \le t \le T$, find the RNN-GARCH parameters that 'best explain' their changing variance. The parameters are: mean level w_k, persistences w_{kl}, $p+1 \le l \le p+q$, moving average coefficients w_{kl}, $1 \le l \le p$, and hidden to output weights w_{ok}, $1 \le k \le K$. We fit the parameters in the maximum likelihood framework.

The likelihood maximisation is equivalent to minimization of the negative log-likelihood, so the instantaneous loss function to be minimized reads [11]:

$$L_t = -\log p(r_t|R_{t-1}) = \frac{1}{2}\left(\log \sigma_t^2 + \frac{r_t^2}{h_t}\right). \qquad (8)$$

where the constant terms are omitted.

As in temporal neural network training by online gradient descent [10], we develop training rules for updating the RNN-GARCH weights as follows:

$$w_{ij} = w_{ij} - \eta \frac{\partial L_t}{\partial w_{ij}} = w_{ij} - \eta \nu_t \frac{\partial h_t}{\partial w_{ij}} \qquad (9)$$

$$\nu_t = \frac{\partial L_t}{\partial h_t} = \frac{1}{2}\left[\frac{1}{h_t} + r_t^2\left(-\frac{1}{h_t^2}\right)\right] = \frac{1}{2h_t}\left[1 - \frac{r_t^2}{h_t}\right] \qquad (10)$$

where w_{ij} is the weight from the j-th source node to the i-th destination node, and η is the learning rate.

The RNN-GARCH temporal derivatives can be computed following the RTRL algorithm [13] for recurrent networks. According to RTRL, the derivative of the output with respect to a weight at time t is obtained as follows:

$$\frac{\partial h_t}{\partial w_{ij}} = f'\left(\sum_{k=1}^{K}\left[w_{ok}\frac{\partial u_{k,t}}{\partial w_{ij}}\right] + \delta_{oi}u_{j,t}\right) \qquad (11)$$

where δ_{oi} is the Kroneker delta function: $\delta_{oi} = 1$ if $o = i$ and 0 otherwise, and f' is the derivative of f defined as follows: $f' = s_{o,t}/|s_{o,t}|$.

The RTRL temporal derivatives of hidden node activations with respect to any weight at time t are obtained analogously:

$$\frac{\partial u_{k,t}}{\partial w_{ij}} = g'\left(\sum_{l=p+1}^{q}\left[w_{kl}\frac{\partial h_{t-l}}{\partial w_{ij}}\right] + \delta_{ik}z_{t-j}\right) \qquad (12)$$

where the initial state is assumed independent from the weights, i.e. $\partial h_0/\partial w_{ij} = 0$, and g' is the derivative of g defined as follows: $g' = (1 - s_{k,t}^2)$.

Although the complexity of this RTRL algorithm for recurrent network training is high ($\mathcal{O}(q^3(q+p))$), it is reasonable to apply it to RNN-GARCH because we typically use small model orders $q = 1$ (or 2) and $p = 1$ (or $p = 2$).

4   Experiments in Volatility Inference

Studied Methods. We compare a variety of GARCH estimation algorithms. Linear GARCH were trained with: an $MCMC$ sampling algorithm [7], and a Maximum Likelihood Estimation (MLE) algorithm using 'static' derivatives [4]. Nonlinear GARCH were trained with: a Maximum likelihood estimation algorithm using 'dynamic' RTRL derivatives ($MRTRL$), the online $RTRL$ and a conjugate-gradients algorithm with static backprop derivatives ($CGBP$) from previous research [12]. We made an RNN-GARCH(1,1) model with $K = 3$ hidden nodes. Learning rate $\eta = 1.0e^{-6}$ and regularization $\lambda = 0.1$, were found using cross-validation. The MLE and $MRTRL$ algorithms were made with a BFGS optimizer, using parameters: $Tolerance = 1.0e^{-10}$, $FunctionEvaluations = 10^2$ and $MaxIterations = 10^2$ (found by cross-validation).

Each of the algorithms started with the same initial values: $\mu = 0.01$, $\beta = 0.85$ and $\alpha = 0.05$. The unconditional variance was taken to initialize the volatility $\sigma_0^2 = \mu/(1 - \alpha - \beta)$. The initial network weights were chosen so as to produce a network response close to one: $w_{10} = w_{20} = w_{30} = 0.5\mu$, $w_{11} = w_{21} = w_{31} = 0.5\alpha$, $w_{13} = w_{23} = 0.0001$, $w_{33} = \beta$, $w_{o1} = 0.2$, $w_{o2} = 0.1$, $w_{o3} = 1.0$.

Experimental Technology. After training with the initial 80% points from the series, the out-of-sample performance was evaluated by rolling over the remaining points to compute one-step-ahead predictions. The model was re-estimated over the next window again of 80% from the next training series, and this process was repeated. The predicted volatilities were taken to evaluate the out-of-sample accuracy with measures from relevant research [12], [9]: normalized mean squared error ($NMSE$), normalized mean absolute error ($NMAE$), hit rate (HR) and weighted hit rate (WHR). The last two HR and WHR compute the accuracy of forecasted directional changes as follows [12], [9]:

$$HR = \frac{1}{T} \sum_{t=1}^{T} \theta_t, \text{ where: } \theta_{t-l} = \begin{cases} 1, & \text{if } (h_t - r_{t-1}^2)(r_t^2 - r_{t-1}^2) \geq 0 \\ 0, & \text{otherwise} \end{cases} \tag{13}$$

$$WHR = \frac{\sum_{t=1}^{T} sgn((h_t - r_{t-1}^2)(r_t^2 - r_{t-1}^2))|r_t^2 - r_{t-1}^2|}{\sum_{t=1}^{T} |r_t^2 - r_{t-1}^2|} \tag{14}$$

Processing the DEM/GBP Series. A series of DEM/GBP currency exchange rates was taken as a benchmark [1]. It consists of 1974 daily observations recorded from 3/1/1984 to 31/12/1991 (divided into 1500 data for training and 474 for testing). Table 1 shows the learned GARCH parameters.

Table 2 reports the testing results calculated with the standardized residuals (produced by passing the squared standardized returns r_t^2/h_t through the normal cumulative density function). It shows that $MCMC$, $RTRL$ and $CGBP$ lead to models with close low skewness and excess kurtosis. Both algorithms

Table 1. Learned linear and nonlinear GARCH(1,1) parameters and their standard errors, obtained over the training series of returns on DEM/GBP exchange rates

	$MCMC$	MLE	$MRTRL$	$RTRL$	$CGBP$
μ	0.01308	0.01352	0.00856	0.01197	0.01056
	(0.00453)	(0.00391)	(0.00204)	(0.00513)	(0.00529)
α	0.14029	0.14185	0.08863	0.11436	0.10385
	(0.03025)	(0.02925)	(0.02258)	(0.02831)	(0.02974)
β	0.80712	0.80857	0.80389	0.80845	0.80751
	(0.04378)	(0.04049)	(0.0365)	(0.04342)	(0.04422)

Table 2. Statistical diagnostics calculated with standardized residuals, obtained by fitting GARCH(1,1) models to the DEM/GBP series with the studied algorithms

	Skewness	Kurtosis	B-S	D-W	B-P	L-B(30)	Log-lik.
$MCMC$	−0.40302	5.09346	314.282	1.89976	0.01975	29.5099	−914.495
MLE	−0.40331	5.08537	311.827	1.89999	0.01978	29.5965	−915.348
$MRTRL$	−0.40472	5.09547	323.589	1.90174	0.01931	28.9338	−914.435
$RTRL$	−0.40237	5.10024	298.473	1.90142	0.01984	29.7496	−914.181
$CGBP$	−0.40485	5.08583	315.286	1.90182	0.01953	29.2453	−914.477

Table 3. Out-of-sample performance of different GARCH(1,1) models, obtained via rolling regression over the unseen testing 474 returns on DEM/GBP exchange rates

	NMSE	NMAE	HR	WHR
$MCMC$	0.75203	0.89187	0.67241	0.57623
MLE	0.75246	0.94271	0.64332	0.57056
$MRTRL$	0.75332	0.89052	0.67305	0.57836
$RTRL$	0.75095	0.88095	0.67944	0.58089
$CGBP$	0.75421	0.89106	0.64551	0.57645

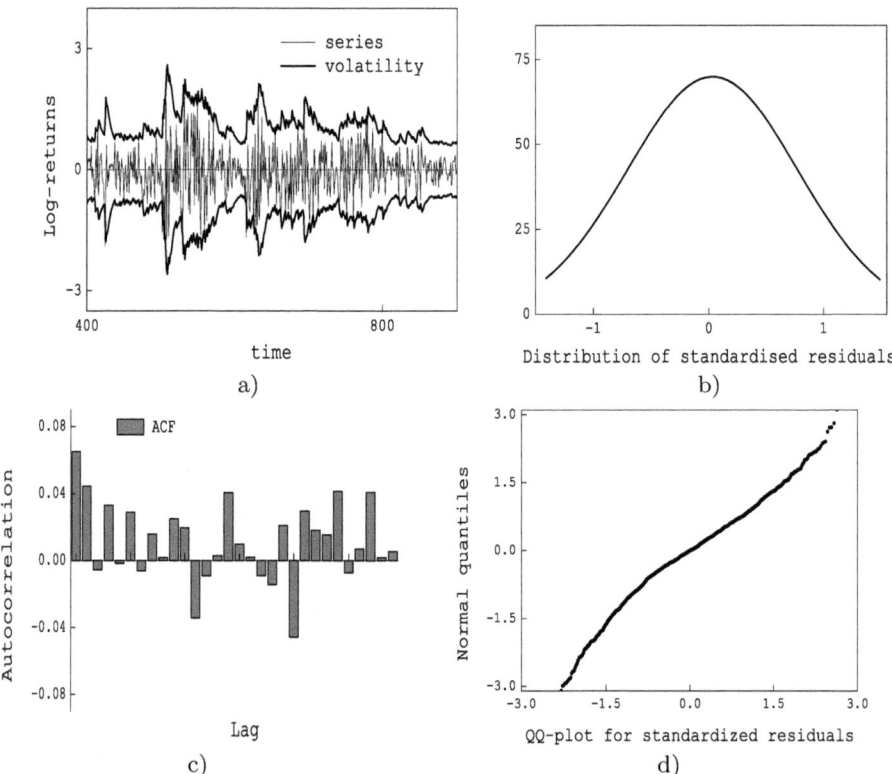

Fig. 2.(a). Returns from DEM/GBP exchange rates and their time-varying volatility (conditional variance) produced by an RNN-GARCH(1,1) model trained by RTRL.
(b). Gaussian fit to the distribution of squared standardized residuals obtained with volatilities learned online by RNN-GARCH(1,1).
(c). Correlogram of the squared standardized residuals obtained with volatilities learned online by RNN-GARCH(1,1).
(d). Quantile-quantile plot of the squared standardized residuals obtained with volatilities learned online by RNN-GARCH(1,1).

$MRTRL$ and $RTRL$ learn models with slightly better statistical characteristics than the other models. All models exhibit similar values of the Durbin-Watson (D-W), Bowman-Shenton (B-S), Box-Pierce (B-P) and Ljung-Box (L-B) statistics, therefore there is no significant autocorrelation in their residuals.

Table 3 shows that indeed using $RTRL$ derivatives leads to best out-of-sample results. The out-of-sample residuals $NMSE$ and $NMAE$ from $MRTRL$ and $RTRL$ training of RNN-GARCH are lower than these from $CGBP$ as well as the other studied models. Both RNN-GARCH models, learned using $MRTRL$ and $RTRL$, demonstrate also better economic performance, in the sense that they achieve better directional forecasting of the future changes in the series as indicated by the higher HR and WHR rates.

Figure 2.a illustrates that the deviations of the RNN-GARCH volatility wrap closely the returns. Figure 2.b shows a Gaussian fit to the distribution of the standardized residuals from RNN-GARCH. Figures 2.c, and 2.d show the correlogram and the quantile-quantile plot of these standardized residuals.

5   Conclusion

This paper presented an RNN approach to nonlinear GARCH modeling of the dynamic evolution of the conditional variance of returns. Empirical investigations showed that this RNN-GARCH yields results with good statistical characteristics and forecasting potential that outperform results from standard alternative approaches. An interesting issue for future research is to develop more sophisticated mechanisms for control of the learning step size.

References

1. Brooks, C., Burke, S.P., Persand, G.: Benchmarks and the Accuracy of GARCH Model Estimation. Journal of Forecasting 17, 45–56 (2001)
2. Donaldson, R.G., Kamstra, M.: An Artificial Neural Network - GARCH Model of International Stock Return Volatility. Journal of Empirical Finance 4, 17–46 (1997)
3. Engle, R.F.: Autoregressive Conditional Heteroscedasticity with Estimates of the Variance of UK Inflation. Econometrica 50, 987–1007 (1982)
4. Fiorentini, G., Calzolari, G., Panattoni, L.: Analytical Derivatives and the Computation of GARCH Estimates. Journal of Applied Econometrics 11, 399–417 (1996)
5. Freisleben, B., Ripper, K.: Volatility Estimation with a Neural Network. In: Proc. of the IEE/IAFE Computational Intelligence for Financial Engineering Conference (CIFEr 1997), pp. 177–181. IEEE Press, Los Alamitos (1997)
6. Hochreiter, S., Schmidhuber, J.: Long Short-Term Memory. Neural Computation 9, 1735–1780 (1997)
7. Kim, S., Shephard, N., Chib, S.: Stochastic Volatility: Likelihood Inference and Comparison with ARCH Models. The Review of Econ. Studies 65, 361–393 (1998)
8. Mandic, D.P., Chambers, J.A.: Recurrent Neural Networks for Prediction. Wiley, New York (2001)
9. Miazhynskaia, T., Dorffner, G., Dockner, E.J.: Risk Management Application of the Recurrent Mixture Density Network Models. In: Kaynak, O., Alpaydın, E., Oja, E., Xu, L. (eds.) ICANN 2003 and ICONIP 2003. LNCS, vol. 2714, pp. 589–596. Springer, Heidelberg (2003)

10. Neuneier, R., Zimmermann, H.G.: How to Train Neural Networks. In: Orr, G.B., Müller, K.-R. (eds.) NIPS-WS 1996. LNCS, vol. 1524, pp. 373–423. Springer, Heidelberg (1998)
11. Nix, D.A., Weigend, A.S.: Estimating the Mean and Variance of the Target Probability Distribution. In: Proc. of the IEEE Int. Conf. on Neural Networks (IEEE-ICNN 1994), pp. 55–60. IEEE Press, Los Alamitos (1994)
12. Schittenkopf, C., Dorffner, G., Dockner, E.J.: Forecasting Time-Dependent Conditional Densities: A Semi Non-parametric Neural Network. Journal of Forecasting 19, 355–374 (2000)
13. Williams, R.J., Zipser, D.: A Learning Algorithm for Continually Running Fully Recurrent Networks. Neural Computation 1, 270–280 (1989)

Historical Consistent Complex Valued Recurrent Neural Network

Hans-Georg Zimmermann[1], Alexey Minin[2,3], and Victoria Kusherbaeva[3]

[1] Siemens AG, Corporate Technology, 81730 Muenchen, Mch-P, R. 53.220, Germany
[2] Technische Universitat Munchen, Institut fur Informatik VI, Boltzmannstrase 3,
85748 Muenchen, Germany
[3] Siemens LLC, Corporate Technology, 191186, St. Petersburg,
Volynskiy lane 3 of. 905, Russia
{Hans_Georg.Zimmermann,Alexey.Minin,Victoria.Kusherbaeva.ext}@Siemens.com

Abstract. Recurrent Neural Networks are in the scope of the machine learning community for many years. In the current paper we discuss the Historical Consistent Recurrent Neural Network and its extension to the complex valued case. We give some insights into complex valued back propagation and its application to the complex valued recurrent neural network training. Finally we present the results for the the Lorenz system modeling. In the end we discuss the advantages of the proposed algorithm and give the outlook.

Keywords: complex valued neural networks, recurrent neural networks, complex valued recurrent neural networks, complex dynamics analysis.

1 Introduction

Historical Consistent Neural Network (further HCNN) was first described in the work of Zimmermann [1]. This architecture is very interesting due to the stability of training and simplicity of the construction. It allows a unique correspondence between the dynamical equations, neural network architecture and the locality of the learning algorithms. This architecture models the behavior of the dynamical system which can be described by the eq.1 below:

$$\begin{cases} s_t = f\left(s_{t-1}, u_t\right) \\ y_t = g\left(s_t\right) \end{cases} \quad (1)$$

where u is a model input, s is an internal state of the model and y is the model output, f and g are some transition functions (recurrent connection is done through the states). Modeling of such systems is of big interest in many application areas. But what happens if there is a need in complex valued neural network inputs? Even with real valued dynamics modeling there are a lot of unsolved problems with the things like stable training, learning and stopping criteria. In the following paper we will try to show the transition from the Real Valued HCNN (further RVHCNN) to the Complex Valued HCNN (further

T. Honkela et al. (Eds.): ICANN 2011, Part I, LNCS 6791, pp. 185–192, 2011.

CVHCNN). We will present our insights in the complex valued back-propagation and its application to the CVHCNN. At the end of the paper we present the results obtained modeling of Lorenz system dynamics.

2   Historical Consistent Complex Valued RNN

2.1   Complex Valued Back-Propagation

Complex Valued Back Propagation (further CVBP) was already discussed in many papers, here we can refer to the papers of Haykin [5], Hirose [6], Nitta [7], Kim [8] etc. One can see that the interest in this topic remains. In this subsection we will rearrange the knowledge in this area and show some insights on complex valued back propagation.

Complex Valued Error Function. The main thing in neural networks approximation problems is to minimize an error function. This function typically selected as a mean squared error MSE, root mean squared error $RMSE$ etc. First let us start with the definition of the error function which we are going to minimize in the complex valued case. Now, all neuron inputs (further *netin*), network outputs (further *netout*), targets (the desired output values) and network weights are complex numbers (consist of real and imaginary parts). The minimization of the complex valued error would be a complicated task due to many reasons discussed below. Therefore, in the majority of the papers mentioned above one can see the following error function (see eq.2):

$$E = \sum_{t=1}^{T} (\text{netout}_\tau - \text{target}_\tau) \overline{(\text{netout}_\tau - \text{target}_\tau)} \rightarrow \min_W \qquad (2)$$

where τ is a pattern number, T is the number of patterns and the bar above the brackets means complex value conjunction ($z = x + iy, z \in \mathbb{C}, \bar{z} = x - iy$). For more types of error function authors refer to the paper of Gangal [9] (in this paper authors describe a lot of different error functions). The property of the presented error function is that it is mapping from $\mathbb{C} \rightarrow \mathbb{R}$. This automatically means that error function is not analytical (see Zimmermann [3]), which means that it does not have neither analytical derivative nor Taylor expansion. Abscence of the Taylor expansion means impossibility to apply Steepest Descent algorithm for the Neural Network training. However, we can treat this error function with the so called Wirtinger calculus; here we refer to Brandwood [4]. Let $f(z) = u(z_r, z_{im}) + iv(z_r, z_{im})$ (here $z \in \mathbb{C}, z_r$ is the real part of z and z_{im} is the imaginary part of z, u and v are some real valued functions), then one can write two real valued variables as $z_r = (z + \bar{z})/2, z_{im} = (z - \bar{z})/2i$. One should consider z and $\bar{z}$ as independent from each other. Then function $f : \mathbb{C} \rightarrow \mathbb{C}$ can be expressed as $f : \mathbb{R} \times \mathbb{R} \rightarrow \mathbb{C}$ by rewriting it as $f(z) = f(z_r, z_{im})$. Using the theorems below when evaluating the gradient, we can directly compute the derivatives with respect to the complex argument, rather than calculating individual real-valued gradients. Here f is our error function written in the eq.2. Let $f : \mathbb{R} \times \mathbb{R} \to \mathbb{C}$ be a function of real variables x and y such that $g(z, \bar{z}) = f(z_r, z_{im})$, where $z = z_r + iz_{im}$ and that g is analytic with respect to z and $\bar{z}$ independently. The requirement for the analyticity of $g(z, \bar{z})$ with respect to z and $\bar{z}$ is equivalent to the condition on real differentiability of $f(z_r, r_{im})$ since we can move from one form of the function to the other using the simple linear transformation given above.

Theorem 1. *Let $f(z, \bar{z})$ be a real-valued function of the vector-valued complex variable z where the dependence on the variable and its conjugate is explicit. By treating z and $\bar{z}$ as independent variables, the quantity pointing in the direction of the maximum rate of change of $f(z, \bar{z})$ is $\nabla_{\bar{z}}(f(z))$.*

This theory has been studied extensively in Brandwood [4]. For us it is important that using Wirtinger calculus we can calculate the gradient for the non analytical error functions, we can calculate the Taylor expansion for the error function $(E(w + \Delta w) = E(w) - \eta g^T \bar{g} + \frac{\eta^2}{2} \bar{g}^T G \bar{g})$ and apply the Steepest Descent learning $\Delta w = -\eta \cdot \bar{g}$ for a small learning rate η. The figure below (see fig.1 shows the overall scheme for the CVBP. Using the presented CVBP one can train complex valued neural networks. Unfortunately, there is another issue which arises during the training of the complex valued neural networks, which is complex valued transition function.

Complex Valued Transition Function. As one can find from the mentioned above papers – analytical transition functions are unbounded due to the Liouville theorem (for example see Haykin [5]). This unboundness of functions can destroy

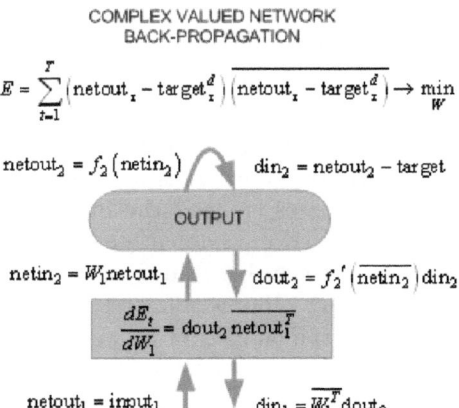

Fig. 1. Complex Valued Back-Propagation. Notations: *netin* - layer inputs, *netout* - layer outputs, *din* -layer derivative input, *dout* -layer derivative output, W_i are network weights, arrows show the information flow, $(\cdot)$ - means complex conjunction. The figure depicts the locality of the CVBP algorithm and independence of the BP from the network architecture.

any computations in few iterations. To solve the problem one can bound the weights, in case the "good" region for the function arguments is known. If not, it is possible to use the so-called "engineered" functions, which are artificial but do not allow unlimited growth of the output amplitude. To calculate the derivative of such functions one should use Wirtinger calculus discussed above. An example of such functions is given further: $f(z) = \tanh(z_r) + i \cdot \tanh(z_{im})$ or $f(z) = \tanh(r)e^{i \cdot \phi}$ (here r is absolute value of z and ϕ is angle of z). One can use the *sin* or *tanh* functions but he or she should take into account the position of singularities or the speed of ascending (descending) of these functions and do not allow the network arguments (weights) to go to infinite regions of these functions.

Now let us describe the architecture of the Complex Valued Historical Consistent Neural Network (further CVHCNN).

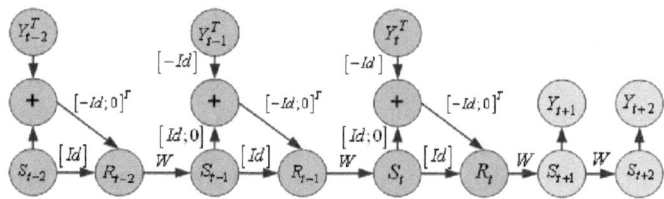

Fig. 2. HCNN architecture. Notations: Y^T is target, R_t is teacher forcing block, S_i is state vector, W is shared weights matrix, $[Id]$ is identity matrix, $(\cdot)^T$ means matrix transpose

2.2   Architecture Description and Insights on Training

The Historical Consistent Neural Network (further HCNN, for more information authors refer to Zimmermann [1]) can do the modeling of the systems which correspond to the eq.1. This architecture is working in the following way (see fig. 2): some bias signal is coming to the most left state of the network (often it is a random noise distributed normally). This network does not have inputs (in the usual sense of this word, states transfer the information from one state to the next one, doing unfolding in time), which means it is autonomous. It tries to model the given outputs with an internal dynamics. To train it one should use the so called Teacher Forcing (Zimmermann [1]) for the time moments from $t-n$ to t (see fig.2), where n is the number of network layers (recurrence layers). One can use the following system of equations to describe the teacher forcing training:

$$\begin{cases} \left[\begin{matrix} \tau \le t : s_{\tau+1} = f(W(s_\tau - [Id;0](y_\tau - y_\tau^d))) \\ \tau > t : s_{\tau+1} = f(Ws_\tau) \end{matrix} \right. \\ \forall t : y_\tau = [Id,0]s_\tau \end{cases} \tag{3}$$

where $[Id, 0] = \begin{bmatrix} \overbrace{1, 1, ..., 1}^{N_s}, \underbrace{0, 0, ..., 0}_{N_o} \end{bmatrix}$, N_o is number of network outputs, N_s is number of network states (number of hidden neurons), f is non linear transition function, W is the weights matrix. Note, that matrix W and function f are every time (at each state of the model) the same matrix and function y_τ is the network output, y_τ^d is the network desired output. To have the forecast one should apply matrix W and then transition function f to the state vector, to obtain the network outputs one has to apply the matrix $[Id; 0]$ to the obtained state vector. Iteratively applying a matrix W and a function f one can obtain the forecast for the needed horizon.

Using this teacher forcing training and the CVBP algorithm we can train the CVHCNN. One should admit the stability of CVHCNN training. The answer to this fact is that due to the teacher forcing we avoid uncontrolled behavior of the information flow inside the CVHCNN which can be rather dangerous for the stability of computations caused by the unlimited functions or function singularities.

2.3   Problem Description and Modeling Results

Problem Description. The Lorenz Problem is an example of a non-linear dynamic system corresponding to the long-term behavior of the Lorenz oscillator. The Lorenz oscillator is a 3-dimensional dynamical system [10]:

$$\begin{cases} \frac{dx}{dt} = \sigma(y - x); \frac{dy}{dt} = x(\rho - z) - y; \frac{dz}{dt} = xy - \beta z \end{cases} \tag{4}$$

here $x, y, z \in \mathbb{C}$, parameters we will take as following: $\beta = 8/3$; $\rho = 28; \sigma = 10$; $h = 0.01$ where h – the step in Euler scheme of differential equation system solving. Complex values can be obtained by multiplying x, y, z by $e^{i \cdot sin(t)}$, where t – time.

Modeling Results. The task was to achieve the maximum possible forecast for all 3 coordinates of Lorenz system development (see eq.4). Let us describe the CVHCNN architecture. The number of layers is 15, the number of states is 15, the matrix weights are randomly initialized in the $[-0.2, -0.2i; 0.2, 0.2i]$ rectangle, the number of outputs is 3 (x, y and z coordinates respectively), the activation function is $f(z) = tanh(z)e^{i \cdot \phi}$, learning rate η was equal to 0.005. The data structure is like following. Training set contains 1400 data points, Test set – 583 and Forecast set – 20. Test set contains 1 step predictions for 583 moments in time. The Forecast set contains 20 steps iterated prediction (network uses forecasted values to predict the next one). All sets follow one after another (time series are historical (dynamical) consistent). To estimate the quality of the network we have used the Root Mean Squared Error and R^2 – is the Determination coefficient. The negative R^2 values arise because of the smooth Lorenz system behavior (desired outputs are close to their average values, which

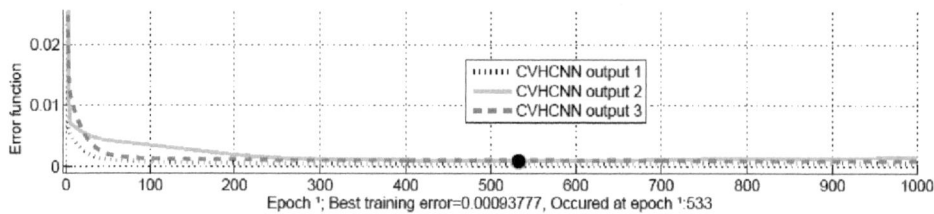

Fig. 3. Training Error Convergence

Table 1. Test set results. Output 1 is x coordinate, Output 2 is y coordinate etc.

RMS for the test set			R^2 for the test set		
output #	absolute	angle	output #	absolute	angle
output 1	0.0005	0.0002	output 1	0.97	0.99
output 2	0.0011	0.0001	output 2	0.90	0.99
output 3	0.0008	0.0001	output 3	0.88	0.99

makes R^2 very negative despite network outputs). Each experiment was repeated 10 times and the results were averaged except the best and the worst.

Training set results are presented at the fig. 3: the error function for all three outputs is exponentially decreasing and is nearly 0. The Test set results are presented for the absolute and angle parts of the CVHCNN output. From the tables below one can see that the Test set results are very promising: all RMS values are close to 0, R^2 values are close to 1. Forecast set results are presented for the absolute part (see fig. 4) and for the angle (phase) part (see fig. 5) of the CVHCNN output. Tables below (see 2) show the statistics for the 20 steps prediction. One should be very careful while treating the $R^2 < 0$. In case desired outputs do not change significantly the denominator of the R^2 is very small, which makes the complete fraction very big. Subtracting this big value from 1 makes the R^2 negative. One should admit that the CVHCNN is giving not only the forecast for the absolute part of the complex output, which contains Lorenz values, but also predicts the sin of time, which stands at the angle (phase) part of the complex output. Therefore by looking at the angle value we can say to which moment in time the prediction is related. In case the prediction for the time (phase of the complex output) starts behaving incorrect (we know this moment

Table 2. Forecast set results. Output 1 is x coordinate, Output 2 is y coordinate etc.

RMS for 20 steps forecast			R^2 for 20 steps forecast		
output #	absolute	angle	output #	absolute	angle
output 1	0.0000	0.0201	output 1	0.86	< 0
output 2	0.0000	0.0059	output 2	0.70	< 0
output 3	0.0007	0.0004	output 3	< 0	< 0

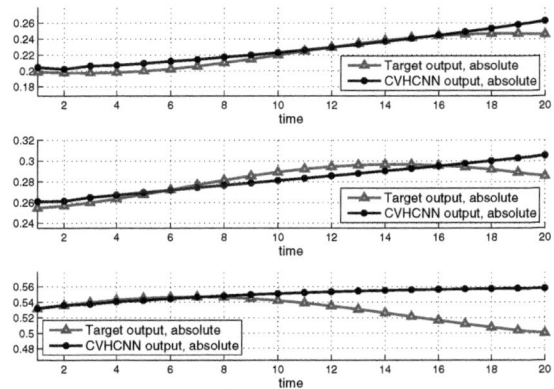

Fig. 4. Forecast for 20 steps, absolute parts of the CVHCNN outputs

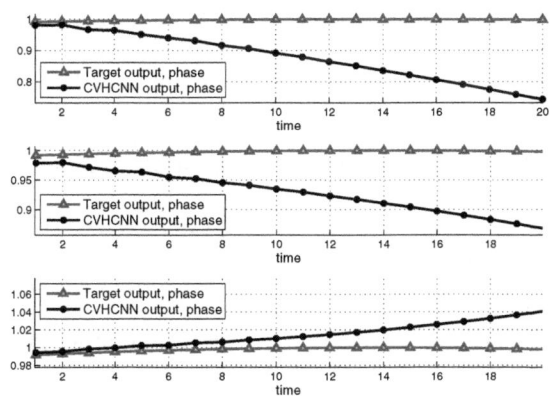

Fig. 5. Forecast for 20 steps, angle parts of the CVHCNN outputs

since time is changing in a linear manner) then we cannot trust our absolute parts predictions any more. The last statement is not proven statistically or theoretically, therefore it should be checked for consistency.

3   Conclusions and Outlook

In the present paper we have shown the back propagation algorithm, presented its locality and extended it for the complex valued case. Then we discussed the CVHCNN which is recurrent. Then we showed that CVHCNN is trainable, moreover the training is robust under certain conditions. We have considered two real world problems and showed the applicability of the CVHCNN for the modeling of such systems (both, real valued and complex valued dynamics).

One of the advantages which arise from the complex representation is the natural representation of time inside the complex valued network which means that we have the prediction not only for the absolute part of the complex (which is for example Lorenz coordinate) but also the time moment to which this prediction is related. This gives us a possibility to think about the continuous dynamics modeling, which was not possible to do to the moment. In the future we are planning to apply CVHCNN for the continuous dynamics modeling and to show, that trained network can give the prediction which includes the moment in time to which this prediction is related. This option is to be investigated in the future.

References

1. Zimmermann, H.G., Grothmann, R., Schafer, A.M., Tietz, C.: Dynamical Consistent Recurrent Neural Networks. In: Proc. of the Int. Joint Conference on Neural Networks (IJCNN), vol. 3, pp. 1537–1541 Montreal (2005)
2. Schaefer, A.M., Zimmermann, H.G.: Recurrent Neural Networks are Universal Approximators. In: Proc. of International Conference on Artificial Neural Networks (ICANN), Athens. LNCS, vol. 17(4), pp. 253–263. Springer, Heidelberg (2006)
3. Zimmermann, H.G., Minin, A., Kusherbaeva, V.: Comparison of the Complex Valued and Real Valued Neural Networks Trained with Gradient Descent and Random Search Algorithms. In: European Symposium on Artificial Neural Networks, ESANN 2011 (to appear 2011)
4. Brandwood, D.H.: A complex gradient operator and its application in adaptive array theory. IEE Proceedings, F: Communications, Radar and Signal Processing 130(1), 1116 (1983)
5. Leung, H., Haykin, S.: The Complex Back Propagation. IEEE Transactions on Signal Processing 39(9), 2101–2104 (1991)
6. Hirose, A.: Continuous Complex-Valued Back-propagation Learning. Electronics Letters 28(20), 1854–1855 (1992)
7. Nitta, T.: An Extension of the Back-Propagation Algorithm to Complex Numbers. Neural Networks 10(8), 1391–1415 (1997)
8. Kim, T., Adali, T.: Fully Complex Multi-Layered Perceptron Network for Nonlinear Signal Processing. VLSI Signal Processing 32, 29–43 (2002)
9. Gangal, A., Kalra, P., Chauhan, S.: Performance Evaluation of Complex Valued Neural Networks Using Various Error Functions. Enformatika 23, 27–32 (2007)
10. Lorenz, E.N.: Deterministic nonperiodic flow. Lecture Supplement 20, 130–141 (1963)

Sparse Spatio-temporal Gaussian Processes with General Likelihoods

Jouni Hartikainen, Jaakko Riihimäki, and Simo Särkkä

Dept. of Biomedical Engineering and Computational Science
Aalto University, Finland
jmjharti@cc.hut.fi, jaakko.riihimaki@tkk.fi, simo.sarkka@tkk.fi

Abstract. In this paper, we consider learning of spatio-temporal processes by formulating a Gaussian process model as a solution to an evolution type stochastic partial differential equation. Our approach is based on converting the stochastic infinite-dimensional differential equation into a finite dimensional linear time invariant (LTI) stochastic differential equation (SDE) by discretizing the process spatially. The LTI SDE is time-discretized analytically, resulting in a state space model with linear-Gaussian dynamics. We use expectation propagation to perform approximate inference on non-Gaussian data, and show how to incorporate sparse approximations to further reduce the computational complexity. We briefly illustrate the proposed methodology with a simulation study and with a real world modelling problem.

Keywords: Gaussian processes, spatio-temporal data, expectation propagation, sparse approximations.

1 Introduction

Over the last decades Gaussian process (GP) based methods [1] have steadily increased popularity as prominent tools for data analysis in several fields, including spatial statistics, epidemiology and machine learning. Although, in the common machine learning setting the modeled phenomena are assumed to be static in time, learning of time dependent spatio-temporal models have recently gained much interest. So far, the application of generic GP techniques to spatio-temporal data has been hindered by the steep increase in computational requirements with respect to the number of data points.

In this article, we show how evolution type stochastic partial differential equations [2] can be used as flexible prior models in spatio-temporal learning. In our approach, the Gaussian spatio-temporal prior processes are modeled as linear time-invariant stochastic partial differential equations, and the measurement models are assumed to be generic conditional distribution models for the measurements. Formulating the model this way enables us to make use of the Markov property inherent in the system to perform inference sequentially. Furthermore, we show how to incorporate the recently proposed sparse GP approximations

T. Honkela et al. (Eds.): ICANN 2011, Part I, LNCS 6791, pp. 193–200, 2011.

[3,4] into the spatio-temporal formulation, which further reduces the computational burden. When combined with expectation propagation (EP) [5] approximate inference scheme the computations are very cheap, enabling accurate inference on large-scale spatio-temporal data sets.

As such, learning of spatio-temporal systems which are modeled as stochastic differential equations is a mature subject and has been much studied in control engineering under the names distributed parameter systems [6] and infinite-dimensional (Kalman) filtering [7]. More recently, the Bayesian Kalman filtering approach to spatio-temporal estimation has been studied, for example, in geostatistics [8,9,10] as well as in statistical inversion theory [11,12]. In machine learning context the usage of differential equations and partial differential equations for encoding prior information into Gaussian process regression models has recently been discussed in [13].

2   Model and Methods

2.1   Spatio-temporal Gaussian Processes

In this paper we consider evolution type stochastic partial differential equations (SPDEs) [2] of the following form:

$$\frac{\partial \mathbf{x}(t, \mathbf{r})}{\partial t} = \mathcal{A}_r \mathbf{x}(t, \mathbf{r}) + \mathcal{L}_r \mathbf{w}(t, \mathbf{r}), \quad \mathbf{y}_k \sim \prod_{i=1}^{n} p(y_{ki} \,|\, \mathbf{x}(t_k, \mathbf{r}_i)), \tag{1}$$

where $\mathbf{x}(t, \mathbf{r})$ denotes the latent spatio-temporal prior Gaussian process depending on the time $t \geq 0$ and spatial location $\mathbf{r} \in \mathbb{D}$ on some bounded domain $\mathbb{D} \subset \Re^d$, and $\mathbf{y}_k = (y_{k1}, \ldots, y_{kn})$ are the measurements. $\mathcal{A}_r$ and $\mathcal{L}_r$ are linear operators acting on the variable $\mathbf{r}$. The noise process $\mathbf{w}(t, \mathbf{r})$ is a Gaussian process with $\mathbf{r}$-dimensional covariance function of the time-white form $k(t, \mathbf{r}; t', \mathbf{r}') = \delta(t - t') \, k(\mathbf{r}, \mathbf{r}')$, where $k(\mathbf{r}, \mathbf{r}')$ is some suitably chosen spatial covariance function. Since $\mathcal{A}_r$ and $\mathcal{L}_r$ are linear operators and $\mathbf{w}(t, \mathbf{r})$ is a Gaussian process, $\mathbf{x}(t, \mathbf{r})$ is also a Gaussian process.

Often in Bayesian inference for Gaussian processes the model is formulated in terms of time-space covariance function $k(t, \mathbf{r}; t', \mathbf{r}')$ instead of a SPDE. However, as shown in [14] there is one-to-one mapping between a large class of temporal covariance functions (including the Matérn class) and linear state space models. Similarly, there is an analogous one-to-one mapping between spatio-temporal covariance functions and SPDEs. In the case of separable covariance functions of the form $k(t, \mathbf{r}; t', \mathbf{r}') = k_t(t, t') \, k_s(\mathbf{r}, \mathbf{r}')$ where k_t and k_s are appropriate temporal and spatial covariance functions, the mapping becomes particularly simple and computationally efficient. In our examples we shall consider models of this form.

After obtaining a set of observations $\mathbf{y}_{1:T} = \{\mathbf{y}, \ldots, \mathbf{y}_T\}$ the aim is to infer the state posterior distribution $p(\mathbf{x}(t, \mathbf{r})|\mathbf{y}_{1:T})$. In practice, $\mathbf{x}(t, \mathbf{r})$ is discretized with respect to space and time to make the model tractable. Additionally, the dynamic model typically has few hyperparameters $\theta = (\theta_1, \ldots, \theta_p)$, which need to be learned. These can include, for instance, the spatial length scales and magnitudes of the noise process $\mathbf{w}(t, \mathbf{r})$ as well as possible parameters of the operators $\mathcal{A}_r$ and $\mathcal{L}_r$.

2.2   Making the Model Tractable

A simple way to convert a stochastic partial differential equation model into tractable form is to use discretization. For example, by using a finite difference or finite basis type of approximation in the spatial dimension, the infinite-dimensional SPDE model can be transformed into finite-dimensional SDE:

$$\frac{d\mathbf{x}(t)}{dt} = \mathbf{F}\,\mathbf{x}(t) + \mathbf{L}\,\mathbf{n}(t), \tag{2}$$

where matrices $\mathbf{F}$ and $\mathbf{L}$ are finite dimensional approximations to the linear operators $\mathcal{A}_r$ and $\mathcal{L}_r$, and $\mathbf{x}(t) = (\mathbf{x}_1(t), \ldots, \mathbf{x}_n(t))$ is the state of the process at a finite set of spatial points $\{\mathbf{r}_1, \ldots, \mathbf{r}_n\}$. GPs with separable covariance functions result also in models of this form, where $\mathbf{n}(t)$ has the covariance function $\delta(t - t')\, k_s(\mathbf{r}, \mathbf{r}')$ and $\mathbf{F}$ is a $hn \times hn$ block diagonal matrix, where the $h \times h$ blocks are constructed in such a way that they determine the desired temporal covariance function $k_t(t, t')$ for the n components (see [14] for more details).

In practice, we are interested in the values of the Gaussian process at discrete points of time, say, $t \in \{t_1, t_2, \ldots\}$. By using the well known methods from linear systems theory [15], the continuous time LTI model above can be transformed into discrete time model of the following form:

$$\mathbf{x}_k = \mathbf{A}_{k-1}\,\mathbf{x}_{k-1} + \mathbf{q}_{k-1}, \quad \mathbf{q}_{k-1} \sim N(\mathbf{0}, \mathbf{Q}_{k-1}), \quad \mathbf{y}_k \sim p(\mathbf{y}_k \,|\, \mathbf{x}_k), \tag{3}$$

where the matrices $\mathbf{A}_{k-1}$ and $\mathbf{Q}_{k-1}$ have analytic solutions (see, e.g., [15]).

2.3   Sparse Approximations

Suppose that we have a GP prior on n latent variables $\mathbf{x} \in \Re^n$ with input features $\{\mathbf{r}_x^i\}_{i=1}^n$ as $\mathbf{x} \sim N(0, \mathbf{K}_{\mathbf{x},\mathbf{x}})$. The problem of this approach is the $\mathcal{O}(n^3)$ scaling of computations in the inference. The recently developed sparse approximations [3,4] are aimed to mitigate these problems by placing a GP prior on a smaller set of m *inducing variables* $\mathbf{u} \in \Re^m$ (with own input features $\{\mathbf{r}_u^i\}_{i=1}^m$) as $\mathbf{u} \sim N(0, \mathbf{K}_{\mathbf{u},\mathbf{u}})$, and then setting a linear-Gaussian relationship between the inducing variables $\mathbf{u}$ and the actual latent variables $\mathbf{x}$ as $\mathbf{x}|\mathbf{u} \sim N(\mathbf{H}\,\mathbf{u}, \mathbf{R})$. Different approximations can be constructed by choosing the matrices $\mathbf{H}$ and $\mathbf{R}$ appropriately. For example, by choosing $\mathbf{H} = \mathbf{K}_{\mathbf{x},\mathbf{u}}\mathbf{K}_{\mathbf{u},\mathbf{u}}^{-1}$ and $\mathbf{R} = \mathrm{diag}(\mathbf{K}_{\mathbf{x},\mathbf{x}} - \mathbf{K}_{\mathbf{x},\mathbf{u}}\,\mathbf{K}_{\mathbf{u},\mathbf{u}}^{-1}\,\mathbf{K}_{\mathbf{u},\mathbf{x}})$ we obtain the *fully independent conditional* (FIC) approximation, which we use as an example during the rest of this paper. Due to linear-Gaussian formulation, the values of $\mathbf{u}$ can always be integrated out analytically during the inference[1], and by using the well-known matrix inverse lemma the computations can be significantly reduced if $\mathbf{R}$ is of such form that it can be inverted easily. For example, if $\mathbf{R}$ is diagonal the complexity is $\mathcal{O}(nm^2)$.

---

[1] The input features of $\mathbf{u}$, however, have an impact on the result.

To translate these ideas to spatio-temporal models we propose to formulate a separable spatio-temporal GP prior model for *inducing process* $\mathbf{u}(t) \in \Re^m$ as

$$\frac{d\mathbf{u}(t)}{dt} = \mathbf{F}_u \mathbf{u}(t) + \mathbf{L}_u \mathbf{n}(t), \tag{4}$$

and the observation model as

$$\mathbf{x}_k|\mathbf{u}_k \sim N(\mathbf{H}_k\mathbf{u}_k, \mathbf{R}_k), \ \mathbf{y}_k \sim p(\mathbf{y}_k|\mathbf{x}_k). \tag{5}$$

This formulation allows also to specify more general models by defining $\mathbf{H}_k$ and $\mathbf{R}_k$ appropriately. For example, we can formulate additive models, in which there are separate spatial, temporal and spatio-temporal components as well as covariates, which have linear or fixed basis effects. This approach allows also to predict the process on arbitrary input $\mathbf{r}$ since we can write the conditional as $\mathbf{x}(t, \mathbf{r})|\mathbf{u}(t) \sim N(\mathbf{H}(\mathbf{r})\mathbf{u}(t), \mathbf{R}(\mathbf{r}))$, which we can easily integrate over the posterior of $\mathbf{u}(t)$ to get the marginal of $\mathbf{x}(t, \mathbf{r})$.

2.4 Expectation Propagation for Dynamic Systems

With generic GPs and non-Gaussian likelihoods expectation propagation (EP) [5] has been shown to give state-of-the-art performance compared to other deterministic inference methods [16]. For dynamic systems EP was first introduced by [17] and later extended for non-linear/Gaussian [18] and non-linear/Poisson smoothing problems [19]. With EP, Gaussian approximations are made only in the state space, avoiding possible difficulties arising with the Kalman filtering type of methods [15]. In this article we apply EP to spatio-temporal GPs with non-Gaussian likelihoods.

The central idea of EP is to factor the smoothing distribution as

$$p(\mathbf{x}_{1:T}|\mathbf{y}_{1:T}) \approx \hat{p}(\mathbf{x}_{1:T}) \propto \prod_{k=1}^{T} \alpha_k(\mathbf{x}_k)\beta_k(\mathbf{x}_k), \tag{6}$$

where the forward and backward messages $\alpha_k(\mathbf{x}_k) \propto p(\mathbf{x}_k|\mathbf{y}_{1:k})$ and $\beta_k(\mathbf{x}_k) \propto p(\mathbf{y}_{k+1:T}|\mathbf{x}_k, \mathbf{y}_{1:k})$ are iteratively refined such that the Kullback-Leibler (KL) divergence from the true posterior $p(\mathbf{x}_{1:T}|\mathbf{y}_{1:T})$ to an approximation $\hat{p}(\mathbf{x}_{1:T})$ is minimized. While the global minimization is intractable, in EP the minimization is performed by sequentially minimizing the KL divergence from $p(\mathbf{x}_{k-1}, \mathbf{x}_k|\mathbf{y}_{1:T}) \propto \alpha_{k-1}(\mathbf{x}_{k-1})p(\mathbf{x}_k|\mathbf{x}_{k-1})p(\mathbf{y}_k|\mathbf{x}_k)\beta_k(\mathbf{x}_k)$ to an approximation $\hat{p}(\mathbf{x}_{k-1}, \mathbf{x}_k)$. The messages $\alpha_k(\mathbf{x}_k)$ and $\beta_k(\mathbf{x}_k)$ are typically chosen to be members of exponential family (in our case un-normalized Gaussians), and such cases the minimization of KL divergence is equivalent to moment matching. In our case this means that the approximation $\hat{p}(\mathbf{x}_{k-1}, \mathbf{x}_k)$ is Gaussian, and in next section we briefly detail how to seek its moments efficiently for the class of models considered here. After obtaining $\hat{p}(\mathbf{x}_{k-1}, \mathbf{x}_k)$, the messages are updated in forward pass as $\alpha_k^{\text{new}}(\mathbf{x}_k) = \int \hat{p}(\mathbf{x}_{k-1}, \mathbf{x}_k)d\mathbf{x}_{k-1}/\beta_k(\mathbf{x}_k)$ and in backward pass as $\beta_{k-1}^{\text{new}}(\mathbf{x}_{k-1}) = \int \hat{p}(\mathbf{x}_{k-1}, \mathbf{x}_k)d\mathbf{x}_k/\alpha_{k-1}(\mathbf{x}_{k-1})$. Usually several forward and backward passes over the data are needed to achieve convergence.

Approximating the Two-Slice Posterior. We now seek to find a Gaussian approximation for $p(\mathbf{x}_{k-1}, \mathbf{x}_k | \mathbf{y}_{1:T})$ via moment matching. First, the product of densities $p_*(\mathbf{x}_{k-1}, \mathbf{x}_k) = \alpha_{k-1}(\mathbf{x}_{k-1}) p(\mathbf{x}_k | \mathbf{x}_{k-1})$ can be written as

$$p_*(\mathbf{x}_{k-1}, \mathbf{x}_k) \propto N(\mathbf{x}_{k-1,k} | \mathbf{m}_{k-1,k}^*, \mathbf{P}_{k-1,k}^*), \tag{7}$$

where

$$\mathbf{m}_{k-1,k}^* = \begin{bmatrix} \mathbf{m}_{k-1}^\alpha \\ \mathbf{m}_k^* \end{bmatrix}, \quad \mathbf{P}_{k-1,k}^* = \begin{bmatrix} \mathbf{P}_{k-1}^\alpha & \mathbf{D}_k^T \\ \mathbf{D}_k & \mathbf{P}_k^* \end{bmatrix} \tag{8}$$

and

$$\mathbf{m}_k^* = \mathbf{A}_{k-1} \mathbf{m}_{k-1}^\alpha, \quad \mathbf{D}_k = \mathbf{A}_{k-1} \mathbf{P}_{k-1}^\alpha, \quad \mathbf{P}_k^* = \mathbf{A}_{k-1} \mathbf{P}_{k-1}^\alpha \mathbf{A}_{k-1}^T + \mathbf{Q}_{k-1}. \tag{9}$$

This can also be decomposed as $p_*(\mathbf{x}_{k-1}, \mathbf{x}_k) \propto p_*(\mathbf{x}_k) p_*(\mathbf{x}_{k-1} | \mathbf{x}_k)$, where

$$p_*(\mathbf{x}_k) = N(\mathbf{x}_k |, \mathbf{m}_k^*, \mathbf{P}_k^*), \quad p_*(\mathbf{x}_{k-1} | \mathbf{x}_k) = N(\mathbf{x}_{k-1} | \mathbf{m}_{k-1|k}^*, \mathbf{P}_{k-1|k}^*),$$
$$\mathbf{m}_{k-1|k}^* = \mathbf{m}_{k-1}^\alpha + \mathbf{D}_k^T [\mathbf{P}_k^*]^{-1} (\mathbf{x}_k - \mathbf{m}_k^*), \quad \mathbf{P}_{k-1|k}^* = \mathbf{P}_{k-1}^\alpha - \mathbf{D}_k^T [\mathbf{P}_k^*]^{-1} \mathbf{D}_k. \tag{10}$$

The backward message can be incorporated by simply using the product rule of Gaussian distribution to get $p_{**}(\mathbf{x}_k) = p_*(\mathbf{x}_k) \beta_k(\mathbf{x}_k) \propto N(\mathbf{x}_k | \mathbf{m}_k^{**}, \mathbf{P}_k^{**})$.

The posterior is now of form $\hat{p}(\mathbf{x}_{k-1}, \mathbf{x}_k) \propto p_*(\mathbf{x}_{k-1} | \mathbf{x}_k) p_{**}(\mathbf{x}_k) p(\mathbf{y}_k | \mathbf{x}_k)$. By using the Bayes' rule we can write $\hat{p}(\mathbf{x}_k) \propto p_{**}(\mathbf{x}_k) p(\mathbf{y}_k | \mathbf{x}_k)$ when we treat $p_{**}(\mathbf{x}_k)$ as a prior for $\mathbf{x}_k$. Generally this is not of an analytically tractable form, but we can seek Gaussian approximations by applying any approximate inference scheme applicable to GPs with non-Gaussian likelihoods. Common approaches are Laplace approximation or EP (see, e.g.,[1]). If we use sparse approximations or other generalized observation models, the dynamic model would be defined for $\mathbf{u}_k$ and the prior for the "moment matching" algorithm is $p_{**}(\mathbf{x}_k) \propto N(\mathbf{H}_k \mathbf{m}_k^{**}, \mathbf{H}_k \mathbf{P}_k^{**} \mathbf{H}_k^T + \mathbf{R}_k)$. Since the covariance of this prior is of same form as in sparse GPs, we can use same tricks as presented, e.g., in [20] to speed up the inference. With this we achieve the overall complexity $\mathcal{O}(NTnm^2)$, where N is the number of EP iterations across the time sequence (in our examples we used $N = 3$, which we empirically observed to be sufficient).

After obtaining an approximation $\hat{p}(\mathbf{x}_k) \propto N(\mathbf{x}_k | \mathbf{m}_k, \mathbf{P}_k)$, the (marginalized) posterior of $\mathbf{x}_{k-1}$ used in updating the backward messages can be obtained by combining $\hat{p}(\mathbf{x}_k)$ with (10), which results in Kalman smoothing like equations that are not stated here due to lack of space.

3   Results

We briefly show how to analyze log-Gaussian Cox process models by using the presented modelling framework. We consider two large sized examples: a simulation study highlighting the properties of our approach, and a real-world example concerning tropical rainforest point process data modelled recently by [21,22].

The log-Gaussian Cox process can be formulated in practice such that the observations y_i in the region w_i are Poisson distributed with mean $|w_i| \exp(\eta(t_i, \mathbf{r}_i))$, where $|w_i|$ is the area of the subregion (in our examples constant), and $\eta(t, \mathbf{r})$ is the latent intensity field, which is given a spatial or spatio-temporal prior.

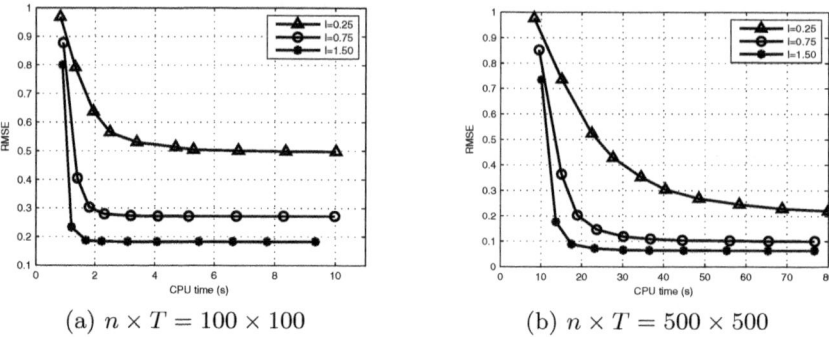

(a) $n \times T = 100 \times 100$ (b) $n \times T = 500 \times 500$

Fig. 1. Simulation study: Comparison of RMSE values versus the used CPU time for the considered data set sizes averaged over several simulation runs. The software was implemented on Matlab and ran on AMD Phenom II 3.5 GHz, 4GB RAM PC.

3.1 The Effect of Sparse Approximations

First we shall test how the sparse approximations affect the accuracy of the posterior estimate. For simplicity we consider here only two dimensional fields such that we treat one coordinate as time and the other as space. We simulate intensity fields η with a GP prior having a separable covariance function $k(t, r; t', r') = k_t(t, t') \, k_s(r, r')$, where both k_t and k_s are Matérn covariance functions with smoothness and magnitude parameters set to $\nu = 3/2$ and $\sigma^2 = 1$. We generate three different cases, in which the length scale parameter (common for both covariance functions) has the values $l \in \{0.25, 0.75, 1.5\}$. We generate data sets of size 100×100 and 500×500, and generate Poisson observations after generating the intensities. Given the observed data, we set the field to have a sparse GP prior and use EP to estimate its posterior. Figure 1 shows the RMSE values plotted against the used CPU time in cases of using different number of inducing variables between 2 and 70. It can be seen that the smoother the field the less number of inducing variables is needed to achieve accurate results.

3.2 Tropical Rainforest Data

We consider tropical rainforest data shown in Panel (a) of Figure 2. The data consists of 3605 trees in a rectangular rainforest area discretized into a 201×101 regular lattice. In each subregion also altitude and norm of the gradient are observed. Similarly as in [21,22], we model the log of the mean parameter in Poisson distribution as

$$\eta_{ij} = \beta_0 + \beta_{\mathrm{alt}} \, \mathrm{alt}_{ij} + \beta_{\mathrm{grad}} \, \mathrm{grad}_{ij} + \mathbf{x}_{ij} + \epsilon_{ij}, \tag{11}$$

where β_0 is a base line effect, β_{alt} and β_{grad} the effects of the elevation and gradient values, $\mathbf{x}_{ij}$ a spatially structured effect and ϵ_{ij} a non-structure random effect. We place a sequential sparse GP prior for $\mathbf{x}_{ij}$ similarly as in previous section and model the random effect as $\epsilon_{ij} \sim N(0, \sigma_\epsilon^2)$. The mean estimate of the

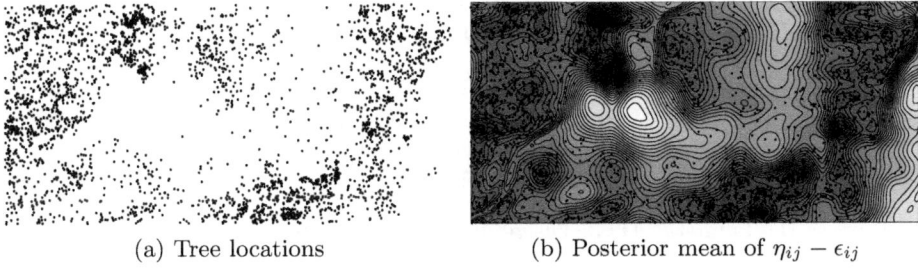

(a) Tree locations   (b) Posterior mean of $\eta_{ij} - \epsilon_{ij}$

Fig. 2. Tropical rainforest data: (a) Data and (b) the mean estimate of $\eta_{ij} - \epsilon_{ij}$ produced by EP. We used Laplace's method with FIC ($m = 60$) in approximating the one-slice posteriors. The horizontal axis was treated as time and the vertical as space.

log intensity produced by EP is shown in Panel (b) of Figure 2. Hyperparameters of the model were optimized w.r.t (approximate) marginal likelihood $p(\mathbf{y}_{1:T}) = \prod_{k:1}^{T} p(\mathbf{y}_k | \mathbf{y}_{1:k-1})$. Although we could use the full spatio-temporal GP prior for the data considered here, by using FIC the computations were significantly faster (the optimization taking only few minutes of CPU time) without affecting result.

4   Conclusions

In this article we have shown how spatio-temporal Gaussian processes can be formed as linear-Gaussian state-space models that can be efficiently inferred by using sequential algorithms. We have shown the key details on how to implement EP for this class of GP priors with non-Gaussian observations. Moreover, we have shown how to incorporate the sparse approximations for further speeding up the computations. In future work we shall study wider class of spatio-temporal Gaussian processes with more general covariance functions and linear operators, implement a finite basis type of approximation to the SPDE by using the sparse approximations, marginalize over the hyperparameters numerically as in [21,22] and apply the developed modelling framework to high dimensional data sets.

Acknowledgments. The authors would like to thank Finnish Doctoral Programme in Computational Sciences (FICS), Centre of Excellence in Computational Complex Systems Research (COSY) and Academy of Finland for financial support, and Aki Vehtari, Pasi Jylänki, Janne Ojanen and Jarno Vanhatalo for helpful discussions during the work.

References

1. Rasmussen, C.E., Williams, C.K.I.: Gaussian Processes for Machine Learning. MIT Press, Cambridge (2006)
2. Da Prato, G., Zabczyk, J.: Stochastic Equations in Infinite Dimensions. Cambridge University Press, Cambridge (1992)

3. Quinonero-Candela, J., Rasmussen, C.E.: A unifying view of sparse approximate Gaussian process regression. Journal Of Machine Learning Research 6, 1939–1959 (2005)
4. Snelson, E., Ghahramani, Z.: Sparse Gaussian process using pseudo-inputs. In: Weiss, Y., Schölkopf, B., Platt, J. (eds.) Advances in Neural Information Processing Systems, vol. 18. MIT Press, Cambridge (2006)
5. Minka, T.: A family of algorithms for approximate Bayesian inference. PhD thesis, Massachusetts Institute of Technology (2001)
6. Ray, W.H., Lainiotis, D.G.: Distributed Parameter Systems. Dekker, New York (1978)
7. Curtain, R.: A survey of infinite-dimensional filtering. SIAM Review 17(3), 395–411 (1975)
8. Wikle, C.K., Cressie, N.: A dimension-reduced approach to space-time Kalman filtering. Biometrika 86(4), 815–829 (1999)
9. Cressie, N., Wikle, C.K.: Space-time Kalman filter. In: El-Shaarawi, A.H., Piegorsch, W.W. (eds.) Encyclopedia of Environmetrics, vol. 4, pp. 2045–2049. John Wiley & Sons, Ltd., Chichester (2002)
10. Gelfand, A.E., Diggle, P.J., Fuentes, M., Guttorp, P.: Handbook of Spatial Statistics. Chapman & Hall/CRC (2010)
11. Kaipio, J., Somersalo, E.: Statistical and Computational Inverse Problems. Applied mathematical Sciences, vol. 160. Springer, Heidelberg (2005)
12. Hiltunen, P., Särkkä, S., Nissilä, I., Lajunen, A., Lampinen, J.: State space regularization in the nonstationary inverse problem for diffuse optical tomography. Inverse Problems 27(2) (2011)
13. Alvarez, M., Lawrence, N.D.: Latent force models. In: van Dyk, D., Welling, M. (eds.) Proceedings of the Twelfth International Workshop on Artificial Intelligence and Statistics, pp. 9–16 (2009)
14. Hartikainen, J., Särkkä, S.: Kalman Filtering and Smoothing Solutions to Temporal Gaussian Process Regression Models. In: Proceedings of IEEE International Workshop on Machine Learning for Signal Processing (MLSP), pp. 379–384 (2010)
15. Bar-Shalom, Y., Li, X.R., Kirubarajan, T.: Estimation with Applications to Tracking and Navigation. Wiley Interscience, Hoboken (2001)
16. Nickisch, H., Rasmussen, C.: Approximations for binary Gaussian process classification. Journal of Machine Learning Research 9, 2035–2078 (2008)
17. Heskes, T., Zoeter, O.: Expectation propogation for approximate inference in dynamic bayesian networks. In: Uncertainty in Artificial Intelligence, pp. 216–223 (2002)
18. Ypma, A., Heskes, T.: Novel approximations for inference in nonlinear dynamical systems using expectation propagation. Neurocomputing 69(1-3), 85–99 (2005)
19. Yu, B.M., Cunningham, J.P., Shenoy, K.V., Sahani, M.: Neural decoding of movements: From linear to nonlinear trajectory models. In: Ishikawa, M., Doya, K., Miyamoto, H., Yamakawa, T. (eds.) ICONIP 2007, Part I. LNCS, vol. 4984, pp. 586–595. Springer, Heidelberg (2008)
20. Vanhatalo, J., Pietiläinen, V., Vehtari, A.: Approximate inference for disease mapping with sparse Gaussian processes. Statistics in Medicine 29(15), 1580–1607 (2010)
21. Rue, H., Martino, S., Chopin, N.: Approximate Bayesian inference for latent Gaussian models by using integrated nested Laplace approximations. Journal of the Royal Statistical Society (Series B) 71(2), 319–392 (2009)
22. Cseke, B., Heskes, T.: Approximate marginals in latent Gaussian models. Journal of Machine Learning Research 12, 417–454 (2011)

Learning Curves for Gaussian Processes via Numerical Cubature Integration

Simo Särkkä

Department of Biomedical Engineering and Computational Science
Aalto University, Finland
`simo.sarkka@tkk.fi`

Abstract. This paper is concerned with estimation of learning curves for Gaussian process regression with multidimensional numerical integration. We propose an approach where the recursion equations for the generalization error are approximately solved using numerical cubature integration methods. The advantage of the approach is that the eigenfunction expansion of the covariance function does not need to be known. The accuracy of the proposed method is compared to eigenfunction expansion based approximations to the learning curve.

Keywords: Gaussian process regression, learning curve, numerical cubature.

1 Introduction

Gaussian process (GP) regression [1,2] refers to a Bayesian machine learning approach, where instead of using a fixed form parametric model such as a MLP neural network [3] one postulates a Gaussian process prior over the model functions. Learning in Gaussian process regression means computing the posterior Gaussian process, which is conditioned to observed measurements. The prediction of unobserved values amounts to computing predictive distributions and their statistics.

This paper is concerned with approximate computation of learning curves for Gaussian process regression. By learning curve we mean the average generalization error $\epsilon(n)$ as function of the number of training samples n. A common way to compute approximations to the learning curves is to express the approximate average learning curve or its bounds in terms of the eigenvalues of the covariance function [4,5,6,7,8]. Upper and lower bounds for one-dimensional covariance functions, in terms of spectral densities and eigenvalues have been presented in [9]. One possible approach is to express the lower bound for the learning curve in terms of the equivalent kernel [10], which leads to similar results as the classical error bounds for Gaussian processes (see, e.g., [11,12]). Statistical physics based approximations to GP learning curves have been considered in [13,14].

In this paper we shall follow the ideas presented in [5,8], but instead of using the eigenfunction expansion, we approximate the integrals over the training and test inputs with multidimensional numerical integration. The advantage of the

T. Honkela et al. (Eds.): ICANN 2011, Part I, LNCS 6791, pp. 201–208, 2011.
© Springer-Verlag Berlin Heidelberg 2011

approach is that the learning curve can be evaluated without the knowledge of the eigenfunctions and eigenvalues of the covariance function. In the numerical integration methods, we shall specifically consider application of multidimensional generalizations of Gauss-Hermite quadratures, that is, Gauss-Hermite cubatures for computation of the multidimensional integrals. The usage of such numerical cubature rules has also recently gained attention in context of nonlinear Kalman filtering and smoothing [15,16,17,18].

2   Recursion for Learning Curve

Consider the following Gaussian process regression model:

$$f(\mathbf{x}) \sim \mathcal{GP}(0, C(\mathbf{x}, \mathbf{x}'))$$
$$y_k = f(\mathbf{x}_k) + r_k, \tag{1}$$

where y_k, $k = 1, 2, \ldots, n$ are the measurements, $r_k \sim \mathrm{N}(0, s^2)$ is the IID measurement error sequence, and the input is $\mathbf{x} \in \mathbb{R}^d$. That is, the unknown function $f(\mathbf{x})$ is modeled as a zero mean Gaussian process with the given covariance function $C(\mathbf{x}, \mathbf{x}')$. Here we shall assume that both the function $f(\mathbf{x})$ and the measurements y_k are scalar valued, but the extension to vector case is straightforward. We shall also assume that the prior Gaussian process has zero mean for notational convenience.

Given n measurements $\mathbf{y} = (y_1, \ldots, y_n)$ at input positions $\mathbf{x}_{1:n} = (\mathbf{x}_1, \ldots, \mathbf{x}_n)$ the posterior mean and covariance functions of f are given as [1,2]:

$$m^{(n)}(\mathbf{x}) = C(\mathbf{x}, \mathbf{x}_{1:n}) \left[C(\mathbf{x}_{1:n}, \mathbf{x}_{1:n}) + s^2 \mathbf{I} \right]^{-1} \mathbf{y}$$
$$C^{(n)}(\mathbf{x}, \mathbf{x}') = C(\mathbf{x}, \mathbf{x}') - C(\mathbf{x}, \mathbf{x}_{1:n}) \left[C(\mathbf{x}_{1:n}, \mathbf{x}_{1:n}) + s^2 \mathbf{I} \right]^{-1} C^T(\mathbf{x}', \mathbf{x}_{1:n}). \tag{2}$$

For the purposes of estimating the learning curves, we shall assume that the input positions in the training set $\mathbf{x}_k$ are random, and form an IID process $\mathbf{x}_1, \ldots, \mathbf{x}_n$ such that $\mathbf{x}_k \sim p(\mathbf{x})$. If we assume that the test inputs have the distribution $\mathbf{x} \sim p^*(\mathbf{x})$, we obtain the following well known expression for the average generalization error of the Gaussian process:

$$\epsilon(n) = \left\langle C(\mathbf{x}, \mathbf{x}) - C(\mathbf{x}, \mathbf{x}_{1:n}) \left[C(\mathbf{x}_{1:n}, \mathbf{x}_{1:n}) + s^2 \mathbf{I} \right]^{-1} C^T(\mathbf{x}, \mathbf{x}_{1:n}) \right\rangle, \tag{3}$$

where the expectation is taken over both the training and test input positions $\mathbf{x}_1, \ldots, \mathbf{x}_n \sim p(\cdot)$ and $\mathbf{x} \sim p^*(\cdot)$, respectively. Note that the error is no longer function of the measurements $y_1, \ldots, y_n$, nor the input positions.

This Gaussian process regression solution (2) can also be equivalently written in the following recursive form:

– **Initialization:** At initial step we have

$$m^{(0)}(\mathbf{x}) = 0$$
$$C^{(0)}(\mathbf{x}, \mathbf{x}') = C(\mathbf{x}, \mathbf{x}'). \tag{4}$$

– **Update:** At each measurement we perform the following update step:

$$m^{(k+1)}(\mathbf{x}) = m^{(k)}(\mathbf{x}) + \frac{C^{(k)}(\mathbf{x}, \mathbf{x}_k)}{C^{(k)}(\mathbf{x}_k, \mathbf{x}_k) + s^2}(y_k - m^{(k)}(\mathbf{x}))$$

$$C^{(k+1)}(\mathbf{x}, \mathbf{x}') = C^{(k)}(\mathbf{x}, \mathbf{x}') - \frac{C^{(k)}(\mathbf{x}, \mathbf{x}_k)\,C^{(k)}(\mathbf{x}', \mathbf{x}_k)}{C^{(k)}(\mathbf{x}_k, \mathbf{x}_k) + s^2}. \tag{5}$$

The result at step $k = n$ will then be exactly the same as given by the equations (2). This recursion can be seen as a special case of the update step of infinite-dimensional distributed parameter Kalman filter (see, e.g., [19,20]) with a trivial dynamic model.

Using these recursions equations, we can now write down the formal recursion formula for the covariance function, which is averaged over n training inputs as follows:

$$\hat{C}^{(k+1)}(\mathbf{x}, \mathbf{x}') = C^{(k)}(\mathbf{x}, \mathbf{x}') - \int_{\mathbb{R}^d} \frac{C^{(k)}(\mathbf{x}, \mathbf{x}_k)\,C^{(k)}(\mathbf{x}', \mathbf{x}_k)}{C^{(k)}(\mathbf{x}_k, \mathbf{x}_k) + s^2} p(\mathbf{x}_k)\,d\mathbf{x}_k. \tag{6}$$

In this article, we shall follow [8] and ignore the dependence from the inputs before the previous step and approximate this as

$$\hat{C}^{(k+1)}(\mathbf{x}, \mathbf{x}') = \hat{C}^{(k)}(\mathbf{x}, \mathbf{x}') - \int_{\mathbb{R}^d} \frac{\hat{C}^{(k)}(\mathbf{x}, \mathbf{x}_k)\,\hat{C}^{(k)}(\mathbf{x}', \mathbf{x}_k)}{\hat{C}^{(k)}(\mathbf{x}_k, \mathbf{x}_k) + s^2} p(\mathbf{x}_k)\,d\mathbf{x}_k. \tag{7}$$

The approximation to the average generalization error is then given as

$$\epsilon(n) = \int_{\mathbb{R}^d} \hat{C}^{(n)}(\mathbf{x}, \mathbf{x})\,p^*(\mathbf{x})\,d\mathbf{x}. \tag{8}$$

3   Eigenfunction Expansion Approximation of Recursion

As done in [8], we can use the eigenfunction expansion method for solving the approximate average generalization error as follows. By Mercer's theorem the input averaged kernel $\hat{C}^{(k)}(\mathbf{x}, \mathbf{x}')$ has the eigenfunction expansion

$$\hat{C}^{(k)}(\mathbf{x}, \mathbf{x}') = \sum_{i=1}^{\infty} \lambda_i^{(k)}\,\phi_i(\mathbf{x})\,\phi_i(\mathbf{x}'), \tag{9}$$

where $\phi_i(\mathbf{x})$ and $\lambda_i^{(k)}$ are the orthonormal set of eigenfunctions and eigenvalues of the kernel such that

$$\lambda_i^{(k)}\,\phi_i(\mathbf{x}) = \int_{\mathbb{R}^d} \hat{C}^{(k)}(\mathbf{x}, \mathbf{x}')\,\phi_i(\mathbf{x}')\,p(\mathbf{x}')\,d\mathbf{x}'. \tag{10}$$

Substituting the series into the recursion (7) now gives

$$\hat{C}^{(k+1)}(\mathbf{x}, \mathbf{x}') = \sum_i \lambda_i^{(k)}\,\phi_i(\mathbf{x})\,\phi_i(\mathbf{x}')$$

$$- \int_{\mathbb{R}^d} \left\{ \frac{\left[\sum_i \lambda_i^{(k)}\phi_i(\mathbf{x})\,\phi_i(\mathbf{x}_k)\right]\left[\sum_j \lambda_j^{(k)}\phi_j(\mathbf{x}')\,\phi_j(\mathbf{x}_k)\right]}{\left[\sum_i \lambda_i^{(k)}\phi_i(\mathbf{x}_k)\,\phi_i(\mathbf{x}_k)\right] + s^2} \right\} p(\mathbf{x}_k)\,d\mathbf{x}_k. \tag{11}$$

If we approximate the latter integral by taking expectations separately in denominator and numerator, then by the orthonormality properties of the eigenfunctions this reduces to:

$$\hat{C}^{(k+1)}(\mathbf{x}, \mathbf{x}') = \sum_i \left(\lambda_i^{(k)} - \frac{\left[\lambda_i^{(k)}\right]^2}{\sum_j \lambda_j^{(k)} + s^2} \right) \phi_i(\mathbf{x})\, \phi_i(\mathbf{x}'), \tag{12}$$

which implies that $\hat{C}^{(k+1)}(\mathbf{x}, \mathbf{x}')$ also has an eigenfunction expansions in terms of the same eigenfunctions. If we denote the coefficients as $\lambda_i^{(k+1)}$, then the approximate recursion equation for the coefficients is given as

$$\lambda_i^{(k+1)} = \lambda_i^{(k)} - \frac{\left[\lambda_i^{(k)}\right]^2}{\sum_j \lambda_j^{(k)} + s^2} \tag{13}$$

If we have $p^*(\mathbf{x}) = p(\mathbf{x})$, then the approximation (8) to the average generalization error now reduces to [8]

$$\epsilon_D(n) = \sum_i \left(\lambda_i^{(n)} - \frac{\left[\lambda_i^{(n)}\right]^2}{\sum_j \lambda_j^{(n)} + s^2} \right). \tag{14}$$

We could then proceed to use further approximations by considering n as continuous, which would lead to UC and LC approximations [8]:

- The upper continuous (UC) approximation has the form

$$\epsilon_{UC}(n) = s^2 \sum_i \frac{\lambda_i}{n' \lambda_i + s^2}, \tag{15}$$

  where λ_i are the eigenvalues of the prior covariance function, and the effective number of training examples n' is the solution to the self-consistency equation

$$n' + \sum_i \ln\left(1 + s^{-2} n' \lambda_i\right) = n. \tag{16}$$

- The lower continuous (LC) approximation is the solution to the self-consistency equation

$$\epsilon_{LC}(n) = s^2 \sum_i \frac{\lambda_i}{n' \lambda_i + s^2}, \tag{17}$$

  where $n' = s^2 n / [s^2 + \epsilon_{LC}(n)]$.

4   Numerical Cubature Approximation of Recursion

Cubature integration refers to methods for approximate computation of integrals of the form

$$\mathrm{E}[g(\mathbf{x})] = \int_{\mathbb{R}^d} g(\mathbf{x}) \, p(\mathbf{x}) \, d\mathbf{x}, \tag{18}$$

where $p(\mathbf{x})$ is some fixed weight function. In particular, cubature integration methods here primarily refer to multidimensional generalizations of Gaussian quadratures, that is, to approximations of the form

$$\mathrm{E}[g(\mathbf{x})] \approx \sum_i W^{(i)} \, g(\mathbf{x}^{(i)}), \tag{19}$$

where the weights $W^{(i)}$ and the evaluation points $\mathbf{x}^{(i)}$ are (known) functionals of the weight function $p(\mathbf{x})$. In particular, when $p(\mathbf{x})$ is a multidimensional Gaussian distribution, we can use multidimensional Gauss-Hermite cubatures or more efficient spherical cubature rules (see, e.g., [21,16,17]). However, because here we need quite high order rules and construction of such efficient higher order spherical rules is quite complicated task, here we have used simpler Cartesian product based Gauss-Hermite cubature rules.

We can now use a multidimensional cubature approximation to the integral in Equation (7) which leads to the following:

$$\hat{C}^{(k+1)}(\mathbf{x}, \mathbf{x}') = \hat{C}^{(k)}(\mathbf{x}, \mathbf{x}') - \sum_i W^{(i)} \frac{\hat{C}^{(k)}(\mathbf{x}, \mathbf{x}^{(i)}) \, \hat{C}^{(k)}(\mathbf{x}', \mathbf{x}^{(i)})}{\hat{C}^{(k)}(\mathbf{x}^{(i)}, \mathbf{x}^{(i)}) + s^2}, \tag{20}$$

where the weights $W^{(i)}$ and sigma points $\mathbf{x}^{(i)}$ correspond to integration over the training set distribution $p(\mathbf{x})$. For arbitrary $\mathbf{x}$ and $\mathbf{x}'$ we thus may now run the recursion (7), apply the above approximation on each step and get an approximation to $\hat{C}^{(n)}(\mathbf{x}, \mathbf{x}')$. Analogously, we can now form approximation to the average generalization error in Equation (8) as follows:

$$\int_{\mathbb{R}^d} \hat{C}^{(n)}(\mathbf{x}, \mathbf{x}) \, p^*(\mathbf{x}) \, d\mathbf{x} \approx \sum_j W^{*(j)} \, \hat{C}^{(n)}(\mathbf{x}^{*(j)}, \mathbf{x}^{*(j)}), \tag{21}$$

where the weights $W^{*(i)}$ and sigma points $\mathbf{x}^{*(i)}$ correspond to integration over the test set distribution $p^*(\mathbf{x})$. The computation of the latter integral can now be done by evaluating the former quadrature based approximation (20) at the quadrature points of the latter integral, that is, at $\mathbf{x} = \mathbf{x}' = \mathbf{x}^{*(j)}$. Note that this procedure might underestimate the generalization error slightly, because the sigma points for the train and test sets are in the same positions. It would be possible to use different sigma points for train and test sets, but then the computation would be slightly more complicated.

We can now compute simple approximation to the learning curve by assuming that $p^*(\mathbf{x}) = p(\mathbf{x})$ and by using the same cubature rule for train and test sets. This leads to a single set of sigma points $\mathbf{x}^{(i)} = \mathbf{x}^{*(i)}$ and weights $W^{(i)} = W^{*(i)}$. The algorithm can be implemented as follows:

- Initialize the elements of matrix $\mathbf{P}^{(0)}$ as follows:

$$P_{ii'}^{(0)} = C(\mathbf{x}^{(i)}, \mathbf{x}^{(i')}).\tag{22}$$

- for $n = 1, \ldots, N$ do

$$\mathbf{P}^{(n)} = \mathbf{P}^{(n-1)} - \sum_i W^{(i)} \frac{\mathbf{P}_{*i}^{(n-1)} \mathbf{P}_{i*}^{(n-1)}}{P_{ii}^{(n-1)} + s^2},\tag{23}$$

where $\mathbf{P}_{*i}$ denotes the ith column of $\mathbf{P}$ and $\mathbf{P}_{i*}$ denotes the ith row.
- The approximate learning curve is given as

$$\epsilon_C(n) = \sum_i W^{(i)} P_{ii}^{(n)}.\tag{24}$$

5   Numerical Comparison

We tested the error bounds presented in this article using 1d and 2d squared exponential (SE) covariance functions $\exp(-|x - x'|^2/(2l^2))$ and with Matérn covariance function $(1 + \sqrt{3}|x - x'|/l)\exp(-\sqrt{3}|x - x'|/l)$. For SE covariance we used the parameters values $l = 1$, $\sigma^2 = 10^{-3}$. The parameters for the Matérn covariance were selected to be $l = 1$, $\sigma^2 = 0.1$. The input and test sets were assumed to have a zero mean unit Gaussian distribution, for which the weights $W^{(i)}$ and evaluation points $x^{(i)}$ can be obtained by using existing methods.

In addition to the bounds $\epsilon_D(n)$ defined in Equation (14), $\epsilon_{UC}(n)$ in (15), $\epsilon_{LC}(n)$ in (17), and the proposed bound $\epsilon_C(n)$ in (24), we also compared to the following well known Opper-Vivarelli (OV) bound [5]:

$$\epsilon_{OV}(n) = s^2 \sum_i \frac{\lambda_i}{n\,\lambda_i + s^2}.\tag{25}$$

For the SE covariance functions we used the known closed form formulas for the eigenvalues, in the 1d Matérn case we computed the eigenvalues numerically. In the 2d Matérn case the eigenvalues were not available, because the eigenvalue problem became too big to be solved with the required numerical accuracy. We used 60th order Gauss-Hermite quadrature for the 1d $\epsilon_C(n)$ calculations and 20th order Gauss-Hermite product-rule cubature for the 2d $\epsilon_C(n)$ calculations. For all the cases, we also computed approximation to the 'true' generalization error curve $\epsilon_{MC}(n)$ using Monte Carlo method with 100 independent training sets for each training set size 1–100, and the generalization error was estimated with test sets of size 100, which were drawn independently for each MC sample.

The learning curves computed using different approximations are shown in Figure 1. As can be seen in the figures, in the 1d and 2d SE cases the proposed approximation $\epsilon_C(n)$ overestimates the error, but is still much better than $\epsilon_{OV}(n)$ and its relative accuracy is close to the other methods. In the 1d and 2d Matérn cases the proposed approximation is very accurate. The overall performance of the proposed method is very good given that it does not need the eigenvalues of the covariance function at all.

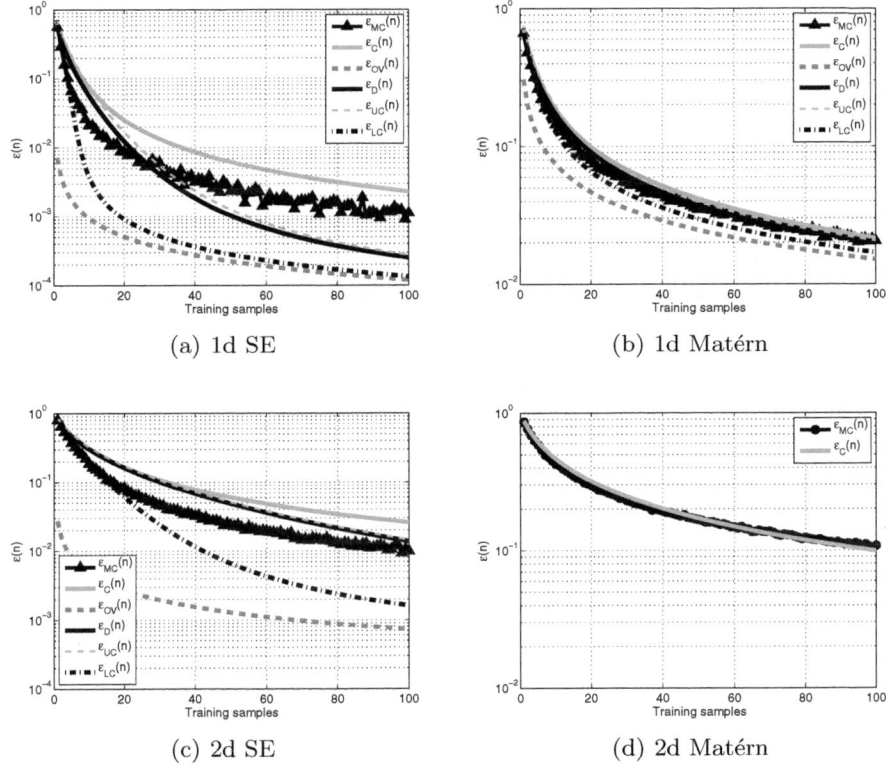

(a) 1d SE

(b) 1d Matérn

(c) 2d SE

(d) 2d Matérn

Fig. 1. Learning curves for squared exponential (SE) and Matérn covariance functions with input dimensions 1 and 2

6   Conclusion

In this article we have presented a new cubature integration based method for approximate computation of learning curves in Gaussian process regression. The advantage of the method is that it does not require availability of eigenvalues of the covariance function unlike most of the alternative methods. The accuracy of the method was numerically compared to previously proposed eigenfunction expansion based methods and the propoposed approach seems to give good approximations to learning curves especially in the case of Matérn covariance function.

Acknowledgments. The author is grateful to the Centre of Excellence in Computational Complex Systems Research of Academy of Finland for the financial support and also likes to thank Aki Vehtari for helpful comments on the manuscript.

References

1. O'Hagan, A.: Curve fitting and optimal design for prediction (with discussion). Journal of the Royal Statistical Society B 40(1), 1–42 (1978)
2. Rasmussen, C.E., Williams, C.K.I.: Gaussian Processes for Machine Learning. The MIT Press (2006)
3. Bishop, C.M.: Pattern recognition and machine learning. Springer, Heidelberg (2006)
4. Opper, M.: Regression with Gaussian processes: Average case performance. In: Theoretical Aspects of Neural Computation. Springer, Heidelberg (1997)
5. Opper, M., Vivarelli, F.: General bounds on bayes errors for regression with gaussian processes. In: NIPS, vol. 11, pp. 302–308. The MIT Press, Cambridge (1999)
6. Sollich, P.: Approximate learning curves for Gaussian processes. In: Proceedings of ICANN 1999, pp. 437–442 (1999)
7. Sollich, P.: Learning curves for Gaussian processes. In: NIPS, vol. 11. The MIT Press, Cambridge (1999)
8. Sollich, P., Halees, A.: Learning curves for Gaussian process regression: Approximations and bounds. Neural Computation 14, 1393–1428 (2002)
9. Williams, C.K.I., Vivarelli, F.: Upper and lower bounds on the learning curve for Gaussian processes. Machine Learning 40, 77–102 (2000)
10. Sollich, P., Williams, C.: Using the equivalent kernel to understand Gaussian process regression. In: NIPS, vol. 17, pp. 1313–1320. MIT Press, Cambridge (2005)
11. Van Trees, H.L.: Detection, Estimation, and Modulation Theory Part I. John Wiley & Sons, New Yark (1968)
12. Papoulis, A.: Probability, Random Variables, and Stochastic Processes. McGraw-Hill, New York (1984)
13. Malzahn, D., Opper, M.: Learning curves for Gaussian process regression: A framework for good approximations. In: NIPS, vol. 13, MIT Press, Cambridge (2001)
14. Malzahn, D., Opper, M.: A variational approach to learning curves. In: NIPS, vol. 14, MIT Press, Cambridge (2002)
15. Ito, K., Xiong, K.: Gaussian filters for nonlinear filtering problems. IEEE Transactions on Automatic Control 45, 910–927 (2000)
16. Wu, Y., Hu, D., Wu, M., Hu, X.: A numerical-integration perspective on Gaussian filters. IEEE Transactions on Signal Processing 54, 2910–2921 (2006)
17. Arasaratnam, I., Haykin, S.: Cubature Kalman filters. IEEE Transactions on Automatic Control 54, 1254–1269 (2009)
18. Särkkä, S., Hartikainen, J.: On Gaussian optimal smoothing of non-linear state space models. IEEE Transactions on Automatic Control 55, 1938–1941 (2010)
19. Curtain, R.: A survey of infinite-dimensional filtering. SIAM Review 17(3), 395–411 (1975)
20. Ray, W.H., Lainiotis, D.G.: Distributed Parameter Systems. Dekker, New York (1978)
21. Cools, R.: Constructing cubature formulae: The science behind the art. Acta Numerica 6, 1–54 Cambridge University Press, Cambridge (1997)

Cross-Species Translation of Multi-way Biomarkers

Tommi Suvitaival[1], Ilkka Huopaniemi[1], Matej Orešič[2], and Samuel Kaski[1,3]

[1] Aalto University School of Science
Department of Information and Computer Science,
Helsinki Institute for Information Technology HIIT
firstname.lastname@tkk.fi
http://research.ics.tkk.fi/mi/
[2] VTT Technical Research Centre of Finland
firstname.lastname@vtt.fi
http://sysbio.vtt.fi/
[3] University of Helsinki
Department of Computer Science,
Helsinki Institute for Information Technology HIIT

Abstract. We present a Bayesian translational model for matching patterns in data sets which have neither co-occurring samples nor variables, but only a similar experiment design dividing the samples into two or more categories. The model estimates covariate effects related to this design and separates the factors that are shared across the data sets from those specific to one data set. The model is designed to find similarities in medical studies, where there is great need for methods for linking laboratory experiments with model organisms to studies of human diseases and new treatments.

Keywords: Bayesian inference, cross-species modeling, multi-way modeling, translational modeling.

1 Introduction

We study the translational modeling problem, where the aim is to integrate data sets which have neither co-occurring samples nor variables. The only known commonality between the sets is that they have been collected from experiments with a similar design.

Translational modeling has an increasingly important application in cross-species analysis of biological experiments, where treatments to human diseases are studied using model organisms. In cross-species analysis, the question is how to integrate data sets with high dimensionality, small sample-size, and potentially structured covariates, as illustrated in Figure 1a.

The basic experimental design in the search for disease biomarkers is one-way comparison of healthy and diseased patient groups. At the simplest, biomarkers can be translated across species by comparing lists of p-values of differential

T. Honkela et al. (Eds.): ICANN 2011, Part I, LNCS 6791, pp. 209–216, 2011.

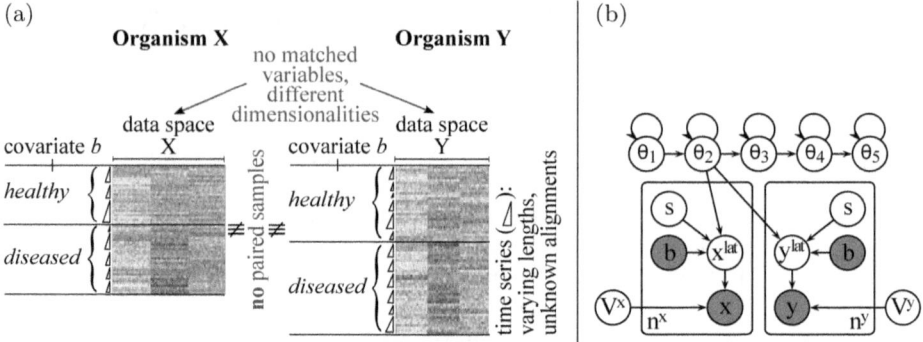

Fig. 1. (a) Data matrix representation of the translational problem. (b) Plate diagram of the proposed Bayesian graphical model. The sets $\boldsymbol{\theta}_s = \{\alpha_s^{\mathrm{sh}}, \alpha_s^{\mathrm{x}}, \alpha_s^{\mathrm{y}}, (\alpha\beta)_{s,b}^{\mathrm{sh}}, (\alpha\beta)_{s,b}^{\mathrm{x}}, (\alpha\beta)_{s,b}^{\mathrm{y}}\}$ contain all latent variables describing the corresponding HMM states. The state (category) of each sample j is determined by an observed covariate b_j and an unobserved covariate s_j.

expression from a t-test. Most existing cross-species analysis tools are limited to these simple designs [6].

Most biological experiments have, however, a multi-way experiment design, where healthy and diseased groups are further divided into subgroups according to additional covariates, such as treatment, gender, age, measurement time, etc. The basic standard statistical methods capable of properly dealing with the multi-way design are analysis of variance (ANOVA) and its multivariate generalization (MANOVA) [8].

Taking all the covariates into account complicates the analysis only slightly, but also allows us to extract considerably more information from the data. There are no earlier tools for utilizing multiple covariates and estimating their effect across data sets with neither co-occurring samples nor variables.

Time series experiments are becoming more and more common in clinical studies searching for disease biomarkers. In our multi-way design, time is one of the covariates, having a special structure. In a clinical follow-up study, such as the Type 1 Diabetes prediction and prevention study [9], measurement times are irregular due to practical reasons of data collection, and there are missing time points. In addition, life spans of organisms, such as human and mouse, are very different, resulting in very different measurement intervals. These complications cause challenges for cross-species data analysis, and call for a possibility to align the time series using machine learning techniques.

In this paper, we show how it is possible to integrate data sets with neither co-occurring samples nor variables, only based on a similar experiment design. We separate and identify shared covariate effects from data set-specific effects. We do this by building on our recent work on high-dimensional multi-way modeling and time series alignment [4]. We test the method on simulated data, and on lipidomic and metabolomic data sets.

2   Previous Work

A few iterative approaches have matched samples without taking covariate information into account. One of the methods matched only samples [10], and another matched both samples and variables [1].

For cross-species analysis, there are methods that use and require side information about the possible matchings of the variables between the data sets. Le & Bar-Joseph [5] utilized sequence similarities as a prior for clustering and matching genes across data sets of two species. Lucas *et al.* [7] inferred a set of factors that are active in one data set and used that as a starting point for the inference in the other data set, requiring at least a subset of variables to be the same across data sets. The model that we present next, does not require any prior match across neither samples nor variables.

3   Model

We address the problem of translating covariate effects across two data sets which have neither co-occurring samples nor variables. We develop a method that handles traditional multi-way experimental designs, where samples have been divided, for instance, into healthy-diseased and treated-untreated categories, or more categories with possibly more levels. In addition, the model extends to time series designs, where one covariate, the time point, is not necessarily matched across the two data sets. Irregular time points are handled by aligning the time series into latent states, which are then matchable across the data sets.

In our previous work [4], we were only able to estimate the covariate effects shared by the data sets. In this paper we present a novel matching algorithm for separating shared covariate effects from effects specific to one data set.

3.1   Dimensionality Reduction and Covariate Effects

We construct a unified multivariate model, where the inference is carried out with Gibbs sampling. It is a single hierarchical Bayesian model capable of handling uncertainty across the levels, in contrast to a straightforward successive dimensionality reduction and MANOVA. In terms of estimation of multi-way covariate effects and dimensionality reduction, the new approach builds on our earlier work on high-dimensional multi-way modeling [3]: we assume that a single latent factor vector $\mathbf{x}^{\text{lat}}$ generates a group of correlated variables in the observed data $\mathbf{x}$, and the latent factors have a covariate-dependent prior structure for each sample. These factors can thus be called clusters (of variables).

The model for sample j explained by K latent factors is

$$\mathbf{x}_j \sim \mathcal{N}\left(\boldsymbol{\mu} + \mathbf{V}\mathbf{x}_j^{\text{lat}}, \boldsymbol{\Lambda}\right)$$
$$\mathbf{x}_j^{\text{lat}} \mid (a_j, b_j) \sim \mathcal{N}\left(\boldsymbol{\alpha}_{a_j} + \boldsymbol{\beta}_{b_j} + (\boldsymbol{\alpha}\boldsymbol{\beta})_{a_j, b_j}, \mathbf{I}\right) , \tag{1}$$

where $\mathbf{x}_j$ is a p-dimensional data sample from the $n \times p$ data matrix, $\boldsymbol{\mu}$ is a p-vector of variable means, $\mathbf{V}$ is a $p \times K$ projection matrix, $\mathbf{x}_j^{\text{lat}}$ the K-vector of latent factors from the $K \times n$ latent space matrix, and $\boldsymbol{\Lambda}$ is a diagonal residual variance matrix with diagonal elements σ_i^2. Covariate effects are estimated in the K-dimensional latent space, and in Equation 1 the prior is presented for the two-way case with particular covariate values a_j and b_j selecting the main effects $\boldsymbol{\alpha}_{a_j}$ and $\boldsymbol{\beta}_{b_j}$, and an interaction effect $(\boldsymbol{\alpha\beta})_{a_j,b_j}$. In the notation, covariates a_j and b_j independently select a corresponding row from the main effect matrices $\boldsymbol{\alpha}$ and $\boldsymbol{\beta}$, respectively, and $(\boldsymbol{\alpha\beta})_{a_j,b_j}$ is an interaction effect vector of the combination a_j, b_j.

3.2   Alignment of Irregular Time Series

When one of the "ways" is irregularly sampled time, underlying states in the time series are inferred in the model by a hidden Markov model (HMM)-type state projection. The learned state allocations $\mathbf{s}$ are used as a covariate and the corresponding HMM latent variable is interpreted as the covariate effect for the sample group [4].

Now, $\mathbf{x}_j^{\text{lat}}$ is assumed to be generated by using the learned covariate s_j instead of a fixed covariate a_j:

$$\mathbf{x}_j^{\text{lat}} | (s_j, b_j) \sim \mathcal{N}\left(\boldsymbol{\alpha}_{s_j} + \boldsymbol{\beta}_{b_j} + (\boldsymbol{\alpha\beta})_{s_j,b_j}, \mathbf{I}\right), \tag{2}$$

where $\boldsymbol{\alpha}_{s_j}$ is the HMM-aligned time effect. We restrict the HMM to a linear chain structure, which is reasonable for the biological patient progression data of our experiment.

3.3   Estimation of Shared and Specific Covariate Effects

Now we have presented the model for dimensionality reduction and estimation of covariate effects in the case of a single data set. Next, we will show how this framework can be extended to the analysis of multiple data sets, and how to identify latent factors that have a match across the data sets. We not only estimate covariate effects of a single data set, but also probabilities of each latent factor being generated either by data set-specific covariate effects or by effects shared with a factor from the other data set. A plate diagram of the model is shown in Figure 1b.

The model makes a flexible assumption [4] that the observed data vectors in the two data sets X and Y are generated by the covariate effects through a transformation f^{x} and f^{y}, respectively:

$$\mathbf{x}_j | (s_j, b_j) = \boldsymbol{\mu}^{\text{x}} + f^{\text{x}}\left(\boldsymbol{\alpha}_{s_j}^{\text{sh}} + \boldsymbol{\beta}_{b_j}^{\text{sh}} + (\boldsymbol{\alpha\beta})_{s_j,b_j}^{\text{sh}}\right) + f^{\text{x}}\left(\boldsymbol{\alpha}_{s_j}^{\text{x}} + \boldsymbol{\beta}_{b_j}^{\text{x}} + (\boldsymbol{\alpha\beta})_{s_j,b_j}^{\text{x}}\right) + \boldsymbol{\varepsilon}^{\text{x}}$$

$$\mathbf{y}_i | (s_i, b_i) = \boldsymbol{\mu}^{\text{y}} + f^{\text{y}}\left(\boldsymbol{\alpha}_{s_i}^{\text{sh}} + \boldsymbol{\beta}_{b_i}^{\text{sh}} + (\boldsymbol{\alpha\beta})_{s_i,b_i}^{\text{sh}}\right) + f^{\text{y}}\left(\boldsymbol{\alpha}_{s_i}^{\text{y}} + \boldsymbol{\beta}_{b_i}^{\text{y}} + (\boldsymbol{\alpha\beta})_{s_i,b_i}^{\text{y}}\right) + \boldsymbol{\varepsilon}^{\text{y}},$$

$$\tag{3}$$

where symbols with superscript ^{sh} represent covariate effects shared by the two data sets, and symbols with superscripts ^{x} and ^{y} represent data set X and Y-specific covariate effects, respectively. The variable spaces of data sets X and Y are different, and therefore also the latent factor spaces $\mathbf{x}^{lat}$ and $\mathbf{y}^{lat}$ representing groups of correlated variables need not match. For this reason, the covariate effects have to be projected into the actual observed data spaces $\mathbf{x}$ and $\mathbf{y}$ through the previously unknown projections f^x and f^y, which will be learned jointly.

Earlier, we have learned covariate effects from multiple data sets, where samples co-occur across the sets (views) [2]. The translational problem is now more complicated, and we have to solve it in a different way.

The modeling question for two non-co-occurring data sets with a multi-way experiment design becomes the following: Does some dimension of $\mathbf{x}^{lat}$ respond to the covariates $\mathbf{s}$ and $\mathbf{b}$ similarly as one of $\mathbf{y}^{lat}$? If it does, one can represent this pattern with *shared* covariate effects $\boldsymbol{\theta}^{sh} = \{\boldsymbol{\alpha}^{sh}, \boldsymbol{\beta}^{sh}, (\boldsymbol{\alpha\beta})^{sh}\}$. The interpretation is that a group of correlated variables in data set X matches with a group in data set Y, represented by a dimension of $\mathbf{x}^{lat}$ and $\mathbf{y}^{lat}$, respectively. In biology, such factors can be considered as multi-species biomarkers. If there is no match, the response to the covariates is modeled by species-specific covariate effects $\boldsymbol{\theta}^x = \{\boldsymbol{\alpha}^x, \boldsymbol{\beta}^x, (\boldsymbol{\alpha\beta})^x\}$, and similarly for Y. Our modeling framework estimates the confidence of the shared effects.

3.4   Matching

We propose the following measure for quantifying the quality of the match between two factors from different data sets: whether the matching is better than an average matching (over other pairs). On a meta-level the measure is intuitively appealing in the spirit of permutation tests, and it can be formulated more exactly by specifying what we mean by "better." We will use probabilistic modeling to measure the relative goodness below.

The matching problem of the clusters is a combinatorial problem, where possible configurations of pairs need to be evaluated, judging for each pair how similarly they respond to multi-way covariates. We resort to an iterative algorithm that attempts to change the matching of one cluster at a time.

After selecting a candidate pair, we compare its goodness to an average pair (uniformly selected having one same endpoint), and accept forming a link between them by a Metropolis criterion that compares the likelihoods of the two pairings. A reverse operation is to attempt to break a link by comparing an existing link between two clusters to an average (random) pair. The goodness (likelihood) of the linked pair is evaluated by comparing likelihoods of the two shared covariate effect structures. Factors with no pairs are modeled by data set-specific covariate effects. Averaging over sampling iterations, we can estimate the probability for matchings and the patterns of the covariate effects. High probability of a particular pair indicates a found matching. Low probability of any pair indicates that there might not be suitable match for the factor in the other data set.

4   Experiments

In this section, we demonstrate how the model works on high-dimensional toy data, and on biological data from human blood samples.

4.1   Generated Data

We generated from the model two data sets X and Y with no pairing of samples but only a shared two-way covariate structure. There are 11 separate time series ("patients") in both of the two data matrices, each series consisting of 5 to 15 time points. This results in 100 and 112 samples in total, and data matrices are 200- and 210-dimensional. The latent factors x_j^{lat} and y_j^{lat} are 3- and 4-dimensional, respectively. Two latent factors in each data set were generated from a shared HMM chain with five states.

We used the proposed model to simultaneously align the samples into matchable HMM states, learn the clusters of variables, search for the possible matches of the clusters between the two data sets, and model the ANOVA-type covariate

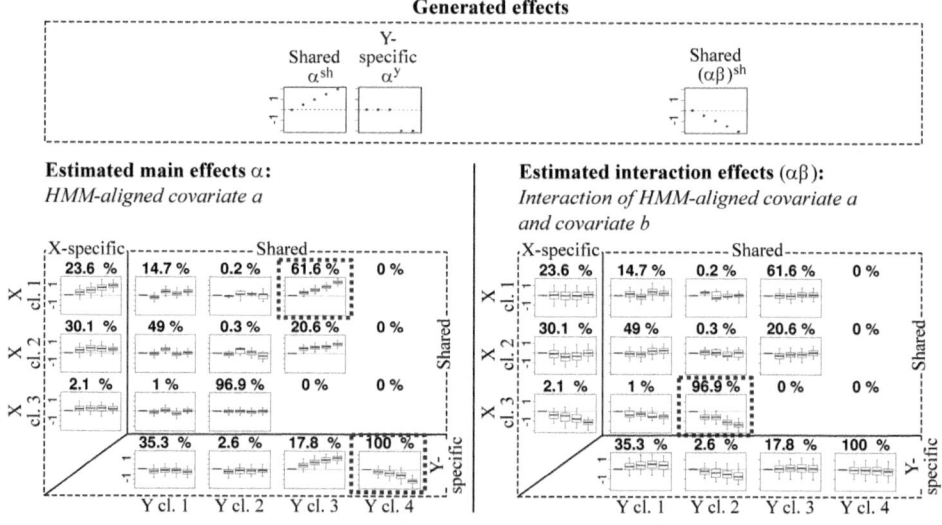

Fig. 2. Matching results from generated time-series data. Shown are the main effects of the HMM-aligned covariate a (α; left), and interaction effects of covariates a and b (($\alpha\beta$); right). Topmost, the generated effects are illustrated. In both the lower parts, the table of estimated covariate effects shows shared (top-right area) and data set-specific (left column and bottom row) effects for both α and ($\alpha\beta$). Rows and columns in the area of shared effects correspond to clusters in data sets X and Y, respectively. The found true pairing is highlighted by a red box. The value on top of each plot shows the percentage of posterior samples, where the matching was found. The boxplots within each subplot represent posterior distributions of effects at different levels of the covariate. A distribution above or below zero with 95 % confidence is considered significant.

effects acting on the found clusters. We *a priori* chose a model with five HMM states. During sampling, 150,000 burn-in samples and 150,000 posterior Gibbs samples were collected, and every 50th sample was collected. The generated effects and the results are shown in Figure 2. Our model found the previously generated clusters without mistakes and matched clusters across the datasets correctly.

4.2   Biological Data

We analysed biological data from a follow-up study of type 1 diabetes, where 53 lipid and 74 metabolite concentrations from blood samples were measured from two sets of human patients, respectively [9]. In total, we had 1153 and 417 samples from 124 and 37 patients, respectively.

We separated the normal development of young individuals from progression of the disease by labeling samples of patients, who acquired the disease, into four stages of progression of the disease using additional information of the antibody levels in blood. These stages were fixed as the levels of covariate b_j, while the temporal alignment a_j of all patients was learned within the model by the HMM. We used a five-state HMM, and 6- and 15-dimensional latent variables to explain the correlated groups of lipids and metabolites in the data, respectively.

Comparison of Matchings of Lipids to the Ground Truth. First, we tested how the model finds matching, when the variables are actually co-occurring across the data sets. We split the lipidomic data set into two groups of patients and used the groups as data sets X and Y.

As a result, we found out that the three strongest matches out of the six were correct.

Integration of Lipidomic and Metabolomic Data Sets. Next, we searched for matching groups between the lipidomic and metabolomic data sets. Some of the patients were the same in the two data sets, but we did not utilize this information to help the model.

Table 1. The best-matched pair of a lipid and a metabolite cluster

Lipids	Metabolites
GPCho(14:0/18:2)	X4.7.10.13.16.19.Docosahexaenoic.acid
GPCho(18:2/16:1)	X9.Octadecenoic.acid..Z.
GPCho(16:0/20:5)	Hexadecanoic.acid
	Phosphoric.acid

The main result was that the best match was a group of three glycerophospho-choline (GPCho) lipids to a group of four metabolites with probability of 19.7 % (see Table 1). Three first of the metabolites in the list are fatty acids, which are building blocks for GPCho lipids. The found lipid and metabolite groups had a similar covariate effect pattern in time (up-regulation) and in the stages of the disease (down-regulation).

5   Conclusion

We presented a novel method for translating biomarkers between multiple species from multi-way, time series experiments, which is applicable even in the extremely hard case of no *a priori* known matching between neither variables nor samples across the two data sets, but only a similar experiment design. The method estimates ANOVA-type multi-way covariate effects for clusters of variables, and identifies and separates covariate effects that are shared between the data sets and effects that are specific to one data set.

Acknowledgements. T.S., I.H. and S.K belong to the Finnish Centre of Excellence in Adaptive Informatics Research. The work was funded by Tekes MASI program and by Tekes Multibio project. I.H. is funded by the Graduate School of Computer Science and Engineering. S.K. is partially supported by EU FP7 NoE PASCAL2, ICT 216886.

References

1. Gholami, A.M., Fellenberg, K.: Cross-species common regulatory network inference without requirement for prior gene affiliation. Bioinformatics 26(8), 1082–1090 (2010)
2. Huopaniemi, I., Suvitaival, T., Nikkilä, J., Orešič, M., Kaski, S.: Multivariate multiway analysis of multi-source data. Bioinformatics 26, i391–i398 (2010)
3. Huopaniemi, I., Suvitaival, T., Nikkilä, J., Orešič, M., Kaski, S.: Two-way analysis of high-dimensional collinear data. Data Mining and Knowledge Discovery 19(2), 261–276 (2009)
4. Huopaniemi, I., Suvitaival, T., Orešič, M., Kaski, S.: Graphical multi-way models. In: Balcázar, J.L., Bonchi, F., Gionis, A., Sebag, M. (eds.) ECML PKDD 2010. LNCS (LNAI), vol. 6321, pp. 538–553. Springer, Heidelberg (2010)
5. Le, H.S., Bar-Joseph, Z.: Cross species expression analysis using a Dirichlet process mixture model with latent matchings. In: Lafferty, J., et al. (eds.) Advances in Neural Information Processing Systems 23, pp. 1270–1278 (2010)
6. Lu, Y., Huggins, P., Bar-Joseph, Z.: Cross species analysis of microarray expression data. Bioinformatics 25(12), 1476–1483 (2009)
7. Lucas, J., Carvalho, C., West, M.: A Bayesian analysis strategy for cross-study translation of gene expression biomarkers. Statistical Applications in Genetics and Molecular Biology 8(1), 11 (2009)
8. Mardia, K.V., Bibby, J.M., Kent, J.T.: Multivariate analysis. Academic Press, London (1979)
9. Orešič, M., et al.: Dysregulation of lipid and amino acid metabolism precedes islet autoimmunity in children who later progress to type 1 diabetes. Journal of Experimental Medicine 205(13), 2975–2984 (2008)
10. Tripathi, A., Klami, A., Orešič, M., Kaski, S.: Matching samples of multiple views. Data Mining and Knowledge Discovery (2011)

An Evaluation of the Image Recognition Method Using Pulse Coupled Neural Network

Masato Yonekawa and Hiroaki Kurokawa

School of Computer Science, Tokyo University of Technology,
1404-1, Katakura, Hachioji, Tokyo, Japan
mstyonekawa1@gmail.com, hkuro@bs.teu.ac.jp

Abstract. A technique for the image recognition is major issue in the image processing and the image recognition method using pulse coupled neural network (PCNN) have been studied as one of the valid method. The most outstanding feature of the method using PCNN is that the method is valid for the rotation, magnification and shrinking of the image. Also, the good compatibility to the hardware implementation is significant feature of the PCNN. In our previous study, we proposed the GA based learning method for the PCNN parameters which enable the reliable results of image recognition. In this study, we evaluate the image recognition method using PCNN with our learning method. In the simulation results, we clarify the characteristics of recognition rate to the number of the images to be learned using our proposed learning method.

Keywords: Pulse coupled neural network, image recognition.

1 Introduction

The pulse coupled neural network (PCNN)[1] is a numerical model of the visual cortex grounded in some physiological works[2] which describes the temporary synchronous dynamics of neurons' firings in the visual cortex. This synchronous phenomenon is considered as an important mechanism to achieve visual information processing in the brain. The most important feature of the PCNN is that the model can reproduce the temporary synchronous dynamics in the visual cortex.

On the other hand, using the synchronous pulse dynamics of the PCNN, many engineering applications of the PCNN have been proposed especially in the fields of image processing, *e.g.* image segmentation, edge detection, image/pattern recognition and so on[3][4][5][6][7]. The image recognition is the major issue in the image processing. A lot of methods to achieve the image recognition have been studied and the method using PCNN had also been proposed in conventional studies[4][8][9]. The method is based on the characteristics of the PCNN that a number of firing neurons in every time step shows a temporal pattern corresponding to the input image. This firing temporal pattern is defined as a "PCNN icon" and this PCNN icon shows unique characteristics for every image to be recognized[4].

T. Honkela et al. (Eds.): ICANN 2011, Part I, LNCS 6791, pp. 217–224, 2011.

The outstanding feature of the image recognition method using PCNN is that the method shows good performance to recognize a rotated and scale modified images. Also, in general, the PCNN is highly compatible to the hardware implementation, *i.e.* the model is easy to achieve real-time processing. A hardware implementation of PCNN is described in recent study[10].

To achieve the image recognition using PCNN icon, the parameters of the PCNN are necessary to be optimized. In our previous study, we had proposed the parameter learning method for the PCNN[11]. The proposed learning rule is a kind of supervised learning using real coded genetic algorithm.

In this study, we evaluate a recognition rate of the image recognition method using the PCNN with our learning method. Here, we assume that the objective of the image recognition is to find the "original image" of the input image which is rotated and scale modified images of the original image. The main objective of the evaluation is to reveal how many images will be learned properly. In the simulation, we show the results using the monochrome images of standard image database(SIDBA) and evaluate how the recognition rate will be changed with increasing learned images. According to the results, we discuss the performances of image recognition using PCNN in practical use.

2   The Image Recognition Using PCNN

2.1   The Pulse Coupled Neural Network Model

Fig. 1 shows a schematic of the neuron in the PCNN. The model consists of the dendrite model and the soma model. In the PCNN, dendrite model forms connections among neurons and input from an environment, and soma model functions as a spike generator. In general, the PCNN to achieve image processing has two-dimensional structure with latticed connection among neurons and each neuron in the PCNN receives information from each corresponding pixel via feeding input. The two-dimensional PCNN model is mathematically described as follows. The internal state of the neuron N_{ij} is given by,

$$U_{ij}(t) = F_{ij}(t)(1 + \beta_{ij}L_{ij}(t)). \tag{1}$$

Note that the indices ij denote neuron number in the two dimensional PCNN.

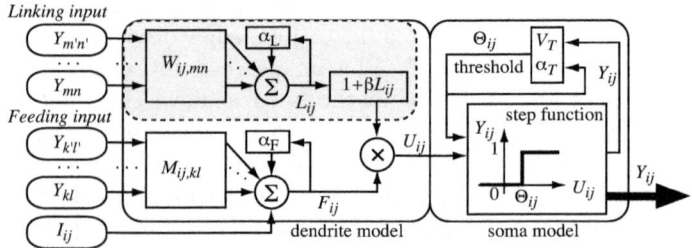

Fig. 1. The schematic of the neuron in Pulse Coupled Neural Network [11]

The neuron model of the PCNN has feeding and linking input as shown in Fig. 1. However, in this study, we assumed that the feeding input of the neuron accepts only an external input, *i.e.*, pixel intensity, as assumed in conventional studies[4].This assumption is widely used in an application for the image processing. Thus the each feeding and linking input is described as follows.

$$F_{ij}(t+1) = I_{ij} = \frac{X_{ij}}{255}, \tag{2}$$

$$L_{ij}(t+1) = L_{ij}(t)\exp(-1/\tau_L) + V_L \sum_m \sum_n W_{ij,mn} Y_{mn}(t). \tag{3}$$

Where X_{ij} denotes 8-bit intensity of the pixel P_{ij}, $W_{ij,mn}$ are weight matrix which define a receptive field of the neuron N_{ij}, I_{ij} is a constant input to the neuron, and $Y_{kl}(t)$ and $Y_{mn}(t)$ are spike output of the neuron N_{kl} and N_{mn}, respectively.

This spike output is defined as a step function which is given by,

$$Y_{kl}(t) = \begin{cases} 1 & \text{if} \quad U_{kl}(t) > \Theta_{kl}(t) \\ 0 & \text{else} \end{cases}. \tag{4}$$

Where $\Theta_{kl}(t)$ is a threshold of the action potential of the neuron N_{kl} which is given by,

$$\Theta_{kl}(t+1) = \Theta_{kl}(t)\exp(-1/\tau_T) + V_T Y_{kl}(t) \tag{5}$$

Through Eq.(1)−Eq.(5), parameters, β_{ij}, τ_L, τ_T, V_L, V_T and $W_{ij,mn}$ are unknown parameters and they have to be decided appropriately.

2.2   The Pattern Recognition Using PCNN Icons

The image recognition using the PCNN is achieved by using the PCNN icon[4]. The PCNN icon is defined as the time series of the number of the firing neurons. To obtain the PCNN icon, a number of the firing neurons are observed in every time step from $t = 0$ to $t = t_{\max}$, where $t_{\max}$ is defined arbitrary. Namely, the PCNN icon is also defined as a $t_{\max}$-dimensional vector of integers. Where we assumed that the $t_{\max}$ is 100 in this study.

The PCNN icon is unique to the input image and its form is almost independent of the rotation and magnification or shrinking of the pattern. This is the most outstanding feature of PCNN icon and this characteristics achieves good performance for the image recognition. The PCNN icon has been applied to various issues in image processing e.g. for the object detection[8], for the human face recognition[9] and so on. These conventional studies certify the validity of the PCNN icon for image processing. Fig. 2 shows examples of the pattern images and their PCNN icons. As shown in the figures, unique PCNN icons are obtained corresponding to each of the input images and images will be discriminated with the form of the PCNN icons.

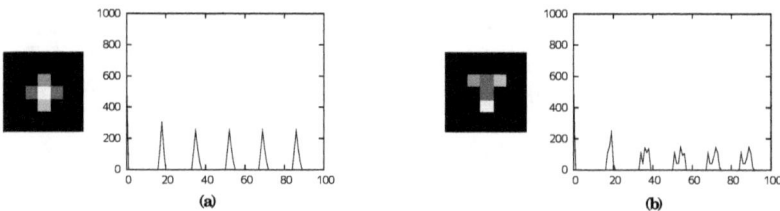

Fig. 2. Examples of the images and their PCNN icons; (a) An input image of pattern "+" and its PCNN icon, (b) An input image of pattern "T" and its PCNN icon[11]

2.3   Parameter Optimization Using Real Code Genetic Algorithm

In our previous study, we proposed the learning method to optimize parameters in the PCNN to achieve the image recognition accurately[11]. Our proposed method use the real coded genetic algorithm. Here, we assumed that the parameters to be optimized are β_{ij}, τ_L, τ_T, V_L, and V_T. To apply the real coded genetic algorithm to the parameter optimization, a set of real numbers of the 5 parameters β_{ij}, τ_L, τ_T, V_L, and V_T are defined as a chromosome. Here, the ranges of the parameters are assumed to be $0 \sim 20.48$ and the discretized value of the parameter is considered, where the minimum difference of the values is 0.000001. Initially, 17 chromosomes are generated randomly as an initial population.

The chromosomes are evaluated in each generation using the fitness which is calculated based on the normalized correlation coefficient. Here the normalized correlation coefficient between the PCNN icons of images X and Y is given by,

$$correlation = \frac{\sum_{t=0}^{t_{\max}}(x_t - \bar{x})(y_t - \bar{y})}{\sqrt{\sum_{t=0}^{t_{\max}}(x_t - \bar{x})^2}\sqrt{\sum_{t=0}^{t_{\max}}(y_t - \bar{y})^2}}. \tag{6}$$

Where, x_t and y_t are the number of the firing neurons at time step t, and $\bar{x}$ and $\bar{y}$ are the average of x_t and y_t through $t = 0$ to $t = t_{max}$.

The fitness is calculated based on the correlation as shown in following procedure. Where we assumed that the images to be learned are P_1, P_2, $\cdots$, P_n, and the procedure requires $m(m \geq 2)$ images for every image to be learned. Note that a rotation angle or a scale factor of these m images is assumed to be different each other. Thus our algorithm requires $n \times m$ images for the learning of n images. In this study, we use the original image and 3 modified images for the learning, *i.e.*, $m = 4$.

1. Set a parameters of PCNN according to the jth chromosome C_j
2. Calculate the PCNN icons for all learning images.
3. Calculate the normalized correlation coefficient among PCNN icons of all learning images.

4. Search the minimum correlation coefficient among m learning images for P_i and substitute it for a_i.
5. Search the maximum correlation coefficient among different images, *i.e.*, among any image of P_i and $P_k (k \neq i)$, and substitute it for b_i.
6. Repeat 4 and 5 for every $P_i (i = 1, 2, ...n)$
7. Calculate the difference between the minimum a_i and the maximum b_i and substitute it for C_j
8. Repeat 1-7 for every $C_j (j = 1, 2, ..., 17)$ and sort the C_js in ascending order.
9. Use the order which is obtained in 8 as a fitness of the chromosome.

To breed a new generation, two chromosomes are selected depending on the fitness using roulette-wheel selection. In our algorithm, the one-point crossover is applied to the selected chromosomes. The mutation is also applied to the selected chromosomes. In the mutation, one randomly selected parameter in the chromosome changes to random value. Here, the probability of the crossover and mutation are 0.6 and 0.2, respectively.

These procedures of breeding the next generation will continue until 16 chromosomes are produced. Also, in our algorithm, elitist strategy is used. The chromosome which has largest fitness is selected and carries over to the next generation. Then 17 chromosomes are produced as a population for the next generation. We assumed that the procedure of breeding the next generation is terminated in 500th generation.

In this study, as an extension of our proposed method, we consider the optimization of the weight matrix of the linking input $W_{ij,mn}$. Here we define the weight matrix $W_{ij,mn}$ as follows.

$$W_{ij,mn} = \begin{cases} \frac{1}{h\sqrt{(i-m)^2+(j-n)^2}} & \text{if} \quad \sqrt{(i-m)^2+(j-n)^2} \leq r \\ 0 & \text{else} \end{cases} \tag{7}$$

We add these parameters h and r to the chromosome, *i.e.*, the 7 parameters of the PCNN are defined as a chromosome in this study.

3 Simulation Results

In this section, we show the simulation results of image recognition using the PCNN with our parameter learning method. Fig. 3 (a)-(u) shows the "original images" used in the simulation. These images are from the standard image database(SIDBA). We prepare a lot of rotated and scale modified images from these original images for the recognition test. Where the rotation angles are 0, 15, 30, 45, 60, 75, 90 degrees, and the scale factors are 0.1 ~ 2.0 at intervals of 0.1. Also we assume that the data only in the image area of 256 × 256 pixels is used, *i.e.*, the image data which is out of the image area is ignored. Some examples of modified images of image (a) is shown in Fig. 3 (v) and (w). As a result, we obtained 139 modified images and a original image from one original image. We assume that the original image and 3 modified images are used as the

(a) LENNA.png (b) mandrill.png (c) Aerial.png (d) Airplane.png (e) Balloon.png (f) BARBARApng

(g) BOAT.png (h) BRIDGE.png (i) Building.png (j) Cameraman.png (k) couple.png (l) Earth.png

(m) girl.png (n) LAX.png (o) Lighthouse.png (p) milkdrop.png (q) Parrots.png (r) Pepper.png

(s) Sailboat.png (t) Text.png (u) WOMAN.png (v) (w)

Fig. 3. (a)-(u) 21 "*original images*" used in the simulations. These images are monochrome image and the resolution of all images is 256×256 pixels. (v) An example of modified image of (a). the rotation angle is 45 degrees and scale factor is 1.0. (w) The rotation angle is 30 degrees and scale factor is 1.5.

"learning image" and the other 136 images are assumed to be a "test image" to calculate the recognition rate. In the simulation, the required number of images is selected from 21 original images and its learning images and test images are used for the simulation.

In the recognition procedure, to select the corresponding image to the input test image, we calculate the correlations of the PCNN icons among the test image and each of the original images. Then the original image with largest correlation is selected as an image to be recognized.

Fig. 4 shows the characteristics of the recognition rate depending on the number of learning images. In Fig.4, the solid line shows the average of recognition rate of all the test images and two kinds of dotted lines show the maximum and minimum recognition rate corresponding to certain original image. Where Fig.4 (a) shows the results using the PCNN with our learning method and (b) shows the results using the PCNN without learning. In these results, the validity of our learning method for the image recognition is obviously illustrated.

From the results in Fig.4 (a), we can find that the average of the recognition rate decreases as increasing of a number of the learning images. Here, we consider that this characteristics is depending on the large amount of data loss of the

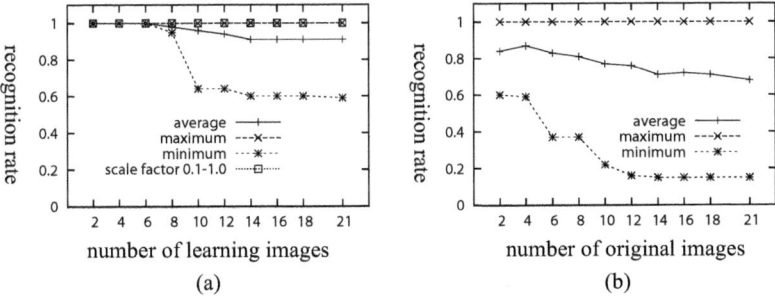

Fig. 4. The characteristics of the recognition rate depending on the number of learning images. (a) Learning method is applied. (b) Learning method is not applied

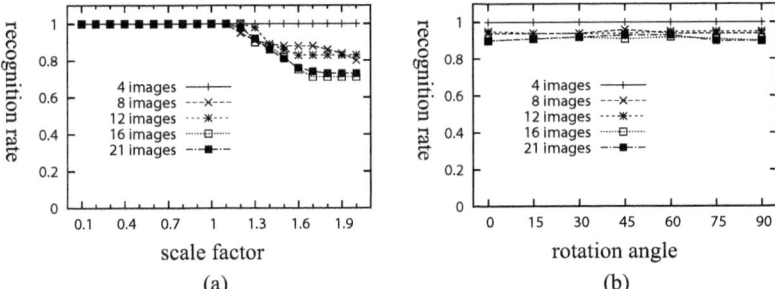

Fig. 5. The characteristics of recognition rate depending on the input test images. (a) varying the scale factor (b) varying the rotation angle

magnified images such as shown in Fig.3 (w). To ensure this consideration, in Fig.4 (a), we also show the characteristics of the average of the recognition rate of all images in the case that the range of the scale factor is 0.1 ∼ 1.0. In this case, the recognition rate always keeps 100% as increasing of the number of the learning images. Then we can conclude that the method achieves good performance in the case of small data loss of input images. Also from the results shown in Fig.4, the maximum recognition rate corresponding to certain original image also keeps 100%. Thus we can know that the decreasing of recognition rate depends on the image characteristics.

These characteristics are ensured in another point of view. Fig. 5 shows the characteristics of recognition rate to the scale factor and the rotation angle. Where, the number of the learning image is 4, 8, 12, 16, and 21. From the results shown in Fig.5(a), the recognition rate for the magnified images decreases as increasing of learning images and it for the shrinking images keeps almost 100%. Also, the recognition rate decreases as increasing of scale factor.

On the other hand, from the results shown in Fig.5(b), the recognition rate is almost independent of the rotation angle. Therefore the results show the validity of the method using PCNN which shows a good performance in the image recognition of the rotated images. These results suggest that only the large amount of data loss in magnified test images can be cause of decreasing of the recognition rate in the image recognition method using PCNN with our learning method.

4   Conclusion

The image recognition is a major issue in the image processing and the method using PCNN have been studied as one of the valuable method for the image recognition. In this study, we evaluated the image recognition method using the PCNN with GA based learning method which proposed in our previous study. In the simulation, we showed the characteristics of recognition rate to the number of the learning images and it to the feature of the input test images. The results showed a good performance for the large number of learning images and the validity of the method using PCNN in practical use is clarified.

Acknowledgments. A part of this work was supported by a Grant-in-Aid for Challenging Exploratory Research from JSPS. (No. 22650046).

References

1. Echorn, R., Reitboeck, H.J., Arndt, M., Dicke, P.: Feature linking via synchronization among distributed assemblies: Simulations of results from cat visual cortex. Neural Computation 2, 293–307 (1990)
2. Engel, A.K., Kreiter, A.K., König, P., Singer, W.: Synchronization of oscillatory neuronal responses between striate and extrastriate visual cortical areas of cat. Proc. Natl. Acad. Sci. 88, 6048–6052, USA (1991)
3. Echorn, R.: Neural Mechanisms of Scene Segmentation: Recording from the Visual Cortex Suggest Basic Circuits for Liking Field Model. IEEE Trans. Neural Network 10(3), 464–479 (1999)
4. Johnson, J.L., Padgett, M.L.: PCNN Models and Applications. IEEE Trans. Neural Network 10(3), 480–498 (1999)
5. Ranganth, H.S., Kuntimad, G.: Image segmentation using pulse coupled neural networks. In: Proc. Int. Conf. Neural Networks, Orlando,FL, vol. 2, pp. 1285–1290 (1994)
6. Kurokawa, H., Kaneko, S., Yonekawa, M.: A Color Image Segmentation Using Inhibitory Connected Pulse Coupled Neural Network. In: Köppen, M., Kasabov, N., Coghill, G. (eds.) ICONIP 2008. LNCS, vol. 5507, pp. 776–783. Springer, Heidelberg (2009)
7. Lindblad, T., Kinser, J.M.: Image processing using Pulse-Coupled Neural Networks, 2nd edn. Springer, Heidelberg (2005)
8. Gu, X.-D., Wang, Y.-y., Zhang, L.-M.: Object detection using unit-linking PCNN image icons. In: Wang, J., Yi, Z., Żurada, J.M., Lu, B.-L., Yin, H. (eds.) ISNN 2006. LNCS, vol. 3972, pp. 616–622. Springer, Heidelberg (2006)
9. Mahgoub, A.G., et al.: An Intersecting Cortical Model Based Framework for Human Face Recognition. Journal of Systemics, Cybernetics and Informatics 6(2), 88–93 (2008)
10. Vega-Pineda, J., Chacon-Murguia, M.I., Camarillo-Cisneros, R.: Synthesis of Pulse-Coupled Neural Networks in FPGAs for Real-Time Image Segmentation. In: Proc. of IJCNN, pp. 8167–8171 (2006)
11. Yonekawa, M., Kurokawa, H.: The parameter optimization of the pulse coupled neural network for the pattern recognition. In: DILS 2010, vol. 6254, pp. 110–113 (2010)

Using the Leader Algorithm with Support Vector Machines for Large Data Sets

Enrique Romero*

Departament de Llenguatges i Sistemes Informàtics
Universitat Politècnica de Catalunya
eromero@lsi.upc.edu

Abstract. One of the main drawbacks of Support Vector Machines (SVM) is their high computational cost for large data sets. We propose the use of the Leader algorithm as a preprocessing procedure for SVM with large data sets, so that the obtained leaders are used as the training set for the SVM. The result is an algorithm where the Leader algorithm allows to construct a sample of the data set whose granularity level and computational cost are controlled by the threshold parameter. Despite its apparent simplicity, the proposed model obtains similar accuracies to *standard LIBSVM* with fewer number of support vectors and less execution times.

1 Introduction

Support Vector Machines (SVM) have been highly successful in several machine learning problems [25,19]. However, one of the main drawbacks of SVM is their computational complexity, leading to long training times for large data sets.

The optimization problem related to SVM is typically formulated as a quadratic programming problem. Given N training examples, standard quadratic programming solvers take $O(N^3)$ training time and $O(N^2)$ space to obtain a solution. Several approaches have been proposed for SVM to reduce time and space complexities. Chunking and decomposition methods [26,15] optimize the SVM with respect to subsets of the data. The Sequential Minimal Optimization algorithm [17] obtains the analytical solution of the subproblem with only two examples, and then heuristically choices the best pairs of parameters to optimize in a sequential process. Other incremental algorithms have also been described [4,7,9]. Another family of algorithms modify the objective function to apply efficient algorithms [6,13] or transform the problem to an equivalent one [23]. In general, these methods suffer from slow convergence when the number of support vectors is large [14].

A different approach aims to reduce the number of support vectors either directly or by reducing the size of the training set while keeping all the necessary information for the construction of a good model. Likelihood-based squashing is used in [16] to remove examples that contribute in a similar way to the likelihood of the SVM parameters. Active learning methods for SVM [18,22] try to sequentially add examples

---

* This work was supported in part by the Ministerio de Ciencia e Innovación (MICINN), under project TIN2009-13895-C02-01.

T. Honkela et al. (Eds.): ICANN 2011, Part I, LNCS 6791, pp. 225–232, 2011.

near the boundaries. Several sampling techniques are also based in similar idea [10,1]. The model proposed in [20] proposes a preprocessing algorithm that tries to select the examples near the decision boundaries by looking at the classes of their neighbors.

A third class of algorithms are based on clustering. The algorithm proposed in this paper also takes this approach. The intrinsic nature of SVM, which is a function only on the support vectors, makes clustering algorithms suitable for preprocessing and obtain a representative sample of the data set. By changing the parameters of the clustering algorithm, the number and shapes of the clusters change, leading to different granularity levels for the training set. In [27], the centroids of a hierarchical clustering tree are recursively selected to train a SVM at every step, where the examples near the boundaries are declustered. The k-means clustering algorithm is used in [21] to select the examples near the cluster boundaries as the input data for a SVM. A similar approach is taken in [3,28] where, starting from a clustering algorithm, the clusters are split or shrinked depending on a SVM trained with the centroids of the clusters. In [11] the learning problem of SVM is redefined assuming that the clusters have a Gaussian distribution in the feature space, and using a probability product kernel.

In this work we propose to use the Leader algorithm [8] as a preprocessing procedure for large data sets. The obtained leaders are used as the training set for SVM. In order to maintain the coherency between distances and inner products, the distance within the Leader algorithm is computed with the kernel function, which is equivalent to run the Leader algorithm in the feature space induced by the kernel. The proposed algorithm consists of two decoupled phases, allowing to control the execution times.

The advantages of using the Leader algorithm are threefold. First, it is a very fast clustering algorithm, compared to most common clustering algorithms such as k-means or hierarchical clustering methods. Second, all the areas of the input space with any example in the data set are represented by, at least, one leader. Finally, the leaders are always a subset of the original data set. Despite its apparent simplicity, the proposed model gives good experimental results on large data sets, obtaining similar accuracies to *standard LIBSVM* with fewer number of support vectors and less execution times.

2   Support Vector Machines

SVMs for classification can be described as follows [25]: the input vectors are mapped into a (usually high-dimensional) inner product space through some non-linear mapping ϕ, chosen *a priori*. In this space (the *feature space*), a maximal margin hyperplane is constructed. By using a (positive definite) kernel function $K(u, v)$ the mapping becames implicit, since the inner product defining the hyperplane can be evaluated as $\langle \phi(u), \phi(v) \rangle = K(u, v)$ for every two vectors $u, v \in \mathbb{R}^D$.

When the data set is not separable by a hyperplane (neither in the input space nor in the feature space), some tolerance to noise is allowed. Using Lagrangian and Kuhn-Tucker theory, the maximal margin hyperplane for a binary classification problem given by a data set X is a linear combination of simple functions depending on the data:

$$f(x) = b + \sum_{i=1}^{N} y_i \alpha_i K(x_i, x) \tag{1}$$

where the vector $(\alpha_i)_{i=1}^N$ is the (1-norm soft margin) solution of the following constrained optimization problem in the dual space:

$$\begin{aligned}
&\text{Maximize}_\alpha \ \sum_{i=1}^N \alpha_i - \tfrac{1}{2} \sum_{i,j=1}^N y_i \alpha_i y_j \alpha_j K(x_i, x_j) \\
&\text{subject to} \quad \sum_{i=1}^N y_i \alpha_i = 0 \qquad \text{(bias constraint)} \\
&\qquad\qquad\quad 0 \leqslant \alpha_i \leqslant C \qquad\quad i = 1...N.
\end{aligned} \tag{2}$$

for a certain constant C. The parameter C allows to control the trade-off between the margin and the errors in the data set. By setting $C = \infty$, the hard margin hyperplane is obtained. The points x_i with $\alpha_i > 0$ (active constraints) are named *support vectors*. The most usual kernel functions $K(u, v)$ are polynomial, Gaussian-like or sigmoidal functions. It is worth noting that the kernel function depends on a certain parameter γ.

3   The Leader Algorithm as a Preprocessing Procedure for SMVs

3.1   The Leader Algorithm

Clustering algorithms divide data into groups (clusters) that are meaningful, useful, or both. Among the many clustering algorithms, the Leader algorithm [8] is one of the fastest ones, and it has been used in many successful applications (see [24], for example).

The Leader algorithm works with a distance or similarity measure and a predetermined threshold T. It constructs a partition of the data into clusters, assigning an example for each cluster (the leader), such that every example in a cluster is within a distance (or similarity) T of the leading example. The algorithm makes a single pass through the data set. For every example, it looks for the first cluster whose leader is close enough (or similar enough) to the current example with respect to the specified measure and threshold T. If such matching leader is found, then the current example is assigned to that cluster. Otherwise, the algorithm will add a new cluster whose leader is the current example. Several variations of the Leader algorithm have been described elsewhere (see [2], for example).

3.2   The Proposed Approach

To fix notation, consider the classification task given by a data set $X = \{(x_i, y_i)\}_{i=1}^N$, where each example $x_i \in \mathbb{R}^D$, $y_i \in \{-1, +1\}$. Let us define X^+ and X^- as the subsets of positive and negative examples, respectively.

The main idea of the proposed approach is to use the Leader algorithm as a preprocessing procedure to select a subset of the data (the leaders) for the subsequent training of the SVM. In order to lose as little information as possible (namely, possible support vectors), the Leader algorithm is applied independently to every class. In this way, examples of different classes (near the decision boundaries, for example) will always be represented by different leaders. Once the leaders of every class have been obtained, they are joined in a single data set that will be the input training set of a standard SVM algorithm. The proposed algorithm is summarized in Figure 1. We will call this scheme *Leader + SVM*. Extension to multiple-class problems is straightforward.

Given a data set X, a threshold T, a kernel function K and learning parameters for the SVM,

Phase 1: Computing the leaders
$L^+ = \text{LeaderAlgorithmKernel}(X^+, T, K)$
$L^- = \text{LeaderAlgorithmKernel}(X^-, T, K)$
$Y = L^+ \cup L^-$

Phase 2: Training the SVM
$\text{Model} = \text{TrainSVM}(Y, K, \text{learning parameters})$

The function $\text{LeaderAlgorithmKernel}(Z, T, K)$ runs the Leader algorithm on the data set Z with threshold T and distance $D(x, y) = \sqrt{K(x, x) - 2K(x, y) + K(y, y)}$

Fig. 1. Algorithm proposed for the *Leader + SVM* scheme

Note that, in order to maintain the coherency between distances within the Leader algorithm and inner products within the training of the SVM, the distance within the Leader algorithm is computed with the kernel function. This is equivalent to run the Leader algorithm in the feature space induced by the kernel K.

Different from other approaches (see [27,3,28], for example), the proposed algorithm consists of two decoupled phases. Therefore, the execution times can be roughly controlled by looking at the number of leaders obtained by the Leader algorithm (which, in turn, is controlled by the threshold T). The accuracy of the trained SVM will also depend on the leaders obtained in the first phase.

The advantages of using the Leader algorithm are threefold. First, it is a very fast algorithm, compared to most common clustering algorithms such as k-means or hierarchical clustering methods. Second, all the areas of the input space with any example in the data set are represented by, at least, one leader. This is a very important property when combined with SVM, since if there exist areas of the input space not covered by the clusters (represented by their centroids, for example), several potential support vectors could be lost. Finally, the leaders are always a subset of the original data set, so that there is no need to work with data subsets in the feature space as if they were an only point (the centroid of a cluster), as in [27,3,28].

In summary, the Leader algorithm allows to construct a sample of the data set whose granularity level and computational cost are controlled by the threshold T. Therefore, it is a suitable preprocessing procedure for SVM with large data sets. A similar approach has been presented in [12], with several important differences. First, the work in [12] is mostly focused on the comparison with other sub-sampling techniques. Second, the threshold T is fixed during the process, so that the computational cost is not controlled. Finally, it is only tested on small data sets (less than $1,000$ examples).

4   Experiments

We performed several experiments on benchmark data sets in order to validate the proposed model. For comparison, we also run a standard LIBSVM implementation [5].

Table 1. Description of the benchmark data sets, kernel and learning parameters. Column 'Frequencies' indicates the frequencies of the examples of every class in the training set.

Data Set	# Variables	# Ex.Train	# Ex.Test	Frequencies	γ	C
KDDCUP-99	127	4,898,431	311,029	0.801 / 0.199	0.1	10,000
Forest Cover	54	522,910	58,102	0.512 / 0.488	0.0001	10,000
Extended USPS	676	266,079	75,383	0.543 / 0.457	0.0078	10

4.1   Data Sets

Several benchmark data sets were used for the experiments: *KDDCUP-99*, *Forest Cover* and *Extended USPS*. These data sets are available at http://www.cse.ust.hk/ ~ivor/cvm.html. A brief description of these data sets is provided in Table 1.

4.2   Experimental Setting

Data Preprocessing. No preprocessing was applied to the data.

Kernel and kernel parameter. We used the Gaussian kernel $K(x, y) = e^{-\gamma \|x - y\|^2}$. In the Leader algorithm, the Gaussian function was normalized dividing by the number of input variables. The values of the γ parameter used for every data set are those of [14], and can be found in Table 1.

Threshold of the Leader algorithm. Different values of the threshold T were tested, ranging from 0.002 to 1.0.

Learning parameters. The values of the C parameter used for every data set are those of [14], and can be found in Table 1. The rest of parameters were used with their default values.

Software. For LIBSVM, we used the C++ implementation available at http://www. cse.ust.hk/~ivor/cvm.html. For the Leader algorithm, we used our own C implementation. Previous to every run, the examples in the data set were randomly shuffled.

Hardware. All the executions were run on an Intel Xeon CPU X3220 at 2.40GHz.

4.3   Results

Figure 2 shows the comparative results between *Leader + LIBSVM* and *standard LIBSVM* (i.e., trained with the whole training set) on the benchmark data sets studied as a function of the threshold value. Blue lines correspond to *Leader + LIBSVM* and red ones correspond to *standard LIBSVM*. We only show the results for the threshold values whose total execution time of *Leader + LIBSVM* (summing up the training times for the Leader algorithm and LIBSVM) was less than the training time of *standard LIBSVM*. Obviously, for threshold values near zero the computational cost of the *Leader + LIBSVM* scheme is larger than that of *standard LIBSVM*, since the leaders selected by the Leader algorithm are the whole data set. Table 2 shows a comparison between the best results obtained by the *Leader + LIBSVM* scheme and those of *standard LIBSVM*.

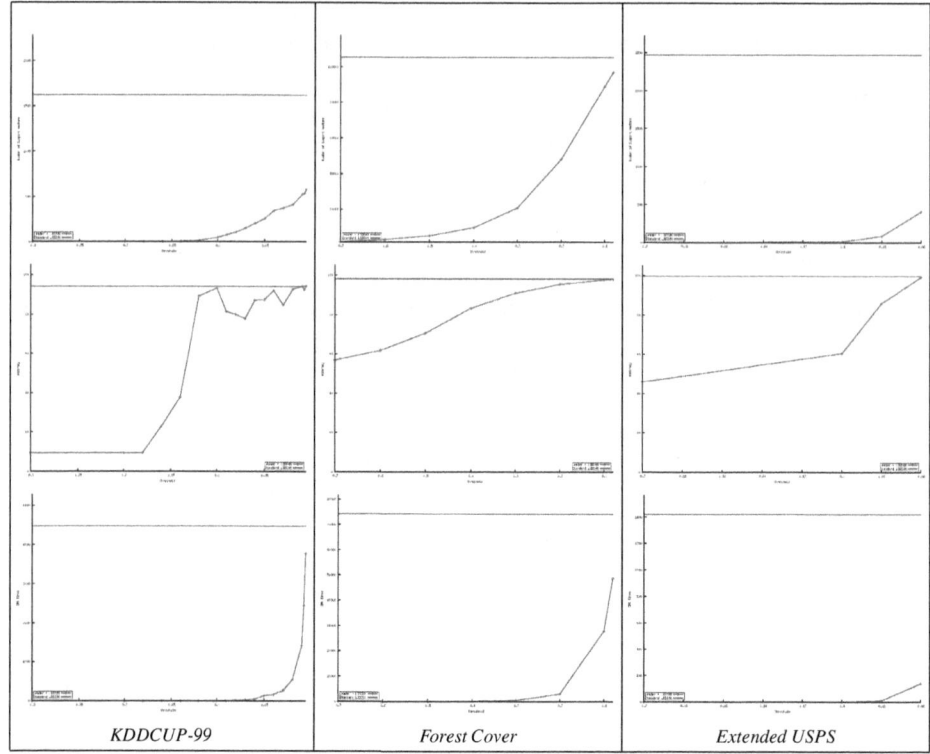

Fig. 2. Comparison between *Leader + LIBSVM* (blue) and *standard LIBSVM* (red) on the *KDDCUP-99* (left), *Forest Cover* (middle) and *Extended USPS* (right) data sets. Top row: number of support vectors. Middle row: test accuracies. Bottom row: execution times

The first thing to note from Figure 2 is that, except for the accuracies in the *KDDCUP-99* data set, the number of support vectors, the accuracies and the execution times increase as far a the threshold T decreases. This is as expected. More interestingly, the *Leader + LIBSVM* scheme is able to obtain similar accuracies to *standard LIBSVM* with fewer number of support vectors and less execution times. This is particularly remarkable for the *Extended USPS* and *KDDCUP-99* data sets (see Table 2).

Note that the behavior on the *Forest Cover* and *Extended USPS* data sets is extremely regular. The non-increasing behavior in the accuracies of the *KDDCUP-99* data set in Figure 2 is probably due to the highly unbalanced classes (see Table 1), that may need different granularity levels for the Leader algorithm. Anyway, very good accuracies can be obtained with very low execution times (see Table 2)

For the *KDDCUP-99* and *Extended USPS* data sets, most of the execution time of the *Leader + LIBSVM* scheme was spent in computing the leaders. For the *Forest Cover* data set, in contrast, the *LIBSVM* software took most of the time. This can be explained by looking at the number of support vectors of the obtained models, which is highly correlated with the number of leaders (see top row in Figure 2 and Table 2): when the number of examples is large and the number of leaders is small, *LIBSVM* may be faster

Table 2. Comparison between *standard LIBSVM* and the best results of the *Leader + LIBSVM* scheme. Columns 'Thr', '# Leads', '# SVs', 'Test' and 'Time' indicate the threshold, number of leaders, number of support vectors, test accuracy and execution times (in seconds), respectively.

Data Set	Standard LIBSVM			Leader + LIBSVM				
	# SVs	Test	Time	Thr	# Leads	# SVs	Test	Time
KDDCUP-99	1,624	94.20%	4,476.8	0.01	7,187	531	94.26%	1,431.1
				0.1	53	48	93.34%	6.2
Forest Cover	105,541	98.23%	74,135.9	0.1	176,102	88,916	97.75%	28,055.9
Extended USPS	2,468	99.53%	1,419.7	0.06	1,605	410	99.21%	139.5

than the Leader algorithm. Therefore, it is better to test high values of the threshold T first, since the number of leaders may be large for low values of T.

5   Conclusions and Future Work

This paper experimentally shows that, for large data sets, selecting a subset of the training set with the Leader algorithm may lead to an important decrease in the training and test times of SVM, without affecting the accuracies.

It could be worth modifying the Leader algorithm so that there were more leaders in the expected boundaries (for example, by comparing the distance to the current leader with the leaders of the other classes). If an example is suspected to be near a boundary, the threshold can be decreased. Similarly, a different threshold T can be used for every class, specially for data sets with highly unbalanced classes.

References

1. Balcázar, J.L., Dai, Y., Tanaka, J., Watanabe, O.: Provably Fast Training Algorithms for Support Vector Machines. Theory of Computing Systems 42(4), 568–595 (2008)
2. Barton, A.: Modelling Variability in the Leader Algorithm Family: A Testable Model and Implementation. Tech. Rep. NRC 47429, Institute for Information Technology, National Research Council Canada (2004)
3. Boley, D., Cao, D.: Training Support Vector Machine using Adaptive Clustering. In: International Conference on Data Mining, pp. 126–137 (2004)
4. Cauwenberghs, G., Poggio, T.: Incremental and Decremental Support Vector Machine Learning. In: Advances in Neural Information Processing Systems, vol. 12, pp. 409–415. MIT Press, Cambridge (2000)
5. Chang, C.C., Lin, C.J.: LIBSVM: A Library for Support Vector Machines (2002), http://www.csie.ntu.edu.tw/~cjlin/libsvm
6. Fung, G., Mangasarian, O.L.: Proximal Support Vector Machine Classifiers. In: ACM SIGKDD International Conference on Knowledge Discovery and Data Mining, pp. 77–86 (2001)
7. Fung, G., Mangasarian, O.L.: Incremental Support Vector Machine Classification. In: International Conference on Data Mining, pp. 247–260 (2002)
8. Hartigan, J.: Clustering Algorithms. John Wiley & Sons, Chichester (1975)
9. Keerthi, S.S., Chapelle, O., DeCoste, D.: Building Support Vector Machines with Reduced Classifier Complexity. Journal of Machine Learning Research 7, 1493–1515 (2006)

10. Lee, Y.J., Mangasarian, O.L.: RSVM: Reduced Support Vector Machines. In: International Conference on Data Mining (2004)
11. Li, B., Chi, M., Fan, J., Xue, X.: Support Cluster Machine. In: 24th International Conference on Machine Learning, pp. 505–512 (2007)
12. Li, D., Simke, S.: Training Set Compression by Incremental Clustering. Journal of Pattern Recognition Research 1, 56–64 (2011)
13. Mangasarian, O.L., Musicant, D.R.: Lagrangian Support Vector Machines. Journal of Machine Learning Research 1, 161–177 (2001)
14. Nguyen, D.D., Matsumoto, K., Takishima, Y., Hashimoto, K.: Condensed Vector Machines: Learning Fast Machine for Large Data. IEEE Transactions on Neural Networks 21(12), 1903–1914 (2010)
15. Osuna, E., Freund, R., Girosi, F.: Improved Training Algorithm for Support Vector Machines. In: IEEE Workshop on Neural Networks for Signal Processing, pp. 276–285 (1997)
16. Pavlov, D., Chudova, D., Smyth, P.: Towards Scalable Support Vector Machines using Squashing. In: ACM SIGKDD International Conference on Knowledge Discovery and Data Mining, pp. 295–299 (2000)
17. Platt, J.: Fast Training of Support Vector Machines using Sequential Minimal Optimization. In: Schölkopf, B., Burges, C., Smola, A. (eds.) Advances in Kernel Methods - Support Vector Learning, pp. 185–208. MIT Press, Cambridge (1999)
18. Schohn, G., Cohn, D.: Less is More: Active Learning with Support Vector Machines. In: 17th International Conference on Machine Learning, pp. 839–846 (2000)
19. Schölkopf, B., Smola, A.J.: Learning with Kernels. MIT Press, Cambridge (2002)
20. Shin, H., Cho, S.: Fast Pattern Selection for Support Vector Classifiers. In: Fagerholm, J., Haataja, J., Järvinen, J., Lyly, M., Råback, P., Savolainen, V. (eds.) PARA 2002. LNCS, vol. 2367, Springer, Heidelberg (2002)
21. Sun, S.Y., Tseng, C.L., Chen, Y.H., Chuang, S.C., Fu, H.C.: Cluster-based Support Vector Machines in Text-independent Speaker Identification. In: International Joint Conference on Neural Networks, vol. 1, pp. 729–734 (2004)
22. Tong, S., Koller, D.: Support Vector Machine Active Learning with Applications to Text Classification. Journal of Machine Learning Research 2, 45–66 (2001)
23. Tsang, I.W.H., Kwok, J.T.Y., Zurada, J.A.: Generalized Core Vector Machines. IEEE Transactions on Neural Networks 17(5), 1126–1140 (2006)
24. Valdés, J.J., Barton, A.J.: Virtual Reality Visual Data Mining via Neural Networks Obtained from Multi-objective Evolutionary Optimization: Application to Geophysical Prospecting. In: International Joint Conference on Neural Networks, pp. 4862–4869 (2006)
25. Vapnik, V.N.: The Nature of Statistical Learning Theory. Springer, Heidelberg (1995)
26. Vapnik, V.N.: Statistical Learning Theory. John Wiley & Sons, NY (1998)
27. Yu, H., Yang, J., Han, J.: Classifying Large Data Sets using SVMs with Hierarchical Clusters. In: ACM SIGKDD International Conference on Knowledge Discovery and Data Mining, pp. 306–315 (2003)
28. Yuan, J., Li, J., Zhang, B.: Learning Concepts from Large Scale Imbalanced Data Sets using Support Cluster Machines. In: 14th Annual ACM International Conference on Multimedia, pp. 441–450 (2006)

Automatic Seizure Detection Incorporating Structural Information

Borbala Hunyadi[1,2], Maarten De Vos[1,2,3], Marco Signoretto[1,2],
Johan A. K. Suykens[1,2], Wim Van Paesschen[4], Sabine Van Huffel[1,2]

[1] Department of Electrical Engineering (ESAT), Division SCD, Katholieke
Universiteit Leuven, Leuven, Belgium
[2] IBBT-K.U.Leuven Future Health Department, Leuven, Belgium
[3] Neuropsychology Lab, Department of Psychology, University of Oldenburg,
Oldenburg, Germany
[4] Department of Neurology, University Hospital Gasthuisberg, Leuven, Belgium
{borbala.hunyadi,maarten.devos,marco.signoretto,
johan.suykens,sabine.vanhuffel}@esat.kuleuven.be,
wim.vanpaesschen@uz.kuleuven.ac.be

Abstract. Traditional seizure detection algorithms act on single channels ignoring the synchronously recorded, inherently interdependent multichannel nature of EEG. However, the spatial distribution and evolution of the ictal pattern is a crucial characteristic of the seizure. Two different approaches aiming at including such structural information into the data representation are presented in this paper. Their performance is compared to the traditional approach both in a simulation study and a real-life example, showing that spatial and structural information facilitates precise classification.

1 Introduction

Epilepsy is the second most common neurological disorder after stroke. Over 0.5% of the worldwide population is affected with epilepsy, and approximately 20% of them are not responding to anti-epileptic drugs. The manifestation of this disease is the epileptic seizure. It is an abnormal, synchronous activity of the neurons in the brain. An automatic seizure detection system could help the diagnosis of epilepsy, reducing the workload of clinicians by supporting visual inspection of EEG. Several seizure detection algorithms have been developed in the past decades, applying various methods including time-frequency analysis [5], [4], nonlinear time series analysis [6], feature extraction and machine learning techniques [8], [3], [7].

The drawback of the existing algorithms is the fact that they act on single channel data, however, the spatial distribution and evolution of the ictal pattern are crucial characteristics of the seizure. A two-step system could overcome this issue, where, in the first step a decision is made for each channel by a separate classifier, and in the second step the outputs of these classifiers serve as the input of a combined, final decision procedure. Greene et al. [3] compared such a *late*

T. Honkela et al. (Eds.): ICANN 2011, Part I, LNCS 6791, pp. 233–240, 2011.

integration method to an *early integration method*, where the features extracted from each channel are sorted and stacked into a long feature vector, which is then used to train a single classifier. The *early integration method* is proved to be superior in performance, by "treating the channels as related, exploiting their statistical inter-relationship and the synchronously recorded nature of the EEG" [3]. Shoeb et al. [8] developed a patient-specific seizure detector, which relies on features describing the temporal evolution, the spectral and the spatial structure of the EEG. In order to capture spatial information, the features of each channel are concatenated to form one feature vector. As opposed to the former study, where the sorting operation was intended to remove spatial information, the goal of the stacking in this case is to drive the attention to the locations corresponding to the channels consistently showing seizure activity.

In the present paper a novel alternative solution is investigated. The features extracted from the multichannel data are represented in the form of a matrix as an input to a classifier. The matrix representation of the data helps preserving and exploiting the inherent spatial structure of the multichannel EEG data. Moreover, recent studies ([1], [12]) show that higher-order representation of signals reduces the small sample-size problem, facilitating a precise classification performance even for low number of training points and outperforms traditional vector representation.

We investigate long-term recordings containing EEG data from refractory epilepsy patients undergoing presurgical evaluation. The immediate intervention after seizure onset is necessary to collect information about the seizure and is a key to successful localization of the seizure focus. After sufficient information has been acquired the patient can leave the hospital. Thus, it is essential that the algorithm can learn the seizure pattern after a few occurrences. Moreover, a low number of training points may be provided by seizures of possibly short length. However, the training of a traditional classifier might need a relatively high number of data points. We will show here that the proposed approach performs well when relatively little information is available.

2   Materials and Methods

2.1   EEG Data

EEG recordings from 14 patients with refractory partial epilepsy were included in the study. The patients were selected based only on the criterion that at least 4 seizures were recorded during their stay in the epilepsy monitoring unit. Data were sampled at 250Hz, an average referenced electrode montage was used and the electrodes were placed according to the standard 10-20 % 19 electrode system with two additonal electrodes placed over the sphenoidal temporal region.

2.2   Feature Extraction

EEG was segmented into 2s long non-overlapping windows. A total number of 19 features were extracted from each channel of each segment. Thus, one data

Table 1. Extracted Features

Frequency domain features	Total power, Peak frequency, Spectral edge frequency (80% , 90% , 95%), Mean and normalized power in the frequency bands (1-3 Hz, 4-8 Hz, 9-13 Hz and 14-20 Hz)
Time domain features	Number of zero crossings, maxima and minima, skewness, kurtosis, root mean square amplitude

point represents the multichannel EEG window in the form of a 19×21 matrix. The features are listed in Table 1 and are selected from the features used in [13].

2.3   Classification Approaches

Single-channel Classification with Late Integration. Traditional seizure detection systems analyze EEG channels independently and integrate the decision outputs of the single channels into a global decision during a separate step. There are several different strategies to follow. The outputs of the channel classifiers can be binary or probabilistic; post-processing can be performed applying a moving average filter on the outputs from the consecutive epochs [14]; the channel outputs can be integrated via mean, max, or min score, or majority vote [3]. The number of channels contributing to the global score might as well be limited [7]. In the current study the length of the feature vectors corresponds to the number of extracted features. The single-channel feature vectors are fed to a least-squares support vector machine (LS-SVM) [11]. Finally, the binary outputs of single epochs are integrated by a simple OR function.

LS-SVM was chosen because of its low computation costs due to solving a set of linear equations instead of quadratic programming. Moreover, the model is based on all data (all support values are nonzero), which can be beneficial in case of small samples. We use LS-SVMlab toolbox (www.esat.kuleuven.be/ sista/lssvmlab, [2]), which performs automatic tuning of the model parameters applying coupled simulated annealing [10].

Including Spatial Information via Early Integration of Feature Vectors. In this approach the feature vectors extracted from each EEG channel are stacked into one long feature vector of length $I \times J$, where I is the number of channels and J is the number of extracted features. One LS-SVM is trained and used for classification. As explained above, the concatenation of the channels in fixed order aims at including spatial information and exploiting the synchronously recorded and inter-dependent nature of multichannel EEG.

In both approaches applying LS-SVM a linear kernel was chosen considering the high dimensionality of input data and the small sample size. Moreover, the choice of linear kernel facilitates a meaningful comparison with the linear model used in the nuclear norm learning approach (see below).

Including Structural Information via Nuclear Norm Regularization.
We consider the following model:

$$\hat{y} = \langle A, X \rangle + b, \tag{1}$$

where X is the input pattern, A is a matrix of the same size, $\langle \cdot, \cdot \rangle$ indicates the inner product, and b is a bias term. Decisions are made according to $\text{sign}(\hat{y}) \in \{-1, 1\}$.

Such formulation allows to keep the natural matrix representation of the EEG data: $X \in R^{I \times J}$, where I is the number of channels, and J the number of features. The classifier (namely the pair (A, b)) is found solving a non-smooth convex optimization problem using a nuclear norm penalty:

$$\min_{(A,b)} F(A, b) = f(A, b) + \mu \|A\|_{\Sigma,1}, \tag{2}$$

where $f(A, b)$ is the quadratic error function accounting for the misclassification. This choice was made specifically because the same loss function is used in LS-SVM classification. Further, μ is a tuning parameter and $\|A\|_{\Sigma,1}$ is the nuclear norm of the matrix A with singular values σ_i :

$$\|A\|_{\Sigma,1} = \sum_i \sigma_i. \tag{3}$$

The tuning parameter μ, as well as the tuning parameters of LS-SVM formulation were chosen according to the 5-fold cross-validation of the misclassification error. Regularization via nuclear norm conveys structural information from the matrix by ensuring a low-rank solution. In the current application the low-rank classifier matrix represents the features and spatial distribution characteristic for the patient. Theoretical background and motivation behind the use of nuclear norms as heuristic ensuring low-rank solution, and details of the convex optimization algorithm can be found in [9] and references therein.

3   Results

3.1   Simulation on Randomized Training and Test Set

Performance of the matrix nuclear norm learning (NNL) algorithm was compared to the early integration (EI-LSSVM) and late integration (LI-LSSVM) solution. The test set consisted of 50 % of the available positive data points randomly selected from all segments of all recorded seizures of the given patient, and negative data points randomly selected from all non-seizure segments. The positive to negative ratio was fixed to 1:50 keeping into account the intrinsic unbalanceness of the problem. Classifiers were built based on increasing sizes of training sets, and were all tested on the same fixed test dataset. In total 5 training sets were randomly generated for each of the 14 patients and each training set size, using all available EEG segments during the random selection, excluding the ones in the test set. Performances are reported as the mean area under the

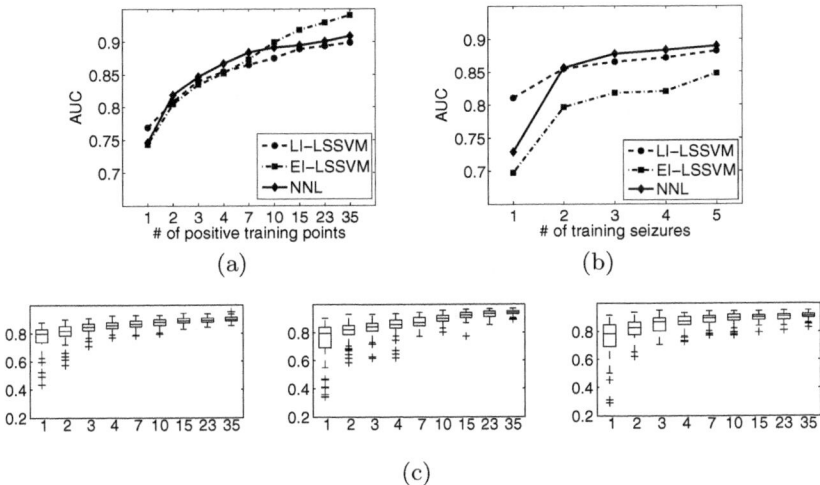

Fig. 1. Results of the simulation on randomized trainingset: (a) mean AUC over all trials in function of the training set size and (c) boxplots of AUC showing the variability in performance between the individual trials. Results of the real-life setting: (b) mean AUC values in function of the number of seizures included in the training set.

curve (AUC) of the 5×14 trials (ordinate) for each training set size (abscissa) as seen on Figure 1(a). The variability of AUC among the trials is depicted on Figure 1(c).

NNL approach is able to capture useful information after a few training points, and performs the best for small sizes of training sets. This advantage is not yet seen in case of one training point, although good generalization from only one training point is obviously not feasible for any learning algorithm. On the contrary, EI-LSSVM benefits the most from including additional training points, and it performs the best if greater number of training points are available.

3.2 Real-life Setting

The results of the above simulation are revised in the analysis of the performances of NNL and EI/LI-LSSVM in a real-life setting. A patient-specific seizure detection system first records EEG until the first seizure occurs, and then builds a classifier based on the collected data. Afterwards it goes on with recording and classifying each new data segment in parallel. Once an other seizure occurs, the classifier is updated in order to reach better classification performance based on the additional information.

In order to simulate such an environment, the available seizures are ordered based on the time of their occurrence, seizures occurring later on time serve as test set, together with the appropriate number of non-seizure segments. The first classifier is now built based on the segments of the seizure occurring first in time,

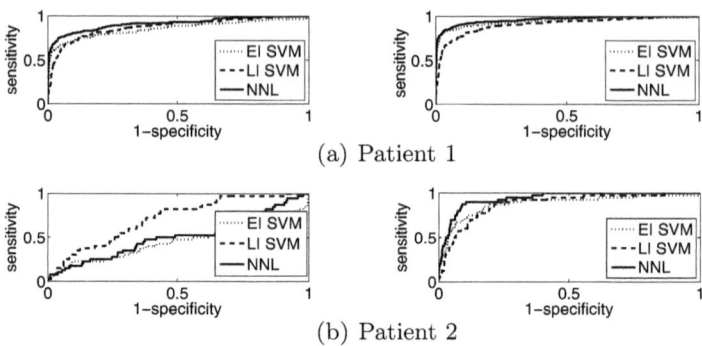

Fig. 2. ROC of the different approaches including one and two seizures in the training set (left and right panel respectively)

then new classifiers are built adding the segments of the consecutive seizures to the training set.

However, in a patient-specific setting, if the first seizure occurs shortly after the start of the recording, there might not be enough diversity of negative training points. Brain activity in different physiological brain state and artifacts have peculiar patterns, and some of them might resemble seizures. In order to include a more complete and representative set of non-seizure segments alpha activity, sleeping and drowsiness patterns, muscle artifacts, chewing artifacts, rapid eye movement and repeated blinking patterns were collected from 29 different patients and were included in a semi-patient-specific training set.

The mean AUC of the three approaches over all the patients with at least five training seizures is depicted on Figure 1(b). NNL proves to be superior when two or more seizures are included in the training set, while LI-LSSVM performs better when only one seizure is available.

Figure 2 illustrates two different scenarios regarding patient-by-patient performance. The receiver operating characteristic (ROC) curves of the different classification approaches are depicted for two patients given one and two training seizures. In the former case NNL and EI-LSSVM are able to capture enough information after one seizure, while in the latter case they require two seizures for their optimal performance. They are outperformed by LI-LSSVM when only one training seizure is available.

3.3 Computational Costs

The computational costs using the three different approaches are compared in Table 2. The computational times were tested given different sizes of training sets. Ten positive datapoints correspond to a 20s long seizure, thus the chosen training set sizes represent training sets including increasing number of seizures from one up till five. For small training set sizes EI-LSSVM has the shortest running time, however, its running time increases at a faster rate and exceeds

Table 2. Computational times (s)

# of positive datapoints	10	20	30	40	50
EI-LSSVM	2.7	12.6	37.8	79.8	151.1
LI-LSSVM	44.2	248.4	769.7	1652.1	3153.4
NNL	49.8	74.1	96.3	118.0	145.5

NNL running time given five training seizures. Nevertheless, they both remain within practical limits, unlike LI-LSSVM.

4 Discussion

The results acquired in the simulation study show clear superiority of the two approaches incorporating spatial/structural information over the traditional single-channel method. However, EI-LSSVM performance clearly decreases in the real-life experiment. Moreover, LI-LSSVM shows higher mean performance than NNL given one training seizure. The principal difference between the two studies is that data points from different seizures are included in the training set in the simulation study, while the data points of the same seizure are included in the real-life example. Given a patient with certain variability in spatial distribution among the seizures, EI-LSSVM fails to generalize, while LI-LSSVM easily overcomes this problem due to the simple OR function integrating the channel decisions. NNL nevertheless outperforms EI-LSSVM, suggesting that the structural information exploited by its learning algorithm is more flexible than the spatial information encoded in the concatenated feature vector, i.e. the input of EI-LSSVM. Moreover, given multiple seizure patterns, NNL is capable of exploiting additional information and performs slightly better than the independent single-channel LI-LSSVM.

Determining the optimal set of features might improve classification performance, but is beyond the scope of this paper. Furthermore, a future study applying the classifiers as on-line seizure detectors should be carried out and evaluated by clinically relevant measures such as sensitivity, false detection rate over time and alarm delay.

Extensive analysis is to be carried out aiming at defining the exact circumstances under which one classification approach is favorable over the other. A final seizure detection system may be developed, which automatically selects the most appropriate learning and classification technique given the actually available training set.

Acknowledgments. Research supported by Research Council KUL: GOA MaNet, CoE EF/05/006 Optimization in Engineering (OPTEC), PFV/10/002 (OPTEC), IDO 05/010 EEG-fMRI, IOF-KP06/11 FunCopt; Flemish Government: FWO G.0302.07 (SVM), FWO G.0427.10N (Integrated EEG-fMRI); IWT: TBM080658-MRI, IBBT; Belgian Federal Science Policy Office: IUAP P6/04 (DYSCO, 2007-2011); EU: Neuromath (COST-BM0601)

References

1. Cai, D., He, X., Weng, J.R., Han, J., Ma, W.Y.: Support tensor machines for text categorization. Tech. rep., Computer Science Department, UIUC, UIUCDCS-R-2006-2714 (April 2006)
2. De Brabanter, K., Karsmakers, P., Ojeda, F., Alzate, C., De Brabanter, J., Pelckmans, K., De Moor, B., Vandewalle, J., Suykens, J.: LS-SVMlab toolbox user's guide version 1.7. Tech. rep., ESAT-SISTA, K.U.Leuven (2011)
3. Greene, B., Marnane, W., Lightbody, G., Reilly, R., Boylan, G.: Classifier models and architectures for eeg-based neonatal seizure detection. Physiol. Meas. 29(10), 1157 (2008)
4. Guerrero-Mosquera, C., Malanda Trigueros, A., Iriarte Franco, J., Navia-Vazquez, A.: New feature extraction approach for epileptic eeg signal detection using time-frequency distributions. Med. Biol. Eng. Comput. 48, 321–330 (2010)
5. Meier, R., Dittrich, H., Schulze-Bonhage, A., Aertsen, A.: Detecting epileptic seizures in long-term human eeg: A new approach to automatic online and real-time detection and classification of polymorphic seizure patterns. J. Clin. Neurophysiol. 25(3), 119–131 (2008)
6. Polychronaki, G.E., Ktonas, P.Y., Gatzonis, S., Siatouni, A., Asvestas, P.A., Tsekou, H., Sakas, D., Nikita, K.: Comparison of fractal dimension estimation algorithms for epileptic seizure onset detection. J. Neural Eng. 7(4), 46007 (2010)
7. Saab, M., Gotman, J.: A system to detect the onset of epileptic seizures in scalp eeg. Clin. Neurophysiol. 116(2), 427–442 (2005)
8. Shoeb, A., Guttag, J.: Application of machine learning to epileptic seizure detection. In: Fürnkranz, J., Joachims, T. (eds.) Proceedings of the 27th International Conference on Machine Learning (ICML 2010), pp. 975–982, Omnipress, Haifa (2010)
9. Signoretto, M., De Lathauwer, L., Suykens, J.: Nuclear norms for tensors and their use for convex multilinear estimation. Tech. rep., ESAT-SISTA, K.U.Leuven (2010)
10. Xavier de Souza, S., Suykens, J., Vandewalle, J., Bollé, D.: Coupled simulated annealing. IEEE Trans. Syst. Man Cybern. Part B Cybern. 40(2), 320–335 (2010)
11. Suykens, J.A.K., Vandewalle, J.: Least squares support vector machine classifiers. Neural Process. Lett. 9(3), 293–300 (1999)
12. Tao, D., Li, X., Wu, X., Hu, W., Maybank, S.J.: Supervised tensor learning. Knowl. Inf. Syst. 13, 1–42 (2007)
13. Temko, A., Thomas, E., Boylan, G., Marnane, W., Lightbody, G.: An svm-based system and its performance for detection of seizures in neonates. In: Annual International Conference of the IEEE Eng. Med. Biol. Mag. EMBC 2009. pp. 2643–2646 (September 2009)
14. Thomas, E., Temko, A., Lightbody, G., Marnane, W., Boylan, G.: A comparison of generative and discriminative approaches in automated neonatal seizure detection. In: IEEE International Symposium on Intelligent Signal Processing 2009, pp. 181–186. IEEE Computer Society Press, Los Alamitos (August 2009)

The Grouped Author-Topic Model for Unsupervised Entity Resolution

Andrew M. Dai and Amos J. Storkey

Institute for Adaptive and Neural Computation, School of Informatics,
University of Edinburgh, U.K.
{a.dai,a.storkey}@ed.ac.uk

Abstract. This paper describes a generative approach for tackling the problem of identity resolution in a completely unsupervised context with no fixed assumption regarding the true number of identities. The problem of entity resolution involves associating different references to authors (in a paper's author list, for example) with real underlying identities. The references may be written in differing forms or may have errors, and identical references may refer to different real identities. The approach taken here uses a generative model of both the abstract of a document and its list of authors to resolve identities in a corpus of documents. In the model, authors and topics are associated with latent groups. For each document, an abstract and an author list are generated conditioned on a given group. Results are presented on real-world datasets, and outperform the best performing unsupervised methods.

Keywords: Bayesian nonparametrics, Dirichlet processes, nested Dirichlet processes, author disambiguation.

1 Introduction

Entity resolution is a problem encountered widely in the literature and is referred to by a variety of names that vary depending on the domain area it is used in, including record linkage, deduplication and coreference resolution. The focus of the problem is essentially to discover duplicate entities in a dataset in the absence of unique identifiers. These entities may be things that are referenced in different ways in a document, duplicate records from merging customer databases or people being referenced within multiple documents in a single corpus. It is this latter task that we focus on. One common approach to tackling this problem includes the use of clustering, such as hierarchical agglomerative clustering and k-means clustering, where each cluster represents an entity. However, a problem with many of these existing approaches is that they require the number of clusters or a cut-off threshold to be set in advance.

Models where the number of clusters is unknown a priori, and which are flexible enough to incorporate a range of likelihood models are attractive for this problem. Additionally, since very little labelled data exists for entity resolution, unsupervised and generative approaches are useful. One class of models

T. Honkela et al. (Eds.): ICANN 2011, Part I, LNCS 6791, pp. 241–249, 2011.

which satisfy these requirements are Bayesian nonparametric models, of which the Dirichlet process (DP) [1] has been especially widely-used. The DP is a probability distribution on the space of probability measures. Since a sample from the DP is a discrete distribution, such a sample is a natural representation for clusters. Infinite mixture models that are based on the DP are not restricted to a finite number of latent classes and so offer extra modelling flexibility. A draw from a Dirichlet process (which we will denote by $G \sim \mathrm{DP}(\alpha, H)$), is dependent on two parameter terms H and α. H is called the base measure and gives the expectation of G, and α is called the concentration. For a definition of the DP we refer the reader to Ferguson [1] or one of the many introductory texts on the subject. Structured variations of the DP include both the nested Dirichlet process (NDP) [2] and the hierarchical Dirichlet process (HDP) [3].

The model described in this paper is a hierarchal generative nonparametric model for document abstracts and author lists that differs from current approaches in a number of ways. It is the first approach (to our knowledge) to integrate both topic and co-author information for tackling the task of unsupervised identity resolution. Co-author information is captured through a concept of research groups that forms part of the generative model. Each group also has a number of topics on which they write. This integration of both topic and group information enables improved performance over methods that only consider individual information sources. Furthermore, unlike earlier methods we make no assumptions regarding the equivalence of authors with names that have the same transcription in the corpus. The approach here is compared to state of the art unsupervised models and is able to both separate identical references that refer to different identities as well as combine different references that refer to the same identity, while still performing better than the current state of the art.

The remainder of this paper is set out as follows. In Section 3, we develop our framework used to tackle this problem with a description of the generative story. In Section 4, we describe inference in this framework. We then describe results on real world datasets in Section 5 and conclude in Section 6 with a discussion.

2   Previous Work

One way to attack the entity resolution problem is via an agglomerative approach where references are merged according to some criterion until a threshold is reached. Recently, approaches for entity resolution have aimed at avoiding the need to set a threshold at which to stop merging clusters or the number of author entities in advance. To avoid this problem, several approaches have been applied. Bhattacharya and Getoor [4] describe an entity-resolution approach (LDA-ER) based on latent Dirichlet allocation (LDA), that is able to infer the number of author entities in the data. However, the number of co-authorship groups need to be pre-specified and they require labelled data for setting the parameters.

Often, models which use information from other attributes perform better than those that solely disambiguate based on names. The author-topic model, proposed by Rosen-Zvi et al. [5], associates latent topics with authors and

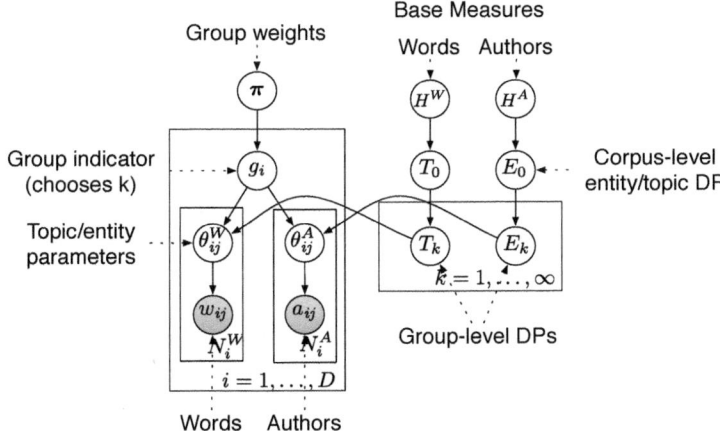

Fig. 1. Our generative model in plate notation. Filled in nodes are observed variables. The concentration parameters for the DPs have been omitted.

identifies the topics that authors frequently write on. In this work, a latent topic is characterised by a distribution over words in the corpus. However, rather than entity resolution, their goal was to model the tendencies of authors to write on certain topics or subject areas assuming the authors for each document are already known. Their model allocates words in the document to one of the known authors and does not use co-author information. However, this approach can require a large amount of data. An author must appear numerous times in the corpus for its topic distribution to be sufficiently tight for the purpose of disambiguation. Instead, in the model introduced in this paper, groups of authors are associated with topics rather than individual authors. This eliminates the difficult problem of associating authors with topics when data is limited.

3   Grouped Author-Topic Model

In this paper we aim to use as much of the commonly-shared information that is available for the purposes of entity resolution. This information is typically the words in the abstract, as well as the author list. This information is organised via the latent concept of a research group (which characterises which authors might be co-authors) along with topic information associated with each group (which helps disambiguate authors which could be members of a number of research groups). This leads to a model which we call the grouped author-topic model.

In the grouped author-topic model each real-world author identity will be represented by a latent *author entity*. Although a single entity, a real-world author may have a number of different names by which he or she is referred. These are known as *references* and different variants of the author's name occur due to variation in initialing, transcription errors, typographical errors, transliteration differences etc. These varying forms can be viewed as being generated by a name corruption process which, for each author, corrupts an underlying *canonical name* associated with that particular author. Any potential corruption model can be used in the context of the grouped author-topic model. We tested a generative bigram model, a trigram model and a previously-used pair hidden Markov model [4]. This last model uses domain knowledge that author names are often written with first or middle names initialled or middle name removed. We found that this corruption model performed the best.

To describe the model we need to introduce two concepts, that of *group* and that of *topic*. The idea of topic is common to other papers on topic modelling, where a topic is a mixture component defining a distribution of words. An individual abstract will only contain a small number of topics out of the total possible number. Intuitively, the idea of a group conceptualises authors who work/publish together and the associated topics they publish on. For each particular group, we define a Dirichlet process over author entities (to capture the authors that work together), and over topics (to capture the topics the group publishes on). This Dirichlet process is drawn hierarchically from a global author and topic DP. Hence author entities and topics can be shared between groups so that an author entity has non-zero probability of occurring in multiple groups, and similarly for the topics. In contrast to the author-topic model, the authors are not associated with topics directly. This model is depicted in Figure 1.

To complete the generative model we need to describe the process of generating the actual abstracts. Each abstract is associated with a group (again drawn from a DP). The group associated with the document determines which authors are potentially represented in a document and which topics are written about (i.e. those given significant probability by the associated group). Intuitively, this can be thought of as a document being authored by a single research group, which has a number of particular topics which they may choose to publish on, and which may be represented in the current document. The structure is loosely similar to the nested Dirichlet Process (NDP) of Rodriguez et al. [2]. However, due to the hierarchical structure in our framework, the clusters are shared between groups so that an author entity may be allocated to multiple groups. In contrast, in the standard NDP, clusters are not shared between groups.

The generative process for a whole corpus is as follows, where γ and α denote concentration parameters for the global and lower level DPs respectively, the superscripts W and A denote the parameters or distributions for the topics and the author entities respectively. H denotes the base measure, π_k denotes the weight from the stick-breaking construction for each group k, and GEM represents the distribution from the stick-breaking construction [3]. These stick breaking weights determine the group DP over entities and topics E_k, T_k respectively. θ denotes the parameters for the likelihood models for the authors and topics and finally $f(a|\theta^A)$ is the probability the name a is corrupted from the canonical name θ^A by the name corruption model.

1. Draw (from their prior distributions) the concentration parameters for the global DPs, $\gamma^W, \gamma^A, \gamma^G$ for the topics, authors and groups respectively. Likewise, draw the concentration parameters for the lower-level DPs, α^W, α^A from their priors.
2. Draw a global distribution over topics $T_0 \sim \mathrm{DP}(\gamma^W, H^W)$ and author entities $E_0 \sim \mathrm{DP}(\gamma^A, H^A)$. Draw a distribution over groups $\boldsymbol{\pi} \sim \mathrm{GEM}(\gamma^G)$.
3. For each group k, draw a distribution over topics $T_k \sim \mathrm{DP}(\alpha^W, T_0)$ and author entities $E_k \sim \mathrm{DP}(\alpha^A, E_0)$.
4. Now for each document $i = 1, \ldots, D$:
   (a) Draw a group to generate the document $g_i | \boldsymbol{\pi} \sim \boldsymbol{\pi}$.
   (b) For each word $w_{ij}, j = 1, \ldots, N_i^W$:
      i. Draw a topic $\theta_{ij}^W | g_i, T_{g_i} \sim T_{g_i}$. Draw a word $w | \theta_{ij}^W \sim \mathrm{Mult}(w | \theta_{ij}^W)$.
   (c) For each author reference $a_{ij}, j = 1, \ldots, N_i^A$:
      i. Draw an author entity $\theta_{ij}^A | g_i, E_{g_i} \sim E_{g_i}$. Draw a (possibly corrupted) author's name from the corruption model $a | \theta_{ij}^A \sim f(a | \theta_{ij}^A)$.

In the grouped author-topic model, H^W is a symmetric Dirichlet(η) prior distribution over topic parameters, where a topic is parameterised by the probabilities of each word appearing in a corpus. Since this is conjugate to the likelihood (a multinomial distribution), during inference θ^W can be integrated out.

4   Inference

Since calculating the exact posterior under DP models is intractable, we use approximate algorithms. Due to the ease of implementing and verifying a Markov chain Monte Carlo approach, we use collapsed Gibbs sampling based on the Polya urn scheme for inference. Collapsed Gibbs sampling is described in Teh et. al [3] and involves Gibbs sampling while integrating out over conjugate distributions and random measures. The group allocations can be sampled given the word and author allocations and vice versa. As noted earlier, we integrate out the parameters for each topic, which are the multinomial distributions over the words. Since the base measure for the author names is not conjugate, we use Algorithm 8 described by Neal [6] for the author name parameters.

The true names in the corpus are considered latent variables in the grouped author-topic model. However, for practical purposes, to avoid the search over all possible canonical names, we make the computationally simplifying assumption that the true name can be sufficiently well represented by one of the references in the corpus. Every unique author name that appears in the corpus is therefore given a uniform prior probability of being the canonical name for an entity, $H^A = \mathrm{Multinomial}(1/A_N)$ where A_N is the number of unique names observed. This is equivalent to using an empirical prior for the space of canonical names.

5   Experiments

We tested the grouped author-topic model on the author lists and abstracts from several standard publicly available citation databases. We chose the real-world

Table 1. B^3 results on Rexa and CiteSeer datasets. Means and standard deviations are across 10 parallel chains, each with a 1,000 iteration burn-in. *Grouped A-T* is the grouped author-topic model, *group per word* relaxes the model allowing abstracts to be allocated to multiple groups, *words with authors* is the model similar to the author-topic model where words are allocated to entities without groups and *without abstracts* is a simple HDP model that ignores abstracts and does not use groups.

Model	Rexa			CiteSeer		
	Recall	Precision	F1	Recall	Precision	F1
Grouped A-T	95.6	99.7	**97.6** ($\pm$ **0.3**)	98.7	99.5	**99.2** ($\pm$ **0.1**)
Group per word	95.2	99.5	97.3 ($\pm$ 0.3)	99.3	85.7	92.0 ($\pm$ 0.9)
Words with authors	93.6	97.3	95.4 ($\pm$ 1.0)	95.1	39.3	55.6 ($\pm$ 0.4)
Without abstracts	93.0	99.3	96.0 ($\pm$ 0.3)	97.2	97.4	97.3 ($\pm$ 0.2)
LDA-ER	92.6	99.4	95.9 ($\pm$ 1.2)	97.0	100	98.4 ($\pm$ 0.1)
Baseline distance	57.4	99.6	72.8	78.5	100	88.0

CiteSeer and Rexa databases as their ground truth is publicly available. The CiteSeer dataset, created by Giles [7] with ground truth compiled by Culotta and McCallum, consists of citations to four areas in machine learning. After removing duplicate documents in the CiteSeer dataset, it contains 1,695 references to 1,158 authors across 862 documents. The Rexa dataset [8] contains 9,366 author references in total with 1,972 of those labelled, by Culotta, to 105 author identities across 2,697 documents. Compared to the Rexa dataset, the CiteSeer dataset contains many more singleton author entities, authors that only appear once in the corpus. We applied a standard stoplist and stemming.

We compare the grouped author-topic model with other similar approaches. The *words with authors* model can be seen as a non-parametric version of the author-topic model [5] adapted for author disambiguation. We implemented the LDA-ER model [4], which uses the concept of groups to perform disambiguation but does not use any abstract or title information. We also evaluate against a baseline distance measure that assigns identical names to the same identity. η was set to 0.01 in common with the author-topic model and for the entities we placed an uninformative Gamma$(1, 0.01)$ prior on the global concentration parameter and a Gamma$(1, 0.1)$ prior on the lower-level concentration parameter and updated by sampling from their posterior. These priors and similar priors on concentration parameters were chosen to give a uniform prior on the number of clusters following the algorithm in Dorazio [9]. Changing the priors by an order of magnitude did not significantly influence the results. We calculated the standard B^3 score [10] used for coreference and the results are shown in Table 1.

The sampler converged in terms of the log likelihood of each chain and between chains after 200 iterations. It took 40 minutes to sample 1,000 iterations running on a single core of an Intel Xeon server for the CiteSeer dataset. We burned-in for 1,000 iterations and sampled for a further 1,000, evaluating on the posterior author entity assignments. For each round of sampling the entity and topic

Table 2. Macro-averaged B^3 disambiguation results on the WePS 2 dataset

Model	Recall	Precision	F1
Unsupervised grouped Author-Topic	50	82	**56**
Supervised bag of words	48	95	59
Baseline (each document in individual cluster)	24	100	34

allocations, we perform 10 iterations of group sampling to improve mixing of groups. An example of an inferred group from the Rexa dataset spread across 20 documents is: *N. Cristianini, Taylor J. Shawe, J. Kandola, J. Platt, H. Lodhi, P. L. Montgomery* with the topics: *spectral, clustering, classification, semantic, kernel, method, extension.* Our results show that the grouped author-topic model performs better than other unsupervised approaches including LDA-ER. Even though LDA-ER performs well in the CiteSeer dataset, their approach assumes that identical author references always refer to the same author identity. As can be seen in the baseline, there is little ambiguity in the CiteSeer dataset. Applying this assumption to the grouped author-topic model can be done by requiring identical references to be assigned to the same entity. However, this would result in a model that would no longer be able to handle ambiguous names, the handling of which was an advantage over LDA-ER. Our results also show that our grouped author-topic model succeeds in integrating abstract and co-author information as compared to the models which do not. The model with words directly assigned to authors likely performs poorer due to the posterior overweighting author entities with many assigned words.

Finally, we show results on a task that LDA-ER cannot tackle due to its assumption that authors with identical names always refer to the same entity. We ran experiments on the dataset from the WePS 2 [11] people clustering task. The goal of the task is to disambiguate person names in web search results. 30 randomly chosen names were searched for on an Internet search engine. The top 150 search results were retrieved and each document was hand annotated to match with a real identity. The dataset is highly ambiguous with an average of 18 different people per name. We extracted the words from each webpage, removed stopwords and ran the result through the Stanford named entity recogniser [12]. We used the extracted named entities in place of the author references in our model and used the Jaro-Winkler distance metric as the name corruption model. This flexible model was chosen to allow matching of name, location and organization entities written in different forms. We used the non-entity words as the observed words for each document. We then performed experiments with priors on the concentration parameters that were scaled logarithmically in proportion to the given real-world frequency of that name. Since identities are at the document level, we evaluate our model using the posterior group assignments. The results in Table 2 show that our unsupervised model almost matches the performance of the supervised bag of words approach. Our model performs well compared to other teams [11] despite the majority of the other teams being reliant on supervised approaches with additional features based on extracted attributes of the person, cutoff distances or additional queries on a search engine.

6   Discussion

Our grouped author-topic model models the authorship of a document through a hierarchical model that combines a topic model with a multiple authorship model. This allows information that comes from a document having multiple authors and the topic specific content in a document to be leveraged to usefully disambiguate the authors that are represented in the corpus. We have evaluated the model against real world data and shown that it performs well in the task of identity resolution against other unsupervised state of the art approaches. The model shows significant improvement over ignoring groups or abstracts in the citation database examples and shows that it can perform well at disambiguating a set of documents where the names are identical.

Our model is versatile in that it can disambiguate identical name references that refer to different entities as well as combine differing references to the same entity. The model is fully automated in that it does not require pre-specification of numbers of entities, research groups, topics etc. This is a result of the model taking a Bayesian non-parametric approach to the problem and allowing broad uninformative priors to be set on the number of entities, etc. while allowing more informative priors over the number of entities to be chosen if needed. Although the base measure for the entities is non-conjugate, using an auxiliary variable Gibbs sampler still resulted in good performance. The name corruption model could be changed to a bigram model or a discriminative name model to simplify inference or to use the model in other settings. For example, the appropriate likelihood and base measure may allow the modelling of co-entity relationships to be used for word sense disambiguation.

References

1. Ferguson, T.S.: A Bayesian Analysis of Some Nonparametric Problems. The Annals of Statistics 1(2), 209–230 (1973)
2. Rodriguez, A., Dunson, D.B., Gelfand, A.E.: The nested Dirichlet process. Journal of the American Statistical Association 103(483), 1131–1154 (2008)
3. Teh, Y.W., Jordan, M.I., Beal, M.J., Blei, D.M.: Hierarchical Dirichlet Processes. Journal of the American Statistical Association 101(476), 1566–1581 (2006)
4. Bhattacharya, I., Getoor, L.: A Latent Dirichlet Model for Unsupervised Entity Resolution. In: The SIAM International Conference on Data Mining (SIAM-SDM), Bethesda, MD, USA (2006)
5. Rosen-Zvi, M., Griffiths, T., Steyvers, M., Smyth, P.: The author-topic model for authors and documents. In: UAI 2004: Proceedings of the 20th Conference on Uncertainty in Artificial Intelligence, pp. 487–494. AUAI Press, Arlington (2004)
6. Neal, R.M.: Markov Chain Sampling Methods for Dirichlet Process Mixture Models. Journal of Computational and Graphical Statistics 9(2), 249–265 (2000)

7. Giles, C.L., Bollacker, K.D., Lawrence, S.: CiteSeer: An Automatic Citation Indexing System. In: Digital Libraries 1998 - The Third ACM Conference on Digital Libraries, pp. 89–98 (1998)
8. Peng, F., Mccallum, A.: Information extraction from research papers using conditional random fields. Information Processing & Management 42(4), 963–979 (2006)
9. Dorazio, R.M.: On selecting a prior for the precision parameter of Dirichlet process mixture models. Journal of Statistical Planning and Inference 139(9), 3384–3390 (2009)
10. Bagga, A., Baldwin, B.: Entity-based cross-document coreferencing using the Vector Space Model. In: Proceedings of the 17th International Conference on Computational Linguistics, Association for Computational Linguistics, pp. 79–85 Morristown (1998)
11. Artiles, J., Gonzalo, J., Sekine, S.: WePS 2 Evaluation Campaign: Overview of the Web People Search Clustering Task. In: Evaluation (2009)
12. Finkel, J.R., Grenager, T., Manning, C.: Incorporating non-local information into information extraction systems by Gibbs sampling. In: Proceedings of the 43rd Annual Meeting on Association for Computational Linguistics ACL 2005, vol. 43, pp. 363–370 (2005)

Kullback-Leibler Divergence for Nonnegative Matrix Factorization*

Zhirong Yang, He Zhang, Zhijian Yuan, and Erkki Oja

Department of Information and Computer Science
Aalto University, P.O.Box 15400, FI-00076, Espoo, Finland,
{zhirong.yang,he.zhang,zhijian.yuan,erkki.oja}@aalto.fi

Abstract. The I-divergence or unnormalized generalization of Kullback-Leibler (KL) divergence is commonly used in Nonnegative Matrix Factorization (NMF). This divergence has the drawback that its gradients with respect to the factorizing matrices depend heavily on the scales of the matrices, and learning the scales in gradient-descent optimization may require many iterations. This is often handled by explicit normalization of one of the matrices, but this step may actually increase the I-divergence and is not included in the NMF monotonicity proof. A simple remedy that we study here is to normalize the input data. Such normalization allows the replacement of the I-divergence with the original KL-divergence for NMF and its variants. We show that using KL-divergence takes the normalization structure into account in a very natural way and brings improvements for nonnegative matrix factorizations: the gradients of the normalized KL-divergence are well-scaled and thus lead to a new projected gradient method for NMF which runs faster or yields better approximation than three other widely used NMF algorithms.

1 Introduction

Nonnegative Matrix Factorization (NMF) is a powerful tool for signal processing, data analysis, and machine learning, that has attracted much research effort recently. The problem was first introduced by Paatero and Tapper [1]. After Lee and Seung [2] presented multiplicative update algorithms for NMF, a multitude of variants of NMF (see e.g. [3] for a survey) have been proposed. Most of these methods can be divided into two categories according to the approximation criterion: least square error or information divergence. For the latter category, the *generalized Kullback-Leibler divergence* or *I-divergence* used in Lee and Seung's algorithm is widely adopted in present applications.

In spite of a number of generalizations (see e.g. [4,5,3]), little research has been devoted to investigating the difference between I-divergence and the original Kullback-Leibler (KL) divergence. Actually the I-divergence difference measure has a number of drawbacks. Firstly, in many applications the data matrix can be

---

* Supported by the Academy of Finland in the project *Finnish Centre of Excellence in Adaptive Informatics Research*.

T. Honkela et al. (Eds.): ICANN 2011, Part I, LNCS 6791, pp. 250–257, 2011.

normalized before input to divergence-based NMF algorithms. This is the case when the relative differences among matrix entries are more important than their individual magnitudes. The normalization structure can provide valuable information for the NMF learning, but I-divergence neglects such information. Secondly, the Poisson noise model that underlies the I-divergence [2] is a discrete distribution defined only for nonnegative integers [6]. Thirdly, the gradients that provide critical information for the updating direction in optimization heavily depend on the scales of factorizing matrices, whose correct values are unknown beforehand. The additive gradient-based optimization of NMF with I-divergence can be very slow because it requires many iterations to recover from wrong initial scales.

In this paper we study the replacement of the I-divergence for NMF with the original KL-divergence for normalized data. Optimizing the new objectives is not trivial, where we are facing the challenge that the KL-divergence is non-separable over the matrix elements. Actually it belongs to the family of γ-divergence (see e.g. [3, Chapter 2]) whose optimization is unseen before. A new projected gradient method is then proposed for NMF based on normalized KL-divergence, which runs faster than two other additive optimization approaches and gives better approximation than the conventional multiplicative updates.

The rest of the paper is organized as follows. We briefly review the NMF problem based on the I-divergence in Section 2. In Section 3, we present NMF based on the normalized KL-divergence, including their objectives and corresponding optimization algorithms. Section 4 shows the empirical results which demonstrate the advantages of using normalized KL-divergence. The conclusions and future work are given in Section 5.

2   NMF Based on I-Divergence

Given a nonnegative input data matrix $\mathbf{X} \in \mathbb{R}_+^{m \times n}$, *Nonnegative Matrix Factorization* (NMF) seeks a decomposition of $\mathbf{X}$ that is of the form $\mathbf{X} \approx \mathbf{WH}$, where $\mathbf{W} \in \mathbb{R}_+^{m \times r}$ and $\mathbf{H} \in \mathbb{R}_+^{r \times n}$ with the rank $r < \min(m, n)$. The matrix $\widehat{\mathbf{X}} = \mathbf{WH}$ is called the unnormalized approximating matrix of $\mathbf{X}$.

In previous work, the approximation has widely been achieved by minimizing one of the two measures: (1) the least square criterion $\varepsilon = \sum_{i,j}(X_{ij} - \widehat{X}_{ij})^2$ and (2) the *generalized Kullback-Leibler divergence* (or *I-divergence*)

$$D_I\left(\mathbf{X}||\widehat{\mathbf{X}}\right) = \sum_{ij}\left(X_{ij}\log\frac{X_{ij}}{\widehat{X}_{ij}} - X_{ij} + \widehat{X}_{ij}\right). \tag{1}$$

In this paper we focus on the second approximation criterion, which is particularly useful for sparse counting data of small occurrences. In what follows, we call NMF based on the I-divergence I-NMF, to distinguish it from the one based on the original KL-divergence described below.

3   NMF Based on KL-Divergence

In many applications, the input data matrix is or can be normalized before its nonnegative matrix factorization. The normalization scheme can provide valuable information for NMF algorithms and should be taken into account. This motivates us to improve NMF by using the original or normalized KL-divergence.

3.1   Normalized Kullback-Leibler Divergence

Let $\mathbf{X}$ denote the normalized input data matrix. According to the original KL-divergence definition, the NMF approximation should be $\mathbf{X} \approx \widetilde{\mathbf{X}}$ by the criterion

$$D_{KL}\left(\mathbf{X}||\widetilde{\mathbf{X}}\right) = \sum_{i,j} X_{ij} \log \frac{X_{ij}}{\widetilde{X}_{ij}}, \tag{2}$$

where $\widetilde{\mathbf{X}}$ is obtained from $\widehat{\mathbf{X}} = \mathbf{WH}$ using the same normalization scheme that was used for $\mathbf{X}$. Common normalization schemes include

- matrix-wise normalization: $\sum_{ij} X_{ij} = 1$. Then $\widetilde{X}_{ij} = \widehat{X}_{ij}/\sum_{ab} \widehat{X}_{ab}$;
- row-wise normalization: for all i, $\sum_j X_{ij} = 1$. Then $\widetilde{X}_{ij} = \widehat{X}_{ij}/\sum_b \widehat{X}_{ib}$;
- column-wise normalization: for all j, $\sum_i X_{ij} = 1$. Then $\widetilde{X}_{ij} = \widehat{X}_{ij}/\sum_a \widehat{X}_{aj}$.

The following derivations will focus on the matrix case to avoid notational clutter, but the discussions can easily be extended to the other two cases. The empirical advantages of row-wise normalized KL-NMF is shown in Section 4.

Normalized data matrices exist widely in applications. A matrix-wise normalization example is to approximate a symmetric affinity matrix [7]. For row-wise or column-wise normalization, a good example is the document-term occurrence matrix commonly used in information retrieval.

We choose the original KL-divergence also because it can bring us better stability. Let us take the matrix-wise normalization for example. Writing out (2), one can see that up to a constant the KL-divergence

$$D_{KL}^{\text{mat}}\left(\mathbf{X}||\widetilde{\mathbf{X}}\right) = \sum_{ij} X_{ij} \log \frac{X_{ij}}{\widehat{X}_{ij}} + \log \sum_{ij} \widehat{X}_{ij} \tag{3}$$

differs from the I-divergence with a logarithm before $\sum_{ij} \widehat{X}_{ij}$. As we shall see, this logarithm plays a key role in efficiently adjusting the scale of $\widehat{\mathbf{X}}$ for both additive and multiplicative optimization.

It has recently been shown that at the stationary points the I-NMF also preserves the column-wise and row-wise sums of the input matrix [8]. However, so far there is no optimization algorithm that theoretically guarantees to achieve such exact stationary points. In practice, the learning with I-divergence can still be inconsistent with the normalization of input matrix.

3.2   Equivalence to pLSI

It has been shown that I-NMF is equivalent to the *Probabilistic Latent Semantic Indexing* (pLSI) under certain conditions [9]. Actually NMF based on KL-divergence (KL-NMF) has closer relationship to pLSI than I-NMF. KL-NMF optimizes exactly the same objective as pLSI by its definition. The requirement of unitary column sum in pLSI can be fulfilled by applying column normalization only once after the iterative learning.

The I-divergence is separable over the matrix elements, but pLSI requires unitary sum of the input matrix and of its approximate. I-divergence belongs to the family of α- or β-divergences, while pLSI and KL-divergence belong to the family of γ-divergences which are non-separable (see e.g. [3, Chapter 2]).

In I-NMF, the equivalence to pLSI can be enforced by employing column normalization as shown by Proposition 2 in [9]. However, the extra normalization steps are not included in the convergence proof. The normalization step itself can indeed often violate the monotonic decrease of the objective. By contrast, both additive and multiplicative algorithms for nonnegative matrix factorizations based on KL-divergence do not require such an extra normalization step, which facilitates their convergence analysis.

3.3   Projected Gradient Algorithms for NMF

The most popular solution for I-NMF is alternatively applying two multiplicative update rules [10]. Such EM-like multiplicative algorithms for NMF do not require user-specified optimization parameters and thus are widely used. However, Gonzales and Zhang [11] as well as Lin [12] found that the monotonicity guaranteed by the proof of multiplicative updates may not imply the full Karush-Kuhn-Tucker conditions. Therefore, it remains possible to find a better objective by using some other optimization methods instead of multiplicative updates. In addition, multiplicative updates are often slower in the long-run training compared with gradient approaches such as [13]. This also motivates the use of additive updates based on the gradient information.

The most commonly used additive approach for I-NMF is the *Projected Gradients* [13], where the new estimate is obtained by first calculating the unconstrained steepest-descent update and then zeroing its negative elements. Lin [13] employed a line search method with the Armijo rule for selecting the learning step size η. Their method alternates the minimization over either $\mathbf{W}$ or $\mathbf{H}$, with the other matrix fixed. Denote $f(\mathbf{W}, \mathbf{H})$ the NMF objective, i.e. I-divergence or KL-divergence in this paper. When minimizing f over $\mathbf{H}$, the Armijo's rule tries to find the largest η that satisfies the *sufficient decrease condition*

$$f(\mathbf{W}, \mathbf{H}^{\mathrm{new}}) - f(\mathbf{W}, \mathbf{H}) \leq \sigma \mathrm{Tr}\left(\nabla_{\mathbf{H}} f(\mathbf{W}, \mathbf{H})(\mathbf{H}^{\mathrm{new}} - \mathbf{H})^T\right), \qquad (4)$$

where $0 < \sigma < 1$. The concrete form of the gradient $\nabla_{\mathbf{H}} f$, depending on the divergence used, is given by Eqs (5) and (7) below. Assuming that η does not vary too much in consecutive iterations, the improved minimization is described

Algorithm 1. Projected gradients with Armijo's rule

Initialize **H**. Set $\eta = 1$.
for $i = 1$ to k **do**
  if η satisfies Eq. (4) **then**
    repeatedly increase it by $\eta \leftarrow \eta/\rho$ until either ρ does not satisfy Eq. (4) or
    $\mathbf{H}(\eta/\rho) = \mathbf{H}(\eta)$
  else
    repeatedly decrease η by $\eta \leftarrow \eta \cdot \rho$ until η satisfies Eq. (4)
  end if
  Set $\mathbf{H}^{\text{new}} = \max(\mathbf{0}, \mathbf{H} - \eta \nabla_{\mathbf{H}} f(\mathbf{W}, \mathbf{H}))$.
end for

in Algorithm 1 [13], in which ρ is the dilation/shrinkage base for line search. The same algorithm applies to the minimization over $\mathbf{W}$ with $\mathbf{H}$ fixed.

Although a number of projected gradient algorithms (e.g. [14,15,3], Chapter 4-6) have been proposed for NMF based on least squared errors, the speedup advantage is more difficult to obtain for the approximation based on the I-divergence. The major reason is that the gradients of I-NMF

$$\nabla_{\mathbf{H}} D_I(\mathbf{X}||\mathbf{WH}) = -\mathbf{W}^T \mathbf{Z} + \mathbf{W}^T \bar{\mathbf{Z}} \tag{5}$$

$$\nabla_{\mathbf{W}} D_I(\mathbf{X}||\mathbf{WH}) = -\mathbf{Z}\mathbf{H}^T + \bar{\mathbf{Z}}\mathbf{H}^T \tag{6}$$

heavily depend on the scaling of $\mathbf{W}$ and $\mathbf{H}$, where $\mathbf{Z}$ and $\bar{\mathbf{Z}}$ are of size $m \times n$ with $Z_{ij} = X_{ij}/(\mathbf{WH})_{ij}$ and $\bar{Z}_{ij} = 1$. For example, if the entries of initial $\mathbf{W}$ are overly large, the second term in Eq. (5) will dominate the gradient because in the first term the scale of $\mathbf{W}$ cancels out. Unlike multiplicative updates which can remedy for an improper scale by alternation between $\mathbf{W}$ and $\mathbf{H}$, the projected gradient algorithm requires many more iterations to recover from such a wrong guess of scales. This is especially problematic for large-scale factorization tasks. The badly scaled gradients also make the second order optimization methods such as Newton or quasi-Newton algorithms ill-posed and even fail to converge, as shown in Section 4.

By contrast, the normalized Kullback-Leibler divergence does not suffer from such a scaling problem. Consider first matrix-wise normalization. Then the logarithm in the second term of Eq. (3) leads to an inverse normalization factor $\alpha = \sum_{ab} (\mathbf{WH})_{ab}$ in the gradients:

$$\nabla_{\mathbf{H}} D_{KL}^{\text{mat}}(\mathbf{X}||\widetilde{\mathbf{X}}) = -\mathbf{W}^T \mathbf{Z} + \frac{1}{\alpha}\mathbf{W}^T \bar{\mathbf{Z}} \tag{7}$$

$$\nabla_{\mathbf{W}} D_{KL}^{\text{mat}}(\mathbf{X}||\widetilde{\mathbf{X}}) = -\mathbf{Z}\mathbf{H}^T + \frac{1}{\alpha}\bar{\mathbf{Z}}\mathbf{H}^T. \tag{8}$$

Such normalization factors can automatically stabilize gradient-based optimization. The learning can thus focus on adjusting the relative values among entries of factorizing matrices, which results in more efficient algorithms.

4   Experiments

The normalized KL-divergence for NMF leads to well-scaled gradients which favor stable additive optimization approaches. We have compared the projected gradient method using the Armijo rule based on the gradients of I-divergence and row-normalized KL-divergence, as well as the multiplicative I-NMF algorithm [2] and a quadratic programming method based on I-divergence [3]. We refer to the four compared methods as *I-Armijo*, *KL-Armijo*, *I-multiplicative*, and *I-quadratic*, respectively.

We have used four datasets med^1 (1033×5831), $cran^1$ (1398×4612), $cisi^1$ (1460×5609), and $webkb4^2$ (4193×1000). The document-term matrices are preprocessed according to the TF-IDF weighting scheme, which is widely used in information retrieval and text mining, and then normalized to unit row-sum. We selected these datasets because (1) our contribution addresses the normalization structure of input data and (2) the Armijo rule can be efficiently performed for large-scale but sparse matrices.

It is important to notice that $D_{KL}(\mathbf{X}||\widetilde{\mathbf{X}}) = D_I(\mathbf{X}||\widetilde{\mathbf{X}})$ if both $\mathbf{X}$ and $\widetilde{\mathbf{X}}$ are normalized in the same scheme. On the other hand, generally $D_I(\mathbf{X}||\widetilde{\mathbf{X}}) \neq D_I(\mathbf{X}||\widehat{\mathbf{X}})$. This enables us to compare the approximation performance of the four selected methods for normalized matrices using $D_I(\mathbf{X}||\widetilde{\mathbf{X}})$.

Following [13], we set the line search base ρ to 0.1. The factor σ for determining sufficient decrease is set to 10^{-5} in our experiments. Each method terminates if maximal time (3600 seconds) or maximal number of iterations (1000, 1000, 10000, 100, respectively) is reached. Maximal ten iterations for inner loops have been used in I-Armijo and KL-Armijo. We repeated 50 times for every method on each dataset and recorded their resulting I-divergences and KL-divergences.

Figure 1 shows the evolution curves of I-divergences versus learning time. The I-quadratic method violates the monotonicity quite often and seems to diverge in the experiment. Another projected gradient method based on the I-divergence, I-Armijo, requires about ten minutes to decrease the objective below 10^4 and is then stuck around 3800. The objectives using the other two methods, I-multiplicative and KL-Armijo, become smaller than 3400 in less than two minutes. The multiplicative algorithm seems faster in early iterations but gives little improvement after one minute, which ends up with the objective value 3378. By contrast, the proposed projected gradient method based on KL-divergence steadily minimizes the objective until it becomes stable at 3314 after about four minutes.

More extensive results are shown in Table 1. The two methods using projected gradients of I-divergence perform poorly in terms of both objectives. Their resulting mean divergences are much higher than the other two approaches. In practice, we find that I-quadratic often yields extremely bad results, which leads to drastically high variance across different tries. I-multiplicative and KL-Armijo are free of such instability, where they both converge with reasonable divergences.

---

[1] http://www.cs.utk.edu/~lsi/
[2] http://www.cs.cmu.edu/afs/cs.cmu.edu/project/theo-20/www/data/

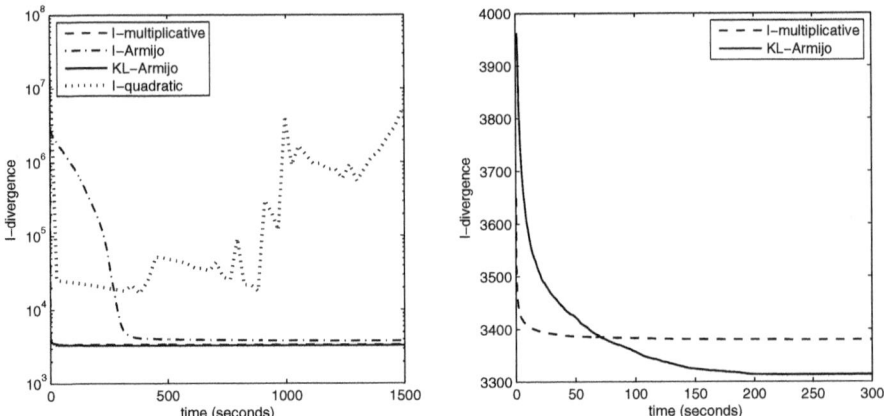

Fig. 1. (Left) I-divergence evolutions using the four compared methods on the *med* dataset. (Right) The zoom-in comparison between I-multiplicative and KL-Armijo.

Table 1. I-divergences shown in format $\mu \pm \sigma$, where μ is the mean and σ the standard deviation. Boldface table cells contain the smallest mean divergences.

	I-multiplicative	I-Armijo	KL-Armijo	I-quadratic
med:	3376.11 ± 15.34	3915.41 ± 117.25	$\mathbf{3337.97 \pm 21.25}$	$1.7 \times 10^{14} \pm 4.2 \times 10^{14}$
cran:	5008.25 ± 12.13	5555.26 ± 85.49	$\mathbf{4961.89 \pm 12.43}$	$4.0 \times 10^{17} \pm 1.1 \times 10^{18}$
cisi:	4058.06 ± 7.43	4697.35 ± 129.76	$\mathbf{4023.99 \pm 12.64}$	$6.4 \times 10^{15} \pm 9.1 \times 10^{15}$
webkb4:	9145.38 ± 42.81	10528.07 ± 367.50	$\mathbf{9113.02 \pm 43.28}$	$1.9 \times 10^{7} \pm 1.3 \times 10^{7}$

By contrast, the latter using KL-divergence and projected gradient descent can find even better objectives. This is probably because monotonicity guaranteed by multiplicative updates may not imply the full KKT condition.

5   Conclusions

We have studied the Kullback-Leibler divergence versus I-divergence in NMF for normalized input data. Using the gradients of the former results in a faster additive optimization algorithm that yields better approximation than three other existing methods. Actually, both theoretical and practical advantages indicate that there would be good reasons to replace the I-divergence with KL-divergence for NMF and its variants.

More advanced optimization algorithms beyond the simple Armijo rule, for example, conjugate gradient descent, could be constructed by using the proposed gradients that provide better learning directions. In addition, the improvement towards uniqueness of KL-NMF needs further investigation. Appropriate constraints or priors could significantly reduce ambiguity between factorizing matrices. For extensions, the proposed method can readily include penalizations such as additional L1 or L2 norms of the factorizing matrices. Other extensions such as the use of Automatic Relevance Determination to automatically select the low rank in approximation can also be implemented as in conventional NMF.

References

1. Paatero, P., Tapper, U.: Positive matrix factorization: A non-negative factor model with optimal utilization of error estimates of data values. Environmetrics 5, 111–126 (1994)
2. Lee, D.D., Seung, H.S.: Learning the parts of objects by non-negative matrix factorization. Nature 401, 788–791 (1999)
3. Cichocki, A., Zdunek, R., Phan, A.-H., Amari, S.: Nonnegative Matrix and Tensor Factorizations: Applications to Exploratory Multi-way Data Analysis. John Wiley, Chichester (2009)
4. Dhillon, I.S., Sra, S.: Generalized nonnegative matrix approximations with bregman divergences. Advances in Neural Information Processing Systems 18, 283–290 (2006)
5. Févotte, C., Bertin, N., Durrieu, J. L.: Nonnegative matrix factorization with the Itakura-Saito divergence: With application to music analysis. Neural Computation 21(3), 793–830 (2009)
6. Gullberg, J.: Mathematics: From the Birth of Numbers. W. W. Norton & Company, New York (1997)
7. van der Maaten, L., Hinton, G.: Visualizing data using t-SNE. Journal of Machine Learning Research 9, 2579–2605 (2008)
8. Ho, N. D., Dooren, P.V.: Non-negative matrix factorization with fixed row and column sums. Linear Algebra and its Applications 429(5-6), 1020–1025 (2008)
9. Ding, C., Li, T., Peng, W.: On the equivalence between non-negative matrix factorization and probabilistic laten semantic indexing. Computational Statistics and Data Analysis 52(8), 3913–3927 (2008)
10. Lee, D.D., Seung, H.S.: Algorithms for non-negative matrix factorization. Advances in Neural Information Processing Systems 13, 556–562 (2001)
11. Gonzales, E.F., Zhang, Y.: Accelerating the lee-seung algorithm for non-negative matrix factorization. Technical report, Dept. of Computational and Applied Mathematics. Rice University (2005)
12. Lin, C. J.: On the convergence of multiplicative update algorithms for nonnegative matrix factorization. IEEE Transactions on Neural Networks 18(6), 1589–1596 (2007)
13. Lin, C.J.: Projected gradient methods for non-negative matrix factorization. Neural Computation 19, 2756–2779 (2007)
14. Kim, D., Sra, S., Dhillon, I.S.: Fast projection-based methods for the least squares nonnegative matrix approximation problem. Statistical Analysis and Data Mining 1(1), 38–51 (2008)
15. Kim, H., Park, H.: Nonnegative matrix factorization based on alternating non-negativity-constrained least squares and the active set method. SIAM Journal on Matrix Analysis and Applications 30(2), 713–730 (2008)

Distributed Deterministic Temporal Information Propagated by Feedforward Neural Networks

Yoshiyuki Asai[1,3] and Alessandro E.P. Villa[2,3]

[1] Open Biology Unit, Okinawa Institute of Science and Technology. Okinawa, Japan
yoshiyuki.asai@oist.jp
[2] INSERM UMRS 836; Université Joseph Fourier, Grenoble, France
[3] Neuroheuristic Research Group, HEC-ISI, University of Lausanne, Switzerland
avilla@neuroheuristic.org
http://www.neuroheuristic.org/

Abstract. A ten layers feedforward network characterized by diverging/converging patterns of projection between successive layers is activated by an external spatio-temporal input pattern fed to layer 1 in presence of stochastic background activities fed to all layers. We used three dynamical systems to derive the external input spike trains including the temporal information, and two types of neuron models for the network, i.e. either a simple spiking neuron (SSN) or a multiple-timescale adaptive threshold neuron (MAT). We observed an unimodal integration effect as a function of the order of the layers and confirmed that the MAT model is likely to be more efficient in integrating and transmitting the temporal structure embedded in the external input.

Keywords: preferred firing sequences, synfire chain, spatio-temporal firing patterns.

1 Introduction

Spike trains are sequences of the exact timing of the occurrences of neuronal action potentials. Experimental evidence of deterministic chaotic properties in spike trains obtained from *in vivo* extracellular recordings [1] suggest that a neuronal network can be considered as a complex nonlinear dynamical system able to exhibit chaotic dynamics. Each neuron of the network is also likely to receive background activities whose origin is unspecified or unknown and its activity is often represented by stochastic occurrences of spikes. Thus, it is possible to assume that in addition to stochastic background activity a network may receive inputs characterized by an embedded temporal structure, which is somehow associated to a deterministic nonlinear system. Diverging/converging feedforward neuronal networks are able to transmit information with great temporal accuracy, in particular synchronous firing in one layer for they were termed synfire chains [2]. The question is whether complex asynchronous temporal structure can be propagated in a reliable way. Previous studies[3,4] showed that spikes related to a deterministic nonlinear dynamics embedded in noisy time series could

T. Honkela et al. (Eds.): ICANN 2011, Part I, LNCS 6791, pp. 258–265, 2011.

be detected by applying algorithms aimed at finding preferred firing sequences with millisecond order time precision. Moreover, the characteristics of the transfer function of the neuron model and the statistical feature of the background activity may affect heavily the propagation of temporal information through the synapses [5].

In the current paper we extend our previous analysis [6]. Each neuron in the input layer of the synfire chain receives only randomly selected fractions of the spike train associated to deterministic chaotic dynamics. The detection of preferred firing sequences by pattern grouping algorithm (PGA) in all layers of the network revealed a reliable propagation of temporal information. In addition we present evidence that adaptive threshold neurons can maintain and integrate the distributed temporal structures better than simple spiking neurons.

2   Methods

2.1   Spiking Neuron Model

We adopted two neuron models to simulate the dynamics of *regular spiking neurons*. The first is a simple spiking neuron (SSN) model[7] described as:

$$\frac{dv}{dt} = 0.04v^2 + 5v + 140 - u + I_{ext}(t) \ , \qquad \frac{du}{dt} = a(bv - u) \ ,$$

where v represents the membrane potential $[mV]$, u is a membrane recovery variable, a and b control the time scale of the membrane potential dynamics. When $v \geq +30 \ mV$, a discontinuous resetting $v \leftarrow c$ and $u \leftarrow u + d$ follows as a hyperpolarization after a spike. Parameters were set as $a = 0.02$, $b = 0.2$, $c = -65$, $d = 8$ [7].

The second model is a multiple-timescale adaptive threshold (MAT) neuron [8] whose membrane potential dynamics follows a non-resetting leaky integrator,

$$\tau_m \frac{dV}{dt} = -V(t) + R \ A \ I_{ext}(t) \ ,$$

where τ_m, V, R and A are the membrane time constant, membrane potential, membrane resistance, and scaling factor, respectively. A spike is generated when $V(t) \geq \theta(t)$, $\theta(t) = \omega + H_1(t) + H_2(t)$, $\frac{dH_1}{dt} = -H_1/\tau_1$, $\frac{dH_2}{dt} = -H_2/\tau_2$, where ω is the resting value. H_1 and H_2 are components of the fast and slow threshold dynamics (characterized by decaying time constants τ_1 and τ_2, respectively) which have a discrete jump when $V(t) \geq \theta(t)$, $H_1 = H_1 + \alpha_1$, $H_2 = H_2 + \alpha_2$. Parameters were set to values $\tau_m = 5$ ms, $R = 50$ MΩ, $A = 0.106$, $\omega = 19$ mV, $\tau_1 = 10$ ms, $\tau_2 = 200$ ms, $\alpha_1 = 37$ mV, $\alpha_2 = 2$ mV.

2.2   Neural Network

We consider a diverging/converging neural network composed of ten layers (Fig. 1). Each layer includes 20 neurons. All neurons in a network are identical and

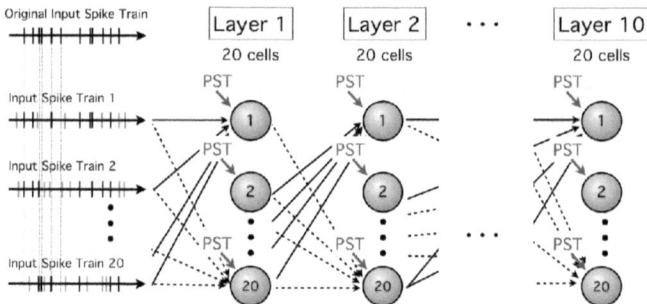

Fig. 1. A schema of the convergent/divergent feedforward circuit formed by ten neuron layers. Each cell receives 15 afferences and a PST (independent Poissonian spike train)

are either SSN or MAT models, and receive background activity represented by an independent Poissonian spike train with a mean firing rate of 425 $spikes/s$, in order to keep valanced excitatory inputs able to sustain the steady level of activity for each neuron. Each neuron of Layer 1 receives an external input represented by 15 spike trains derived from selected dynamical systems described below. From 2nd to downward layers each neuron receives afferences from 15 neurons randomly selected among those of the immediately upstream layer. All connections were hardwired, and no synaptic plasticity was taken into account. Explicit synaptic transmission delays were in 0.7-1.3 ms range. Once we created a network model, we used it for all simulations in order to avoid side effects produced by different, even if statistically similar, connectivities.

A synaptic current I given to a post-synaptic neuron was defined as follows: $I = -A \sum_k g_{syn}(t - t_k)$, where A is an intensity of the synaptic transmission ($A = 0.9$), and t_k represents time when the k-th spike arrives to the neuron. g_{syn} is the post synaptic conductance represented by $g_{syn}(t) = C_0 \frac{e^{-t/\tilde{\tau}_1} - e^{-t/\tilde{\tau}_2}}{\tilde{\tau}_1 - \tilde{\tau}_2}$, where $\tilde{\tau}_1$ and $\tilde{\tau}_2$ are rise and decay time constants given by 0.17 and 4 ms, respectively. C_0 is a coefficient used to normalize the maximum amplitude of $g_{syn}(t)$ to 1. Numerical integration was done by the 4th order Runge-Kutta numerical integration method with 0.01 ms time steps for all cases and the total simulation duration corresponded to $2,000$ s.

2.3   Dynamical Systems for Generation of the Input Spike Trains

We considered three dynamical systems as exemplars exhibiting chaotic dynamics with certain parameter values to create input spike trains.
(1) The Zaslavskii map is defined by

$$x_{n+1} = x_n + v(1 + \mu y_n) + \varepsilon v \mu \cos x_n \ (mod. \ 2\pi) \ , \ y_{n+1} = e^{-\gamma}(y_n + \varepsilon \cos x_n) \ ,$$

where $x, y \in \mathbf{R}$, and $\mu = \frac{1-e^{-\gamma}}{\gamma}$, $v = \frac{4}{3} \cdot 100, \gamma = 3.0, \varepsilon = 0.1$. The initial conditions were set to $x_0 = y_0 = 0.3$. The iterative calculation generated the time series $\{x_n\}$ which is used for the external input.

(2) The Ikeda map is the quadratic mapping defined as follows,

$$x_{n+1} = p + \mu(x_n \cos\theta - y_n \sin\theta) , \quad y_{n+1} = \mu(y_n \cos\theta + x_n \sin\theta)$$

where $\theta = k - a/(1 + x_n^2 + y_n^2)$, and $a = 6.0, k = 0.4, p = 1.0, \mu = 0.9$. Initial conditions were $x_0 = y_0 = 0.3$. The sequence $\{x_n\}$ is used for the external input.
(3) The Chen's equations are formulated by three equations,

$$\frac{dx}{dt} = a(y - x) , \quad \frac{dy}{dt} = (c - a)x - xz + cy , \quad \frac{dz}{dt} = xy - bz ,$$

where $a = 35.0, b = 3.0, c = 28.0$, and $x(0) = y(0) = 3.0$ for initial conditions. We considered a Poincaré map where the Poincaré section was defined by $\frac{dx}{dt} = 0$, and the sequence of $z(t)$ on the section was traced, referred to as $\{x_n\}$ hereinafter.

2.4   Simulated Input Spike Trains

A new time series $\{w_n\}$ corresponding to the sequence of the inter-spike-intervals was derived from $\{x_n\}$ following $w_n = x_{n+1} - x_n + C$, where $C = \min\{(x_{n+1} - x_n)\} + 0.1$ is a constant to make sure $w_n > 0$. The sequence $\{w_n\}$ was rescaled to an average rate of 5 *events/s* for the sake of comparison with neurophysiological firing rates of 5 *spikes/s*. We calculated $N = 10,000$ points of time series corresponding to a duration $L = 2,000$ s. This was the original input.

The original input as such was never used to activate a neuron of the upstream layer (Layer 1). Instead, the original input was used to generate sparse input spike trains as follows. $D \times N$ ($0 \leq D \leq 1$) spikes were selected at random (uniformly distributed) from the original input and the remaining spikes were deleted, thus yielding a sparse input spike train, where D is a dynamical information ratio taking a value from 0 to 1. The sparse input spike train was merged with a Poissonian spike train with mean firing rate $N(1 - D)/L$ *spikes/s*. The average rate of the resultant spike train was close to 5 *spikes/s* and its duration is 2,000 s. This is an input spike train. For a given dynamical information ratio D this procedure is repeated 20 times to generate 20 different input spike trains. Notice that if $D = 1$ all input spike trains are identical to the original input spike train, and if $D = 0$ all input spike trains are independent Poissonian spike trains. In this study we used $D = 1, 0.5$ and 0.7. Return maps, a plot of the $(n+1)$-st inter-spike-interval against the n-th inter-spike-interval, of input spike trains were shown at upper pannels in Fig. 2.

2.5   Pattern Detection and Reconstruction of Time Series

Subsets of spike trains were obtained by using the Pattern Grouping Algorithm (PGA)[9,10,11] as follows. Firing sequences repeating at least 5 times and above the chance level ($p = 0.05$) are detected by PGA. The maximun interval between the first and the last spike of the pattern was set to ≤ 600 *ms*. Given a maximum allowed jitter in spike timing accuracy (± 3 *ms*) clusters of firing sequences are represented by a template pattern. For example, if 9 triplets (*i.e.*, spike sequences

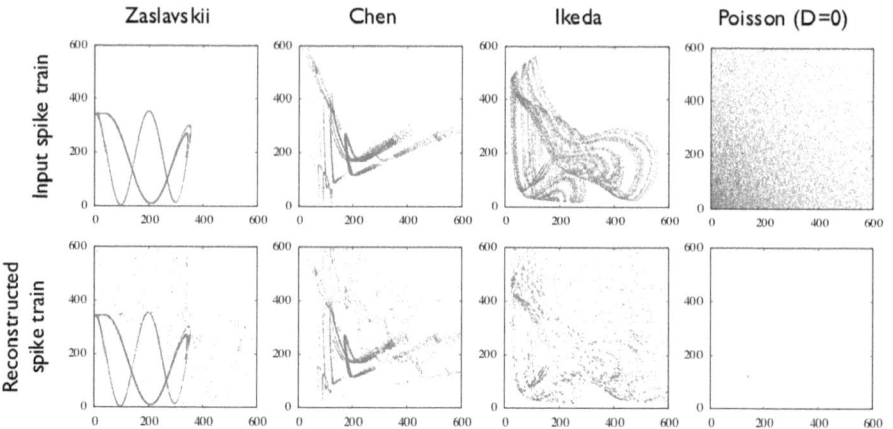

Fig. 2. (Upper) Return maps of input spike trains derived from three dynamical systems with dynamical information ratio $D = 1$ (the original input spike train) are presented with the axes scaled in ms time units. The rightmost return map is derived from a pure Poissonian spike train (i.e. $D = 0$). (Lower) Return maps of reconstructed spike trains from the original input spike trains.

formed by 3 spikes) belonging to the same cluster were detected by PGA, a subset of the original spike train that includes 27 spikes ($= 9 \times 3$) can be determined, which is referred to as "reconstructed spike train"[4]. 92% of the original input spike train derived from Zaslavskii map are included in the reconstructed spike train. Similarly 86 % and 58% were reconstructed in the cases of Chen and Ikeda maps, respectively. In a case of a Poissonian spike train with an average rate of 5 $spikes/s$ the reconstructed spike train included only 0.4% spikes of the original series. Figure 2 shows the return map of reconstructed spike trains.

2.6   Similarity between Two Spike Trains

Following [12,8] let us assume that spike trains A and B contain N_A and N_B spikes, and M spikes occur at the same time in A and B with jitter Δ. Then, the similarity between A and B is defined by the coincidence factor Γ: $\Gamma = \frac{100}{C} \frac{2(M-P)}{N_A+N_B}$ where $P = 2f\Delta N_B$ is the expected number of coincidences generated by a Poisson process with the same mean firing rate f of spike train B. The jitter Δ is 0.003 s here. C is a normalization coefficient given by $(1 - 2f\Delta)$ so that $\Gamma = 100$ for two identical spike trains.

3   Results

We investigated the dynamics of the membrane potential of neurons modeled by SSN and MAT and analyzed their output spike trains at all layers. Table 1

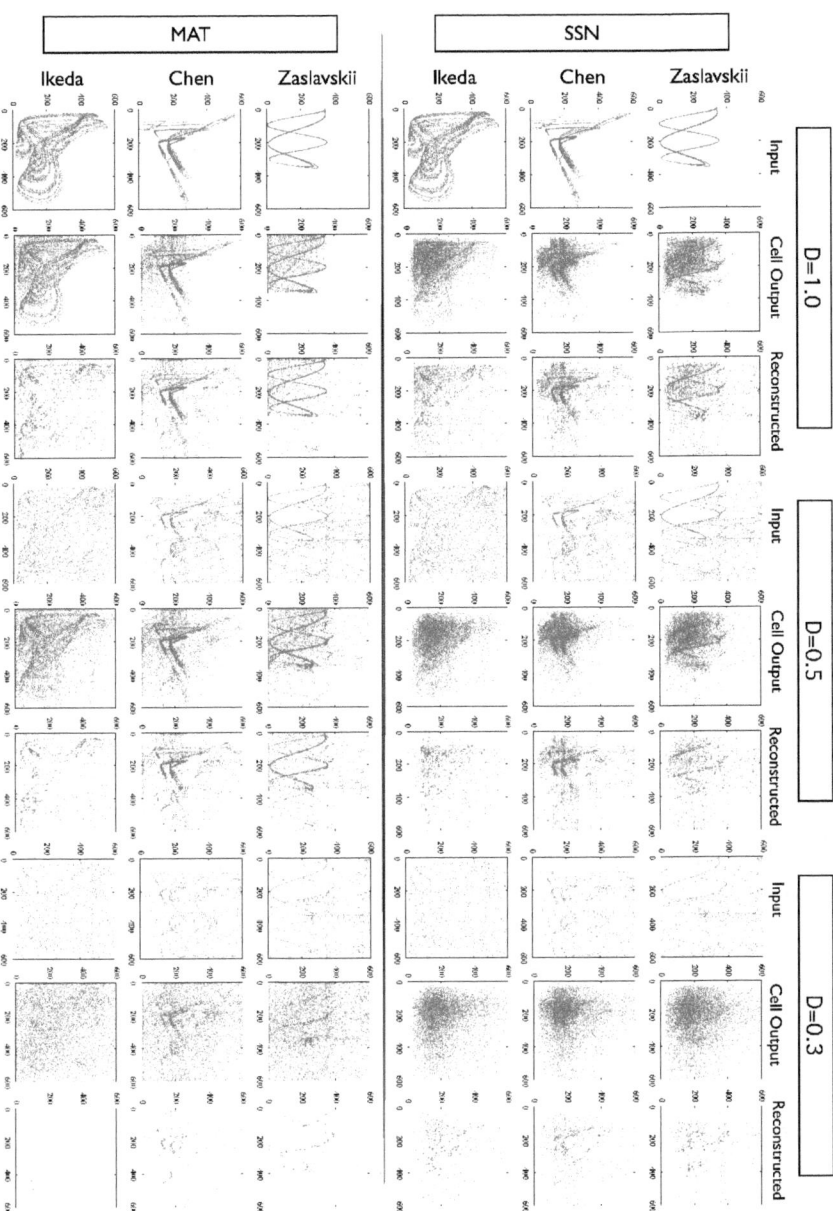

Fig. 3. Firing dynamics at Layer 5 for SSN and MAT models as a function of Ikeda, Chen and Zaslasvskii dynamical systems for several dynamical information ratio D. Return maps of an input spike train fed to Layer 1 (Input), of an output spike train at Layer 5 (Cell Output) and its corresponding reconstructed time series (Reconstructed).

Table 1. Mean firing rate (*spikes/s*) and coincidence factor between the original input spike trains and reconstructed spike trains of neurons modeled by SSN and MAT as a function of the order of the layer and of the dynamical information ratio D for three dynamical systems used to generate input spike trains.

	SSN model						MAT model					
	Zaslavskii			Chen			Ikeda			Zaslavskii			Chen			Ikeda		
Layer	$D=$ 1.0	0.5	0.3	1.0	0.5	0.3	1.0	0.5	0.3	1.0	0.5	0.3	1.0	0.5	0.3	1.0	0.5	0.3
	Mean firing rate																	
1	5.4	4.8	4.1	5.6	5.2	4.3	5.6	4.9	4.1	5.5	4.6	3.4	5.5	4.7	3.5	5.5	4.6	3.4
2	5.5	5.1	4.2	5.8	5.5	4.4	5.7	5.1	4.2	5.5	4.8	3.3	5.5	5.0	3.4	5.4	4.8	3.3
3	5.5	5.2	4.4	5.8	5.6	4.6	5.8	5.2	4.3	5.6	4.9	3.4	5.6	5.1	3.5	5.5	5.0	3.4
5	5.6	5.3	4.6	5.9	5.7	4.8	5.8	5.3	4.5	5.6	5.0	3.5	5.6	5.2	3.6	5.5	5.0	3.5
7	5.7	5.4	4.7	5.9	5.8	5.0	5.8	5.4	4.7	5.6	5.0	3.6	5.6	5.3	3.7	5.5	5.1	3.5
10	5.8	5.6	4.2	6.0	5.9	5.1	6.0	5.6	4.9	5.7	5.1	3.7	5.6	5.3	3.7	5.6	5.1	3.6
	Coincidence factor																	
1	81	40	9	86	45	14	66	21	10	93	48	5	91	47	6	69	22	1
2	73	42	10	80	54	14	60	28	8	93	68	10	91	69	10	68	39	1
3	70	40	10	79	54	14	56	25	7	94	70	12	91	72	17	70	42	2
5	65	36	9	76	49	12	52	26	7	93	68	11	89	73	15	68	43	1
7	59	32	8	69	45	11	48	26	6	93	69	10	90	72	16	66	39	1
10	49	24	7	62	39	10	41	24	6	89	66	12	89	69	13	62	31	1

shows that the mean firing rate was only slightly increased through the downstream layers for both neuronal models and for all dynamical information ratio D. Notice that small values of D provoked fewer spikes for all dynamical systems. On the opposite to SSN in the MAT model it is interesting to observe that the coincidence factor for dynamical information ratio $D = 0.5$ increased going downstream throughout the layers.

Figure 3 exemplifies return maps of input (layer 1), output and reconstructed spike trains of SSN and MAT neurons in layer 5. In the case of SSN, notice that significant amount of preferred firing sequences were detected by PGA even for $D = 0.3$, but the return maps do not show the attractor contour seen in the original input spike train, as confirmed by the small values of the coincidence factor. Those spurious events can be attributed to the intrinsic dynamics of the model. On the opposite, the MAT model did not tend to introduce a spurious temporal structure associated to its intrinsic dynamics.

4   Discussion

We observed the ability of partially convergent/divergent feedforward neural networks to integrate and transmit distributed fractions of temporally organized spikes in presence of the stochastic background activities. This network structure appears to be very efficient beyond its well known feature of propagating synchronous firing [2], because it was able to preserve much of the asynchronous temporal information at least up to layer 10 even for values of dynamical information ratio $D = 0.5$. This performance depended on the neuronal model and the spike coincidence analysis showed that a MAT model could integrate and retain the embedded temporal information much better than a SSN model. We cannot discard that a fine tuning of the parameters of the SSN could improve the result. However, both models reproduced the dynamics of regular spiking neurons and the difference in performance is likely to persist in favor of MAT models. Notice that with large values of D a neuron receives almost all spikes derived from the original input and the short interval occurrences are likely to trigger a post-synaptic neuron's firing. Conversely with small values of D, spikes with stochastic timing are dominant and the short intervals embedded in the temporal information tend to be lost, thus leading to lower firing rates.

We consider that this work may be viewed as seminal because it suggests that MAT class of models might represent the good candidate for integrating a distributed deterministic temporal information and preserve its dynamics through networks of cell assemblies. Our further work is aimed to determine the limits and robustness of this performance by designing inhomogeneous and diverging/converging networks with recurrent connections, the introduction of synaptic plasticity and the effect of the wide range of the background activity.

References

1. Celletti, A., Villa, A.E.P.: Determination of chaotic attractors in the rat brain. J. Stat. Physics 84, 1379–1385 (1996)
2. Abeles, M.: Local Cortical Circuits. Springer, Heidelberg (1982)
3. Tetko, I.V., Villa, A.E.: A comparative study of pattern detection algorithm and dynamical system approach using simulated spike trains. In: ICANN 1997. LNCS, vol. 1327, pp. 37–42. Springer, Heidelberg (1997)
4. Asai, Y., Yokoi, T., Villa, A.E.P.: Detection of a dynamical system attractor from spike train analysis. In: Kollias, S.D., Stafylopatis, A., Duch, W., Oja, E. (eds.) ICANN 2006. LNCS, vol. 4131, pp. 623–631. Springer, Heidelberg (2006)
5. Asai, Y., Guha, A., Villa, A.E.P.: Deterministic neural dynamics transmitted through neural networks. Neural Networks 21, 799–809 (2008)
6. Asai, Y., Villa, A.E.P.: Transmission of distributed deterministic temporal information through a diverging/converging three-layers neural network. In: Bosse, T., Geller, A., Jonker, C.M. (eds.) MABS 2010. LNCS, vol. 6532, Springer, Heidelberg (2011)
7. Izhikevich, E.M.: Which model to use for cortical spiking neurons? IEEE Transactions on Neural Networks 15, 1063–1070 (2004)
8. Kobayashi, R., Tsubo, Y., Shinomoto, S.: Made-to-order spiking neuron model equipped with a multi-timescale adaptive threshold. Front Comput. Neurosci. 3 (2009), doi:10.3389/neuro.10.009.2009
9. Villa, A.E.P., Tetko, I.V.: Spatiotemporal activity patterns detected from single cell measurements from behaving animals. In: Proceedings SPIE, vol. 3728, pp. 20–34 (1999)
10. Tetko, I.V., Villa, A.E.P.: A pattern grouping algorithm for analysis of spatiotemporal patterns in neuronal spike trains. 1. detection of repeated patterns. J. Neurosci. Meth. 105, 1–14 (2001)
11. Abeles, M., Gat, I.: Detecting precise firing sequences in experimental data. J. Neurosci. Meth. 107, 141–154 (2001)
12. Jolivet, R., Kobayashi, R., Rauch, A., Naud, R., Shinomoto, S., Gerstner, W.: A benchmark test for a quantitative assessment of simple neuron models. J. Neurosci. Meth. 169, 417–424 (2008)

Chaotic Complex-Valued Multidirectional Associative Memory with Variable Scaling Factor

Akio Yoshida and Yuko Osana

Tokyo University of Technology,
1404-1 Katakura Hachioji, Tokyo, Japan
osana@cs.teu.ac.jp

Abstract. In this paper, we propose a Chaotic Complex-valued Multidirectional Associative Memory (CCMAM) with variable scale factor which can realize one-to-many associations of M-tuple multi-valued patterns. The proposed model is based on the Multidirectional Associative Memory, and is composed of complex-valued neurons and chaotic complex-valued neurons. In the proposed model, associations of multi-valued patterns are realized by using complex-valued neurons, and one-to-many associations are realized by using chaotic complex-valued neurons. Moreover, in the proposed model, the appropriate parameters of chaotic complex-valued neurons can be determined easily than in the original Chaotic Complex-valued Multidirectional Associative Memory. We carried out a series of computer experiments and confirmed that the proposed model has superior one-to-many association ability than that of the conventional model.

Keywords: Chaotic Complex-valued Neuron, Multidirecional Associative Memory, One-to-Many Association, Variable Scaling Factor.

1 Introduction

Recently, neural networks are drawing much attention as a method to realize flexible information processing. And, some associative memories have been proposed. However, most of these models can not deal with multiple-valued patterns and one-to-many associations. As the model which can deal with multi-valued patterns, the complex-valued neuron model has been proposed[1]. In the complex-valued neuron model, input, output and internal states of neurons have complex-value. The network is composed of complex-valued neurons can deal with multi-valued pattern[1].

On the other hand, chaos is drawing much attention as a method to realize flexible information processing. In order to mimic the real neurons, a chaotic neuron model has been proposed by Aihara et al.[2]. It is known that the dynamic (chaotic) association is realized in the associative memories composed of the chaotic neurons.

T. Honkela et al. (Eds.): ICANN 2011, Part I, LNCS 6791, pp. 266–274, 2011.
© Springer-Verlag Berlin Heidelberg 2011

The chaotic complex-valued neuron model[3] which is based on the complex-valued neuron model[1] and the chaotic neuron model[2] has been proposed. The chaotic complex-valued associative memory[3] composed of chaotic complex-valued neuron models can realize dynamic associations of multi-valued patterns. And the Chaotic Complex-valued Bidirectional Associative Memory (CCBAM) [4][5] which can realize one-to-many associations of multi-valued patterns has been proposed. The CCBAM is based on the Bidirectional Associative Memory[6], and is composed of complex-valued neurons and chaotic complex-valued neurons. Moreover, the Chaotic Complex-valued Multidirectional Associative Memory (CCMAM) [7] which can realize one-to-many associations of multi-valued N-tuple patterns. In these models, the property of the network composed of chaotic complex-valued neurons is very sensitive to the parameters of chaotic complex-valued neurons. Moreover, in most cases, chaotic complex-valued neuron parameters are determined based on the designer's experiments or trial and errors.

In this paper, we propose the Chaotic Complex-valued Multidirectional Associative Memory (CCMAM) with variable scale factor which can realize one-to-many associations of M-tuple multi-valued patterns. The proposed model is based on the Multidirectional Associative Memory[8], and is composed of complex-valued neurons and chaotic complex-valued neurons. In the proposed model, associations of multi-valued patterns are realized by using complex-valued neurons, and one-to-many associations are realized by using chaotic complex-valued neurons. Moreover, in the proposed model, the appropriate parameters of chaotic complex-valued neurons can be determined easily than in the original Chaotic Complex-valued Multidirectional Associative Memory[7].

2   Chaotic Complex-Valued Multidirectional Associative Memory with Variable Scaling Factor

Here, we explain the proposed Chaotic Complex-valued Multidirectional Associative Memory (CCMAM) with variable scaling factor.

2.1   Structure

The proposed model has more than two layers as similar as the conventional Multidirectional Associative Memory[8] and the Chaotic Complex-Valued Multidirectional Associative Memory[7]. Figure 1 shows the structure of the proposed model which has three layers. Each layer has two parts; (1) Key Input Part composed of complex-valued neurons and (2) Context Part composed of chaotic complex-valued neurons.

2.2   Learning Process

Generally, the associative memory which is trained by the correlation matrix can not deal with one-to-many associations because the stored common data cause superimposed patterns. In the Chaotic Bidirectional Associative Memory

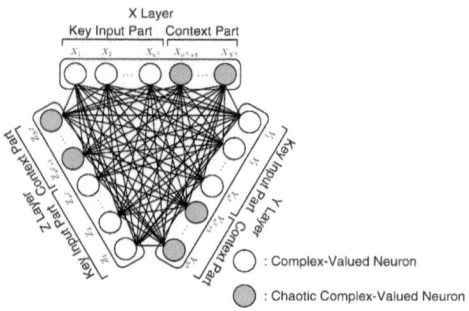

Fig. 1. Structure of Proposed Model

(CBAM)[10], each training pair is memorized together with its own contextual information in order to memorize the training set including one-to-many relations. In the proposed model, we use the same method to memorize the training set including one-to-many relations.

In the proposed model, the patterns with its own contextual information are memorized by the orthogonal learning. The connection weights from the layer y to the layer x, $\boldsymbol{w}^{xy}$ and the connection weights from the layer x to the layer y, $\boldsymbol{w}^{yx}$ are given by

$$\boldsymbol{w}^{xy} = \boldsymbol{X}_y(\boldsymbol{X}_x^*\boldsymbol{X}_x)^{-1}\boldsymbol{X}_x^* \tag{1}$$

$$\boldsymbol{w}^{yx} = \boldsymbol{X}_x(\boldsymbol{X}_y^*\boldsymbol{X}_y)^{-1}\boldsymbol{X}_y^* \tag{2}$$

where * shows the conjugate transpose, and -1 shows the inverse. $\boldsymbol{X}_x$ and $\boldsymbol{X}_y$ are the training pattern matrixes which are memorized in the x layer and the y layer, and are given by

$$\boldsymbol{X}_x = \{\boldsymbol{X}_x^{(1)}, \cdots, \boldsymbol{X}_x^{(p)}, \cdots, \boldsymbol{X}_x^{(P)}\} \tag{3}$$

$$\boldsymbol{X}_y = \{\boldsymbol{X}_y^{(1)}, \cdots, \boldsymbol{X}_y^{(p)}, \cdots, \boldsymbol{X}_y^{(P)}\} \tag{4}$$

where $\boldsymbol{X}_x^{(p)}$ is the pth pattern which is stored in the layer x, $\boldsymbol{X}_y^{(p)}$ is the pth pattern which is stored in the layer y and P is the number of the training pattern sets.

2.3   Recall Process

Since we assume that contextual information is usually unknown for users, in the recall process of the proposed model, only the Key Input Part receives input. For example, in the training sets which is given by

$$\{(\boldsymbol{X}_1\_\boldsymbol{C}_{X1}, \boldsymbol{Y}_1\_\boldsymbol{C}_{Y1}, \boldsymbol{Z}_1\_\boldsymbol{C}_{Z1}), (\boldsymbol{X}_1\_\boldsymbol{C}_{X2}, \boldsymbol{Y}_2\_\boldsymbol{C}_{Y2}, \boldsymbol{Z}_2\_\boldsymbol{C}_{Z2}),$$
$$(\boldsymbol{X}_2\_\boldsymbol{C}_{X3}, \boldsymbol{Y}_3\_\boldsymbol{C}_{Y3}, \boldsymbol{Z}_3\_\boldsymbol{C}_{Z3})\}, \tag{5}$$

$\boldsymbol{X}_1$ is used as an input to the proposed model. Here, $\boldsymbol{C}_{\mathbf{xx}}$ (such as $\boldsymbol{C}_{X1}$ and $\boldsymbol{C}_{Y1}$) shows the contextual information. In the proposed model, when $\boldsymbol{X}_1$ is given to the network as an initial input, since the chaotic complex-valued neurons in the

Contextual Information Part change their states by chaos, we can expect that they can realize one-to-many associations as follows:

$$(\boldsymbol{X}_1\_\boldsymbol{0}, ?, ?) \rightarrow \cdots \rightarrow (\boldsymbol{X}_1\_\boldsymbol{C}_{X1}, \boldsymbol{Y}_1, \boldsymbol{Z}_1) \rightarrow \cdots \rightarrow (\boldsymbol{X}_1\_\boldsymbol{C}_{X2}, \boldsymbol{Y}_2, \boldsymbol{Z}_2) \rightarrow \cdots \quad (6)$$

The recall process of the proposed model has the following procedures when the input pattern is given to the layer x.

Step 1 : Input to Layer x

The input pattern is given to the layer x.

Step 2 : Propagation from Layer x to Other Layers

When the pattern is given to the layer x, the information are propagated to the Key Input Part in the other layers. The output of the neuron k in the Key Input Part of the layer y $(y \neq x)$, $x_k^y(t)$ is given by

$$x_k^y(t) = f\left(\sum_{j=1}^{N^x} w_{kj}^{yx} x_j^x(t)\right) \quad (7)$$

where N^x is the number of neurons in the layer x, w_{kj}^{yx} is the connection weight from the neuron j in the layer x to the neuron k in the layer y, $x_j^x(t)$ is the output of the neuron j in the layer x at the time t. And $f(\cdot)$ is the output function which is given by

$$f(u) = \frac{\eta u}{\eta - 1.0 + |u|} \quad (\eta \in \mathrm{R}) \quad (8)$$

where η $(\eta > 1)$ is the constant.

Step 3 : Propagation from Other Layers to Layer x

The output of the neuron j in the Key Input Part of the layer x $x_j^x(t+1)$ is given by

$$x_j^x(t+1) = f\left(\sum_{y \neq x}^{M}\left(\sum_{k=1}^{n^y} w_{jk}^{xy} x_k^y(t)\right) + vA_j\right) \quad (9)$$

where M is the number of layers, n^y is the number of neurons in the Key Input Part of the layer y, w_{jk}^{xy} is the connection weight from the neuron k in the layer y to the neuron j in the layer x, v is the connection weight from the external input, and A_j is the external input (See **2.4**) to the neuron j in the layer x.

The output of the neuron j of the Contextual Information Part in the layer x, $x_j^x(t+1)$ is given by

$$x_j^x(t+1) = f\left(\sum_{y \neq x}^{M}\left(\sum_{k=1}^{n^y} w_{jk}^{xy} \sum_{d=0}^{t} k_m^d x_k^d(t-d)\right) - \alpha(t)\sum_{d=0}^{t} k_r^d x_j^x(t-d)\right) \quad (10)$$

where k_m, k_r are damping factors. And, $\alpha(t)$ is the scaling factor of the refractoriness at the time t, and is given by

$$\alpha(t) = a + b \cdot \sin(c \cdot t) \quad (11)$$

where a, b and c are coefficients.

Step 4 : Repeat

Steps **2** and **3** are repeated.

2.4　External Input

In the proposed model, the external input A_j is always given so that the key pattern does not change into other patterns.

If the pattern is given to the layer x and the initial input does not include noise, we can use the initial input pattern $A_j = x_j^x(0)$ as the external pattern. However, the initial input pattern sometimes includes noise. So we use the following pattern $\hat{x}_j^x(t_{in})$ when the network becomes stable t_{in} as an external input.

$$t_{in} = \min \left\{ t \,\middle|\, \sum_{j=1}^{n^x} (\hat{x}_j^x(t) - \hat{x}_j^x(t-1)) = 0 \right\} \tag{12}$$

where n^x is the number of neurons in the Key Input Part of the layer x. $\hat{x}_j^x(t)$ is the quantized output of the neuron j in the layer x at the time t, and is given by

$$\hat{x}_j^x(t) = \arg\min(\omega^s - x_j^x)^*(\omega^s - x_j^x) \qquad (s = 1, 2, ..., S-1) \tag{13}$$

where S is the number of states and ω is given by

$$\omega = \exp(i2\pi/S) \tag{14}$$

where i is the imaginary unit.

3　Computer Experiment Results

Here, we show the computer experiment results to demonstrate the effectiveness of the proposed model.

3.1　One-to-Many Associations of Multi-valued Patterns $(S = 4)$

Here, we show the association result of the proposed model for 4-valued patterns. In this experiment, the training set shown in Fig.2 including one-to-many relations were memorized.

Figure 3 shows the association result by the direction cosine between the recalled pattern and each stored pattern. In this experiment, the pattern A (*panda*) was given to the 1st layer at $t=0$, and the corresponding patterns (Pattern Sets 1 and 2) were recalled. At $t=30$, the new pattern E (*cow*) was given to the 2nd layer, and the corresponding patterns (Pattern Sets 2 and 3) were recalled. Then, at $t=60$, the pattern I (*bear*) was given to the 3rd layer, and the corresponding patterns (Pattern Sets 3 and 4) were recalled. At $t=85$, the pattern J (*snake*) was given to the 4th layer, the corresponding patterns (Pattern Sets 1 and 4) were recalled.

We carried out the similar experiments using various patterns, and confirmed that the proposed model can realize one-to-many associations of 4 or 8-valued patterns.

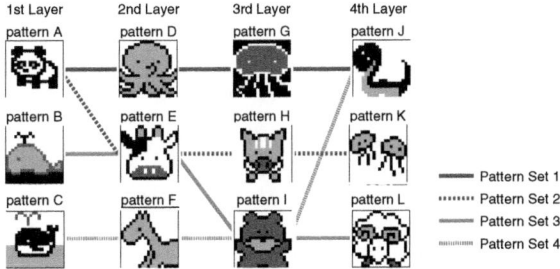

Fig. 2. Training Patterns ($S = 4$)

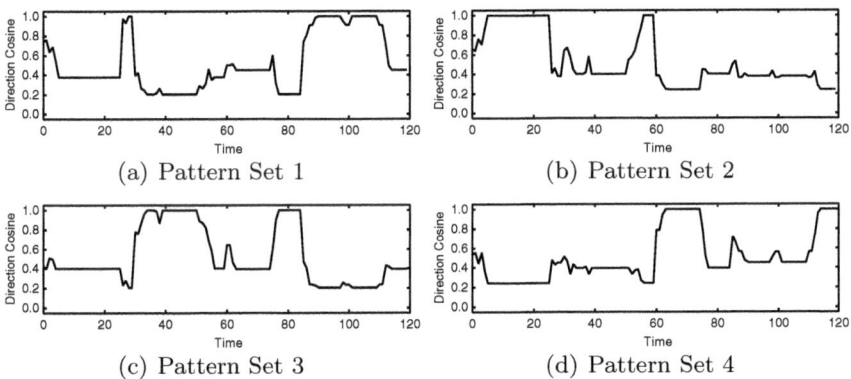

Fig. 3. Association Result (Direction Cosine)

Table 1. Parameters of Variable Scaling Factor

# of Layers M	3			4			5			6		
N (in 1-to-N)	4	5	6	4	5	6	4	5	6	4	5	6
a in Eq.(11)	2.5	2.5	1.5	2.5	2.5	2.5	2.5	2.5	2.5	2.5	2.5	2.5
b in Eq.(11)	2.0	2.0	1.0	2.0	2.0	2.0	2.0	2.0	2.0	1.0	2.0	2.0
c in Eq.(11)	$\pi/3$	$\pi/3$	$\pi/3$	$\pi/3$	$\pi/3$	$\pi/3$	$\pi/3$	$\pi/3$	$\pi/3$	$\pi/3$	$\pi/3$	$\pi/3$

3.2 Comparison of One-to-Many Associations Ability

Here, we examined the one-to-many association ability of the proposed model and the conventional Chaotic Complex-valued Multidirectional Associative Memory[7] using random 4 or 8-valued patterns. In this experiment, N patterns including 1-to-N relation ($N = 4 \sim 6$) were memorized in the network, and the common pattern was given to the network as an initial input. Figure $4 \sim 7$ shows the recall rate in each model based on 100 trials of the experiments. In these figures, the horizontal axis indicates the scaling factor α in the conventional

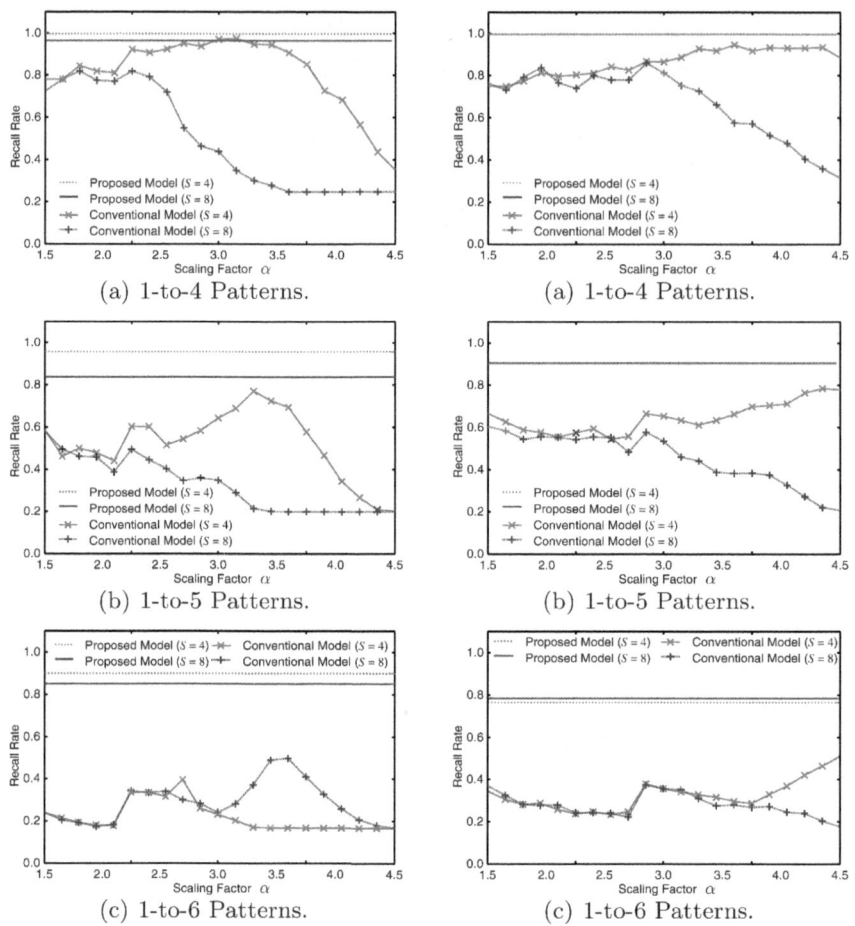

Fig. 4. Association Ability $(M = 3)$ **Fig. 5.** Association Ability $(M = 4)$

model[7], and the vertical axis indicates the recall rate. In the proposed model, the parameters of the variable scaling factor $\alpha(t)$ shown in Table 1 were used.

From these figures, the recall rate of the proposed model is higher than that of the conventional model.

4   Conclusion

In this paper, we have proposed the Chaotic Complex-valued Multidirectional Associative Memory (CCMAM) with variable scaling factor which can realize one-to-many associations of N-tuple multi-valued patterns. We carried out a series of computer experiments and confirmed that the proposed model can realize one-to-many associations of M-tuple multi-valued patterns and has superior one-to-many association ability than that of the conventional model.

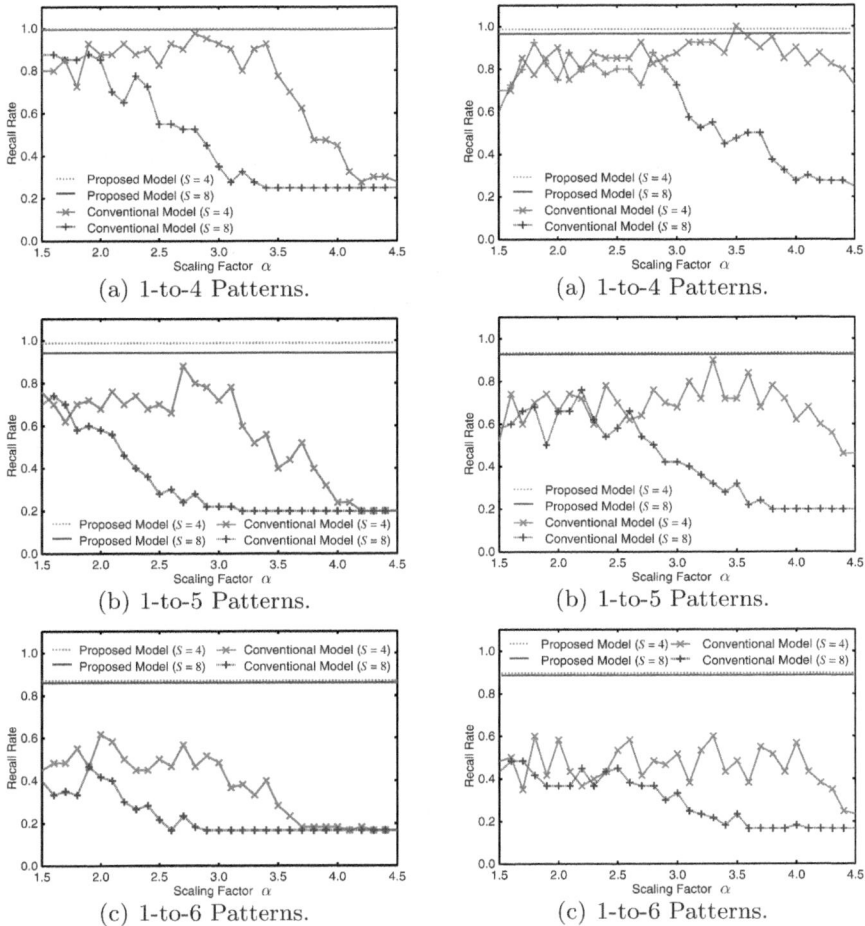

Fig. 6. Association Ability ($M = 5$)   **Fig. 7.** Association Ability ($M = 6$)

References

1. Jankowski, S., Lozowski, A., Zurada, J.M.: Complex-valued Multistate Neural Associative Memory. IEEE Trans. Neural Networks 7(6), 1491–1496 (1996)
2. Aihara, K., Takabe, T., Toyoda, M.: Chaotic Neural Networks. Physics Letter A 144(6 & 7), 333–340 (1990)
3. Nakada, M., Osana, Y.: Chaotic Complex-valued Associative Memory. In: International Symposium on Nonlinear Theory and its Applications (2007)
4. Yano, Y., Osana, Y.: Chaotic Complex-valued Bidirectional Associative Memory. In: IEEE and INNS International Joint Conference on Neural Networks (2009)

5. Yano, Y., Osana, Y.: Chaotic Complex-valued Bidirectional Associative Memory – One-to-Many Association Ability –. In: International Symposium on Nonlinear Theory and its Applications (2009)
6. Kosko, B.: Bidirectional Associative Memories. IEEE Trans. Systems Man and Cybernetics 18(1), 49–60 (1988)
7. Shimizu, Y., Osana, Y.: Chaotic Complex-valued Multidirectional Associative Memory. In: IASTED Artificial Intelligence and Applications (2010)
8. Hagiwara, M.: Multidirectional Associative Memory. In: IEEE and INNS International Joint Conference on Neural Networks, vol. 1, pp. 3–6 (1990)
9. Osana, Y.: Recall and Separation Ability of Chaotic Associative Memory with Variable Scaling Factor. In: IEEE and INNS International Joint Conference on Neural Networks (2002)
10. Osana, Y., Hattori, M., Hagiwara, M.: Chaotic Bidirectional Associative Memory. In: IEEE International Conference on Neural Networks, pp. 816–821 (1996)

Predicting Reaction Times in Word Recognition by Unsupervised Learning of Morphology

Sami Virpioja[1], Minna Lehtonen[2,3,4], Annika Hultén[3,4],
Riitta Salmelin[3], and Krista Lagus[1]

[1] Department of Information and Computer Science,
Aalto University School of Science
[2] Cognitive Brain Research Unit, Cognitive Science,
Institute of Behavioural Sciences, University of Helsinki
[3] Brain Research Unit, Low Temperature Laboratory,
Aalto University School of Science
[4] Department of Psychology and Logopedics, Åbo Akademi University

Abstract. A central question in the study of the mental lexicon is how morphologically complex words are processed. We consider this question from the viewpoint of statistical models of morphology. As an indicator of the mental processing cost in the brain, we use reaction times to words in a visual lexical decision task on Finnish nouns. Statistical correlation between a model and reaction times is employed as a goodness measure of the model. In particular, we study Morfessor, an unsupervised method for learning concatenative morphology. The results for a set of inflected and monomorphemic Finnish nouns reveal that the probabilities given by Morfessor, especially the Categories-MAP version, show considerably higher correlations to the reaction times than simple word statistics such as frequency, morphological family size, or length. These correlations are also higher than when any individual test subject is viewed as a model.

1 Introduction

The processing of morphologically complex words is a central question in the study of the mental lexicon. Theoretical models have been put forward that suggest that morphologically complex words are recognized either through full-form representations [3], full decomposition (e.g. [17]) or a combination of the two (e.g. [11]). For example, Finnish words can be combined of several morphemes, and one single noun can, in principle, attain up to 2000 different forms [7]. Having separate neural representations for each of these forms would seem unnecessarily demanding compared to a process where words would be analyzed based on their compound morphemes. In behavioral word recognition tasks, a processing cost (i.e., long reaction times and high error rates) has been robustly associated with inflected Finnish nouns in comparison to matched monomorphemic nouns [11,10]. This has been taken as evidence for the existence of morphological decomposition for most Finnish inflected words, with the possible exception of very high frequency inflected nouns [15].

T. Honkela et al. (Eds.): ICANN 2011, Part I, LNCS 6791, pp. 275–282, 2011.

Statistical models of language learning would be attractive both conceptually and because they yield quantitative predictions that may be tested against measured values of performance and, eventually, of brain activation. In this first feasibility test, we use reaction times as a proxy, providing an indirect measure of the underlying mental processing. In previous studies, several factors, including the cumulative base frequency (i.e., the summative frequency of all the inflectional variants of a single stem, [16]), surface frequency (i.e., whole form frequency, [1]), and morphological family size (i.e., the number of derivations and compounds where the noun occurs as a constituent, [2]), have been found to affect the recognition times of morphologically complex words. However, we do not know of any previous work that would use statistical models of morphology as models of the reaction times. In the proposed evaluation setting, we examine how well they predict the average reaction times for individual inflected and monomorphemic words in a word recognition task. As a particular morphological model we examine an unsupervised method for word segmentation, Morfessor, that induces a compact lexicon of morphs from unannotated text data.

2   Experimental Setup

Our experimental setup can be summarized as follows: (1) *Data recording:* Measurement data from humans is obtained, namely reaction times recorded on test subjects in a lexical decision task with inflected and monomorphemic words. (2) *Model estimation:* Using training data of varying size and type, we estimate statistical models of morphology that can be used to predict the recognition times of words. In addition, we collect such statistics of the words that are known to affect the reaction times. (3) *Model evaluation:* We calculate linear correlation between model predictions and the average reaction times of the test subjects. A good model is one which produces costs that have high correlation to the reaction times. Also any of the human test subjects can be viewed as a model, and their reaction times thus correlated with those of the rest of the subjects.

2.1   Reaction Time Data and Model Evaluation

We use the reaction time data reported in [9]. Sixteen Finnish-speaking university students participated in the experiment. The task was to decide as quickly and accurately as possible whether the letter string appearing on the screen was a real Finnish word or not, and to press a corresponding button. The stimuli consisted of 320 real Finnish nouns and 320 pseudowords. The words were taken from an unpublished Turun Sanomat newspaper corpus of 22.7 million word tokens and divided into four groups of 80 words according to their frequency in the corpus (high or low) and morphological structure (monomorphemic or inflected). There were four kinds of pseudowords (monomorphemic, real stem with pseudosuffix, pseudostem with real suffix, and incorrect combination of real stem and suffix) and their lengths and bigram frequencies (i.e., the average frequency of letter bigrams in the word) were similar to the real words.

As preprocessing, we exclude all incorrect responses and reaction times of three standard deviations longer or shorter than the individual's mean. For the remaining data, we take the logarithm of the reaction times, normalize them to zero mean for each subject, and calculate the average across subjects per each word. To evaluate the predicted costs, we calculate the Pearson product-moment correlation coefficient ρ between the costs and the average reaction times, with $\rho \in [-1, +1]$ and $\rho = 0$ for uncorrelated variables. This is equilavent to calculating linear regression, as ρ^2 corresponds to the coefficient of determination, i.e., the fraction of variance of the predicted variable explained by the predictor.

2.2   Statistics and Computational Models

Several statistics are calculated for each stimulus word: length, surface frequency, base frequency, morphological family size, and bigram frequency. As logarithmic frequencies often correlate with reaction times better than direct frequencies, we also test those. The computational models examined here give a probability distribution $p(W)$ over the words. Thus, we can use the cost or self-information $-\log p(W)$ to explain the reaction times in a similar manner as with the word frequencies: a high probability is assumed to correlate with a low reaction time.

N-gram Models. We use n-gram models to get a good estimate on how common the form of the word (sequence of letters l_i) is among all the words in the language. An n-gram model of order n is a $(n-1)$:th order Markov model, thus approximating $p(W = l_1 l_2 \ldots l_N)$ as $\prod_{i=1}^{N} p(l_i \mid l_{i-n+1} \ldots l_{i-1})$. For estimating the n-gram probabilities $p(l_i \mid l_{i-n+1} \ldots l_{i-1})$, the standard techniques include smoothing of the maximum likelihood distributions and interpolation between different lengths of n-grams. We apply one of the state-of-the-art methods, Kneser-Ney interpolation [4], implemented in VariKN toolkit [14].

Morfessor Baseline. Morfessor [6] is a method for unsupervised learning of concatenative morphology. It does not limit the number of morphemes per word, and is thus suitable for modeling complex morphology such as that in Finnish. The basic idea can be explained using the Minimum Description Length (MDL) principle [13], where modeling is viewed as a problem of encoding a data set efficiently in order to transmit it. In two-part MDL coding, one first transmits the model $\mathcal{M}$, and then the data set by referring to the model. Thus the task is to find the model that minimizes the sum of the coding lengths $L(\mathcal{M})$ and $L(\text{corpus}|\mathcal{M})$. In the case of segmenting words into morphs, the model simply consists of a lexicon of unique morphs, and a pointer assigned for each. The corpus is then transmitted by sending the pointer of each morph as they occur in the text. Using $L(X) = -\log p(X)$, the task is equivalent to probabilistic *maximum a posteriori* (MAP) estimation, where $p(\mathcal{M}|\text{corpus})$ is maximized.

In Morfessor Baseline, the lexicon consists of the strings and frequencies of the morphs. The cost of the lexicon increases by the number and length of the morphs. Each pointer in the corpus corresponds to a maximum likelihood probability set according to the morph frequency. Thus, for a known segmentation, the likelihood for corpus is simply the product of the morph probabilities. During training, Morfessor applies a greedy algorithm for finding simultaneously the morph lexicon and a segmentation for the training corpus. After training, a Viterbi-like algorithm can be applied to find the segmentation with the highest probability—the product of the respective morph probabilities—for any single word. For details, see, e.g., [6] and [5].

Morfessor Categories-MAP. The assumption of the independence between the morphs in a word is an obvious problem in Morfessor Baseline. For example, the model gives an equal probability to "s + walk" and "walk + s". The later versions of Morfessor extend the model by adding another layer of representation, namely a Hidden Markov Model (HMM) model of the segments [6]. In Morfessor Categories-MAP, the HMM has four categories (states): prefix, stem, suffix, and non-morpheme. While the model allows hierarchical segmentation to non-morphemes, the final analysis of a word is restricted by the regular expression (`prefix* stem+ suffix*`)+. Context-sensitivity of the model has lead to improved segmentation results when compared to a linguistic gold standard segmentation of words into morphemes [6].

2.3   Data for Learning Computational Models

The main corpus in our experiments is the one used in the Morpho Challenge 2007 competition [8]. It is part of the Wortschatz collection [12] and contains three million sentences collected from World Wide Web. To observe the effect of the training corpus, we also use 30 000, 100 000, 300 000 and one million sentence random subsets of the corpus. In addition, we use three smaller corpora: "Book" (4.4 million words) and "Periodical" (2.1 million words) parts of Finnish Parole corpus [18], subtitles of movies from OpenSubs corpus [19] (3.0 million words), and their combination.

It is often unclear whether intra-word models should be trained on a corpus (word tokens), a word lexicon (types), or something in between. For example, Morfessor Baseline gives segments that correspond better to linguistic morphemes when trained on types rather than tokens [6,5]: with token counts, many inflected high-frequency words are not segmented. Morfessor Categories-MAP, however, is by default trained on tokens [6]: the context-sensitivity of the Markov model reduces the effect of direct corpus frequencies. We compare models trained on types, tokens, and an intermediate approach, where the corpus frequencies c are reduced using a logarithmic function $f(c) = \log(1 + c)$.

3   Results

Table 1 shows the correlations of the different statistics and logarithmic probabilities of the models to the average reaction times for the stimulus words. All values, except for the bigram frequency, showed statistically significant correlation ($p(\rho = 0) < 0.01$). Among the statistics, logarithmic frequencies gave higher

Table 1. Correlation coefficients ρ of different word statistics and models to average human reaction times. Surface frequency I and other statistics are from the Turun Sanomat newspaper corpus. Surface frequency II is from the Morpho Challenge corpus used for training the models. The last row shows correlations for reaction times of individual subjects. The highest correlations are marked with an asterisk.

Word statistics		Logarithmic	Linear
Surface frequency I		−0.5108	−0.2806
Surface frequency II		−0.5353*	−0.2376
Base frequency		−0.4453	−0.1901
Morphological family size		−0.4233	−0.2916
Bigram frequency		−0.0211	+0.0221
Length (letters)		+0.2180	+0.2158
Length (morphemes)		+0.5417*	+0.5417*
Models	*Types*	*Log-frequencies*	*Tokens*
Letter 1-gram model	+0.1818	+0.1816	+0.1799
Letter 5-gram model	+0.5394	+0.5380	+0.5160
Letter 9-gram model	+0.6952*	+0.6920	+0.6358
Morfessor Baseline	+0.6605	+0.6765*	+0.5817
Morfessor Categories-MAP	+0.6620	+0.6950*	+0.5474
Other	*Minimum*	*Median*	*Maximum*
Reaction times of a single subject	+0.2030	+0.4774	+0.5681*

correlations than linear frequencies, and the highest ones were obtained for the number of morphemes in the word and the surface frequency. Among the models, the n-grams were best trained with word types, while training with the logaritmic frequencies gave the highest correlations for Morfessor. The highest correlation was obtained for the letter 9-gram model trained with word types—any longer n-grams did not improve the results. Categories-MAP correlated almost as well as the 9-gram model, while Baseline did somewhat worse. All of them had markedly higher correlations than the maximum correlation obtained for an single test subject to the average reaction times of the others.

With logarithmic counts, the Categories-MAP model segmented 135 of the 160 inflected nouns, but also 33 of the 160 monomorphemic nouns. The Baseline model segmented less: 39 of the inflected and 5 of the monomorphemic nouns.

Figure 1 shows how the reaction times and probabilities given by Categories-MAP model match for individual stimulus words. Observing the words that have poor match between the predicted difficulty and reaction time led us to suspect that some of the unexplained variance is due to a training corpus that does not match the material that humans are exposed to. Thus we next studied the effect of the training corpus for the morphological models (Fig. 2). Increasing the amount of word types in the corpus clearly improved the correlation between model predictions and measured reaction times. However, the data from books, periodicals and subtitles gave usually higher correlations than the same amount of the Morpho Challenge data.

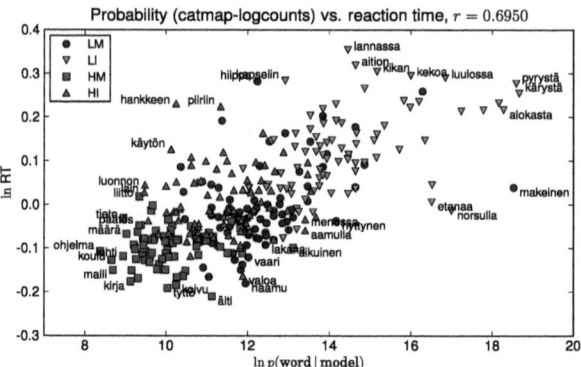

Fig. 1. Scatter plot of reaction times and log-probabilities from Morfessor Categories-MAP. The words are divided into four groups: low-frequency monomorphemic (LM), low-frequency inflected (LI), high-frequency monomorphemic (HM), and high-frequency inflected (HI). Words that have faster reaction times than predicted are often very concrete and related to family, nature, or stories: *tyttö* (girl), *äiti* (mother), *haamu* (ghost), *etanaa* (snail + partitive case), *norsulla* (elephant + adessive case). Words that have slower reaction times than predicted are often more abstract or professional: *ohjelma* (program), *tieto* (knowledge), *hankkeen* (project + genitive case), *käytön* (usage + genitive case), *hiippa* (miter), *kapselin* (capsule + genitive case).

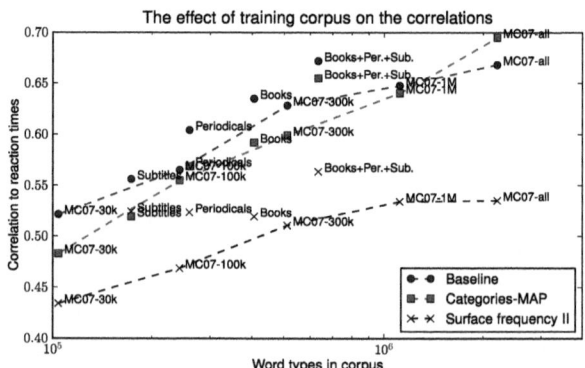

Fig. 2. The effect of training corpus on correlations of Morfessor Baseline (blue circles), Categories-MAP (red squares), and logarithmic surface frequencies (black crosses). The dotted lines show the results on subsets of the same corpus. Unconnected points show the results using different types of corpora.

4   Discussion

We studied how language models trained on unannotated textual data can predict human reaction times for inflected and monomorphemic Finnish words in a lexical decision task. Three models, the letter-based 9-gram model and the

Morfessor Baseline and Categories-MAP models, provided not only higher correlations than the simple statistics of words previously identified as important factors affecting the recognition times in morphologically complex words (cf. [16,1,2]), but also higher than the correlations of reaction times of individual subjects to the average times of the others. The level of correlation was surprisingly high especially because the training corpus is likely to differ from the material humans encounter during their course of life. Based on the results using several training corpora, we assume that even higher correlations would be obtained with more realistic training data.

The highest correlations were obtained for the letter 9-gram model. However, its number of parameteres—almost 6 million n-gram probabilities—was very large. As the estimates of the word probabilities are very precise, we assume that they are good predictors especially for early visual processing stages.

The Categories-MAP model had almost as high correlation as the 9-gram model with much fewer parameters (178 000 transition and emission probabilities). It has three important aspects: First, it applies morpheme-like units instead of words or letters. Second, it finds units that provide a compact representation for the data. Third, the model is context-sensitive: the cost of next unit depends on the previous unit. It is still unclear which contributes more to the high correlations: the morpheme lexicon learned by minimizing the description length, or the underlying probabilistic model. One way to study this question further is to apply a similar model to a linguistic morphological analysis of a corpus.

While behavioral reaction times necessarily incorporate multiple processing stages, brain activation measures could provide markedly more precise markers of the different stages of visual word processing. At the level of the brain, effects of morphology have been previously detected in neural responses that have been associated with later stages of word recognition such as lexical-semantic, phonological and syntactic processing [9,20]. Future work includes finding out whether the predictive power of the models stems from some of these stages, or from an earlier one related to the processing of visual word forms.

Acknowledgments. This work was funded by Academy of Finland, Graduate School of Language Technology in Finland, Sigrid Jusélius Foundation, Finnish Cultural Foundation, and Stiftelsen för Åbo Akademi.

References

1. Alegre, M., Gordon, P.: Frequency effects and the representational status of regular inflections. Journal of Memory and Language 40, 41–61 (1999)
2. Bertram, R., Baayen, R., Schreuder, R.: Effects of family size for complex words. Journal of Memory and Language 42, 390–405 (2000)
3. Butterworth, B.: Lexical representation. In: Butterworth, B. (ed.) Language Production, pp. 257–294. Academic Press, London (1983)
4. Chen, S.F., Goodman, J.: An empirical study of smoothing techniques for language modeling. Computer Speech & Language 13(4), 359–393 (1999)

5. Creutz, M., Lagus, K.: Unsupervised morpheme segmentation and morphology induction from text corpora using Morfessor 1.0. Tech. Rep. A81. Publications in Computer and Information Science. Helsinki University of Technology (2005)
6. Creutz, M., Lagus, K.: Unsupervised models for morpheme segmentation and morphology learning. ACM Transactions on Speech and Language Processing 4(1) (January 2007)
7. Karlsson, F.: Suomen kielen äänne- ja muotorakenne (The Phonological and Morphological Structure of Finnish). Werner Söderström, Juva (1983)
8. Kurimo, M., Creutz, M., Varjokallio, M.: Morpho challenge evaluation using a linguistic gold standard. In: Peters, C., Jijkoun, V., Mandl, T., Müller, H., Oard, D.W., Peñas, A., Petras, V., Santos, D. (eds.) CLEF 2007. LNCS, vol. 5152, pp. 864–872. Springer, Heidelberg (2008)
9. Lehtonen, M., Cunillera, T., Rodríguez-Fornells, A., Hultén, A., Tuomainen, J., Laine, M.: Recognition of morphologically complex words in Finnish: evidence from event-related potentials. Brain Research 1148, 123–137 (2007)
10. Lehtonen, M., Laine, M.: How word frequency affects morphological processing in monolinguals and bilinguals. Bilingualism: Language and Cognition 6, 213–225 (2003)
11. Niemi, J., Laine, M., Tuominen, J.: Cognitive morphology in Finnish: foundations of a new model. Language and Cognitive Processes 9, 423–446 (1994)
12. Quasthoff, U., Richter, M., Biemann, C.: Corpus portal for search in monolingual corpora. In: Proceedings of the Fifth International Conference on Language Resources and Evaluation, LREC 2006, Genoa, Italy, pp. 1799–1802 (2006)
13. Rissanen, J.: Modeling by shortest data description. Automatica 14, 465–471 (1978)
14. Siivola, V., Hirsimäki, T., Virpioja, S.: On growing and pruning Kneser-Ney smoothed n-gram models. IEEE Transactions on Audio, Speech & Language Processing 15(5), 1617–1624 (2007)
15. Soveri, A., Lehtonen, M., Laine, M.: Word frequency and morphological processing revisited. The Mental Lexicon 2, 359–385 (2007)
16. Taft, M.: Recognition of affixed words and the word frequency effect. Memory and Cognition 7, 263–272 (1979)
17. Taft, M.: Morphological decomposition and the reverse base frequency effect. The Quarterly Journal of Experimental Psychology A 57, 745–765 (2004)
18. The Department of General Linguistics, University of Helsinki and Research Institute for the Languages of Finland (gatherers): Finnish Parole Corpus (1996–1998), available through CSC, http://www.csc.fi/
19. Tiedemann, J.: News from OPUS — A collection of multilingual parallel corpora with tools and interfaces. In: Recent Advances in Natural Language Processing, vol. 5, pp. 237–248. John Benjamins, Amsterdam (2009)
20. Vartiainen, J., Aggujaro, S., Lehtonen, M., Hultén, A., Laine, M., Salmelin, R.: Neural dynamics of reading morphologically complex words. NeuroImage 47, 2064–2072 (2007)

An Examination of the Dynamic Interaction within Metaphor Understanding Using a Model Simulation

Asuka Terai[1], Saori Hirose[2], Naoko Kuriyama[1], and Masanori Nakagawa[1]

[1] Tokyo Institute of Technology, 2-12-1 O-okayama, Meguro-ku, Tokyo, Japan
[2] Business Consultant Co., Ltd., Sapia Tower 18F, 1-7-12 Marunouchi,
Chiyoda-ku, Tokyo, Japan
asuka@nm.hum.titech.ac.jp, s-hirose@bcon.co.jp,
kuriyama@hum.titech.ac.jp, nakagawa@hum.titech.ac.jp

Abstract. The purpose of this study is to examine the understanding mechanism for metaphors represented in the form of "A is like B" (simile) using model simulation. In a previous experimental study[1] , the priming effects of visual images on metaphor processing were demonstrated in a psychological experiment. In that experiment, the presentation of a picture of a vehicle ("B") interfered with metaphor comprehension, even when the picture did not directly inhibit features that relate to metaphor interpretation. The previous research has suggested that priming effects arise from interaction among features. In this research, in order to elucidate the dynamic interaction among features within metaphor understanding, the priming effect is examined by simulating computational models that do and do not incorporate detailed processes of dynamic interaction. Furthermore, the strengths of the dynamic interactions among features are estimated as the parameters of the model.

Keywords: metaphor, priming effect, recurrent neural network.

1 Introduction

This study examines the dynamic interaction among features within the understanding process for metaphors, represented in the form of "A (target) is like B (vehicle)" (simile). Interaction among features has been assumed by many models of metaphor understanding (e.g. [2][3][4]). However, few previous studies have examined experimentally this interaction. One previous study [1]conducted an experiment using visual priming and obtained results that support the existence of such interaction. Many previous studies have examined priming effects for metaphor understanding using word priming. McGlone & Manfredi [5] reported that presenting the sentence "VEHICLE is (vehicle's) IRRELEVANT FEATURE" inhibits metaphor understanding. The (vehicle's) irrelevant features are properties of the vehicle but are ones that are irrelevant to the metaphoric interpretation.

T. Honkela et al. (Eds.): ICANN 2011, Part I, LNCS 6791, pp. 283–290, 2011.

On the other hand, another experimental study[1] used pictures of the vehicle as the primes in order to examine the more complicated priming effects of the vehicle. In that experiment, two types of pictures were used: irrelevant pictures and relevant pictures. The irrelevant pictures usually included more vehicle-term properties that were irrelevant to the metaphoric interpretation. In contrast, relevant pictures included fewer irrelevant properties than the irrelevant picture, and had properties that were relevant to the metaphoric interpretation. That study reported that, in addition to the presentation of irrelevant pictures inhibiting metaphor understanding, the presentation of relevant pictures also caused inhibition. The priming effects of the irrelevant picture are consistent with the sentence priming effect [5], however, the effects from the relevant pictures are not. The study argued that the inhibition from relevant pictures was caused by interaction among the features. A subsequent study [6] sought to examine the priming effects with a model simulation. However, the mechanism was not investigated in detail and the strengths of dynamical interactions among the features were not examined.

We have constructed a simulation model of metaphor understanding using a recurrent neural network in order to verify the interaction among features within metaphor understanding. As mentioned above, a number of previous models (e.g. [2][3][4]) have been constructed that assume interaction among features. However, the parameters for the models were statistically estimated from relationships among features based on either human judgments or language statistical analysis. In this research, the model parameters are estimated by applying a generalized method of back-propagation to the recurrent neural network[7] based on data obtained from the previous experiment. By this method, the strengths of the dynamic interactions among features can be estimated as parameter values.

2   Experiment Using Visual Primes

This experiment[1] was conducted in order to examine the visual priming effect on metaphor comprehension.

2.1   Method

Six metaphors in Japanese were used (e.g. "ballerinas are like butterflies"). Four types of features (total 17 features) are used for each metaphor: target's features, which are relevant only to the basic-level meaning of the target (e.g. "are human-beings" "stand on the toes"), vehicle's features, which are relevant only to the basic-level meaning of the vehicle (e.g. "suck honey", "are insects"), common features which are relevant to the meaning of the vehicle and the target (e.g. "fluttering", "dance", "fly"), neutral abstract features (e.g. "beautiful", "light"). Two types of pictures for the vehicle were used as a prime for each metaphor: a relevant picture and an irrelevant picture. The participants were 70 undergraduates (native Japanese speakers). They were divided into two groups. One group ($N = 33$) was the relevant-picture group and the other ($N = 37$) was the irrelevant-picture group.

The participants were asked to undertake two kinds of task: one task with a picture and one task without a picture. The procedure of the with-picture task was as follows: Step 1: The participants were asked to evaluate the relationships between the features and the target-term (or the vehicle-term) (7-point scales). Step 2: They were presented with the picture (relevant picture to relevant-picture group and irrelevant picture to irrelevant-picture group) as a prime for 5000 msec. Step 3: They were asked to rate the understandability of the metaphor (5-point scales). Step 4: They were asked to evaluate the relationships between the features and the metaphor. Step 5: They were asked to evaluate the relationships between the features and the presented picture. The without-picture task consisted of Step 1, Step 3 and Step 4. In the task without pictures, the participants were not presented with a picture and were not asked to evaluate the picture. In order to avoid the influence of individual differences, the participants undertook both of the tasks, with and without pictures.

2.2   Results of the Experiment

Comparing the understandability ratings of the metaphor with a picture and without a picture. While the results indicated that both relevant and irrelevant pictures significantly inhibited understanding for the metaphor "ballerinas are like butterflies" (p < .01) [1]. In order to investigate the process of the priming effect of the relevant picture on "ballerinas are like butterflies", the ratings for the metaphor were compared to those for the target-term. The shift from a image of the target's term[2] o to one of the metaphor reflects the process of metaphor understanding. Participants who rated the understandability of a metaphor lower in the with-picture task than in the without-picture task exhibited priming effects, such that their metaphor understanding processes were inhibited. In order to examine the priming effect clearly, the ratings of 19 participants were analyzed.

Three types of rating sets relating to the relevant-picture group are presented here. First, ratings for the target and for the metaphor (target in the metaphor) in the with- and without-picture tasks are shown in Fig.1. The ratings for the without-picture task show a pattern of change from target-term images to metaphor images when the metaphor makes sense. The pattern of changes reflects the process of metaphor understanding. The ratings in the with-picture task indicate the pattern of change when the participants do not understand the sentence as a metaphor. In order to compare the processes of the metaphor understanding in these with- and without-picture tasks, the differences between the target-term ratings and the metaphor ratings in the respective tasks were examined. There was a significant difference for the feature of "beautiful " (number of figure is 13 in Fig.1) (p<0.05) between two tasks. The results show that the

---

[1] Only significant priming effects for irrelevant pictures were observed on the understanding of the "rage like a volcano" metaphor (p < .01), with no priming effect observed for the relevant picture. There is no priming effects about the other 4 metaphors.

[2] The image of the target's term means the relationships between features and target terms.

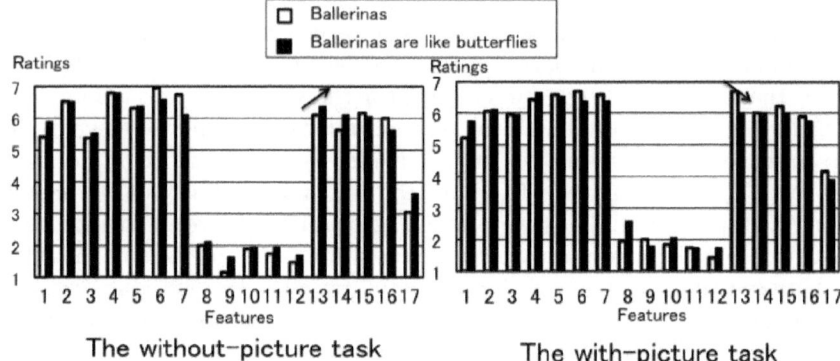

Fig. 1. Average ratings (relevant-picture group - "ballerinas like butterflies" N=19). Numbers of features means as follows, 1:fluttering, 2:dance, 3:fly, 4:are human-beings, 5:stand on the toes, 6:wear the toe-shoes, 7:wear the costume, 8:suck honey, 9: are insects, 10:scale-winged, 11:become pupae, 12:become specimens, 13:beautiful, 14:light, 15:soft, 16:dynamic, 17:strong.

"beautiful" feature was significantly influenced by the presentation of a picture. Thus, metaphor understanding was inhibited. Furthermore, the ratings for the vehicle's relevant picture in the with-picture task are compared with the ratings for the vehicle-term. If there is no difference between these ratings, presentation of a picture might not influence metaphor understanding. However, the differences between the ratings for the vehicle-term and for the picture indicate an influence from presenting the relevant picture. The relevant picture exerted an influence in facilitating the features of "fly" and "suck honey", such that the ratings for the picture were significantly higher than that for the vehicle-term ($p < 0.05$). However, it did not directly influence to the feature of "beautiful". Therefore, the results of priming effects for the relevant picture are consistent with the notion that interaction among features exists.

3   The Model of the Metaphor Understanding

The results of the experiment concerning the priming effects of the relevant picture suggest that there should be interactions among features in the process of metaphor understanding. In order to verify that the mechanism underlying the priming effects of the relevant pictures is due to the interactions among features, a computational model of metaphor understanding is constructed based on the results obtained from the experiment and simulation results for the model with interactions is compared against the simulation results for a model without interactions.

3.1   Architecture of the Model

The model of the metaphor understanding is constructed using a recurrent neural network (Fig.2). The model has feature nodes, which are the input and the output nodes. Each node indicates a feature. There are connections among feature nodes, which represent the interactions among features. The dynamics of the feature nodes are represented using the following formula:

$$\frac{dx_i^k(t)}{dt} = -x_i^k(t) + f(\sum_j w_{ij}x_j^k(t) + I_i^k),$$

(1)

where $x_i^k(t)$ means the activation of the ith feature node concerning the kth participant at time t. Function f means the following sigmoid function, whose range is (-1,1). The initial value of each node is 0. When $\frac{dx_i^k(t')}{dt} = 0$, each node outputs $O_i^k = x_i^k(t')$ as the relationship between each feature and the target of the metaphor. w_{ij} indicates the connection weight to the jth feature node to the ith feature node. I_i^k represents the input value of the ith feature node concerning the kth participant.

The model represents metaphor understanding for the with-picture and without-picture tasks using different input values. In the with-picture task, the input values are computed using the formula2:

$$I_i^k = \alpha\frac{RA_i^k - 4}{3} + \beta\frac{RB_i^k - 4}{3} + \gamma\frac{(RBP_i^k - RB_i^k) - 4}{3},$$

(2)

where, RA_i^k means the kth participant's rating of the relationship between the ith feature and the target term, RB_i^k means the rating of the relationship between the ith feature and the vehicle-term and RBP_i^k indicates the rating of the relationship between the ith feature and the picture of the vehicle. The ratings (RA_i^k, RB_i^k, and RBP_i^k) have 7 grades. Thus, these ratings are changed to values from -1 to 1. And, the influence of the picture is represented using the difference between the ratings of the picture and those of the vehicle-term. That is, the first term represents the influence of the target, the second term represents the influence of the vehicle and the third term indicates the priming effect of a picture within metaphor understanding. The respective strengths of these influence are represented using the parameters α, β, γ. On the other hand, in the without-picture task, the input values are computed using the formula3:

$$I_i^k = \alpha\frac{RA_i^k - 4}{3} + \beta\frac{RB_i^k - 4}{3}.$$

(3)

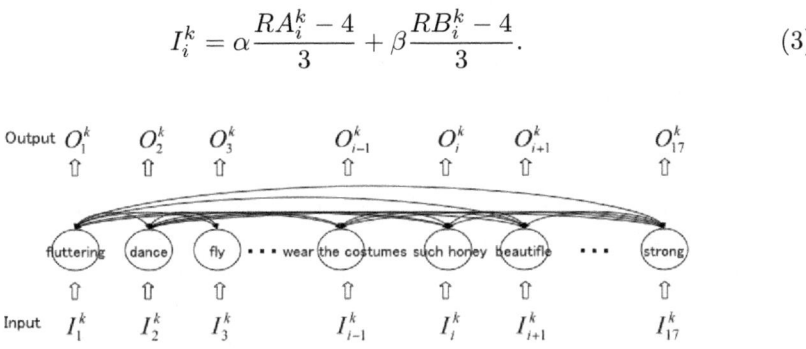

Fig. 2. The architecture of the model with interactions

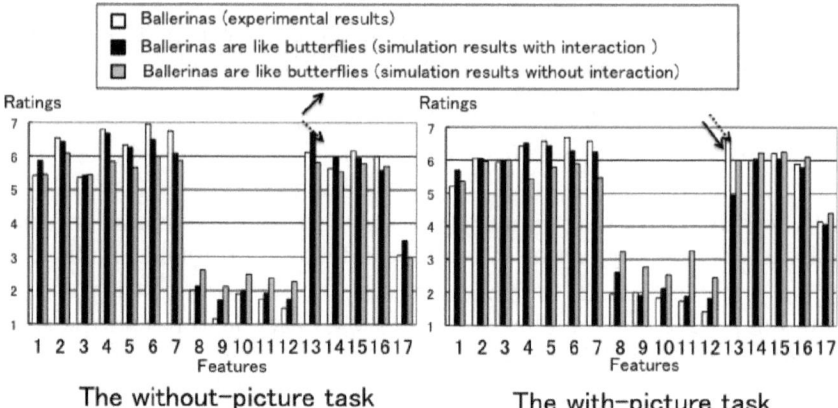

Fig. 3. Results of the model with and without interaction (relevant-picture group - "ballerinas are like butterflies"). Numbers of features means as follows, 1:fluttering, 2:dance, 3:fly, 4:are human-beings, 5:stand on the toes, 6:wear the toe-shoes, 7:wear the costume, 8:suck honey, 9: are insects, 10:scale-winged, 11:become pupae, 12:become specimens, 13:beautiful, 14:light, 15:soft, 16:dynamic, 17:strong.

These are values derived by subtracting the influence of the picture from the input values for the with-picture task.

The connection weights are estimated using generalized back-propagation[7], which can estimate the parameter values for a recurrent neural network model. The connection weighs and the parameters α, β, γ are estimated alternatively. An artificial data set, which is generated from the experimental results, is used to train the model. The artificial data for target-term and vehicle-term ratings are generated by adding an error, which has an average of 0 and a standard deviation of 0.5, to average ratings for the target term and the vehicle-term respectively. The artificial data for the metaphor ratings are generated by adding the average difference between target-term and metaphor ratings with 10% of the errors to the artificial data for the target-term in the with-picture task. Similarly, the artificial data for the picture ratings were generated by added the average difference between the ratings for the vehicle-term and for the picture with 10% of the errors to the artificial data for the vehicle-term in the with-picture task. In total, 1000 sets of artificial data were generated.

3.2   Model Simulation

The simulation results are shown in Fig.3. In this figure, the ratings of the target-term are the average ratings from the experiment results and the ratings of the metaphor are the average output values from the simulation results, which are changed to values from 1 to 7. The change from the ratings for the target-term to the output values represents the metaphor understanding process. Comparing the simulation results to the experimental results, it is clear that the model can represent the priming effect of relevant pictures. The features ("beautiful" (number of figure is 13 in Fig.3)) are emphasized in the without-picture task by the metaphor, while "beautiful" is weakened in the with-picture task. The results show that metaphor understanding is inhibited in the with-picture task. Consequently, the model simulation shows the process of the priming effect in the psychological experiment. Namely, the model with interactions among features can represent the priming effect of the visual stimulus.

In order to explain the effects of interactions, the model whose parameters $w_{ij} = 0$ simulated the process as the model without interactions. The results from the model without interactions are shown in Fig.3. The model does not represent the emphasizing of "beautiful" for the relevant-picture group in the without-picture task. The model does not show the process of metaphor understanding in the task without a picture. Comparing the results of the model without interaction to those of the model with interaction, metaphor comprehension is realized using interaction among features, not only combining the meanings of the target and the vehicle.

3.3   Estimated Parameters

In understanding the metaphor "ballerinas are like butterflies", the results of the psychological experiment suggest that there should be interactions among features. Therefore, the estimated weights among features in the model are examined. Metaphor understanding was interfered with because the feature of "beautiful" was weakened, although the relevant picture did not weaken the feature of "beautiful" directly. The estimated parameters are $\alpha = 3.66$, $\beta = 0.51$ and $\gamma = 5.59$. The connection weights from "fly", "strong" "light" and "suck honey" are -6.78, -6.49, -5.47 and -5.21, respectively. These are bottom four weights to the features of "beautiful". The relevant picture significantly emphasizes the features of "fly" and of "suck honey". Thus, emphasizing these features inhibits the feature of "beautiful" through interactions from these features to "beautiful".

4   Discussion

The model with dynamic interaction among features simulates the priming effect of pictures within the process of metaphor understanding. And, the simulation results of the model without interaction fail to represent the priming effect, which indicates the necessity of including interaction. Furthermore, the parameter values of the model are estimated based on data which was obtained from the previous experiment, using generalized back-propagation[7]. The parameter values represent the strengths of the dynamic interactions among features.

By way of comparison, the relationships among features are estimated statically using a correlation coefficient to represent the priming effect. The correlation coefficient among features are computed using differences between two changes $(\delta_2 - \delta_1)$; δ_1 are the changes from ratings for the target to those for the metaphor in the without-picture task and δ_2 are the respective changes in the with-picture task. The correlation coefficients between the features ("fly", "strong", "light" and "suck honey") and the feature of "beautiful" are -0.39, -0.08, 0.39 and -0.01, respectively. There is some difference between the correlation coefficients between other features and the feature of "beautiful" and the parameter values of the model. Especially, the parameter value between "fly" and "beautiful" is the lowest value in the parameter values for the feature of "beautiful", on the other hand, the correlation coefficient between these features is not the lowest. The correlation coefficient between "scale-winged" and "beautiful" is the lowest value in the correlations for "beautiful". This suggests that the parameter values more accurately represent the relationships between these features.

In previous research, the priming effect of pictures, which suggests an interaction among features, was observed for only one picture for only one metaphor. Accordingly, the present study examined the interaction using only the metaphor of "ballerinas are like butterflies". In order to examine the interactions within metaphor understanding in greater detail, it will be necessary to employ more metaphors.

Acknowledgments. This research is supported by MEXT's program "Promotion of Environmental Improvement for Independence of Young Researchers".

References

1. Terai, A., Hirose, S., Kuriyama, N., Nakagawa, M.: An Experimental Research on the Visual Image Effect on Metaphor Understanding. In: 28th International Congress of Psychology Abstract Book, vol. 1096 (2004)
2. Utsumi, A.: Hiyu no Ninchi / Keisan Moderu. Computer Today 96(3), 34–39 (2000)
3. Terai, A., Nakagawa, M.: A Neural Network Model of Metaphor Understanding with Dynamic Interaction based on a Statistical Language Analysis; Targeting a Human-like Model. International Journal of Neural Systems 17(4), 265–274 (2007)
4. Terai, A., Nakagawa, M.: A Corpus-Based Computational Model of Metaphor Understanding Incorporating Dynamic Interaction. In: Kůrková, V., Neruda, R., Koutník, J. (eds.) ICANN 2008, Part II, vol. 5164, pp. 443–452. Springer, Heidelberg (2008)
5. McGlone, M., Manfredi, D.: Topic-vehicle Interaction in Metaphor Comprehension. Memory and Cognition 29(8), 1209–1219 (2001)
6. Terai, A., Hirose, S., Nakagawa, M.: Neural Networks Model of Metaphor Understanding Influenced by the Visual Image. In: Proc. of Eighth International Conference on Cognitive and Neural Systems, vol. 31 (2004)
7. Pineda, F.J.: Generalization of Back-propagation to Recurrent Neural Networks. Physical Review Letters 59(19), 2229–2233 (1987)

Visual Pathways for Shape Abstraction

Konstantinos A. Raftopoulos and Stefanos D. Kollias

Computer Science Division
National Technical University of Athens
Iroon Polytexneiou 9, 15780 Zografou, Greece
Electrical Engineering Building - 1st Floor - Room 1.1.23
raftop@image.ntua.gr, stefanos@cs.ntua.gr

Abstract. The Medial Axis Transform (MAT) (or skeleton transform) is one of the most studied shape representation techniques with established advantages for general 2D shape recognition. Embedding local boundary information in the skeleton, in particular, has been shown to improve 2D shape recognition capability to state of the art levels. In this paper we present a visual pathway for extracting an analogous to the MAT skeleton abstraction of shape that also contains local boundary curvature information. We refer to this structure with the term *curvature-skeleton*. The proposed architecture is inspired by the biological findings regarding the cortical neurons of the visual cortex and their special purpose Receptive Fields (RFs). Points of high curvature are initially identified and subsequently combined by means of a visual pathway that achieves an analogous to the MAT abstraction of shape but also embeds in the skeleton local curvature information of the shape's boundary. We present experimental results illustrating that such an abstraction can improve the recognition capability of multi layered neural network classifiers.

Keywords: Shape Abstraction, Skeleton Transform, Visual Pathways.

1   Introduction

Our first knowledge about cortical neurons and their receptive fields we owe to the Nobel Prize winners Hubel and Wiesel. Their 25 years of collaboration marked an unprecedented progress in elucidating the responses of cortical neurons. In their papers they define the ways in which area VI receptive fields differ from the Lateral Geniculate Nucleus (LGN) receptive fields by using stimuli of great relevance to vision. The qualitative methods they used for studying the cortex continue to dominate experimental physiology [1]. Hubel and Wiesel recorded the activity of cortical neurons while displaying patterned stimuli, mainly line segments and spots, on a screen that was imaged through the animal's cornea and lens onto the retina. As the micro-electrode penetrated the visual cortex, they presented line segments whose width and length could be adjusted. After they varied the position of the stimulus on the screen, searching for the neuron's receptive field, they measured the response of the neuron to lines, bars

T. Honkela et al. (Eds.): ICANN 2011, Part I, LNCS 6791, pp. 291–298, 2011.

and spots presented individually. One of their main discoveries, regarding simple cells, is that they have oriented receptive fields, and hence they respond to stimuli in some orientations better than others. This receptive field property is called *orientation selectivity*. The orientation of the stimulus that evokes the most powerful response is called the cell's preferred orientation. Other cells are also end-stopped, that is selective for bars of specific lengths. The defining characteristic of end-stopped cells is the presence of inhibitory receptive field (RF) end zones that 'stop' the response of the cell to stimuli which are long enough to intrude into the end zones. This specific arrangement of orientation-specific simple or complex cells *detect* or are specific for the direction of a short line segment. Whether our perception of a line or curve depends on them and how the information from such sets of cells is assembled at subsequent stages in the path, to build up what we call *percepts* of lines or curves, is still an open question.

Our contribution in this paper is in extending the proposed in [2] method for curvature calculation to a complete pathway for transforming a random shape into a skeleton abstraction that also contains curvature information. The extension consists in adding an additional layer that will extract the skeleton of the projected image but at the same time will encode the boundary points of high curvature into the skeleton itself. The proposed pathway abides to the rules regarding orientation selectivity and end-stopping discovered by Hubel and Wiesel. We show that the proposed method achieves extraction of a *curvature-skeleton* that conveys both local and global shape information. Experimental results show that encoding hybrid shape information into the intensity values of the curvature-skeleton location improves the recognition capability of Neural Network (NN) classifiers.

2   Related Work

The concept of landmark points of high curvature for shape summarization has been appreciated by many researchers in many different areas of neuropsychology [3], [4]. A. Dobbins, S.W. Zucker and M.S. Cynader presented evidence that the curvature detection is related to end-stopping neurons, they also presented a supporting mathematical model [5]. In the field of human cognition further research has revealed that the extraction of landmark points is a critical process in human perception and the basis for potential mechanisms of shape identification and recognition [6]. In biology biometrics Bookstein defined landmark points on various biological shape for species classification [7]. The use of landmark points has been appreciated as the most compatible to the human cognition method of representing and encoding shape information. Berreti introduces a decomposition of the shape into primitives based on the curvature [8]. Mokhtarian and Mackworth [9] showed that curvature inflection points extracted using a Gaussian scale space can be used to recognise curved objects. Dudek and Tsotsos [10] presented a technique for shape representation and recognition of objects based on multi-scale curvature information. A similar technique based on the landmark points of high curvature, is also introduced in [11]. The most popular and extensively studied, shape abstraction method, is the medial axis transform (MAT) originally proposed by Blum [12]. The terms *fire transform*, *symmetric axis transform*, and *skeleton transform* have all been used in literature to refer to the same approach [13]. Among the most successful attempts regarding the skeleton representation, T. B. Sebastian et al [14] demonstrated state of the art recognition by editing the shock graphs which is a skeletal representation that contains also local boundary information. A skeletal representation based on shape stable properties that arise as a result of excessive regularization is another recent approach that give successful results on a diverse database of planar shapes [15]. It appears that the most successful recent approaches are based on the incorporation of boundary local shape information as well as global abstractions of shape [16,17,18]. The proposed approach in this paper describes a neural pathway for extracting a skeleton abstraction of the projected shape that also contains boundary curvature information. The proposed approach is compatible to our knowledge regarding the arrangement of the cortical neurons.

3   The Skeleton Extraction Process with Embedded Curvature Information

Orientation selectivity of cortical neurons is a critical receptive-field property. LGN and retinal neurons have circularly symmetric receptive fields, and they respond almost equally well to all stimulus orientations. Orientation-selective neurons are found throughout layers 2 and 3 of the visual cortex, though they are relatively rare in the primary inputs within layer 4C. In [2] it has been shown that continuous successive orientations of an orientation selective filter, like the ones discovered by Hubel and Wiesel in the visual cortex of primates, can be a mechanism of measuring curvature. End-stopped cells, on the other hand, are characterized by the presence of inhibitory receptive field (RF) end zones that 'stop' the response of the cell to stimuli which are long enough to intrude into the end zones.

In this section we will describe the mechanism and the neuron connectivity model that under the above assumptions encodes the skeleton of the planar shape into the intensity values together with curvature measurements available from the previous layer. The cortical cells in layers 2 and 3 of the visual cortex have orientation selective receptive fields and this orientation changes direction continuously in successive layers. Successive rotations of an orientation selective filter we can indeed measure the curvature at every point on the curve as was shown by Raftopoulos at al in [2] and [19]. The idea was to use the orientation selectivity to locate the direction which is tangent to the curve at a specific point and at the same time measure the curvature at this point by accumulating the firings of the successive layers in which the rotated field remains close to the direction of the tangent. This method of calculating curvature was implemented by a layered architecture designed in an analogous way to resemble the arrangement of the cortical sheets [19]. We now extend this architecture by adding another layer with the purpose to extract the skeleton of the projected shape

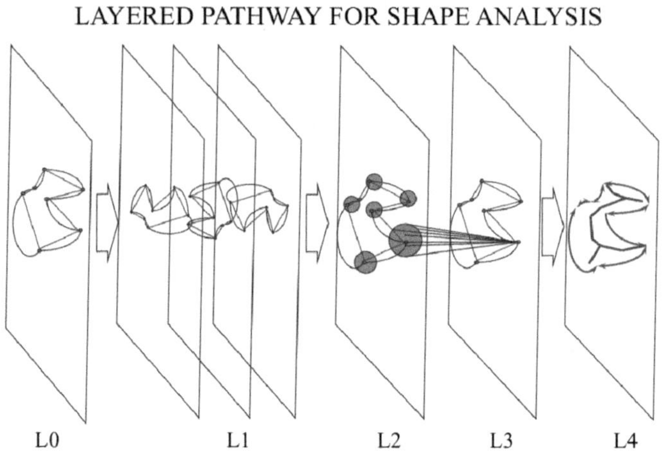

LAYERED PATHWAY FOR SHAPE ANALYSIS

Fig. 1. The complete layered architecture for skeleton extraction together with boundary curvature information. The proposed added mechanism between layers L3 and L4 is illustrated in Figure 2.

and embed the previously calculated points of high curvature into the skeleton representation. The complete layered architecture is shown in figure 1 while the mechanism for skeleton extraction in the added layer is shown in figure 2. The medial axis of a shape is the set of all the inner points having more than one closest point on the object's boundary. Originally referred to as the topological skeleton, it was introduced by Blum as a tool for biological shape recognition.

In 2D, the medial axis of a plane curve S is the locus of the centers of circles that are tangent to curve S in two or more points, where all such circles are contained in S. It is therefore natural to assume the circular RF of the simple neurons as the model of the inscribing disks by assuming an off-center, on-surround type of RF that will ensure firing of the appropriate neuron, located at the center of the circle, only if the curve's boundary falls in the surrounding excitatory zone and not in the central inhibitory zone of the circular RF disk. This ensures that only the circular RFs that are inscribed in the contour will cause firing and not the RFs that cut the boundary in one or more points because in the later case the contour will enter in the RF's inhibitory zone. Furthermore, the firing will be stronger according to the stimulation on the excitatory surrounding zone (perimeter of the disc) in a way that if the disc is tangent to the curve in more than one points the firings of the appropriate neuron, at the center of the disk, will be stronger. Since the disks that are tangent to the curve in more than one points are centered on the shape's skeleton, the respective cells (that have RF on these disks) in the next layer, will receive a stronger stimulation.

At the same time recall that the contour image that appears in layer L3 (figure 2) receives stronger inputs at the points of high curvature, as was explained in [19] and is assumed here. These points are depicted with big dots on the boundary

SKELETON EXTRACTION WITH EMBEDDED CURVATURE
INFORMATION

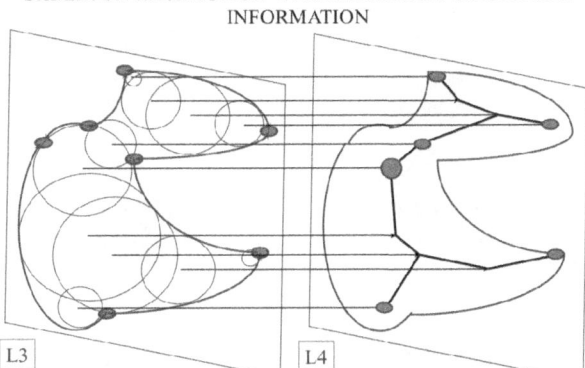

Fig. 2. Points of high curvature receive stronger input from the previous layers and are depicted in L3 with big dots on the boundary. Circular off-center on-surround RFs of different sizes fire at the skeleton points whenever the shape's boundary falls in the circular on-surround region and not in the off-center RF region. The firing is proportional to the curvature at the tangential boundary points. Points of the skeleton that receive stronger input are depicted in L4 with big dots on the skeleton. These points receive stronger input because their corresponding on-surround circular RF in layer L3, falls on points of high boundary curvature.

in L3. A consequence of this is that a circle that is tangent at the points of high curvature will in turn receive a stronger excitation in a way that the respective neuron in L4 , with its RF on this circle, will receive a stronger stimulaiton as well. But this neuron lies at the center of the RF (disk) and therefore the strong signal due to the high curvature detected in layer 3 will appear on the shape skeleton in layer 4. This way, in layer 4, we encode not only the global shape topology (skeleton) but also the local boundary (curvature) information from layer 3 on the skeleton itself. The proposed mechanism for extracting the *curvature-skeleton* of a shape is consistent with the neuroanatomical findings of the visual cortex, as was explained before, regarding the orientation selective, end-stopped but also the circular off center, on surround RFs of various sizes. At the same time the proposed model of shape abstraction is consistent with the most successful attempts in shape representation and recognition as was explained in the related work section.

4   Experimental Results

To evaluate the proposed representation we examined the ability of a neural network trained by an efficient back-propagation scheme [20] to generalize over a set of five hundred shapes in the presence of occlusions and deformations like the ones shown in figure 4. Occlusions and deformations alter the signal significantly therefore traditional classifiers perform poorly under these conditions.

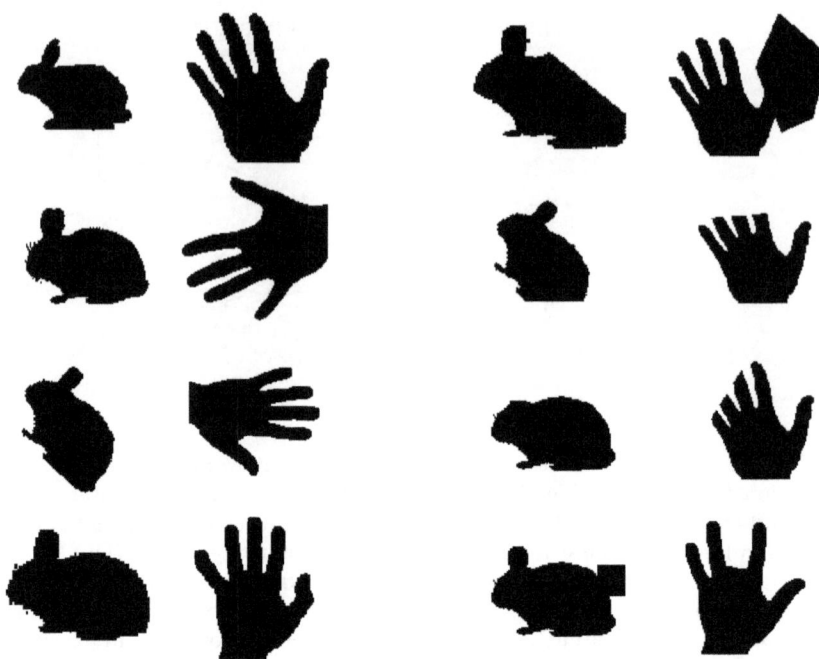

Fig. 3. Training set sample   **Fig. 4.** Test set sample

For the experiment we used 2-D gray scale images of hands and rabbits from the KIMIA shilouette database to be classified in two categories. 500 such images of the two classes, like the ones in figure 3, were first encoded with the proposed skeleton-curvature representation and used to train a network of two hidden layers varying the number of neurons in the first layer between 2 and 8 and the number of neurons in the second hidden layer from 1 to 3, as identified through application of the weight decay pruning methodology [20]. The network was able to learn the correct classification for all the presented 500 images. We then tested the generalization ability of this network by presenting 50 new images like the ones in figure 4 which are versions of the original 500 images after applying partial occlusion, deformations and missing parts. The test set was also encoded by means of the skeleton-curvature representation before presented to the NN classifier. Correct recognition was achieved at 91.6% of these cases which renders the method applicable for real life scenarios. In figure 5 the curvature skeleton image that served as input to the NN classifier is shown for various test and train images. Columns 1 and 3 show the images received from layer 3 (with encoded curvature in the gray scale values), where columns 2 and 4 show the curvature-skeleton image that is produced in layer 4 and is actually used as an input to the NN classifier.

The same NN classifier was also trained using the same 500 images but without encoding the skeleton-curvature representation into the gray scales. The network again was able to learn all the 500 images at the same rate. We then again tested the generalization capability by presenting the same test set of 50 occluded or deformed shapes but also without encoding the skeleton-curvature representation. The recognition in this experiment was correct at 61.5% of these cases which is low compared to the 91.6% achieved by encoding the skeleton-curvature representation into the intensities of the same images.

As a result we can conclude that encoding the shape content of the image through global(skeleton) and local(curvature) descriptors into the signal energy (gray scales) improves the recognition ability of NN classifiers under conditions of occlusion and deformation.

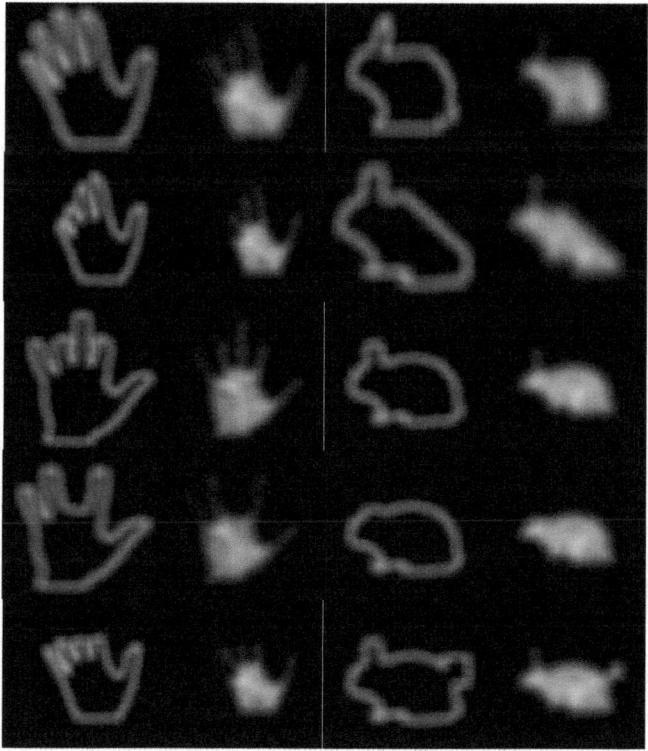

Fig. 5. The curvature image and the curvature-skeleton image for some test and train images. In columns 1 and 3 the curvature images of Layer 3 are shown. In columns 2 and 4, the corresponding skeleton-curvature images, as these are captured in the 4th layer of the proposed pathway, are shown. The skeleton structure can be tracked by the local maxima of the intensity values. The images of the 4th layer serve as inputs to the NN classifier.

References

1. Hubel, D.H., Wiesel, T.: Receptive fields and functional architecture of monkey striate cortex. J. Physiol. 195, 215–243 (1968)
2. Raftopoulos, K.A., Papadakis, N., Ntalianis, K.S.: Visual pathways for detection of landmark points. In: Kollias, S.D., Stafylopatis, A., Duch, W., Oja, E. (eds.) ICANN 2006. LNCS, vol. 4131, pp. 728–739. Springer, Heidelberg (2006)
3. Goodale, M.A., Meenan, J.P., Buelthoff, H.H., Nicolle, D.A., Murphy, K.J., Racicot, C.I.: Separate neural pathways for the visual analysis of object shape in perception and prehension. Current Biol. 4, 604–610 (1994)
4. Ungerleider, L.G., Courtney, S.M., Haxby, J.V.: A neural system for human visual working memory. Proc. Natl. Acad. Sci. USA 95, 883–890 (1998)
5. Dobbins, A., Zucker, S.W., Cynader, M.S.: Endstopped neurons in the visual cortex as a substrate for calculating curvature. Nature 329, 438–441 (1987)
6. Biederman, I.: Recognition-by-components: A theory of human image understanding. Psychological Review 94, 115–147 (1987)
7. Bookstein, F.L.: Landmark methods for forms without landmarks: morphometrics of group differences in outline shape. Med. Im. Anal. 1, 225–243 (1996)
8. Berretti, S., Bimbo, A.D., Pala, P.: Retrieval by shape similarity with perceptual distance and effective indexing. IEEE Trans on Multimedia 2, 225–239 (2000)
9. Mokharian, F.: A theory of multiscale, curvature-based shape representation for planar curves. IEEE Trans. Pattern Anal. Mach. Intell. 14, 789–805 (1992)
10. Dudek, G., Tsotsos, J.K.: Shape representation and recognition from multiscale curvature. Comput. Vis. Image Understand. 68, 170–189 (1997)
11. Super, B.J.: Fast correspondence-based system for shape-retrieval. Patt. Recog. Lett. 24, 217–225 (2004)
12. Blum, H.: A transformation for extracting new descriptors of shape. Models for the Perception of Speech and Visual Forms (1967)
13. Davis, L.: Two-dimensional shape representation. Academic Press, London (1986)
14. Sebastian, T.B., Klein, P.N., Kimia, B.B.: Recognition of shapes by editing their shock graphs. IEEE Transactions on PAMI 26, 550–571 (2004)
15. Aslan, C., Erdem, A., Erdem, E., Tari, S.: Disconnected skeleton: Shape at its absolute scale. IEEE Transactions on PAMI 30, 2188–2203 (2008)
16. Bai, X., Latecki, L.J.: Path similarity skeleton graph matching. IEEE Transactions on PAMI 30, 1282–1292 (2008)
17. Yang, X.W., Bai, X., Latecki, L.J., Tu, Z.W.: Improving shape retrieval by learning graph transduction. In: Forsyth, D., Torr, P., Zisserman, A. (eds.) ECCV 2008, Part IV. LNCS, vol. 5305, pp. 788–801. Springer, Heidelberg (2008)
18. Wang, J., Athitsos, V., Sclaroff, S., Betke, M.: Detecting objects of variable shape structure with hidden state shape models. IEEE Transactions on PAMI 30, 477–492 (2008)
19. Raftopoulos, K.A., Papadakis, N., Ntalianis, K., Kollias, S.D.: A visual pathway for shape-based invariant classification of gray scale images. Integr. Comput.-Aided Eng. 14, 365–378 (2007)
20. Haykin, S.: Neural Networks: A Comprehensive Foundation. PrenticeHall, Englewood Cliffs (1998)

Improving Articulatory Feature and Phoneme Recognition Using Multitask Learning

Ramya Rasipuram[1,2] and Mathew Magimai-Doss[1]

[1] Idiap Research Institute, Martigny, Switzerland
[2] Ecole Polytechnique Fédérale de Lausanne (EPFL), Switzerland
{ramya.rasipuram,mathew}@idiap.ch

Abstract. Speech sounds can be characterized by articulatory features. Articulatory features are typically estimated using a set of multilayer perceptrons (MLPs), i.e., a separate MLP is trained for each articulatory feature. In this paper, we investigate multitask learning (MTL) approach for joint estimation of articulatory features with and without phoneme classification as subtask. Our studies show that MTL MLP can estimate articulatory features compactly and efficiently by learning the inter-feature dependencies through a common hidden layer representation. Furthermore, adding phoneme as subtask while estimating articulatory features improves both articulatory feature estimation and phoneme recognition. On TIMIT phoneme recognition task, articulatory feature posterior probabilities obtained by MTL MLP achieve a phoneme recognition accuracy of 73.2%, while the phoneme posterior probabilities achieve an accuracy of 74.0%.

Keywords: multitask learning, articulatory features, posterior probabilities, multilayer perceptrons.

1 Introduction

In machine learning and neural networks often it is required to learn a set of multiple related tasks. If the tasks can share what they learn, then learning them together may be better than learning them in isolation. Multitask learning (MTL) is an approach of transfer learning where multiple tasks are learned together and what is learned for each task can help other tasks be learned better [2]. MTL is an inductive transfer mechanism which can be used to improve generalization accuracy, speed of learning and intelligibility of learned models. Multitask learning in neural networks allows features learned at the hidden layer for one task to be useful for other tasks.

In the context of speech processing, MTL has been applied to improve ASR performance (a) in noise by incorporating speech enhancement and gender recognition as additional tasks [8], (b) by high level additional tasks such as gender, broad phoneme classification, grapheme classification [12], (c) on meeting data by jointly learning phone classification and feature mapping from farfield microphone to near field microphone [3]. MTL has also been applied for acoustic-articulatory inversion [11].

T. Honkela et al. (Eds.): ICANN 2011, Part I, LNCS 6791, pp. 299–306, 2011.

In this paper, we investigate the use of MTL framework for joint estimation of articulatory features, such as manner of articulation, place of articulation (Section 2). We study this approach on the TIMIT phoneme recognition task and compare it with the traditional approach of estimating articulatory features using independent classifiers (Section 3). As MTL allows addition of new tasks, we also investigate a framework where both articulatory features and phonemes are learned together. Our studies show that (a) MTL not only yields similar or better system but also a system with fewer number of parameters (about 50% less parameters than independent classifier approach), and (b) adding phoneme classification as an additional task helps in improving both articulatory feature and phoneme recognition (Section 4).

2 Articulatory Feature Estimation

Phonological studies suggest that each sound unit of a language (phoneme) can be decomposed into a set of features based on the articulators used to produce the sound. Articulatory features define the properties of speech production. There exist different types of articulatory representations of speech, like: binary features, multi-valued features, and government phonological features [7]. In this work, we are interested in multi-valued articulatory features.

2.1 Previous Work

Traditionally, articulatory features are estimated using a set of multilayer perceptron (MLP) classifiers [4,7,10], dynamic Bayesian networks (DBNs) [5] etc. Stage: 1 of Figure 1 shows estimation of articulatory features using a set of MLP classifiers. The number of independent MLPs depend upon the way phoneme to articulatory feature maps are derived. In literature, it has been shown that the articulatory feature classification accuracies could be improved by modeling inter-feature dependencies [5]. Along this line, in a more recent work, we showed that by modeling the inter-feature dependencies using a hierarchy of MLP classifiers as shown in Stage: 2 of Figure 1, articulatory feature classification accuracy can be improved, and thereby the phoneme recognition accuracy [10] . The hierarchical approach is originally inspired from [9].

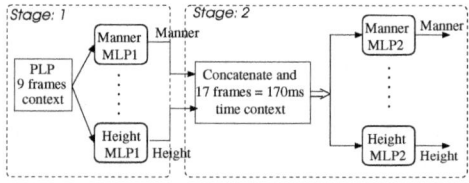

Fig. 1. Hierarchical MLP classifiers for articulatory posterior estimation

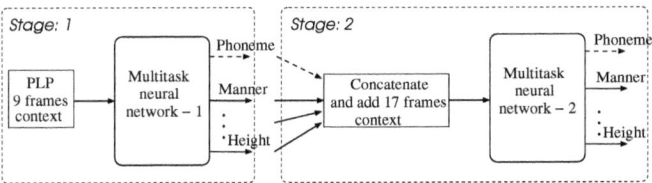

Fig. 2. Hierarchical Multitask MLP classifiers for articulatory (and phoneme) posterior estimation

2.2 Proposed Work

In this work, we investigate the use of multitasking MLP (MTL MLP) for joint estimation of articulatory features (as shown in Stage: 1 of Figure 2). The motivation for this is two fold. Firstly, estimating different articulatory features from the same acoustic signal could be considered as a set of interrelated tasks [5]. Traditional, approach of training independent MLPs does not takes it into consideration. Secondly, a system that has fewer number of parameters can be obtained. Similar to our previous work [10], we also consider a hierarchical approach where a second MTL MLP as shown in Stage: 2 of Figure 2 is trained using the posterior probabilities of articulatory features estimated from Stage: 1 as feature input. In earlier work, it has been observed that articulatory feature probabilities (articulatory posteriors) and phoneme probabilities (phoneme posteriors) when modeled together can yield better system [10]. Motivated from these observations, we also investigate the importance of phoneme classification as one of the tasks (depicted as dotted line in Figure 2) and examine if MTL could exploit shared hidden layer representation to learn the complementary information.

3 Experimental Setup

TIMIT acoustic-phonetic corpus (excluding the SA sentences) is used in all the experiments. The partitioning of the database as specified in the TIMIT corpus is used. The experimental setup is exactly same as the one described in [9]. The targets of articulatory features for MLP training are obtained from phoneme to articulatory feature maps given in John Hopkin's workshop (JHU) [4]. The articulatory features are given in Table 1 along with their cardinality. The different types of MLP classifiers used in this work are:

1. MTL MLP with articulatory features as tasks (*MTL MLP-af*).
2. MTL MLP with articulatory features and phoneme classification as tasks (*MTL MLP-af+ph*).
3. MLP with one articulatory feature as task, i.e. training a separate classifier for each articulatory feature (*MLP-af*).
4. MLP with phoneme classification as task (*MLP-ph*).

These MLPs can be in the first stage or second stage of hierarchical MLP classifiers as shown earlier in Figures 2 and 1. To compare similar systems, phoneme posteriors are also estimated using a hierarchical MLP classifier described in [9]. All the first stage MLPs use PLP cepstral coefficients with a context window of 9 frames as input and the second stage MLPs use posteriors estimated in the first stage with a temporal context of 17 frames as input.

The hidden layer size of *MTL MLP-af* was optimized on the cross-validation dataset. The same hidden layer size was used for the *MTL MLP-af+ph* and *MLP-ph*. This was done to ascertain the benefit of training jointly both articulatory features and phonemes. As it could be noted that after completion of training *MTL MLP-af+ph* can be split into two MLPs which are of the same size of *MTL MLP-af* and *MLP-ph*. In the case of training individual classifiers for each articulatory feature, i.e., *MLP-af*, the size of the hidden layer were determined by fixing the total number of parameters to 35% of the training data following the previous work [10]. The total number of parameters in this system was more than two times of the number of parameters in *MTL MLP-af*.

The stopping criterion of the MLPs during training is the cross-validation frame accuracy. All the tasks in the MTL MLP (including the case where phoneme classification is a subtask) are learned with equal learning rate and equal error weight. It is also observed that the optimal cross-validation performance is obtained for all the articulatory features at the last training epoch. All the MLPs used in this work are trained using a modified version of ICSI Quicknet software[1] with minimum cross entropy error criterion.

The phoneme recognition experiments were carried out using Kullback-Leibler divergence based hidden Markov model (KL-HMM) system. In KL-HMM acoustic modelling [1], posterior probabilities of sub-word units are directly used as features and the state distribution is parameterized by a reference multinomial distribution. Description about the integration of articulatory feature into KL-HMM system can be found in [10].

4   Results

In this section, we first present the results of articulation feature classification studies and then phoneme recognition studies.

4.1   Articulatory Feature Classification

Table 1 compares the frame level articulatory feature and phoneme classification accuracies, when estimated using a set of MLPs and MTL MLPs. The performance of the articulatory features is slightly better when estimated from MTL MLP compared to a set of MLPs. The results also show that along with the articulatory feature classification accuracy, frame level phoneme classification accuracy can also be improved by having phoneme as a subtask in MTL MLP.

---

[1] http://www.icsi.berkeley.edu/Speech/qn.html

Table 1. Frame level articulatory feature and phoneme classification accuracies of individual and MTL MLPs expressed in percentage on the TIMIT cross-validation set

Task	Cardi-nality	Chance rates	MLP-af / MLP-ph		MTL MLP-af		MTL MLP-af+ph	
			First stage	Second stage	First stage	Second stage	First stage	Second stage
Manner	8	34.1	86.0	88.1	86.9	88.4	86.9	88.8
Glottal state	5	61.6	92.9	94.5	93.4	94.5	93.4	94.7
Nasality	4	77.9	96.0	96.8	96.4	96.9	96.4	97.0
Place	11	34.1	86.3	88.5	87.0	88.7	87.2	89.3
Height	9	47.7	82.5	85.1	83.8	86.0	83.8	86.5
Frontedness	8	47.7	84.2	86.6	85.3	87.1	85.3	87.6
Rounding	4	67.8	89.9	91.9	91.2	92.9	91.3	93.1
Vowel	22	47.7	81.3	84.5	82.5	84.8	82.7	85.4
Phoneme	40	–	75.1	78.4	–	–	75.6	79.4

4.2   Phoneme Recognition

In this section we compare phoneme recognition accuracies of the KL-HMM systems obtained by using phoneme posteriors and articulatory posteriors estimated from MLPs described in Section 3 as feature observations.

First Stage Results: Phoneme recognition studies were performed using the posteriors obtained by different first stage of MLPs:

1. *base-ph*: phoneme posteriors estimated from an MLP.
2. *base-af*: articulatory posteriors estimated from a set of independent MLPs (Stage: 1 in Figure 1).
3. *base-mtl-af*: articulatory posteriors estimated from an MTL MLP without phoneme subtask (Stage: 1 in Figure 2).
4. *base-mtl-af+ph*: articulatory posteriors and phoneme posteriors estimated from an MTL MLP with phoneme as one of the subtask (Stage: 1 in Figure 2).

Table 2 presents the phoneme recognition accuracies of the above systems on the test set of TIMIT database. Results show that the phoneme recognition accuracy obtained using articulatory posteriors estimated from MTL MLP is significantly better than the system using posteriors from independent MLPs. The addition of phoneme subtask to the MTL MLP further improves the accuracy of the system using articulatory posteriors as well as the system using phoneme posteriors.

Second Stage Results: The baseline hierarchical posteriors used for comparison are:

1. *hier-af*: articulatory posteriors estimated from a set of hierarchical MLP classifiers (Stage: 2 in Figure 1).
2. *hier-ph*: phoneme posteriors estimated from hierarchical MLP classifier.

Two different posteriors can be obtained from hierarchical MTL MLP systems based on the presence or absence of phoneme subtask:

Table 2. Phoneme recognition accuracy expressed in percentage on the TIMIT test set, using phoneme posteriors and articulatory posteriors as features in KL-HMM. Also given the number of hidden units and output units.

Features	MLP hidden units	MLP output units	Posteriors used	Accuracy
base-ph	3500	40	phoneme	70.2
base-af	Not applicable	71	articulatory	67.4
base-mtl-af	3500	71	articulatory	68.9
base-mtl-ph+af	3500	111	articulatory	**69.2**
			phoneme	**70.4**

1. *hier-mtl-af*: articulatory posteriors estimated from hierarchical MTL MLP classifier without phoneme task.
2. *hier-mtl-af+ph*: articulatory posteriors and phoneme posteriors estimated from hierarchical MTL MLP classifier with phoneme as one of the subtask.

However, the input to the MTL MLPs estimating above posteriors can be the articulatory posteriors obtained from *base-mtl-af* or *base-mtl-af+ph* (shown as inputs *(1)* and *(2)* in Figure 3 respectively). Also, a hierarchical MTL MLP system was built where the input of the second MTL MLP consisted of phoneme posteriors and articulatory posteriors (shown as input *(3)* in Figure 3).

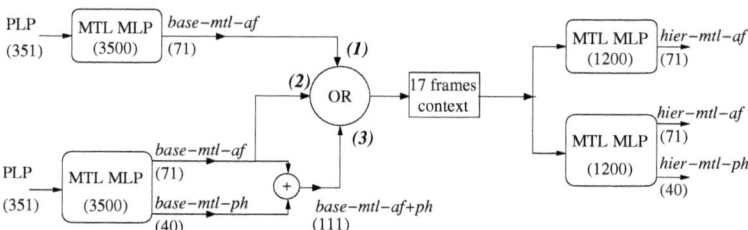

Fig. 3. Hierarchical MTL MLP systems with inputs, hidden and outputs specified

Table 3 presents the phoneme recognition accuracies obtained by using baseline MLP and MTL MLP posteriors as features in KL-HMM system. The results show that performance of the system using articulatory posteriors from MTL MLP without phoneme task is comparable to the system using articulatory posteriors from a set of MLPs. The second stage MTL MLP with input as articulatory posteriors from *base-mtl-af+ph* (discarding phoneme posteriors) further improves the performance slightly. Thus, indicating that articulatory features could be learned better when phoneme classification is also a subtask. Overall, in all the cases MTL MLP with phoneme as subtask improves the phoneme recognition performance of system that uses articulatory posteriors as well as system that uses phoneme posteriors.

Table 3. Phoneme recognition accuracy expressed in percentage on the TIMIT test set, using phoneme posteriors and articulatory posteriors as features in KL-HMM. Also given the number of input and output units of MLPs.

Input to MLP	MLP i/p units	Features	MLP o/p units	Posteriors used	Phoneme accuracy
base-ph	680	*hier-ph*	40	phoneme	73.0
base-af	1207	*hier-af*	71	articulatory	72.0
base-mtl-af	1207	*hier-mtl-af*	71	articulatory	72.2
		hier-mtl-af+ph	111	articulatory	72.3
				phoneme	72.7
articulatory posteriors of *base-mtl-af+ph*	1207	*hier-mtl-af*	71	articulatory	72.4
		hier-mtl-af+ph	111	articulatory	72.5
				phoneme	73.3
base-mtl-af+ph	1887	*hier-mtl-af*	71	articulatory	72.7
		hier-mtl-af+ph	111	articulatory	**73.2**
				phoneme	**74.0**

The MTL MLP with phoneme as subtask at both the stages gave the best performance of 73.2% for articulatory posteriors and 74.0% for phoneme posteriors. It is important to note that the system benefited from both phoneme input and MTL of articulatory and phoneme tasks.

5   Discussion and Conclusions

Our studies show that MTL provides a framework for efficient and compact estimation of articulatory posteriors compared to a set of MLPs. Furthermore, jointly training articulatory features and phoneme improves both articulatory feature classification and phoneme recognition. We hypothesize that *MTL MLP-af+ph* through a shared hidden layer learns to exploit the complementary information present in phoneme and articulatory tasks. This is partly supported by the fact that we do not achieve significant improvement in phoneme recognition accuracy (74.1% compared to 74.0% with phoneme posteriors alone) when concatenating phoneme posteriors and articulatory feature posteriors (as done in our previous work [10]).

In our work, we have used JHU phoneme to articulatory feature maps. However, in literature one could find different phoneme to articulatory feature maps. In the case of MTL MLP, one of the difference it brings in is number of tasks that are learned jointly. Along this line, we have also investigated the representation given in [6] (after making a few modifications, such as adding vowel features resulting in four subtasks). The results showed similar trends in terms of articulatory feature classification and phoneme recognition accuracy irrespective of number of subtasks. Furthermore, in preliminary (ongoing) ASR studies we have observed trends similar to phoneme recognition at word recognition level.

In this work, during the training of MTL MLPs all the tasks were given equal importance. It may be interesting to study the effect of giving one or a few tasks more importance. Future work will also focus on addition of more subtasks, such as gender, rate-of-speech estimation, and performing full-fledged ASR studies.

Acknowledgments. This work was supported by the Swiss NSF through the grants "Flexible Grapheme-Based Automatic Speech Recognition (FlexASR) " and the National Center of Competence in Research (NCCR) on "Interactive Multimodal Information Management" (www.im2.ch). The authors would like to thank Joe Frankel, CSTR, Edinburgh for fruitful discussions as well as providing the multitasking MLP software.

References

1. Aradilla, G., Vepa, J., Bourlard, H.: An Acoustic Model Based on Kullback-Leibler Divergence for Posterior Features. In: Proc. of ICASSP, pp. 657–660 (2007)
2. Caruana, R.: Multitask Learning. Machine Learning 28(1), 41–75 (1997)
3. Frankel, J., Çetin, O., Morgan, N.: Transfer Learning for Tandem ASR Feature Extraction. In: Proceedings of MLMI, pp. 227–236 (2007)
4. Frankel, J., Magimai-Doss, M., King, S., Livescu, K., Çetin, O.: Articulatory Feature Classifiers Trained on 2000 hours of Telephone Speech. In: Proc. of Interspeech (2007)
5. Frankel, J., Wester, M., King, S.: Articulatory feature recognition using dynamic Bayesian networks. Computer Speech & Language 21(4), 620–640 (2007)
6. Hosom, J.P.: Speaker-independent phoneme alignment using transition-dependent states. Speech Communication 51, 352–368 (2009)
7. King, S., Taylor, P.: Detection of Phonological Features in Continuous Speech using Neural Networks. Computer Speech and Language 14(4), 333–353 (2000)
8. Parveen, S., Green, P.: Multitask Learning in Connectionist Robust ASR using Recurrent Neural Networks. In: Proceedings of EUROSPEECH, pp. 1813–1816 (2003)
9. Pinto, J., Sivaram, G., Magimai.-Doss, M., Hermansky, H., Bourlard, H.: Analysis of MLP based Hierarchical Phoneme Posterior Probability Estimator. IEEE Trans. on Audio, Speech, and Language Processing 19(2), 225–241 (2011)
10. Rasipuram, R., Magimai.-Doss, M.: Integrating Articulatory Features using Kullback-Leibler Divergence based Acoustic Model for Phoneme Recognition. In: Proc. of ICASSP (2011)
11. Richmond, K.: A Multitask Learning Perspective on Acoustic-Articulatory Inversion. In: Proc. of Interspeech (2007)
12. Stadermann, J., Koska, W., Rigoll, G.: Multi-task Learning Strategies for a Recurrent Neural Net in a Hybrid Tied-Posteriors Acoustic Model. In: Proc. of Interspeech. pp. 2993–2996 (2005)

OrBEAGLE: Integrating Orthography into a Holographic Model of the Lexicon

George Kachergis, Gregory E. Cox, and Michael N. Jones

Indiana University, Bloomington, IN 47405 U.S.A.
{gkacherg,grcox,jonesmn}@indiana.edu

Abstract. Many measures of human verbal behavior deal primarily with semantics (e.g., associative priming, semantic priming). Other measures are tied more closely to orthography (e.g., lexical decision time, visual word-form priming). Semantics and orthography are thus often studied and modeled separately. However, given that concepts must be built upon a foundation of percepts, it seems desirable that models of the human lexicon should mirror this structure. Using a holographic, distributed representation of visual word-forms in BEAGLE [12], a corpus-trained model of semantics and word order, we show that free association data is better explained with the addition of orthographic information. However, we find that orthography plays a minor role in accounting for cue-target strengths in free association data. Thus, it seems that free association is primarily conceptual, relying more on semantic context and word order than word form information.

Keywords: holographic reduced representation, orthographic priming, semantic priming, word association norms.

1 Introduction

Verbal behavior is a hallmark of humankind, and is thus of great interest to cognitive science. Human adults have command of tens of thousands of words and use them effortlessly each day. As such, words are used in studies of many levels of cognition, from perception to memory to semantics, and many effects have been observed. Descriptive factors such as word frequency, length, part-of-speech, and phonological features have been found to be correlated with these effects, but models have rarely attempted to integrate all of these dimensions. Models of word perception tend to focus on the orthographic and phonological features of a word, yet often ignore semantic information such as word co-occurrence. On the other hand, most models of semantics treat words as atomic units with no overt perceptual features. Fortunately, recent research seeks to bridge this divide from both directions.

The SOLAR model [6,5] uses a spatial coding representation of word forms to account for effects in both masked priming and lexical decision. [3] proposes an alternative orthographic encoding scheme that better captures a set of empirical constraints enumerated by [9]. This encoding scheme uses Holographic Reduced Representations (HRRs) [15], which are neurally-plausible, distributed,

T. Honkela et al. (Eds.): ICANN 2011, Part I, LNCS 6791, pp. 307–314, 2011.

and which result in analytically similar representations for items with similar content or structure. [3] integrates orthographic vectors into BEAGLE, an HRR-based model of lexical semantics and word order [12], and also successfully accounts for lexical decision data. In the present work, after briefly describing HRRs, the Cox et al. orthographic encoding scheme, and BEAGLE, we apply this model to human free-association data [4].

2   Methodology

2.1   Holographic Reduced Representations

HRRs [15] are a form of distributed representation that can hierarchically encode information from diverse sources in a single format. This format is usually a large vector, similar to a layer in an artificial neural network. As in a neural network, it is not the individual vector elements that carry information, but the pattern of values across the vector. The high-dimensional, distributed nature of HRRs thus makes them robust against input noise and memory degradation. Further tightening the connection between HRRs and neural systems, [10] have recently shown that back-propagation neural networks, when trained on location-invariant visual word recognition, produce patterns of stimulus similarity that are equivalent to those derived from HRR representations of the stimuli. HRRs go beyond many simple neural systems, however, in that they can perform variable binding operations (i.e., tracking which items have what properties) and straightforwardly encode hierarchical structure [15].

Although there are other ways of implementing HRRs (including, e.g., binary spatter codes [13]), we focus on the methods introduced by [15] that are based on circular convolution. HRRs begin with a set of "atomic" vectors which are operated upon to produce more structured representations. Each element of these "atoms" is drawn independently from a normal distribution with mean 0 and variance $\frac{1}{n}$, where n is the dimensionality of the vector. There are two operations that enable these atoms to be combined into more structured representations. The first, *superposition* $(+)$, is simply vector addition; it takes two HRR vectors and produces a third vector–still an HRR, and with the same dimensionality– that is partially similar to its components (where "similarity" is defined below).

The second operation, *binding* $(\circledast)$, takes two HRRs and produces a third HRR that is independent of (not similar to) its components. Binding is implemented as circular convolution, which is both neurally plausible [8] and approximately invertible via correlation $(\#)$. If $C = A \circledast B$ is the circular convolution of two vectors, A and B, then each element c_j of C is defined:

$$c_j = \sum_{k=0}^{n-1} a_k b_{j-k \bmod n}.$$

C can be thought of as a compressed version of the outer product of A and B. Note that the output vector of a circular convolution is the same dimensionality as each input vector, unlike techniques in other models that produce outputs with greater dimensionality (e.g., [14,11]). Circular convolution is commutative, associative, and distributes over addition. Implementing circular convolution as defined above is an $O(n^2)$ operation; therefore, in our implementation, we employ the fast Fourier transform, which can be used to approximates circular convolution in $O(n \log n)$ time[1]. In combination, binding and superposition can be used to implement a variety of encoding schemes that simultaneously represent structure at multiple levels. For example, the word *cat* may be represented as the superposition of bound substrings of the word, e.g.: $c + a + t + c \circledast a + a \circledast t$, where each letter is represented by a unique random vector (i.e., they are the "atoms" of the representational scheme). This strategy of chunking long sequences (e.g., letters in words, words in sentences) allows the representation to capture similarity at many resolutions: *cat* will be similar to *catch*, but *catcher* will be more similar to *catch* by virtue of more shared substrings. The similarity between two HRRs is given by their normalized dot product, otherwise known as *cosine similarity*:

$$\text{sim}(A, B) = \frac{A \bullet B}{\|A\|\|B\|} = \frac{\sum_{i=0}^{n-1} a_i b_i}{\sqrt{\sum_{i=0}^{n-1} a_i^2} \sqrt{\sum_{i=0}^{n-1} b_i^2}}.$$

This similarity measure is always in the range $[-1, 1]$. The expected cosine similarity of two i.i.d. random vectors (e.g., letters c and a) is 0—that is, they are orthogonal. Bound items (e.g., $c \circledast a$) are independent of (orthogonal to) their contents (c or a), but superposed vectors (e.g., $c + a$) will have positive similarity to each component. Identical vectors have maximal similarity. The similarity of two HRRs relies not just on the contents of the representations (e.g., *cat* and *catch* both have the letters c, a, and t), but also on the structure of the stored associations (e.g., *cat* can be made more similar to *cut* if the association $c \circledast t$ is included in their HRRs). When using HRRs, researchers must be explicit about what structures they are encoding, allowing simpler interpretation and comparison than the learned correlations in standard neural network models.

2.2 A Holographic Encoding for Word-Form

[3] and [9] investigate several methods of encoding word-form structure as a HRR, evaluating them on the basis of empirical studies of word-form similarity. While all but one of these word-form encoding methods were found unable to account for the entirety of the empirical constraints, [3] introduced a word-form encoding that satisfied the desiderata. Our solution, called "terminal-relative" (TR) encoding, is related somewhat to the simplified word recognition model of [1] and to the SERIOL model [16].

Each individual letter is an "atom" represented by a random vector of dimension n with elements drawn independently from a normal distribution $\mathcal{N}\left(0, \frac{1}{\sqrt{n}}\right)$.

---

[1] This follows from the fact that convolution in the "spatial domain" (i.e., of the raw vectors) is equivalent to elementwise multiplication in the "frequency domain" (the discrete Fourier transforms of each operand).

Thus, the representations for individual letters are orthonormal. To encode a word, e.g., "word", we first superpose vectors for each individual letter and for all contiguous letter bigrams in the word: $word = w+o+r+d+w\circledast o+o\circledast r+r\circledast d$. Here, we wish to form bigrams that are order-specific; to do this, we randomly permute each operand before convolving them according to whether it is on the left or right: $L(w) \circledast R(o)$. To encode larger n-grams, these permutations are applied iteratively: $wor = L(L(w) \circledast R(o)) \circledast R(r)$. Throughout the remainder of this paper, we will use this non-commutative variant of circular convolution (suggested by [15]), although we omit the L and R operators for clarity.

After encoding the individual letters (unigrams) and bigrams, for any n-gram that does not contain one of the terminal letters (either the first or last letter), we encode an additional n-gram that binds the missing terminal letter to that n-gram, including a "space" (just another random vector) to encode a gap in any non-contiguous n-grams. For example,

$$\begin{aligned}
word =&w + o + r + d + w \circledast o + o \circledast r + r \circledast d \\
&+ w \circledast o + (w \circledast \_) \circledast r + (w \circledast \_) \circledast d + (w \circledast o) \circledast r + ((w \circledast \_) \circledast r) \circledast d \\
&+ (w \circledast \_) \circledast d + (o \circledast \_) \circledast d + r \circledast d + ((w \circledast o)\_) \circledast d + (o \circledast r) \circledast d
\end{aligned}$$

Because this last rule is applied iteratively, the first and last bigrams, and the noncontiguous bigram comprising the terminal letters are added into the representation repeatedly, thus increasing their "strength". Although our method possesses the advantage of being parameter-free, the relative weighting of bigrams in TR encoding is similar to the bigram weighting that arises from neural mechanisms in the SERIOL model of word recognition [16].

The overall effect of this encoding scheme is to capture both local (contiguous bigrams) and global (internal n-grams bound to terminal letters) structure in word-forms. Empirical studies of word recognition (see, for a review, [9,7]) show that humans are indeed sensitive to structure on both those levels, and that such sensitivity is required to account for human word recognition capabilities. In addition, TR encoding is capable not just of capturing the relative similarity between isolated pairs of words, but scales to account for orthographic similarity effects within the entire lexicon, as evidenced in lexical decision and speeded pronunciation tasks [3]. In general, TR encoding is a good balance between simplicity (it is parameter free), veracity (it accounts for many word recognition effects), and scalability (orthographic similarity effects across the entire lexicon).

2.3   BEAGLE

BEAGLE (Bound Encoding of the AGgregrate Language Environment) is a convolution-based HRR model that learns word order and meaning information from natural language text corpora [12]. For each word, BEAGLE uses an i.i.d. 2048-dimensional *environmental* vector to represent the word's perceptual characteristics, a *context* vector to store word co-occurrence information, and an *order* vector to encode which words appear before and after the given word. As BEAGLE reads each sentence, the environmental vectors of the neighboring

n (window size) words are superimposed on each word's context vector. Words that have similar meanings grow more similar to one another, since their context vectors tend to hold the same set of superimposed vectors. Thus, BEAGLE learns a semantic space; the semantic similarity of any two words can be found by taking the cosine similarity of the two words' context vectors. BEAGLE learns word order by binding n-grams containing a placeholder vector for the current word (denoted Φ) and superimposing the bound n-grams in the current word's order vector. For example, "dog bites" would be encoded in the order vector for "dog" (o_{dog}) as $\Phi \circledast e_{bites}$ where e_{bites} is the environmental vector for "bites". Thus, an approximate environmental vector for the word(s) following "dog" can be obtained by inverting the convolution via the correlation operator ($\#$), $\Phi \# o_{dog} \approx e_{bites}$; we refer to this inversion of the order vector as "probing".

BEAGLE captures many aspects of syntactic and semantic similarity between words. However, this space is constructed on the basis of random environmental vectors which are, on average, orthogonal to one another. We replaced BEAGLE's random environmental vectors with the TR HRR word-form encoding defined above. In this way, we may capture orthographic similarity (e.g., *cat* and *catch*), and perhaps additional semantic relationships (e.g., *catch* and *catcher*). Because OrBEAGLE builds its knowledge of semantics and word order on the basis of a principled orthographic representation, it may better explain a variety of human data, and can be applied to tasks such as fragment completion that no semantic model has previously been suited to model [3]. In the present paper, we examine how well OrBEAGLE accounts for human free-association data, and compare it to BEAGLE.

3   Experiment

[4] collected free association (FA) data by asking some 6,000 participants to write down the first word (*target*) that came to mind after seeing a *cue* word. Given 5,019 words as cues, participants produced 72,176 responses. In various cases, these responses seem to depend on order (e.g., *aluminum-foil*), semantics (e.g., *aluminum-metal*), or orthography (e.g., *abduct-adduct*). Thus, we chose to examine whether OrBEAGLE—which encodes order, semantic, and orthographic information—can account for this FA data.

As a dependent measure, we use the forward strength (FSG) of each cue-target association, defined as the proportion of participants who generated a particular target when given the cue word ($\Pr(target|cue)$). For example, 17 of 143 participants responded *capability* when given the cue *ability*, so FSG for this pairing is 0.119. We examine how well $logit(\text{FSG})^2$ of each cue-target pairing is predicted by the cosine similarity of these words' representations in BEAGLE and OrBEAGLE.

Using a window size of three and 2048-dimensional vectors, we trained both Or-BEAGLE and BEAGLE on the lemmatized TASA corpus ($\approx 680,000$

---

[2] Because FSG is a probability, the *logit* function is used to transform the domain to all real numbers.

Table 1. Regression terms and coefficients (βs) for predicting *logit*(FSG) on the basis of cosine similarities of a cue's and target's holographic vectors, both in ordinary BEAGLE (left), and using OrBEAGLE's orthography and probe results (right)

Predictor	BEAGLE			BEAGLE + Ortho.		
	β	*t*-value	*p*-value	β	*t*-value	*p*-value
Ortho.	–	–	–	0.249	3.961	<.001***
Context	0.846	28.142	<.001***	0.848	28.188	<.001***
Order	0.207	8.330	<.001***	0.206	8.306	<.001***
Probe	0.598	5.079	<.001***	0.605	5.140	<.001***

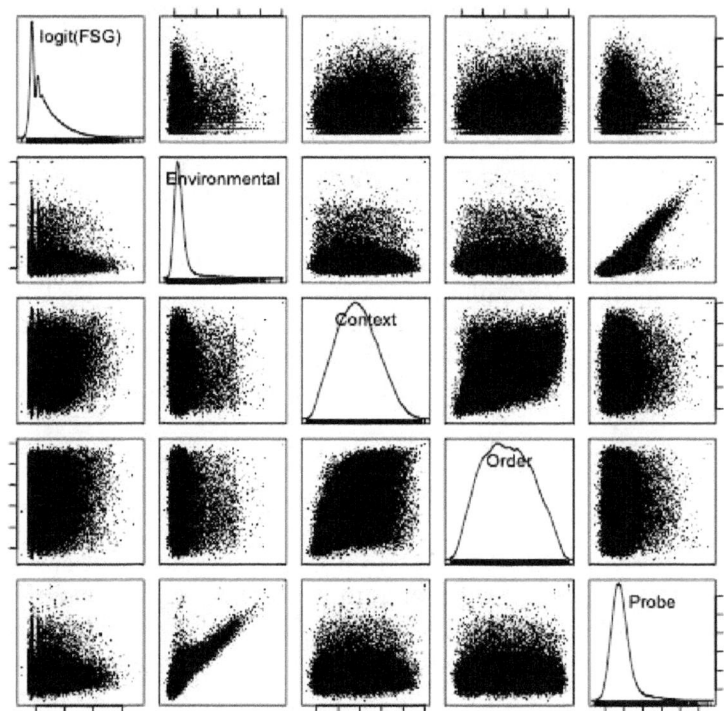

Fig. 1. Cue-target similarities of BEAGLE's context and order vectors and OrBEAGLE's environmental vector and probe results compared to *logit*(FSG)

sentences). Overall, the cosine similarity of the composite OrBEAGLE representation–including semantic context, order, and orthographic information–of cues and targets are significantly correlated with FSG ($r = .087, p < .001$). However, the cue-target similarities computed from BEAGLE's context and order vectors were more strongly correlated with FSG ($r = .199, p < .001$). By examining the separate order, context, and environmental (random or orthographic) vectors comprising BEAGLE and OrBEAGLE, we found that context vectors built from BEAGLE's orthogonal environmental vectors were more highly-correlated with FSG than OrBEAGLE's context vectors ($r = 0.154$ vs. $r = 0.035$).

To determine whether OrBEAGLE can explain any unique variance beyond BEAGLE, we used a linear regression to examine the relative contributions of BEAGLE's context and order similarities, and OrBEAGLE's orthographic similarities. Also included in the regression are the cosine similarities of the target's environmental vector with the results from "probing" the order vector of the cue word as described above. Shown in Table 1 (left), BEAGLE's order, context, and probe similarities are significant positive predictors. Introducing OrBEAGLE's orthographic similarities and probe results significantly increased the regression fit (right; $F(1,47858) = 15.687$, $p < .001$). All correlation coefficients are significantly positive, with context the largest, followed by the probe, orthography, and order. A scatterplot of the cue-target similarities and the probe results used in this regression, along with $logit(\text{FSG})$, are shown in Figure 1.

4   Discussion

We have described OrBEAGLE, a holographic model incorporating orthographic, semantic, and order information, and demonstrated that it can account for significant variance in human free-association data. However, using independent representations for each word, BEAGLE better accounts for this data, and does so primarily due to its context vectors. In different tasks, perceptual (orthography) and conceptual (context) information likely contribute differentially. Masked priming, a perceptual task, shows large effects of orthography. Lexical decision and word naming are less well-accounted for by orthography, and it is not unreasonable to expect that free association would be primarily conceptual. Nonetheless, we also demonstrated that a significant portion of additional variance in FA data can be accounted for by adding OrBEAGLE's orthographic similarities and orthographic probe results to BEAGLE's context and order similarities.

Indeed, the partial independence of orthographic and semantic/syntactic properties of words underlies many theories of verbal processing, including the Dual Route Cascaded model (DRC, [2]). In DRC, orthographic similarity plays a role in *which* semantic representations are activated, but the two types of information are not embodied in a single representation; DRC's semantic representations are akin to the random environmental vectors in the original BEAGLE model, while its orthographic representations are akin to the environmental vectors in OrBEAGLE. While DRC has been implemented as a neural network model, the results in this paper suggest that a holographic approach—with reduced training time and the ability to store a larger lexicon—can capture many of the same theoretical ideas.

OrBEAGLE is a distributed representation system that uses neurally-plausible mechanisms and an empirically-viable encoding scheme for visual word-forms to capture a wide variety of human data, including latencies in word naming and lexical decision, word fragment completion [3], and now, free-association data. OrBEAGLE can be applied to a variety of other experimental paradigms as it stands, and can indicate the relative contributions of word order, context, and orthography. We have shown that it is both possible and useful to begin unifying models that previously operated at different levels and on different tasks.

References

1. Clark, J.J., O'Regan, J.K.: Word ambiguity and the optimal viewing position in reading. Vision Res. 39, 843–857 (1998)
2. Coltheart, M., Rastle, K., Perry, C., Langdon, R., Ziegler, J.: The DRC model: A model of visual word recognition and reading aloud. Psychol. Rev. 108, 204–258 (2001)
3. Cox, G.E., Kachergis, G., Recchia, G., Jones, M.N.: Towards a scalable holographic word-form representation. Behav. Res. Methods (in press)
4. Nelson, D.L., McEvoy, C.L., Schreiber, T.A.: The university of south florida word association, rhyme, and word fragment norms (1998), http://www.usf.edu/FreeAssociation/
5. Davis, C.J.: The spatial coding model of visual word identification. Psychol. Rev. 117(3), 713–758 (2010)
6. Davis, C.J.: The self-organising lexical acquisition and recognition (SOLAR) model of visual word recognition. Ph.D. thesis. University of New South Wales, Sydney, Australia (1999)
7. Davis, C.J., Bowers, J.S.: Contrasting five different theories of letter position coding: Evidence from orthographic similarity effects. J. Exp. Psychol. Human 32(3), 535–557 (2006)
8. Eliasmith, C.: Learning context sensitive logical inference in a neurobiological simulation. In: Levy, S., Gayler, R. (eds.) Compositional Connectionism in Cognitive Science. AAAI Press, Menlo Park (2004)
9. Hannagan, T., Dupoux, E., Christophe, A.: Holographic string encoding. Cognitive Sci. 35(1), 79–118 (2011)
10. Hannagan, T., Dandurand, F., Grainger, J.: Broken symmetries in a location invariant word recognition network. Neural Comput. (in press)
11. Humphreys, M.S., Bain, J.D., Pike, R.: Different ways to cue a coherent memory system: A Theory for episodic, semantic, and procedural tasks. Psychol. Rev. 96(2), 208–233 (1989)
12. Jones, M.N., Mewhort, D.J.K.: Representing word meaning and order information in a composite holographic lexicon. Psychol. Rev. 114(1), 1–37 (2007)
13. Kanerva, P.: The spatter code for encoding concepts at many levels. In: P. Int. Conf. Artif. Neural Networ., vol. 1, pp. 226–229. Springer-Verlag, London (1994)
14. Murdock, B.B.: A theory for the storage and retrieval of item and associative information. Psychol. Rev. 89(3), 609–626 (1982)
15. Plate, T.A.: Holographic Reduced Representations. CSLI Publications, Stanford (2003)
16. Whitney, C.: How the brain encodes the order of letters in a printed word: The SERIOL model and selective literature review. Psychon. B. Rev. 8(2), 221–243 (2001)

On the Problem of Finding the Least Number of Features by L1-Norm Minimisation

Sascha Klement and Thomas Martinetz

Institute for Neuro- and Bioinformatics, University of Lübeck,
Ratzeburger Allee 160, 23538 Lübeck, Germany
{klement,martinetz}@inb.uni-luebeck.de

Abstract. Recently, the so-called Support Feature Machine (SFM) was proposed as a novel approach to feature selection for classification. It relies on approximating the zero-norm minimising weight vector of a separating hyperplane by optimising for its one-norm. In contrast to the L1-SVM it uses an additional constraint based on the average of data points. In experiments on artificial datasets we observe that the SFM is highly superior in returning a lower number of features and a larger percentage of truly relevant features. Here, we derive a necessary condition that the zero-norm and 1-norm solution coincide. Based on this condition the superiority can be made plausible.

Keywords: Support feature machine, L1-SVM, feature selection, zero norm minimisation, classification.

1 Introduction

The ever increasing complexity of real-world machine learning tasks requires more and more sophisticated methods to deal with datasets that contain only very few relevant features but many irrelevant noise dimensions. In practise, these scenarios often arise in the analysis of biological datasets, such as tissue classification using microarrays [2], identification of disease-specific genome mutations or distinction between mental states using functional magnetic resonance imaging [3]. It is well-known that a large number of irrelevant features may distract state-of-the-art methods, such as the support vector machine. Thus, feature selection is a fundamental preprocessing step to achieve proper classification results, to improve runtime, and to make the training results more interpretable.

The recently proposed Support Feature Machine [5,4] relies on approximating the zero-norm of a separating hyperplane. As zero-norm optimisation is computationally infeasible for real world datasets, the SFM approach uses an iterative optimisation scheme based on the one-norm that is closely related to the SVM-based method proposed by Weston et. al [6]. However, in artificial experiments it has been shown that the SFM approach is superior, i.e. it returns a significantly lower number of features and a larger number of truly relevant features. The reason is not obvious, so here, we derive plausibility considerations to explain why the SFM approach finds the zero-norm more frequently.

T. Honkela et al. (Eds.): ICANN 2011, Part I, LNCS 6791, pp. 315–322, 2011.

The following sections are organised as follows. First, we outline the mathematical formulation of the Support Feature Machine and related methods. Then, we compare its performance with the L1-SVM on an artificial dataset. Finally, for the SFM and Weston's method we derive a coincidence condition, i.e. a condition in which zero-norm and one-norm minimising solution coincide. Unfortunately, it is not possible to decide for a specific dataset whether this condition is fulfilled or not. However, we compare both methods in a simple scenario to give a plausible explanation for the superior performance of the SFM.

2   Feature Selection by Zero-Norm Minimisation

We make use of the common notations used in classification and feature selection frameworks, i.e. the training set $\mathcal{D} = \{\boldsymbol{x}_i, y_i\}_{i=1}^n$ consists of feature vectors $\boldsymbol{x}_i \in \mathbb{R}^d$ and corresponding class labels $y_i \in \{-1, +1\}$. We assume the dataset $\mathcal{D}$ to be linearly separable without bias, i.e.

$$\exists \boldsymbol{w} \in \mathbb{R}^d \quad \text{with} \quad y_i \boldsymbol{x}_i^{\mathrm{T}} \boldsymbol{w} \geq 0 \ \forall i \quad \text{and} \quad \boldsymbol{w} \neq \boldsymbol{0}, \tag{1}$$

where the normal vector $\boldsymbol{w} \in \mathbb{R}^d$ describes the separating hyperplane except for a constant factor. Analogous formulations including bias can be found in [5] and [4]. In general, there is no unique solution to (1). A common approach in feature selection is to find a weight vector $\boldsymbol{w}$ which solves

$$\text{minimise} \quad \|\boldsymbol{w}\|_0^0 \quad \text{subject to} \quad y_i \boldsymbol{x}_i^{\mathrm{T}} \boldsymbol{w} \geq 0 \quad \text{and} \quad \boldsymbol{w} \neq \boldsymbol{0} \tag{2}$$

with $\|\boldsymbol{w}\|_0^0 = \text{card}\{w_i | w_i \neq 0\}$. Hence, solutions to (2) solve the classification problem (1) using the least number of features. Some attempts have been made to approximate the above problem with a variant of the Support Vector Machine (SVM), e.g. by Weston et al. [6] who

$$\text{minimise} \quad \sum_{j=1}^d \ln (\epsilon + |w_j|) \quad \text{subject to} \quad y_i \boldsymbol{x}_i^{\mathrm{T}} \boldsymbol{w} \geq 1 \tag{3}$$

with $0 < \epsilon \ll 1$. A local minimum of (3) is found using an iterative scheme based on linear programming. However, the following approach was found to identify relevant features more effectively. Instead of modifying the SVM setting as in [6], we slightly change (2) such that we

$$\text{minimise} \quad \|\boldsymbol{w}\|_0^0 \quad \text{subject to} \quad y_i \boldsymbol{x}_i^{\mathrm{T}} \boldsymbol{w} \geq 0 \quad \text{and} \quad \left(\frac{1}{n} \sum_{i=1}^n y_i \boldsymbol{x}_i\right)^{\mathrm{T}} \boldsymbol{w} = 1. \tag{4}$$

The second constraint excludes $\boldsymbol{w} = \boldsymbol{0}$ and solving (4) yields a solution to the ultimate problem (2). Since we have linear constraints, for solving (4) we can employ the same framework Weston et al. [6] used for solving their problem. However, our experiments show that by

$$\text{minimising} \sum_{j=1}^d \ln (\epsilon + |w_j|) \quad \text{subject to} \quad y_i \boldsymbol{x}_i^{\mathrm{T}} \boldsymbol{w} \geq 0 \text{ and } \left(\frac{1}{n} \sum_{i=1}^n y_i \boldsymbol{x}_i\right)^{\mathrm{T}} \boldsymbol{w} = 1$$

we obtain significantly better solutions to the ultimate problem than by solving (3). It seems that the new cost function is much less prone to local minima. For solving the above problem, we apply a constrained gradient descent technique based on Frank and Wolfe's method [1]:

1. Set $v = (1, \ldots, 1)$.
2. Minimise $|w|$ such that $y_i(x_i * v)^\mathrm{T} w \geq 0$ and $\left(\frac{1}{n} \sum_{i=1}^{n} y_i(x_i * v)\right)^\mathrm{T} w = 1$
3. Set $v = v * w$.
4. Repeat until convergence.

Here, v is the iteratively adapted scaling vector and the operator $*$ denotes the element-wise multiplication. The solution is optimal with respect to feature selection if a solution to (4) is found, i.e. if both solutions coincide.

3   Experiments

We compared the performance of both approaches with respect to k and n. For that purpose, we constructed artificial scenarios with balanced classes. The first k dimensions $x_i, \ldots, x_k$ were drawn as $x_i = \mathcal{N}(c \cdot y, \sigma^2)$. The parameter c controls the distance between both classes. The remaining features $x_{k+1}, \ldots, x_d$ were noise drawn as $x_i = \mathcal{N}(0, \sigma^2)$. Additionally, we ensured that both classes were linearly separable. However, it was possible that both classes were separable with less than k features.

The results are shown in Fig. 1. Obviously, the SFM returns both a lower total number of features and a higher percentage of correct features. So, Weston's method returns more irrelevant features than the SFM. Besides, increasing the number of features (see Fig. 1, bottom) has a different impact on both methods. If we increase the number of data points (in this case to 100), the SFM will identify all relevant features correctly. The SVM-based method fails to converge to the correct number of features even if the number of data points is further increased (e.g. to 1000). So, in this setting the SFM converges for large n to the correct set of features, while the SVM-based approach gets stuck in a local minimum even for large datasets. It is also obvious, that the SFM solution in the first iteration is already very close to the final solution, while the SVM-based method needs more iterations. In scenarios with a large number of data points the SFM converges already after one iteration (see Fig. 1, bottom left).

4   Optimality of the Support Feature Machine

In general, it is not possible to decide whether the zero-norm and one-norm solution coincide. However, one may give some plausibility considerations to show why in most cases the SFM is closer to the ultimate zero-norm solution than the SVM-based approach.

This section is organised as follows. First, we introduce notations to improve the readability of the admittedly complex plausibility considerations. Then, we derive a condition for zero- and one-norm minimising solutions to coincide. This condition holds both for the SFM and the SVM-based approach. Finally, we demonstrate that in certain scenarios it is beneficial to use the SFM.

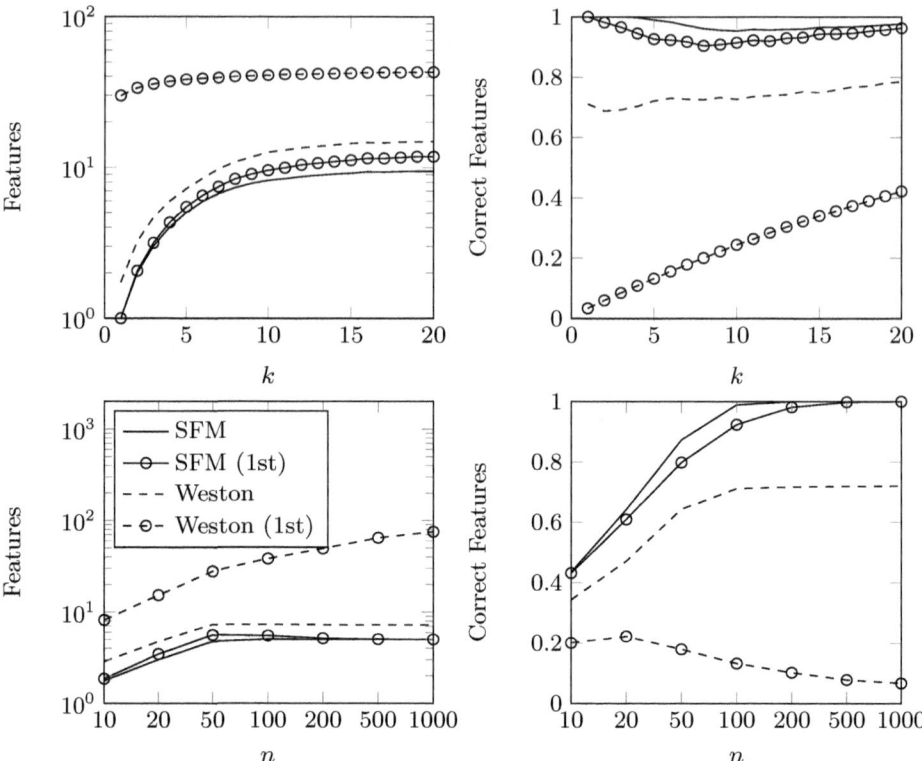

Fig. 1. Feature selection performance depending on k and n. The top row shows the mean number of features and the mean percentage of correctly identified features after the first and after the last iteration depending on k ($k = 1, \ldots, 20, n = 100, \sigma = 1, d = 100, c = 0.3$, 1000 repetitions), while the bottom row shows the same aspects for different values of n ($\sigma = 1, d = 100, k = 5, c = 0.3$, 1000 repetitions).

4.1 Preliminaries

For simplicity, we define $z_i = y_i x_i$ and $Z = (z_1, \ldots, z_n)$ and $\bar{z} = \frac{1}{n} \sum_{i=1}^{n} z_i$. Additionally, $\mathbf{0}$ and $\mathbf{1}$ are vectors that consist of zeros and ones, respectively. For reasons of readability, we omit the length of these vectors where possible. Using this notation, Weston et al. aim to

$$\text{minimise} \quad ||w||_0 \quad \text{subject to} \quad Z^T w \geq 1, \tag{5}$$

while in the SFM setting we aim to

$$\text{minimise} \quad ||w||_0 \quad \text{subject to} \quad Z^T w \geq \mathbf{0} \quad \text{and} \quad \bar{z}^T w = 1. \tag{6}$$

First, we focus on (5) — minor changes will lead us to (6). To simplify a comparison, we consider only results after the very first iteration of the overall optimisation procedure. We denote the solution space with Ω and define the following two weight vectors:

$$\boldsymbol{w}_0 = \underset{\boldsymbol{w} \in \Omega}{\arg\min} \quad ||\boldsymbol{w}||_1 \quad \text{subject to} \quad \boldsymbol{Z}^\mathsf{T}\boldsymbol{w} \geq 1$$

$$\boldsymbol{w}_1 = \underset{\boldsymbol{w} \in \mathbb{R}^d}{\arg\min} \quad ||\boldsymbol{w}||_1 \quad \text{subject to} \quad \boldsymbol{Z}^\mathsf{T}\boldsymbol{w} \geq 1$$

So, among all solutions of (5), $\boldsymbol{w}_0$ is the solution with lowest one-norm. Note that if $\boldsymbol{w}_1$ is in Ω then $\boldsymbol{w}_1 = \boldsymbol{w}_0$. As in practise (5) cannot be solved directly, Ω is in general unknown as well as $\boldsymbol{w}_0$. However, both are well-defined. In contrast, $\boldsymbol{w}_1$ is the solution on the entire $\mathbb{R}^d$ and can efficiently be solved by linear programming. If $\boldsymbol{w}_0 = \boldsymbol{w}_1$ for a specific dataset, then the optimal feature set would be found by optimising for the one-norm.

In the following, we assume $\Omega \neq \emptyset$ and $\boldsymbol{w}_1$ to be unique. This is only a minor restriction as non-uniqueness of $\boldsymbol{w}_1$ will occur only in degenerate cases. Since $\boldsymbol{Z}$ is drawn from a probability distribution, the probability of these cases is of measure zero. The probabilistic nature of the input data also ensures that all quadratic submatrices of $\boldsymbol{Z}$ have full rank.

Without loss of generality, for the following considerations we assume:

1. All entries of the weight vector are positive, i.e. $w_{0,i} \geq 0$. Otherwise, invert the corresponding input dimension.
2. The training data is ordered such that $\boldsymbol{Z} = \begin{pmatrix} \hat{\boldsymbol{Z}} & \check{\boldsymbol{Z}} \end{pmatrix}$ with $\hat{\boldsymbol{Z}}^\mathsf{T}\boldsymbol{w}_0 = 1$ and $\check{\boldsymbol{Z}}^\mathsf{T}\boldsymbol{w}_0 > 1$.
3. The dimensions of $\mathcal{D}$ are sorted, such that exactly the first k dimensions of $\boldsymbol{w}_0$ are non-zero, i.e.

$$w_{0,i} \begin{cases} > 0 & i = 1,\ldots,k \\ = 0 & \text{otherwise} \end{cases} \quad \text{such that} \quad \boldsymbol{w}_0 = \begin{pmatrix} \hat{\boldsymbol{w}}_0 \\ \boldsymbol{0} \end{pmatrix}$$

In total the input data matrix $\boldsymbol{Z}$ has the following structure:

$$\boldsymbol{Z} = \begin{pmatrix} \hat{\boldsymbol{Z}}_1 & \check{\boldsymbol{Z}} \\ \hat{\boldsymbol{Z}}_2 \end{pmatrix} \quad \text{with} \quad \hat{\boldsymbol{Z}}_1 \in \mathbb{R}^{k \times k^*}, \hat{\boldsymbol{Z}}_2 \in \mathbb{R}^{d-k \times k^*}, \check{\boldsymbol{Z}} \in \mathbb{R}^{d \times n - k^*}$$

Lemma 1. *If $\boldsymbol{w}_0$ contains k non-zero entries, exactly k equations in $\boldsymbol{Z}^T\boldsymbol{w}_0 \geq 1$ are active, i.e. $k = k^*$.*

Proof. By definition, the problem is feasible and non-degenerate. Thus, as an optimal solution exists, also a basic optimal solution exist, which is known from linear programming theory. Due to $\hat{\boldsymbol{Z}}^\mathsf{T}\boldsymbol{w}_0 = \hat{\boldsymbol{Z}}_1^\mathsf{T}\hat{\boldsymbol{w}}_0 = 1$, the initial d-dimensional problem is reduced to a k-dimensional one. Thus, in a basic solution k constraints are active and $k^* = k$ follows. □

4.2 Optimality Condition

Theorem 1. *For $\boldsymbol{w}_1 = \boldsymbol{w}_0$, it is necessary that* $\left\| \hat{\boldsymbol{Z}}_2 \hat{\boldsymbol{Z}}_1^\mathsf{T} \left(\hat{\boldsymbol{Z}}_1 \hat{\boldsymbol{Z}}_1^\mathsf{T} \right)^{-1} 1 \right\|_\infty < 1.$

Proof. If $\boldsymbol{w}_0 = \boldsymbol{w}_1$, for each infinitesimal $\boldsymbol{\Delta}$ with $\hat{\boldsymbol{Z}}^{\mathrm{T}}(\boldsymbol{w}_0 + \boldsymbol{\Delta}) = 1$ and $\check{\boldsymbol{Z}}^{\mathrm{T}}(\boldsymbol{w}_0 + \boldsymbol{\Delta}) > 1$ we have

$$||\boldsymbol{w}_0 + \boldsymbol{\Delta}||_1 > ||\boldsymbol{w}_0||_1$$

$$\Leftrightarrow \quad \sum_{i=1}^{d} |w_{0,i} + \Delta_i| > \sum_{i=1}^{d} |w_{0,i}| = \sum_{i=1}^{d} w_{0,i}$$

$$\Leftrightarrow \quad \sum_{i=1}^{k} |w_{0,i} + \Delta_i| + \sum_{i=k+1}^{d} |\underbrace{w_{0,i}}_{=0} + \Delta_i| > \sum_{i=1}^{k} w_{0,i}$$

$$\Leftrightarrow \quad \sum_{i=1}^{k} (w_{0,i} + \Delta_i) + \sum_{i=k+1}^{d} |\Delta_i| > \sum_{i=1}^{k} w_{0,i} \tag{7}$$

$$\Leftrightarrow \quad \sum_{i=1}^{k} \Delta_i + \sum_{i=k+1}^{d} |\Delta_i| > 0. \tag{8}$$

Next, we apply the structure of the matrix $\hat{\boldsymbol{Z}}$ and split the disparity vector, i.e. $\boldsymbol{\Delta}^{\mathrm{T}} = \left(\boldsymbol{\Delta}_1^{\mathrm{T}} \boldsymbol{\Delta}_2^{\mathrm{T}}\right)$ with $\boldsymbol{\Delta}_1 \in \mathbb{R}^k$, $\boldsymbol{\Delta}_2 \in \mathbb{R}^{d-k}$. After some rearrangements, we can derive a closed formulation for $\boldsymbol{\Delta}_1$:

$$\Leftrightarrow \quad \hat{\boldsymbol{Z}}^{\mathrm{T}} \boldsymbol{\Delta} = \hat{\boldsymbol{Z}}_1^{\mathrm{T}} \boldsymbol{\Delta}_1 + \hat{\boldsymbol{Z}}_2^{\mathrm{T}} \boldsymbol{\Delta}_2 = \boldsymbol{0}$$

$$\Leftrightarrow \quad \hat{\boldsymbol{Z}}_1^{\mathrm{T}} \boldsymbol{\Delta}_1 = -\hat{\boldsymbol{Z}}_2^{\mathrm{T}} \boldsymbol{\Delta}_2$$

$$\Leftrightarrow \quad \hat{\boldsymbol{Z}}_1 \hat{\boldsymbol{Z}}_1^{\mathrm{T}} \boldsymbol{\Delta}_1 = -\hat{\boldsymbol{Z}}_1 \hat{\boldsymbol{Z}}_2^{\mathrm{T}} \boldsymbol{\Delta}_2$$

$$\Leftrightarrow \quad \boldsymbol{\Delta}_1 = -\left(\hat{\boldsymbol{Z}}_1 \hat{\boldsymbol{Z}}_1^{\mathrm{T}}\right)^{-1} \hat{\boldsymbol{Z}}_1 \hat{\boldsymbol{Z}}_2^{\mathrm{T}} \boldsymbol{\Delta}_2 \tag{9}$$

$$\Rightarrow \quad \boldsymbol{1}^{\mathrm{T}} \boldsymbol{\Delta}_1 = \underbrace{-\boldsymbol{1}^{\mathrm{T}} \left(\hat{\boldsymbol{Z}}_1 \hat{\boldsymbol{Z}}_1^{\mathrm{T}}\right)^{-1} \hat{\boldsymbol{Z}}_1 \hat{\boldsymbol{Z}}_2^{\mathrm{T}}}_{:=\boldsymbol{\alpha}^{\mathrm{T}}} \boldsymbol{\Delta}_2$$

Finally, (8) can be expressed using $\boldsymbol{\alpha}$ and $\boldsymbol{\Delta}_2$:

$$\sum_{i=1}^{k} \Delta_i + \sum_{i=k+1}^{d} |\Delta_i| = -\boldsymbol{\alpha}^{\mathrm{T}} \boldsymbol{\Delta}_2 + ||\boldsymbol{\Delta}_2||_1 = \sum_{i=k+1}^{d} -\alpha_{i-k} \Delta_i + |\Delta_i| > 0 \tag{10}$$

Equation (10) has to hold for any infinitesimal $\boldsymbol{\Delta}_2$. This is only the case if $|\alpha_i| < 1$ holds for all i, i.e. if

$$||\boldsymbol{\alpha}||_\infty = \left\|\hat{\boldsymbol{Z}}_2 \hat{\boldsymbol{Z}}_1^{\mathrm{T}} \left(\hat{\boldsymbol{Z}}_1 \hat{\boldsymbol{Z}}_1^{\mathrm{T}}\right)^{-1} \boldsymbol{1}\right\|_\infty < 1. \tag{11}$$

(Note: $\boldsymbol{\Delta}_2 = \boldsymbol{0}$ and simultaneously $\boldsymbol{\Delta}_1 \neq \boldsymbol{0}$ is excluded according to (9)).   □

So far, the above observations only apply for the optimisation problem (5). However, with the following minor changes the same condition is derived for (6):

1. The weight vectors $\boldsymbol{w}_0$ and $\boldsymbol{w}_1$ are defined analogously:

$$\boldsymbol{w}_0 = \underset{\boldsymbol{w} \in \Omega}{\arg\min} \quad ||\boldsymbol{w}||_1 \quad \text{subject to} \quad \boldsymbol{Z}^{\mathrm{T}}\boldsymbol{w} \geq \boldsymbol{0} \quad \text{and} \quad \bar{\boldsymbol{z}}^{\mathrm{T}}\boldsymbol{w} = 1$$

$$\boldsymbol{w}_1 = \underset{\boldsymbol{w} \in \mathbb{R}^d}{\arg\min} \quad ||\boldsymbol{w}||_1 \quad \text{subject to} \quad \boldsymbol{Z}^{\mathrm{T}}\boldsymbol{w} \geq \boldsymbol{0} \quad \text{and} \quad \bar{\boldsymbol{z}}^{\mathrm{T}}\boldsymbol{w} = 1$$

2. If $\boldsymbol{w}_0$ contains k non-zero entries, exactly k equations are active. The last of these constraints is the equality constraint $\bar{\boldsymbol{z}}^{\mathrm{T}}\boldsymbol{w} = 1$. To allow a compact notation, we include this constraint into the matrix $\boldsymbol{Z}$, i.e. we append the vector $\bar{\boldsymbol{z}}$.
3. The proof of Theorem 1 works analogously and leads to the same condition.

So, both approaches are very closely connected. However, they are not identical as the matrices $\boldsymbol{Z}$ are not the same.

4.3   Arguments for the Superior Results of the SFM

Due to the complexity of both approaches, it is not possible to give a rigorous mathematical proof for the superior performance of the SFM (6) compared to Weston's approach (5). However, within a simplified scenario and with approximate arguments we can use the result of the above theorem to make the superior performance plausible.

We consider the same scenario as in our experiments and assume the rows of $\boldsymbol{Z}$ to be drawn as $\mathcal{Z}_i$. The first k features are relevant — all others are irrelevant, i.e. the expected value of the first k features differs from zero, all others are exactly zero: $E(\mathcal{Z}_i) = c$ for $i = 1, \ldots, k$ and $E(\mathcal{Z}_i) = 0$ otherwise. For Weston's approach (5) we have $\hat{\boldsymbol{Z}}_1^{\mathrm{T}}\hat{\boldsymbol{w}}_0 = 1$ and obtain

$$\hat{\boldsymbol{Z}}_1\hat{\boldsymbol{Z}}_1^{\mathrm{T}}\hat{\boldsymbol{w}}_0 = \hat{\boldsymbol{Z}}_1 \boldsymbol{1} \approx k \cdot c \cdot \boldsymbol{1} \qquad \Leftrightarrow \qquad \hat{\boldsymbol{w}}_0 \approx k \cdot c \cdot \left(\hat{\boldsymbol{Z}}_1\hat{\boldsymbol{Z}}_1^{\mathrm{T}}\right)^{-1}\boldsymbol{1}$$

such that

$$||\boldsymbol{\alpha}||_\infty \approx \left\|\frac{\hat{\boldsymbol{Z}}_2\hat{\boldsymbol{Z}}_1^{\mathrm{T}}\hat{\boldsymbol{w}}_0}{k \cdot c}\right\|_\infty = \left\|\frac{\hat{\boldsymbol{Z}}_2\boldsymbol{1}}{k \cdot c}\right\|_\infty = \left\|\frac{\boldsymbol{\epsilon}_k}{c}\right\|_\infty \quad \text{with} \quad \boldsymbol{\epsilon}_k := \frac{\hat{\boldsymbol{Z}}_2\boldsymbol{1}}{k} \in \mathbb{R}^{d-k} .$$

Here, the entries of the vector $\boldsymbol{\epsilon}_k$ are distributed as $\mathcal{N}(0, \sigma^2/k)$. In contrast, for the SFM (6), where the last column of $\hat{\boldsymbol{Z}}$ is the mean of all $\boldsymbol{z}_i$, we have $\hat{\boldsymbol{Z}}_1^{\mathrm{T}}\hat{\boldsymbol{w}}_0 = \binom{0}{1}$ and obtain

$$\hat{\boldsymbol{Z}}_1\hat{\boldsymbol{Z}}_1^{\mathrm{T}}\hat{\boldsymbol{w}}_0 = \hat{\boldsymbol{Z}}_1 \binom{0}{1} \approx c \cdot \boldsymbol{1} \qquad \Leftrightarrow \qquad \hat{\boldsymbol{w}}_0 \approx c \cdot \left(\hat{\boldsymbol{Z}}_1\hat{\boldsymbol{Z}}_1^{\mathrm{T}}\right)^{-1}\boldsymbol{1}$$

and

$$||\boldsymbol{\alpha}||_\infty \approx \left\|\frac{\hat{\boldsymbol{Z}}_2\hat{\boldsymbol{Z}}_1^{\mathrm{T}}\hat{\boldsymbol{w}}_0}{c}\right\|_\infty = \left\|\frac{\hat{\boldsymbol{Z}}_2\binom{0}{1}}{c}\right\|_\infty = \left\|\frac{\boldsymbol{\epsilon}_n}{c}\right\|_\infty \quad \text{with} \quad \boldsymbol{\epsilon}_n := \hat{\boldsymbol{Z}}_2\binom{0}{1} \in \mathbb{R}^{d-k+1} .$$

Obviously, for $k \ll n$, the probability that all elements of $\boldsymbol{\alpha}$ stay below 1 and, hence, that the condition in Theorem 1 to successfully find $\boldsymbol{w}_0$ is fulfilled, is much larger for the SFM. As expected, the larger c, the easier it is for both approaches to be successful. Note, that we assumed that the elements of $\hat{\boldsymbol{Z}}_1$ and $\hat{\boldsymbol{Z}}_2$ are independent stochastic variables. Of course, since $\hat{\boldsymbol{Z}}_1$ and $\hat{\boldsymbol{Z}}_2$ are selected by the respective algorithm according to certain criteria, this is not really the case.

5   Conclusions

The recently proposed SFM approach for feature selection identifies relevant features very effectively and may improve the generalisation performance significantly. It is based on the approximation of the weight vector's zero-norm by its one-norm. Here, we derived a condition under which both measures coincide. Unfortunately, in practise it is not possible to decide whether the condition is fulfilled for a specific dataset or not. However, one can compare the SFM approach with other zero-norm approximating methods such as Weston's method.

We found that the coincidence constraint in the SFM approach relies on averaging over n values, while in Weston's approach it relies on averaging over k values. According to this finding, it is beneficial to use the more stable SFM approach in scenarios with $n > k$. In toy experiments, we found that in almost all cases the SFM returns a lower number of features and a higher percentage of truly relevant features than Weston's method.

Further work will include a comparison of the SFM to other zero-norm approximating methods and the derivation of more strict constraints that could possibly be used to judge whether the solution to a specific dataset is close to the optimal one or not.

References

1. Frank, M., Wolfe, P.: An algorithm for quadratic programming. Naval Research Logistics Quarterly 3, 95–110 (1956)
2. Golub, T.R., Slonim, D.K., Tamayo, P., Huard, C., Gaasenbeek, M., Mesirov, J.P., Coller, H., Loh, M.L., Downing, J.R., Caligiuri, M.A., Bloomfield, C.D.: Molecular classification of cancer: class discovery and class prediction by gene expression monitoring. Science 286, 531–537 (1999)
3. Haynes, J.-D., Rees, G.: Decoding mental states from brain activity in humans. Nature Reviews Neuroscience 7, 523–534 (2006)
4. Klement, S., Martinetz, T.: A new approach to classification with the least number of features. In: ICMLA 2010, December 12-14, pp. 141–146. IEEE Computer Society, Washington, D.C, USA (2010)
5. Klement, S., Martinetz, T.: The support feature machine for classifying with the least number of features. In: Diamantaras, K., Duch, W., Iliadis, L.S. (eds.) ICANN 2010. LNCS, vol. 6353, pp. 88–93. Springer, Heidelberg (2010)
6. Weston, J., Elisseeff, A., Schölkopf, B., Tipping, M.: Use of the Zero-Norm with Linear Models and Kernel Methods. Journal of Machine Learning Research 3, 1439–1461 (2003)

Extracting Coactivated Features from Multiple Data Sets

Michael U. Gutmann and Aapo Hyvärinen

Dept. of Computer Science and HIIT
Dept. of Mathematics and Statistics
P.O. Box 68, FIN-00014 University of Helsinki, Finland
{michael.gutmann,aapo.hyvarinen}@helsinki.fi

Abstract. We present a nonlinear generalization of Canonical Correlation Analysis (CCA) to find related structure in multiple data sets. The new method allows to analyze an arbitrary number of data sets, and the extracted features capture higher-order statistical dependencies. The features are independent components that are coupled across the data sets. The coupling takes the form of coactivation (dependencies of variances). We validate the new method on artificial data, and apply it to natural images and brain imaging data.

Keywords: Data fusion, coactivated features, generalization of CCA.

1 Introduction

This paper is about data fusion – the joint analysis of multiple data sets. We propose methods to identify for each data set features which are related to the identified features of the other data sets.

Canonical Correlation Analysis (CCA) is a classical method to find in two data sets features that are related. In CCA, "related" means correlated. CCA can be considered to consist of individual whitening of the data sets, followed by their rotation such that the corresponding coordinates are maximally correlated. CCA extracts features which capture both the correlation structure within and between the two data sets.

CCA has seen various extensions: More robust versions were formulated [2], sparsity priors on the features were imposed [1], it was combined with Independent Component Analysis (ICA) to postprocess the independent components of two data sets [7], and it was extended to find in two data sets related clusters [8]. Here, we propose a new method which generalizes CCA in three aspects:

1. Multiple data sets can be analyzed.
2. The features for each data set are maximally statistically independent.
3. The features across the data sets have statistically dependent variances; the features tend to be jointly activated.

In Section 2, we present our method to find coactivated features. In Section 3, we test its performance on artificial data. Applications to natural image and brain imaging data are given in Section 4. Section 5 concludes the paper.

T. Honkela et al. (Eds.): ICANN 2011, Part I, LNCS 6791, pp. 323–330, 2011.

2   Extraction of Coactivated Features

In Subsection 2.1, we present the general statistical model which underlies our data analysis method. In Subsection 2.2, we show that in some special case our method boils down to CCA. Subsection 2.3 focuses on the analysis of multiple data sets.

2.1   Modeling the Coupling between the Data Sets

As in CCA, we assume that each data set has been whitened. Denote by $\mathbf{z}^i$ the random vector whose i.i.d. observations form data set i. We assume that the total number of data sets is n. We use ICA to find, for each data set, features that are maximally statistically independent. That is, we model the $\mathbf{z}^i$ as

$$\mathbf{z}^i = \mathbf{Q}^i \mathbf{s}^i \quad (i = 1, \dots n), \tag{1}$$

where $\mathbf{z}^i \in \mathbb{R}^d$ and the $\mathbf{Q}^i$ are orthonormal matrices of size $d \times d$. Each vector $\mathbf{s}^i$ contains d independent random variables $s_k^i, k = 1, \dots d$ of variance one which follow possibly different distributions. The unknown features that we wish to identify are the columns of the $\mathbf{Q}^i$. We denote them by $\mathbf{q}_k^i, k = 1, \dots, d$.

We have assumed that the $s_k^i, k = 1, \dots, d$ are statistically independent in order to extract, for each data set i, meaningful features. In order to find features that are related across the data sets, we assume, in contrast, that across the index i, the s_k^i are statistically dependent. The joint density $p_{s_1^1, \dots, s_d^1, \dots, s_1^n, \dots, s_d^n}$ factorizes thus into d factors $p_{s_1^1, s_1^2, \dots, s_1^n}$ to $p_{s_d^1, s_d^2, \dots, s_d^n}$. To model coactivation, we assume that the dependent variables have a common variance component, that is

$$s_k^1 = \sigma_k \tilde{s}_k^1 \qquad s_k^2 = \sigma_k \tilde{s}_k^2 \qquad s_k^3 = \sigma_k \tilde{s}_k^3 \qquad \dots \qquad s_k^n = \sigma_k \tilde{s}_k^n, \tag{2}$$

where the random variable $\sigma_k > 0$ sets the variance, and the $\tilde{s}_k^i$ are Gaussian random variables. Treating the general case where the $\tilde{s}_k^i$ may be correlated becomes quickly complex. We are treating here two special cases: For correlated sources, we consider only the case of $n = 2$. This is done in the next subsection. For larger numbers of data sets, we are additionally assuming that the $\tilde{s}_k^i$ are independent random variables. This is the topic of Subsection 2.3.

2.2   Two Data Sets: A Generalization of Canonical Correlation Analysis

We consider here the case $n = 2$. Let $\mathbf{s}_k = (s_k^1, \ s_k^2)^T$ contain the k-th component of the vectors $\mathbf{s}^1$ and $\mathbf{s}^2$. If $(\sigma_k)^2$ follows the inverse Gamma distribution with parameter ν_k, the variance variable σ_k can analytically be integrated out.[1] The factors $p_{\mathbf{s}_k} = p_{s_k^1, s_k^2}, k = 1, \dots, d$, follow a student's t-distribution,

$$p_{\mathbf{s}_k}(\mathbf{s}_k; \nu_k; \mathbf{\Lambda}_k) = \frac{\Gamma\left(\frac{\nu_k+2}{2}\right)}{(\pi(\nu_k - 2))\Gamma\left(\frac{\nu_k}{2}\right)} |\mathbf{\Lambda}_k|^{\frac{1}{2}} \left(1 + \frac{1}{(\nu_k - 2)} \mathbf{s}_k^T \mathbf{\Lambda}_k \mathbf{s}_k\right)^{-\frac{\nu_k+2}{2}}. \tag{3}$$

---

[1] Proofs are omitted due to a lack of space. Supplementary material is available from the first author.

Here, $\Gamma()$ is the gamma function and $\mathbf{\Lambda}_k$ is the inverse covariance matrix of $\mathbf{s}_k$,

$$\mathbf{\Lambda}_k = \frac{1}{1 - \rho_k^2} \begin{pmatrix} 1 & -\rho_k \\ -\rho_k & 1 \end{pmatrix}. \tag{4}$$

The parameter ρ_k is the correlation coefficient between s_k^1 and s_k^2. As ν_k becomes larger, the distribution $p_{\mathbf{s}_k}$ approaches a Gaussian.

Together with Eq. (1), the density $p_{\mathbf{s}_k}$ leads to the log-likelihood ℓ,

$$\ell(\mathbf{q}_1^1, \mathbf{q}_2^1, \ldots, \mathbf{q}_d^1, \mathbf{q}_d^2, \rho_1, \ldots, \rho_d, \nu_1, \ldots, \nu_d) = \sum_{t=1}^{T} \sum_{k=1}^{d} \log p_{\mathbf{s}_k}(\mathbf{y}_k(t)), \tag{5}$$

where $\mathbf{y}_k(t) = (\mathbf{q}_k^{1T} \mathbf{z}^1(t), \ \mathbf{q}_k^{2T} \mathbf{z}^2(t))^T$ contains the two inner products between the feature vectors $\mathbf{q}_k^i$ and the t-th observation of the white random vector $\mathbf{z}^i$. As denoted in the equation, maximization of the log-likelihood ℓ can be used to find the features $\mathbf{q}_k^i$ (the columns of the orthonormal matrices $\mathbf{Q}^i$), the correlation coefficients ρ_k, as well as the parameters ν_k. If the learned ν_k have small values there are higher-order statistical dependencies between the features; large values mean that the correlation coefficient ρ_k captures already most of the dependency.

We show now that maximization of Eq. (5) generalizes CCA. More specifically, we show that for large values of ν_k, the vectors $\mathbf{q}_k^i$ which maximize ℓ are those found by CCA: The objective ℓ considered as function of the $\mathbf{q}_k^i$ is

$$\ell(\mathbf{q}_1^1, \ldots, \mathbf{q}_d^2) = \text{const} - \sum_{t=1}^{T} \sum_{k=1}^{d} \frac{\nu_k + 2}{2} \log \left(1 + \frac{1}{\nu_k - 2} \mathbf{y}_k(t)^T \mathbf{\Lambda}_k \mathbf{y}_k(t) \right). \tag{6}$$

For large ν_k the term $1/(\nu_k - 2)\mathbf{y}_k(t)^T\mathbf{\Lambda}_k\mathbf{y}_k(t)$ is small so that we can use the first-order Taylor expansion $\log(1 + x) = x + O(x^2)$. Taking further into account that the $\mathbf{z}^i$ are white and that the $\mathbf{q}_k^i$ have unit norm, we obtain with Eq. (4)

$$\ell(\mathbf{q}_1^1, \mathbf{q}_1^2, \ldots, \mathbf{q}_d^1, \mathbf{q}_d^2) \approx \text{const} + T \sum_{k=1}^{d} \frac{1}{1 - \rho_k^2} \left(\rho_k \mathbf{q}_k^{1T} \widehat{\mathbf{\Sigma}}_{12} \mathbf{q}_k^2 \right), \tag{7}$$

where $\widehat{\mathbf{\Sigma}}_{12}$ is the sample cross-correlation matrix between $\mathbf{z}^1$ and $\mathbf{z}^2$. Since $1 - \rho_k^2$ is positive, ℓ is maximized when $|\mathbf{q}_k^{1T} \widehat{\mathbf{\Sigma}}_{12} \mathbf{q}_k^2|$ is maximized for all k under the orthonormality constraint for the matrices $\mathbf{Q}^i = (\mathbf{q}_1^i \ldots \mathbf{q}_d^i)$. We need here the absolute value since ρ_k can be positive or negative. This set of optimization problems is solved by CCA, see for example [3, ch. 3]. Normally, CCA maximizes $\mathbf{q}_k^{1T} \widehat{\mathbf{\Sigma}}_{12} \mathbf{q}_k^2$ so that for negative ρ_k, one of the $\mathbf{q}_k^i$ obtained via maximization of ℓ would have switched signs compared to the one obtained with CCA.

2.3   Analysis of Multiple Data Sets

We return now to Eq. (2), and consider the case where the $\tilde{s}_k^i$ are independent random variables which follow a standard normal distribution. The random variables $s_k^1, \ldots, s_k^n$ are then linearly uncorrelated but have higher order

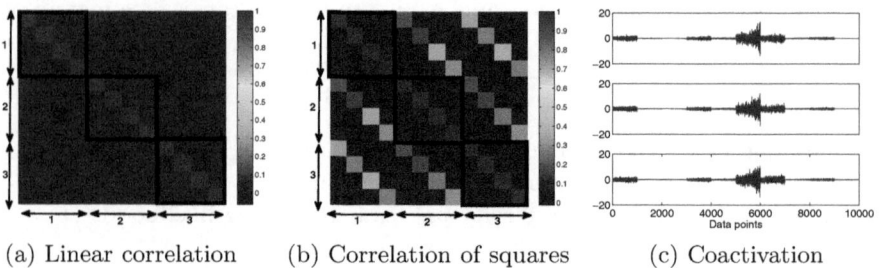

(a) Linear correlation   (b) Correlation of squares   (c) Coactivation

Fig. 1. We illustrate with artificial data the coactivation of the features across the data sets. (a) Correlation coefficients between the s_k^i. (b) Correlation coefficients between the squared s_k^i. The black rectangles indicate each data set. In this example, there are three data sets ($n = 3$), each has four dimensions ($d = 4$). (c) Illustration of the dependencies between the s_1^i. Row i shows s_1^i, $i \in \{1, 2, 3\}$. Correlation of squares means that the sources tend to be concurrently activated. Note that the data points $s_k^i(t)$, $t = 1, \ldots, 10000$ do not have an order. To visualize coactivation, we chose the order in the figure.

dependencies. The dependencies can be described by the terms "coactivation" or "variance-coupling": whenever one variable is strongly nonzero the others are likely to be nonzero as well. Figure 1 illustrates this for the case of three coupled data sets ($n = 3$) with dimensionality four ($d = 4$).

Under the assumption of uncorrelated Gaussian $\tilde{s}_k^i$, the log-likelihood ℓ to estimate the features $\mathbf{q}_k^i$ is

$$\ell(\mathbf{q}_1^1, \ldots, \mathbf{q}_d^n) = \sum_{t=1}^{T} \sum_{k=1}^{d} G_k \left(\sum_{i=1}^{n} (\mathbf{q}_k^{i\,T} \mathbf{z}^i(t))^2 \right), \qquad (8)$$

where $\mathbf{z}^i(t)$ is the t-th data point in data set $i = 1, \ldots, n$, and G_k is a nonlinearity which depends on the distribution of the variance variable σ_k.

This model is closely related to Independent Subspace Analysis (ISA) [5, ch. 20]. ISA is a generalization of ICA; the sources are not assumed to be statistically independent but, like above, some groups of sources (subspaces) are dependent through a common variance variable. ISA was proposed for the analysis of a single data set but by imposing constraints on the feature vectors we can relate it to our model: Denote by $\mathbf{z}$ and $\mathbf{s}$ the vectors in $\mathbb{R}^{dn}$ which are obtained by stacking the $\mathbf{z}^i$ and $\mathbf{s}^i$ on each other. Eq. (1) can then be written as $\mathbf{z} = \mathbf{Qs}$. The matrix $\mathbf{Q}$ is orthonormal and block-diagonal, with blocks given by the $\mathbf{Q}_i$. Our dependency assumptions for the sources s_k^i in this subsection correspond to the dependency assumptions in ISA. This means that our model corresponds to an ISA model with a block-diagonality constraint for the mixing matrix. This correspondence allows us to maximize the log-likelihood in Eq. (8) with an adapted version of the FastISA algorithm [6].

3   Simulations with Artificial Data

In this section, we use artificial data to both illustrate the theory and to test our methods. To save space, we only show results for the method in Subsection 2.3. We generated data which follows the model of Subsection 2.1 and 2.3; the dependencies for that kind of data were illustrated in Figure 1. As in the figure, we set the number of data sets to three ($n = 3$), and the dimension of each data set to four ($d = 4$). The variance variables σ_k in Eq. (2) were generated by squaring Gaussian random variables. The sources s_k^i were then normalized to unit variance. The three orthonormal mixing matrices $\mathbf{Q}_i$ were drawn at random. This defined the three random variables $\mathbf{z}_i$. For each, we drew $T = 10000$ observations, which gave the coupled data sets.

Given the data sets, we optimized the log-likelihood ℓ in Eq. (8) to estimate the coupled features (the columns $\mathbf{q}_i^k$ of the mixing matrices $\mathbf{Q}_i$). As nonlinearity, we chose $G_k(u) = G(u) = -\sqrt{0.1 + u}$, as in [6]. Comparison of the estimates with the true features allows to assess the method. In particular, we can assess whether the coupling is estimated correctly. The ICA model for each of the data sets, see Eq. (1), can only be estimated up to a permutation matrix. That is, the order of the sources is arbitrary. However, for the coupling between the features to be correct, the permutation matrix for each of the data sets must be the same. Comparison of the permutation matrices allows to assess the estimated coupling.

We tested the algorithm for ten toy data sets (each consisting of three coupled data sets of dimension four). In each case, we found the correct coupling at the maximum of the objective in Eq. (8). However, we observed that the objective has local maxima. Figure 2 shows that only the global maximum corresponds to the

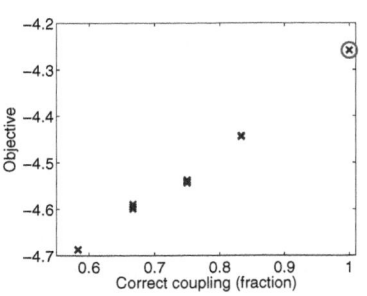
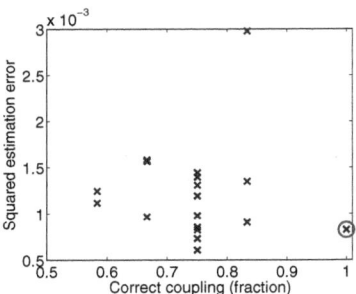

(a) Correct coupling vs. objective   (b) Correct coupling vs. estim. error

Fig. 2. Local maxima in the objective function in Eq. (8). The figures show simulation results where, for the same data, we started from 20 different random initializations of the $\mathbf{Q}_i$. The red circle indicates the trial with the largest objective. (a) We plot the value of the objective function versus the fraction of the correct learned coupling. The larger the value of the objective, the better the estimated coupling. (b) We plot the sum of the estimation errors in the $\mathbf{Q}_i$ versus the learned coupling. The estimation error can be very small but the estimated coupling can be wrong. This happens when the $\mathbf{Q}_i$ are individually well estimated but they do not have the same permutation matrix.

correct estimates of the coupling. We have used the adapted FastISA algorithm to maximize Eq. (8). It has been pointed out that FastISA converges to local maxima [6]. When we used a simple gradient ascent algorithm to maximize Eq. (8), we observed also the presence of local maxima – the results were as in Figure 2.

Simulations with the method for two data sets, outlined in Subsection 2.2, showed that local maxima also exist in that case (results not shown).

4 Simulations with Real Data

In Subsection 4.1, we apply our new method to the analysis of structure in natural images; we are learning from image sequences (video clips) features that are related over time. In Subsection 4.2, we apply the method to brain imaging data.

4.1 Simulations with Natural Images

We use here the method outlined in Subsection 2.3 for the analysis of $n = 2$ and $n = 5$ coupled data sets. First, we consider the case of two data sets, and compare our results with those obtained with CCA. The two data sets were constructed from natural image sequences. The database consisted of the 129 videos used in [4].[2] From this data, we extracted $T = 10000$ image patches of size 25px $\times$ 25px at random locations and at two time points. The first time points were also random; the resulting image patches formed the first data set. The second time points were 40ms after the first time points; these image patches formed the second data set. As preprocessing, we whitened each data set individually and retained in both cases 50 dimensions (98% of the variance). This gave our data $\mathbf{z}^i(t) \in \mathbb{R}^{50}, i \in \{1,2\}$ and $t = 1,\ldots,10000$, for the learning of the $\mathbf{q}_k^i, k = 1,\ldots,50$. We run the algorithm five times, and picked the features giving the highest log-likelihood.

Figure 3 shows the learned features where we included the whitening matrices in the visualization: the features $(\mathbf{q}_k^i{}^T\mathbf{V}^i)^T$ are shown, where $\mathbf{V}^i$ is the whitening matrix for the i-th data set. The learned features are Gabor-like. The features are arranged such that the k-th feature of the first data set is coupled with the k-th feature of the second data set. It can be clearly seen that the coupled features are very similar. This shows that, for natural video, the Gabor features produce temporally stable responses. This result is in line with previous research on natural images which explicitly learned temporally stable features from the same database [4]. This shows that the presence of local maxima in the objective ℓ is not really harmful; our learned features, which most likely correspond to a local maximum, also produced meaningful insight into the structure of the investigated coupled data sets.

As a baseline for this simulation, we also applied CCA to the two coupled data sets. The extracted features were highly correlated but they did not identify meaningful structure in the data. The features were noise-like (results not shown). This shows the advantages of having a method at hand which takes both within and across the data sets higher-order statistics into account.

---

[2] For more details on the database, see [4], and references within.

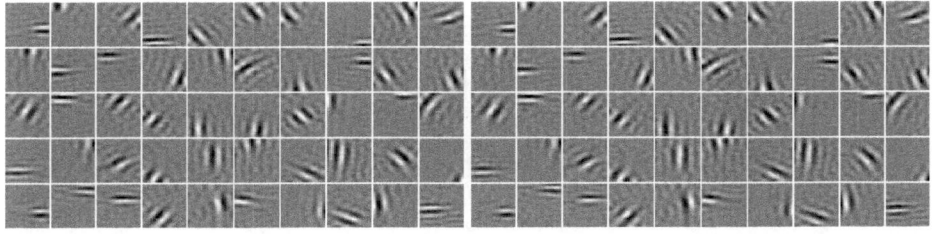

(a) Features, first data set   (b) Features, second data set

Fig. 3. Activity-coupled features in natural image sequences. The natural image patches in the second data set showed the same image sections as those in the first data set but 40ms later. The k-th feature of the first data set is coupled with the k-th feature of the second data set. The coupled features are very similar. This shows that Gabor features produce temporally stable responses [4].

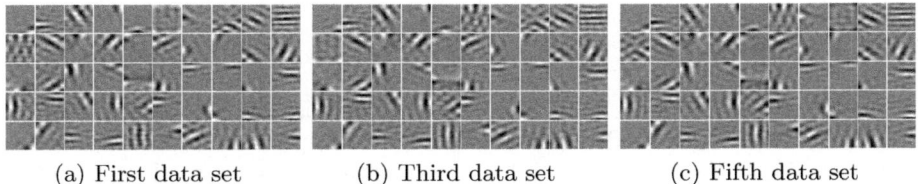

(a) First data set   (b) Third data set   (c) Fifth data set

Fig. 4. Activity-coupled features in natural image sequences. The image patches in the five data sets showed the same image sections at different time points, each 40ms apart. The features for only three of five data sets are shown.

Next, we consider the case of $n = 5$ data sets. The image patches in the different data sets showed the same image sections at different time points, each 40ms apart. Figure 4 shows the results. The learned coupled features are again very similar, albeit less localized than those in Figure 3. The similarity of the features in the different data sets means that, for natural image sequences, the Gabor features tend to be active for a longer time period, see also [4].

4.2   Simulations with Brain Imaging Data

Finally, we apply the method of Subsection 2.2 to magnetoencephalography (MEG) data. [3] A subject received alternating visual, tactile and auditory stimulation interspersed with rest [9]. We estimated sources by a blind source separation method and chose for further analysis two sources which were located close to each other in the somatosensory or motor areas. We took at random time points windows of size 300ms for each source. This formed the two data sets which we analyzed with our method.

Figure 5 shows three selected pairs of the learned coupled features. The results indicate the presence of highly synchronized activity in the brain. The correlation

---

[3] We thank Pavan Ramkumar and Riitta Hari from the Brain Research Unit of Aalto University for the access to the data.

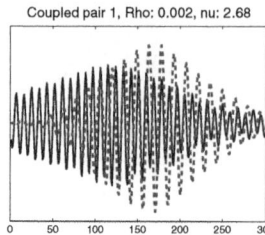 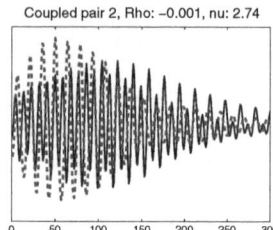 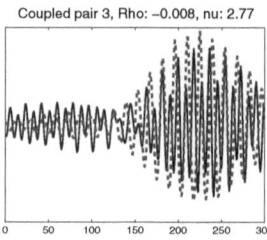

Fig. 5. Coupled features in MEG data. The feature outputs show no linear correlation $(\rho_k \approx 0)$ but are nonlinearly correlated $(\nu_k \approx 2.7)$.

coefficients ρ_k between the feature outputs are practically zero which shows that higher-order dependencies need to be detected in order to find this kind of synchronization.

5   Conclusions

We have presented a data analysis method which generalizes canonical correlation analysis to higher-order statistics and to multiple data sets. The method finds independent components which, across the data sets, tend to be jointly activated ("coactivated features"). The method was tested on artificial data, and its applicability to real data was demonstrated on natural images and brain imaging data.

References

1. Archambeau, C., Bach, F.: Sparse probabilistic projections. In: Advances in Neural Information Processing Systems (NIPS), vol. 21 (2009)
2. Archambeau, C., Delannay, N., Verleysen, M.: Mixtures of robust probabilistic principal component analyzers. Neurocomputing 71(7-9), 1274–1282 (2008)
3. Hastie, T., Tibshirani, R., Friedman, J.: The Elements of Statistical Learning. Springer, Heidelberg (2009)
4. Hurri, J., Hyvärinen, A.: Simple-cell-like receptive fields maximize temporal coherence in natural video. Neural Computation 15(3), 663–691 (2003)
5. Hyvärinen, A., Karhunen, J., Oja, E.: Independent Component Analysis. John Wiley & Sons, Chichester (2001)
6. Hyvärinen, A., Köster, U.: FastISA: A fast fixed-point algorithm for independent subspace analysis. In: 14th European Symposium on Artificial Neural Networks, ESANN (2006)
7. Karhunen, J., Ukkonen, T.: Extending ICA for finding jointly dependent components from two related data sets. Neurocomputing 70(16-18), 2969–2979 (2007)
8. Klami, A., Kaski, S.: Probabilistic approach to detecting dependencies between data sets. Neurocomputing 72(1-3), 39–46 (2008)
9. Ramkumar, P., Parkkonen, L., Hari, R., Hyvärinen, A.: Characterization of neuromagnetic brain rhythms over time scales of minutes using spatial independent component analysis. Human Brain Mapping (in press)

Single Layer Complex Valued Neural Network with Entropic Cost Function

Luís A. Alexandre

Dept. Informatics, Univ. Beira Interior
R. Marquês d'Ávila e Bolama, 6201-001 Covilhã
and IT - Instituto de Telecomunicações, Covilhã, Portugal
lfbaa@ubi.pt

Abstract. This paper presents the adaptation of a single layer complex valued neural network (NN) to use entropy in the cost function instead of the usual mean squared error (MSE). This network has the good property of having only one layer so that there is no need to search for the number of hidden layer neurons: the topology is completely determined by the problem. We extend the existing stochastic MSE based learning algorithm to a batch MSE version first and then to a batch minimum error entropy (MEE). We present experiments showing the the proposed algorithms are competitive with other learning machines.

Keywords: Complex valued NN, Entropic cost function, MSE, MEE.

1 Introduction

Complex valued neural networks (CVNNs) have been gaining considerable attention [1,2,3,4]. The benefits of using a complex valued NN come when dealing with specific types of data, such as wave phenomena [1,5] where there is the need of processing phase and amplitude information.

The key feature of these networks is related to how the product of complex numbers work. Let's compare what happens if we consider a 2D input to a neuron in the following two cases: first, the traditional real valued case where the neuron has a weight associated with each input; second the complex value case where a single complex weight is used for a single complex valued input. The two cases are represented in figure 1. Consider the real numbers a, b, w_1 and w_2. In a real value neuron the 2D input consisting of values a and b gets multiplied by the respective weights w_1 and w_2 giving an input to the neuron of $aw_1 + bw_2$. In the case represented in the lower part of the figure, we have the same input values a and b but now as real and imaginary parts of a complex input $z = a + ib$. The weight are also part of a single complex weight $w = w_1 + iw_2$. The neuron now sees this input as the product $zw = aw_1 - bw_2 + i(aw_2 + bw_1)$. If we write this result using amplitude and phase representation of complex numbers, say, $z = \sqrt{a^2 + b^2}e^{i\tan^{-1}(b/a)}$ and $w = \sqrt{w_1^2 + w_2^2}e^{i\tan^{-1}(w_2/w_1)}$, we get $zw = \sqrt{a^2 + b^2}\sqrt{w_1^2 + w_2^2}e^{i(\tan^{-1}(b/a) + \tan^{-1}(w_2/w_1))}$. This means that the product of complex numbers is really just multiplying the amplitudes and adding the phases.

T. Honkela et al. (Eds.): ICANN 2011, Part I, LNCS 6791, pp. 331–338, 2011.

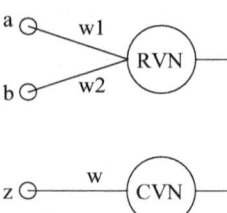

Fig. 1. Example of how a real valued (above) and a complex valued (below) neuron deal with a 2D input. $z = a + ib$ and $w = w_1 + iw_2$. See the text for details.

Traditionally, neural networks have used mean squared error as cost functions [6]. Recently however, it has been shown [7,8] that there may be advantages in using a cost function based on an information theoretical approaches, such as the minimization of the entropy of the errors (MEE). A concrete example is the increase in convergence during the training of recurrent NNs that were observed in [9,10].

In this paper we show a batch learning algorithm for the single layer complex value neural network proposed in [3] and proceed to derive the MEE based learning algorithm for this network.

The rest of the paper is organized as follows: the next section contains a presentation of the single layer complex valued NN, section 3 contains the derivation of the batch versions of the learning algorithm (with MSE and MEE); the following sections contains experiments and section 5 contains the conclusions.

2   Complex Valued NN

2.1   One Layer CVNN

In this subsection we follow closely [3].

Consider an input space with m features. The neuron input is the complex vector $x = x^R + ix^I$ where x^R is the real and x^I is the imaginary part, such that $x \in \mathbb{C}^m$. The complex unit is $i = \sqrt{-1}$. The weight matrix $w \in \mathbb{C}^m$ can also be written as $w = w^R + iw^I$. The net input of neuron k is given by

$$z_k = \theta_k + \sum_{j=1}^{m} w_{kj} x_j \tag{1}$$

where $\theta_k \in \mathbb{C}$ is the bias for neuron k and can be written as $\theta_k = \theta_k^R + i\theta_k^I$.

Given the complex multiplication of $w_k x$, this can be further written as

$$z_k = z_k^R + iz_k^I = \left(\theta_k^R + x^R w_k^R - x^I w_k^I\right) + i\left(\theta_k^I + x^R w_k^I + x^I w_k^R\right) \tag{2}$$

Note that,

$$x^R w_k^R = \sum_{j=1}^{m} x_j^R w_{kj}^R \tag{3}$$

The k neuron output is given by $y_k = f(z_k)$ where $f : \mathbb{C} \to \mathbb{R}$ is the activation function and $y_k \in \mathbb{R}$. The activation function used is $f(z_k) = (s(z_k^R) - s(z_k^I))^2$ where $s(\cdot)$ is the sigmoid function $s(x) = \frac{1}{1+\exp(-x)}$.

Given the form of this activation function, it is possible to solve non-linear classification problems whereas in the case of a real valued neural network with only one layer (such as a simple perceptron) this would not be possible.

Now that we know how a single neuron obtains its output, we will see how to train a network composed of a single layer with N of these complex valued neurons.

To train the network in a stochastic learning approach we need to obtain the weights that minimize the following error functional

$$E(w) = \frac{1}{2} \sum_{k=1}^{N} (t_k - y_k)^2 \tag{4}$$

where $t_k \in \mathbb{R}$ represents the target output for neuron k. This is the mean squared error functional (MSE) that is traditionally used in the learning algorithm of NNs, only in this case it depends on a complex weight matrix, w.

To minimize (4) we find its derivative w.r.t. the weights:

$$\frac{\partial E}{\partial w_{kj}^R} = -2e_k(s(z_k^R) - s(z_k^I)) \left(s'(z_k^R)x_j^R - s'(z_k^I)x_j^I \right) \tag{5}$$

The previous expression is the derivative w.r.t. the real weights but a similar one should be made w.r.t. the imaginary weights.

To obtain the weights we use the gradient descent rule, and update the weights at each iteration (t), that is, after the presentation of each training pattern to the network, using

$$w_{kj}^R(t) = w_{kj}^R(t-1) + \Delta w_{kj}^R(t) \tag{6}$$

with (gradient descent: go opposite to the derivative of E w.r.t. the weights)

$$\Delta w_{kj}^R(t) = -\eta \frac{\partial E}{\partial w_{kj}^R} = 2\eta e_k(s(z_k^R) - s(z_k^I)) \left(s'(z_k^R)x_j^R - s'(z_k^I)x_j^I \right) \tag{7}$$

A similar derivation can be made for the case of the imaginary part of the weights, yielding

$$\Delta w_{kj}^I(t) = -\eta \frac{\partial E}{\partial w_{kj}^I} = 2\eta e_k(s(z_k^I) - s(z_k^R)) \left(s'(z_k^R)x_j^I + s'(z_k^I)x_j^R \right) \tag{8}$$

It is possible to show that the final expressions for the adjustment of the real and imaginary parts of the bias are

$$\Delta \theta_k^R = 2\eta e_k(s(z_k^R) - s(z_k^I))s'(z_k^R) \tag{9}$$

and

$$\Delta \theta_k^I = 2\eta e_k(s(z_k^I) - s(z_k^R))s'(z_k^I) \tag{10}$$

3   Batch Learning

In this section we present the batch version of the algorithm presented in the previous section.

First change is on the functional that should be minimized: now it contains the error contributions from all the L patterns in the training set:

$$E(w) = \frac{1}{2L} \sum_{l=1}^{L} \sum_{k=1}^{N} (t_k - y_k)^2 \tag{11}$$

The only difference to the stochastic approach presented earlier is that instead of updating the weights after each pattern is presented to the network, we sum the values of Δw_{kj} and $\Delta \theta_k$ obtained after each pattern is presented to the network and only update the weights after all patterns have been shown to the network (after an epoch).

3.1   MEE for Learning in Batch Mode

Now we propose the use of the minimization of the entropy of the errors (MEE) instead of the minimization of the mean squared error (MSE) as the optimization principle behind the learning for this network.

This type of training needs a batch mode algorithm because we have to estimate the distribution of the errors for updating the weights, so we need several of these errors to obtain a good estimate.

In [11] it is shown that the minimization of the error entropy (in particular, Renyi's entropy) results in the minimization of the divergence between the joint pdfs of input-target and input-output signals. This suggests that the distribution of the output of the system is converging to the distribution of the targets. Also, when the entropy is minimized, for the classification case and under certain mild conditions, implies that the error must be zero (see proof in [12]).

As we saw above, the error $e_j = t_j - y_j$ represents the difference between the target t_j of the j neuron and its output y_j. We will replace the MSE of the variable e_j for its MEE counterpart. First it is necessary to estimate the pdf of the error. For this we use the Parzen window approach $\hat{f}(e_j) = \frac{1}{Lh} \sum_{i=1}^{L} K\left(\frac{e_j - e_i}{h}\right)$ where h represents the bandwidth of the kernel K and L is the number of patterns in the training set. The kernel used is the Gaussian kernel given by $K(x) = \frac{1}{\sqrt{2\pi}} \exp\left(-\frac{x^2}{2}\right)$. Renyi's quadratic entropy is given by $H_{R2}(x) = -\log\left(\int_C (f(x))^2 dx\right)$ where C is the support of x and $f(\cdot)$ is its density function. Note that this last equation can be seen as the logarithm of the expected value of the pdf: $-\log E[f(x)]$. This justifies the use of the following estimator for H_{R2}: $\hat{H}_{R2}(x) = -\log\left(\frac{1}{L} \sum_{i=1}^{L} f(x_i)\right)$.

Once we plug the estimator of the pdf into this last expression, we get the final expression of the entropy of the error (the cost function)

$$\hat{H}_{R2}(e_j) = -\log\left(\frac{1}{L^2 h}\sum_{i=1}^{L}\sum_{u=1}^{L}K\left(\frac{e_i - e_u}{h}\right)\right) \tag{12}$$

Note that instead of the time complexity for the MSE which is $O(L)$, the MEE approach has $O(L^2)$ complexity.

To find how to minimize this cost function, we follow a similar approach to the one done above for the MSE. Note first that to minimize equation (12) is the same as to maximize the argument of the logarithm, which we call J (ignoring the constant factors):

$$J = \sum_{i=1}^{L}\sum_{u=1}^{L}K\left(\frac{e_i - e_u}{h}\right) \tag{13}$$

First we find the derivative of J w.r.t. the real weights:

$$\frac{\partial J}{\partial w_{kj}^R} = \frac{1}{h}\sum_{i=1}^{L}\sum_{u=1}^{L}K'\left(\frac{e_i - e_u}{h}\right)\left(\frac{\partial e_i}{\partial w_{kj}^R} - \frac{\partial e_u}{\partial w_{kj}^R}\right) \tag{14}$$

The term $\frac{\partial e_i}{\partial w_{kj}^R}$ is given by $-\frac{\partial y_i}{\partial w_{kj}^R}$. This gives the following

$$\frac{\partial J}{\partial w_{kj}^R} = \frac{2}{h}\sum_{i=1}^{L}\sum_{u=1}^{L}K'\left(\frac{e_i - e_u}{h}\right)((s(z_i^R) - s(z_i^I))(s'(z_i^R)x_j^R - s'(z_i^I)x_j^I) - \tag{15}$$
$$(s(z_u^R) - s(z_u^I))(s'(z_u^R)x_j^R - s'(z_u^I)x_j^I))$$

We will again use the gradient to guide the search for the weights, but in this case it is a gradient ascent since we wish to maximize J. So, the weight update at each iteration (t) will be guided by

$$\Delta w_{kj}^R(t) = \eta\frac{\partial J}{\partial w_{kj}^R} \tag{16}$$

A similar derivation can be done for the case of the imaginary weights. The expression equivalent to (15) is

$$\frac{\partial J}{\partial w_{kj}^I} = \frac{2}{h}\sum_{i=1}^{N}\sum_{u=1}^{N}K'\left(\frac{e_i - e_u}{h}\right)((s(z_i^I) - s(z_i^R))(s'(z_i^R)x_j^I + s'(z_i^I)x_j^R) - \tag{17}$$
$$(s(z_u^I) - s(z_u^R))(s'(z_u^R)x_j^I + s'(z_u^I)x_j^R))$$

The update equations for the thresholds can be obtained by finding $\frac{\partial J}{\partial \theta_k^R}$ and $\frac{\partial J}{\partial \theta_k^I}$. These equations are

$$\frac{\partial J}{\partial \theta_k^R} = \frac{2}{h}\sum_{i=1}^{N}\sum_{u=1}^{N}K'\left(\frac{e_i - e_u}{h}\right)((s(z_i^R) - s(z_i^I))s'(z_i^R) - \tag{18}$$
$$(s(z_u^R) - s(z_u^I))s'(z_u^R))$$

and

$$\frac{\partial J}{\partial \theta_k^I} = \frac{2}{h} \sum_{i=1}^{N} \sum_{u=1}^{N} K' \left(\frac{e_i - e_u}{h} \right) ((s(z_i^I) - s(z_i^R))s'(z_i^I) - \\ (s(z_u^I) - s(z_u^R))s'(z_u^I)) \tag{19}$$

4   Experiments

4.1   Datasets

We tried to find datasets were measurements were made with real and imaginary parts (complex numbers) because we suspected that these would be the most adequate settings for the type of network we are studying. Unfortunately it is very hard to find this type of data. We used an artificial dataset to simulate complex data and a real one, with actual complex measurements.

The artificial generated problem (Checkerboard) is a 2 by 2 grid of points with alternate classes (similar to the XOR problem). It contains 400 points, 100 per grid position and 200 per class. In this case we consider that the value of the X coordinate of a point is the real part of a complex measurement and the Y coordinate is the imaginary part.

The second is a breast cancer dataset. It consists of electrical impedance measurements that were performed on 120 samples of freshly excised breast tissue. The problem has 6 classes, 120 points and 24 features (real and imaginary parts of 12 measurements of impedance at different frequencies) [13].

The data was centered and reduced for all algorithms with the exception of the SVM where a normalization in the interval [-1,1] was done for each feature. We used the LIBSVM [14] implementation.

4.2   Results

The results are in table 1. This table contain the average error and standard deviation of 30 repetitions of a two-fold cross-validation. We show also the results using SVM with RBF kernel (best value obtained for g varying from 2.2 to 0.8 in steps of 0.2, for C=10 and C=100), k-NN (best value from k=1, 3, 5 and 7) and the C4.5 decision tree. For the MEE version there were 3 results for each value of the learning rate, one for each of values of the kernel bandwidth used (1.0, 1.2 and 1.4). We only show the best to save space. The presented results for the CVNNs were the best values obtained when the training run for 4000 epochs, which were evaluated at 20 epochs intervals on the test set.

The results for the Checkerboard problem are very impressive: the CVNN is able to attain almost perfect classification and the second best method, the SVM with RBF, is still a bit behind. In this dataset, the batch MEE version is also the best for the tested values of the parameters, when compared with the other two versions. For the Checkerboard problem we also show the more informative balanced error rate since this is a two class problem (we cannot show this value for the second dataset since it has 6 classes).

Table 1. Average error and balanced error (BER), in percentage, with standard deviation for 30 repetitions of a two fold-cross validation for both datasets

Dataset ->		Checkerboard			Breast cancer	
Method	Parameters	Error (std)	BER (std)	Parameters		Error (std)
SVM RBF	g=1.8, C=10	2.92 (0.60)	5.37 (1.14)	g=1.0, C=10		31.83 (3.23)
k-NN	$k = 1$	4.48 (0.98)	7.18 (1.38)	$k = 5$		34.42 (2.99)
C4.5	-	25.22 (0.29)	49.91 (0.55)	-		35.28 (5.28)
Stochastic	$\eta = 0.09$	0.51 (0.38)	0.38 (0.34)	$\eta = 0.09$		32.11 (5.68)
Batch MSE	$\eta = 0.09$	0.60 (0.43)	0.47 (0.39)	$\eta = 0.09$		33.25 (6.05)
Batch MEE	$\eta = 0.09, h = 1.0$	0.30 (0.22)	0.22 (0.21)	$\eta = 0.09, h = 1.0$	33.14 (5.55)
Stochastic	$\eta = 0.07$	0.43 (0.26)	0.32 (0.29)	$\eta = 0.07$		32.69 (5.30)
Batch MSE	$\eta = 0.07$	0.48 (0.39)	0.37 (0.33)	$\eta = 0.07$		33.25 (6.05)
Batch MEE	$\eta = 0.07, h = 1.4$	0.32 (0.31)	0.24 (0.28)	$\eta = 0.07, h = 1.4$	33.47 (6.19)
Stochastic	$\eta = 0.05$	0.57 (0.50)	0.46 (0.54)	$\eta = 0.05$		33.64 (5.07)
Batch MSE	$\eta = 0.05$	0.45 (0.30)	0.33 (0.26)	$\eta = 0.05$		33.03 (5.26)
Batch MEE	$\eta = 0.05, h = 1.4$	0.33 (0.24)	0.22 (0.16)	$\eta = 0.05, h = 1.0$	33.00 (4.94)
Stochastic	$\eta = 0.03$	0.72 (0.55)	0.59 (0.51)	$\eta = 0.03$		33.17 (6.18)
Batch MSE	$\eta = 0.03$	0.58 (0.36)	0.44 (0.34)	$\eta = 0.03$		32.94 (5.74)
Batch MEE	$\eta = 0.03, h = 1.4$	0.37 (0.22)	0.27 (0.21)	$\eta = 0.03, h = 1.0$	33.50 (4.43)
Stochastic	$\eta = 0.01$	0.68 (0.32)	0.57 (0.34)	$\eta = 0.01$		33.28 (5.66)
Batch MSE	$\eta = 0.01$	0.68 (0.54)	0.59 (0.57)	$\eta = 0.01$		33.61 (5.29)
Batch MEE	$\eta = 0.01, h = 1.0$	0.23 (0.31)	0.18 (0.27)	$\eta = 0.01, h = 1.0$	34.58 (3.84)

For the Brest Cancer problem, the SVM with RBF was the best classifier. The CVNN came in second place. Within the 3 variants of the CVNN, the best results were obtained by the stochastic version. The MEE based version showed in general (4 out of 5) smaller standard deviations in the results. The exception was for $\eta = 0.07$.

5   Conclusions

In this paper we showed how to extend the previous existing single layer complex valued neural network to batch MSE training and batch MEE training. We present some experiments showing the validity of the proposals. It is interesting to see that in one of the experiments (Checkerboard), the CVNN improves substantially the results of other approaches. It would be important to try to understand what are the features of this dataset that make CVNNs so adequate to it, but this is beyond the scope of the present work. As future work, we would like to try to accelerate the MEE based algorithm, since it is quadratic in the number of data points. A possibility is the application of a mixed batch-sequential approach as in [15].

Acknowledgments. We acknowledge Prof. Marques de Sá for providing the datasets used in the experiments.

References

1. Hirose, A.: Complex-valued neural networks: The merits and their origins. In: Proceedings of the 2009 International Joint Conference on Neural Networks, pp. 1209–1216 (2009)
2. Mandic, D.P., Goh, V.S.L.: Complex valued nonlinear adaptive filters. John Wiley & Sons, Chichester (2009)
3. Amin, M., Murase, K.: Single-layered complex-valued neural network for real-valued classification problems. Neurocomputing 72, 945–955 (2009)
4. Savitha, R., Suresh, S., Sundararajan, N., Saratchandran, P.: A new learning algorithm with logarithmic performance index for complex-valued neural networks. Neurocomputing 72, 3771–3781 (2009)
5. Hirose, A.: Complex-Valued Neural Networks. Springer, Heidelberg (2006)
6. Haykin, S.: Neural Networks: A Comprehensive Foundation. MacMillan College Publishing Company, Inc., Basingstoke (1994)
7. Silva, L., Felgueiras, C., Alexandre, L., Marques de Sá, J.: Error entropy in classification problems: A univariate data analysis. Neural Computation **18**(9) (September 2006) 2036–2061
8. Silva, L.M., Marques de Sá, J., Alexandre, L.A.: The MEE principle in data classification: A perceptron-based analysis. Neural Computation 22(10), 2698–2728 (2010)
9. Alexandre, L., Marques de Sá, J.: Error Entropy Minimization for LSTM Training. In: Kollias, S.D., Stafylopatis, A., Duch, W., Oja, E. (eds.) ICANN 2006. LNCS, vol. 4131, pp. 244–253. Springer, Heidelberg (2006)
10. Alexandre, L.: Maximizing the zero-error density for RTRL. In: 8th IEEE International Symposium on Signal Processing and Information Technology - ISSPIT 2008. IEEE Press, Sarajevo (December 2008)
11. Erdogmus, D., Principe, J.: An error-entropy minimization algorithm for supervised training of nonlinear adaptive systems. IEEE Trans. Signal Processing 50(7), 1780–1786 (2002)
12. Santos, J., Alexandre, L., Marques de Sá, J.: The error entropy minimization algorithm for neural network classification. In: Lofti, A. (ed.) Proceedings of the 5th International Conference on Recent Advances in Soft Computing, Nottingham, United Kingdom, pp. 92–97 (December 2004)
13. Silva, J., Sá, J., Jossinet, J.: Classification of breast tissue by electrical impedance spectroscopy. Medical & Biological Engineering & Computing 38(1), 26–30 (2000)
14. Chang, C.C., Lin, C.J.: LIBSVM: a library for support vector machines (2001), Software, http://www.csie.ntu.edu.tw/~cjlin/libsvm
15. Santos, J., Marques de Sá, J., Alexandre, L.: Neural networks trained with the EEM algorithm: Tuning the smoothing parameter. In: 6th WSEAS Int. Conference on Neural Networks, Lisbon, Portugal, vol. 4, pp. 295–300 (June 2005)

Batch Intrinsic Plasticity
for Extreme Learning Machines

Klaus Neumann and Jochen J. Steil

Research Institute for Cognition and Robotics (CoR-Lab)
Bielefeld University, Universitätsstr. 25, 33615 Bielefeld
{kneumann,jsteil}@cor-lab.uni-bielefeld.de,
www.cor-lab.de

Abstract. Extreme learning machines are single-hidden layer feed-forward neural networks, where the training is restricted to the output weights in order to achieve fast learning with good performance. The success of learning strongly depends on the random parameter initialization. To overcome the problem of unsuited initialization ranges, a novel and efficient pretraining method to adapt extreme learning machines task-specific is presented. The pretraining aims at desired output distributions of the hidden neurons. It leads to better performance and less dependence on the size of the hidden layer.

Keywords: extreme learning machine, pretraining, neural network, learning, intrinsic plasticity, batch, regression.

1 Introduction

In [1], Huang proposes the extreme learning machine (ELM) which is an efficient learning algorithm based on random projections. Its task performance depends on the size of the hidden layer and the initialization ranges of the parameters. A good performance is usually achieved by manually tuning these parameters to a task-suitable regime.

Although, recently some improvements to the ELM have been developed, that are based on the idea to change the hidden layer size, an automatic and efficient task-specific optimization method for ELMs is still missing.

Feng presents a method which adds random neurons to the ELM - the error minimized extreme learning machine (EMELM) [2]. Whereas recomputation of the pseudo inverse is necessary, the computational time for solving the regression task is reduced to a minimum by using fast update rules derived in the original paper. Another idea to improve ELMs is to decrease the size of the hidden layer - the optimally pruned extreme learning machine (OPELM) [3]. The OPELM method starts with a large hidden layer and a ranking of the neurons. The learning results are improved by pruning the OPELM using a leave-one-out criterion. There is no need to specify the size of the hidden layer in advance without knowledge of the task complexity by using these methods. However, the

T. Honkela et al. (Eds.): ICANN 2011, Part I, LNCS 6791, pp. 339–346, 2011.

results still strongly depend on the random initialization - i.e. the biases and input weights. Methods controlling the network size are insufficient in tuning the neurons to a good regime, where the encoding is optimal.

It is shown in [4], that a biologically inspired online learning rule called intrinsic plasticity (IP) published by Triesch in [5] is able to enhance the encoding in recurrent neural networks. The output is forced by IP to produce exponential distributions. This maximizes the network's information transmission, caused by the high entropy of the distribution. Inspired by IP, we propose a novel method to pretrain ELMs, which also aims on achieving desired output distributions. In contrast to IP, the pretraining works in batch fashion by creating imaginary targets and will therefore be called batch intrinsic plasticity (BIP). The method adapts the hidden layer analytically by a pseudo inverse technique instead of performing a computationally expensive gradient-descent. This idea makes BIP highly efficient.

The following experiments show that the new method leads to better results for randomly initialized ELMs. In particular the generalization ability of the networks is improved significantly.

2   Extreme Learning Machine

The ELM consists of three different layers: $u \in \mathbb{R}^{I \times 1}$ collects the input, $h \in \mathbb{R}^{R \times 1}$ the hidden, and $\hat{y} \in \mathbb{R}^{O \times 1}$ the output neurons. The input is connected to the hidden layer through the input matrix $W^{\text{in}} \in \mathbb{R}^{R \times I}$, while the read-out matrix $W^{\text{out}} \in \mathbb{R}^{O \times R}$ contains the read-out weights. The ELM as it is proposed by Huang is created by randomly initializing the input matrix, the slopes a_i and the biases b_i $(i = 1, \ldots R)$ in the - typically sigmoid - activation function. Usually the slopes are set to one. When denoting the weights from the input layer to a specific hidden layer neuron i with $W_i^{\text{in}} \in \mathbb{R}^{1 \times I}$, the ELM scheme then becomes

$$\hat{y} = W^{\text{out}} h = W^{\text{out}} \left(\ldots, f\left(a_i W_i^{\text{in}} u + b_i \right), \ldots \right)^T . \tag{1}$$

2.1   Supervised Read-Out Learning by Ridge Regression

Supervised learning for ELMs is restricted to the read-out weights W^{out}. In order to infer a desired input-output mapping from a set of N_{tr} training samples $(u(k), y(k))$ with $k = 1 \ldots N_{\text{tr}}$, the read-out weights W^{out} are adapted such that the mean square error for the training set is minimized:

$$E = \frac{1}{N_{\text{tr}}} \sum_{k=1}^{N_{\text{tr}}} ||y(k) - \hat{y}(k)||^2 \to \min . \tag{2}$$

The paper focuses on batch training and uses a standard linear ridge regression method to control the size of the output weights. This is different to the approach in the original ELM paper where the pseudo inverse is used. The generalization ability of the networks is improved by that technique. The network's states

$h(k)$ belonging to the inputs $u(k)$ as well as the desired output targets $y(k)$ are collected in a state matrix $H = (h(1) \ldots h(N_{\mathrm{tr}}))^T \in \mathbb{R}^{N_{\mathrm{tr}} \times R}$ and a target matrix $Y = (y(1) \ldots y(N_{\mathrm{tr}}))^T \in \mathbb{R}^{N_{\mathrm{tr}} \times O}$. The optimal read-out weights are then determined by the least squares solution

$$(W^{\mathrm{out}})^T = \left(H^T H + \varepsilon \mathbf{1}\right)^{-1} H^T Y, \tag{3}$$

where the factor $\varepsilon \geq 0$ was identified by Tikhonov in [6] as output regularization strength.

2.2   Batch Intrinsic Plasticity

The task performance of an ELM strongly depends on the random initialization of the input matrix and the biases. Without expert-tuning by means of additional task knowledge, a random initialization can lead to the problem of saturated, almost linear or constant neurons. This can be avoided by finding activation functions which are in a favorable regime. Thus, we introduce a novel method to adapt activation functions such that certain output distributions are achieved. An invertible activation function and a random number generator which produces numbers drawn from the desired distribution are assumed.

Only the inputs $u = (u(1), u(2) \ldots u(N_{\mathrm{tr}})) \in \mathbb{R}^{I \times N_{\mathrm{tr}}}$ stimulating the network are used for optimization. The goal is to adapt slope a_i and bias b_i of the activation function such that the desired distribution f_{des} for the neuron's outputs $h_i(k) = f(a_i s_i(k) + b_i)$ is realized. The synaptic sum arriving at neuron i is given by $s_i(k) = W_i^{\mathrm{in}} u(k)$ and collected in $s_i = W_i^{\mathrm{in}} u$.

Therefore, a linear regression problem is formulated, where random targets $t = (t_1, t_2 \ldots t_{N_{\mathrm{tr}}})^T$ are drawn in ascending order $t_1 < \cdots < t_{N_{\mathrm{tr}}}$ from the desired output distribution. Since the stimuli need to be mapped onto the right targets, a rearrangement of the stimuli in ascending order $s_i(1) < \cdots < s_i(N_{\mathrm{tr}})$ is done by sorting $s_i \leftarrow \mathrm{sort}(s_i)$. This is necessary because a monotonically increasing activation function f is used to map all incoming training stimuli on the right targets and infer the desired distribution f_{des} for the neuron's output. The model $\Phi(s_i) = \left(s_i^T, (1 \ldots 1)^T\right)$ and the parameter vector $v_i = (a_i, b_i)^T$ are built to reduce the learning for the i-th neuron to a linear and over-determined regression problem, where the outputs are mapped onto the targets $h_i(k) \approx t_k$:

$$\|\Phi(s_i) \cdot v_i - f^{-1}(t)\| \to \min \ . \tag{4}$$

The solution for the optimal slope a_i and bias b_i is obtained by computation of the Moore-Penrose pseudo inverse [7]:

$$v_i = (a_i, b_i)^T = \Phi^\dagger(s_i) \cdot f^{-1}(t) \ . \tag{5}$$

Typically Fermi and tangens hyperbolicus functions are used as activation functions. The learning is done in one-shot fashion and summarized in Alg. 1.

The pretraining is of the same order of complexity than the supervised read-out learning, since only the least squares solutions of the linear model Φ have to

---

Algorithm 1. Batch intrinsic plasticity (BIP)

Require: get inputs $u = (u(1), u(2) \ldots u(N_{tr}))^T$
    for all hidden neurons i **do**
        get stimuli $s_i = W_i^{in} \cdot u$
        draw targets $t = (t_1, t_2 \ldots t_{N_{tr}})^T$ from desired distribution f_{des}
        sort targets $t \leftarrow \text{sort}(t)$ and stimuli $s_i \leftarrow \text{sort}(s_i)$
        build $\Phi(s_i) = (s_i^T, (1 \ldots 1)^T)$
        calculate (pseudo-)inverse $(a_i, b_i)^T = v_i = \Phi(s_i)^\dagger \cdot f^{-1}(t)$
    end for
    return $v = (v_1, v_2 \ldots v_R)^T$

---

be calculated. In the experiments, the pretraining and the supervised learning showed no significant difference in the computational time.

3   Results

In Sect. 3.1 the impact of BIP-learning is considered and single-neuron behavior is illustrated for different input and desired output distributions. Sect. 3.2 demonstrates the performance of the ELMs after pretraining on a robotics task. Sect. 3.3 shows that the performance is less dependent on the size of the hidden layer after pretraining the ELMs with BIP on the Abalone task from the UCI machine learning repository [8] and compares the method to other state of the art models.

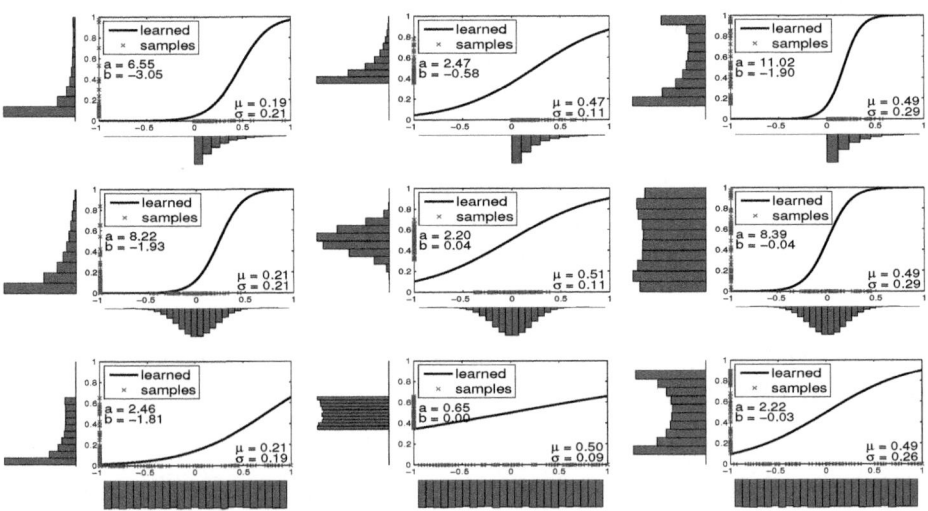

Fig. 1. A neuron's activation function adapted by BIP to approximate the output distributions f_{des} while starting from the input distributions f_s. The input distribution is varied over the rows, while the output distributions varies column-wise.

Table 1. Fits of output distributions. A cell contains mean and standard deviation of the χ^2-value, μ and σ.

$\chi^2/\mu/\sigma$	exp	norm	uni
exp	0.49±0.36	1.04±1.04	1.83±0.37
	0.18±0.02	0.49±0.01	0.46±0.04
	0.21±0.03	0.08±0.01	0.25±0.02
norm	0.08±0.06	0.05±0.04	0.27±0.11
	0.20±0.02	0.50±0.01	0.49±0.04
	0.19±0.02	0.09±0.01	0.29±0.01
uni	0.27±0.11	0.25±0.09	1.14±0.13
	0.19±0.02	0.49±0.01	0.49±0.03
	0.18±0.02	0.09±0.01	0.31±0.01

Table 2. Test errors on the robotics task. Comparison of randomly initialized and BIP-pretrained ELMs.

rnd	ld(ε)=-15	−12	−9
BIP			
R=50	.062±.003	.062±.003	.060±.002
	.062±.004	.063±.004	.059±.002
100	.094±.034	.093±.032	.077±.017
	.073±.014	.072±.013	.061±.002
150	.149±.076	.148±.076	.107±.042
	.073±.013	.073±.013	.062±.003
200	.229±.160	.227±.158	.153±.085
	.075±.015	.075±.015	.062±.003

3.1   Batch Intrinsic Plasticity and Single Neuron Behavior

To illustrate the behavior of the BIP-learning, a single-neuron model with different fixed input distributions f_s is considered. $N_{tr} = 50$ samples are used for training and $N_{te} = 1000$ samples are used for testing - both drawn from f_s.

Three different input and output distributions are taken into account: $f_{des} = f_s = $ exp(onential), norm(al), and uni(form). The moments of the distributions are: $\mu(\exp) = 0.2$, $\sigma(\exp) = 0.2$, $\mu(\text{norm}) = 0.5$, $\sigma(\text{norm}) = 0.1$, $\mu(\text{uni}) = 0.5$, and $\sigma(\text{uni}) = 0.3$.

Fig. 1 illustrates the result of adapting the neuron's nonlinear transfer function. The input distribution is assigned to the rows of the figure, while the desired output distribution is assigned column-wise. The incoming training stimuli are visualized by the crosses on the x-axis, while the corresponding targets are on the y-axis. The x-axis shows a histogram of the synthetically created test stimuli while the y-axis shows a histogram of the outputs produced by the learned activation function transforming the inputs. Especially when stimulated with Gaussian input, the neuron is able to achieve the three desired output distributions very accurately - illustrated by the second row in Fig. 1. It is demonstrated in the first column of Fig. 1 that the exponential distribution is approximated for all inputs. However, since the sigmoid activation function has only two degrees of freedom, the match is typically not perfect. The figure shows that large deviations from the optimal output distribution can sometimes be observed.

Further statistics are summarized in Tab. 1. The table shows a neuron which is trained by BIP for 100 trials. After each trial, the mean and the standard deviation of the output distribution are collected as well as the χ^2-value over 100 trials which determines the deviation of samples from the desired probability distribution. The χ^2-value is given by $\chi^2 = \sum_{i=1}^{\#bins} \frac{(O_i - E_i)^2}{E_i}$, where $\#bins = 20$ is the number of bins equidistantly distributed in the interval $[0, 1]$. E_i is the analytically given value of the integral in the i-th bin-range, and O_i is the observed value divided by the number of test samples $N_{te} = 1000$. The table

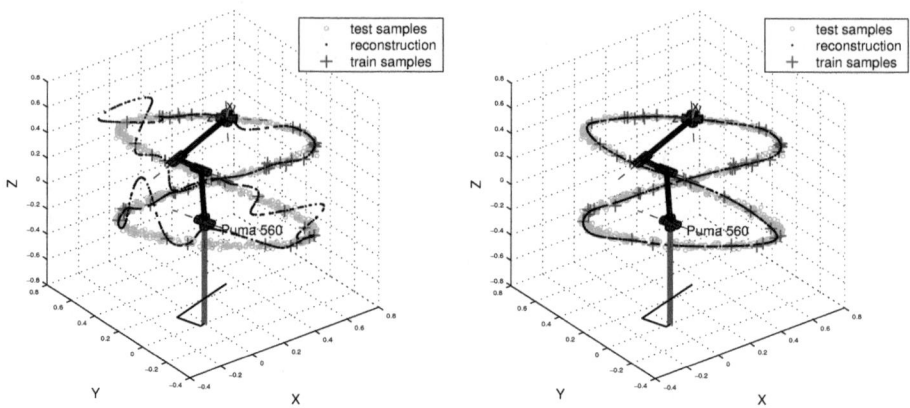

Fig. 2. Robotics task for ELMs with: $R = 150$ and $\varepsilon = 10^{-12}$. Left: performance of the randomly initialized ELM. Right: performance of the ELM which was first trained with the BIP method.

shows, that μ and σ of the output distribution are always approximated very well with low variance.

3.2 Robotics Regression Task

In the following two sections the experiments are described, where the networks' input matrix components W_{ij}^{in} and the biases b_i are drawn from a uniform distribution in the interval $[-10, 10]$ while the slopes a_i are set to unity. In the experiments, the Fermi-function $f(x) = 1/(1 + \exp(-x))$ is used as activation function and the desired output is the exponential distribution $f_{\text{des}} = f_{\text{exp}}$ with a fixed mean $\mu = 0.2$. It was already shown that this choice of desired output distribution can lead to an improvement of the generalization ability [4].

The network models are applied to learn the observed inverse kinematics mapping between joint and task space of a redundant six degrees-of-freedom (DOF) robot arm shown in Fig. 2. $N_{\text{tr}} = 100$ training samples are generated by projecting a task trajectory specified in Cartesian end-effector coordinates into the joint space of the robot arm by means of the analytically calculated inverse kinematics function $F : \mathbb{U} \rightarrow \mathbb{Y}$, where $\mathbb{U}$ is the task and $\mathbb{Y}$ the joint space. For each task space input $(u_1(k) \ldots u_6(k))^T$ containing the end-effector position and orientation the six-dim target vector $(y_1(k) \ldots y_6(k))^T$ is computed and additionally corrupted with Gaussian-noise ($\sigma_N = 0.1$). The generated trajectory forms an eight - see Fig. 2. The left plot images the learned inverse kinematics for a randomly initialized ELM, which apparently overfits the data. The right plot shows the result of the supervised learning for an ELM which was first trained with BIP. The learned part of the inverse kinematics is approximated very well.

Additionally, $N_{\text{te}} = 1000$ test samples are created to verify the generalization capability for different hidden layer sizes R and output regularization strengths ε. The results of the experiments are summarized in Tab. 2 and done for 10 different ELMs and 10 different data sets for each cell. The results show that the ELMs trained with BIP perform significantly better than the randomly initialized networks over the whole range of the parameters. Even ELMs with a big hidden layer and low output regularization (e.g. with $R = 200$, $\varepsilon = 10^{-15}$) do not tend to overfit the data after BIP-pretraining. Also the variance in the performance is much less after pretraining, a robust solution from the learning can be guaranteed.

3.3   Abalone Regression Task

In this section, the performance is tested on the well known Abalone task comprising $N_{tr} = 2000$ samples for training and $N_{te} = 2177$ for testing. The performance results of some popular optimization techniques (resource allocation network (RAN) [9], minimum resource allocation network (MRAN) [10], incremental extreme learning machine (IELM) [11], and error minimized extreme learning machine (EMELM) [2]) on the Abalone regression task quoted from [2] are given in Tab. 4. 20 BIP-pretrained ELMs are used with different hidden layer sizes R, the results are summarized in Tab. 3. The input was normalized to $[-1, 1]$ and the output to $[0, 1]$, the weights were drawn uniformly from $[-1, 1]$ and linear regression where used for supervised learning as it was done in Feng's work to make the results comparable. Since the mentioned models are focusing on incremental growth of the hidden layer, which is different to the BIP scheme, a direct comparison seems difficult. However, Tab. 3 shows that the ELMs of size $R = [40, 49]$ perform better in most of the cases than the other models without incrementally searching for good performing networks.

Table 3. Test-RMSEs on Abalone task

R	40	41	42	43	44
mean	.0748	.0754	.0749	**.0745**	.0756
std	.0005	.0014	.0012	**.0004**	.0020
R	45	46	47	48	49
mean	.0751	.0761	.0747	.0745	.0748
std	.0004	.0014	.0008	.0008	.0005

Table 4. Abalone results, [2]

model	EMELM	IELM
mean	**.0755**	.0920
std	**.0032**	.0046
model	RAN	MRAN
mean	.1183	.0906
std	.0076	.0065

4   Conclusion

This contribution introduces BIP, a novel and unsupervised scheme to pretrain ELMs. Since the algorithm works in batch fashion, it is independent of learning dynamics. It was shown that the new learning method produces the desired output distributions to some extend and leads to an improvement of the learning for randomly initialized ELMs by task-specific pretraining - no excessive expert-tuning is needed anymore. The method is efficient and can therefore be used to initialize the networks input weights and biases without detailed knowledge about the task. In addition, BIP is compared to other optimization techniques and show that it leads to better and stable results for a specific network size.

Only the desired distribution f_{des} and the inverse of the activation f^{-1} is needed for the method, which points out the high flexibility of the method. The generic formulation might be used to analyze the performance of the method with respect to other desired output distributions and activation functions. This will lead to different codes in the hidden layer and has a huge impact on the network's performance.

Most of the methods used for optimizing ELMs - like the ones mentioned - focus on the size of the hidden layer. BIP complements those methods and could - combined with other optimization methods - lead to even better learning results for ELMs.

References

1. Huang, G.-B., Zhu, Q.-Y., Siew, C.-K.: Extreme Learning Machine: A New Learning Scheme of Feedforward Neural Networks. In: International Joint Conference on Neural Networks (IJCNN 2004), Budapest, Hungary (July 2004)
2. Feng, G., Huang, G.-B., Lin, Q., Gay, R.: Error Minimized Extreme Learning Machine with Growth of Hidden Nodes and Incremental Learning. Trans. Neur. Netw. 20, 1352–1357 (2009)
3. Miche, Y., Sorjamaa, A., Bas, P., Simula, O., Jutten, C., Lendasse, A.: OP-ELM: Optimally Pruned Extreme Learning Machine. IEEE Transactions on Neural Networks 21(1), 158–162 (2010)
4. Steil, J.J.: Online Reservoir Adaptation by Intrinsic Plasticity for Backpropagation-Decorrelation and Echo State Learning. Neural Networks, Special Issue on Echo State and Liquid State Networks, 353–364 (2007)
5. Triesch, J.: Synergies beween Intrinsic and Synaptic Plasticity in Individual Model Neurons. In: NIPS (2005)
6. Tikhonov, A.N., Arsenin, V.Y.: Solutions of Ill-Posed Problems. Soviet Math. Dokl. (4), 1035–1038 (1963)
7. Penrose, R.: A Generalized Inverse for Matrices. Mathematical Proceedings of the Cambridge Philosophical Society, pp. 406–413 (1955)
8. Frank, A., Asuncion, A.: UCI machine learning repository (2010)
9. Platt, J.: Resource-Allocating Network for Function Interpolation. Neural Computation 3(2) (1991)
10. Yingwei, L., Sundararajan, N., Saratchandran, P.: A Sequential Learning Scheme for Function Approximation using Minimal Radial Basis Function Neural Networks. Neural Comput. 9, 461–478 (1997)
11. Huang, G.-B., Chen, L., Siew, C.-K.: Universal Approximation using Incremental Constructive Feedforward Networks with Random Hidden Nodes. IEEE Transactions on Neural Networks 17(4), 879–892 (2006)

An Empirical Study on the Performance of Spectral Manifold Learning Techniques

Peter Mysling, Søren Hauberg, and Kim Steenstrup Pedersen

The eScience Center,
Dept. of Computer Science, University of Copenhagen,
Universitetsparken 5, 2100 Copenhagen Ø, Denmark
{mysling,hauberg,kimstp}@diku.dk

Abstract. In recent years, there has been a surge of interest in spectral manifold learning techniques. Despite the interest, only little work has focused on the empirical behavior of these techniques. We construct synthetic data of variable complexity and observe the performance of the techniques as they are subjected to increasingly difficult problems. We evaluate performance in terms of both a classification and a regression task. Our study includes Isomap, LLE, Laplacian eigenmaps, and diffusion maps. Among others, our results indicate that the techniques are highly dependent on data density, sensitive to scaling, and greatly influenced by intrinsic dimensionality.

1 Introduction

In recent years, the development of techniques for nonlinear dimensionality reduction has generated much interest. Spectral manifold learning, in which the data is assumed to lie near an embedded manifold, has emerged as a particularly prominent approach. These techniques compute a low-dimensional representation based on the structure of the manifold, while also guaranteeing a globally optimal solution. During the last decade, a vast number of manifold learning techniques were proposed [1–7].

Surprisingly, only little work has focused on the empirical behavior and performance of these techniques. To our knowledge, only three such studies exist, namely (1) the work of Yeh et al. [8], in which LLE, Kernel PCA, and Isomap are compared in terms of a clustering task; (2) the work of Niskanen & Silven [9] in which five techniques are evaluated on several low-density data sets; and (3) the technical report of van der Maaten et al. [10] in which twelve techniques are compared on a range of both artificial and natural data sets. In the case of the two latter studies, performance is only evaluated in terms of neighborhood preservation. All previous studies only consider problems of fixed difficulty.

Our study deviates from the previous work in two critical ways. First of all, the techniques are evaluated in terms of both a local and a global measure of structure preservation. Secondly, and more importantly, we construct data sets in which the complexity can be controlled by a single parameter, allowing us to study the performance as a function of the problem difficulty. By systematically

T. Honkela et al. (Eds.): ICANN 2011, Part I, LNCS 6791, pp. 347–354, 2011.

applying this scheme to several types of complexity, we are able to identify scenarios under which the techniques break down. Moreover, we are able to highlight strengths and weaknesses, not only of each technique individually, but also of the methods in general. Furthermore, we believe that, by visualizing the performance as a function of the data complexity, we give an intuitive understanding of characteristic behavior not found in previous studies.

We have designed 5 data set variants, each of which can be scaled in complexity, in terms of a certain data property. The suite contains data sets in which (1) the density can be varied, (2) the amount of noise can be varied, (3) the embedded manifold contains a hole of variable size, (4) the scaling can be varied, (5) the intrinsic dimensionality can be varied. All data sets are modifications of the classical swiss roll [2], which has traditionally been applied in qualitative evaluation of manifold learning techniques. Our data sets are synthetic, because natural data sets would have an unknown or at least poorly estimated manifold structure, which would render our study impossible. We have confined our analysis to four canonical manifold learning techniques, namely Isomap [2], LLE [1], Laplacian eigenmaps [3], and diffusion maps [7]. In order to evaluate the discovered embeddings, we construct quality measures based on two common supervised learning tasks—classification and regression. The quality measure based on regression is sensitive to global deformations in data structure and, to our knowledge, this measure is novel in the analysis of manifold learning techniques.

2   Techniques

In the following, we provide a brief review of the applied manifold learning techniques. Due to space constraints, we refer to the original papers for details.

The manifold learning problem is stated as follows. Let $\{\mathbf{x}_i \in \mathbb{R}^D : i \in 1, \ldots, n\}$ be a collection of data points lying near a possibly nonlinear d-dimensional manifold. The aim is to determine a low-dimensional representation in the form of a mapping $\mathbf{x}_i \in \mathbb{R}^D \mapsto \mathbf{y}_i \in \mathbb{R}^d$ which preserves the structure of the embedded manifold. We let $\mathbf{X}$ and $\mathbf{Y}$ denote corresponding design matrices.

The evaluated techniques represent each data point as a node in a similarity graph G. The graph is constructed in one of three ways: i) by an ϵ-neighborhood approach, in which each point is connected to all points within a ball of radius ϵ; ii) by connecting each point to its k nearest neighbors; iii) by similarity weighting, in which G is a fully connected, weighted graph and weights are assigned according to a Gaussian function of width σ^2.

All techniques compute a low-dimensional representation which retains some measure of the data structure, based on the similarity graph. The optimization amounts to an eigendecomposition of a matrix which is quadratic in the number of data examples.

Isomap [2] estimates the pair-wise geodesic distances by the shortest paths distances in G. The low-dimensional representation is chosen such that the geodesic distances are retained. LLE [1] characterizes the local data structure using linear models and uncovers an embedding which can be described by the same model. Laplacian eigenmaps [3] compute a low-dimensional embedding in which neighboring nodes are proximate, under the weighting of a Gaussian kernel of width σ^2. Diffusion maps [7] apply similarity weighting and treats the distances between data points as transition probabilities in a Markov chain. The similarity between data points is estimated by simulating a Markov random walk between the nodes for t time steps.

3 Synthetic Data Sets

In this study, we construct data sets which vary in complexity as a function of a single argument, which we will refer to as the *data* argument. We evaluate the selected techniques by applying them to data sets of increasing complexity. All constructed data sets are modifications of the traditional swiss roll [2]. The swiss roll data set is a natural basis for several reasons: 1) it is visualizable; 2) it has a simple shape which cannot be modeled by PCA; 3) the chosen techniques are known to perform well on this data set.

A synthetic data set $\mathbf{X}$ is constructed by a mapping $f : \mathbb{R}^d \to \mathbb{R}^D$ of n data points $\{\hat{\mathbf{y}}_i \in \mathbb{R}^d : i = 1, \ldots, n\}$, where $\hat{\mathbf{y}}_i = [\hat{y}_{i,1}, \ldots, \hat{y}_{i,d}]^T$. $\hat{y}_{i,j}$ is sampled from a uniform distribution with finite support $[c_j^{min}, c_j^{max}]$. We refer to these points as the *true* embedding. Letting $\hat{y}_{i,1} \in \left[\frac{3\pi}{2}, \frac{9\pi}{2}\right]$ and $\hat{y}_{i,2} \in [0, 100]$, each data point of the embedded swiss roll is calculated by

$$\mathbf{x}_i = f(\hat{\mathbf{y}}_i) = [\hat{y}_{i,1}\cos(\hat{y}_{i,1}),\ \hat{y}_{i,2},\ \hat{y}_{i,1}\sin(\hat{y}_{i,1})]^T.$$

Below we motivate and describe the five data set variants. We provide visualizations when the structure of the data set is nontrivial.

Density: Machine learning data sets are often of low density and it is unknown how severely this affects the discovered embeddings. We construct data sets which vary in density by varying n, the number of data points.

Noise: Natural data often exhibit irregular structure and contains noisy measurements. We model this by adding Gaussian noise sampled from $\mathcal{N}(0, \sigma^2)$ to

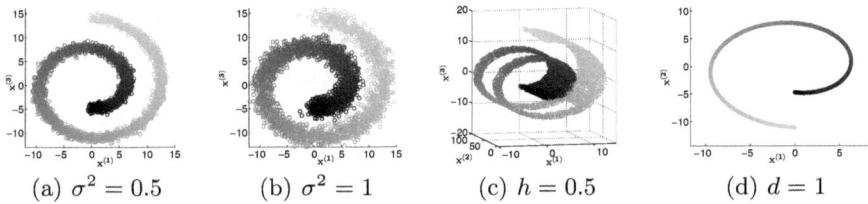

(a) $\sigma^2 = 0.5$ (b) $\sigma^2 = 1$ (c) $h = 0.5$ (d) $d = 1$

Fig. 1. Visualizations of a selection of the applied data sets. (a) 2-dimensional visualization of the noise data set for $\sigma^2 = 0.5$. (b) 2-dimensional visualization of the noise data set for $\sigma^2 = 1$. (c) Visualization of the hole data set for $h = 0.5$ (50%). (d) Visualization of the intrinsic dimensionality data set for $d = 1$.

each component of the swiss roll data points $\mathbf{x}_i$. Realizations of this data are visualized in Fig. 1(a) and 1(b).

Hole: Some concern has been expressed regarding the inability of Isomap to model nonconvex manifolds [5]. Motivated by this, we apply the techniques to data where the manifold has a hole. A manifold which contains a square hole, centered in the true embedding and spanning h percent of each true embedding axis, is constructed by rejecting all samples within the hole. Fig. 1(c) shows a realization of this data.

Scaling: Natural data is often a product of a number of measurements; these measurements are frequently not directly comparable and must be rescaled appropriately for analysis. We investigate the sensitivity of the techniques with respect to scaling. Rescalings of the swiss roll data set are constructed by rotating the manifold 45 degrees around each coordinate axis and scaling the first component of the resulting data points by a factor of s.

Intrinsic dimensionality: We investigate the performance of the techniques when subjected to data of variable intrinsic dimensionality. A data set containing one intrinsic dimension is defined to be the 2-dimensional swiss roll. Each additional intrinsic dimension is simply added by including a linear component sampled from $U(0, 100)$. Note that, under this simple scheme, the empirical performance of the techniques degenerate to that of PCA when $d = 3$ and higher. Because of this, we simplify the swiss roll by only sampling $\hat{y}_{i,1}$ from $U\left(\frac{3\pi}{2}, \frac{7\pi}{2}\right)$. A visualization of this is given in Fig. 1(d).

4   Quality Measures

Motivated by the applicability of spectral manifold learning techniques to data analysis, we evaluate the embeddings discovered by these techniques in terms of two common supervised learning tasks—classification and regression. Under this scheme, we associate to each data point $\mathbf{y}_i$ a target value t_i based on its position in the true embedding. In the classification setting, where $t_i^{clas} \in \{0, 1\}$, target values are assigned in a checkerboard pattern. In the regression setting we have $t_i^{reg} \in \mathbb{R}$ and target values are assigned linearly along the first coordinate axis in the true embedding, i.e. $t_i^{reg} = \hat{y}_{i,1}$. Visualizations are given in Fig. 2.

In principle, any classification technique can be applied in the classification setting. In this study, we employ a Nearest Neighbour (NN) classifier for simplicity. Letting p_i^{clas} denote the NN prediction of t_i^{clas} under leave-one-out cross-validation, we define the quality Q_{clas} of $\mathbf{Y}$ as the misclassification rate [10, 9]. The classification measure determines how well the local structure is preserved in the discovered embeddings.

Since the target values were chosen as a linear component in the true embedding, it is reasonable to expect that they can approximately be reconstructed linearly in the embedded coordinate system. Thus, we define the quality Q_{reg} of the embedding $\mathbf{Y}$ wrt. the data $\mathbf{X}$ as the root mean squared error

$$Q_{reg} = \sqrt{n^{-1} \sum_{i=1}^{n} (p_i^{reg} - t_i^{reg})^2},$$

where p_i^{reg} is the predicted target value under a linear least squares regression model using leave-one-out cross-validation. The regression measure responds to deformations in both global and local data structure. To our knowledge, this measure is novel.

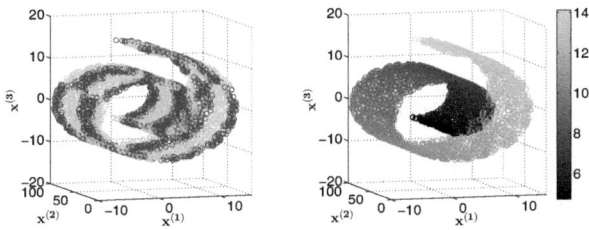

Fig. 2. Target value assignment in the classification and regression settings. Color denotes target value. Left: Classification setting. Right: Regression setting.

5 Experimental Results

Each technique has a number of parameters which must be fixed. We estimate the optimal parameters in a practical manner, by exhaustively searching a fixed range of viable parameters, and retaining the parameters which maximize quality measures. For Isomap, LLE, and Laplacian eigenmaps, k is varied in $k \in \{4, \ldots, 20\}$. For diffusion maps, the parameters are varied in $t \in \{1, 2, 3, 5, 10, 15, 25\}$ and $\sigma^2 \in \{0.75, 1, 2, 3, 5\}$. Note that we avoid fixing the σ^2 parameter of Laplacian eigenmaps by letting $\sigma^2 \to \infty$, as proposed by Belkin & Niyogi [3].

Having fixed the parameters for each data set, we estimate the mean performance over a series of 10 trials; each trial uses a new realization of the data set. The results are plotted along with the standard error. We report the performance of PCA as a baseline measure. Except for the density experiment, each data set is constructed with a density of 3500 data points. We remind the reader that, for both quality measures, a lower score is indicative of better performance.

The experimental results are given in Fig. 3–7. For clarity, the markers have been slighty displaced. Before inspecting each experiment in turn, we make two general observations. First, we note that the two quality measures are highly correlated; when the measures disagree, it is an indication that a global deformation of the embedded manifold has occurred. Secondly, we observe that LLE tends to perform less stable than the remaining techniques, especially in the regression setting. We do, however, not believe that this is an effect of attempting

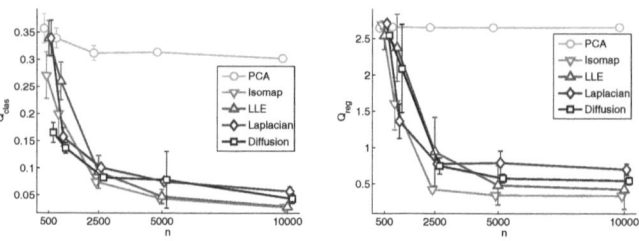

Fig. 3. Results of the density experiment. Left: Classification measure. Right: Regression measure.

to uncover global manifold structure from models of local geometry; our results show that Laplacian eigenmaps is capable of this with considerable stability. Rather, we speculate that this is a weakness of modeling the local geometry by reconstruction weights.

Density (Fig. 3): We make two key observations. First, the performance of the techniques does not converge until $n \geq 2500$; note that this is a fairly densely sampled manifold. Additionally, we observe that diffusion maps, in the low-density cases, outperform the remaining techniques with significant stability, according to the classification measure. Since this is not the case in the regression setting, we conclude that only the local manifold structure is preserved.

Noise (Fig. 4): We note that the performance of the techniques deteriorates as the noise is increased beyond $\sigma^2 = 0.5$. Surprisingly, the sensitivity of Isomap with respect to short-circuiting does not result in more rapid deterioration than the remaining techniques. Diffusion maps and Laplacian eigenmaps tend to be especially robust when subjected to low noise data. We also observe that diffusion maps are capable of preserving the local structure, even noise levels increase.

Hole (Fig. 5): We observe that holes on the manifold, regardless of the size, does not significantly affect the performance of the applied techniques. Note that this is not necessarily an indication that the applied techniques accurately determine the structure of the true embedding, but rather that the discovered embeddings are satisfactory in terms of the classification and regression tasks.

Scaling (Fig. 6): We observe that, generally, the techniques more easily reconstruct an embedding which is satisfactory in terms of the classification measure than the regression measure. Again, this gives an indication that the local structure is more easily retained than the global structure. Additionally, we observe that the techniques struggle to recover the global manifold structure when the data is scaled beyond $s \in [0.5; 2]$. This effect is most pronounced for LLE, Laplacian eigenmaps, and diffusion maps.

Intrinsic Dimensionality (Fig. 7): We observe that the performance of the techniques begins to deteriorate when $d > 3$ and that the techniques do not have a significant advantage over PCA when $d > 4$.

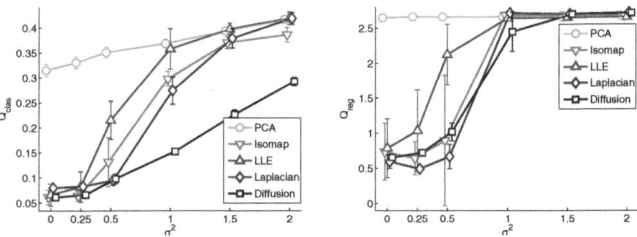

Fig. 4. Results of the noise experiment. Left: Classification measure. Right: Regression measure.

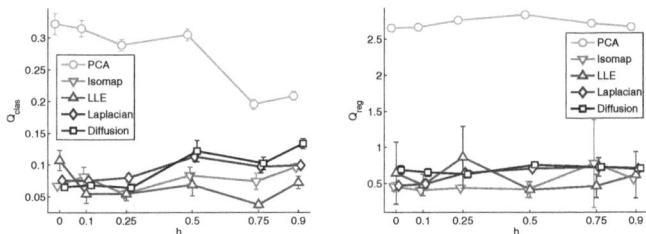

Fig. 5. Results of the hole experiment. Left: Classification measure. Right: Regression measure.

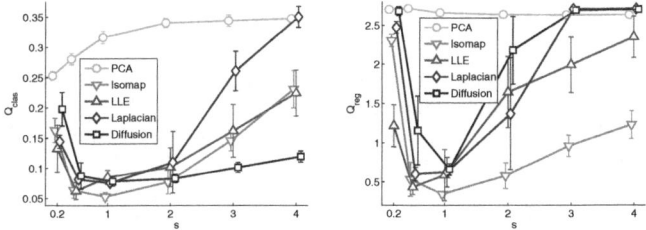

Fig. 6. Results of the scaling experiment. Left: Classification measure. Right: Regression measure.

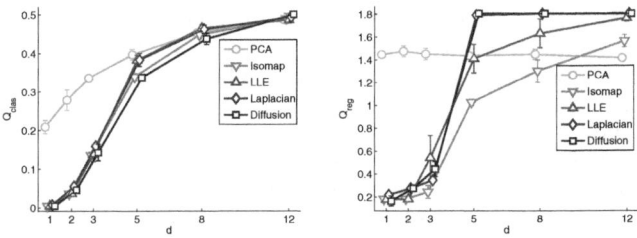

Fig. 7. Results of the intrinsic dimensionality experiment. Left: Classification measure. Right: Regression measure.

6   Discussion

In summary, our experiments indicate that the evaluated techniques are 1) highly dependent on data density, 2) invariant to holes on the manifold with respect to the classification and regression tasks, 3) sensitive to scaling, and 4) highly dependent on intrinsic dimensionality. Clearly, 1) and 4) are tightly related.

Although it is expected that high intrinsic dimensionality and low data density have a negative impact on the discovered embeddings, the severity of these effects is nevertheless surprising. As limited amounts of data is the rule rather than the exception, we consider this a severe problem. Note that these techniques require quadratic memory in the amount of data examples, making problems of more than 10.000 examples virtually infeasible on modern computers.

The experiments showed that the methods were sensitive to scaling of the original data. This is a problem of practical concern as it questions the use of e.g. whitening as a pre-processing step. Such pre-processing does not take the manifold structure into account, which is why we see performance drops when data is scaled.

We believe that our study provides four important contributions to the community: 1) we have presented a novel quality measure which is sensitive to global deformations in data structure; 2) we exemplify how to view performance as a function of complexity; 3) we facilitate an intuitive understanding of manifold learning performance; 4) our study can help practitioners evaluate whether spectral manifold learning is applicable for a certain data set.

References

1. Roweis, S., Saul, L.: Nonlinear Dimensionality Reduction by Locally Linear Embedding. Science 290, 2323–2326 (2000)
2. Tenenbaum, J., de Silva, V., Langford, J.: A Global Geometric Framework for Nonlinear Dimensionality Reduction. Science 290, 2319–2323 (2000)
3. Belkin, M., Niyogi, P.: Laplacian Eigenmaps for Dimensionality Reduction and Data Representation. Neural Computation 15, 1373–1396 (2003)
4. Brand, M.: Charting a Manifold. In: NIPS, vol. 15, pp. 977–984. IEEE Press, Los Alamitos (2003)
5. Donoho, D.L., Grimes, C.: Hessian Eigenmaps: Locally Linear Embedding Techniques for High-dimensional Data. In: PNAS, vol. 100, pp. 5591–5596. National Academy Sciences, Washington (2003)
6. Zhang, Z., Zha, H.: Principal Manifolds and Nonlinear Dimensionality Reduction via Tangent Space Alignment. SIAM J. Sci. Comput. 26, 313–338 (2004)
7. Coifman, R.R., Lafon, S.: Diffusion Maps. Applied and Computational Harmonics Analysis 21, 5–30 (2006)
8. Yeh, M.C., Lee, I.H., Wu, G., Wu, Y., Chang, E.Y.: Manifold Learning, a Promised Land or Work in Progress. In: Proc. of IEEE Intl. Conf. on Multimedia and Expo, pp. 1154–1157. IEEE Press, New York (2005)
9. Niskanen, M., Silven, O.: Comparison of Dimensionality Reduction Methods for Wood Surface Inspection. In: Proc. of the 6th Intl. Conference on Quality Control by Artificial Vision, pp. 179–188 (2003)
10. van der Maaten, L., Postma, E.O., van den Herik, H.J.: Dimensionality Reduction: A Comparative Review. Technical report, Tilburg Uni (2009)

Semi-supervised Learning for WLAN Positioning

Teemu Pulkkinen, Teemu Roos, and Petri Myllymäki

Helsinki Institute for Information Technology HIIT
PO Box 68, FI-00014 University of Helsinki, Finland
{firstname.lastname}@cs.helsinki.fi

Abstract. Currently the most accurate WLAN positioning systems are based on the fingerprinting approach, where a "radio map" is constructed by modeling how the signal strength measurements vary according to the location. However, collecting a sufficient amount of location-tagged training data is a rather tedious and time consuming task, especially in indoor scenarios — the main application area of WLAN positioning — where GPS coverage is unavailable. To alleviate this problem, we present a semi-supervised manifold learning technique for building accurate radio maps from partially labeled data, where only a small portion of the signal strength measurements need to be tagged with the corresponding coordinates. The basic idea is to construct a non-linear projection that maps high-dimensional signal fingerprints onto a two-dimensional manifold, thereby dramatically reducing the need of location-tagged data. Our results from a deployment in a real-world experiment demonstrate the practical utility of the method.

Keywords: non-linear projection, manifold learning, wlan positioning, Isomap.

1 Introduction

The need for special-purpose positioning systems for indoor use arises from the failure of established technologies, such as GPS, to properly locate and track objects in an indoor environment [8]. GPS signals tend to be weak when blocked by building walls, and even when a position is triangulated the accuracy is not sufficient for indoor use [4]. Several systems have been proposed that rely on the localized object carrying some kind of transceiver (RFID) [9] or infrared sensors built into the environment [14].

Recently, the interest in positioning based on wireless local area networks (WLANs), in particular, has grown significantly. This can be attributed to their wide use and distribution as well as the open standard which allows for requesting of signal strength information without separate authentication. WLAN-based systems have come a long way since the pioneering work of Bahl and Padmanabhan, who applied a nearest neighbor method on fingerprints composed of received signal strength indicator (RSSI) values [1]. Many of the most successful methods currently used in the field are probabilistic in nature ([6],[17], [23]). For a survey

T. Honkela et al. (Eds.): ICANN 2011, Part I, LNCS 6791, pp. 355–362, 2011.

on indoor positioning techniques, see [8]; for recent work, we refer the reader
to [12],[22],[25].

Though WLAN fingerprinting approaches have achieved relatively good accuracy, and have found their way into some commercial services (e.g. [5]), the
majority of location-based services are still based on GPS and other technologies [15]. One of the reasons to this is probably the manual effort required in
calibrating fingerprinting-based methods: before the system can be used, fingerprints need to be recorded everywhere in the deployment area. Since the radio
map created through this effort needs to be tied to real-world coordinates, it
is also necessary to record the location of every fingerprint. This invariably requires human presence or other external location information (e.g., GPS, camera
arrays) for the entirety of the calibration process.

We present a method for WLAN positioning wherein the fingerprinting approach is augmented with non-linear dimension reduction techniques. The main
idea is to learn a low-dimensional, non-linear manifold that can represent the radio map, enabling better statistical modeling of the signal properties in complex
multi-path environments. Once the manifold is constructed, we further propose
a very simple method for mapping observation points attached to the manifold
into geographical coordinates. Our approach is semi-supervised as the manifold
learning phase is based on observing plain RSSI vectors without their geographical coordinates. A small sample of *key points* whose location is recorded are
needed only to fix the mapping from the coordinate system of the manifold to
geographical coordinates.

Earlier related work has focused on localization in sensor-networks. In the
sensor-network localization problem a large set of sensor nodes communicate
with other nodes in their proximity: Shang et al. [19] use the Isomap algorithm [21], and Patwari and Hero [13] use Laplacian eigenmaps to process binary connectivity data from each of the sensor nodes. Pan et al. [10,11] apply
Laplacian regularized least squares regression [2], without explicitly constructing
a low-dimensional manifold; the drawback of this method is that the outcome is
highly sensitive to the choice of the parameters controlling the regularization [24].

The rest of this paper is organized as follows. In Section 2, we lay out the
basic concepts in semi-supervised learning, and in particular, manifold learning,
including the specific non-linear approach (Isomap) used in this paper. In Section
3, we present the empirical framework and the details of the testing environment.
Conclusions are summarized in Section 4.

2   The Semi-supervised Approach

Manifold learning methods attempt to find the defining features of a high-
dimensional data set by reducing the dimensions (number of features) of the data
to a more manageable level, usually two or three. The underlying assumption
is that most of the variability in the data is concentrated on a low-dimensional
(possibly non-linear) manifold embedded in the high-dimensional space. In our
case, this is natural assuming that the signal characteristics are determined by

the location of the receiver, and that the dependency is smooth. If the possible locations are constrained to a flat two-dimensional surface, the resulting manifold is then two-dimensional as well. The crux of this approach is maintaining the pairwise distances between the fingerprints, at least locally, when they are mapped from the high-dimensional signal space to the low-dimensional manifold.

2.1 Isomap

One of the established manifold learning methods is the Isomap algorithm [21]. Isomap is based on the same principle as multidimensional scaling (MDS) in that, given a dissimilarity matrix, it tries to find a lower dimensional representation of the data such that the pairwise distances between the points are distorted as little as possible. One way to cast this as an optimization problem is to minimize the sum of squared deviations between the actual distances $d_X(i,j)$, and the distances in the new representation $d_Y(i,j)$:

$$\min_Y \sum_{i=1}^{t} \sum_{i=1}^{t} (d_X(i,j) - d_Y(i,j))^2, \tag{1}$$

If the original distances, $d_X(i,j)$, are Euclidean, MDS reduces to principal component analysis (PCA) [3]. Due to space limitations, we omit further details and refer the interested reader to [7].

Given a set of m-dimensional column vectors $X = (\mathbf{x}'_1, \ldots, \mathbf{x}'_n)$, we denote by $D = [d_X(i,j)]$ the matrix defined by their Euclidean distances. Further, we define $B = HDH$, where H is the symmetric centering matrix $H = I_n - \frac{1}{n}\mathbf{1}\mathbf{1}^T$, where $\mathbf{1}$ denotes the all-ones column matrix, and $\mathbf{1}^T$ its transpose. This implies that both the vector and column sums of B are null. Letting $B = V\Lambda V^T$, where Λ is a diagonal matrix, be the eigendecomposition of B, we obtain the eigenvectors as the columns of V, and the eigenvalues as the diagonal elements of Λ. The reconstruction obtained by using the $l \geq 1$ largest eigenvalues, $Y = V_p \Lambda_p^{\frac{1}{2}}$ is optimal in the sense of Eq. (1). An important observation is that if we replace the Euclidean distances $d_X(i,j)$ by arbitrary dissimilarity values, which may or may not satisfy the properties of a valid distance metric, a solution can still be obtained by setting all negative eigenvalues (if any) to zero.

In the Isomap algorithm, the distances $d_X(i,j)$ are obtained by constructing a neighborhood graph where each point $\mathbf{x}_i$ is connected to its K nearest neighbors (in Euclidean distance). The length of an edge connecting two points is defined as their distance, and the distance $d_X(i,j)$ between two points (that need not be neighbors) is then calculated as the sum of edge lengths along the shortest path connecting them. Applying the MDS algorithm as outlined above to the resulting distance matrix, yields a low-dimensional representation where the pairwise distances approximate path lengths along the neighborhood graph.

2.2 Manifold-Based Radio Map Learning

We now describe the application of Isomap in WLAN-based positioning. Consider a sample $S = (\mathbf{s}'_1, \ldots, \mathbf{s}'_n)$ of *fingerprints*, each of which is represented as a vector $\mathbf{s}_i = (s_{i1}, \ldots, s_{ip})$ of RSSI values. The length of the vector, p, is defined as the number of access points (APs) in the WLAN network. The distance matrix X is then given by the Euclidean distance between the fingerprint vectors, $d_X(i, j) = \|\mathbf{s}_i - \mathbf{s}_j\|_2$. One of the practical problems that need to be solved is treating the occasionally unobserved RSSI values that show up as missing entries in the fingerprint vectors. Since the unobserved values are usually caused by too weak received signal, one reasonable solution is to replace all missing values by a small dummy value. In practice, we found that missing values typically result when the signal power drops below -100 dBm, and hence, we replaced all missing values by the constant -100 dBm, see [10,17].

Another technical detail, albeit one that has a dramatic effect on the quality of the radio map produced by Isomap, is the choice of the neighborhood size, K. There is no universally good value, as appropriate values are determined by the variance of the observations perpendicular to the manifold relative to its curvature, and the sparseness of the available data [18,20]. For too small a neighborhood, the neighborhood graph will not properly capture the geodesic distances on the manifold. Too large a neighborhood, on the other hand, risks creating "short circuits" that distort the topological properties of the manifold and make the algorithm unstable.

We propose to solve the neighborhood selection problem by exploiting additional information available in a set of fingerprints that are labelled by their geographical coordinates, which we call the *key points*. The method we propose below depends on being able to map points on the manifold onto a geographical coordinate system; we first describe a method for doing this.

2.3   Calibrating the Manifold to Geographical Coordinates

While the manifold learned by Isomap will reflect the topological structure of the area from which the data was collected, see Fig. 1a, it will usually not correctly match its metric properties such as lengths, angles, and curvature, which makes it unsuitable for positioning. This is corrected in what we call the *calibration* phase. We have found that the following very straightforward method is effective.

Assume that we have access to the precise location of n_{key} fingerprints, which we can without loss of generality assume to be the first n_{key} out of the total sample size of n. We denote the geographical coordinates of these *key points* by $(g_i^{(x)}, g_i^{(y)})_{1 \leq i \leq n_{key}}$. Denoting the manifold coordinates of the fingerprints by $(m_i^{(x)}, m_i^{(y)})_{1 \leq i \leq n}$, we map the manifold coordinates to geographical coordinates via

$$
\begin{aligned}
g_i^{(x)} &= \boldsymbol{\beta}_x \tilde{\mathbf{m}}_i' + \epsilon_i^{(x)} \\
g_i^{(y)} &= \boldsymbol{\beta}_y \tilde{\mathbf{m}}_i' + \epsilon_i^{(y)},
\end{aligned}
\tag{2}
$$

where $\boldsymbol{\beta}_x$ and $\boldsymbol{\beta}_y$ are both parameter vectors of length five, and

$$
\tilde{\mathbf{m}}_i = (1, m_i^{(x)}, (m_i^{(x)})^2, m_i^{(y)}, (m_i^{(y)})^2),
\tag{3}
$$

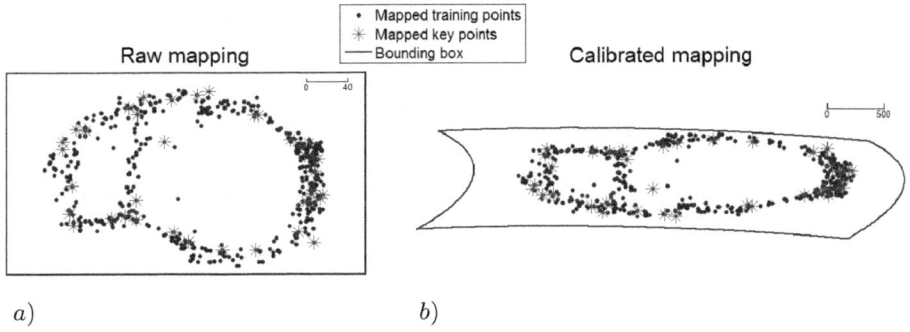

Fig. 1. *a*) Manifold discovered by Isomap with the fingerprints on it, and *b*) the same manifold calibrated with geographical coordinates of a subset of key points (fingerprints marked with red stars)

are the regressor variables where we include the constant (intercept) term, both the manifold coordinates, as well as their squares. Note that the labeling of the manifold coordinates as x and y has no significance. The parameters β_x and β_y can be estimated by the standard least squares technique to minimize the sum of squares of the respective errors $\epsilon_i^{(x)}$ and $\epsilon_i^{(y)}$ for the key points $1 \leq i \leq n_{key}$. This provides an efficient way to map any point on the manifold, expressed as $(m^{(x)}, m^{(y)})$ onto the corresponding geographical coordinates $(g^{(x)}, g^{(y)})$.

Figure 1 illustrates the process. The fact that the squares of the manifold coordinates are involved in Eq. (3) allows non-linear (namely quadratic) mappings, which is important since there is no guarantee that the correspondence between the learned manifold and the actual locations is linear. The non-linearity of the fit is clearly visible in the distortion of the bounding box in Fig. 1b. If a more generous set of key points is available, it may be useful to consider even more flexible mappings such as nonparametric regression, see [16].

Finally, we can use the error in the calibration mapping (2) to adjust the Isomap neighborhood size, K. We do this by trying different values between one and the total number of fingerprints (minus one), and choosing the one that leads to the mapping with the smallest error between the embedded key points and their actual (known) geographical coordinates:

$$\frac{1}{n_{key}} \sum_{i=1}^{n_{key}} \left((g_i^{(x)} - \hat{\beta}_x \tilde{\mathbf{m}}_i')^2 + (g_i^{(y)} - \hat{\beta}_y \tilde{\mathbf{m}}_i')^2 \right).$$

2.4   Positioning

Positioning new fingerprints is relatively straightforward once the manifold has been learned and calibrated with the key points. There are various ways to map new fingerprints onto the manifold, and thence to geographic coordinates. We choose to use the *k-nearest neighbors* method, selecting the k nearest fingerprints

Fig. 2. Plot of embedded fingerprints

(not necessarily any of the key points), and then letting the manifold coordinates of the new fingerprint be given by the average of the coordinates of the selected k fingerprints. The latter are directly obtained from Isomap output. The resulting manifold coordinates are then mapped to geographical coordinates, providing the position estimate, by Eq. (2). A comparison of alternative positioning methods in combination with manifold approaches is an interesting topic for future work.

3   Deployment and Results

We deployed the system in a real-world office building at the Department of Computer Science, University of Helsinki. The deployment area covered hall-ways and an adjoining open space used as a meeting space. The total area of the environment was about 24 m × 7 m. The data recording, processing, and most positioning tests were performed with a Samsung NC10 Netbook, running Ubuntu Linux 9.10, equipped with an Atheros AR5007EG Wireless network adapter, complying to the 802.11b/g standard. The total number of fingerprints used for learning and calibrating the manifold was $n = 437$, of which $n_{key} = 38$ were used as key points. We reserved an additional $n_{test} = 66$ points for testing purposes.

The Isomap neighborhood size that was found to minimize the error in map-ping the key points was 15. This left the average error of 1.9 m. Among the 66 test fingerprints collected separately, the mean positioning error was 2.0 m, and the median error was 1.5 m. Plotting the calibrated points onto the floor plan, we can clearly see the shape of the hallway in the mass of points, see Fig. 2. A majority of the points mapped to the hallway respect the infrastructure. It is clear that the hallways insulate the WLAN signal and create unique signatures. The mapping of fingerprints in the open space was not as distinct, however. This was most likely caused by the lack of attenuating infrastructure, making it hard to distinguish between the fingerprints from different ends of the space.

We have also carried out experiments in other environments with somewhat varying results; details are omitted due to space restrictions. Future research will benefit from an investigation of the factors most affecting the outcome.

4   Conclusion

We presented a WLAN positioning approach where high-dimensional signal fingerprints are represented as points on a two-dimensional manifold. For the manifold learning phase, we used the Isomap algorithm. Our contributions include a straightforward method for mapping points on the Isomap manifold to a geographical coordinate system by taking advantage of a relatively small subset of the fingerprints whose precise location is known. This also allowed us to choose the neighborhood size, a central (and only) parameter in Isomap, in a principled way by minimizing the error in the resulting coordinate mapping.

The main benefits of our method are: more robust estimation of the RSSI variability due to the lower dimensionality of the estimated model, and even more importantly, reduction in the effort required to collect measurement data. The latter feature boosts the cost-effectiveness of the fingerprinting approach both in terms of initial set-up as well as maintenance, which may finally enable WLAN-based indoor positioning to become the method of choice for future location-based services. Exploring the exact tradeoff between the number of labelled examples (and thus the deployment cost), and accuracy is a most urgent topic for investigation, which, however, is beyond the scope of this paper.

Acknowledgments. This work was supported in part by the European Commission under the PASCAL Network of Excellence.

References

1. Bahl, P., Padmanabhan, V.N.: RADAR: An In-building RF-based User Location and Tracking system. In: 19th Conference of IEEE Computer and Communications Societies, pp. 775–784. IEEE Computer Society, Piscataway (2000)
2. Belkin, M., Niyogi, P., Sindhwani, V.: On Manifold Regularization. In: 10th International Workshop on Artificial Intelligence and Statistics, pp. 17–24. IOS Press, Amsterdam (2005)
3. Cox, T.F., Cox, M.A.A.: Multidimensional Scaling. Chapman & Hall, London (2001)
4. Dedes, G., Dempster, A.: Indoor GPS: Positioning Challenges and Opportunities. In: 62nd Vehicular Technology Conference, pp. 412–415. IEEE Press, Piscataway (2005)
5. Ekahau, Inc. RTLS, http://www.ekahau.com
6. Ferris, B., Hahnel, D., Fox, D.: Gaussian Processes for Signal Strength-Based Location Estimation. In: Robotics: Science and Systems, pp. 1–8. MIT Press, Cambridge (2006)
7. Ghodsi, A.: Dimensionality Reduction – A Short Tutorial. Technical report. University of Waterloo (2006)
8. Liu, H., Darabi, H., Banerjee, P., Liu, J.: Survey of Wireless Indoor Positioning Techniques and Systems. IEEE T. Syst. Man. Cyb. 37, 1067–1080 (2007)
9. Ni, L.M., Liu, Y., Lau, Y.C., Patil, A.P.: LANDMARC: Indoor Location Sensing Using Active RFID. Wireless Networks 10, 701–710 (2004)

10. Pan, J.J., Yang, Q., Chang, H., Yeung, D.-Y.: A Manifold Regularization Approach to Calibration Reduction for Sensor-Network Based Tracking. In: 21st National Conference on Artificial Intelligence, pp. 988–993. AAAI Press, Menlo Park (2006)
11. Pan, J.J., Yang, Q.: Co-localization from Labeled and Unlabeled Data Using Graph Laplacian. In: 20th International Joint Conference on Artificial Intelligence, pp. 2166–2171. Morgan Kaufmann, San Francisco (2007)
12. Papapostolou, A., Chaouchi, H.: WIFE: Wireless Indoor Positioning Based on Fingerprint Evaluation. In: Fratta, L., Schulzrinne, H., Takahashi, Y., Spaniol, O. (eds.) NETWORKING 2009. LNCS, vol. 5550, pp. 234–247. Springer, Heidelberg (2009)
13. Patwari, N., Hero, A.O.: Adaptive Neighborhoods for Manifold Learning-based Sensor Localization. In: IEEE 6th Workshop on Signal Processing Advances in Wireless Communications, pp. 1098–1102. IEEE Press, Piscataway (2005)
14. Petrellis, N., Konofaos, N., Alexiou, G.: A Wireless Infrared Sensor Network for the Estimation of the Position and Orientation of a Moving Target. In: Third International Mobile Multimedia Communications Conference, pp. 1–4. ICST, Brussels (2007)
15. Raper, J., Gartner, G., Karimi, H., Rizos, C.: Applications of Location-based Services: A Selected Review. J. Location-based Services 1, 89–111 (2007)
16. Rasmussen, C.E., Williams, C.K.I.: Gaussian Processes for Machine Learning. MIT Press, Cambridge (2005)
17. Roos, T., Myllymäki, P., Tirri, H., Misikangas, P., Sievänen, J.: A Probabilistic Approach to WLAN User Location Estimation. Int. J. Wireless Information Networks 9, 155–164 (2002)
18. Samko, O., Marshall, A.D., Rosin, P.L.: Selection of the Optimal Parameter Value for the Isomap Algorithm. Pattern Recogn. Letters 27, 968–979 (2006)
19. Shang, Y., Ruml, W., Zhang, Y., Fromherz, M.P.J.: Localization from Mere Connectivity. In: 4th ACM International Symposium on Mobile Ad Hoc Networking & Computing, pp. 201–212. ACM Press, New York (2003)
20. Shao, C., Huang, H., Wan, C.: Selection of the Suitable Neighborhood Size for the Isomap Algorithm. In: International Joint Conference on Neural Networks, pp. 300–305. IEEE Press, Piscataway (2007)
21. Tenenbaum, J.B., de Silva, V., Langford, J.C.: A Global Geometric Framework for Nonlinear Dimensionality Reduction. Science 290, 2319–2323 (2000)
22. Yeung, W.H., Zhou, J.-Y., Ng, J.K.: Enhanced Fingerprint-Based Location Estimation System in Wireless LAN Environment. In: Denko, M.K., Shih, C.-s., Li, K.-C., Tsao, S.-L., Zeng, Q.-A., Park, S.H., Ko, Y.-B., Hung, S.-H., Park, J.-H. (eds.) EUC-WS 2007. LNCS, vol. 4809, pp. 273–284. Springer, Heidelberg (2007)
23. Youssef, M., Agrawala, A., Shankar, A.U.: WLAN Location Determination via Clustering and Probability Distributions. In: 1st IEEE International Conference on Pervasive Computing and Communications, pp. 1–8. IEEE Press, Piscataway (2003)
24. Yuan, J., Li, Y., Liu, C., Zha, X.F.: Leave-One-Out Cross-Validation Based Model Selection for Manifold Regularization. In: Yuan, J., Li, Y.-M., Liu, C.-L., Zha, X.F. (eds.) ISNN 2010. LNCS, vol. 6064, pp. 457–464. Springer, Heidelberg (2010)
25. Zhang, M., Zhang, S.: An Accurate and Fast WLAN User Location Estimation Method Based on Received Signal Strength. In: Shi, Y., van Albada, G.D., Dongarra, J., Sloot, P.M.A. (eds.) ICCS 2007. LNCS, vol. 4489, pp. 58–65. Springer, Heidelberg (2007)

Ensemble-Teacher Learning through a Perceptron Rule with a Margin

Kazuyuki Hara[1] and Seiji Miyoshi[2]

[1] College of Industrial Technology, Nihon University,
1-2-1, Izumi-cho, Narashino, Chiba 275-8575, Japan
hara.kazuyuki@nihon-u.ac.jp
[2] Faculty of Engineering Science, Kansai University,
3-3-35, Yamate-cho, Suita, Osaka, 564-8680, Japan
miyoshi@ipcku.kansai-u.ac.jp

Abstract. In ensemble-teacher learning, a student learns from a quasi-optimal-teacher selected randomly from a pool of many quasi-optimal-teachers, and the student performs better than the quasi-optimal teachers after the learning. The student performance is improved by using many quasi-optimal-teachers when a Hebbian rule is used. However, a perceptron rule cannot improve the student performance. We previously proposed a novel ensemble-teacher learning using a perceptron rule with a margin. A perceptron rule with a margin is mid-way between a Hebbian rule and a perceptron rule. We have found through computer simulation that a perceptron rule with a margin can improve student performance. In this paper, we provide theoretical support to the proposed method by using statistical mechanics methods.

1 Introduction

Ensemble learning improves the performance of a learning machine by using a majority vote of many weak-learners. The majority vote is obtained by calculating the average of the weak-learners output. Bagging[1] or boosting[2] is a kind of ensemble learning. Ensemble learning is classified with respect to the way a new weak learner is added and the way weak learners are combined. In particular, when the weak learners are non-linear perceptrons, the space spanned by combining weak learners differs from the original space, so ensemble learning improves the learning machine performance. [3].

Miyoshi and Okada proposed ensemble-teacher learning as an alternative method [4]. This method employs a true-teacher, quasi-optimal-teachers, and a student. Quasi-optimal-teachers learn from the true-teacher beforehand and are not a subject of learning. In this method, the student learns from a quasi-optimal-teacher selected randomly from a pool of many quasi-optimal-teachers, and the student performs better than the quasi-optimal-teachers after the learning. The student performance is improved by using many quasi-optimal-teachers when a Hebbian rule is used. However, a perceptron rule cannot improve the student performance. [5]. Okada et al. showed theoretically that the student

T. Honkela et al. (Eds.): ICANN 2011, Part I, LNCS 6791, pp. 363–370, 2011.

used in ensemble-teacher learning mimics an averaging mechanism of ensemble learning [6].

We earlier proposed ensemble-teacher learning using a perceptron rule with a margin[7] to overcome the problem. A perceptron rule with a margin is identical to a perceptron rule when the margin is zero, and to a Hebbian rule when the margin is infinity. Otherwise, it is somewhere between a Hebbian rule and a perceptron rule. We have shown through computer simulation that student performance is related to the number of quasi-optimal-teachers when a small margin is added to a perceptron rule. However, we have not previously provided a theoretical background to explain why this is so.

In this paper, we provide theoretical support to the effectiveness of ensemble-teacher learning through a perceptron rule with a margin. We first review the theory of the ensemble-teacher learning given by Miyoshi and Okada[4]. We then point out some theoretical insights, and derive coupled differential equations which depict the learning behavior by using statistical mechanics methods. After that, we solve the order parameter equations in a numerical way and show the behavior of the generalization error. Last, we show the validity of the proposed method.

2   Model

In this section, we formulate a true-teacher (latent teacher), quasi-optimal-teachers (ensemble-teachers), and a student network. Then we formulate ensemble-teacher-learning through a perceptron rule.

We assume the latent teacher network, ensemble-teacher networks and the student network receive N-dimensional input $\boldsymbol{x}(m) = (x_1(m), \ldots, x_N(m))$ at the m-th learning iteration. We also assume that the elements $x_i(m)$ of the independently drawn input $\boldsymbol{x}(m)$ are uncorrelated Gaussian random variables with zero mean and $1/N$ variance; that is, the i-th element of input is drawn from a probability distribution $P(x_i)$. At the limit of $N \to \infty$, the norm of input vector $\|\boldsymbol{x}\|$ becomes one.

The latent teacher network is a non-linear perceptron. The ensemble-teacher networks are K non-linear perceptrons, and the student is a non-linear perceptron. The latent teacher network and the ensemble-teacher networks are not subject to training. Thus, the weight vectors of these networks are fixed in the learning process. The latent teacher output is $\mathrm{sgn}(y(m)) = \mathrm{sgn}(\sum_{i=1}^N A_i x_i(m))$, the ensemble-teacher output is $\mathrm{sgn}(v_k(m)) = \mathrm{sgn}(\sum_{i=1}^N B_{ki} x_i(m))$, and the student output is $\mathrm{sgn}(u(m)) = \mathrm{sgn}(\sum_{i=1}^N J_i(m) x_i(m))$. Each element of the latent teacher weight vector A_i, those of the ensemble-teacher weight vector B_{ki}, and those of the initial student weight vector $J_i(0)$ are drawn from a Gaussian distribution of zero mean and unit variance. Assuming the thermodynamic limit of $N \to \infty$, $\|\boldsymbol{A}\|$, $\|\boldsymbol{B}_k\|$ and $\|\boldsymbol{J}(0)\|$ become $\sqrt{N}$. At the limit, the distribution of the input potential of the latent teacher $P(y)$, that of the ensemble-teacher

$P(v_k)$, and that of the student $P(u)$ follow a Gaussian distribution of zero mean and unit variance. $\boldsymbol{B}_k$ and $\boldsymbol{A}$ are correlated with each other. The direction cosine between $\boldsymbol{J}$ and $\boldsymbol{A}$ is R_J, that between $\boldsymbol{J}$ and $\boldsymbol{B}_k$ is R_{BkJ}, that between $\boldsymbol{A}$ and $\boldsymbol{B}_k$ is R_{Bk}, and that between $\boldsymbol{B}_k$ and $\boldsymbol{B}_{k'}$ is $q_{kk'}$.

Generally, the norm of student weight vector $\|\boldsymbol{J}(m)\|$ changes as the time step proceeds. Therefore, the ratio l of the norm to $\sqrt{N}$ is considered and is called the length of student weight vector $\boldsymbol{J}$. The norm at the m-th iteration is $l(m)\sqrt{N}$, and the size of $l(m)$ is $O(1)$. The distribution of the input potential of the student $P(u)$ follows a Gaussian distribution of zero mean and unit variance in the thermodynamic limit of $N \to \infty$. The distribution of the input potentials of the latent teacher $P(y)$ and that of the sub-optimal teacher $P(v_k)$ follow a Gaussian distribution of zero mean and unit variance.

We then introduce the ensemble-teacher learning[4]. This learning uses a latent teacher, ensemble-teachers that are quasi-optimal-teachers, and the student. The student learns from an ensemble-teacher that is randomly selected from K ensemble-teachers. Here, a perceptron rule is used. The learning equation is

$$\boldsymbol{J}(m+1) = \boldsymbol{J}(m) + \eta \Theta\left(-u(m)\, \mathrm{sgn}(v_{k'(m)})\right) \mathrm{sgn}(v_{k'(m)})\boldsymbol{x}(m). \tag{1}$$

Here, subscript $k'(m)$ denotes an ensemble-teacher selected at the m-th iteration. $\Theta(x)$ is a step function defined as $+1$ when $x \geq 0$, or defined as -1 when $x < 0$. Equation (1) shows that the student learns many semi-optimal-teachers within a microscopic interval when we assume that time t is defined as $t = m/N$ and $N \to \infty$, so there are N iterations in a microscopic interval of $t \to t + \Delta t$. Okada et al. showed theoretically that the student used in ensemble-teacher learning mimics an averaging mechanism of ensemble learning [6].

3   Theory of Ensemble-Teacher Learning with a Perceptron Rule

Next, we show theoretical results for ensemble-teacher learning through a perceptron rule[5]. The generalization error ϵ_g is given by error ϵ averaged over the possible input.

$$\epsilon_g = \int d\boldsymbol{x}\, P(\boldsymbol{x})\epsilon = \int dy du P(y, u)\epsilon(y, u) = \frac{1}{\pi} \arccos(R_J) \tag{2}$$

$$\epsilon = \Theta(-yu) \tag{3}$$

Here, y is output of the latent teacher, and u is output of the student. $P(\boldsymbol{x})$ is the distribution of input $\boldsymbol{x}$, and $P(y, u)$ is the joint distribution of y and u.

Next, we introduce closed differential equations of the order parameters which depict dynamics of the learning system[5]. $r_{BkJ} = R_{BkJ}l$ and $r_J = R_J l$ are used to simplify the analysis.

$$\frac{dr_{BkJ}}{dt} = \frac{\eta}{K} \sum_{k'=1}^{K} \langle f_{k'} v_k \rangle \tag{4}$$

$$\frac{dr_J}{dt} = \frac{\eta}{N} \sum_{k=1}^{K} \langle f_k y \rangle \tag{5}$$

$$\frac{dl}{dt} = \frac{1}{K} \sum_{k=1}^{K} \left\{ \eta \langle f_k \rangle + \frac{\eta^2}{2l} \langle f_k^2 \rangle \right\} \tag{6}$$

Here, $f_k = \Theta(-uv_k)\mathrm{sgn}(v_k)$. We treat the case $R_{BkJ} = R_{BJ}$, $R_{Bk} = R_B$, and $q_{kk'} = q$. $q_{kk'} = q$ when $k \neq k'$ and is $q_{kk} = 1$ when $k = k'$. K ensemble-teachers are used. Utsumi et al. calculate the four averages $\langle f_{k'} v_k \rangle$, $\langle f_k y \rangle$, $\langle f_k \rangle$ and $\langle f_k^2 \rangle$ and substitute to Eqs. (4) to (6); then

$$\frac{dr_{BJ}}{dt} = \frac{\eta}{\sqrt{2\pi}} \left(\frac{1 + (K-1)q}{K} - R_{BJ} \right), \tag{7}$$

$$\frac{dr_J}{dt} = \eta \frac{R_B - R_J}{\sqrt{2\pi}}, \tag{8}$$

$$\frac{dl}{dt} = \eta \frac{R_{BJ} - 1}{\sqrt{2\pi}} + \eta^2 \frac{1}{\pi} \arccos(R_{BJ}), \tag{9}$$

are obtained[5] . Here, time $t = m/N$ and we assume $N \to \infty$. K is the number of sub-optimal teachers. R_B and q are constant values. From Eqs. (7) to (9), only dr_{BJ}/dt depends on K. Note that in Eq. (9), the second term of the right-hand side represents the generalization error of ensemble-teachers. By solving Eqs. (7) to (9) numerically at each time t, we can obtain the generalization error by substituting $R_J(t)$ into Eq. (2).

Figure 1 shows time dependence of the generalization error of ensemble-teacher learning through a perceptron rule. Analytical solutions are used. The horizontal axis is normalized time $t = m/N$, where m is the learning iteration. The vertical axis is the generalization error. In Figure 1(a), learning step size $\eta = 0.05$ and in (b), $\eta = 1$. Initial conditions are $R_{BJ}(0) = R_J(0) = 0$. We set $R_B = 0.6$ and $q = 0.2$. As shown in Fig. 1(a), the generalization error decreased with larger K and overshot in the early stage of learning, but the errors eventually became the same regardless of K. However, in Fig. 1(b), the decrease in the generalization error was almost the same for $K = 1, 2$ or 3. In both cases, the effect of majority voting obtained from many ensemble-teachers asymptotically disappeared.

We next consider the reason for the difference between Figs. 1 (a) and (b). From Eq. (9), the term η^2 will be negligible when η is small. This term is the generalization error of the ensemble-teachers, so the generalization error of the ensemble-teachers need not be taken into account when η is small. Then, the student length l becomes shorter and $R_J = r_J/l$ becomes larger. Therefore, the generalization error $\epsilon_g = \arccos(R_J)/\pi$ for a small learning step size becomes smaller in the early stage of the learning. This mechanism may cause overshooting in the early stage of learning.

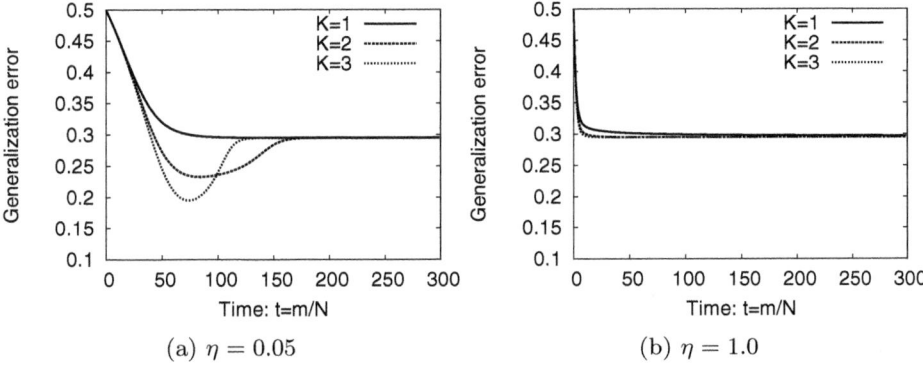

Fig. 1. Time dependence of generalization error of ensemble-teacher learning through a perceptron rule

The generalization error of the ensemble-teachers may be relatively large compared to the first term of Eq. (9) since the overshooting disappears when η is large.

4   Theory of Proposed Method

In this section, we describe ensemble-teacher learning through a perceptron rule with a margin[7], and then we build a theory supporting this method.

As discussed in [7], the cause of the diminishing effect of using many ensemble-teachers is that the perceptron rule does not learn from ensemble-teachers whose output sign is the same as that of the student. To avoid this problem, we introduce a perceptron rule with a margin. The learning equation is

$$J(m+1) = J(m) + \eta\Theta\left(\kappa - u(m)\ \mathrm{sgn}(v_{k'(m)})\right)\mathrm{sgn}(v_{k'(m)})x(m). \qquad (10)$$

Here, κ is a positive constant, and subscript $k'(m)$ denotes an ensemble-teacher selected at the m-th iteration. As shown in Eq. (10), a perceptron rule with a margin expands the learnable region in the input space, thus changing the dynamics of ensemble-teacher learning and improving the learning ability. When $\kappa \to \infty$, this learning rule is identical to a Hebbian rule, and when $\kappa \to 0$, it is identical to a perceptron rule. In other words, a perceptron rule with a margin is a middle way between a Hebbian rule and a perceptron rule.

Next, we derive differential equations of the method's order parameters. We can use the same differential equations in Eqs. (7) to (9) instead of using different $f_k = \Theta\left(\kappa - u(m)\ \mathrm{sgn}(v_k)\right)\cdot\mathrm{sgn}(v_k)$. The following equations are then obtained:

$$\langle f_{k'}v_k \rangle = \sqrt{\frac{2}{\pi}} \left[q_{kk'} \mathrm{H}\left(\frac{-\frac{\kappa}{l}}{\sqrt{1 - R_{Bk'J}^2}} \right) \right.$$
$$\left. - R_{BkJ}\exp\left(-\frac{\kappa^2}{2l^2}\right) \mathrm{H}\left(\frac{-\frac{\kappa}{l}R_{Bk'J}}{\sqrt{1 - R_{Bk'J}^2}} \right) \right]$$

$$\langle f_k y \rangle = \sqrt{\frac{2}{\pi}} \left[R_{Bk}\mathrm{H}\left(\frac{-\frac{\kappa}{l}}{\sqrt{1 - R_{BkJ}^2}} \right) - R_J\exp\left(-\frac{\kappa^2}{2l^2}\right) \mathrm{H}\left(\frac{-\frac{\kappa}{l}R_{BkJ}}{\sqrt{1 - R_{BkJ}^2}} \right) \right]$$

$$\langle f_k u \rangle = \sqrt{\frac{2}{\pi}} \left[R_{BkJ}\mathrm{H}\left(\frac{-\frac{\kappa}{l}}{\sqrt{1 - R_{BkJ}^2}} \right) - \exp\left(-\frac{\kappa^2}{2l^2}\right) \mathrm{H}\left(\frac{-\frac{\kappa}{l}R_{BkJ}}{\sqrt{1 - R_{BkJ}^2}} \right) \right]$$

$$\langle f_k^2 \rangle = 2 \int_0^\infty Du \mathrm{H}\left(\frac{R_{BkJ}v_k - \frac{\kappa}{l}}{\sqrt{1 - R_{BkJ}^2}} \right).$$

Here,

$$\mathrm{H}(x) = \int_x^\infty Dx = \int_x^\infty \frac{dx}{\sqrt{2\pi}} \exp\left(-\frac{x^2}{2}\right).$$

We treat the case $R_{BkJ} = R_{BJ}$, $R_{Bk} = R_B$, and $q_{kk'} = q$ when $k \neq k'$ and $q_{kk'} = 1$ when $k = k'$. K ensemble-teachers are used. Then we get

$$\frac{dr_{BJ}}{dt} = \eta\sqrt{\frac{2}{\pi}} \left[\frac{1 + (K-1)q}{K}\mathrm{H}\left(\frac{-\frac{\kappa}{l}}{\sqrt{1 - R_{BJ}^2}} \right) \right.$$
$$\left. - R_{BJ}\exp\left(-\frac{\kappa^2}{2l^2}\right) \mathrm{H}\left(\frac{-\frac{\kappa}{l}R_{BJ}}{\sqrt{1 - R_{BJ}^2}} \right) \right] \tag{11}$$

$$\frac{dr_J}{dt} = \eta\sqrt{\frac{2}{\pi}} \left[R_B\mathrm{H}\left(\frac{-\frac{\kappa}{l}}{\sqrt{1 - R_{BJ}^2}} \right) - R_J\exp\left(-\frac{\kappa^2}{2l^2}\right) \mathrm{H}\left(\frac{-\frac{\kappa}{l}R_{BJ}}{\sqrt{1 - R_{BJ}^2}} \right) \right] \tag{12}$$

$$\frac{dl}{dt} = \eta\sqrt{\frac{2}{\pi}} \left[R_{BJ}\mathrm{H}\left(\frac{-\frac{\kappa}{l}}{\sqrt{1 - R_{BJ}^2}} \right) - \exp\left(-\frac{\kappa^2}{2l^2}\right) \mathrm{H}\left(\frac{-\frac{\kappa}{l}R_{BJ}}{\sqrt{1 - R_{BJ}^2}} \right) \right]$$
$$+ \frac{\eta^2}{l} \int_0^\infty Dv_k \mathrm{H}\left(\frac{R_{BJ} - \frac{\kappa}{l}}{\sqrt{1 - R_{BJ}^2}} \right) \tag{13}$$

5   Results

We solved closed order parameter equations of the proposed method (Eqs. (11) to (13)) numerically and then substituted into Eq. (2) to obtain the generalization error. We compared the errors with those of computer simulations. Figure 2 shows the time dependence of the generalization error. The horizontal axis is normalized time $t = m/N$, where m is the learning iteration. The vertical axis is the generalization error. Initial conditions are $R_{BJ}(0) = R_J(0) = 0$. We set

$R_B = 0.6$ and $q = 0.2$. The number of ensemble-teachers was $K = 1, 2$ or 3. The margin κ was 0.2. The learning step size $\eta = 0.05$. Figure 2(a) shows analytical solutions, and (b) shows computer simulation results. For the computer simulations, $N = 1000$ and 1000 samples were used to calculate the mean error. Figure 2 shows that the analytical solutions agreed with those of the computer simulations, confirming the validity of the analytical solutions. The generalization error decreased with larger K, so our objective is sufficiently achieved.

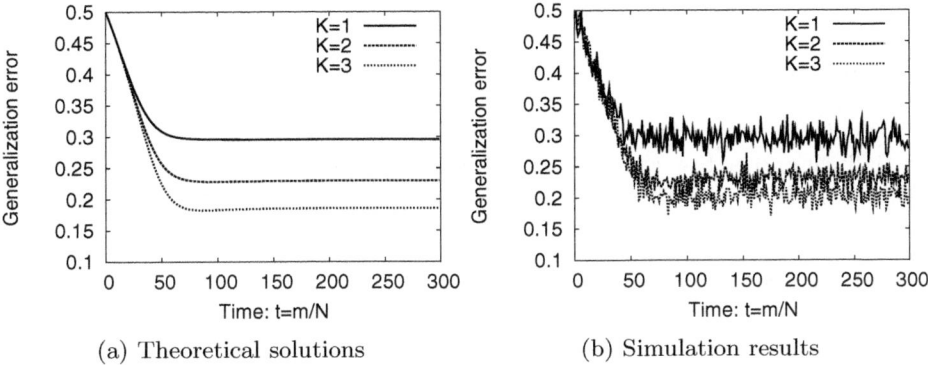

(a) Theoretical solutions   (b) Simulation results

Fig. 2. Time dependence of generalization error for proposed method. The margin κ is 0.2.

Next, we consider the case of $K \to \infty$. From Eqs. (11), (12) and (13), Eq. (11) depend on K and remained two does not depend on K. So, we consider the effect of K using Eq. (11). When the number of output K goes to infinity, $1 + (K - 1)q)/K$ approaches to q as shown in Fig. 3. q is set to 0.5. From this fact, the generalization error using many ensemble-teachers converges into the generalization error replacing $1 + (K - 1)q/K$ by q with respect to the order of $1/K$.

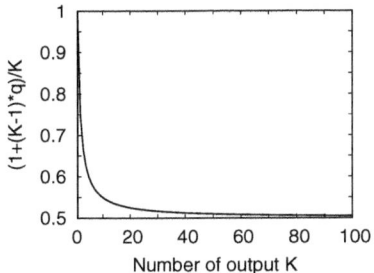

Fig. 3. K dependence in ensemble-teacher learning. ($q = 0.5$)

6   Conclusion

In this paper, we have theoretically analyzed ensemble-teacher learning through a perceptron rule with a margin. We derived the order parameter equations using a statistical mechanics method. The generalization error was obtained by using solutions of the order parameter equations. The analytical results show that this learning method has achieved our objectives and the generalization error decreased with larger K. Note that a random margin for every learning iteration may also work well.

Acknowledgments

We thank Professor Masato Okada for his fruitful discussions. This research was partially supported by the Ministry of Education, Culture, Sports, Science, and Technology of Japan, through Grant-in-Aid for Scientific Research 21500228.

References

1. Breiman, L.: Bagging predictors Machine Learning, vol. 24, pp. 123–140 (1996)
2. Freund, Y., Shapire, R.E.: A decision-theoretic generalization of on-line learning and an application to boosting. J. Comp. Sys. Sci. 55, 119–139 (1997)
3. Murata, N., Takenouchi, T., Kanamori, T., Eguchi, S.: Information Geometry of U-Boost and Bregman Divergences. Neural Computation 16(7), 1437–1481 (2004)
4. Miyoshi, S., Okada, M.: Statistical mechanics of online learning for ensemble-teachers. Journal of the Physical Society of Japan 75(4), 044002 (6 Pages) (2006)
5. Utsumi, H., Miyoshi, S., Okada, M.: Statistical Mechanics of Nonlinear On-line Learning for ensemble-teachers. J. Phys. Soc. Jpn. 76, 114001 (2007)
6. Okada, M., Hara, K., Miyoshi, S.: Quasi-supervised learning and ensemble learning. Meeting Abstracts of the Physical Society of Japan (2007) (in Japanese)
7. Hara, K., Ono, K., Miyoshi, S.: On-Line Ensemble-Teacher Learning through a Perceptron Rule with a Margin. In: Diamantaras, K., Duch, W., Iliadis, L.S. (eds.) ICANN 2010. LNCS, vol. 6354, pp. 339–344. Springer, Heidelberg (2010)
8. Hara, K., Okada, M.: On-line learning through simple perceptron with a margin. Neural Networks 17, 215–223 (2004)

Topic-Dependent Document Ranking: Citation Network Analysis by Analogy to Memory Retrieval in the Brain

Hiroshi Okamoto[1,2]

[1] Research & Development Group, Fuji Xerox Co., Ltd.
6-1 Minatomirai, Nishi-ku, Yokohama-shi, Kanagawa 220-8668, Japan
[2] RIKEN Brain Science Institute
2-1 Hirosawa, Wako, Saitama 351-0198, Japan
hiroshi.okamoto@fujixerox.co.jp

Abstract. We propose a method of citation analysis for evaluating the topic-dependent importance of individual scientific papers. This method assumes spreading activation in citation networks with a multi-hysteretic input/output relationship for each node (paper). The multi-hysteretic property renders the steady state of spreading activation continuously dependent on the initial state. Given a topic represented by the initial state, the importance of individual papers can be defined by the activities they have in the steady state. We have devised this method inspired by memory retrieval in the brain, where the multi-hysteretic property of single cells or neuronal networks is considered to play an essential role for cue-dependent retrieval of memory. Quantitative evaluation using a restoration problem has revealed that the performance of the proposed method is considerably higher than that of the benchmark method. We demonstrate the practical usefulness of the proposed method by applying it to a citation network of neuroscience papers.

Keywords: Bibliometrics. Scientometrics. Citation network. PageRank. Memory retrieval. Continuous attractor. Graded persistent activity.

1 Introduction

Citation of a scientific paper in another scientific paper means that research activity described in the latter was under the influence of that in the former (Fig. 1, left). Some papers, which have had broad impact upon subsequent studies, are cited many times. Accordingly, the simplest way of evaluating the importance of a paper in terms of citation is to count how many times it is cited. The importance of a paper defined in this way is exactly proportional to the number of citation. The impact factor, a measure for the influence of a journal, is also calculated with the same idea [1].

Nevertheless, we believe that a citation in a more important paper is more valuable than that in a less important paper. So, taking account of the value of each citation will provide a more appropriate definition of the importance of individual papers [2]. The most sophisticated method employing such an idea is the PageRank algorithm

T. Honkela et al. (Eds.): ICANN 2011, Part I, LNCS 6791, pp. 371–378, 2011.

used by the Google internet search engine [3, 4]. This algorithm assigns higher scores of importance to web pages that are linked from more numerous and more important pages.

The PageRank algorithm defines the importance of individual web pages only from the graph structure of the World Wide Web. However we often consider the 'importance' of a paper as what varies depending on the context or user's interest [5-7]. Here we propose a novel method of citation analysis to evaluate the topic-dependent importance of individual papers. We have devised this method inspired by recent liens of evidence in neuroscience suggesting biophysical mechanisms of cue-dependent retrieval of memory in the brain [8].

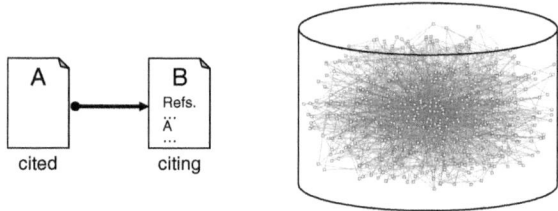

Fig. 1. *Left:* Document B cites document A. *Right:* Citation network.

2 Methods

2.1 Citation Network and Spreading Activation

Consider a large network consisting of documents as nodes and citation relations between documents as links (Fig. 1, right). Each node has an instantaneous value of 'activity'. Activities spread along links from nodes to nodes; this process is referred to as 'spreading activation' [9, 10]. We define the importance of a document by the value of activity finally acquired by this document. It should be noted that the PageRank algorithm [3] also uses the idea of spreading activation. (The difference between the PageRank algorithm and ours will be described later.)

2.2 Algorithm: Initial-State-Dependent Retrieval of Information

Let $\mathbf{A} = (A_{nm})$ $(n, m = 1, \cdots, N)$ be an adjacency matrix defining the citation network of N documents. If document m cites document n, $A_{nm} = 1$; otherwise $A_{nm} = 0$. Let $x_n(t)$ denote the activity (output) of node n corresponding to document n. The input to node n at time t is given by $I_n(t) = \sum_{m=1}^{N} T_{nm} x_m(t)$, where $T_{nm} \equiv A_{nm} / \sum_{l=1}^{N} A_{lm}$ corresponds to the transition matrix in the PageRank algorithm [3].

We assume a multi-hysteretic input/output (I/O) relationship (Fig. 2) for each node. The time evolution of spreading activation is hence defined by the following rule:

(1a)   If $x_n(t) < I_1$, $x_n(t+1) = I_n(t)/\alpha$;

(1b)   if $I_1 \le x_n(t) \le I_2$, $x_n(t+1) = x_n(t)$;

(1c)   if $I_2 < x_n(t)$, $x_n(t+1) = \alpha I_n(t)$.

Here, α is a parameter whose value ranges from 0 to 1 and controls the magnitude of hysteresis; $I_1 = \alpha I_n(t)$ and $I_2 = I_n(t)/\alpha$.

Because of the hysteretic property of the I/O relationship, the spreading activation results in the steady state that continuously depends on the initial state [8]. So, if a given 'topic' is represented by the initial state $\vec{x}(0)$, information specific to this topic can be retrieved as a continuous attractor $\lim_{t \to \infty} \vec{x}(t) = \vec{x}(\infty)$ [8]. Note that, at the limit $\alpha \to 1$, the topic dependence (i.e. the continuous dependence of attractors on the initial state) disappears and the procedure (1a-c) is identical to the PageRank algorithm.

The multi-hysteretic property (Fig. 2) of single cells [11, 12] or neuronal networks [13, 14] was originally proposed by computational neuroscientists to explain a type of neuronal activity whose magnitude depends on the transient cue signal in a graded manner (graded neuronal activity) [15, 16]. The multi-hysteretic system can generate robust continuous attractors; this well accounts for the experimentally observed property of graded neuronal activity. We have hypothesized that graded neuronal activity is the neural substrate of cue-dependent retrieval of memory [8]. Thus the proposed algorithm using spreading activation with the multi-hysteretic I/O relationship replicates cue-dependent retrieval of memory in the real brain.

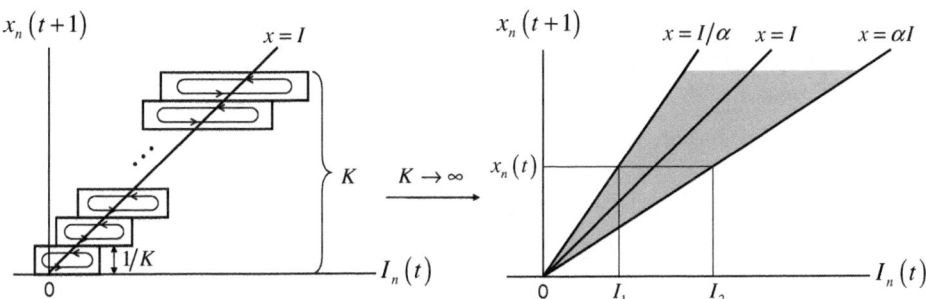

Fig. 2. The multi-hysteretic input/output relationship is implemented by stacking K hysteresis units as described in the *left* diagram. In the limit $K \to \infty$ (*right*), the relationship between $I_n(t)$ and $x_n(t+1)$ can be expressed by the simple rule (1) given in the text.

2.3 Expressing a Topic by Seed Documents

A given topic is fed into the algorithm through 'seed documents', which are prepared by a user as a set of documents judged to be relevant to this topic. Since user's knowledge about the topic is incomplete beforehand, seed documents might lack some documents that are truly relevant to the topic or include irrelevant ones. Even so, high restoration performance of the proposed algorithm will retrieve truly relevant documents and remove irrelevant ones.

Let $\vec{\tau}$ be a vector representing a 'seed state', which is defined as:

(2a) $\tau_n = 1$ if document n is a seed document;

(2b) $\tau_n = 0$ otherwise.

Hence the initial state of spreading activation is set as

$$\vec{x}(0) = \vec{\tau} . \tag{3}$$

2.4   Comparison Experiment: Evaluation of the Performance

To evaluate the performance of the proposed algorithm, we carry out a comparison experiment taking the personalized PageRank (PPR) algorithm [3, 7] as a benchmark. The PPR algorithm, unlike the original PageRank algorithm, can allocate activities to individual nodes in a topic-dependent manner in the steady state of spreading activation. The PPR algorithm is defined by the formula

$$x_n(t+1) = \rho I_n(t) + (1-\rho)\tau_n , \tag{4}$$

where $0 \leq \rho \leq 1$. In the right-hand side, $\vec{\tau}$ behaves as a bias force, rendering the steady state dependent on the topic represented by $\vec{\tau}$.

The comparison experiment is conducted using a restoration problem set as follows. First, we adopt a mathematical model for complex networks proposed by Klemn and Eguiluz (KE model) [17]. Among existing network models, the KE model most appropriately reproduces characteristics of real citation networks. The KE model used in the present experiment is defined with the notations in [17] as follows: $N = 5000$, $m = 5$ and $\mu = 0.1$.

Next, we define a 'correct state' $\vec{\xi}$ as the steady state of the PPR algorithm,

$$x_n(t+1) = \lambda I_n(t) + (1-\lambda)b_n \tag{5}$$

with $\lambda = 0.8$; $b_n = 1$ if $n_1 < n \leq n_2$, and $b_n = 0$ otherwise. Here, n_1 and n_1 are integers satisfying $1 \leq n_1 < n_1 \leq N$, and 100 sets of (n_1, n_2) are chosen (randomly but with the constraint $50 \leq n_2 - n_1 \leq 150$) to generate 100 different $\vec{\xi}$'s. The PPR algorithm (5) is used only to generate $\vec{\xi}$'s and should not be confused with the PPR algorithm (4) to be compared with the proposed algorithm.

Each $\vec{\xi}$ is quantized to a vector $\vec{d}$ as follows: if ξ_n is larger than the $L = 50$ th largest component, $d_n = 1$ (document n with $d_n = 1$ will be referred to as 'correct document'); otherwise $d_n = 0$ ('non-correct document'). Then we produce a 'seed state' $\vec{\tau}$ according to the following probabilistic rule (Fig. 3):

(6a) If $d_n = 1$, $\tau_n = 0$ with probability p and $\tau_n = 1$ with probability $1-p$;

(6b) if $d_n = 0$, $\tau_n = 1$ with probability q and $\tau_n = 0$ with probability $1-q$.

The rule (6a) models the event that some correct documents might be dropped from the seed state, while (3b) states that non-correct documents (noise) might enter the seed state. For each of the 100 $\vec{\xi}$'s, we produce corresponding $\vec{\tau}$ with p and q that are chosen each time randomly from uniform distributions $0.05 \leq p \leq 0.95$ and $0 \leq q \leq 0.02$. The above procedure of generating $\vec{\tau}$ includes several parameters such as λ, n_1, n_2, L, p and q. Quantitatively, however, the results of comparison experiment do not strongly depend on the values of these parameters.

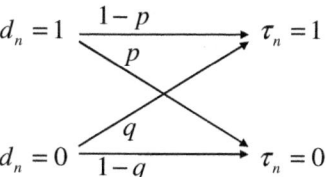

Fig. 3. Production of seed documents ($\vec{\tau}$) from correct documents ($\vec{d}$)

We examine how accurately $\vec{\xi}$ is restored in the steady state $\vec{x}(\infty)$. For this we calculate the correlation coefficient between $\vec{x}(\infty)$ and ξ:

$$r = \frac{\sum_{n=1}^{N}(x_n(\infty) - \bar{x}(\infty))(\xi_n - \bar{\xi})}{\sqrt{\sum_{n=1}^{N}(x_n(\infty) - \bar{x}(\infty))^2}\sqrt{\sum_{n=1}^{N}(\xi_n - \bar{\xi})^2}}, \tag{6}$$

where $\bar{x}(\infty) = \sum_{n=1}^{N} x_n(\infty)/N$ and $\bar{\xi} = \sum_{n=1}^{N} \xi_n/N$. The larger r the more accurate restoration; especially when $r = 1$, restoration is complete. The correlation coefficient for each value of the unique parameter involved in each algorithm (α for the proposed algorithm and ρ for the PPR algorithm (4)) is averaged over the 100 $\vec{\xi}$'s.

2.5 Bibliographic Data

To demonstrate the practical usefulness of the proposed method, we examine its application to real citation networks. For this, we prepared bibliographic information of papers published in major neuroscience journals. This includes for each paper: Identification data (ID); author(s); title; journal; volume; pages; year; IDs of cited papers; abstract; and so forth. Among them, only IDs of citing and cited papers are necessary to construct a citation network (Fig. 1, right).

2.6 Topic-Dependent Ranking

Documents that are highly activated in the steady state are regarded as what are truly relevant to the topic. Sorting these documents in descending order of acquired values of activity gives a topic-dependent document ranking.

2.7 Visualization

Documents highly activated in the steady state tend to form a connected graph because the activation of these documents is maintained by mutual exchange of their activities via citation links. So, visualizing such a connected graph will give an overview of a 'genealogy' in the research field of the topic.

3 Results

Using the restoration problem defined in Methods, we compared the performances of the proposed algorithm with that of the PPR algorithm taken as a benchmark. How accurately these algorithms restore correct states $\vec{\xi}$ from seed states $\vec{\tau}$ was evaluated by calculating the correlation coefficient (6). The average correlation coefficient $\bar{r}$ was plotted as a function of the unique parameter in each algorithm (α for the proposed algorithm and ρ for the PPR algorithm). Remind that $\vec{\xi}$ itself is generated by the PPR algorithm (5); this appears to be more advantageous to the PPR algorithm than to the proposed algorithm. Despite that, the performance of the proposed algorithm turned out to be considerably higher than that of the PPR algorithm (Fig. 4). To our best knowledge, the PPR algorithm [3, 7], except for the proposed algorithm, is the only method that achieves topic-dependent allocation of activities to individual nodes by spreading activation. Therefore, the proposed algorithm is currently the best for achieving such a function.

Next we empirically demonstrate the use and the benefit of the proposed method by applying it to a real citation network. A citation network (Fig. 1, right) was constructed from papers published in major neuroscience journals. Then we took for example an emerging topic in neuroscience, expressed by the phrase "graded persistent activity and neural integrator". A set of 10 papers with abstracts showing high scores of word matching to this phrase was chosen as seed documents.

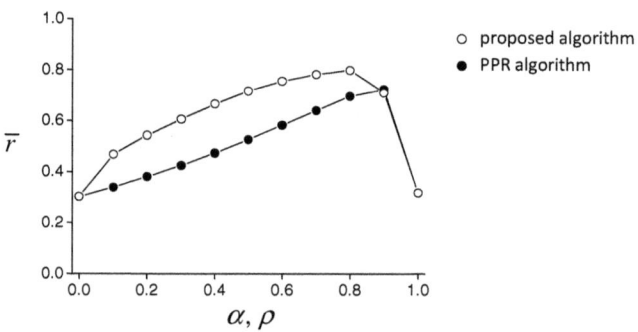

Fig. 4. The restoration performance, expressed by the average correlation coefficient $\bar{r}$, is plotted as a function of the unique parameter in each algorithm (α for the proposed algorithm and ρ for the PPR algorithm)

Table 1. The top 20 in the topic-dependent ranking

Rank	Title	Authors	Activity	Seed? 1(Y)/0(N)	Journal Vol. pages year
1	STABILITY OF THE MEMORY OF E	SEUNG HS,LEE DD,REIS BY,T	0.073831	0	NEURON 26 259–271 2000
2	IN VIVO INTRACELLULAR RECORD	AKSAY E,GAMKRELIDZE G,SI	0.073822	1	NAT NEUROSCI 4 184–193 2001
3	MODEL FOR A ROBUST NEURAL I	KOULAKOV AA,RAGHAVACH	0.069003	1	NAT NEUROSCI 5 775–782 2002
4	SYNAPTIC MECHANISMS AND NET	COMPTE A,BRUNEL N,GOLD	0.06481	0	CEREB CORTEX 10 910–923 2000
5	SYNAPTIC REVERBERATION UNDE	WANG XJ	0.061916	0	TRENDS NEUROSCI 24 455–463 2001
6	A MODEL OF VISUOSPATIAL WOR	CAMPERI M,WANG XJ	0.058597	0	J COMPUT NEUROSCI 5 383–405 1998
7	ROBUST PERSISTENT NEURAL AC	GOLDMAN MS,LEVINE JH,MA	0.057205	1	CEREB CORTEX 13 1185–1195 2003
8	A RECURRENT NETWORK MODEL	MILLER P,BRODY CD,ROMO	0.056	1	CEREB CORTEX 13 1208–1218 2003
9	BRAIN CALCULUS: NEURAL INTEG	MCCORMICK DA	0.055254	0	NAT NEUROSCI 4 113–114 2001
10	TIMING AND NEURAL ENCODING (	BRODY CD,HERNANDEZ A,ZA	0.055159	0	CEREB CORTEX 13 1196–1207 2003
11	HISTORY DEPENDENCE OF RATE	AKSAY E,MAJOR G,GOLDMA	0.052381	1	CEREB CORTEX 13 1173–1184 2003
12	SYNAPTIC BASIS OF CORTICAL P	WANG XJ	0.050142	0	J NEUROSCI 19 9587–9603 1999
13	MATCHING PATTERNS OF ACTIVI	CHAFEE MV,GOLDMAN–RAK	0.048867	0	J NEUROPHYSIOL 79 2919–2940 1998
14	BASIC MECHANISMS FOR GRADE	BRODY CD,ROMO R,KEPECS	0.047541	0	CURR OPIN NEUROBIOL 13 204–211 2003
15	ROBUST SPATIAL WORKING MEM	RENART A,SONG PC,WANG X	0.042419	0	NEURON 38 473–485 2003
16	NEURAL BASIS OF A PERCEPTUA	SHADLEN MN,NEWSOME WT	0.04152	0	J NEUROPHYSIOL 86 1916–1936 2001
17	CORRELATED DISCHARGE AMON	AKSAY E,BAKER R,SEUNG H	0.040958	1	J NEUROSCI 23 10852–10858 2003
18	TEMPORAL STRUCTURE IN NEUR	PESARAN B,PEZARIS JS,SAH	0.040258	0	NAT NEUROSCI 5 805–811 2002
19	TURNING ON AND OFF WITH EXCI	GUTKIN BS,LAING CR,COLBY	0.038298	0	J COMPUT NEUROSCI 11 121–134 2001
20	DYNAMICS AND PLASTICITY OF S	BRUNEL N	0.037095	0	CEREB CORTEX 13 1151–1161 2003

Table 1 shows the top 20 in the ranking obtained by our algorithm. With this table, one can learn a list of papers to read in order of priority. It is noticeable that the paper by Seung et al. (2000), which is not highly ranked by word matching and is dropped from the seed documents, is ranked first by our algorithm. Indeed, this paper is acknowledged as what has marked the beginning of the research field.

Fig. 5 visualizes citation relations among the top 30 in the ranking. Each document icon symbolizes a paper and its size expresses the activity, namely, the topic-dependent importance assigned to this paper. Icons are sorted in chronological order from the top to the bottom. Thin arrowed lines represent citation relations between the papers. The arrow is directed from a citied to a citing paper, denoting that the latter is under the influence of the former (Fig. 1, left). When an icon is clicked (as indicated by the block arrow), bibliographic information of the corresponding paper is displayed in a pop-up window. Interacting with this visualized graph, one can find out which papers are central or subsidiary and which relations between papers are mainstream or tributary; he/she will thereby figure out how this research field has developed.

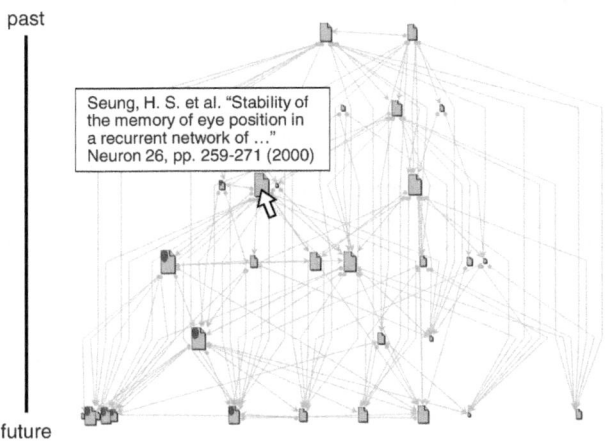

Fig. 5. Visualization of citation relations between the top 30 papers

4 Discussion

One problem overwhelming modern scientists is a tremendous number of papers being published every year. Even for a narrowed topic, what one has to read often exceeds what one can read. Hence, it is crucial to efficiently select papers to read from a pile of papers and prioritize them. Using the topic-dependent ranking proposed here, one can get a list of papers to read in order of priority (Table 1).

The benefit and performance of the proposed algorithm might be so high (Fig. 4) because it models excellent functions of the real brain. We believe that exploring the real brain will be helpful for creating new information-processing technology.

Acknowledgments. We used the bibliographic information (Science Citation Index Expanded) purchased from Thomson Scientific (presently Thomson Reuters). This study was partly supported by KAKENHI (20500279).

References

1. Garfield, E.: Citation Indexes for Science: A New Dimension in Documentation through Association of Ideas. Science 122, 108–111 (1955)
2. Davis, P.M.: Eigenfactor: Does the principle of repeated improvement result in better estimates than raw citation counts? J. Am. Soc. Info. Sci. Tech. 59, 2186–2188 (2008)
3. Page, L., et al.: The PageRank Citation Ranking: Bringing Order to the Web. Technical Report, Stanford InfoLab (1998),
   http://www-db.stanford.edu/~backrub/pageranksub.ps
4. Maslov, S., Redner, S.: Promise and Pitfalls of Extending Google's PageRank Algorithm to Citation Networks. J. Neurosci. 28, 11103–11105 (2008)
5. Kleinberg, J.: Authoritative sources in a hyperlinked environment. J. ACM 46, 604–632 (1999)
6. Woodruff, A., et al.: Enhancing a Digital Book with a Reading Recommender. In: Proceedings of CHI 2000, pp. 153–160. ACM Press, New York (2000)
7. Haveliwala, T.: Topic-Sensitive PageRank: A Context-Sensitive Ranking Algorithm for Web Search. IEEE Trans. Knowledge Data Eng. 15, 784–796 (2003)
8. Tsuboshita, Y., Okamoto, H.: Graded information extraction by neural-network dynamics with multihysteretic neurons. Neural Netw. 22, 922–930 (2009)
9. Collins, A.M., Loftus, E.F.: Spreading-Activation Theory of Semantic Processing. Psychol. Rev. 82, 407–428 (1975)
10. Anderson, J.R., Pirolli, P.L.: Spread of activation. J. Exp. Psychol. 10, 791–798 (1984)
11. Egorov, A.V., et al.: Graded persistent activity in entorhinal cortex neurons. Nature 420, 173–178 (2002)
12. Goldman, M.S., et al.: Robust persistent neural activity in a model integrator with multiple hysteretic dendrites per neuron. Cereb. Cortex 13, 1185–1195 (2003)
13. Koulakov, A.A., et al.: Model for a robust neural integrator. Nat. Neurosci. 5, 775–782 (2002)
14. Okamoto, H., et al.: Temporal integration by stochastic recurrent network dynamics with bimodal neurons. J. Neurophysiol. 97, 3859–3867 (2007)
15. Romo, R., et al.: Somatosensory discrimination based on cortical microstimulation. Nature 399, 470–473 (1999)
16. Aksay, E., et al.: In vivo intracellular recording and perturbation of persistent activity in a neural integrator. Nat. Neurosci. 4, 184–193 (2001)
17. Klemm, K., Eguiluz, V.M.: Growing scale-free networks with small-world behavior. Phys. Rev. E 65, 057102 (2002)

PADDLE: Proximal Algorithm for Dual Dictionaries LEarning

Curzio Basso[1], Matteo Santoro[1], Alessandro Verri[1], and Silvia Villa[2]

[1] Dipartimento di Informatica e Scienze dell'Informazione
Università degli Studi di Genova
Genova, 16128 Italy
{curzio.basso,santoro,verri}@disi.unige.it
[2] Dipartimento di Matematica
Università degli Studi di Genova
Genova, 16128 Italy
{silvia.villa}@dima.unige.it

Abstract. Recently, considerable research efforts have been devoted to the design of methods to learn from data overcomplete dictionaries for sparse coding. However, learned dictionaries require the solution of a sparse approximation problem for coding new data. In order to overcome this drawback, we propose an algorithm aimed at learning both a dictionary and its *dual*: a linear mapping directly performing the coding. Our algorithm is based on proximal methods and jointly minimizes the reconstruction error of the dictionary and the coding error of its dual; the sparsity of the representation is induced by an ℓ_1-based penalty on its coefficients. Experimental results show that the algorithm is capable of recovering the expected dictionaries. Furthermore, on a benchmark dataset the image features obtained from the dual matrix yield state-of-the-art classification performance while being much less computational intensive.

1 Introduction

The goal of this paper is to introduce an algorithm – that we called PADDLE – capable of learning from examples a dictionary as well as its (approximate) *dual*: a linear operator that decomposes new signals to their optimal sparse representations, without the need for solving any further optimization problem.

Over the years considerable effort has been devoted to the design of methods for learning optimal dictionaries from data. The seminal work of Olshausen and Field [13] was the first to propose an algorithm for learning an overcomplete dictionary in the field of natural image analysis. Recent advances in compressed sensing and feature selection led to use an ℓ_1 penalty on the decomposition coefficients, as in [8,10].

Within this framework, given N training vectors $\boldsymbol{x}_i \in \mathbb{R}^d$, the goal is to minimize the functional

$$\sum_{i=1}^{N} \|\boldsymbol{x}_i - \boldsymbol{D}\boldsymbol{u}_i\|^2 + \tau \sum_{i=1}^{N} \|\boldsymbol{u}_i\|_1 \quad s.t. \quad \|\boldsymbol{d}_i\|^2 \leq 1, \tag{1}$$

T. Honkela et al. (Eds.): ICANN 2011, Part I, LNCS 6791, pp. 379–386, 2011.

where $D = [d_1, \ldots, d_K] \in \mathbb{R}^{d \times K}$ is the dictionary whose columns are the atoms, the vectors $u_i \in \mathbb{R}^K$ are the decompositions over D of the training vectors x_i, and $\tau \geq 0$ weights the sparsity penalty.

Although the use of the decompositions u_i as features for subsequent supervised tasks has proved to be very successful, e.g. [15], it has one major drawback. Each decomposition requires the minimization of the functional in (1) with fixed D, which may turn out to be impractical in real-life settings. To address this problem, in [14] and subsequent works [7,4] the authors proposed to learn, as well as the dictionary, a non-linear encoding transformation. For settings with large amounts of data and/or budgeted computational resources, purely linear approaches may be preferable and as an additional advantage can be easily and efficiently implemented in hardware.

In the present paper we look for an optimal pair of linear operators D and $C = [c_1, \ldots, c_K]^T \in \mathbb{R}^{K \times d}$ (the *encoding* or *analysis* operator) that minimize

$$E(D, C, U) = \|X - DU\|_F^2 + \eta \|U - CX\|_F^2 + \tau \|U\|_1 \quad s.t. \quad \|d_i\|^2, \|c_i\|^2 \leq 1, \quad (2)$$

where $X \in \mathbb{R}^{d \times N}$ is the matrix whose columns are the training vectors and $U \in \mathbb{R}^{K \times N}$ is the matrix holding the encodings. The c_i can be seen as filters that are convolved with an input signal x to approximate its optimal encoding u.

The minimization of the proposed functional may be achieved by block coordinate descent, and we rely on proximal methods to perform the three resulting inner optimization problems. Indeed, in recent years different authors provided both theoretical and empirical evidence that proximal methods may be used to solve the optimization problems underlying many algorithms for ℓ_1-based regularization and structured sparsity. A considerable amount of work has been devoted to this topic within the context of signal recovery and image processing. An extensive list of references and an overview of several approaches can be found in [2], and in [3] for the context of machine learning. Proximal methods have been recently used in the context of dictionary learning by [6] for imposing a hierarchical structure into a dictionary using a structured sparsity penalty.

Experimental results show that PADDLE can recover the expected dictionaries and duals, and that codes based on the dual matrix yields state-of-the-art classification performance while being much less computational intensive.

2   Proximal Methods for Learning Dual Dictionaries

Since the functional in 2 is separately convex in each variable, we proceed by block coordinate descent (also known as block nonlinear Gauss-Seidel method) [9], iteratively minimizing first with respect to the encoding variables U (*sparse coding* step), and then to the dictionary D and its dual C (*dictionary update* step). Such approach has been shown to be empirically successful [8], and its convergence towards a critical point of E is guaranteed by Corollary 2 of [5].

The minimization steps both with respect to U and w.r.t. D and C are solved by proximal methods. In summary, a proximal (or forward-backward splitting) algorithm minimizes a function of type $E(\xi) = F(\xi) + J(\xi)$, where F is convex and differentiable, with Lipschitz continuous gradient, while J is lower semicontinuous, convex and coercive. These assumptions on F and J, required to ensure the existence of a solution, are fairly standard in the optimization literature (see e.g. [2]) and are always satisfied in the setting of dictionary learning for visual feature extraction. In the following we will denote by F the differentiable terms of the functional $E(D, C, U)$, and by J the sparsity penalty and the constraints on D and C.

The non-smooth term J is involved via its proximity operator P, which can be seen as a generalized version of a projection operator:

$$P(x) = \operatorname*{argmin}_{y}\{J(y) + \frac{1}{2}\|x - y\|^2\}. \tag{3}$$

The proximal algorithm is given by combining the projection step with a forward gradient descent step, as follows

$$\xi^p = P\left(\xi^{p-1} - \frac{1}{2\sigma}\nabla F(\xi^{p-1})\right). \tag{4}$$

The step-size of the inner gradient descent is governed by the coefficient σ, which can be fixed or adaptive, and whose choice will be discussed in Section 2. In particular, it can be shown that $E(\xi^p)$ converges to the minimum of E if σ is chosen appropriately [2].

Sparse Coding. Applying the algorithm (4) to the minimization of the functional (2) with fixed D and C, the gradient of the (strictly convex) differentiable term F is

$$\nabla_U F = -2D^T(X - DU) + 2\eta(U - CX),$$

while the proximity operator corresponding to J is the well-known soft-thresholding operator S_λ defined component-wise as

$$(S_\lambda[U])_{ij} = \operatorname{sign}(U_{ij})\max\{|U_{ij}| - \lambda, 0\}.$$

Plugging the gradient and the proximal operator into the general equation (4), we obtain the following update rule:

$$U^p = S_{\tau/\sigma_U}\left[\left(1 - \frac{\eta}{\sigma_U}\right)U^{p-1} + \frac{1}{\sigma_U}\left(D^T(X - DU^{p-1}) + \eta CX\right)\right] \tag{5}$$

Dictionary Update. When U is fixed, the optimization problems with respect to D and C are decoupled and can be solved separately.

The quadratic constraints on the columns of D and the rows of C are equivalent to an indicator function J. Denoting by B the unit ball in $\mathbb{R}^d$, the constraint on D (respectively C) is formalized with J being the indicator function of the set of matrices whose columns (resp. rows) belong to B. In both cases the proximity operator is a projection operator. Denoting by $\pi(d) = d/\max\{1, \|d\|\}$ the projection on the unit ball in $\mathbb{R}^d$, let π_D be the operator applying π to the columns of D and π_C the operator applying π to the rows of C.

Plugging the appropriate gradients and projection operators into Eq. (4) leads to the update steps

$$D^p = \pi_D(D^{p-1} + \frac{1}{\sigma_D}(X - D^{p-1}U)U^T), \qquad (6)$$

$$C^p = \pi_C(C^{p-1} + \frac{1}{\sigma_C}(U - C^{p-1}X)X^T). \qquad (7)$$

Gradient Descent Step. The choice of the step-sizes σ_U, σ_D and σ_C is crucial in achieving fast convergence.

In general, for $E = F + J$, one can choose the step-size to be equal to the Lipschitz constant of ∇F for all iterations. These constants can be evaluated explicitly, leading to $\sigma_U = 2\|D^T D + \eta I\|_F$, $\sigma_D = 2\|UU^T\|_F$ and $\sigma_C = 2\|XX^T\|_F$.

Faster rates can be obtained in two ways: either through adaptive step-size choices (e.g. the Barzilai-Borwein method), or by slightly modifying the proximal step as in FISTA [1]. The PADDLE algorithm makes use of the latter approach.

The FISTA update rule is based on evaluating the proximity operator with a weighted sum of the previous two iterates. More precisely, defining $a_1 = 1$ and $\phi^1 = \xi^1$, the proximal step (4) is replaced by

$$\xi^p = P\left(\phi^p - \frac{1}{2\sigma}\nabla F(\phi^p)\right), \qquad (8)$$

$$a_{p+1} = (1 + \sqrt{1 + 4a_p^2})/2 \qquad (9)$$

$$\phi^{p+1} = \xi^p + \frac{a_p - 1}{a_{p+1}}(\xi^p - \xi^{p-1}). \qquad (10)$$

Choosing σ as in the fixed step-size case, this simple modification allows to achieve quadratic convergence rate with respect to the values [1]. Although convergence of the sequences D^p, C^p and U^p is not proved theoretically, there is empirical evidence that it holds in practice. Our experiments confirm this observation.

The PADDLE Algorithm. Let us summarize the complete algorithm. As previously explained, PADDLE alternates between optimizing with respect to U, D and C. These three optimizations are carried out employing the iterative projections defined in equations (5), (6) and (7), respectively, adapted according to equations (8–10). After the first iteration of the algorithm, the three inner optimizations are initialized with the results obtained at the previous iteration. This can be seen as an instance of the popular *warm-restart* strategy.

During the iterations it may happen that, after the optimization with respect to U, some atoms of D are used only for few reconstructions, or not at all. If the i-th atom d_i is under-used, meaning that only few elements of the i-th row of U are non-zero, we can replace it with an example that is not reconstructed well. If x_j is such an example, this can be achieved by simply setting u_j to the canonical vector e_i, since at the next step D and C are estimated from U and X. In our experiments we only replaced atoms when not used at all.

The iterative procedure is stopped either upon reaching the maximum number of iterations, or when the energy decreases only slightly with respect to the last H iterations. In our experiments we found out that, in practice, after a few hundreds of outer iterations the convergence was always reached. Indeed, in many cases only a few tens of iterations were required.

It is worth noting that in our implementation the algorithm optimizes with respect to all codes $\boldsymbol{u}_i$ simultaneously. Although not strictly necessary, it is a possibility we opted for, since we are confident it could prove advantageous in future hardware-accelerated implementations. However, the algorithm can be easily implemented with a sequential optimization of the $\boldsymbol{u}_i$.

A reference implementation in Python, together with scripts for replicating the experiments of the following sections, are available online at the address http://slipguru.disi.unige.it/Research/PADDLE.

3   Experiments

The natural application of PADDLE is in the context of learning discriminative features for image analysis. Therefore, in the following we report the experiments on standard datasets of digits and natural images, in order to perform qualitative and quantitative assessments of the recovered dictionaries for various choices of the parameters. Furthermore, we discuss the impact of the feature vectors obtained from a learned C on the accuracy of an image classifier.

Berkeley Segmentation Dataset. Following the experiment in [14, Sec. 4], we have extracted a random sample of 10^5 patches of size 12x12 from the Berkeley segmentation data set [11]. The images intensities have been centered by their mean and normalized dividing by half the range (125). The patches have been separately recentered too.

We have run PADDLE over a range of values for τ, with $K = 200$ and both with coding error ($\eta = 1$) and without ($\eta = 0$). The relative tolerance for stopping has been set to 10^{-4}. The reconstruction error achieved at the various level of sparsity (τ), both with and without the coding error, have been constantly lower than the reconstruction error achievable with as many principal components as the number of non-zero elements of the encodings.

In Figure 1 we show images of the recovered dictionary. An interesting effect we observed is that different levels of sparsity in the coding coefficients also affects the visual patterns of the dictionary atoms. The sparser the representation, the closer the atoms are to simple partial derivatives of a $2D$ Gaussian kernel, i.e. the dictionary tends to adapt poorly to the specific set of data. On the contrary, with a less sparse representation, a larger number of the atoms seem to encode for more structured local patterns or specific textures present in the dataset.

MNIST Dataset. Next we have tested the algorithm on the $50,000$ training images of the popular MNIST data set [12], which is a collection of 28×28 quasi binary images of handwritten digits. According to the experiments described

Fig. 1. Dictionary learned from the Berkley segmentation dataset with different values of τ: from left to right, 1, 0.1 and 0.02. The atoms are in column-major order from the most used to the least one. The codes corresponding to the three dictionaries pairs uses on average 6.6, 65.9 and 139.8 atoms, respectively.

in [14], we have trained the dictionary with 200 atoms. All the images have been pre-processed by mapping their range into the interval $[0, 1]$. The results obtained are consistent with those already reported in the literature. In particular, the learned dictionary D comprises the most representative digits from which it is possible to reconstruct all the others with a low approximation error. In Figure 2 (bottom) we show how the exemplar digit on the left can be expressed in terms of the small subset of the atoms in the middle, obtaining the approximate image on the right. As expected, the actual number of non-zero coefficients is extremely low if compared with the size of the dictionary. In the two rows in the middle, we first report all the dictionary atoms with non-zero coefficients and then we weight them with respect to their relevance in the reconstruction.

A second, more interesting aspect is the fast empirical convergence of the algorithm with such a well-structured dataset, as shown in Figure 2 (top). The initial dictionary has been built with random patches. After the first iteration it was already possible to inspect some digits, and the amount of change decreased rapidly reaching a substantial convergence after only a few iterations. The dictionary after 20 iterations (corresponding to the full convergence) was almost identical to the one after 4 iterations only.

Classification. In this last group of experiments we have focused on the impact of using the dictionaries learned with the PADDLE algorithm in a classification context. More specifically, we have investigated the discriminative power of the sparse coding associated to the dictionary D and its dual C when used to represent the visual content of an image. The goal of the experiments has been to build a classifier to assign each image to a specific semantic class. In practice, we replicated the experimental setting of [15], using the authors' software package ScSPM (available at http://www.ifp.illinois.edu/~jyang29/ScSPM.htm). According to our experiments, the classifcation accuracy we have obtained using a representation computed with PADDLE, 98.4% (SD=0.8%), is essentially the

Initialization   After 1 iteration   After 4 iterations   At convergence

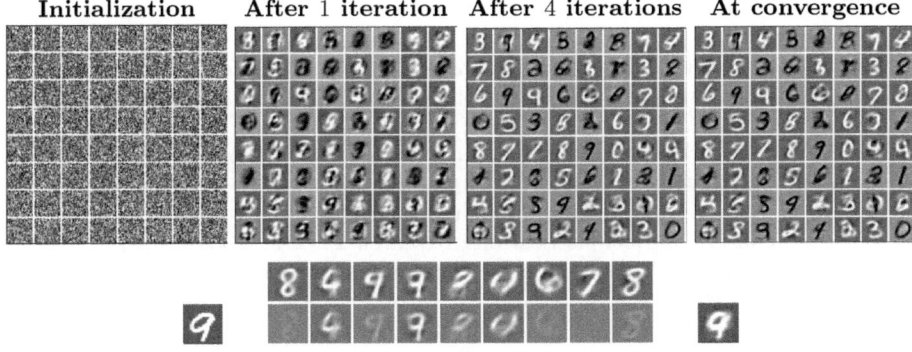

Fig. 2. Experiments on MNIST dataset. See text for details.

same as the one obtained with the learned dictionary used by the authors in the original paper: 98.5% (SD=0.8%).

The results obtained with the dictionary C are especially encouraging if one consider the substantial gain in the computational time required to compute the sparse codes, with a fixed dictionary, for each new input image. In our classification experiments (i.e. after learning the dictionary), processing an image took less than 0.21 seconds on average if the representations where computed with the matrix C, compared to 2.3 seconds using the original implementation of the feature-sign search algorithm [8] provided with ScSPM. Indeed, regardless the specific implementation of the sparse optimization method, it is easy to see that using C is always the best choice since it requires just one matrix-vector multiplication.

4   Conclusion

We have proposed a novel algorithm based on proximal methods to learn a dictionary and its dual, that can be used to compute sparse overcomplete representations of data. Although there may be other methods for solving the inner optimization steps, we believe that using proximal methods allows for an additional flexibility that may be useful in employing more complex penalities, as in [6]. The experiments have shown that for image data the algorithm yields representations with good discriminative power. In particular, the dual dictionary can be used to efficiently compute the representations by means of a simple matrix-vector multiplication, without any loss of classification accuracy. We believe that our method is a valid contribution towards building robust and expressive dictionaries of visual features.

Acknowledgments. The authors wish to gratefully thank A. Barla, G. Chiusano, M. Esposito, A. Staglianó.

References

1. Beck, A., Teboulle, M.: Fast gradient-based algorithms for constrained total variation image denoising and deblurring problems. IEEE Transactions on Image Processing 18(11), 2419–2434 (2009)
2. Combettes, P.L., Wajs, V.R.: Signal recovery by proximal forward-backward splitting. Multiscale Model. Simul. 4(4), 1168–1200 (2005) (electronic)
3. Duchi, J., Singer, Y.: Efficient online and batch learning using forward backward splitting. Journal of Machine Learning Research 10, 2899–2934 (2009)
4. Gregor, K., LeCun, Y.: Learning fast approximations of sparse coding. In: Proc. ICML 2010 (2010)
5. Grippo, L., Sciandrone, M.: On the convergence of the block nonlinear Gauss-Seidel method under convex constraints. Oper. Res. Lett. 26(3), 127–136 (2000)
6. Jenatton, R., Mairal, J., Obozinski, G., Bach, F.: Proximal methods for sparse hierarchical dictionary learning. In: Proc. of the 27th International Conference on Machine Learning, Haifa, Israel (2010)
7. Kavukcuoglu, K., Ranzato, M., LeCun, Y.: Fast inference in sparse coding algorithms with applications to object recognition. Tech. rep., Computational and Biological Learning Lab, Courant Institute, NYU (2008)
8. Lee, H., Battle, A., Raina, R., Ng, A.: Efficient sparse coding algorithms. In: Advances in Neural Information Processing Systems 19 (NIPS 2006), pp. 801–808 (2006)
9. Luenberger, D.G.: Linear and nonlinear programming, 2nd edn. Kluwer Academic Publishers, Boston (2003)
10. Mairal, J., Bach, F., Ponce, J., Sapiro, G.: Online learning for matrix factorization and sparse coding. Journal of Machine Learning Research 11, 19–60 (2010)
11. Martin, D., Fowlkes, C., Tal, D., Malik, J.: A database of human segmented natural images and its application to evaluating segmentation algorithms and measuring ecological statistics. In: Proc. 8th Int'l Conf. Computer Vision, July 2001, vol. 2, pp. 416–423 (2001)
12. The MNIST database of handwritten digits, http://yann.lecun.com/exdb/mnist/ (1998)
13. Olshausen, B., Field, D.: Sparse coding with an overcomplete basis set: A strategy employed by V1? Vision Research 37(23), 3311–3325 (1997)
14. Ranzato, M., Poultney, C., Chopra, S., LeCun, Y.: Efficient learning of sparse representations with an energy-based model. In: Advances in Neural Information Processing Systems 19, NIPS 2006 (2006)
15. Yang, J., Yu, K., Gong, Y., Huang, T.: Linear spatial pyramids matching using sparse coding for image classification. In: Proc. of Computer Vision and Pattern Recognition Conference (CVPR 2009) (2009)

Author Index

GPSR Compliance

*The European Union's (EU) General Product Safety Regulation (GPSR)
is a set of rules that requires consumer products to be safe and our
obligations to ensure this.*

*If you have any concerns about our products, you can contact us on
ProductSafety@springernature.com*

In case Publisher is established outside the EU, the EU authorized
representative is:

Springer Nature Customer Service Center GmbH
Europaplatz 3
69115 Heidelberg, Germany

Batch number: 09467203

Printed by Printforce, the Netherlands